Critical Essays on American Transcendentalism

Critical Essays on American Transcendentalism

Philip F. Gura
and
Joel Myerson

G. K. Hall & Co. • Boston, Massachusetts

Library of Congress Cataloging in Publication Data
Main entry under title:
Critical essays on American transcendentalism.

(Critical essays on American literature)
Includes index.
1. American literature—History and criticism—Addresses,
essays, lectures. 2. Transcendentalism in literature—Addresses,
essays, lectures. I. Gura, Philip F., 1950–   . II. Myerson, Joel.
III. Series.
PS217.T7C7   810'.9'13   81-7269
ISBN 0-8161-8466-6   AACR2

This publication is printed on permanent/durable acid-free paper
MANUFACTURED IN THE UNITED STATES OF AMERICA

CRITICAL ESSAYS ON AMERICAN LITERATURE

This series seeks to publish the most important reprinted criticism on writers and topics in American literature along with, in various volumes, original essays, interviews, bibliographies, letters, manuscript sections, and other materials brought to public attention for the first time. *Critical Essays on American Transcendentalism*, by Philip F. Gura and Joel Myerson, is the most ambitious collection of scholarship on this topic ever assembled. They have presented over fifty important documents on Transcendentalism, including statements by Charles Dickens, Thomas Carlyle, Oliver Wendell Holmes, Edgar Allan Poe, and Louisa May Alcott, and more recent critical assessments by George Santayana, René Wellek, Perry Miller, Lawrence Buell, and Joel Porte, among others. Professor Gura is Associate Professor of English and Director of Graduate Studies at the University of Colorado. He is the author of *The Wisdom of Words: Language, Theology, and Literature in the New England Renaissance* (1981) and of many articles on colonial and nineteenth-century American literature. Professor Myerson, Professor of English at the University of South Carolina, has published nearly fifty articles and a dozen books on American Transcendentalism. He is also the editor of the annual *Studies in the American Renaissance*. We are confident that this collection will make a permanent and significant contribution to American literary scholarship.

James Nagel, GENERAL EDITOR

Northeastern University

CONTENTS

INTRODUCTION

From the 1830s on, the abiding difficulty in discussing the American Transcendental movement has been that of definition, a problem augmented by the posture of the Transcendentalists themselves. As hyperbolic as it now may sound, Charles Dickens' quip that "On inquiring what this appellation [transcendental] might be supposed to signify," he "was given to understand that whatever was unintelligible would be certainly transcendental," succinctly expressed the confusion of many nineteenth-century thinkers as they tried to understand the many-headed monster fertilized within the Unitarian Church.[1]

The movement's earliest critics, in particular, delighted in lampooning the opaque language in which New England's rebellious sons expressed their allegiance to Germanic and Platonic ideas. But while such philosophical plum-puddings gained respectability in France and Germany under the banner of Cousin's Eclecticism, and Schelling's and Fichte's Idealism, across the Atlantic comparable pronouncements drew the kind of ridicule epitomized in the mock-transcendental jargon of one "Moonshine Milkywater," who in a letter to *Brother Jonathan* in 1841 refused an invitation to Boston's famous dinner for Dickens by maintaining, among other things, that "Surely Rag, Tag, and Bobtail are but a dualism; for it is only the Me and the Not-Me, that exist even in Committees and Corporations, pluripersonal enough although."[2] As it became apparent, especially after the publication of the *Dial* in 1840, that as an intellectual movement Transcendentalism was not going to disappear quickly, countless New Englanders asked the question an anonymous author posed to a fictional Transcendentalist in the *New Englander* in 1843: "Is there any prospect that the community will ever understand your new system of philosophy and faith?"[3]

In his essay on "Transcendental Antics" included in this collection, Joel Porte points out that many members of the movement had wit enough to treat such criticism good-naturedly, for they regarded their extravagant declarations as a necessary component of their mission to awaken America from the materialistic slumber into which the age of steam rapidly was carrying it. People had to be shocked into an awareness that intuition, spirit, and Reason had been too much neglected; and most Transcendentalists would have been pleased to know that after speaking with a man or woman of their persuasion Lydia Maria Child always had to bite her finger, "to know whether it exists or not."[4]

So much the better, if thus she was brought to contemplate the worlds of matter and spirit. Even a seemingly high-minded minister like Theodore Parker was not above provocative self-parody in his descriptions of the Transcendental movement, as long as his final counterthrusts served the spiritual and intellectual reformation he supported. His pose as a homespun Levi Blodgett is well-known, but less so is the piece he published anonymously in the *Christian Register* for 1840, in which he described an old man's dream after reading *Two Articles from the Princeton Review, Concerning the Transcendental Philosophy of the Germans and of Cousin,* and which we might take as a light-hearted key to the concerns of early commentators on the movement.[5]

As Parker's old man stood "on the extreme point of Cape Cod" he saw rapidly approaching from the horizon a misty cloud "extending many miles in breadth, and with a depth he could not measure," composed, he soon learned, of all the Transcendentalists of past ages driven thither from Germany by a "Mr. Hengstenberg." The list of luminaries—from Plato to Goethe—is itself revealing as an acknowledgement of Parker's intellectual lineage, but more important here is the author's mockery of the exaggerated fear to which the old man is brought by his vision of the Transcendental Huns: "'Alas,' said I, 'alas for the churches of New England. We be all dead men, for the Transcendentalists have come! They say there is no Christ; no God; no soul; only 'an absolute nothing,' and Hegel is the Holy Ghost. Our churches will be pulled down; there will be no Sabbath; our wives will wear the breeches, and the Transcendentalists will ride over us rough shod.'" So far the piece reads like anti-Transcendentalist propaganda, with the men all babbling in strange tongues and loudly disagreeing among themselves as they come ashore and divide into Right and Left, "Centres and Extremes." But Parker finally shows his hand as the old man learns that New England can be providentially "delivered" only by Mr. Hengstenberg himself, who soon appears astride a gigantic broom to tell the terrified man how to combat the invasion. "We must go back to the thirteenth century," he declares. "We must take the whole of the Old Testament, letter for letter, and believe it . . . we must never consult Reason, but bow to the letter, and reckon doubt as the sin not to be pardoned." "Least of all," Mr. Hengstenberg concludes, "should we make the slightest attempt to reconcile Faith and Reason, Religion and Philosophy, for this would be like marrying Christ and Belial." The reader finally understands that Mr. Hengstenberg is nothing but a ridiculous anachronism, his fear of the Transcendentalists based on a combination of philosophical misconception and medieval superstition. If the Transcendental hordes were indeed arriving, wise men knew that only such ideas as they brought could rescue America from its aimless drift into the modern age.

Parker's amusing sketch moves us to the heart of early criticism of the Transcendental movement, for in its earliest form the significant commentary focused not so much on the Idealistic philosophy *per se* as on the group's theological radicalism. In early nineteenth-century New England, philosophy still served as the handmaiden of the Christian religion, and, even leaving aside the frequent diatribes against Emerson, Parker, and their cohorts by conservative Unitarians, much that was published about the movement between 1840 and 1870 took the form of debate about intended Transcendental reform of American Christianity.

For example, writing in the *Magnolia* in 1842, J. E. Snodgrass defended the New Thought as part and parcel of the renewal of faith rampant in Methodist and Quaker congregations. Like members of those groups, Transcendentalists looked "away from man and his scholastic acquirements" and "listen[ed] to the God within." Snodgrass took the word "transcendental" to be a mere "scapegoat" for ideas and attitudes its critics did not understand; he decried the fact that members of other Christian bodies joined the general condemnation of the New Thought while, in truth, like the Transcendentalists, they too were only "struggling to catch a view of the true and the beautiful."[6] Similarly, James Kennard, answering the question, "What is Transcendentalism?" in *The Knickerbocker* for 1844, maintained that if the movement's tenets were presented clearly enough, any intelligent man had to consider himself a Transcendentalist, for anyone who "amid the apparent contradictions with which we are surrounded, strives to reconcile appearances and discover principles" and to "learn the inward and spiritual" from "the outward and visible," already had accepted the central beliefs of the movement.[7] Even Lydia Maria Child, for all her finger-biting, had to admit that many Transcendentalists she met most reminded her of members of the Society of Friends, for "the doctrine of perpetual revelation, heard in the quietude of the soul," was common to both groups. If Transcendentalists sometimes alienated potential sympathizers by talking in oracular or mystical strains, "that which is really uttered," Child noted, "has deeper significance than is usually apprehended by intelligent minds unaccustomed to similar habits of thought."[8]

To be sure, these and other sympathetic writers greeted Transcendentalism's message a bit hesitantly, but their commentaries are linked by an agreement that the Transcendentalists' defense of the intuitive basis of religion offered a necessary restorative to the corpse-cold Unitarianism of the day. By far a more common response to the group, however, stressed the dangers inherent in accepting their subjective and emotional definitions of religious experience. The often-noted Transcendentalist tendency toward exaggeration, what one writer called "an outlandish and affected mode of expression," was closely linked in many eyes to an egotism seemingly incompatible with true Christianity.[9]

Theophilus Parsons, for example, a Swedenborgian writing in 1840 in the *New Jerusalem Magazine*, declared Transcendentalism part of the "universal unloosening of all opinion and belief" that presaged the New Heaven and New Earth and admitted that its ideas were particularly attractive to "those minds who are stirred by the great desire of comprehending their origin and destiny." But like his fellow New Churchman, Sampson Reed, who by the 1840s was struggling to dissociate himself from radicals like Emerson who had proclaimed him a herald of their faith, Parsons vigorously denied the Transcendentalists' legitimacy because they acknowledged no authority above them to hold their speculations in check. "Its whole religion is self-worship," Parsons declared, for "with Transcendentalism, the pride of self-intelligence is itself the beginning and end of all wisdom."[10] The Church of the New Jerusalem offered seekers the same emotional gratification in an age of religious unrest, but it added the discipline of the Word of God, interpreted by Emanuel Swedenborg. The Transcendentalists may have placed the proper stress on faith and emotion in the religious life, but Parsons knew that in the not too distant future Transcendentalism, like Unitarianism, was destined to pass away with all things belonging to the old, corrupt order.

Parsons spoke as a member of a minority sect and so had much to fear (as did many liberal Unitarians) from association in the public mind with Transcendentalism. In their appraisals of the movement, however, members of the conservative Trinitarian churches mounted a less self-conscious offensive. All through the 1820s and 1830s they had warned that the "liberal Christianity" of ministers like William Ellery Channing and Andrews Norton would result in the kinds of frightening doctrinal errors that finally appeared in the sermons of Parker and George Ripley. Simeon Doggett, for example, a minister in the town of Wrentham, Massachusetts, vigorously condemned Parker's *Discourse of Matters Pertaining to Religion* in a sermon he delivered on a day of public fast in 1843. Linking Parker to such notorious infidels as Voltaire and Thomas Paine, Doggett was aghast at the Transcendentalists' rejection of the miraculous interpretation of the Bible and declared, as Parsons did, that mankind needed "a higher authority than that of man, to enforce the truth." By exalting man's conscience above the Bible, Parker had shorn the scriptures of all their glory, and Doggett fervently prayed that God might "allay this moral infection that has lit upon our shores, that its deleterious influence spread no farther."[11]

Noah Porter, Jr., one of the Trinitarians' most respected intellectual work-horses, was more restrained in his response to the movement but still felt that Parker's works, especially the notorious sermon on the transient and permanent in Christianity, greatly "dishonored" religion "under the guise of philosophy" and made God's revelation into a "poor tattered thing of shreds and patches." But Porter, who by 1849 could praise the contribution of James Marsh and other of Coleridge's American disciples for the new vigor they had brought to the orthodox churches, also was able to distinguish the different segments of the Transcendentalist movement—in particular among the "Pantheists" like Emerson, who preached a "natural theology without a personal God," the Transcendentalists "in the Unitarian communion" like Parker and Ripley, who rejected the historical evidences of Christianity and instead "planted themselves on the moral evidence" for God, and, finally, those Transcendentalists "who are known and acknowledged as men, strenuous for evangelical and spiritual Christianity," presumably those like Marsh who found in the Idealistic philosophy the basis for a truly spiritual reinvigoration of orthodoxy. Porter's lengthy essay, "Transcendentalism," published in an 1842 number of the *American Biblical Repository,* emerges, like his later effort on Coleridge, as one of the most restrained and judicious assessments of the movement, for unlike others who received the Transcendentalists' tenets with the same fears an earlier generation had reserved for "free-thinkers," Porter knew that these radicals had something important to offer American Protestants. "Read, study, and ponder these writers as much as you will," he urged; "used aright, they will reward you well." But, he added, "let them not lead you captive as partisans."[12]

As late as 1857 a few churchmen persisted in their efforts to exorcise the troublesome spirit of Transcendentalism from their midst. George E. Ellis, for example, assessing *A Half-Century of the Unitarian Controversy,* claimed that while "the differences between Orthodoxy and Unitarianism arise from questions of interpretation," the Transcendentalists had rejected all historical evidences for the biblical miracles and so no longer had any connection to true Christianity. Most ministers, though, were enough preoccupied with the vertiginous political events of the period to stop worrying about the specific theological reforms of a Parker or a Ripley.[13] And by the post-Civil War era, with the specter of Darwinian science at their study doors, many clergymen became willing to take what they could from the Transcendental church reformers to buttress their arguments for the existence of Christianity as a system still worthy of men's allegiance. Accepting any help they could receive to combat the materialistic view of the universe that Darwinism implied, enlightened Protestant clergymen praised the Transcendentalists' belief in Christianity as an intuitively valid faith.

This reconciliation among hitherto divergent viewpoints was evident, for example, in the Congregationalist Horace Bushnell's various calls for a "Christian comprehensiveness" in doctrine, but it was visible as well in Cyrus Bartol's *Radical Problems,* published in 1872.[14] A Unitarian who frequently flirted with the ideas of Transcendentalism, Bartol also maintained close friendships with enlightened Trinitarians like Bushnell. In an essay in *Radical Problems* he assessed the importance of Transcendentalism to the development of contemporary liberal theology, and in particular he lauded the movement for its much-needed reinvigoration of American Protestantism. In the early nineteenth century "liturgy had become lethargy," he declared, and such events as Emerson's sermon on the Lord's Supper and his Divinity School address hardly contained, as his critics had maintained, "upstart" or "bastard" doctrines. Rather, "while Andover and Cambridge responded to each other with paper pop-guns," men like Emerson witnessed "the return of the Holy Ghost with voice."[15]

Arguing further that Transcendentalism "did not foul its nest, or, as is continually charged, despise its mother," Bartol appealed to a shattered nation's patriotism to defend the movement's worth. Transcendentalism, he maintained, merely "unfolded the faith implied in every act of the settlers of the land," and thus the Transcendentalist revolt was nothing less than "a new vessel, a better Mayflower for the Truth's escape from her foes."[16] Because of the particular spiritual doctrines men like Parker, Ripley, and Emerson brought to the forefront of the churches' attention, Protestantism was better able to meet the challenges of the post-War era, a time when very different demands were made of those who defended the faith once delivered to the saints.

With this absorption of the Transcendentalists' subjective view of the religious life into the main current of American Christianity, the movement's theological radicalism ceased to be discussed seriously in any except historical accounts of its rise and progress. Instead, by the late 1870s Transcendentalism became of most interest as a particular philosophical movement. Even a liberal minister like Octavius Brooks Frothingham, for example, whose *Transcendentalism in New England* stands as the first full-scale account of the phenomenon, devoted a significant part of his volume to a discussion of the German and French antecedents of this American manifestation of Idealism; and seven years later, in the *Atlantic*, he further reminisced about "Some Phases of Idealism in New England."[17] Of course Emerson himself, in his early lecture on "The Transcendentalist," had stressed that he and his friends were only taking sides in the age-old battle between Materialism and Idealism, an assessment echoed by Charles Mayo Ellis in his *An Essay on Transcendentalism* (1842), but in the later nineteenth century, with philosophical circles abuzz with talk of "positivism" and "naturalism," what the New England school said in defense of spiritual Idealism acquired new significance.[18]

John Orr, in an essay on "The Transcendentalism of New England," spoke directly to this new interest in philosophical Idealism when in the *International Review* for 1882 he reminded readers that while the leading ideas in philosophy "are now the doctrines of evolution as formulated by Darwin" and Herbert Spencer's belief that "experience deposits results in the texture of the brain, which are transmitted from generation to generation," Transcendentalism, in the various forms New Englanders pursued it, encouraged "a stern reaction against . . . materialism, formalism and utilitarianism in its lower aspects." Correcting what he believed a too facile characterization of the movement as essentially vapid mysticism, Orr also went out of his way to note that Transcendentalism offered a philosophical system that bore fruits in practical reform. It was not "Oriental," he declared, "taking the soul away into solitudes of profitless contemplation." Nor was it "sentimental, finding in emotion the point of union with God." It was, he concluded, "practical and reformatory," and to those tired of the materialistic grip in which the new science held mankind, Transcendentalism was, "par excellence, a *stimulus,* and to some a revelation, morally and spiritually." Quite simply, it "purified the air and amplified the horizon."[19]

The "recent materialists" now took the brunt of the attack from those who praised the spiritual, intuitive dimensions of man's existence. For example, Samuel Johnson, using John Stuart Mill and John Locke as philosophical straw men, complained bitterly that his contemporaries declared Transcendentalism "unscientific" because it was based on "faith rather than reason." To his chagrin, Johnson found that while Transcendentalism embodied "a far stronger reaction against the old theology than scientific induction can be without it," everywhere around him he saw that "in the very impetus of their reaction [against Transcendental Idealism]" scientists were confounding "this indispensable ally with the foe they would destroy." Like Parker and Horace Bushnell, both of whom sought to effect a fruitful marriage between science and religion, Johnson understood that Kant's true challenge to Locke and his disciples had gone unanswered. Thus, "a war upon the Transcendental method . . . would simply divorce science from that sense of the unlimited and universal" that was its chief "motive force." To Johnson, the transcendental implied nothing less than the "recognition of the inevitable step beyond experience or observation by which man lives and grows."[20]

Perhaps even more important to an age in which increasing social stratification threatened to verify the pessimistic appraisals of the capitalist economy made by Karl Marx and other social theorists, Johnson asked his readers to consider that once scientific materialists were brought to accept the mind's intuitive acknowledgment of "universal conceptions and principles of order," they also had to see that "Justice, Humanity, Universal Rights and Duties, on which progress moves," themselves were transcendental ideas. Just as Kant had understood that such concepts as Unity, Universe, Law, Cause, Substance, and Permanence could only be affirmed intuitively, so, too, the ideals of social justice that were held by enlightened liberals, particularly in America. The "idea of a unity of races and religions," the notion of "a true State, combining personal with public freedom," the belief in "equal opportunities for race and sex"—all such dreams of mankind were transcendentally inspired. How, then, could John Stuart Mill fancy that Transcendentalism stood in the way of the social progress in which he and other utilitarians so fervently believed? Sounding like a latter-day Henry Thoreau taking to task his degenerate and desperate townsmen, Johnson proclaimed that to combat the materialistic temper of the age "we want the personal ideal . . . inward dignities . . . a self-respect and self-reliance that require new starting points in the philosophy of culture." We want, he concluded, "training in principles instead of dissipation in details," and only the philosophical Idealism that had flourished during the New England Renaissance could "stay" America in its "downward tracks."[21]

The whole subject of the renewed interest in Transcendentalism in the Gilded Age needs more exploration, especially in its philosophical and ideological ramifications, for the pragmatism of such philosophers as C. S. Peirce and William James did not sweep the country unchallenged. To be sure, between 1870 and 1890 many assessments of the movement were linked to the fact that by then the Transcendental flowering was enough a part of history to insure that Emerson (who had died in 1882) and his friends were fit material for literary reminiscence. More significantly, though, popular essays like those of Frothingham in the *Atlantic* and Louis James Block in the *New England Magazine* suggest the profound concern of many citizens about the ideological direction in which their material prosperity was taking them. A prime example here is the work of Joseph Cook, whose published series of "Boston Monday Lectures" found their way into countless homes. In his discussion of "Transcendentalism" he admitted to disliking the Concord school's undue emphasis on extreme individualism, but he praised the European Transcendentalists for preserving the notion that "transcendental truths are simply those necessary, self-evident, axiomatic truths which transcend experience," and which supported a morality of which he approved. In Germany, he declared, "is a vast stretch of modern philosophical discussion" from Leibnitz to Kant to Lotze, "all on the line of intuitive truth" and which "never has broken with Christianity, nor been drawn into either the Charybdis of materialism or the Scylla of pantheism."[22] Only this philosophical structure could counter America's rampant degeneracy in an age of robber-barons and social darwinists.

Indeed, this distinction between scientific materialism and philosophical Idealism also provided the starting point for discussions of Transcendentalism in the early twentieth century, for whatever pragmatism's utility as a rationalization for America's chauvinistic views of its destiny, some thinkers continued to question the values of a nation that persisted in defining itself primarily through economic achievement. These critics saw Transcendentalism not only as part of the age-old struggle between Materialists and Idealists, Aristotelians and Platonists, but as another phase of a particularly *American* tale. Such characterizations, which made much of the empirical, pragmatic, mensurative traits in the American character, had begun at least as far back as de Tocqueville's *Democracy in America* but assumed a major role in the philosophical challenge to utilitarianism in the 1880s and 1890s. John Orr, for example, had noted that because America was "engaged so much with the measurable and ponderable," it was not at all interested "in that which cannot be seen and handled." "The sensible," he concluded, "rather than the rational, horizon bounds its vision."[23]

In the early twentieth century George Santayana's description of "The Genteel Tradition in American Philosophy" permanently enshrined in the American imagination the distinction between the "American Will," which "inhabits the skyscraper," and the "American intellect," which still dwelled, in Santayana's marvelous phrase, in "the colonial mansion." "The one is all aggressive enterprize," he continued; "the other is all genteel tradition."[24] Santayana's near-contemporary, Van Wyck Brooks, would go even farther, marking these as differences between the "highbrow" and "lowbrow" in American culture, but Santayana's famous lecture at Berkeley better addressed the New Englanders' philosophical positions and their relationship to the schizophrenia that marked the American mind as Calvinism's tenets gradually were diluted into the saccharine moralism of James Russell Lowell and Henry Wadsworth Longfellow.

While Transcendentalism proper—what Santayana defined as "systematic subjectivism," a study of "the perspectives of knowledge as they radiate from the self"—offered a restoration of the balance between will and intellect, too many American Transcendentalists (so-called) had attempted to turn a method of deriving knowledge into an entire *system* of knowledge itself, thus miring themselves further in the subjective landscape of the genteel.[25] Santayana singled out such thinkers as Emerson and William James, and the poet Walt Whitman, as men who had strained against the bounds by which the Genteel Tradition had yarded them, and he argued that in Whitman's "Bohemian temperament, with its poetry of crude naturalism," and James' "impassioned empiricism" and belief that the universe was "wild and young, and not to be harnessed by the logic of any school," Americans could discover the fruition of Emerson's best thought.[26] Santayana believed that some good finally had come from all the Transcendental jabbering around Concord and Boston, and he genuinely hoped that the day of the Genteel finally was passing.

Santayana's invocation of Whitman also should remind us that, even if many critics ignored it, there was a literary dimension to the Transcendentalist movement. Thus, in the nineteenth and the early twentieth century discussions of the group's literary production quickly narrowed to analyses of individual authors, and apart from a lampooning of the Transcendentalists' adoption of Teutonic vocabulary there was little talk of a Transcendentalist aesthetic. For example, an anonymous "J." writing in *Arcturus* for 1841 declared that the Transcendentalists united only to differ; "they must maintain," he continued, "a contrariety of belief, a mixture of systems." As to the "tone of the sect," it was "at once mystical, aphoristic [and] oracular," and their "style" was defined by "transposition, involution, a conciseness approaching obscurity."[27]

Of course, to this writer Emerson himself epitomized these characteristics, and it was no doubt he, too, whom Poe had in mind when he parodied "the tone transcendental": "Eschew . . . big words; get them as small as possible, and write them upside down. Look over Channing's poems and quote what he says about a 'fat little man with delusive show of Can.' Put in something about the Supernal Oneness. Don't say a syllable about the Infernal Twoness. Above all, study innuendo. Hint everything—assert nothing."[28] Few of the movement's earliest literary critics understood that, as Elizabeth Meese and Catherine Albanese argued later in the twentieth century, the Transcendentalists' style in particular best characterized the tension and resolution of ideas within their philosophical system.[29] But through the 1920s such insights were few, and Transcendentalism continued to be understood primarily as a philosophical movement in America's intellectual history.

This implicitly negative assessment of the Transcendentalists' literary accomplishment began to change in 1926 with the publication of Lewis Mumford's *The Golden Day*, a volume that marked an important expansion of studies of the individuals who participated in the New England Renaissance and in Transcendentalist literature as a whole. Like Santayana, Mumford regarded the Transcendentalists as expressing particularly American concerns in their literature, but his analysis of "The Morning Star" that rose over Concord and Boston in the 1840s suggested that, contrary to what Santayana and Brooks thought, the Transcendental mind contributed to a profound reinvigoration and extension of the American myths of progress, of which the literature of the American Renaissance was the most dynamic example. In the 1930s V. L. Parrington treated Transcendentalism similarly, as a moment of extreme expansiveness in Jacksonian America, and in 1941 F. O. Matthiessen, in his magisterial *American Renaissance,* worked from a similar premise, while providing what is still the finest account of the literary production of that period. These critics argued that, because America's finest writers were embedded solidly within the context of the movement—even if, like Hawthorne and Melville, they finally reacted against it—Transcendentalism and its literary fruits provided the greatest artistic feast in American literary history.[30]

Even as such wide-ranging critics as Mumford, Parrington, and Brooks were focusing their concentrated attention on the archetypally American qualities of the Transcendentalists, other scholars, not yet satisfied with reports of its rise and progress, investigated the notion that the movement was a many-faceted experiment whose shape, both in its indigenous and acquired characteristics, had not yet been definitively ascertained. As early as 1908 Harold C. Goddard's *Studies in New England Transcendentalism* dealt with just such problems, and in 1918 Woodbridge Riley, the dean of historians of American philosophy, published an essay distinguishing "Two Types of Transcendentalism in America," the French and the German.[31] Such critics—and later ones like Georges Joyaux and René Wellek—did not deny the peculiarly American flavor of Transcendentalist thought, but they did wish to settle definitively the mixture and measure of philosophical ingredients that provided its composition. More than a single-minded search after origins, at its best this scholarship provided historians and literary critics alike with better ways of comprehending the originality of the participants in the literary flowering of New England. Thus, even as recently as the 1960s Perry Miller claimed that "New England Transcendentalism will always signify the effect upon American provinciality of a European sophistication with which it was not entirely competent to deal," and this as he himself continued to give so many hours to an appreciation of the American Transcendentalists' contribution to the American mind.[32]

Moreover, after the syntheses of Mumford, Parrington, and Brooks, most studies of the movement—with the important exception of Matthiessen's *American Renaissance*—became increasingly particularized. Even as critics brought to their subject new insights and a sharp refinement of knowledge—Arthur Christy's *The Orient in American Transcendentalism* (1932) and Clarence Gohdes' *The Periodicals of American Transcendentalism* (1931) immediately come to mind—hardly any studies were truly synthetic, willing to embrace the Transcendentalists on their own terms to assess the lasting importance of their thought.[33] Rather, in the late 1930s and early 1940s, Transcendentalism became enshrined as a literary and historical artifact, worthy of study primarily in almost antiquarian terms. Thus we have such efforts as Zoltan Haraszti's *The Idyll of Brook Farm* (1937), Clarence Faust's "The Background of the Unitarian Opposition to Transcendentalism" (1938), and Lucile Gafford's "Transcendentalist Attitudes Toward Drama and the Theatre" (1940), all worthwhile studies, but not animated by the desire, as in Frothingham or Parrington, to describe affirmatively the larger significance of the movement.[34] A few studies of individual figures—Henry S. Commager's *Theodore Parker* (1936) and Arthur Schlesinger, Jr.'s *Orestes A. Brownson* (1939)—attempted to resurrect interest in the primary subject of Transcendental Idealism during the depths of the Depression, but the movement as a whole suffered from a neglect that originated in a concern with more apparently relevant subjects like proletarian literature and the social fiction produced in those troubled decades.[35]

Since World War II studies of Transcendentalism have been marked by an increased willingness to attempt just what was neglected in the 1930s, to take the movement on its own merits and in so doing to break down the walls of convention that had prevented investigation of certain topics with which Transcendentalists had been concerned but which did not necessarily dovetail with contemporary scholarly interests. Most successful here have been those studies that have explored how the movement drew upon and itself provided nourishment for other significant developments in American intellectual history. Thus, for example, the work of William R. Hutchison on the relationship of Transcendentalism to church reform (1959) and Lawrence Buell's related studies of the linkage of Unitarian and Transcendentalist theology and aesthetics to larger questions within American Romanticism (1972) have paved the way for an understanding of the Transcendentalists' role in the liberalization of the American Protestant tradition.[36] Then, too, essays like Charles R. Crowe's " 'This Unnatural Union of Phalansteries and Transcendentalists' " (1959), Richard Francis' "The Ideology of Brook Farm" (1979), and Duane E. Smith's "Romanticism in America: The Transcendentalists" (1973) have allowed scholars to assess the paradoxical nature of the movement's radical demands for America's social rehabilitation.[37] Caught between a desire to maintain the primacy of the individual's sacred rights of conscience and their equally powerful wish for an America based on full social justice, the Transcendentalists now can be understood as playing out roles that American liberals continue to assume as they wrestle with similar problems.

Another important result of the post-war generation's willingness to investigate the Transcendentalists' thought in its full complexity has been the increase in studies that have explained more fully the aesthetic renovation of American literature that the group had proclaimed as part of its agenda. Unlike the first tentative efforts to define and assess the Transcendentalist aesthetic, many of which partook more of ridicule or skepticism than comprehension, some recent studies have focused on the Transcendentalists' almost obsessive concern with language and its relationship to both philosophy and literary style. Hence, the two important essays on the subject that appeared in 1975—Elizabeth A. Meese's "Transcendentalism: The Metaphysics of the Theme" and Catherine Albanese's "The Kinetic Revolution: Transformation in the Language of the Transcendentalists"—provoke critics to take more seriously the complex development of an aesthetic that derived from the Transcendentalists' important philosophical positions.[38] Other essays like John T. Irwin's "The Symbol of the Hieroglyphics in the American Renaissance" and Philip F. Gura's "The Transcendentalists and Language: The Unitarian Exegetical Background," open areas of inquiry regarding the Transcendentalists' interests in establishing through their language theory a response to the nineteenth-century philologists' disturbing challenge to hitherto sacrosanct notions of logocentricity.[39] Though implied in such pioneering work as Charles Feidelson's *Symbolism and American Literature* (1953), the uniqueness of the Transcendentalists' exploration of the larger questions of language and meaning that confronted their contemporaries only now are beginning to receive the attention they deserve.[40]

A word remains to be said about the best overviews of the movement, for if the middle- and late-twentieth century has seen a progressively more sophisticated understanding of the various facets of Transcendentalism, on occasion some commentators have risen to the standard earlier established by such works as Ellis's *An Essay on Transcendentalism* (1842), Frothingham's *Transcendentalism in New England* (1876), and Goddard's *Studies in New England Transcendentalism* (1908), and have been able to assimilate and synthesize the best current scholarship about the movement. Alexander Kern's "The Rise of Transcendentalism, 1815–1860" is worthy of inclusion in this company, and in its entirety his essay, too lengthy to reprint here, remains perhaps the best introduction to this complex phase of American thought. Equally informative is George Hochfield's "New England Transcendentalism," an essay included in Marcus Cunliffe's *American Literature to 1900* (1973), and which may be read profitably with Hochfield's introduction to his edition of Transcendentalist writings, *The Transcendentalists* (1966). In their pages both these essays capture not only the essence, but also the rich variety of ideas and personalities that contributed to this colorful moment in America's cultural history. Among other, larger, attempts to describe the movement, none comes close to approaching Perry Miller's *The Transcendentalists: An Anthology* (1950), a rich volume whose headnotes to its various selections of and about the Transcendentalists remain the most penetrating introduction to the movement. While we still lack a companion for the early nineteenth century to Miller's *The New England Mind: From Colony to Province*, it is no exaggeration to say that a significant portion of such a study is outlined in this splendid anthology.[41]

Despite one hundred forty years of commentary upon it, then, the Transcendentalist movement seems assured of receiving even more attention, a fact attested to by the impending publication of *The Transcendentalists: A Guide to Research and Criticism*, edited by Joel Myerson and supported by the Modern Language Association. And, if the most recent essays in this collection are any indication, we may look forward not so much to studies that center on the background to and sources of the movement, but to more subtle analyses of the relationships among both the movement's members themselves and their theological, philosophical, and literary formulations. Despite the important work of William Hutchison, for example, we still know too little about Transcendentalism's impact on ministers who remained within the Unitarian faith; or, to cite another example, how the emergence of novel conceptions of language and meaning affected not only the movement's literary productions, but also its members' response to the epistemological crisis within American Protestantism.

We also can anticipate more detailed studies of second and third generation Transcendentalists, those men and women who grew up in the luxurious shade of Emerson, Parker, Ripley, and other charismatic leaders of the first generation, but who themselves witnessed, and, in some cases, participated in, the gradual eclipse of the Transcendental mind. As yet, for example, we have no thorough analysis of how Transcendentalism devolved into the sentimentality of the Genteel Tradition, nor of the kinds of resistance the movement's sons and grandsons encountered as they tried to preach its optimism in the face of those who believed in an ethic of social darwinism and material progress. By 1917 a new class of intellectuals began to explain America to itself, but between the Civil War and the onslaught of modernism in art, literature, and politics, the Transcendentalists maintained a visible, if often wraithlike, presence, one which we must strive to illuminate. Contrary to many popular accounts, Transcendentalism did not cease to exist after the national trauma of the 1860s, and it well may be that in those later years of the nineteenth century we will discover the true extent of the movement's influence on, and the truth of its criticism of, American thought. Its literary and philosophical currents well-charted, it is time to learn what we can about Transcendentalism's lesson for the proper organization of our social priorities.

Because of its general complexity—including the wide range of literary, philosophic, and religious interests it embodied, as well as the varied backgrounds and concerns of its members—the Transcendentalist movement has not encouraged the writing of a single work covering its multi-faceted history. As a result, most studies of the movement tend to deal with individual aspects of it. The following bibliographical essay selectively presents those books and articles which the editors consider to be the more helpful in studying American Transcendentalism.

Movements, unlike authors, do not generate editions of "collected works." There are, however, four general anthologies of writings by the Transcendentalists. The best is Perry Miller's *The Transcendentalists: An Anthology* (Cambridge: Harvard University Press, 1950), a selection of the essential documents by those both for and against the Transcendentalists, arranged topically with informative and often opinionated headnotes. Miller's shorter anthology, *The American Transcendentalists: Their Prose and Poetry* (Garden City, N.Y.: Doubleday, 1957), and George Hochfield's *Selected Writings of the American Transcendentalists* (New York: New American Library, 1966), are also useful. More selective, but still of value, is *The Poets of Transcendentalism,* ed. George Willis Cooke (Boston: Houghton, Mifflin, 1903).

There is no single bibliography of Transcendentalism. Theresa Layton Hall, "A Bibliography of the New England Transcendental Movement," M.A. thesis, Columbia University, 1929, is an ambitious attempt to list the writings by and about the members of the movement, but is of course now outdated. Although lacking focus, its wide scope does pick up a number of items not listed in other works. The Modern Language Association is currently preparing *The Transcendentalists: A Review of Research and Criticism,* ed. Joel Myerson, for publication, but until it appears students of Transcendentalism will have to go to a number of sources for their bibliographical information.

For writings by the Transcendentalists, one should consult *Bibliography of American Literature,* ed. Jacob Blanck, 6 vols. to date (New Haven: Yale University Press, 1955–), *First Printings of American Authors,* ed. Matthew J. Bruccoli et al., 4 vols. to date (Detroit: Gale, 1977–), *Literary Writings in America: A Bibliography,* 8 vols. (Millwood, N.Y.: KTO Press, 1977), and the *National Union Catalog of Pre-1956 Imprints.* The most convenient source for locating manuscripts by the Transcendentalists is *American Literary Manuscripts,* 2d ed., ed. J. Albert Robbins (Athens: University of Georgia Press, 1977).

For writings about Transcendentalism, the three volumes of *Articles in American Literature,* edited by Lewis Leary and covering the periods 1900–1950, 1950–1967, and 1968–1975 (Durham: Duke University Press, 1954, 1970, 1979), are essential starting points, and should be supplemented by the essays on "Emerson, Thoreau, Transcendentalism" in the annual *American Literary Scholarship* (Durham: Duke University Press, 1965–), the quarterly bibliography in *American Literature,* and the annual bibliographies in *PMLA* and *Studies in the American Renaissance.* A useful source for locating contemporary responses is Daniel A. Wells, *The Literary Index to American Magazines, 1815–1865* (Metuchen, N.J.: Scarecrow, 1980).

There are two collections of reprinted essays on Transcendentalism, both hampered in their usefulness by limitations of space: *The Transcendentalist Revolt Against Materialism,* ed. George F. Whicher

(Boston: D. C. Heath, 1949; rev. ed. as *The Transcendentalist Revolt,* ed. Whicher and Gail Kennedy [Boston: D. C. Heath, 1968]), and *American Transcendentalism: An Anthology of Criticism,* ed. Brian M. Barbour (Notre Dame: University of Notre Dame Press, 1973), which also contains a good bibliography. The original articles in *Transcendentalism and Its Legacy,* ed. Myron Simon and Thornton H. Parsons (Ann Arbor: University of Michigan Press, 1966), and *The Minor and Later Transcendentalists,* ed. Edwin Gittleman (Hartford, Conn.: Transcendental Books, 1969), are of varying quality, and are more often concerned with a single author than with the movement as a whole. The numerous compilations by Kenneth Walter Cameron, published by Transcendental Books, are also a useful if diffuse body of reprintings of contemporary writings on Transcendentalism.

With few general studies of Transcendentalism available (to be discussed below), it is important to consider what the movement's participants and contemporaries wrote about it. The essential documents of the 1836–1844 period are assembled in Miller's *The Transcendentalists.* Probably the most valuable works by participants are Ralph Waldo Emerson's 1842 lecture, "The Transcendentalist" (collected in *Nature; Addresses, and Lectures* [1849]), and "Historic Notes on Life and Letters in Massachusetts," *Atlantic Monthly Magazine,* 52 (October 1883), 529–543 (collected in *Lectures and Biographical Sketches* [1884]); Caroline Dall, *Margaret and Her Friends* (Boston: Roberts Brothers, 1895), an eyewitness account of a "Conversation"; *Memoirs of Margaret Fuller Ossoli,* ed. Emerson, William Henry Channing, and James Freeman Clarke, 2 vols. (Boston: Phillips, Sampson, 1852); Theodore Parker's *Experience as a Minister* (Boston: Rufus Leighton, Jr., 1859), and *Transcendentalism: A Lecture* (Boston: Free Religious Association, 1876); and George Ripley and George P. Bradford, "Philosophic Thought in Boston," in *The Memorial History of Boston,* ed. Justin Winsor, 4 vols. (Boston: Ticknor, 1881), IV, 295–330.

Works by participants and sympathizers which comment on Transcendentalism include: Cyrus Bartol, "Transcendentalism," *Radical Problems* (Boston: Roberts Brothers, 1872), pp. 61–97; Caroline Dall, *Transcendentalism: A Lecture* (Boston: Roberts Brothers, 1897), an interesting feminist view of the movement; Charles Mayo Ellis, *An Essay on Transcendentalism* (Boston: Crocker and Ruggles, 1842), a good contemporary detailed explanation of Transcendentalism; Cornelius C. Felton, "Modern Transcendentalism," *Knickerbocker,* 17 (June 1841), 469–475; Octavius Brooks Frothingham, "Some Phases of Idealism in New England," *Atlantic Monthly Magazine,* 52 (July 1883), 13–23; William B. Greene, *Transcendentalism* (West Brookfield, Mass.: Oliver Cooke, 1849), revised as "New-England Transcendentalism," *Blazing Star* (Boston: A. Williams, 1872), pp. 145–180; Frederic Henry Hedge, "The

Destinies of Ecclesiastical Religion," *Christian Examiner,* 82 (January 1867), 1–15; Samuel Johnson "Transcendentalism," *Radical Review,* 1 (November 1877), 447–478, and reprinted in his *Essays, Lectures, and Sermons* (Boston: Houghton, Mifflin, 1883), pp. 416–460; Charles Lane, "Transatlantic Transcendentalism," *Union* [England], 1 (1 August 1842), 166–168; F. B. Sanborn, *Recollections of Seventy Years,* 2 vols. (Boston: Richard G. Badger, 1909), and his numerous columns in the *Springfield Republican* and other contemporary newspapers and periodicals, which are being collected by Kenneth Walter Cameron in a series of reprints from Transcendental Books; and J. A. Saxton, "Prophecy—Transcendentalism—Progress," *Dial,* 2 (July 1841), 83–121, an account praised by its contemporary readers.

Particularly useful comments by other contemporaries, not all favorable, are: Alden Bradford, *An Address Delivered . . . in Bowdoin College, September 2, 1841* (Boston: S. G. Simpkins, 1841), subtitled "Historical Learning Favourable to true Religion: But the Transcendental Theory hostile to the Christian Revelation"; George W. Burnap, "Transcendentalism," *Monthly Religious Magazine,* 3 (February 1846), 66–71; Joseph Cook, "After Emerson, What? or, the Consequences of Concord Theism," *The Boston Monday Lectures. Ninth Series* (London: R. D. Dickinson, n.d.), pp. 1–13, and *Transcendentalism, With Preludes on Current Events* (Boston: James R. Osgood, 1878), both conservative attacks on the lingering effects of the movement; Charles Dickens, *American Notes* (1842); Simeon Doggett, *A Sermon on Transcendentalism* (Taunton, Mass.: J. W. D. Hall, 1843), mainly an attack on Parker; Evert A. Duyckinck, "Bad News for Transcendental Poets," *Literary World,* 1 (20 February 1847), 53; J. E. G., "The Latterlights and Their Progeny: or Doings in the City of the Savans," *Knickerbocker,* 17 (June 1841), 499–506; Nathaniel Hawthorne, "The Celestial Railroad," *United States Magazine, and Democratic Review,* 12 (May 1843), 515–523, and "Hall of Fantasy," *Pioneer,* 1 (February 1843), 49–55; James Kennard, Jr., "What is Transcendentalism?," *Knickerbocker,* 23 (March 1844), 205–211; J. M. Manning, "Pantheism in the Form of Self-Worship," *Half Truths and the Truth* (Boston: Lee and Shepard, 1872), pp. 268–361; James Murdock, "American Transcendentalism," *Sketches of Modern Philosophy* (Hartford, Conn.: John C. Wells, 1842), pp. 167–188; Theophilus Parsons, "Transcendentalism," *New Jerusalem Magazine,* 14 (December 1840, June 1841)), 137–140, 380–388; Enoch Pond, "Pantheism," *American Biblical Repository,* 3d ser., 6 (April 1850), 243–272; James Porter, *Three Lectures on . . . Come-Out-Ism, as Connected with Non-Resistance, Transcendentalism, The Old Massachusetts Anti-Slavery Society . . . Shewing By Numerous Facts That It Is Infidelity* (Boston: Reid and Rand, 1844; rev. ed. as *Modern Infidelity, Alias Come-Out-Ism, As Taught by Ultra Non-Resistants, Transcendentalists, Garrisonians, and*

Other Revolutionists [Boston: Waite and Peirce, 1845]); Noah Porter, Jr., "Transcendentalism," *American Biblical Repository*, n.s. 8 (July 1842), 195–218; Merrill Richardson, "A Plain Discussion with a Transcendentalist," *New Englander*, 1 (October 1843), 502–516; J. E. Snodgrass, "Transcendentalism. A Miniature Essay," *Magnolia*, 4 (April 1842), 214–215; William Silsbee, "The Transcendental Doctrine of Self-Reliance," *Christian Examiner*, 37 (November 1844), 331–349, and Alfred S. Rosa, " 'Aesthetic Culture': A Lyceum Lecture by William Silsbee," *Essex Institute Historical Collections*, 107 (January 1971), 35–61; Giles B. Stebbins, "Transcendentalism," *Upward Steps of Seventy Years* (New York: United States Book Company, 1890), pp. 51–71; Moses George Thomas, *A Rejected Article* (Boston: Benjamin H. Greene, 1844), an attack on Parker; James B. Walker, *Philosophy of Skepticism and Ultraism* (New York: Derby and Jackson, 1857); and Daniel Whitaker, "Transcendentalism," *Southern Quarterly Review*, 2 (October 1842), 437–471, a review of the first two volumes of the *Dial*. An examination of the response to one Transcendentalist work is Joel Myerson, " 'In the Transcendental Emporium': Bronson Alcott's 'Orphic Sayings' in the *Dial*," *English Language Notes*, 10 (September 1972), 31–38.

The first book-length study of Transcendentalism was by a contemporary of the movement: Octavius Brooks Frothingham's *Transcendentalism in New England: A History* (New York: Putnams, 1876) has moments of insight but is too unfocused to be truly satisfactory. Three reviews of this book place it in its historical context: Isaac Hecker, "The Transcendental Movement in New England," *Catholic World*, 23 (July 1876), 528–537; Samuel Osgood, "Transcendentalism in New England," *International Review*, 3 (November 1876), 742–763; and Henry Holbeach, "Transcendentalism in England, New England, and India," *Contemporary Review*, 29 (February 1877), 469–488. Harold Clarke Goddard's *Studies in New England Transcendentalism* (New York: Columbia University Press, 1908) surveys the major figures of Transcendentalism but is disappointing in its comments on the movement in general.

Nearly half a century later, Alexander Kern examined "The Rise of Transcendentalism, 1815–1860," in *Transitions in American Literary History*, ed. Harry Hayden Clark (Durham: Duke University Press, 1954), pp. 245–314. Kern's excellent essay identifies the figures in the movement and examines in depth its major literary, philosophic, and religious concerns. It is an essential starting point for the study of Transcendentalism. Hochfield's introduction to *Selected Writings of the American Transcendentalists* and his revised "New England Transcendentalism," in *American Literature to 1900*, ed. Marcus Cunliffe (London: Barrie and Jenkins, 1973), pp. 160–196, are fine critical overviews of the movement. Longer but less satisfactory are Nathaniel Kaplan and Thomas

Natsaros, *Origins of American Transcendentalism in Philosophy and Mysticism* (New Haven: College and University Press, 1975), a rambling study of sources, and two general and somewhat skimpy introductory works: Paul E. Boller, *American Transcendentalism, 1830–1860: An Intellectual Inquiry* (New York: Putnams, 1974), and Donald N. Koster, *Transcendentalism in America* (Boston: Twayne, 1975). Three dissertations are also of use: John Byron Wilson, "Activities of the New England Transcendentalists in the Dissemination of Culture," University of North Carolina, 1941; Lawrence Charles Porter, "New England Transcendentalism: A Self-Portrait," University of Michigan, 1964; and Anne Carver Rose, "Transcendentalism as a Social Movement, 1830–1850," Yale University, 1979.

A number of articles try to survey the entire movement. Those of some value are Edward Dowden, "The Transcendental Movement and Literature," *Contemporary Review*, 30 (July 1877), 297–318, and reprinted in his *Studies in Literature 1799–1877* (London: Kegan Paul, Trench, Trübner, 1909), pp. 44–84; John Orr, "The Transcendentalism of New England," *International Review*, 13 (October 1882), 381–398; Annie Wall, "Early Transcendentalism in New England," *New England Magazine*, 5 (December 1886), 162–170; Francis Tiffany, "Transcendentalism: The New England Renaissance," *Unitarian Review*, 31 (February 1889), 97–117 (rpt. in *Unitarianism: Its Origins and History* [Boston: American Unitarian Association, 1890], pp. 196–219); Louis James Block, "Thoughts on the Transcendental Movement in New England," *New England Magazine*, 15 (January 1897), 564–570; Woodbridge Riley, "Two Types of Transcendentalism in America," *Journal of Philosophy*, 15 (23 May 1918), 281–292; Frederic I. Carpenter, "The Transcendental Dream," *American Literature and the Dream* (New York: Philosophical Library, 1955), pp. 11–18; Chester E. Eisinger, "Transcendentalism—Its Effect Upon American Literature and Democracy," in *The American Renaissance*, ed. George Hendrick (Berlin: Verlag Moritz Diesterweg, 1961), pp. 22–38; and Elizabeth A. Meese, "Transcendentalism: The Metaphysics of the Theme," *American Literature*, 47 (March 1975), 1–20. Other articles, of little or no value, but which appear in bibliographies and must therefore be warned about, are Charles A. Ingraham, "Transcendentalism," *Americana*, 15 (April 1921), 169–181; V. Krishnamachari, "Transcendentalism in America," *Calcutta Review*, 116 (June 1950), 10–27; C. D. Narasimhaiah, "Transcendentalism in American Literature: An Introductory Essay," *Literary Criterion*, 5 (Winter 1962), 48–65; Georg Friden, "Transcendental Idealism in New England," *Neuphilologische Mitteilungen*, 69 (June 1968), 256–271; and S. P. Das, "Beginnings of American Transcendentalism," *Indian Journal of American Studies*, 1 (July 1970), 15–22.

Transcendentalism occupies a prominent position in histories of

American literature. Some of the more valuable are Evert A. and George L. Duyckinck, *Cyclopædia of American Literature*, 2 vols. (New York: Scribner, 1855), the closest we have to a literary history from this early period; John Nichol, *American Literature: An Historical Sketch 1620–1880* (Edinburgh: Adam and Charles Black, 1882), pp. 254–286, an early if unsympathetic foreign appraisal; Fred Lewis Pattee, *A History of American Literature* (New York: Silver, Burdett, 1896), pp. 208–238, more of a listing of members than an interpretation of the movement; Donald G. Mitchell, *American Lands and Letters: Leather-Stocking to Poe's "Raven"* (New York: Scribners, 1899), an anecdotal account; Barrett Wendell, *A Critical History of American Literature* (New York: Scribners, 1900), pp. 290–310, an informed though not completely sympathetic account; William P. Trent, *A History of American Literature* (New York: D. Appleton, 1903), pp. 285–348; Harold Clarke Goddard, "Transcendentalism," in *The Cambridge History of American Literature*, ed. William Peterfield Trent et al., 3 vols. (New York: Macmillan, 1917), I, 326–348, an excellent early work; Bliss Perry, *The American Spirit in Literature* (New Haven: Yale University Press, 1918), pp. 109–142; Vernon Lewis Parrington, *The Romantic Revolution in America 1800–1860* (New York: Harcourt, Brace, 1927), pp. 379–434, especially good on the social orientation of Transcendentalism; V. F. Calverton, *The Liberation of American Literature* (New York: Scribners, 1932), a socialist study; Grant C. Knight, *American Literature and Culture* (New York: Ray Long and Richard R. Smith, 1932), pp. 171–224, a bemused look; Ludwig Lewisohn, *Expression in America* (New York: Harpers, 1932), pp. 105–152, a psychoanalytic overview; Stanley T. Williams, *American Literature* (Philadelphia: J. B. Lippincott, 1933), pp. 53–76; F. O. Matthiessen, *American Renaissance: Art and Expression in the Age of Emerson and Whitman* (New York: Oxford University Press, 1941), the first look at Transcendentalism by a "new critic"; Randall Stewart, *American Literature and Christian Doctrine* (Baton Rouge: Louisiana State University Press, 1958), a late unsympathetic approach; and Leon Howard, *Literature and the American Tradition* (Garden City, N.Y.: Doubleday, 1960), pp. 136–166. Of help in evaluating the history of histories of American literature is Richard Ruland, *The Rediscovery of American Literature: Premises of Critical Taste, 1900–1940* (Cambridge: Harvard University Press, 1967).

Other studies of Transcendentalism tend to focus more upon particular aspects of the movement, especially as they relate to similar developments in American philosophy, religion, social history, and literature.

The philosophic underpinnings of Transcendentalism have long been recognized and studied. General histories of philosophy which have good sections on Transcendentalism are Woodbridge Riley, *Amer-*

ican Thought: From Puritanism to Pragmatism and Beyond (New York: Henry Holt, 1915), pp. 140–171; Kenyon Rogers, English and American Philosophy Since 1800 (New York: Macmillan, 1922), pp. 207–219; Herbert W. Schneider, A History of American Philosophy (New York: Columbia University Press, 1946), pp. 259–318; Joseph L. Blau, Men and Movements in American Philosophy (Englewood Cliffs, N.J.: Prentice-Hall, 1952), pp. 110–150; and Elizabeth Flower and Murray G. Murphey, A History of Philosophy in America, 2 vols. (New York: Putnams, 1977), I, 397–435. Particular aspects of Transcendentalist thought are dealt with in Clarence Gohdes, "Aspects of Idealism in Early New England," Philosophical Review, 39 (November 1930), 537–555; Herbert W. Schneider, "American Transcendentalism's Escape from Phenomenology," in Transcendentalism and Its Legacy, ed. Simon and Parsons, pp. 215–228; Edward H. Madden, Civil Disobedience and Moral Law in Nineteenth-Century American Philosophy (Seattle: University of Washington Press, 1968), pp. 85–102; Morton White, "Transcendentalism: 'Hallelujah to the Reason Forever More,'" Science and Sentiment in America (New York: Oxford University Press, 1972), pp. 71–96; Everett Carter, The American Idea: The Literary Response to American Optimism (Chapel Hill: University of North Carolina Press, 1977); and Merle Curti, "The Romantic Impulse," Human Nature in American Thought: A History (Madison: University of Wisconsin Press, 1980), pp. 148–185.

Because nearly all the Transcendentalists were ministers, the religious backgrounds of the movement have been studied in detail. Early studies often mistook Transcendentalism to be its own religion, rather than in its true relation as a dissenting faction of Unitarianism; fortunately, later studies have restored a proper perspective. The best overview of religion in America is Sydney E. Ahlstrom, A Religious History of the American People (New Haven: Yale University Press, 1972). Useful histories of American Unitarianism include Unitarianism: Its Origins and History (Boston: American Unitarian Association, 1890); Joseph Henry Allen and Richard Eddy, A History of the Unitarians and the Universalists in the United States (New York: Christian Literature Company, 1894), pp. 195–246; George Willis Cooke, Unitarianism in America (Boston: American Unitarian Association, 1902); Conrad Wright, The Beginnings of Unitarianism in America (Boston: Starr King Press, 1955); and A Stream of Light: A Sesquicentennial History of American Unitarianism, ed. Conrad Wright (Boston: Beacon Press, 1975), especially the chapter by Daniel Walker Howe, pp. 33–61. Specialized studies of nineteenth-century Unitarianism of use are Jane Maloney Johnson, " 'Through Change and Through Storm': A Study of Federalist-Unitarian Thought, 1800–1860," Ph.D. dissertation, Radcliffe College, 1958; Daniel Walker Howe, The Unitarian Conscience: Harvard Moral Philosophy, 1805–1861 (Cambridge: Harvard University Press, 1970), a brilliant interpretation of the times; and Douglas C. Stange, *Patterns of Antislavery Among the American Unitarians, 1831–1860* (Rutherford, N.J.: Fairleigh Dickinson University Press, 1970). Unitarianism is placed within the context of contemporary religious reform in Ralph H. Gabriel, "Evangelical Religion and Popular Romanticism in Early Nineteenth-Century America," *Church History*, 19 (March 1950), 34–47, and Timothy L. Smith, *Revivalism and Social Reform in Mid-Nineteenth-Century America* (New York: Abington Press, 1957). Biographies of contemporary Unitarians (including Transcendentalists) are in *Heralds of a Liberal Faith*, ed. Samuel A. Eliot, 3 vols. (Boston: American Unitarian Association, 1910), especially volume three. A number of hymns by Transcendentalists are included in *Singers and Songs of the Liberal Faith*, ed. Alfred P. Putnam (Boston: Roberts Brothers, 1874). Transcendentalism's influence on later Unitarianism can be traced in the Free Religious Association's *Freedom and Fellowship in Religion* (Boston: Roberts Brothers, 1875); George Willis Cooke, "The Free Religious Association," *New England Magazine*, n.s. 28 (June 1903), 484–499; Raymond Bennett Bragg, "Principles and Purposes of the Free Religious Association," B.Div. thesis, Meadville Theological School, 1930; and Stow Persons, *Free Religion: An American Faith* (New Haven: Yale University Press, 1947). Two general studies are also of value: Rod W. Horton and Herbert W. Edwards, *Backgrounds of American Literary Thought* (New York: Appleton-Century-Crofts, 1952), pp. 108–121, briefly outlines the similarities and differences between Unitarianism and Transcendentalism; Lawrence Buell, "The Unitarian Movement and the Art of Preaching in 19th-Century America," *American Quarterly*, 24 (May 1972), 166–190, provides solid background on what for most of the Transcendentalists was the first literary form to which they were formally exposed.

The rift between the Unitarians and the Transcendentalists is documented in Miller's *The Transcendentalists*. An important discussion of the subject is C. H. Faust, "The Background of the Unitarian Opposition to Transcendentalism," *Modern Philology*, 35 (February 1938), 297–324. An absolutely essential work is William R. Hutchison, *The Transcendentalist Ministers: Church Reform in the New England Renaissance* (New Haven: Yale University Press, 1959), an insightful and lucid discussion of the Unitarian-Transcendentalist controversy. Also of use are the chapters on "The Transcendental Pattern of Religious Liberalism" in *American Christianity*, ed. H. Shelton Smith, Robert T. Handy, and Lefferts A. Loetscher, 2 vols. (New York: Scribners, 1963), II, 119–166, and Jerry Wayne Brown's solid study of *The Rise of Biblical Criticism in America 1800–1870: The New England Scholars* (Middletown, Conn.: Wesleyan University Press, 1969). Valuable memoirs of the Unitarian-Transcendentalist period by contemporaries are Joseph Henry Allen,

Our Liberal Movement in Theology (Boston: Roberts Brothers, 1882); Octavius Brooks Frothingham, *Boston Unitarianism 1820–1850* (New York: Putnams, 1890) and *Recollections and Impressions 1822–1890* (New York: Putnams, 1891); and Joseph Henry Allen, *Sequel to "Our Liberal Movement"* (Boston: Roberts Brothers, 1897).

More specialized studies of Transcendentalism and religion are Henry G. Fairbanks, "Theocracy to Transcendentalism in America," *Emerson Society Quarterly*, no. 44 (3d Quarter 1966), 45–58; F. S. Darrow, "The Transcendentalists and Theosophy," *New Outlook*, 11 (March 1958), 9–18, an interesting if all too brief comparison of the writings of the two groups; Harriet Elizabeth Knight, "Two Streams of Mysticism in America: Quakerism and Transcendentalism," M.A. thesis, Columbia University, 1929, and Stephanie Ann Reeck, "Transcendentalism and Quakerism," M.A. thesis, University of Washington, 1970; Sister Mary Helena Sanfilippo, "The New England Transcendentalists' Opinions on the Catholic Church," Ph.D. dissertation, University of Notre Dame, 1972; James R. Hodges, "Christian Science and Transcendentalism: A Comparative Study," M.A. thesis, Vanderbilt University, 1942; and Frank Sewell, "The New Church and the New-England Transcendentalists," *New Church Review*, 10 (October 1903), 535–539, a skimpy treatment of Swedenborgianism.

Transcendentalism gained momentum in a period of American history marked by the rise of the common man and a general interest in reforms of all kinds. Not surprisingly, then, there were many social manifestations of Transcendentalism, some of which are discussed in Rose's "Transcendentalism as a Social Movement." Good bibliographies of the period are *Harvard Guide to American History*, 2d ed., ed. Frank Freidel, 2 vols. (Cambridge: Harvard University Press, 1974), and Gerald N. Grob, *American Social History Before 1860* (New York: Appleton-Century-Crofts, 1970).

Works which help modern readers to understand American life during the Transcendental period are Carl Russell Fish, *The Rise of the Common Man 1830–1850* (New York: Macmillan, 1927); Gilbert Seldes, *The Stammering Century* (New York: John Day, 1928); Van Wyck Brooks, *The Flowering of New England 1815–1865* (New York: E. P. Dutton, 1936); Ralph Henry Gabriel, *The Course of American Democratic Thought: An Intellectual History Since 1815* (New York: Ronald Press, 1940); Alice Felt Tyler, *Freedom's Ferment* (Minneapolis: University of Minnesota Press, 1944), pp. 47–67; Arthur M. Schlesinger, Jr., *The Age of Jackson* (Boston: Little, Brown, 1945); Robert E. Riegel, *Young America 1830–1840* (Norman: University of Oklahoma Press, 1949); Harvey Wish, *Science and Thought in Early America* (New York: Longmans, Green, 1950); Martin L. Abbott, "Historical and Social Backgrounds of the American Renaissance II.—Jacksonian Democracy," in *The American Renaissance*, ed. Hendrick, pp. 64–76; Irving H. Bartlett, *The American Mind in the Mid-Nineteenth Century* (New York: Thomas Y. Crowell, 1967); Jerome L. Clark, *1844*, 3 vols. (Nashville: Southern Publishing Association, 1968); Edward Pessen, *Jacksonian America: Society, Personality, and Politics* (Homewood, Ill.: Dorsey Press, 1969); Russel Blaine Nye, *Society and Culture in America 1830–1860* (New York: Harpers, 1974); and Rush Welter, *The Mind of America 1820–1860* (New York: Columbia University Press, 1975). Amusing anecdotal histories are Meade Minnegerode, *The Fabulous Forties 1840–1850* (Garden City, N.Y.: Garden City Publishing Company, 1924); E. Douglas Branch, *The Sentimental Years 1836–1860* (New York: D. Appleton-Century, 1934); Fred Lewis Pattee, *The Feminine Fifties* (New York: D. Appleton-Century, 1940); and Grace Adams and Edward Hutter, *The Mad Forties* (New York: Harpers, 1942). An interesting collection of documents is in *American Life in the 1840s*, ed. Carl Bode (Garden City, N.Y.: Doubleday, 1967). A good sense of the reform-mindedness of the period can be seen in Wendell Phillips Garrison, "The Isms of Forty Years Ago," *Harper's New Monthly Magazine*, 60 (January 1880), 182–192; Martin L. Abbott, "Historical and Social Backgrounds of the American Renaissance I.–The Generation of Reform," in *The American Renaissance*, ed. Hendrick, pp. 52–63; Lawrence Lader, *The Bold Brahmins: New England's War Against Slavery: 1831–1863* (New York: E. P. Dutton, 1961); *The Antislavery Argument*, ed. William H. and Jane H. Pease (Indianapolis: Bobbs-Merrill, 1965); John L. Thomas, "Romantic Reform in America, 1815–1865," *American Quarterly*, 17 (Winter 1965), 656–681; C. S. Griffin, *The Ferment of Reform, 1830–1860* (New York: Thomas Y. Crowell, 1967); Jane H. and William H. Pease, *Bound Them in Chains: A Biographical History of the Antislavery Movement* (Westport, Conn.: Greenwood, 1972); Charles A. Barker, *American Convictions: Cycles of Public Thought* (Philadelphia: J. B. Lippincott, 1973), pp. 495–532; *The Perfectionists: Radical Social Thought in the North, 1815–1860*, ed. Laurence Veysey (New York: John Wiley, 1973); and Stephen Nissenbaum, *Sex, Diet, and Debility in Jacksonian America: Sylvester Graham and Health Reform* (Westport, Conn.: Greenwood, 1980). For the rise of science, see Herbert Hovenkamp, *Science and Religion in America 1800–1860* (Philadelphia: University of Pennsylvania Press, 1978). The fine arts are discussed in Neil Harris, "Art and Transcendentalism," *The Artist in American Society: The Formative Years, 1790–1860* (New York: George Braziller, 1966), pp. 170–186. Other useful background studies are Arthur Hobson Quinn, "American Literature and American Politics," *Proceedings of the American Antiquarian Society*, 54 (April 1944), part 1, 59–112; Richard D. Mosier, *The American Temper: Patterns of Our Intellectual Heritage* (Berkeley: University of California Press, 1952), esp. "The Transcendental Temper," pp. 159–170; Carl Bode, *The American Lyceum: Town Meeting of the Mind* (New York: Oxford University Press, 1956); Aaron Kramer, *The Prophetic Tradition in American Poetry* (Rutherford, N.J.: Fairleigh Dickinson University Press, 1968), a catalogue of poetic responses to current events; Russel Nye, *The Unembarrassed Muse: The Popular Arts in America* (New York: Dial Press, 1970); and Donald S. Spencer, *Louis Kossuth and Young America: A Study of Sectionalism and Foreign Policy 1848–1852* (Columbia: University of Missouri Press, 1977).

The Transcendentalists responded to much within this labyrinth of social movements and reforms. Some idea of the diversity of this response can be seen in William Girard, "Du Transcendentalisme Considere Sous Sons Aspect Social," *University of California Publications in Modern Philology*, 8 (6 August 1918), 153–226; George M. Frederickson, *The Inner Civil War* (New York: Harpers, 1965); Robert C. Albrecht, "The Theological Response of the Transcendentalists to the Civil War," *New England Quarterly*, 38 (March 1965), 21–34; Saul Lerner, "History, Progress and Perfectability in Nineteenth-Century American Transcendentalist Thought," Ph.D. dissertation, University of Kansas, 1966; David Herreshoff, "Marx and the Transcendentalists," *American Disciples of Marx* (Detroit: Wayne State University Press, 1967), pp. 11–30 (rpt. as *The Origins of American Marxism from the Transcendentalists to De Leon* [New York: Pathfinder Press, 1973]); Daniel Aaron, *The Unwritten War* (New York: Alfred A. Knopf, 1973), pp. 4–38; Taylor Stoehr, "Transcendentalist Attitudes Toward Communitism and Individualism," *ESQ: A Journal of the American Renaissance*, 20 (2d Quarter 1974), 65–90; A. Robert Caponigri, "Individual, Civil Society, and State in American Transcendentalism," in *American Philosophy from Edwards to Quine*, ed. Robert W. Shahan and Kenneth R. Merrill (Norman: University of Oklahoma Press, 1977), pp. 49-77; and Yves Carlet, " 'Respectables iniquites': le transcendentalisme et l'ordre social," *Revue Francaise d'Etudes Americaines*, 3 (April 1978), 19–31. Brief and uninformative, yet somewhat tantalizing discussions are in the following M.A. theses: Harriet Elaine Cunningham, "The Economic Ideas of the New England Transcendentalists," University of Texas, 1941; William C. Walter, "American Transcendentalism and Social Theory," State University of Iowa, 1952; James Miller McCutcheon, "American Society in the World-View of the Transcendentalists," University of Wisconsin, 1955; John Anthony Doon, "Transcendentalism and Labor Reform," Clark University, 1959; and Sister Mary Ancillita Jarvis, "Personalism Vs. Individualism in the Concord Transcendentalists," Boston College, 1964. We can also pinpoint some areas that were of primary concern to the Transcendentalists: educational reform, natural history, clubs, communities, and publishing, particularly periodicals.

Despite the interests of many Transcendentalists, especially Bronson

Alcott and Elizabeth Palmer Peabody, in educational reforms, little of quality has been done on this subject outside of studies of those two authors. Good general discussions are Abraham Blinderman, *American Writers on Education Before 1865* (Boston: Twayne, 1975), and Rüdiger C. Schlicht, *Die Pädagogischen Ansätze Amerikanischer Tranzendentalisten* (Frankfurt am Main: Peter Lang, 1977). A number of brief studies exist, all of which are unsatisfactory: Myrle James, "Contributions of the Transcendental Group to the Educational Theory in the United States," M.A. thesis, University of Washington, 1934; Henry Arlo Anderson, "The Contribution of Transcendentalism to Education," M.A. thesis, Cornell University, 1936; John B. Wilson, "The Transcendentalists and Women's Education," *AAUW Journal*, 59 (March 1966), 118, 121–124; and John B. Wilson, "The Transcendentalists' Idea of a University," *Educational Forum*, 33 (March 1969), 343–354. For the later expression of Transcendentalism in the Concord School of Philosophy, see *Concord Lectures in Philosophy*, ed. Raymond L. Bridgman (Boston: Moses King, 1883), and Austin Warren, "The Concord School of Philosophy," *New England Quarterly*, 2 (April 1929), 199–233.

America's Edenic setting is discussed in R. W. B. Lewis, *The American Adam: Innocence, Tragedy, and Tradition in the Nineteenth Century* (Chicago: University of Chicago Press, 1955); David W. Noble, *The Eternal Adam and the New World Garden* (New York: Grosset and Dunlap, 1968); and Edward Halsey Foster, *The Civilized Wilderness: Backgrounds to American Romantic Literature, 1817–1860* (New York: Free Press, 1975). Particularly useful in tracing the Transcendentalists' responses to natural history are Philip Marshall Hicks, *The Development of the Natural History Essay in American Literature* (Philadelphia: University of Pennsylvania Press, 1924), pp. 63–99, and Hans Huth, *Nature and the American: Three Centuries of Changing Attitudes* (Berkeley: University of California Press, 1957), pp. 87–96. Accounts of the opposite reactions of industrialization and urbanization are in Leo Marx, *The Machine in the Garden: Technology and the Pastoral Ideal in America* (New York: Oxford University Press, 1964), and Thomas Bender, *Toward an Urban Vision: Ideas and Institutions in Nineteenth-Century America* (Lexington: University Press of Kentucky, 1975).

The Transcendental Club was the most important forum for the social meetings of the Transcendentalists: it was at these meetings that they talked—and argued—about their ideas. The only published accounts by a participant are Bronson Alcott's "Reminiscences of the Transcendental Club," *Boston Book Bulletin*, 1 (December 1877, March 1878), 3–5, 30, and Clarence Gohdes, "Alcott's 'Conversation' on the Transcendental Club and *The Dial*," *American Literature*, 3 (March 1931), 14–27. Two modern studies by Joel Myerson are essential: "A Calendar of Transcendental Club Meetings," *American Literature*, 44 (May 1972), 197–207, and "A History of the Transcendental Club," *ESQ: A Journal of the American Renaissance*, 23 (1st Quarter 1977), 27–35. Information on the Semi-Colon Club of Cincinnati, which some of the Transcendentalists also attended, can be found in Frank R. Shivers, Jr., "A Western Chapter in the History of American Transcendentalism," *Bulletin of the Historical and Philosophical Society of Ohio*, 15 (April 1957), 117–130, and Louis L. Tucker, "The Semi-Colon Club of Cincinnati," *Ohio History*, 73 (Winter 1964), 13–26. As the Transcendentalists dispersed, some of them became members of the Town and Country Club, the more social Saturday Club, and the Radical Club: see Kenneth Walter Cameron, "Emerson, Thoreau, and the Town and Country Club," *Emerson Society Quarterly*, no. 8 (3d Quarter 1957), 2–17; Edward Waldo Emerson, *The Early Years of the Saturday Club 1855–1870* (Boston: Houghton Mifflin, 1918); and Mary T. Sargent, *Sketches and Reminiscences of the Radical Club* (Boston: James R. Osgood, 1880), for histories of these groups.

The other purely social manifestation of Transcendentalism was in communities started by George Ripley and Bronson Alcott. The literature on Brook Farm is ably surveyed in Joel Myerson, *Brook Farm: An Annotated Bibliography and Resources Guide* (New York: Garland, 1978), which also catalogues major manuscript collections. Of particular use are John Thomas Codman, *Brook Farm: Historic and Personal Memoirs* (Boston: Arena, 1894); Lindsay Swift, *Brook Farm* (New York: Macmillan, 1900); Marianne Dwight, *Letters from Brook Farm 1844–1847*, ed. Amy L. Reed (Poughkeepsie, N.Y.: Vassar College, 1928); *Autobiography of Brook Farm*, ed. Henry W. Sams (Englewood Cliffs, N.J.: Prentice-Hall, 1958), a superb collection of primary documents; Edith Roelker Curtis, *A Season in Utopia: The Story of Brook Farm* (New York: Thomas Nelson, 1961); Charles Crowe, *George Ripley: Transcendentalist and Utopian Socialist* (Athens: University of Georgia Press, 1967); and Richard Francis, "The Ideology of Brook Farm," *Studies in the American Renaissance 1977*, ed. Joel Myerson (Boston: Twayne, 1978), pp. 1–48.

The short and unhappy history of Fruitlands is discussed in Annie M. L. Clark, *The Alcotts in Harvard* (Lancaster, Mass.: J. C. L. Clark, 1902); Clara Endicott Sears, *Bronson Alcott's Fruitlands* (Boston: Houghton Mifflin, 1915); Odell Shepard, *Pedlar's Progress: The Life of Bronson Alcott* (Boston: Little, Brown, 1938); David Palmer Edgell, "The New Eden: A Study of Bronson Alcott's Fruitlands," M.A. thesis, Wesleyan University, 1939; Roger William Cummins, "The Second Eden: Charles Lane and American Transcendentalism," Ph.D. dissertation, University of Minnesota, 1967; Robert Howard Walker, "Charles Lane and the Fruitlands Utopia," Ph.D. dissertation, University of Texas, 1967; and Richard Francis, "Circumstances and Salvation: The Ideology of the Fruitlands Utopia," *American Quarterly*, 25 (May 1973), 202–234. A humorous portrait of the community is in Louisa May Alcott, "Transcendental Wild Oats," *Independent*, 25 (18 December 1873), 1569–1571.

Another, logical outlet for Transcendentalism was in the print media. A good sense of the American literary scene in the 1830–1860 period can be gleaned from Robert W. Flint, "The Boston Book Trade, 1835–1845: A Directory," Library School thesis, Simmons College, n.d.; Frank Luther Mott, *A History of American Magazines 1741–1850* (Cambridge: D. Appleton-Century, 1930); Frank Luther Mott, *Golden Multitudes: A History of Best-Sellers in the United States* (New York: Macmillan, 1947); J. Albert Robbins, "Fees Paid to Authors by Certain American Periodicals, 1840–1850," *Studies in Bibliography*, 2 (1949–1950), 95–104; William Charvat, *Literary Publishing in America: 1790–1850* (Philadelphia: University of Pennsylvania Press 1959); William Charvat, *The Profession of Authorship in America, 1800–1870*, ed. Matthew J. Bruccoli (Columbus: Ohio State University Press, 1968); Edward E. Chielens, *The Literary Journal in America to 1900* (Detroit: Gale, 1975); and Jayne K. Kribbs, *An Annotated Bibliography of American Literary Periodicals, 1741–1850* (Boston: G. K. Hall, 1977). Only two publishers of the Transcendentalists have been studied in depth for their connection with the movement; see Raymond L. Kilgour, *Messrs. Roberts Brothers, Publishers* (Ann Arbor: University of Michigan Press, 1952), and Madeleine B. Stern, "James P. Walker and Horace B. Fuller: Transcendental Publishers," *Boston Public Library Quarterly*, 6 (July 1954), 123–140 (rpt. in her *Imprints on History: Book Publishers and American Frontiers* [Bloomington: Indiana University Press, 1956], pp. 45–59).

The starting point for any study of Transcendentalist journalism is Clarence L. F. Gohdes, *The Periodicals of American Transcendentalism* (Durham: Duke University Press, 1931). Specialized studies are available on three periodicals: the *Dial*, the major journal of the movement; the *Harbinger*, Brook Farm's publication; and the *Western Messenger*, published in the Ohio Valley by the Western Transcendentalists and their sympathizers. For the *Western Messenger*, see Charles E. Blackburn, "James Freeman Clarke: An Interpretation of the Western Years (1833–1840)," Ph.D. dissertation, Yale University, 1952, and "Some New Light on the *Western Messenger*," *American Literature*, 26 (November 1954), 320–336. The *Harbinger* is discussed in Marjorie Ruth Kaufman, "The Literary Reviews of the *Harbinger* During Its Brook Farm Period 1845–1847," M.A. thesis, University of Washington, 1947, and Sterling F. Delano, "*The Harbinger*: A Portrait of Associationism in America," Ph.D. dissertation, Southern Illinois University, 1963. Of the large body of literature on the *Dial*, the best works are George Willis Cooke, *An Historical and Biographical Introduction to Accompany The*

Dial, 2 vols. (Cleveland: Rowfant Club, 1902); Helen Hennessy, "The *Dial*: Its Poetry and Poetic Criticism," *New England Quarterly*, 31 (March 1958), 66–87; Joel Myerson, "An Annotated List of Contributions to the Boston *Dial*," *Studies in Bibliography*, 26 (1973), 133–166; Donald F. Warders, " 'The Progress of the Hour and the Day': A Critical Study of the *Dial*," Ph.D. dissertation, University of Kansas, 1973; Joel Myerson, "The Contemporary Reception of the Boston *Dial*," *Resources for American Literary Study*, 3 (Autumn 1973), 203–220; and Joel Myerson, *The New England Transcendentalists and the* Dial: *A History of the Magazine and Its Contributors* (Rutherford, N.J.: Fairleigh Dickinson University Press, 1980).

Studies of Transcendentalism as a literary movement nearly all concentrate on a particular aspect of the literature, such as criticism, use of language, writings on music, or poetry. However, an excellent overview is Lawrence Buell, *Literary Transcendentalism: Style and Vision in the American Renaissance* (Ithaca: Cornell University Press, 1973), a detailed study of the various literary forms—conversation, moral essay, catalogue rhetoric, symbolic excursion, and autobiography—adopted by individual Transcendentalists. Buell's earlier "Transcendentalist Catalogue Rhetoric: Vision Versus Form," *American Literature*, 40 (November 1968), 325–339, is incorporated into his book, though with a shift in emphasis. Attention to the visionary aspects of Transcendentalist writing is paid by Tony Tanner, "The Transcendentalists," *Reign of Wonder: Naivety and Reality in American Literature* (Cambridge, England: Cambridge University Press, 1965), pp. 19–96, and Roger Asselineau, " 'Dreaming on the Grass,' or the Transcendentalist Constant in American Literature," *Forum* [Houston], 14, no. 1 (Spring 1976), 31–37. A general essay, placing Transcendentalism in context, is Richard P. Adams, "The American Renaissance: An Epistemological Problem," *Emerson Society Quarterly*, no. 35 (2d Quarter 1964), 2–7. Also of interest is an original approach taken by John T. Irwin in "The Symbol of the Hieroglyphics in the American Renaissance," *American Quarterly*, 26 (May 1974), 103–126, and expanded in his *American Hieroglyphics: The Symbol of the Egyptian Hieroglyphic in the American Renaissance* (New Haven: Yale University Press, 1980).

The literary criticism of the Transcendentalists is usually mentioned in passing in studies of Margaret Fuller. General studies, some with chapters on the Transcendentalists, include William Charvat, *The Origins of American Critical Thought 1810–1835* (Philadelphia: University of Pennsylvania Press, 1936); Bernard Smith, *Forces in American Criticism: A Study in the History of American Literary Thought* (New York: Harcourt, Brace, 1939); Robert E. Spiller, "Critical Standards in the American Romantic Movement," *College English*, 8 (April 1947), 344–352; Richard H. Fogle, "Organic Form in American Criticism: 1840–1870," in *The Development of American Literary Criticism*, ed. Floyd Stovall (Chapel Hill: University of North Carolina Press, 1955), pp. 75–112; John Paul Pritchard, *Criticism in America* (Norman: University of Oklahoma Press, 1956), pp. 43–69; John W. Rathbun, "The Historical Sense in American Associationist Criticism," *Philological Quarterly*, 40 (October 1961), 553–568; René Wellek, "American Criticism," *A History of Modern Criticism: 1750–1950. Volume Three: The Age of Transition* (New Haven: Yale University Press, 1965), pp. 150–181; Max I. Baym, *A History of Literary Aesthetics in America* (New York: Frederick Ungar, 1973); and John W. Rathbun, *American Literary Criticism, 1800–1860* (Boston: Twayne, 1979). Specialized studies are Lucile Gafford, "Transcendentalist Attitudes Toward Drama and the Theatre," *New England Quarterly*, 13 (September 1940), 442–466; John B. Wilson, "The Aesthetics of Transcendentalism," *Emerson Society Quarterly*, no. 57 (4th Quarter 1969), 27–34; and Closept N. Srinath, "Aspects of Transcendental Literary Criticism," Ph.D. dissertation, University of Utah, 1974.

The ways in which the Transcendentalists used language have recently become the subject of much valuable scholarship. B. Damodar Rao's "Transcendental Dialectic and Literature," *Literary Criterion*, 4 (Summer 1960), 24–33, has easily been surpassed by Albert Gilman and Roger Brown, "Personality and Style in Concord," in *Transcendentalism and Its Legacy*, ed. Simon and Parsons, pp. 87–122; Irving Jacob Rein, "The New England Transcendentalists: Rhetoric of Paradox," Ph.D. dissertation, University of Pittsburgh, 1966; Richard Poirier, "Is There an I for an Eye? The Visionary Possession of America," *A World Elsewhere: The Place of Style in American Literature* (London: Chatto and Windus, 1967), pp. 50–92; Irving J. Rein, "The New England Transcendentalists: Philosophy and Rhetoric," *Philosophy and Rhetoric*, 1 (Winter 1968), 103–117; Jesse Bier, "Weberism, Franklin, and the Transcendental Style," *New England Quarterly*, 43 (June 1970), 179–192; Catherine L. Albanese, "The Kinetic Revolution: Transformation in the Language of the Transcendentalists," *New England Quarterly*, 48 (September 1975), 319–340; Phillip K. Tompkins, "On 'Paradoxes' in the Rhetoric of the New England Transcendentalists," *Quarterly Journal of Speech*, 62 (February 1976), 40–48; Catherine L. Albanese, *Corresponding Motion: Transcendental Religion and the New America* (Philadelphia: Temple University Press, 1977); Philip F. Gura, "The Transcendentalists and Language: The Unitarian Exegetical Background," *Studies in the American Renaissance 1979*, ed. Joel Myerson (Boston: Twayne, 1979), pp. 1–16; and Philip F. Gura, *The Wisdom of Words: Language, Theology, and Literature in the New England Renaissance* (Middletown, Conn.: Wesleyan University Press, 1981). (The articles by Albanese and Gura are incorporated into their books.) Gura's book is especially interesting since it relates language to other philosophical concerns. The influence of Charles Kraitsir is discussed in two articles on "Grimm's Law and the Brahmins" by John B. Wilson in *New England Quarterly*, 16 (March 1943), 106–109, and 38 (June 1965), 234–239.

The Transcendentalists' writings about music are ably discussed in Charmenz S. Lenhart, "Music and the Transcendentalists," *Musical Influences on American Poetry* (Athens: University of Georgia Press, 1956), pp. 105–117; Irving Lowens, "Writings About Music in the Periodicals of American Transcendentalism (1835–1850)," *Journal of the American Musicological Society*, 10 (Summer 1957), 71–85 (rpt. in his *Music and Musicians in Early America* [New York: W. W. Norton, 1964], pp. 249–263, 311–321); Daniel E. Rider, "The Musical Thought and Activities of the New England Transcendentalists," Ph.D. dissertation, University of Minnesota, 1964; and Earl Walter Booth, "Beethoven and the American Transcendentalists," M.A. thesis, University of Utah, 1970.

Nearly all of the Transcendentalists wrote poetry, with varying degrees of success. Particularly useful in studying this aspect of their writings are Elsie Furbush Brickett, "Studies in the Poets and Poetry of New England Transcendentalism," Ph.D. dissertation, Yale University, 1937; Stanley T. Williams, *The Beginnings of American Poetry (1620–1855)* (Uppsala: Almquist and Wiksells, 1951), pp. 65–94; Roy Harvey Pearce, *The Continuity of American Poetry* (Princeton: Princeton University Press, 1961); Edwin Fussell, "The Meter-Making Argument," in *Aspects of Modern Poetry*, ed. Richard M. Ludwig (Columbus: Ohio State University Press, 1962), pp. 3–31; Paul Osborne Williams, "The Transcendental Movement in American Poetry," Ph.D. dissertation, University of Pennsylvania, 1962; A. D. Van Nostrand, *Everyman His Own Poet: Romantic Gospels in American Literature* (New York: McGraw-Hill, 1968), pp. 28–62, 92–112; Hyatt H. Waggoner, *American Poets from the Puritans to the Present* (Boston: Houghton Mifflin, 1968); Harold Bloom, "Bacchus and Merlin: The Dialectic of Romantic Poetry in America," *The Ringers in the Tower* (Chicago: University of Chicago Press, 1971), pp. 291–321; and Donald Barlow Stauffer, *A Short History of American Poetry* (New York: E. P. Dutton, 1974), pp. 93–113.

Other aspects of Transcendentalist literary practices have been studied in Elizabeth A. Meese, "Transcendental Vision: A History of the Doctrine of Correspondence and Its Role in American Transcendentalism," Ph.D. dissertation, Wayne State University, 1972; Ann-Mari Peirce "The Transcendentalists and Fiction," M.A. thesis, University of Utah, 1969; Joel Porte, "Transcendental Antics," in *Veins of Humor*, ed. Harry Levin (Cambridge: Harvard University Press, 1972), pp. 167–184; Cleon Holmes, "The Use of Myth by the American Transcendentalists," M.A. thesis, University of New Hampshire, 1950, now superseded by Robert D.

Richardson, Jr., *Myth and Literature in the American Renaissance* (Bloomington: Indiana University Press, 1978), a striking and original work; John B. Wilson, "Phrenology and the Transcendentalists," *American Literature*, 28 (May 1956), 220–225; Donna Evelyn Davis, "Spiritualism and American Transcendentalism," M.A. thesis, University of Texas, 1957; and Russell M. and Clare R. Goldfarb, *Spiritualism and Nineteenth-Century Letters* (Rutherford, N.J.: Fairleigh Dickinson University Press, 1978). Although dealing primarily with Emerson, Charles Feidelson, *Symbolism and American Literature* (Chicago: University of Chicago Press, 1953), pp. 119–161, is a fine starting point for understanding the movement as a whole.

As a literary movement, Transcendentalism is most often compared to English Romanticism. Valuable background for discovering the reasons for this comparison is given in G. Harrison Orians, "The Rise of Romanticism, 1805–1855," in *Transitions in American Literary History*, ed. Clark, pp. 161–244, and Tony Tanner, "Notes for a Comparison Between American and European Romanticism," *Journal of American Studies*, 2 (April 1968), 83–103. The best critical perspective is provided in R. A. Yoder, "The Equilibrist Perspective: Toward a Theory of American Romanticism," *Studies in Romanticism*, 12 (Fall 1973), 705–740. Other useful studies are Paul Kaufman, "The Romantic Movement," in *The Reinterpretation of American Literature*, ed. Norman Foerster (New York: Harcourt, Brace, 1928), pp. 114–138; George Boas, "Romantic Philosophy in America," in *Romanticism in America*, ed. Boas (Baltimore: Johns Hopkins University Press, 1940), pp. 191–202; R. P. Adams, "Romanticism and the American Renaissance," *American Literature*, 23 (January 1952), 419–432; Norman Foerster, "The Romantic Movement," *Image of America: Our Literature from Puritanism to the Space Age* (Notre Dame: University of Notre Dame Press, 1962), pp. 45–87; James Early, *Romanticism and American Architecture* (New York: A. S. Barnes, 1965); William Charvat, "American Romanticism and the Depression of 1837," *Science and Society*, 2 (Winter 1937), 67–82 (rpt. in his *The Profession of Authorship in America*, ed. Bruccoli, pp. 49–67); Richard P. Adams, "Permutations of American Romanticism," *Studies in Romanticism*, 9 (Fall 1970), 249–268; and Jesse Bier, "The Romantic Coordinates of American Literature," *Bucknell Review*, 18 (Fall 1970), 16–33. Of particular interest is Duane E. Smith, "Romanticism in America: The Transcendentalists," *Review of Politics*, 35 (July 1973), 302–325.

A depressingly large number of studies diligently search for sources of American Transcendentalism in the literature of other countries, particularly those of England, France, Germany, and Oriental literatures in general. True, the Transcendentalists did read widely, but they selectively adopted whatever they liked to their own purposes. An important essay in this regard is Perry Miller, "New England's Transcendentalism: Native or Imported?," in *Literary Views: Critical and*

Historical Essays, ed. Carroll Camden (Chicago: University of Chicago Press, 1964), pp. 115–130. A collection of source materials used by the Transcendentalists is in Kenneth Walter Cameron, *Emerson the Essayist,* 2 vols. (Raleigh, N.C.: Thistle Press, 1945); see also George Ripley's fourteen-volume series, *Specimens of Foreign Standard Literature* (1839–1842).

General works on Anglo-American literary relations which provide a background against which to place other, more specialized studies are William Charvat, *The Origins of American Critical Thought;* Merle Curti, "The Great Mr. Locke: America's Philosopher, 1783–1861," *Huntington Library Bulletin,* no. 11 (April 1937), 107–151; George Stuart Gordon, *Anglo-American Literary Relations* (London: Oxford University Press, 1942); Clarence Gohdes, *American Literature in Nineteenth Century England* (New York: Columbia University Press, 1944); Wendell Glick, "Bishop Paley in America," *New England Quarterly,* 27 (September 1954), 347–354; Sydney E. Ahlstrom, "The Scottish Philosophy and American Theology," *Church History,* 24 (September 1955), 257–272; George H. Daniels, "An American Defense of Bacon: A Study in the Relations of Scientific Thought," *Huntington Library Quarterly,* 28 (August 1965), 321–339; Robert N. Hertz, "English and American Romanticism," *Personalist,* 46 (Winter 1965), 81–92; James J. Barnes, *Authors, Publishers and Politicians: The Quest for an Anglo-American Copyright Agreement, 1815–1854* (Columbus: Ohio State University Press, 1974); and Stephen Spender, *Love-Hate Relationships: English and American Sensibilities* (New York: Random House, 1974). Studies of particular borrowings or similarities are in Miller's *The Transcendentalists;* Noah Porter, Jr., "Coleridge and His American Disciples," *Bibliotheca Sacra,* 4 (February 1847), 117–171; Samuel C. Chew, "Byron in America," *American Mercury,* 1 (March 1924), 335–344; Julia Power, *Shelley in America in the Nineteenth Century* (Lincoln: University of Nebraska Press, 1940); John Olin Eidson, *Tennyson in America: His Reputation and Influence from 1827 to 1858* (Athens: University of Georgia Press, 1943); Merrell R. Davis, "Emerson's 'Reason' and the Scottish Philosophers," *New England Quarterly,* 17 (June 1944), 209–228; Hyder Edward Rollins, *Keats' Reputation in America to 1848* (Cambridge: Harvard University Press, 1946); Richard J. Peterson, "The Influence of Scottish Common Sense Philosophy on New England Transcendentalism with Special Attention to James Walker," M.A. thesis, American University, 1956; Terrence Martin, *The Instructed Vision: Scottish Common Sense Philosophy and the Origins of American Fiction* (Bloomington: Indiana University Press, 1961); Cameron Thompson, "John Locke and New England Transcendentalism," *New England Quarterly,* 35 (December 1962), 435–457; Richard J. Peterson, "Scottish Common Sense Philosophy in America, 1768–1850," Ph.D. dissertation,

American University, 1963; John B. Wilson, "Darwin and the Transcendentalists," *Journal of the History of Ideas*, 26 (April–June 1965), 286–290; Jean Martin Clinton, "The American Transcendentalists' View of the Major English Romantics," M.A. thesis, University of Southern Mississippi, 1967; Arthur S. Pfeffer, "The Instauration of Spirit: Transcendentalism and Francis Bacon," Ph.D. dissertation, City University of New York, 1968; and George Mills Harper, "Thomas Taylor in America," in *Thomas Taylor the Platonist*, ed. Kathleen Raine and Harper (Princeton: Princeton University Press, 1969), pp. 49–102, a masterful discussion of how neo-Platonism came to America from England.

French sources of American Transcendentalism are briefly discussed in these general studies: Woodbridge Riley, "La philosophie francaise en Amerique," *Review Philosophique*, 84 (November 1917), 393–428; Howard Mumford Jones, *American and French Culture 1750–1848* (Chapel Hill: University of North Carolina Press, 1927); Howard Mumford Jones, "American Comment on George Sand, 1837–1848," *American Literature*, 3 (January 1932), 389–407; Leo Lemchen, "A Summary View of the Vogue of French Electicism in New England—1829–1844," M.A. thesis, Columbia University, 1936; Georges Jules Joyaux, "French Thought in American Magazines, 1800–1848," Ph.D. dissertation, Michigan State University, 1951; C. M. Lombard, "The American Attitude Towards the French Romantics (1800–1861)," *Revue de Litterature Comparee*, 39 (July–September 1965), 358–371; and Henry Blumenthal, *American and French Culture, 1800–1900: Interchanges in Art, Science, Literature, and Society* (Baton Rouge: Louisiana State University Press, 1975). For an interesting contemporary statement, see J. A. Heraud's articles on Cousin, under the general title of "Continental Philosophy in America," *Monthly Magazine* [England], 3d ser., 4 (July, August, October, December 1840), 1–14, 112–128, 331–338, 628–637. Studies dealing especially with Transcendentalism are Walter L. Leighton, *French Philosophers and New England Transcendentalism* (Charlottesville: University of Virginia, 1908); William Girard, "Du Transcendentalisme Considere Essentiellment Dans Sa Definition et Ses Origines Francaises," *University of California Publications in Modern Philology*, 4 (18 October 1916), 351–498; Albert Schinz, "French Origins of American Transcendentalism," *American Journal of Psychology*, 29 (January 1918), 50–65; Ruth Amerman, "Journalistic Evidence of French Influence on Transcendentalism in America," M.A. thesis, Columbia University, 1929; Ruth S. Fielden, "Cousin's Vogue During the American Transcendental Period," M.A. thesis, Columbia University, 1941; Georges J. Joyaux, "Victor Cousin and American Transcendentalism," *French Review*, 29 (December 1955), 117–130; and John B. Wilson, "A Fallen Idol of the Transcendentalists: Baron de Gerando," *Comparative Literature*, 19 (Fall 1967), 334–340.

Studies of the German sources of American Transcendentalism are particularly interested in the influences of Goethe and Kant. The contemporary controversy over these authors is well represented in Miller's *The Transcendentalists*. Good general background reading is in James Murdock, "German Philosophy in America," *Sketches of Modern Philosophy*, pp. 156–166; Joseph Henry Allen, "The Contact of American Unitarianism and German Thought," in *Unitarianism: Its Origin and History*, pp. 97–115; and Philip Allison Shelley, "A German Art of Life in America: The American Reception of the Goethean Doctrine of Self-Culture," in *Anglo-American and American-German Crosscurrents*, ed. Shelley, Arthur O. Lewis, Jr., and William W. Betts, Jr. (Chapel Hill: University of North Carolina Press, 1957), pp. 241–292. The American reception of particular authors is studied in Henry A. Brann, "Hegel and His New England Echo," *Catholic World*, 41 (April 1885), 56–61; J. H. Muirhead, "How Hegel Came to America," *Philosophical Review*, 37 (May 1928), 226–240; Edward V. Brewer, "The New England Interest in Jean Paul Friedrich Richter," *University of California Publications in Modern Philology*, 27 (1943), 1–25; Joseph L. Blau, "Kant in America," *Journal of Philosophy*, 54 (11 November 1954), 874–880; Siegfried B. Puknat, "De Wette in New England," *Proceedings of the American Philosophical Society*, 102 (August 1958), 376–395; and *The American Hegelians: An Intellectual Episode in the History of Western America*, ed. William H. Goetzmann (New York: Alfred A. Knopf, 1973). The essential work for studying the larger question of German literary influence is Henry A. Pochmann, *German Culture in America: Philosophical and Literary Influences 1600–1900* (Madison: University of Wisconsin Press, 1956), an encyclopedic and scrupulously annotated commentary. More specialized but just as valuable is Stanley M. Vogel, *German Literary Influences on the American Transcendentalists* (New Haven: Yale University Press, 1955). Interesting complements to Pochmann and Vogel are John Henry Christopher Groth, "German Backgrounds of American Transcendentalism: Prologomena to the Study of Influence," Ph.D. dissertation, University of Washington, 1940, and Henry A. Pochmann, *New England Transcendentalism and St. Louis Hegelianism* (Philadelphia: Carl Schurz Foundation, 1948). While most studies of German literary influence deal with Emerson and Margaret Fuller, René Wellek has studied "The Minor Transcendentalists and German Philosophy," *New England Quarterly*, 15 (December 1942), 652–680. A useful examination of the reverse flow of ideas is Kaspar T. Locher, "The Reception of American Literature in German Literary Histories in the Nineteenth Century," Ph.D. dissertation, University of Chicago, 1949.

Possible Oriental influences on American Transcendentalism have fascinated writers for years, though the results of their studies are probably more suggestive than conclusive. The major works are Frederic Ives

Carpenter, *Emerson and Asia* (Cambridge: Harvard University Press, 1930); Arthur Christy, *The Orient in American Transcendentalism* (New York: Columbia University Press, 1932); Roger Chester Mueller, "The Orient in the Periodicals of American Transcendentalism (1835–1886)," Ph.D. dissertation, University of Minnesota, 1968; and Shoei Ando, *Zen and American Transcendentalism* (Tokyo: Hokuseido, 1970); see also W. E. Washburn, "The Oriental 'Roots' of American Transcendentalism," *Southwestern Journal*, 4 (Fall 1949), 141–155; John T. Reid, "The Great Transcendentalists," *Indian Influences in American Literature and Thought* (N.p.: Indian Council for Cultural Relations, 1965), pp. 18–43; and J. P. Rao Rayapati, *Early American Interest in Vedanta: Pre-Emersonian Interest in Vedic Literature and Vedantic Philosophy* (London: Asia Publishing House, 1973), pp. 1–23, 93–106.

Finally, Italian influences and responses are examined in Angelina La Piana, *Dante's American Pilgrimage: A Historical Survey of Dante Studies in the United States 1800–1914* (New Haven: Yale University Press, 1948), and Polish influences in Francis J. Whitfield, "Mickiewicz and American Literature," in *Adam Mickiewicz in World Literature*, ed. Waclaw Lednicki (Berkeley: University of California Press, 1956), pp. 339–352.

A useful complement to studies of foreign influences on American Transcendentalism might be an examination of its more native origins. One particularly fruitful area of inquiry is American religious history. The Puritan antecedents to Transcendentalism are traced in Perry Miller, "Jonathan Edwards to Emerson," *New England Quarterly*, 13 (December 1940), 589–617; Van-Diem Le, "Puritan Idealism and the Transcendental Movement," Ph.D. dissertation, University of Minnesota, 1960; Ursula Brumm, *American Thought and Religious Typology*, trans. John Hoagland (New Brunswick, N.J.: Rutgers University Press, 1970), pp. 86–108; William H. Parker, "Jonathan Edwards: Founder of the Counter-Tradition of Transcendental Thought in America," *Georgia Review*, 27 (Winter 1973), 543–549; William Shurr, "Typology and Historical Criticism of the American Renaissance," *ESQ: A Journal of the American Renaissance*, 20 (1st Quarter 1974), 57–63; Sacvan Bercovitch, *The Puritan Origins of the American Self* (New Haven: Yale University Press, 1975); Sacvan Bercovitch, *The American Jeremiad* (Madison: University of Wisconsin Press, 1978); Charles Berryman, *From Wilderness to Wasteland: The Trial of the Puritan God in the American Imagination* (Port Washington, N.Y.: Kennikat, 1979), pp. 104–121; and Mason I. Lowance, Jr., *The Language of Canaan: Metaphor and Symbol in New England from the Puritans to the Transcendentalists* (Cambridge: Harvard University Press, 1980), pp. 277–295. The Unitarian background has already been discussed above.

The importance of Boston as the setting for Transcendentalism should not be underestimated. Interesting works in this respect are *The Memorial History of Boston,* ed. Justin Winsor, 4 vols. (Boston: Ticknor, 1881); Helen M. Winslow, *Literary Boston of To-Day* (Boston: L. C. Page, 1903); Lilian Whiting, *Boston Days* (Boston: Little, Brown, 1911); M. A. DeWolfe Howe, "The Boston Religion" and "The 'Literary Centre,'" *Atlantic Monthly Magazine,* 91 (June 1903), 729–738, and 92 (September 1903), 346–355; Cleveland Amory, *The Proper Bostonians* (New York: E. P. Dutton, 1947); Martin Green, *The Problem of Boston: Some Readings in Cultural History* (New York: W. W. Norton, 1966); and Paul Goodman, "Ethics and Enterprise: The Values of a Boston Elite, 1800–1860," *American Quarterly,* 18 (Fall 1966), 437–451. And one must not forget that most of the Transcendentalists were educated at Harvard College and Harvard Divinity School. Useful in examining these particular connections are Andrew P. Peabody, *Harvard Reminiscences* (Boston: Ticknor, 1888); Edgeley Woodman Todd, "Philosophical Ideas at Harvard College, 1817–1837," *New England Quarterly,* 16 (March 1943), 63–90; *The Harvard Divinity School: Its Place in Harvard University and In American Culture,* ed. George Hunston Williams (Boston: Beacon, 1954), esp. Sydney E. Ahlstrom's "The Middle Period (1840–1880)," pp. 78–147; Daniel Walker Howe, *The Unitarian Conscience,* an essential work; and Ronald Story, *The Forging of an Aristocracy: Harvard and the Boston Upper Class, 1800–1870* (Middletown, Conn.: Wesleyan University Press, 1980) .

Emerson and Thoreau lived most of their lives in Concord, and many of the Transcendentalists visited there, some dwelling in the town for extended periods of time. Two good histories of the town are Allen French, *Old Concord* (Boston: Little, Brown, 1915), and Townsend Scudder, *Concord: American Town* (Boston: Little, Brown, 1947). Reminiscences of Concord during the Transcendentalist period are in Julia R. Anagnos, *Philosophiæ Quæstor; or, Days in Concord* (Boston: D. Lothrop, 1885), about the time of the Concord School of Philosophy; Margaret Sidney, *Old Concord: Her Highways and Byways,* rev. ed. (Boston: D. Lothrop, 1893); Frank Preston Stearns, "Concord Thirty-Odd Years Ago," *Sketches from Concord and Appledore* (New York: Putnams, 1895), pp. 1–28; Mary Hosmer Brown, *Memories of Concord* (Boston: Four Seas, 1926); L. D. Geller, *Between Concord and Plymouth: The Transcendentalists and the Watsons* (Concord: Thoreau Foundation; Plymouth: Pilgrim Society, 1973); and *Remembrances of Concord and the Thoreaus: Letters of Horace Hosmer to Dr. S. A. Jones,* ed. George Hendrick (Urbana: University of Illinois Press, 1977). Interesting studies of the Concord authors and their relations are Randall Stewart, "The Concord Group: A Study in Relationships," *Sewanee Review,* 44 (October–December 1936), 434–446, and Taylor Stoehr, *Nay-Saying in Concord* (Hamden, Conn.: Archon, 1979). A thought provoking article is Robert A. Gross, "'The Most Estimable Place in All the World': A Debate on Progress in Nineteenth-Century Concord," *Studies in the American Renaissance 1978*, ed. Joel Myerson (Boston: Twayne, 1978), pp. 1–15.

The importance of Transcendentalism to the development of American literature has been much discussed. As an indigenous literary movement, it had much to do with the overall concerns that existed at the time for a truly American literature. In this latter respect, the following works provide a useful context: Benjamin T. Spencer, "A National Literature, 1837–1855," *American Literature,* 8 (May 1936), 125–159; Benjamin Spencer, "The Spur of Transcendentalism (1820–1860)," *The Quest for Nationality: An American Literary Campaign* (Syracuse: Syracuse University Press, 1957), pp. 156–194; John T. Frederick, "American Literary Nationalism: The Process of Definition, 1825–1850," *Review of Politics,* 21 (January 1959), 224–238; Yehoshu Arieli, *Individualism and Nationalism in American Ideology* (Cambridge: Harvard University Press, 1964); Donald Vincent Gawronski, "Transcendentalism: An Ideological Basis for Manifest Destiny," Ph.D. dissertation, St. Louis University, 1964; and Robert Lemelin, *Pathway to the National Character 1830–1861* (Port Washington, N.Y.: Kennikat, 1974). The Transcendentalists' connection with the New York-based "Young America" movement can be found in John Stafford, *The Literary Criticism of "Young America": A Study in the Relationship of Politics and Literature 1837–1850* (Berkeley: University of California Press, 1952); Perry Miller, *The Raven and the Whale: The War of Words and Wits in the Era of Poe and Melville* (New York: Harcourt, Brace, and World, 1956); Heyward Bruce Ehrlich, "A Study of the Literary Activity in New York City During the 1840-Decade," Ph.D. dissertation, New York University, 1963; and John Paul Pritchard, *Literary Wise Men of Gotham: Criticism in New York, 1815–1860* (Baton Rouge: Louisiana State University Press, 1963).

Transcendentalism's move westward is followed in Lucy Lockwood Hazard, "The Golden Age of Transcendentalism," *The Frontier in American Literature* (New York: Thomas Y. Crowell, 1927), pp. 147–180; Henry A. Pochmann, *New England Transcendentalism and St. Louis Hegelianism;* Edwin Fussell, *Frontier: American Literature and the American West* (Princeton: Princeton University Press, 1965); Walter Allen, *The Urgent West: The American Dream and Modern Man* (New York: E. P. Dutton, 1969); and *The American Hegelians,* ed. Goetzmann; see also the articles on the Semi-Colon Club of Cincinnati discussed above. The best study of the Transcendentalism in the West is Elizabeth R. McKinsey, *The Western Experiment: New England Transcendentalists in the Ohio Valley* (Cambridge: Harvard University Press, 1973). The standard study for the Southern reaction to Transcendentalism is Jay B.

Hubbell, *The South in American Literature 1607–1900* (Durham: Duke University Press, 1954). Transcendentalism in Salem is the subject of Alfred Rosa, *Salem, Transcendentalism, and Hawthorne* (Rutherford, N.J.: Fairleigh Dickinson University Press, 1980), and in Rhode Island of two articles by Charles R. Crowe: "Transcendentalism and 'The Newness' in Rhode Island" and "Transcendentalism and the Providence Literati," *Rhode Island History,* 14 (April, July 1955), 33–46, 65–78.

Modern scholarship has recognized that Transcendentalism has greatly influenced the major writers of the American Renaissance period, especially Emily Dickinson, Nathaniel Hawthorne, Herman Melville, Edgar Allan Poe, and Walt Whitman. Moreover, references to Transcendentalism and the Transcendentalists can be found in the letters and journals of nearly all the important writers of the time. A complete survey of such references will be found in the forthcoming *The Transcendentalists: A Review of Research and Criticism,* ed. Joel Myerson.

Mr. Gura has been responsible for the preliminary selection of twentieth-century criticism and for writing the first part of the introduction; Mr. Myerson for the preliminary selection of the nineteenth-century criticism and for writing the bibliographical part of the introduction. The final selection of criticism and the introduction are the work of both editors. Mr. Gura would like to thank James R. Kincaid, past chairman of the Department of English, University of Colorado at Boulder, for his hearty encouragement, and the administrative committee of the Charles Warren Center, Harvard University, for providing time and space for this project to be completed. Mr. Myerson is grateful to the Department of English of the University of South Carolina, and especially the chairman, George L. Geckle. We are both grateful to James Nagel for establishing the *Critical Essays* series and for his help in preparing our contribution to it. For various assistance, we thank Lawrence Buell, Carol Johnston, Caroline Bokinsky, and Stephen Garrison.

P. F. G.

Boulder, Colorado

J. M.

Columbia, South Carolina

Notes

1. Charles Dickens, *American Notes for General Circulation* (London: Chapman and Hall, 1842), I, 133.
2. [Samuel Kettell] "Quozziana," *Brother Jonathan,* 1 (26 March 1842), 354.

3. Anonymous, "A Plain Discussion with a Transcendentalist," *New Englander*, 1 (October 1843), 502.

4. Joel Porte, "Transcendental Antics," in *Veins of Humor*, ed. Harry Levin (Cambridge: Harvard University Press, 1972), pp. 167–183; L. Maria Child, *Letters from New York: Second Series* (New York: C. S. Francis, 1845), p. 129.

5. "Senex" [Theodore Parker], "Transcendentalism," *Christian Register*, 25 April 1840, pp. 66–67.

6. J. E. Snodgrass, "Transcendentalism. A Miniature Essay," *Magnolia*, 4 (April 1842), 214–215.

7. J[ames]. K[ennard]., Jr., "What is Transcendentalism," *Knickerbocker*, 23 (March 1844), 207.

8. Child, *Letters from New York*, p. 127.

9. [Daniel K. Whitaker], "Transcendentalism," *Southern Quarterly Review*, 2 (October 1842), 440.

10. T[heophilus]. P[arsons]., "Transcendentalism," *New Jerusalem Magazine*, 14 (December 1840), 137, and 14 (June 1841), 383, 386.

11. Simeon Doggett, *A Sermon on Transcendentalism* (Taunton, Mass.: J. W. D. Hall, 1843), pp. 6, 10.

12. Noah Porter, Jr., "Transcendentalism," *American Biblical Repository*, n.s. 8 (July 1842), 195–218.

13. George E. Ellis, *A Half-Century of the Unitarian Controversy* (Boston: Crosby, Nichols, 1857), p. 412.

14. Cyrus Bartol, *Radical Problems* (Boston: Roberts Brothers, 1872), pp. 78–97.

15. Bartol, *Radical Problems*, pp. 67–68.

16. Bartol, *Radical Problems*, p. 73.

17. Octavius Brooks Frothingham, "Some Phases of Idealism in New England," *Atlantic Monthly Magazine*, 58 (July 1883), 13–23.

18. [Charles Mayo Ellis], *An Essay on Transcendentalism* (Boston: Crocker and Ruggles, 1842).

19. John Orr, "The Transcendentalism of New England," *International Review*, 13 (October 1882), 396, 390, 397.

20. Samuel Johnson, "Transcendentalism," *Radical Review*, 1 (November 1877), 473, 448, 471, 469.

21. Johnson, "Transcendentalism," pp. 468, 477.

22. Louis James Block, "Thoughts on the Transcendental Movement in New England," *New England Magazine*, 15 (January 1897), 564–570; Joseph Cook, *Transcendentalism, with Preludes on Current Events* (Boston: James R. Osgood, 1878), pp. 49, 38.

23. Orr, "The Transcendentalism of New England," p. 382.

24. George Santayana, "The Genteel Tradition in American Philosophy," *University of California Chronicle*, 13 (October 1911), 357–380.

25. Santayana, "The Genteel Tradition in American Philosophy."

26. Santayana, "The Genteel Tradition in American Philosophy."

27. "J.," *Arcturus*, 1 (April 1841), 279.

28. Edgar Allan Poe, "How to Write a Blackwood Article," *Broadway Journal*, 2 (12 July 1845), 1–7.

29. Elizabeth A. Meese, "Transcendentalism: The Metaphysics of the Theme," *American Literature*, 47 (March 1975), 1–20; Catherine Albanese, "The Kinetic Revolution: Transformation in the Language of the Transcendentalists," *New England Quarterly*, 48 (September 1975), 319–340.

30. Lewis Mumford, *The Golden Day* (New York: Boni and Liveright, 1926); Vernon Louis Parrington, *The Romantic Revolution in America 1800–1860* (New York: Harcourt, Brace, 1927); F. O. Matthiessen, *American Renaissance: Art and Expression in the Age of Emerson and Whitman* (New York: Oxford University Press, 1941).

31. Harold Clarke Goddard, *Studies in New England Transcendentalism* (New York: Columbia University Press, 1908); Woodbridge Riley, "Two Types of Transcendentalism in America," *Journal of Philosophy*, 15 (23 May 1918), 281–292.

32. Perry Miller, "New England's Transcendentalism: Native or Imported?" in *Literary Views: Critical and Historical Essays*, ed. Carroll Camden (Chicago: University of Chicago Press, 1964), pp. 115–130; Georges Joyaux, "Victor Cousin and American Transcendentalism," *French Review*, 29 (December 1955), 117–130; René Wellek, "The Minor Transcendentalists and German Philosophy," *New England Quarterly*, 15 (December 1942), 652–680.

33. Arthur Christy, *The Orient in American Transcendentalism* (New York: Columbia University Press, 1932); Clarence L. F. Gohdes, *The Periodicals of American Transcendentalism* (Durham: Duke University Press, 1931).

34. Zoltan Haraszti, *The Idyll of Brook Farm* (Boston: Boston Public Library, 1937); C. H. Faust, "The Background of the Unitarian Opposition to Transcendentalism," *Modern Philology*, 35 (February 1938), 297–324; Lucile Gafford, "Transcendentalist Attitudes Toward Drama and the Theatre," *New England Quarterly*, 13 (September 1940), 442–466.

35. Henry Steele Commager, *Theodore Parker* (Boston, Little, Brown, 1936); Arthur M. Schlesinger, Jr., *Orestes A. Brownson* (Boston: Little, Brown, 1939).

36. William R. Hutchison, *The Transcendentalist Ministers: Church Reform in the New England Renaissance* (New Haven: Yale University Press, 1959); Lawrence Buell, *Literary Transcendentalism: Style and Vision in the American Renaissance* (Ithaca: Cornell University Press, 1973).

37. Charles R. Crowe, " 'This Unnatural Union of Phalansteries and Transcendentalists,' " *Journal of the History of Ideas*, 20 (October-December 1959), 495–502; Richard Francis, "The Ideology of Brook Farm," *Studies in the American Renaissance 1977*, ed. Joel Myerson (Boston: Twayne, 1978), pp. 1–48; Duane E. Smith, "Romanticism in America: The Transcendentalists," *Review of Politics*, 35 (July 1973), 302–325.

38. See note 29.

39. John T. Irwin, "The Symbol of the Hieroglyphics in the American Renaissance," *American Quarterly*, 26 (May 1974), 103–126; Philip F. Gura, "The Transcendentalists and Language: The Unitarian Exegetical Background," *Studies in the American Renaissance 1979*, ed. Joel Myerson (Boston: Twayne, 1979), pp. 1–16.

40. Charles Feidelson, *Symbolism and American Literature* (Chicago: University of Chicago Press, 1953).

41. Alexander Kern, "The Rise of Transcendentalism, 1815–1860," in *Transitions in American Literary History*, ed. Harry Hayden Clark (Durham: Duke University Press, 1954), pp. 245–314; George Hochfield, Introduction, *Selected Writings of the American Transcendentalists* (New York: New American Library, 1966), and "New England Transcendentalism," in *American Literature to 1900*, ed. Marcus Cunliffe (London: Barrie and Jenkins, 1973), pp. 160–196; *The Transcendentalists: An Anthology*, ed. Perry Miller (Cambridge: Harvard University Press, 1950).

ESSAYS

"Transcendentalism"

"Senex" [Theodore Parker]*

'It shall be my pride
'That I have dared to tread this holy ground.
Speaking no dream, but things oracular,
Matter not lightly to be heard by those,
Who to the letter of the outward promise,
Do read the invisible soul.'

I have been a dreamer of dreams for nearly fourscore years, Mr. Reader, and now see visions like a young man. The first thing I can remember is a sleep; and the next, in point of age, is a dream. What is remarkable, my visions almost always prove true. I relate this to my friends, who usually laugh at my odd conceit, as *they* call it; but the event always fulfils the prediction. 'Coming events cast their *shadows* before;' or their splendors, as the case may be. I dreamed of the battle of Lexington (just sixty five years ago yesterday) thirteen days before it happened; of the Declaration of Independence; and the treaty of Peace, and various other matters all came just as I had dreamed them. I have even learned when the greatest event in modern history is to take place, and General Jackson is to die. These things I state, to show you that 'old men dream dreams' as the prophet foretold—another proof that we have fallen on good times. Now one of my most remarkable visions occurred after this wise.

I was sitting after dinner, in the great oaken arm-chair,—which was brought over from Devonshire by my ancestors in the time of the Long-Parliament, and in which three generations of them have dreamed their sermons after dinner, and I read that remarkable tract lately edited by 'A. N.' which relates to Transcendentalism.[1] It was the first time I had ever seen the word in print, and I never yet have heard it pronounced except by myself, with the accent on the second syllable,

*Reprinted from *Christian Register*, 25 April 1840, pp. 66–67. We are grateful to Carol Johnston, who is editing Parker's journals, for pointing this out to us and attributing it to Parker on the basis of entries in his journal.

Trans-*cend*-ent-al-ism. (Is that right?) and I wondered what it meant. I thought of *Trans*-sylvanian, and *Trans*substantiation, but found no light, though I consulted my Dictionary, which did not contain it; so I resolved to read the Pamphlet. Then to my great surprise I learned that Trans-cendentalism, was a very naughty thing. I was very much surprised, to hear there were such men as we find there; and such men even in America, and some of them near Cambridge it seemed. I never closed the book till I read the last word, 'Hegel.' Then while I was resolving to go to Cambridge, and consult with my old friends there, as to this great evil, about to fall on the churches I fell into a profound sleep, and was visited with a dream so remarkable that I will write it down for the edification of the churches.

I thought I stood on the extreme point of Cape Cod, and the ocean lay before me, rolling like a great giant in his sleep. The waves rolled in upon the beach, with that sweet sound so soothing to the ear of an old man. I looked out on the porpoises tumbling heavily along, in their uncooth gambols, and the distant sails moving swiftly or slowly, as the wind favored or opposed them. Far away in the East, while I looked, I saw a little misty speck, on the ocean, no bigger than a man's hand. It increased rapidly in size, and seemed to approach. Then it became a large cloud, extending for many miles in breath, and with a depth that I could not measure.

It came nearer and nearer, and seemed larger and larger. At last I observed it was divided into several clouds. There was a large division into two bodies, the Right and Left; each of which was again parted in two smaller bodies, the Centre and Extreme. On the cloud came, and when within a mile of the shore, for old men are far-sighted, I saw each of these divisions was composed of countless smaller parties, which, as they came still nearer I found were men, flying swiftly along, who made up this immense cloud. They spoke to one another, and seemed to laugh, and chatter, and I could now and then catch the word '*Begriff*,' which I took to be Hebrew, (*Be Geriff*, i.e. in *sweeping away*.) What it meant I could not devise. Presently the men all alighted on the shore and sat down, some on great Books, which they brought under their arms, some on nothing that I could see, others on kegs, wine-skins, and fifteen-gallon jugs,—still keeping their relative position, of Right and Left, Centre and Extreme. They kept chatting, and I could now and then catch the words, '*Menschhiet*,' '*Idee*,' '*Vorstellang*,' '*Gegensatz*,' but knew not what they meant. One of them often repeated the Greek word 'To-Hori,' another said 'Kehabilitation' continually. Presently they all fell a smoking, with large tobacco pipes, but kept talking as fiercely as before. But they did not seem to agree, for the Centres, often made insulting gestures towards the Extremes, and which were very promptly returned.

While I wondered what these things should mean, one of them, the only one who saw me, stepped up, and relieved my wonder, by telling me in good English, 'These are the Transcendentalists.' I asked him to go on and tell me all about them, and inform me if he was one of them. He said he was not, but was a good Christian; a deacon, who kept a green and white grocery in Munchon, and had been sent by Mr. Hengstenberg, as a spy upon their actions. He affected to be a Transcendentalist and repeated 'Begriff,' as often as the others, and passed for a very profound Philosopher. But he heard all he could, and should write it home to his master. He then told me the names of the men in that great army. I will mention only a few. Some had been taken from the tombs; some from Pulpits, or professorial chairs; some from Parlors, others from Beer-shops, and some from places still worse. Among these were Plato, and Proclus Plotinus, Ammonius with his old bag, Stilpo, Strato, Zeno, Camedes, Basilides, and Bardesanes; Pelagius, Borthius, Rabanus-Maurus, Erigena; the St. Victors, Dyonisius the Areopagite, Albertus Magnus, Thomas a Kempis; Ficinus and Picus; Cardanus, Agrippa and Roger Bacon. There was Melancthon and Jordano Bruno, Savonorola, Campanella, Dr. Faustus, Scotus and Ramus; Behme, and Helmont, Grotius and Leclerc, Kepler and Spinoza, Bayle, Berkely, Samuel Clarke, and Cudworth and Parker and More; Leibnitz and Wolff, Kant, Jacobi, Schleiermacher, Reinhold, Fichte, Schelling, Tiedeman, Krause, Hegel, de Wette, Fries, Eichhorn, Gesenius, Strauss, Weisse, Schiller, the Schlegels, Heine, Borne, Schafer, Goethe, Richter, Rosenkrantz, Ammon, Herbart and Vatke, Paulus and Rohr, and Ullmann, Lucke and Tholuck.

All these men and countless others were thrown together in the greatest confusion, without any regard to age, opinion or character. My deacon of Munchon, told me that Mr Hengstenberg had been making a great stir in Germany; had 'harried the land,' and rendered it too hot for these men, dead or alive, so that he had driven them clean across the ocean.

'Alas' said I, 'alas for the churches in New England. We be all dead men, for the Transcendentalists have come! They say there is no Christ; no God; no soul; only 'an absolute nothing,' and Hegel is the Holy Ghost. Our churches will be pulled down; there will be no Sabbath; our wives will wear the breeches, and the Transcendentalists will ride over us rough shod. How shall we be delivered, from these desperate fellows; this 'mixed multitude of devils?' 'Fear not,' said he, 'they will work desolation only for a time. I have come to save the Faith of the Land, and Mr Hengstenberg will soon be here.'

Again I looked, and far away in the East, I saw a giant figure, like a man, approaching. It was Mr. Hengstenberg himself, mounted on a monstrous broom, alike his weapon, and his chariot. He looked worn with toil, and eager haste, and devoured by self-consuming fires, Wonderful to tell, he grew smaller, and smaller as he came near us, till at last he was an homunculus, 'no bigger than a tobacco-seed,' still he made a great cry. But soon he recovered his original size, and seemed a mere mortal like ourselves. I asked 'what help, oh mighty man!'

He told us, 'we must go back, to the *thirteenth century*; must take the whole of the Old Testament, letter for letter, and believe it; must admit that a special Revelation was made to Balaam's ass; and to Jonah's whale. That Joshua really stopped the sun a whole day, and Elisha's bones raised up a dead man; that Samson drank water out of the jaw bone of an ass. That we must never consult Reason, but bow to the letter, and reckon a doubt as the sin not to be pardoned,—instigated by the Devil. Least of all should we make the slightest attempt to reconcile Faith and Reason, Religion and Philosophy, for this would be like marrying Christ and Belial.' 'We will do it all,' said I, 'illustrious sage, or angel if such thou art!' Thereupon I awoke, and there was nothing before me but the 'pamphlet of 100 pages' and my pipe, broken at my feet.

Notes

1. Parker's sketch was introduced by the following editorial note (the reference to "A. N." is to *Two Articles from the Princeton Review, Concerning the Transcendental Philosophy of the Germans and of Cousin* . . . [Cambridge: John Owen, 1840], with an introduction by Andrews Norton):

> We insert the following article on Transcendentalism for two reasons; first, because, 'Senex' is a frequent contributor to the Register and has often enriched its columns with valuable matter; and secondly, because, being only temporarily in charge of the paper during the absence, for a few weeks, of the regular Editor, we feel it incumbent upon us to exercise sparingly, in relation to old contributors especially, the right of rejection. We feel it to be due to ourselves however to say, that we do not altogether approve of the style or spirit of the article. We have no objection to a little wit if it be good, or to a little badinage if it be sprightly,—though in general they are out of place in our columns. But, (the remark perhaps is only proof of our own dullness,) we do not see much wit in the piece, and certainly no argument, for none is attempted. We are disposed to think that it really is, what it purports to be, a *'dream'* and that our friend 'Senex,' who has done some things excellently well when wide awake, must have been dozing a little when he wrote it. A full and fair criticism on the Pamphlet, whose publication has been procured by 'A. N.' setting forth its misrepresentations, if it make any, the weakness and fallacy of its reasoning and its conclusions, if there be weakness and fallacy in them, we should be very glad to receive and very willing to publish. It is a grave pamphlet,

relating to matters of great moment to the interests of religious truth. If it deserve any, it deserves and demands a grave reply. It is not to be met and put down by ridicule, a weapon commonly regarded as the last resort of weakness.

"Transcendentalism"

T[heophilus]. P[arsons].*

There are many reasons why the New Church should examine, and, if possible, understand, that system of thought, of belief and of expression, which is known as transcendentalism. The fact that it has enlisted in its service some men of energetic and active minds; that many who do not call themselves its disciples and who stand aloof from its sanctuary, do nevertheless turn their faces thitherward; and that it is one of the ways by which inquiring minds seek to solve the problems of our nature and destiny,—in this alone there would be reason enough for us to wish to know what that really is, which is certainly one among the elements which together make up public opinion. But other and stronger reasons may be found in the relation between transcendentalism and the church. Many of the doctrines and principles of that school,—so far as they can be seen through the cloudy veil which seems not their ornament or vesture, but their very body,—claim affinity with leading truths of the church. It is well known that the adversaries of both class them together, as if to deepen the disgrace of each by contact with the other. And although we acknowledge no relationship between the doctrines of the New Church and transcendentalism, still there may be some, who, though still lingering in that land of glittering mists and ever-shifting shadows, seem to be finding their way out of it in a direction which will lead them to the solid land and the clear sky of the true Church.

In an age which differs in so many respects from the whole past, there is no one point of difference more striking, or more often adverted to, than the universal unloosening of all opinion and belief. The foundations of the great deep, of every deep in every thinking mind, are heaving, as if the powers within and beneath were stirring with a new force and life. The characteristic of the age is *unrest;* and transcendentalism is one of the effects and one of the symptoms of the wide

*Reprinted from *New Jerusalem Magazine,* 14 (December 1840, June 1841), 137–140, 380–388.

fermentation of thought. Nothing is positive about it, but its negation. It denies and rebukes old and established systems and habits clearly and sharply enough; but it asserts only loosely, in the way of suggestion and by all sorts of figures and metaphors. It wields for the purpose of attack, of destruction, a weapon of the hardest steel, wrought to the finest edge, and beautifully polished; but when it comes to construct and establish, it has no materials but cloud and mist, and it works with no instrument but fantasy. For those therefore who are prone to live a life of imagination, it has great charms. It lifts them off from the earth, and they do not stop to ask whether it lifts them towards heaven. They look down upon the fixed realities and duties of daily life from such an elevation and through such a medium, that the whole earth seems to them flat and tame. But there are not many who can sustain themselves for a great while in this unnatural condition. And thus there are but few who are known as settled and thorough in their devotion to transcendentalism, while there are many who are and many who have been more or less under its influence. There are very few who would like to live all their life in a balloon, although when we see one floating over our heads like a painted cloud, most of us would be willing to be up there for a little while, if we could be sure of coming back in safety.

They who thus go up by the help of transcendentalism, do not always come back in safety. And in the fact, that its supposed and seeming resemblance to the religious philosophy of the New Church, entices some away, and delays others who are still in the right road, we find the strongest reason, for wishing to form a distinct and just opinion of it.

The transcendentalism which prevails in our neighborhood, may be regarded either as a new thing, or as a very old one. There are those who suppose it an original invention of these days of discovery; who point it out as a proof that we have reached that stage of human progress, when we may hope to see, for the first time, the real truths which shall explain all mysteries; and they hold this system to be at once the evidence and the effect of a new day-spring. But it is not quite so new as this would imply. Far back before the Grecian philosophy, far in the eastern twilight of mystical theosophy, there are to be discerned clear traces of notions concerning man's relation to the First Cause and to surrounding nature, which are,—so far as things so hard to define can be compared,—identical with the essential principles of transcendentalism. Nor have they ever disappeared from the schools of philosophy; for they have always found among restless and imaginative minds, some to receive and pass along the tradition of these fantasies. But, it is also true, that they have assumed a shape, a semblance of system and coherence, a peculiar dress and form, here, and in these days, which may well be called new. The word transcendental was used in mathematics; and from this science, Kant, the German philosopher, who was also a great mathematician, borrowed the term and introduced it into his metaphysics. It had then a sufficiently precise meaning, which may be briefly described thus. The English philosophy founded by Locke, completed by Frenchmen, and generally taught until very recently in all our colleges, is based upon the proposition that all our knowledge and all our ideas originate in and from the senses; and hence its common name of the sensual philosophy. According to this system, for instance, we get the idea of *causation*, by seeing one thing follow another until we form the notion that they are necessarily connected, and thus we generate the idea of *causation;* and so of *power,* from seeing one thing act upon and change another. Kant taught, that we might see things follow each other forever and changes of all sorts occur, without ever getting the idea of causation or of power *from* what we saw; and therefore all these ideas belong to the *reason,* and are only developed and called forth to consciousness, by the operations and evidences of the senses. These ideas therefore *transcend* or go beyond the senses; and so a transcendental philosophy, instead of beginning with the senses, and seeking mainly to analyze and recombine their operations, occupies itself first and most in investigating the laws and powers of the mind by which all knowledge is possible, and without which the senses prove nothing. "I call all knowledge *transcendental*," says he, in one of his principal works, "which occupies itself not so much with objects as with the way of knowing these objects." There is nothing very difficult to understand in all this, and nothing to which any would object but those who cling to the sensual philosophy; which we certainly do not. But it soon went much farther. Kant himself was one of the most unintelligible of writers. Complaining that the old words would not express his new notions, he invented new terms in philosophy and employed in fact a new language. In his own life time there were hot disputes among his disciples as to what he had taught or meant; and he never interfered to decide such questions; perhaps because he did not himself see very clearly what he did mean. One thing, however, was certain. He had with great boldness and equal ability, opened the way for a philosophy which should appeal but seldom to the senses, and manifest no great respect for their authority. And his successors—if so they may be called—went much farther than he. He was a close thinker and reasoner; but it became a sort of fashion to philosophize in a wild and random way; definitions were sneered at, all limitations were looked upon as signs of feebleness; and it seemed as if a whole class of writers, some of whom were very able men, had set to work under the conviction that whatever was unintelligible was therefore profound.

In England this did not spread much; partly from the remaining influence of the sensual philosophy, and partly because that is a very busy and practical nation; and therefore it made no great progress here, because the readers of this country were, until very lately, almost confined to English books. There were however some men in England in love with transcendentalism; men like the late Mr. Coleridge, whose extraordinary genius seemed often on the point of breaking down into insanity, for the plain reason that he was not protected by any clearly defined and deeply seated principles of thought and belief. Such men began to excite the most excitable minds of this country; and the study of German, which is now quite common, came in aid of this new influence. And transcendentalism, thus imported, thus planted here, grew, as our country itself and every thing in it grows. That is to say, it cast off all restraint, and expanded in every direction, and indulged itself in just that extravagance of speculation and expression, which might be expected where there was no acknowledged allegiance to established truths, no reverence for anything, to hold it in check and mature its products. Our transcendentalists have pushed this fashion of reasoning and composing, as far as it can go. Some of them not only write as fast as they can *think*, without pausing to *reflect*, but sometimes much faster than they think; and they never seem to suspect that their words are, of course, meaningless.

The peculiar style of the transcendentalists is their most obvious absurdity, and it has been abundantly ridiculed and caricatured. It indicates the very common folly of supposing one says a new thing when he says only an old thing in a new way. Originality,—is their perpetual aim. They claim for their own system the freshness and beauty of a new creation; and it is not strange that they should feel as if they, of all men, must be always original. Now this is not easy; that is, it is not easy to find sentiments, opinions, principles, which none have found and uttered before. But it is comparatively easy to use new words, or old words in new ways; and when they can make their phrases startling and picturesque, and hint at the vast treasury of truth which they have behind the veil, it is natural that their followers should believe, and accordingly be lost in admiration. All this is exceedingly silly; but it is also *significant;* it affords one indication of the real nature and character of transcendentalism. Truth is light, not darkness. Its spontaneous form is simple, direct and transparent language. It sometimes happens, that an individual has a clear thought, and is unable to express it clearly: but this will not often occur if he thinks less of himself and more of the truth. And when a system of thought loves and seeks obscurity, it is a very bad sign, to say no more. Nevertheless, transcendentalism possesses and presents some principles, and some qualities, which may be seen, and ought to be seen and known for what they are; and we propose to consider them in subsequent numbers of our magazine.

Upon every observer of this age, the remark forces itself, that opinions and principles are losing their authority, and the foundations of belief are shaken and shattered. There are those who regard this with joy and hope; they read in it a promise that the oppressions of the past will be avenged, that darkness and night, and the violence which is wrought in darkness are fleeing away; that freedom and the rights of man, freedom of thought and freedom of life are about to be established upon sure foundations. In this there is much folly and some wickedness. But not more folly than theirs, who suppose that all change must be for the worse; who execrate or despise every thing that is new, and diligently labor to beat back the sunbeams which are breaking in through the opening chinks of those walls upon which the doom of destruction is written. There is folly, and great folly, in both of these extremes. But they are just such extremes and there is in them just such folly as are proper to the circumstances of the age.

We are witnessing the formation of a new earth under the influence of a new heaven; for the old earth and the old heaven have passed and are passing away. This we know from the revelations which have been made for the instruction of the New Church; but we do not learn from them the fact alone. We learn also the causes which are producing this great change; the principles which must govern and the influences which will modify their operation; the end for which the change is wrought and towards which it proceeds; and, in some degree, the circumstances which must accompany the steps of its progress. But they who are without this information can form only obscure anticipations of coming events; and these anticipations will receive shape and color from the temperament and habits of individuals. Hence it is, that the fearful, and they who believe that the world has already degenerated, and who would gladly give up all hope of improvement for the comfortable security and external peace which they dearly love,—they regard the universal commotion around them, like the first heavings of an earthquake, which will throw down and mingle in a common ruin all that man has constructed or God has given. While they who are sanguine and of a restless nature, and they who, deeply moved by some of the mischiefs and corruptions of the past or present day, have looked at them till, in their morbid enthusiasm, they can see nothing else, and above all, the vain and turbulent, who love to catch attention and be thought the founders and the rulers of new schools,—these love the universal disturbance of the present day, as a healthy mind loves calm and order.

We have made these remarks, because they may be illustrated by the course and the character of what is called Transcendentalism amongst us. Of the "school" which professes or approves that system, there are persons of the kinds we have sketched; and their motives and ends are as diverse as can well be imagined. Often one common object will bring and hold together those who have on other grounds little sympathy or similarity; and often is that object sought, for wholly different purposes. The history of opinion and of society in all ages proves this. But we know no instance more striking than in this matter of Transcendentalism. Among its disciples are those whose piety we have reason to regard as fervent and sincere, and those whose whole sense of religion would easily evaporate in a rhapsody on a rosebud. There are those of a still and contemplative temper, with little love of exhibition, and those who are unhappy if they are not always saying or doing something which shall mark a difference between them and common men, and are therefore always pressing before the public in books or lectures. What then is the common end of all these? In it we shall find their common bond; and not this only, but it must disclose to us that essential thing, which, common to it in all its forms, and in all the minds which embrace it, must qualify and characterize the whole system.

We think it obvious, what this one thing is, which Transcendentalism in all its forms seeks, and, with more or less of positiveness, asserts itself to have accomplished: it is,—to solve the problem of man's relation to the First Cause which produced him, and to the spiritual influences and laws which pervade and vivify and govern him. Here then is one cause of its attractiveness. It speaks for, as well as to, those whose minds are stirred by the great desire of comprehending their origin and their destiny. All persons who have a strong tendency to reflective thought, and who are not immersed in the cares or toils of life, have this desire. It varies in its form as well as its degree in various persons; but to them in whom it is most earnest, who, feeling that before an infinite future our poor present is nothing, and that the concerns and the knowledges of temporal and material things are worthless in comparison with the truths which, treating of an eternity, may qualify its character, and are in themselves the greatest and the highest the mind can contemplate,—and who are not restrained by settled notions of religious doctrines,—to them Transcendentalism has a peculiar charm, and among them it finds its disciples.

But this problem has always been before the minds of men; it has always been the leading object of all religious philosophy; how then has this old question given birth to this new system? One answer, and but a partial answer, is, that Transcendentalism is not altogether a new thing; in some respects it is, as we said in a former number, as old as human inquiry. Still, in its present form and aspect, it is a new thing; and the reason is, that the great questions which it seeks to answer stand now in the world under new auspices. They are asked with a freedom, and in a spirit unknown before. The ancient philosophies were free enough, and were as profound as the utmost efforts of the strongest understandings could make them; but they were confined to very limited classes. There was then no press, no interchange of thought between nations, no

general education. And since the Christian era, philosophy has either acknowledged the control and guidance of the Church, or been marked and
oppressed by its anathema. Not so is it now. *There is no Church*; there
is none in Christendom, save that which is in the feebleness of infancy.
The old church has lost its power. It no longer holds public opinion as
its subject and its instrument. Hence men may hold almost any doctrine,
and express it in almost any way, and yet claim to be religious men and
Christians, because there is no fixed and acknowledged standard whereby
to try this claim. We see, both here and in Europe, a latitude of belief
allowed which would have been formerly impossible; and principles and
opinions advanced and defended from pulpits, which would have been
heretofore excommunicated with the universal assent of the church as
mere infidelity,—or, rather, they who chose to hold and declare such doctrines in past ages, would not have thought for a moment of retaining the
name or profession of church members, or of Christians. Where the
Catholic church retains its temporal power, and where the established
Church of England controls by authority or by interest, there is less of
this freedom manifested. But in this country, where every thing is unrestrained to a degree unknown upon earth before or elsewhere, and in
this part of our country, where, without more restraint, there is more than
the average amount of reading and literary speculation, this kind of liberty
is rushing rapidly towards license. And here is the peculiar province of
what we call Transcendentalism.

The great growth of free inquiry, and the relief from the bonds
which have hitherto confined it, are not accidental. They are the legitimate result of the ecclesiastical condition of the world; or, in other words,
of the condition of its church. We use this word now in its broadest sense,
and are aware that but little which we can say of it can be received or
indeed understood out of the New Church, for elsewhere all true idea of
a church has faded from men's minds as the church itself has faded from
the earth. But if there were no church upon earth there could be no life;
for the church is its soul. It is the medium of conjunction with the source
of life; and it is the medium by which all truth is given to men. The
constant effort of Divine Providence is to give all truth to all men; but
this effort is always limited by the capacity of the world to receive truth.
In the days of the first christian church, truth was veiled; and then a
thousand restraints upon inquiry were permitted or imposed, because inquiry could not be answered. The time had not come when the truth itself
was or could be given; the time had not come when the "veil which was
cast over all nations" could be taken away. But that time has now come,
and the prophecy is fulfilled which declared that the veil itself *should* be
taken away. And while they who know only of the old church look with
dismay upon the advancing tread of this freed giant of inquiry, and feel
as if his every step crushed some ancient belief and his hands were out-

stretched to desolate every altar and heap upon it the ruins of every temple,—they who know that a new day is dawning, recognise in this very work of destruction one more sign that new truths are being given. Their trust in the Divine Providence teaches them that the questioning spirit of the age would not be let loose, if there were no answer to its questions. And we believe that the Church which is now being established can give this answer. Let us then compare its answer with that of Transcendentalism.

The question concerns the relation of man to his Maker; of the finite to the infinite; of the Human to the Divine. And this relation comprehends all of man's origin, faculty, duty and destiny. It is plain, that so far as we understand it, we understand how man receives life from the source of life; how he may best conform and correspond to this influent life, to its laws or its commands, and what he may hope for, by way of a renewed or continued life, after the form and matter which being conditions of his earthly existence are taken away by death. All this, and infinitely more is comprehended in this relation. And moreover the relation must be in some way a relation of union, of conjunction. Thought itself is spiritual; every hope, and reason, and argument, are all of the spirit, and are all manifested through bodily life. The soul and the body, the immortal and the mortal, make the man. An inquiry therefore into the relation of the finite to the infinite, is in fact an inquiry into the conjunction of the finite with the infinite; of that which is created with that which creates; of the Human with the Divine; and the object of the inquiry is, to understand how the Divine and the Human are One.

In our Lord and Saviour Jesus Christ, the Human was made Divine; He assumed the Human, and wholly glorified it, and thereby made it wholly divine; and thus, in Him, the Divine and the Human are perfectly one. In one way of viewing this doctrine, it cannot be considered as new, or as belonging exclusively to the New Church. On the contrary, it is most expressly and repeatedly asserted in the gospels, and forms a part of the belief of nearly all Christendom, in every age. Not only so, but it entered into heathenism, by a kind of anticipation. Until the event itself occurred, "priests and prophets longed for it." And that looking forward to the coming of the external fact, and inward to the internal truths and doctrines and principles of which it is the soul, constituted in such schools as those of Pythagoras and Plato a most profoundly religious philosophy, and through them exercised a salutary influence upon all surrounding religions. A similar thing may be said of the oriental nations, for learned men have found such indisputable proofs of a similar belief as to lead to the theory of one common origin of the whole. But, in another way of viewing the subject, the doctrine is new in the New Church. Its aspect is new, and its extent. The "veil" is taken from it; it is fully disclosed; and,—what is in the present connection most important,—it is no longer a doctrine of religion only; it is now seen to be a doctrine of philosophy also, and of all philosophy, and the chief and central doctrine of all philosophy. We know now that the fact was one for which all preceding time was preparing and from which all succeeding time takes a new beginning. We know too that in the glorification of the Human by the Divine, of the Son by the Father, and in the oneness of the Son with the Father, are gathered all the truths and all the laws of all creation, life and action. And from this we know, consequently, that in proportion as we understand that fact, so we may understand these laws and truths; and therefore, if we would comprehend the mysteries of our being,—of our origin, our nature, our duty and our destiny,—if we would comprehend all that is embraced in the relation which binds us as human beings to our God and Father, we must *begin* with the great fact in which this relation is realized, perfected and fulfilled; which took place in the fullness of time as the great medium of all human good, and is recorded in the gospels and now more fully explained in the revelations made for the New Church, as the great medium for all improvement in true wisdom. And it is because of these revelations thus supplying this source of infinite instruction, that a freedom of inquiry is *now* permitted in the world, which was unknown to former ages.

And now, without stopping to consider at all what these revelations have disclosed, let us turn to Transcendentalism; and we shall find at once an extreme contrast. The New Church teaches, that, to be wise, man should look *from* himself; Transcendentalism teaches him to look always *to* himself. The New Church derives from that great act wherein the infinite love and the infinite wisdom and the infinite power of our Lord were equally and fully displayed, not only a reason for the deepest humiliation, not only a ground for humble but unlimited hope, but a truth which will fill with light an understanding that lies open to it, as a sun illuminates a world; while Transcendentalism holds itself above all this, declares that the mind of man is self-luminous, and gropes or dances over the face of things as if it were a living and conscious Will-o'-the-wisp flitting over a desolate and murky waste. The New Church declares, that, as the renunciation of self-love is the beginning of all goodness, so the renunciation of the pride of self-intelligence is the beginning of all true wisdom; but, with Transcendentalism, the pride of self-intelligence is itself the beginning and the end of all wisdom. "I," says one who is its hierophant in this region, "I, the finite, worship in myself, myself the infinite." And so it always is, though not always so expressed. Its whole religion is self-worship.

We do not propose to attempt a statement of what the doctrines of the New Church teach on this subject, and contrast them with the teachings of Transcendentalism. We have not room, nor time for this work; nor is there any need of it. In fact there is no definite doctrine of Transcendentalism. There is nothing like system, order, connection or defini-tion about it; and this is one thing which some of its disciples boast and are proud of:—they call it freedom!

It is quite enough to examine the principles and the methods of Transcendentalism in its inquiries, to know whither they must lead. He who has no care nor thought, nor hope that an educated animal might not have, will find nothing in his own nature which arrests his attention, nothing in the possibilities of the future which may move him to fear and solemn awe. But whoever has reflected upon the soul within him and felt the weight of the great mystery of life, cannot but hunger and thirst for an answer to the questions which come from the depths of his heart. And there is one right way to seek, to find, to have this answer. It is to go to the great event which solved the problem in point of fact; to go in humility and a docile spirit as a little child to Him in whom there is an Humanity once infested by tendencies to all that could limit, lower or pollute it, but by perfect victory over these, glorified, and filled with the Divine, and made Divine. To this, the one right way, all, of every religious name, do go, whose faces are towards the light; all go, but each in his or her own way, and with more or less clearness of vision, and more or less comfort and instruction; but all go thither, and in one respect alike, for unless they go as little children, they cannot have the wisdom which belongs to the kingdom of heaven. And if they go in this right way, they may be learned or simple, man or woman, able to tell by words all that they learn, or only showing it forth in the peace and order of a useful and quiet life; in one thing they will be alike; they will show how well they have learnt that the very best instruction is that which teaches how to do our daily duty and that the very highest wisdom consists in doing it, as our duty, in order, industry and peace.

So too there is one wrong way; for the thousand errors on this subject of the past and present time are as one in this; they begin with self; their first effort is to construct God in the image and after the likeness of man; they make pride a duty; the dignity of our nature is the one thing they will never forget; and religious duty is summed up in the constant and regular observance of the worship of self. But as all this is hostile to the habits of reverence and the common feelings of religious faith and prac-tice which yet prevail not only around all, but in the minds of almost all, it must put on a disguise; and many are its masks and names; but that concealment which it most depends upon, it borrows from a robe of glit-tering mist that constantly enwraps it, and so blinds the eye, that we can see nothing distinctly and imagine that we see just what we please. Never has this been carried so far, as now and here. Never has a system been so openly and professedly self-seeking and egotistical, never so glittering, shapeless and impalpable. It would seem as if the law that all things must have their opposites, could alone account for this. And we understand it better when we look upon it as the opposite of that New Church, which now preaches a doctrine that goes beyond all former doctrine in its promise of a clear and definite explanation of the mysteries of life and in its command to fill every moment of life with religious duty; not a duty which can be helped out by talk, intention and speculation, but the duty which is to be faithfully done, day by day, in just the way that Providence appoints to us.

The difference between these two ways is practical; and not only practical as it affects the life and conduct, but as it affects the understanding. There is no greater enemy to clear thoughts and just conclusions than indulged self-conceit. The very word vanity indicates this; originally meaning emptiness, nothingness, and sometimes used so now, its more common meaning is the love of indulging self-conceit and self-display; and the same word means these two things, because they are so closely connected. Now, Transcendentalism holds, that the mind of man is itself infinite, and has within its depths all mysteries, and has moreover the power, by self-inspection, of insight into these mysteries. And there is nothing whatever to check, restrain, or humble it, in this career. It acknowledges no principle which can guide it; no feeling of reverence which would oppose, and might mitigate its inflation; no established truth, no acknowledged standard, by which it could determine what notion was and what was not the mere phantasm of a stimulated imagination; no rules of reason, by which it might discriminate between mere words, polished and glittering words,—and distinct, apprehensible thoughts. On the other hand, in the New Church we have the Word of God, and the duties of life; they are with us at every moment and in every work as guides, and, where needful, as restraints; and, however imperfect our conformity or obedience may be, yet we know we cannot forget or neglect them, without danger not only of sin, but of foolishness.

But let it not be supposed that we think the disciples of this school are therefore to be condemned or dreaded. Far from it. Over this school as over each one of its disciples, a judgment will pass. And it will sift the good from the evil *in* each one. Those of them whose conscience and religious sense demand a reality, and ask that the Word which God has given should be held in some reverence, and who, when they cry aloud for truth cannot accept a shining vapor in its stead,—all such are passing through experiences which may not be pleasant but will be wholesome; and we believe there are many such. Transcendentalism offers much of charm and enticement to honest but enthusiastic seekers after truth. It is often compared to Swedenborgianism; it is commonly thought to be near of kin with it, and almost the same thing. And there are respects in which they are much alike. Both proclaim the utter degeneracy of the church and the world; both declare that all man's life needs to be purified, renewed, and lifted from the ground; both declare that infinite measures of truth lie within our reach; both profess to teach how new life, religious, moral, intellectual, civil and social, may be poured forth upon the world, to vivify and re-create it. But here the analogy stops; here the likeness gives place to contrast and opposition; for when they both seek for the instruction which they profess to give,—the one turns towards light and the source of light,—the other towards thick darkness.

"Transcendentalism"

"J"*

Mr. Emerson is the leader of the new Boston school of philosophy—the sect of wise men from the east; a school which has a certain daring transcendental spirit of its own, but (so far as we can discover) holding no very precise doctrines, and without any one bond of union. Its sub-leaders and separate teachers, each, declare a modification of the grand doctrine for themselves, each are their own instructors. They compose an independency of opinion. They unite to differ. Referring every thing to the individual soul, they must entertain, within themselves, a contrariety of belief, a mixture of systems. They are now shrewd and practical, again absurd and visionary; at last, high and spiritual.

The tone of the sect, is at once mystical, aphoristic, oracular. They are stiff dogmatists. In treating with them, you must have a large share of faith, or rather credulity. By it they seek to move mountains of meta-physical difficulty, to unriddle the darkest problems of humanity, to dis-close the secrets of the universe. Vain endeavor! to do them justice, they have high aims, spiritual views, but they rush in with boldness, where—'angels fear to tread.'

They are hardly as clear and practical, as they are daring and pre-sumptuous. Their success is doubtful; their tendency, injurious. Injurious, especially in point of religious creed. For, the certain effect, the sure end of their philosophizing, is Pantheism. This, by making every thing God, destroys the very idea of a Deity, distinct from matter and from the creatures of his plastic hand.

The sect has a narrowing influence, not only from the very fact of its being a *sect*, but also from the reiteration of its favorite topics. These are of progress, of insight, of the individual soul. Most true and weighty are they; yet, by being eternally harped on and insulated, they lose their effect; and out of their proper place, like figures transposed, their force and complexion is entirely altered. In this way the highest truths may be

*Reprinted in part from "Ralph Waldo Emerson," *Arcturus*, 1 (April 1841), 278–284.

converted into, may be made to assume, the appearance of the rankest falsehoods.

The style of these writers deserves to be noticed. Their favorite method of composition seems to be transposition, involution, a conciseness approaching to obscurity, and sometimes actually obscuring the thought. They are writers of maxims, thinking to make old thoughts appear new, by the striking form in which they are moulded. On the tritest topics, they are on the look-out for some grand discovery. They will not believe truth *has been* and *is*; they think it is to come. They look for a revelation. They seek a sign. But their oracles are not always veracious. There are lying prophets among them. In all probability, they employ this form to hide the truth. It is easy to speak falsely in enigmas: it is almost impossible to lie in plain phrase.

[Boston Transcendentalism]

Charles Dickens*

The fruits of the earth have their growth in corruption. Out of the rottenness of these things, there has sprung up in Boston a sect of philosophers known as Transcendentalists. On inquiring what this appellation might be supposed to signify, I was given to understand that whatever was unintelligible would be certainly transcendental. Not deriving much comfort from this elucidation, I pursued the inquiry still further, and found that the Transcendentalists are followers of my friend Mr. Carlyle, or, I should rather say, of a follower of his, Mr. Ralph Waldo Emerson. This gentleman has written a volume of Essays, in which, among much that is dreamy and fanciful (if he will pardon me for saying so), there is much more that is true and manly, honest and bold. Transcendentalism has its occasional vagaries (what school has not?) but it has good healthful qualities in spite of them; not least among the number a hearty disgust of Cant, and an aptitude to detect her in all the million varieties of her everlasting wardrobe. And therefore if I were a Bostonian, I think I would be a Transcendentalist.

*Reprinted from *American Notes for General Circulation* (London: Chapman and Hall, 1842), I, 133–134.

"American Transcendentalism"

James Murdock*

That species of German Philosophy which has sprung up among the Unitarian Clergy of Massachusetts, and which is advocated especially in a recent periodical called the Dial, is known by the appellation TRANSCENDENTALISM. The propriety however of the appellation, may be questioned. KANT, who, so far as I know, first brought the term Transcendental into philosophy, would certainly not apply it to this or to any similar system. He would denominate it TRANSCENDENT, not Transcendental. The difference, according to his views, is immense. Both terms indeed denote the *surpassing* or transcending of certain limits; but the limits surpassed are entirely different. That is called *Transcendental*, which surpasses the limits of sensible or empirical knowledge and expatiates in the region of pure thought or absolute science. It is therefore truly scientific; and it serves to explain empirical truths, so far as they are explicable. On the other hand, that is called *Transcendent*, which not only goes beyond empiricism, but surpasses the boundaries of human knowledge. It expatiates in the shadowy region of imaginary truth. It is, therefore, falsely called science: it is the opposite of true philosophy. A balloon sent up by a besieging army to overlook the ramparts of a fortification, if moored by cables, whereby its elevation, its movements, and its safe return into camp are secured, is a *transcendental* thing; but if cut loose from its moorings and left to the mercy of the winds, it is *transcendent*; it has no connection with any thing stable, no regulator; it rises or descends, moves this way or that way, at hap-hazard, and it will land, no one knows where or when. Now, according to the Critical Philosophy, all speculations in physical science that attempt to go beyond phenomena, and all speculations on supersensible things which attempt to explain their essential nature, are *transcendent*; that is, they overleap the boundaries of human knowledge. In violation of these canons, Fichte, Schelling, and Hegel

*Reprinted from *Sketches of Modern Philosophy* (Hartford, Conn.: John C. Wells, 1842), pp. 167–188. Omitted are lengthy quotations from George Ripley, Orestes A. Brownson, Emerson, and William Dexter Wilson.

plunged head-long into such speculations, and yet called them Transcendental; and the new German Philosophers of Massachusetts follow their example.

Waiving however this misnomer,—as every real Kantian must regard it, we will call this philosophy *Transcendental*; since its advocates choose to call it so, and seeing the name has become current in our country. And we will first inquire into its origin among us, and then proceed to notice its prominent characteristics.

ORIGIN OF TRANSCENDENTALISM AMONG US.

According to their own representations, the believers in this philosophy are Unitarian clergymen, who had for some time been dissatisfied with the Unitarian system of theology. They tell us, they found it to be a meagre, uninteresting system, which did not meet the religious wants of the community. While laboring to improve their system of theology, or to find a better, they cast their eyes on foreign countries. There they discovered a different philosophy prevailing; a philosophy which gives an entirely new version to Christianity, invests it with a more spiritual character, with more power to move the soul, to call forth warm emotions, and to produce communion with God. This philosophy they have now embraced. Such, they inform us, was the origin of Transcendentalism among them.—But it may be more satisfactory to give their own statements on this head. . . .

CHARACTERISTICS OF THE TRANSCENDENTAL PHILOSOPHY.

None of the Transcendentalists of this country are Philosophers by profession. Nearly all of them are clergymen, of the Unitarian school; and their habits of thought, their feelings, and their aims, are manifestly theological. Nor do they give us proof that they have devoted very great attention to philosophy as a science. They have produced, I believe, no work professedly on the subject, not even an elementary treatise; and, if I do not mistake, they have brought forward no new views or principles in philosophy. So far as I can judge, they have merely taken up the philosophy of Victor Cousin, and, after comparing it according to their opportunity with that of the more recent German schools, have modified a little some of its dicta, and applied them freely to scientific and practical theology. At the same time they take little pains, to elucidate and explain the principles of their new philosophy. They address us, as if we all read and understood their favorite Cousin, and were not ignorant of the speculations of the German pantheists: and their chief aim seems to be, to shew us how much better this Gallo-Germanic philosophy explains the religion of nature and of the bible, than the old philosophy of Locke and the Scottish school. Whoever, therefore, would understand the Transcendental writers, must first understand, if he can, the French philosopher Cousin and the German pantheists.

The philosophy of Cousin, as well as that of the modern Germans, we have attempted to describe very briefly, in the preceding chapters; and to them the reader is referred.

Cousin maintains that, by taking a higher point of observation, he has brought all previous systems of philosophy to harmonize with each other. [See his Introd. to Hist. of Phil. by Linberg, page 414.] He therefore adopts, and uses at pleasure, the peculiar phraseology of all the systems, as being all suited to express his own new views. This causes his writings to exhibit, not only great variety, but apparently, if not really, great inconsistency of terminology. And hence different persons, aiming to follow him as a guide, may easily mistake his meaning, and adopt different principles; or, if they adopt the same principles, they may express themselves in a very different manner. And, if we suppose the same persons, with only a moderate share of philosophic learning and philosophic tact, to attempt to re-construct the philosophy of Cousin, by comparing it with the German systems from which it is taken, and at the same time to adopt Cousin's lax use of language; we may easily conceive, what confusion of thought and obscurity of statement may appear on their pages. Now the Transcendentalists, if I do not mistake, have thus followed Cousin. Of course, they differ considerably from one another; some following Cousin more closely, and others leaning more towards some German; some preferring one set of Cousin's terms, and others another, or coining new ones to suit their fancy. After all, Linberg's translation of Cousin's Introduction to the History of Philosophy may be considered as the great store house, from which most of them—e.g. Brownson, Emerson, Parker, &c.—have derived their peculiar philosophical opinions, their modes of reasoning, and their forms of thought and expression.

The radical principle of the Transcendental philosophy, the corner stone of the whole edifice, is, Cousin's doctrine that *Spontaneous Reason* acquaints us with the true and essential nature of things. According to this doctrine, Reason, when uncontrolled by the Will, or when left free to expatiate undirected and uninfluenced by the voluntary faculty, always apprehends things as they are, or has direct and absolute knowledge of the objects of its contemplation. This *clairvoyance* of Reason, Cousin calls "an instinctive perception of truth, an entirely instinctive development of thought,"—"an original, irresistible, and unreflective perception of truth," "pure apperception, and spontaneous faith,"—"the absolute affirmation of truth, without reflection,—inspiration,—veritable revelation."—[Introd. &c. pages 163, 167, 172, 166.] The characteristics of this kind of knowledge, as being *immediate*, and *infallible*, though not always perfectly distinct at first, and as being *divine*, or as coming from God either directly or indirectly, all Transcendentalists maintain. But in what manner, or by what mode of action, our Reason acquires this knowledge, they do not distinctly inform us. Whether our Creator has endowed us with an intellectual *instinct*, a power of rational intuition; or whether the rational soul, as itself partaking of the divine nature, has this *inherent sagacity* in and of itself; or whether the divine Being, God himself, is always present in the soul and acting in it by way of *inspiration*, these philosophers seem not to have decided. They use terms, however, which fairly imply each and all of these hypotheses, and specially the last. But however undecided on this point, which is of so much importance in a philosophic view, on the general fact that all rational beings do possess this knowledge, they are very explicit; and some of them attempt to prove it, by reasoning from the necessity of such knowledge to us, and from the current belief of mankind. [See Cousin's Psychology, Chap. vi and a writer in the Dial, vol. ii. page 86, &c.]

The effects of this principle, when carried into theology, are immense. It dispels all mysteries and all obscurities from this most profound of all sciences, and gives to human Reason absolute dominion over it. For, it makes the divine Being, his government and laws, and our relations to him, and all our religious obligations and interests,—every part of theology, theoretical or practical,—perfectly comprehensible to our Reason in its spontaneous operation. It makes all the doctrines of *natural religion* the objects of our direct, intuitive knowledge: we need no explanations and no confirmations from any books or teachers; we have only to listen to the voice of spontaneous Reason, or to the teachings of our own souls, the light that shines within us, and all will be perfectly intelligible and absolutely certain. And hence, we need no *external revelation*, no inspired teacher, to solve our doubts and difficulties, or to make any part of natural religion, or any principle of moral duty, either more plain or more certain. We are, all of us, prophets of God, all inspired through our Reason, and we need no one to instruct and enlighten us. The great Seers of ancient times, Moses and the prophets, Christ and the apostles, were no otherwise inspired than we all are; they only cultivated and listened to spontaneous Reason more than ordinary men; and this enabled them to see further and to speak and write better than other men on religious subjects. If we would determine whether the *bible* was written by inspired men, we need not pore upon the so called external evidences, miracles, prophecies, &c. but merely listen to the testimony of our own souls, the teachings of spontaneous Reason, or what is called the internal evidence, and we shall at once see the clear and infallible marks of inspiration. And *to understand the bible*, we need no aid from learned interpreters. Only give us the book in a language we can read, and the suggestions of our own inspired minds will enable us to comprehend perfectly the import of every sentence, and to see clearly what is divine and what is human, or what originated from spontaneous Reason and what from human infirmity, in the holy scriptures. And of course, every man is competent to decide, definitely and infallibly, all the controversies among theologians and all the disputes between sects of Christians, respecting the *doctrines taught in the bible*. In short, not only the profound researches of philologists, antiquarians, and biblical commentators, but also the elaborate discussions of didactic theologians, polemic, apologetic, and metaphysical, are all of little or no value in theology. Instead of depending on them, the theological inquirer should rather retire to solitude and silence, and while musing on religious subjects, with the bible and the book of nature before him, he should refrain from giving any determinate direction to his thoughts, and allowing them to flow on spontaneously, he should listen to the voice of Reason as she expatiates freely in the open field of visions; then he will be caught up, as it were, to the third heaven, and will see all that the inspired prophets saw; his knowledge will be superhuman and divine.

But to understand more fully the metaphysics of the Transcendental writers, we must not overlook their *ontological* doctrines. If Reason acquaints us with the true and essential nature of all things, then the field of ontology is open fully to our inspection, and we may form there a perfectly solid and safe science. Accordingly, all Transcendentalists, on both sides of the Atlantic, assume some system of ontology as the basis of their speculations. The prevailing system among the modern Germans, and that to which Cousin and his American followers assent, is *pantheistic*: that is, it resolves the universe into one primordial Being, who develops himself in various finite forms: in other words, it supposes God and the developments of God, to be the only real existences, the το παν, the entire universe. But when they attempt to explain this general statement, the Germans bring forward different hypotheses. Some, following *Spinoza*, invest the primordial Being with the essential attributes of both a substance and a person; and they suppose him to create from himself, or to form out of his own substance, all rational and sentient beings and all material things. Others, with *Schelling*, suppose him to be originally neither a person nor a substance, but the elementary principle of both, which, in developing itself, becomes first a person and a substance, and then a universe of beings and things. Others follow *Hegel*, and adopt a system of pure *idealism*. They suppose concrete ideas to be the only real existences, and the logical genesis of ideas to be the physical genesis of the universe. Take the simple idea of existence, and abstract from it every thing conceivable, so that it shall become evanescent; and in that evanescent state, while fluctuating between something and nothing, it is the primitive, the generative principle of all things. For it is the most comprehensive or generical of all ideas, including all other ideas under it as subordinate genera and species; and therefore, when expanded or drawn out into the subordinate genera and species, it becomes the το παν, the universe of beings and things. Vacillating among all these theories, especially between the two last, and trying to amalgamate them all in one, Cousin, without exhibiting any very definite ideas, merely declares the Infinite to be the primitive, and all that is finite to be derivative from the Infinite, while yet both the Infinite and the finite are so inseparable that neither can exist without the other.—The appellation *Pantheists*, it appears, is unacceptable to Cousin, and to most of his American followers; but some of the latter voluntarily assume it; and they unscrupulously apply it to all Transcendentalists. That the doctrines of the Transcendentalists, as well as those of Spinoza, Schelling, and Hegel, are really and truly *pantheistic*, appears from the fact that they hold to but *one essence*, or *one substance*, in the universe. They expressly deny, that God created or produced the world *out of nothing*, or that he gave existence to beings and things the substance or matter of which had no previous existence: they say, he created or brought forth the world *from himself*, or formed it out of *his own substance*; and also, that he still exists in the created universe, and the created universe in him, thus constituting an *absolute unity*, as to essence or substance. That the epithet *pantheistic* may properly be applied to such doctrines, seems not to be deniable. [See Krug's Philos. Lexikon; art. *Pantheismus*.]

As Pantheists, the Transcendentalists must behold God, or the divine nature and essence, in every thing that exists. Of course, none of them can ever doubt the *existence of God*, or be in the least danger of atheism; for they cannot believe any thing to exist, without finding God in it: they see him, they feel him, they have sensible perception of his very substance in every object around.—Moreover, if our souls are only portions of the Divinity, if they are really God working in us, then there is solid ground for the belief that *spontaneous Reason* always sees the true nature of things, or has divine knowledge of the objects of its contemplation.— And again, if it is the Divine Nature which lives and acts in all creatures and things, then all *their action* is *Divine action*. All created intelligences think, and feel, and act, as God acts in them; and of course, precisely as He would have them. There can, then, be nothing *wrong*, nothing *sinful*, in the character or conduct of any rational being. There may be imperfection, or imperfect action, because the whole power of God is not exerted; but every act, so far as it goes, is just what it should be, just such as best pleases God. And hence, though men may sigh over their imperfections, or may ardently desire and strive to become more perfect, yet they can have no reason for *repentance*, for sorrow and shame and self-condemnation, for any thing they have done or have omitted to do. Neither can they feel themselves to need any radical *change of character*, to make them acceptable to God; or any *Redeemer*, to rescue them from impending perdition. All they need, is, to foster the divinity within, to give it more full scope and more perfect action; then they will become all that it is possible they should be, and all they can reasonably desire.—These inferences from their principles, are not palmed upon Transcendentalists by their adversaries, but are admitted and defended by their ablest writers. Says one of them, whom we have before quoted, [Dial, vol. i. pages 423–4,] "Holding as they do but one essence of all things, which essence is God, Pantheists must deny the existence of essential evil. All evil is negative,—it is imperfection, non-growth. It is not essential, but modal. Of course there can be no such thing as hereditary sin,—a tendency positively sinful in the soul. Sin is not a wilful transgression of a righteous law, but the difficulty and obstruction which the Infinite meets with in entering into the finite. *Regeneration* is nothing but an ingress of God into the soul, before which sin disappears as darkness before the rising sun. Pantheists hold also to the atonement, or at-one-ment between the soul and God. This is strictly a unity or *oneness of essence*, to be brought about by the incarnation of the spirit of God, [in us,] which is going on in us as we grow in holiness. As we grow wise, just, and pure,—in a word, holy,—we grow to be one with him in mode, as we always were in essence. This atonement is effected by *Christ*, only in as far as he taught the manner in which it was to be accomplished more fully than any other, and gave us a better illustration of the method and result in his own person than any one else that has ever lived."

"Quozziana"

"Moonshine Milkywater"
[Samuel Kettell]*

Some restless wag in Boston, or rather some wags have got up a burlesque upon the pamphlet account of the Boz Dinner, in the city. Curry & Co. have it here for sale, and as a specimen of its style, we give the following letter from a transcendentalist, to the Committee, declining an invitation dinner. It is rich:

SUNDIAL AVENUE, Feb. 1, 1842.

Gentlemen of the Committee:

The wonder-sign of Great Goslington's furibundity is world-absorbing, Quozdom yawns abysmal. Lionized humanity, ephemeral though, floats upon the time-stream of newspapers, and peradventure may avoid fuliginous obliviscity. Scaturient are editor-paragraphs: committee-letters no less. Ancient Nicholas shall have his due; why not Liondom? and if Liondom then Quozdom. Penny-trumpetism is orbed:—small-talkism is cubed:—in the abyss of Quozdom ingulfed are both—re-nascent nevertheless. A dinner is, and it is not.

Savory, committee-gentlemen, is the order of the fried smelts, pork-fat in potatoism pan-borne, harmoniously liquidating. But wherefor fried? Are not gridirons extant in perennial parallelism? Is there lack of culinary capacity in copper stew-pans? Skillets—stand they no longer on three legs in *rerum natura?* Chimneys, methinks, are still redolent of smoke. Nay—Penobscot herrings, even, are world-pickled. Humanity, fish-wise enclined, esurient withal, but antagonizing chowder, might yearn stomach-borne, towards salt mackerel, though ensconced in Barreldom and branded Cargo No. 3.

Truly a world-wonder! But jubilating Quozdom cries, "get out of that!" Patience! O Quozdom—coals are black as ever and will not water run down hill—Taunton to the contrary notwithstanding? Surely Tag, Rag, and Bobtail are but a dualism: for it is only the Me and the Not-Me, that exist even in Committees and Corporations, pluripersonal although. A pound of butter is the sole type of exis-

*Reprinted from *Brother Jonathan*, 1 (26 March 1842), 354. The "Boz Dinner" was the dinner in honor of Charles Dickens in Boston during his visit there.

tence in the life actual, for cheesedom is but a formula. There is no cow, there is no calf; skim-milk alone is. Firkindom is the sappy recipient;—Polly Smallfry the old woman that sells it for ninepence a pound. Avoirdupois is the weight, but don't grease your fingers.

On the time-trodden subject of old shoes, what metaphysics have been expended!—Erebus-like, nevertheless, it frowns repellent; leaving respectable humanity to go barefoot or "toe the mark" in coriaceous integuments. Since calf-skin was made into knapsacks, cobblers have gone in leather aprons. But to Quozdom what avails this? Gentlemen I incline not dinner-wise. And why?—I have dined already. *Pransi;—* enough.

> I remain, gentlemen,
>
> MOONSHINE MILKYWATER.

PAUL PIPPS, Esq.
ELI SMALLCORN, Esq. } Committee.
ALLELUIA BUNCH, Esq.

"Transcendentalism.
A Miniature Essay"

J. E. Snodgrass*

How readily mankind—even the most enquiring and candid—are deceived by new styles and new forms. One half of what passes, now-a-days, for novelty in religion and literature, is no such thing in reality, but only in *appearance*. Such is the fact with respect to the cardinal and central doctrine of "Transcendentalism." Now we do not profess to be Transcendentalist, but we are sure of one thing; those who prate much about the "absurdities" of those bearing the name, are, for the greater number, totally ignorant of the true meaning of the word—and hence the laughable displays of ignorance made by some sectarian papers we meet with. Metaphysical science has had its day of ridicule from those who did not understand its designs any more than they discriminated between the legitimate fruits of its mode of reasoning, and the rediculous results of its *abuse*. Now "Transcendentalism" is the scape-goat, which is laden with all the sins of those who pretend to understand, and would use it, if they could, as a stepping stone to literary or theological fame. Let all systems, and creeds, and schools, receive a fair judgment from their opposers, and that they cannot expect until honest investigation *precedes* judgment.

It is not our design to give our notions on the subject just now. We may do that at some future time. We only desire to say a word or two, in relation to the meaning of the word "transcendental," as applied by the class of theologicians, of whom it is an appelative. In Germany (where the true and unadulterated view of the school are to be found) the term indicates that there are certain mental (or psychological) views of God and man and their relations generally, which mere reason, or logic if you please, cannot attain. In other words, that man who relies on processes of reasoning to arrive at truth, cannot depend, with certainty, on securing the prize. Hence the real Transcendentalist scouts *mere* reasons in morals. He looks *within*, and speakes and writes. He obeys the injunction of the poet, "Look into thy heart and write." He looks away from man and his

*Reprinted from *Magnolia*, 4 (April 1842), 214–215.

scholastic acquirements, and listens to the GOD within, as He teaches views of right and wrong, of truth and goodness. He believes that there are moments when thoughts flash upon the soul, unbidden or searched for by reason. These our moral consciousness proclaims true. Such are they which come to the humble and patient christian seated before his family hearth, or reposing "oft in the stilly night," upon a sleep-forsaken couch. Such are the inspirations of the true poet, when communing silently and alone with nature, when at twilight, for example, he gazes upon the sky with the lamps of Heaven hung out to light his course to God. Reason could not attain to these thoughts. They are not mere *uncertain opinions*. They are clearest perceptions, "transcending," the highest graspings of mere ratiocination. Argument, logical tho' it be, cannot lead to certainty. After the process is finished, we come to a conclusion and adopt a belief, but it is a mere opinion at last. There is no knowing for one's self. Truth from error the transcendentalist *does* know, for he has relied on his moral consciousness—which is to religion the "divinity within"—the "light within."

Now does it not seem strange that we find any christian with his Bible before him, scouting and ridiculing Transcendentalism, because many aspiring writers have suffered the language employed for teaching the views of this school, to run into unmeaning jargon. But is it not still more surprising to find the Methodist and the Quaker denouncing the system as absurd in whole as well as parts. The latter sectarian, particularly declaims against *reliance* upon education or arguments derived from collegiate investigations, in proclamations of gospel truth. He professes to preach as one sent of God—needing only spiritual enlightenment to direct the way to what is profitable to man's moral nature. The primitive Quakers taught that human reason cannot attain to the knowledge of divine truth, and that logic is unbecoming the preacher of *religious* knowledge. He waited for the intuitions of the divine teacher within. Now, we ask, what is there in the cardinal views of the real TRANSCENDENTALIST, so incongruous with the QUAKER or the METHODIST? Nothing, when their views are examined with the naked eye of candor, instead of the spectacles which ancient prejudice always wears upon his nose! What is there between them when names are *looked through,* to catch the designs of parties? Nothing! The fact is, all are struggling to catch a view of the true and the beautiful, (if honest in their religion) and there is something good in all the (apparently) clashing theological notions of mankind.

But we have said more already than we designed at this time. What we have written, has been dictated not by prejudice, but love of fair dealing. The article has been suggested by certain remarks which we have lately met with in a religious Journal that appeared to denounce "Transcendentalism," because certain writers of the school in this country, have mistaken *words* for ideas, and run themselves into the labyrinths of nonsense, leaving *terra firma* of thought, they have suffered themselves to attempt a sail over the ocean of the sky, without the ballast of truth, to protect them from the gales of speculation.

"Transcendentalism"

Noah Porter, Jr.*

What is Transcendentalism? This question is often asked by intelligent men, and sometimes with great earnestness. As the movement indicated by the word is without doubt extensively to prevail, the question is constantly becoming a question of greater interest, and will force itself upon the attention of thinking men throughout the country.

We make no apology, therefore, for attempting to answer the question—which we shall aim to do with all possible honesty and truth, and in a direct and business-like manner.

The word Transcendentalism, as used at the present day, has two applications, one of which is popular and indefinite, the other, philosophical and precise. In the former sense it describes men, rather than opinions, since it is freely extended to those who hold opinions, not only diverse from each other, but directly opposed, not only in their statements, but in their bearings upon the most important interests of man. In its precise and strictly appropriate application, it denotes a class of philosophical opinions, concerning the principles of human knowledge, or the grounds of our faith in the world of sense, and also in those higher truths which make us capable of science and of religion, those truths which impart to our being, as men, all its dignity, and to our hopes and fears for the future, their interest. Our first concern will be with the term in its looser and more general sense, or rather with the men, who, in current phrase, are called Transcendentalists. And here it will doubtless be asked, how can such a term be applied to them at all, and especially with what propriety can it be used in respect to those who differ so widely in their intellectual and moral position and influence? To this we answer, that while we cannot feel ourselves bound to defend, or even to explain the popular use of every epithet, which may originate only in ignorance or confusion of thought, it is yet more frequently true, that such use is owing to a sufficient reason, which it is not difficult to detect and state. In the present instance this reason is obvious. Those called transcenden-

*Reprinted from *American Biblical Repository*, n.s. 8 (July 1842), 195–218.

talists, while on the one hand they are Pantheists or social Reformers, receivers or rejectors of Christianity, unitarian or evangelical in their views of Christian truth, and in these respects, strangely unlike, are yet, in other points, as strikingly similar. These points are their intellectual and moral predispositions, their favorite philosophical and literary authors, and of consequence, their general cultivation and literary sympathies, with a strong family likeness in their modes of thought and expression. These striking and strong affinities make them of one school, and secure to its peculiar name, while within that school, are heard the voices of many discordant and contending teachers.

Among these we mention the Pantheistic variety, with whom the name of Mr. Emerson is too intimately connected, to require that it should be concealed. This school, though not claiming to be learnedly or profoundly metaphysical, and apparently despising the logical processes, the acute criticism, and the scientific research of a Kant or Cousin, and in many respects, not to say in most, very unlike to Plato, do yet follow in their train and call themselves by their name. Seizing upon a fragment of the Platonic or Transcendental formula, that the ideas which the reason reveals to man are objectively the laws by which the universe subsists and proceeds, they boldly and dogmatically affirm that these forces constitute the supreme Reason, that besides these there is no Deity; that the Deity is no living person, no Eternal Jehovah. These eternal and unchanging laws, both physical and moral, thus revealing themselves to man and regulating his happiness here and deciding his destiny hereafter, are the only God whom their philosophy acknowledges or their religion adores. This doctrine they propound, rather than prove. They utter it forth with the sage solemnity, the authoritative wisdom, and the affected phrase of the mysterious oracle or the inspired prophet. When ridiculed, they will not condescend to retort, for it would be inconsistent with their dignity as prophets. When questioned, they will not give a reason, but emit other mysterious utterances, which, according to the mood of the listener, are received either as the voice of divinest wisdom, or the ravings of men inspired by no other afflatus than that of their own self-complacency.

Other peculiarities they have which are innocent, or rather which almost makes them innocent, in the ancient sense of the word. They remove themselves from the stirring enterprises and the active benevolence of a bustling age, and can find in its science, its literature, and its religion, but little that suits their taste, or is worthy their notice. The transcendentalist, says their master and oracle, is content to wait in silence and seclusion for an age which shall be worthy of himself. From the past, also, he severs himself, by rejecting the record of its facts, when these facts contradict his philosophy, especially by denying the historic truth of the Christian revelation, by accounting for its miracles, by transmuting them into myths, arising out of occurrences not in the least supernatural, and by making Christianity itself but the highest of all symbols of the higher and purer Pantheistic Truth. Indeed, all past ages and all by-gone enterprises, all the prayers and praises, the high aspirations, the deeds of overcoming faith and daring heroism which had distinguished the great men of other times—all these are worthy of consideration only as they faintly shadow forth the age which is to come, the times of "the restitution of all things," on the true foundations of Pantheism in Theology, of mysterious enigmas in science, and of unnatural energy and affected phrase in literature. With all these vagaries, there are intermingled, in their writings, many just and many striking sayings concerning man, many most worthy and noble principles in relation to the aims of life and follies of artificial society, expressed oftentimes with a delightful freshness of language. These give to their writings a high interest to ardent and youthful minds, and to the writers an influence that has no connection with the truth or error of their opinions. When this is termed the Pantheistic variety of the Transcendental school, it would be unjust, were the impression to be conveyed to our readers, that the dogma concerning the Deity, holds a conspicuous place in their writings. It is not properly a school in philosophy, as it is a school in literature. Its inspiring genius is rather Carlyle in his criticism on books and men, than Straus in his mythical exegesis, or Hegel in his philosophical chaotics. And yet Carlyle has a system in science, theology and exegesis, which, even if he has not dared to utter it to his own thoughts, or to propound it to his readers, does yet exist in its elements and principles, and which gives to his writings their spirit, their meaning, and, we fear, much of their attraction. We care not to call his writings infidel writings, or their author a Pantheist or an unbeliever. In a certain sense he deserves neither of the appellations, while yet the influence of his writings and of the man pleases and fosters that current of feeling which is even now pressing on, with a silent, yet deep and powerful tide, which we call the practically infidel feeling of the literary men of the age. This infidelity is not metaphysical; it does not preach atheism with D'Holbach, nor Pantheism with Spinosa, nor man's irresponsibility with Hume; for metaphysics is not to its taste. It does not concern itself with the infidel exegesis of the German students of the Scriptures, for this is a study which it despises. Nor does it dishonor the moral effects of Christian truth or the record of its religious experience, as many an infidel churchman has done, for even Carlyle discourses of the regeneration of Cromwell, and with so much earnestness in *his* interpretation of the event, that many a Christian might not see the sneer behind. What, then, is it? How can it be infidelity? We reply; It is natural theology without a personal God. It is moral philosophy without a responsible agent. It is Christianity without the belief of its historic truths, acknowledging some of its effects, even those called spiritual, yet without connecting them with its facts, the government of a Holy God, and the redemption of a revealed Redeemer, and the cleansing of a Holy Spirit. It is rather unbelief than disbelief. Subtle, refining, symbolizing all living truths and real facts into inert and powerless myths, and yet exerting its influence unconsciously to the man himself. Let the dreamers of Oxford, on both sides the Atlantic, understand it and ask themselves, whether Christianity has no work for them to do, except to make her more offensive to such men, by hanging about her neck other mill-stones than those which have well nigh sunk her already; and whether the Church has no demand for them, except to fill her courts with grotesque and chattering priests, and to busy their brains with inquiring what are the dimensions of that surplice which makes the wearer most devout, and what the size of the cross upon the back of the priest, that leads the spectator most effectually to put on Christ. Let hair-splitting and angry theologians ask themselves, whether Christianity and the Church had nothing for them to do, but to contract their influence, and narrow their minds, and exhaust their energies. Amateur divines also, and petit maitres in the pulpit, may inquire with profit, whether, as they have to do with men, they had not best act the part of men, and arm themselves for manly contests.

As next in order, we name the Transcendentalists in the Unitarian communion, of the different sorts of which class, Mr. Ripley and Mr. Parker may be taken as specimens. They are not Pantheists, and hence, deserve not to be classed with Mr. Emerson; while they are too decidedly theologians to be named with Carlyle. They take their character as a school, and perhaps their name, from the fact that while in the Unitarian connection they have gone widely aside from that exclusive reliance on the historical evidences of Christianity, which has been so characteristic of those divines, and have planted themselves on the moral evidence, not only as superior, but as supreme and decisive. The truth of its doctrines and its facts, they ground upon their fitness to the reason of man, and only so far as the reason sees and feels them to be true, so far are they to be received. So also they prove the being of God, from the wants and aspirations of our nature, rather than the fact of his existence from the visible universe, and the principals of his moral administration and his own moral attributes, from the course of his own actual providence with man. From the fact that they have rejected and labored to depreciate the only species of proof for the Christian system, which Unitarians have been accustomed to acknowledge, they have seemed to many Unitarians of the older stamp to be no less than rejectors of the system, and their principles have been called "The latest form of Infidelity."

In the writings and general course of thought of some of them, there is certainly much to approve, and we cannot but hail that distinct recognition which they allow to the facts of Christian experience, and to its authority and importance in interpreting the word of God, as well as the honor which they give to man's moral nature,—the greatness of its wants, and the greatness also of the change within which it must experience—to be the omen of a purer theology and a more spiritual religion. As far as they constitute reason, the voucher for all truth, both in Natural and Revealed Theology, so that of truths that are within her province, none are to be received to which she does not consent—and of truths but partially revealed, nothing is to be believed which plainly contradicts her voice, and as far also, as they give the highest place and the most convincing energy to those truths, which make themselves manifest to the conscience, so far are they to be commended, as holding truth, and important truth. But when they exalt reason to the seat of judgment, and flatter her vanity till she forgets the limits within which she is competent to judge, and yields herself to the perverting influences of an evil heart, then do they dishonor the truth which suffers by their perversion, and send out the words of God's revelation, a poor, tattered thing of shreds and patches, stripped of its venerable authority, and robbed of its aspect of benignant love. Surely religion was never more dishonored, under the garb of philosophy, than in that noted discourse "On the Transient and Permanent in Christianity," by Mr. Parker, a disciple of this school. All that is characteristic of the Christian system, or that could be deemed such, has he taken away, under the name of the Transient, except the name of "the Galilean Youth," to whom he renders no higher honor than more than one of the English Deists have done. Under the name of "the Permanent," has he left a poor caput mortuum, which is spiritless, impotent and contemptible. In his own words, "Christianity is a simple thing; very simple. It is absolute, pure morality; absolute, pure religion, the love of man; the love of God, acting without let or hindrance. The only creed it lays down, is the great truth which springs up spontaneous in the holy heart—there is a God. Its watch-word is, be perfect as your Father in Heaven. The only form it demands is a divine life, doing the best thing, in the best way, from the highest motives; perfect obedience to the great law of God. Its sanction is the voice of God in your heart; the perpetual presence of Him who made us, and the stars over our head; Christ and the Father abiding within us." Did not Tindal say as much as this in his "Christianity as old as the Creation." Surely if the name of a Christian, in its most superficial meaning, and its largest extension, signifies anything, on the ground of past or present usage, he whose creed is nothing more than this, ought not to claim it to himself. This is but a more distinct and decided avowal of the infidelity of the age. An infidelity that admits "the moral" of the Christian system, but denies its facts on earth, and the facts which it reveals from heaven; which honors the regenerate man, but honors not those truths, by the beliefs of which, and those influences by whose power and aid his regeneration is secured.

Mr. O. A. Brownson might here be naturally named, as being himself a variety altogether peculiar. But we shall not attempt to describe him. A preacher and a politician—a critic and theologian—a determined reformer of all the present forms of society, and a stern defender of the powers that be—a vulgar demagogue and a teacher of aesthetics—a philosopher of the spiritual and of the experimental school—he is beyond the powers of any one who would seek to portray him. As he is manifestly and avowedly in a state of continued transition,—in a condition of perpetually *becoming*, but of never *being*—of unquestioned vigor of intellect, of no inferior capacity for investigation in the moral and intellectual sciences— possessed of surpassing facility and force in stating and defending his opinions,—we can barely give his name as one of those who bear the name of Transcendentalists, without giving a history of his past transformations, or venturing upon a prophecy of what he is yet to be.

We come now to speak more at length of those Transcendentalists, who are known and acknowledged as men, strenuous for evangelical and spiritual Christianity. In remarking upon the opinions which they hold, and the influence which they exert, we shall present certain suggestions which apply with equal force to all who call themselves *par eminence*, spiritual philosophers, and others which are appropriate to the common position which we hold as believers in the same system of Christian faith. It will not be forgotten that they are Transcendentalists rather in popular phraseology and by common usage, than in the strict and scientific sense. They do not profess to be deeply and learnedly metaphysical. Many would say of themselves, that they are mere disciples and beginners in the school, which yet they are satisfied is the school where truth is most purely taught. Others would tell you that they neither wish nor expect to master all the heights and depths of the spiritual philosophy, while yet they know that it is the only philosophy that is the friend of poetry, and of noble sentiment, and of true and spiritual religion; the fount of manly principles, of self-sacrificing benevolence, and of pure and reverential worship. They point you with confidence to the opposing classes of opinions which have ever divided the scientific world, which are represented by the two great masters of Grecian philosophy, and called after their names; and affirm that according to the structure of their minds and the divinity of earthliness of their original genius, and perhaps according to their moral dispositions, all men have, and all men must be the followers, either of the shrewd, severe, and unbelieving Aristotle, or of the divine and believing Plato. The systems are contradictory, and tend to opposite directions. The one is earth-born, and has its sphere and its limits in the understanding, while it tends to sensuality, selfishness and unbelief; —the other is from heaven, and carries the soul upward, and in its direct and remoter influences, elevates the spirit above the world of sense, purifies benevolence, and blends in delightful harmony with the faith and love of the believer.

Of the prevailing English philosophy, and of the system of Locke in particular, they express their hearty dislike, not merely on account of individual opinions which Locke, or certain of his disciples have held, but because of the inevitable tendency of its spirit, and its master principles. They trace its fatal consequences, in the struggle which philosophy has been maintaining with Christian truth ever since its prevalence, in the enfeebling and corrupting influences which the sensual philosophy has ever imparted to scientific theology. They find its appropriate results in the Socinianism of Priestly, the Pyrrhonism of Hume, and the Atheism of the French Revolution. They regard with no friendly eye the metaphysical theology of New England, based as it is on the sensual philosophy, and would substitute in its stead the more spiritual Platonism of Germany and of a better age in the past. Our description we acknowledge to be incomplete, but it will answer its design if it indicates with sufficient precision the class of men of whom it affirms, and with whose spirit and opinions many of our readers are familiar.

Others there are, who are Transcendentalists, as the result of close investigation and scientific research; and who, while they would consent to all that is affirmed by their brethren, do yet rest with firm conviction on their opinions, because, as *philosophers*, they have proved them true. With them, at present we have no concern. The arena of strictly scientific discussion, is the only arena on which we would wish to meet them, and the examination of their principles of science and faith, on scientific grounds, the only one on which we would rest the question of their truth or error. We trust, however, that the considerations which we shall urge, will not be deemed impertinent, even by them, in their general bearings upon the subject.

Much is made by the spiritualists of all classes, and most of all by those who are now before us, of the inevitable necessity by which all those who attempt to philosophize, become either Platonists or Aristotelians, whether the cause is found in their intellectual tendencies, their moral disposition, or the influence of favorite authors. The distinction between the schools is represented as so great, that the one employs certain faculties, and appeals to their decision, which the other neither recognizes nor believes to exist, that in consequence, the two cannot confer together, nor can they comprehend each other,—that the one is the school of science, and the other of empiricism,—the one, a sanctuary of faith, and a temple of worship,—the other, a dwelling place of unbelief and a nursery of irreligion. It is easy to see that if these claims be admitted as true, they carry with them the most sweeping conclusions, and give to the spiritualists, not only the field in argument, but occasion for earnest and devout attachment to their own philosophy, and for serious alarm at the prevalence of the opposite. Nor ought it to be a matter of wonder, that much importance should be attached by them to this general fact, and that it should be often used in the argument.

It cannot be intended by this doctrine, merely, that there was a wide dissimilarity in the intellectual structure of these great philosophers, nor that their modes of announcing and defending their doctrines were so unlike, that if they held precisely the same opinions, one would express them in the Aristotelian fashion, and the other in the Platonic way; but that the school of the one is a school of scepticism and of unbelief—while the other is a nursery of faith and devotion; that the one invests the mind with the mists of error, and perplexes it in the intricate labyrinth of doubt, while the other causes it to breathe the pure ether, where forgotten truths of heavenly origin are brought back to the delighted memory, and the soul holds communion with her divine original.

The former of these opinions—the one *not* held by our spiritualists, we regard as correct;—the latter which they hold and propagate, we think is defective and false. It is defective and untrue in its judgment of the two philosophers, who are made the representatives of the opposing systems. Who then, was Aristotle, and who was Plato? Aristotle was a man who thought severely, and expressed his thoughts in language, condensed, precise and purely philosophical. Plato also thought severely, but in giving expression to his thoughts, presents processes rather than results,—hence, in contrast to Aristotle, he is diffuse rather than concise, suggestive rather than precise, rambling rather than condensed, useful rather in setting the mind upon a course of thinking, than satisfying it at the conclusion by a result briefly expressed and skillfully elaborated. Above all, while Aristotle is naked and abstract in his diction, Plato is illustrative, warm, and poetical, while that of the one is rough, often obscure and always repulsive, aiming to present the thought alone, that of the other is wrought into the finest harmonies of a most delightful style, which is as clear as amber, and musical as the lute of Apollo. The one marches you right on to his conclusion; and often by strides so tremendous that you must follow, *haud passibus æquis*, the other takes you by the hand, and leads you in a devious way, now along a still stream, then beneath a cool and balmy shade, not forgetting now and then to try you with a tangled thicket, and to perplex you with the intricacy of nice distinctions in the way—till at length, having carried you as far as he thinks well to do, he leaves you to review the way you have gone, and to guess out the remainder alone—being satisfied with the exercise which you have received, and apparently having aimed at this as his only object. The one seeks to grasp and understand all the things that are, or which have sprung from the mind of man—the laws of nature, the principles of government, society, and education, the elements of logic, rhetoric, and poetry, and subjects them alike to an analysis marvellously subtle, and a process that is wonderfully exhausting, till he arrives at conclusions which are admirable for the justness of their good sense. He seeks alike to collect the facts which were known in natural history, then a science in its embryo, and discourses also in the same calm and unpretending way of the mysteries of the Deity and of the human soul. He would penetrate all nature by the searching eye of his analysis, or cause her to reveal herself in her primeval elements, by the powerful solvent of his own scientific method. The favorite field of the other is the moral, the religious, and metaphysical—into the darker recesses of which departments he loves to penetrate; and having gone with you to a certain depth, he prefers then to worship, rather than farther to explore, to pause in mute wonder, or to relieve himself of the mystery under which he labors, by some splendid and lofty mythus, or ornate and finished description. Hence, his doctrine of truths forgotten in a former state, but recalled in this, of men confined in a cave to the view of their own shadow, as cast by the light above upon the farthest wall, of the chariot drawn by unequal steeds, etc., which are sometimes taken by his more devout, not to say, credulous disciples, in a sense somewhat more scientific than the master designed.

Such are some of the contrasts between these venerable masters of Grecian science. Opposite in many intellectual characteristics, and fitted by their modes of instruction, and the intellectual training which they impart, to produce philosophers who will differ, and that most widely, but still in no sense deserving to be set over against each other, the one as constituting the school of empiricism and of unbelief, and the other, that of science and of faith.

Rather should we style them, the one, the imaginative and mythical school, the other, the analytic, and we will not yet say, the more purely philosophical. We grant also, that each have their peculiar exposures to error,—that while that of the Aristotelian is to deny that to exist which does, in fact—that of the Platonist is to bring into being that which is not; in a word, the besetting sin of the one is unbelief, that of the other, is idolatry and superstition. Which is the more hostile to science we do not hesitate to affirm. Which is the more a foe to true religion, it would be hard to decide. The spirit of both is equally a spirit of science and of faith. Yet the Aristotelian, often, when he arrived at a great first truth,—principium et fons congnoscendi,—deems it important to survey it with a more careful exactness, and to test the certainty of its being one of the truths, for which faith alone, or rather intuition, must vouch, or whether it is susceptible of a still nicer division. As the naturalist, when the nucleus of the crystal has been uncovered, and presents its brilliant surfaces to his view, still must search for a new cleavage, till he sometimes batters its fair face with his chisel, or it breaks in pieces under his hammer, so does the analytical philosopher, with the primal elements of knowledge—either refining them till they cease to be objects of faith, or denying that any can be attained on which the mind may fasten. So did Hume; and others besides him have thus destroyed the elements which make possible either science or faith. Hume was altogether an Aristotelian, it is true, but the results to which he arrived are in no sense the legitimate consequences of the Aristotelian philosophy, but only their possible perversion.

The Platonist on the other hand, has his exposures. From his disposition to believe rather than to question, to wonder or worship rather than to analyze, he receives as general laws, and primal elements, those facts which a closer examination would lead him to refer to a law still more general. He imposes upon himself, as facts, the merest figments of words. He multiplies first truths, and thus destroys the simplicity of science, and does dishonor to the simplicity of nature. So also, through his fondness for certain mysterious entities, which he calls ideas, is he tempted to render them a vague and almost idolatrous worship, to substitute them as objects of love and honor, in the stead of his brother-man, and his sovereign God. Not unfrequently does he thus fall into a demon-worship of the powers of nature, or referring them back to one grand idea, to bow before it, as το παν, an entity, not personal nor yet material, not living nor yet unconscious; the supreme reason,—the great idea,—the vital force,—the fount of being,—or whatever be the name under which he chooses to veil his pantheistic divinity.

The different methods in which the opposite schools use language, has been adverted to in passing; there are in it consequences, which it is much to our purpose to notice. The Aristotelian employs the language of abstraction, which, though clear and precise, and not without interest to the reflecting mind, is yet the most remote from the looser language of common life, and not less unlike the diction of the excited orator, or the rapt poet. He employs images indeed, but they are briefly presented, and instead of withdrawing the mind from the scientific truth, reflect a stronger light upon the argument, and set it forth in a finer relief. He presents, from common life, facts and illustrations, but such only as carry the mind back again, with a freshened interest to the truths which they illustrate. The Platonist adopts with freedom, the poetical and figurative diction, and is solicitous to avoid the lifeless and naked style of the follower of Aristotle. Nay, often when the severest simplicity of scientific statement is required, and all the powers of a strictly philosophical expression should be tasked, he is content darkly to show forth what he deems the truth by an allegory or an image, and thinks that he has given a triumphant solution, when he has only hit upon a happy illustration, and covered the knot of the problem by a veil of graceful diction. Even if the two should possess the same scientific truth, and should see with a metaphysical exactness equally nice, they would adopt a method so different, and forms of language so entirely unlike, that the truths propounded might seem scarcely the same. Then, too, the associations which they awaken, the emotions which they kindle, the allusions in which they are at home, and the nomenclature with which they are familiar, are all so different, that they often seem to be combatants, even when they are fellow-soldiers, for the same great truths. We are quite certain that truths have been propounded by Locke and Reid, on which Kant and Coleridge have prided themselves as peculiar to their own system, and as giving it an indisputable advantage over the opposite school. More than one determined partizan of Coleridge has been unable to see such a truth in a plainer style and under a different form of expression, through the merest trickery of language, and the splendid fascinations of a portico-philosophical diction.

Indeed, to the spiritualist of our day, the naked and abstract language of mental and moral science, is most offensive, contrasted with the gorgeous coloring of his own favorite authors and their warmer and more moving style. He counts it reason enough, for his rejection of any writer, that his speculations are dead; that they have not that living force which of itself wakes up the intellect and warms the heart. His language of them all is, "Let the dead bury their dead," while he directs you to his own adopted teachers, and asks no other reason for the excellence of their philosophy than its influence on the minds of those who study it.

We are not insensible to the fascinations and the power of that style which delights to invest some grand truth, concerning God or man, in the splendid drapery of a creating imagination, and to awaken a new and startled interest in facts, over which man is ever prone to slumber.

We do not object that any truth which deeply concerns man should be presented by the philosopher in such a way as to take the strongest hold of his faith and his feelings. But it should be remembered that the attitude of the philosopher, in investigating truth and announcing to others the results, is essentially different from that of the meditative believer, or the devout worshipper. When, then, it is insisted that he shall be both at once, that he shall use the language both of worship and of science, the attempt is made to combine elements more unlike than oil and water. Let the philosopher use the language of the schools, when he is in the schools; when he is a poet, let him chant the language which the muses shall teach him; when he worships let him pray; when he summons his fellow man from his sleep of death and sin, let him startle him with the awakening tones of the prophet. But let every thing be done in its place, and let the language of the place be adhered to. True it is, that much philosophical truth can be, and doubtless is, conveyed in a style thus fascinating to the imagination. It would be bigotted folly to deny that many profound observations, on intellectual, moral and theological science, on the history of opinions and of man are thus presented. It is even granted that the entire circle of principles that are received in metaphysical science, may be announced in such language, and there be no important error. We certainly do not value the truth the less, nor do we deny that it is philosophical truth, because it is presented in a poetical garb. We deem works thus written to be of the highest interest and importance, at certain stages of mental progress, and would recommend them as of the highest use, in awakening a philosophical spirit, and in calling into action the reflecting faculty. But we must contend, the while, that it shows a most limited acquaintance with the nature of real science and the kind of language it demands, to suppose that such a diction can be employed in its more refined and attenuated investigations, or can express and make permanent the results of its more refined analyses; that because it can convey certain general facts, concerning the soul, in its wants, and aspirations, and immortality, that it can name all its powers, and allot their functions, and distinguish between false and sound logic, and make new investigations, and leave the results graven on the page of science, in distinct and legible characters, for coming generations. It is more bigotted still to demand that no other than a style so unnatural shall be employed, and to be incapable of discerning in the homely phraseology of a Locke or Reid, the truth that sparkles and entrances as uttered by Coleridge or Cousin. And yet, if all this were understood as it should be, what an end it would bring to a vast deal of fine writing about vital metaphysics, and the necessity of a spiritual philosophy, and the blight which the common philosophy breathes upon the life of faith.

We are far from defending the homely diffuseness, and the loose inconsistencies of Locke and certain of his English followers, and farther still from expressing any complacency in that hardest of all metaphysical styles, the ungraceful and untutored diction of the New England metaphysicians. A perfect philosophical style is not unsusceptible of sparkling vivacity or of graceful ease. Nor does it entirely forbid the rising from the even progression of its ordinary course into the excited ardor of lofty emotion. Still it should ever be remembered that the mien of science is chastened and severe, that her distinctions are many, and to all but her devotees, they seem excessively minute and over-refined; that the language which she employs is not that of ordinary life, and must be a naked and lifeless thing to him, who has not himself known the thoughts which the words describe. When, then, the spiritualist will have no other than what he terms vital metaphysics, i.e., a philosophy which employs a diction, which will waken the intellect by its electric impulses, and stir the emotions, and is in no way contrasted with a style that is concerned with the realities of nature, rather than the names of science, he demands an impossibility. He even seeks an element, the very presence of which proves the metaphysics to be, at best, but very general, and, perhaps, very superficial philosophizing. Science in all her departments, and, most of all, mental science, begins with abstraction. Her very first effort is to give generic names—names which must be divested of that interest which pertains to the picture language of the senses. As she prosecutes her work, one of her highest attainments is to keep to her terminology with a severe precision, and to guard it with a determined caution; and on this depends, in a great degree, her continued progress and her successful achievements.

Were we in a word to speak of our spiritualists, as philosophers, we should say that they are in danger, while declaiming against the superficial and sensual philosophy which prevails, of becoming themselves more superficial, by adopting the dicta of their favorite authors, with too little severity of thinking of their own. While they claim independence of thought, they may find themselves hanging with a servile dependence on the writings of their own inspiring genius, or looking back with an awful reverence on something admirably profound in the past which yet is in nothing admirable except for its obscurity. While they propose to themselves a course of scientific pursuit which shall be continually progressive, they need to see it, lest they are revolving in the same charmed circle of sounding words, and incomprehensible yet lofty phraseology, and making progress only as they drive on in greater familiarity with the same recurring round. There is a danger, lest interpretation should usurp the place of reasoning, and the admiration with which they dwell upon the mythi of Plato, or the effort with which they labor to put some comprehensible meaning into the sayings "hard to be understood" of Coleridge or Schelling, should be mistaken for the clear yet penetrating gaze by which true science sees into the life of things, and wrests from Nature the secret of her mystery. To our view, many of these professed spiritualists appear to be an earnest group of disciples lingering in the vestibule of the temple of science, who are ever pointing with a fervent admiration to the mysterious recesses within, and shuddering with a holy reverence at her consecrated shrines that disclose themselves in the distance; ever seeming to be just about to enter, but never crossing the threshold.

We have contemplated the spiritualists of the day, so far, as philosophers. But they present themselves in another attitude. As Theologians, they claim unquestioned merits, and an undisputed superiority. "Our mode of studying truth," they tell us, "is not to contemplate her in the lifeless abstractions, or the dim and dead conceptions through which alone she reveals herself to the understanding, but in the living ideas, with which she ever stands before the Reason in her native beauty and commanding majesty. The arguments by which we commend her to others, are not those which argue with the intellect, but those which command the soul. We wait not for the slow and sceptical induction of the doubting understanding, but we possess at once the citadel of the heart. We degrade not truth to the attitude of a suppliant entreating for admission, but we gird her with the armor of a conqueror. As we believe that there are mysteries in science, so we are not offended at mysteries in Theology, and they do not awaken within us a perpetual struggle between our philosophy and our faith. While the prevailing philosophy leads the mind away from faith, ours carries us to its very borders, and easily blends with it, so that we can scarcely discern the line where Science terminates and Faith begins."

Natural Theology, as an independent science, with its own principles, its laws of evidence, its cautious admissions, in short, in all its researches concerning the being of God, its deductions as to the nature of man and his hopes and fears, under the light of nature, is pronounced a useless and almost an unchristian science, as though it cast implied dishonor on the truth of the Scriptures to meet the question of their falsehood or truth. So also the effort to reconcile the records of science with the page of revelation, is scouted as of evil tendency, as having no other effect than to place Christianity in a false position, as reduced to straits in her defences, rather than as demanding to be obeyed. All this apparatus of logic, and this cautious nicety of investigation, is useless, and worse than useless. The ideas of the soul, of immortality, and of God, are made known to the Reason, and the Reason commands the man to receive them as true. So also Christian Truth shines by its own light, and needs only to be seen by a spirit rightly attuned to be believed.

There is a sense in which all this is true. There is a sense in which it is not only false, but fraught with evil, not only to the progress of the intellect, but also to the moral feelings and character. If nothing more were intended by it than that the moral nature in man is to be recognized in all our reasonings concerning God and his government over man, and that it should ever be regarded as of the highest dignity and worth, and from it should be drawn the most convincing arguments, in speculations as to the light of nature, it would not only be true, but truth of the highest moment. For the lack of this respect to conscience in man, and to the will of God as it there reveals itself, and the demands of God as he thus makes himself heard in the fears of conscience unenlightened, Natural Theology has too often, not to say more usually, been a barren and unconvincing speculation, and the defences of Christianity which rest upon it have been tame and powerless in their reasonings, and often impotent in their appeals. Speculators concerning the material works of God, and collators of evidences from profane history, have seemed to reason as if theirs were the arena on which the contest was to be decided, rather than by reasonings concerning the soul in its moral constitution and wants, and the government of God as likely to meet its capacities and needs, and as tending to perfect this his noblest work. But we must protest against the conclusion, that because our reasonings in Natural Theology and in the defence of Christianity, ought to take another direction, and to employ the most effective arguments, that therefore we are to cease to reason; or that because the mind of man will respond to these truths when made to see them, that therefore there is no need that they be set before the mind by a process of severe deduction, and driven home by an irresistible logic.

But when, asks one, "Oh, when shall Christianity be regarded as proved? After eighteen hundred years, is it still a question to be debated? Must it again and again be brought into the lists by every combatant, who in this way aspires to a literary reputation—who takes upon himself to affect a spurious candor, and to make unauthorized concessions, as though the whole defence of revealed truth had been by the church universal committed to his keeping? How long are young men to be taught that nothing has yet been settled—that all established opinions are fetters upon the human mind, or that a standing miracle of eighteen centuries is to be called in question in each succeeding generation? Oh, when shall that truly believing age fully come, when we shall have again a *teaching*, and not merely a *reasoning* church—cultivating a believing spirit, and laying so deep the foundations of faith, that the after structure of human science shall not disturb them, without wrenching away all that imparts vigor to the intellect, or life to the affections?"

To *the truth* involved in these inquiries we heartily respond—in its quackery and confusion of error with truth we have not so entire a sympathy. Never will the necessity cease for a reasoning church. The laws of God's providence, the conditions of man's probation, both forbid that it should. So long as new minds shall come into being, and must go through the same struggle with doubt and unbelief, which is a part of the discipline and trial allotted to man's depravity and weakness, so long will their teachers need to meet them with convincing logic—so long will their sluggish torpor need to be awakened by giving life to the intellect, so long will it be required to tear them from their refuges of lies, that the truth be armed with convincing light and resistless energy. As long as each successive generation shall grow up from ignorance to knowledge, and grope its way from darkness to light, and shake off the envelopments of its unexpanded, blinded energies, into the clearness of well established convictions, and the firmness of undoubting faith, so long must the truth be sustained by argument, and that argument be set home to the intellect, and through the intellect to the conscience of man. Error, too, will be ever awake; and if, through a pious dread of calling in question the claims of religion, or the vague pretensions of a confident philosophy, the believer ceases to reason, error will not. The aspects and arguments of Error will change with each changing age. From each advancing science, from the fickle and capricious phases of a morbid literary taste, she will derive new arguments, and cast up new defences; and if Truth will only let her defences alone, and proclaim herself of the celestial empire, she will be as well satisfied as the English are with each new issue of contemptuous bravado from Pekin.

Nor is it desirable that this necessity for a reasoning church should terminate. When its teachers imagine that that time has come, then will they sink into sluggish and animalized torpor, or bask in the luxurious sunshine of spiritual quietism, or amuse themselves in literary trifling, or forge and hurl anathemas for those who dare to knock about their ears any of the mistaken and defenceless outworks of their Faith. Then, too, will their disciples yield a supine and tame submission to church authority, or a lifeless faith to the dogmas of an orthodoxy out-worn and dead, instead of resorting for themselves to the living word, to learn the will of God from his own mouth, not only awed but quickened by the responsibility under which they reason, as they know it is for their lives. The moment that the church ceases to be a reasoning church, that moment does she cast forth the element which marks the character of Protestantism. For Protestantism has been what she is, by her logical and instructive ministry, and by the quickening energies of the Word of God, as they have reasoned out of it to the aroused understandings of their flocks. Thus only have they made the people what they are, possessed of manly growth and an independent life—men able to give a reason for the hope that is within them, and in their turn instructors of their own households, and holders forth of the word of life unto all. The instant that this is to cease, and the intellect of the teacher and the taught is no longer tasked and aroused that faith and hope may also live, then let him who was appointed a teacher turn a priest, and as the intellect is stupified, let him dazzle and amuse the senses; and in token of the change which is to come upon his flock, let him turn his back upon them in the ministration of the sanctuary. Let those, also, who find it easier to believe, than to know why they believe, and to give a reason for their faith to others, rather by bold and vague generalities than by clear and progressive reasonings, understand where their affinities connect them. If they want a believing church, there is one at Rome, with a branch at Oxford, which, the last especially, grieved at the unbelieving spirit of the age, and with the progress of reasoning without, urges itself to more daring heroics in faith, as the rude and glaring light drives into remoter darkness the birds of night, disturbed in their dim retreat. Nothing should be less surprising than the tendency of this undefined and morbid spiritualism, to those churches in which authority is the prevailing element, in which faith is nourished rather by the impressive solemnity of sensible rites, than by that animated and convincing reasoning which sways the man. It is natural that the confusion of thought with which it is often accompanied, with its morbid aspirations after the high and holy, and its desire to rest upon fixed belief, without that expense of thought which the nature of things requires, has led some of its disciples who had been nurtured in a communion more purely Protestant, to seek a rest and refuge under the authority of prelacy, where the thinking has been done up in past generations, and faith may occupy all the energies of the man.

"But the moral and religious tendency of spiritualism is still most happy, and especially needed in an age of prevalent unbelief." We are aware that it commends itself to the favor of many men of refined sensibilities and high moral feeling, as springing from a devout and believing spirit in those who originate it, and as suited to exert a healthful influence on the character of those who adopt it. To it, therefore, they give their adhesion and their sympathy, as men of taste and of piety, rather than as philosophers. We have naught to affirm against the moral elevation and amiable feelings of many who are ardently enlisted in its favor, nor do we care to offend the enthusiasm for good, of any right-hearted man. But our convictions, and our observation, too, compel us to say, that this indiscriminate admiration of whatever tends *to faith*, this seeking to believe without the clear and rigid insight into the grounds of what we believe, is far from tending wholly to moral or religious good. Nor is it, as a token of good in character, worth so much as it often passes for. Often, very often, the very zeal for faith signifies simply this—that there is less of calm conviction and of firm reliance, than there is of a perturbed desire after more, which calls upon the will to supply what is lacking in the intellect and heart. So, instead of the soul which is fixed and at peace because it has proved and understands its foundations, there is the pretension and cant of a school, and the being certain merely for the comfort of certainty. This is bigotry—it is not faith—no matter with what literary accomplishments it is associated, or with what intellectual grace, or with what words or songs of pious fervor. It is *wilful*—defending its position to itself, because it has taken it, and repelling others that it may be let alone to enjoy it. True, while it is cloistered in the schools, or buoyed up by the consenting sympathies of an admiring clique of like-minded spirits, or nursed in the artificial air of affected sentiment, it will be confident to itself, and scornful and repellant to the last degree, to those who differ. But let it be summoned to endure the severer struggles of life, or to grapple with its sterner duties, or to bring out its own faith into collision with the opposing faith of another,—let it measure itself with the brawny strength of some coarse but intellectual assailant, or face the sneer of some rude scoffer or some discerning sceptic, and the trial will not only detect intellectual incapacity, but uncover a moral weakness; and as doubt and despair rush thickly in upon the soul, it will see that pretension to faith in excess, is not faith, and the cant about believing, is not believing. By such a trial is it shown that Truth is the only food of faith; and the more clearly Truth is seen, and the more distinctly is it held in the method of its proof, the deeper downward does Faith strike its roots, and the fairer, and richer, and more abundant are the fruits which she yields in profit to man, and in honor to God. So, too, is the weakness of this affected Faith made manifest, as she sinks for a time in despondency, because her cherished arguments, and high pretensions, and accustomed plaudits, are gone, and she finds herself compelled to meet argument with dogmatism, and to bestow her splenetic contempt upon the adversary whom she cannot face. Happy if the consequence be not a misanthropic and moody anger with the vulgar herd, and a hasty abandonment of the defence of truth, because they are too obtuse to be moved by the high and spiritual arguments of a transcendentalizing theology. "He who begins by loving Christianity better than truth, will proceed by loving his own sect or church better than Christianity, and end in loving himself better than all."

Not such has been the faith of the real martyrs to principle, in church and state. They who have faced danger with that high-minded peace, which was too calm to scoff or dogmatize, they who have bled upon the scaffold of martyred patriotism, or have been burned in the fires of Christian piety, have been made of other stuff than this. They have acted no heroics in sentiment or profession, but have been truly heroes. They saw the truth in her deep and strong foundations, upon them rested their souls, with all the energy of men convinced, and for the truth they cared not if they were called to die. We would not then cultivate faith for the sake of faith, for then do we turn spiritual mountebanks, and actors, and are in danger of doing mockery to the holiest thing, but we would that she should be nurtured by the truth, her vital element and her appropriate life.

Of the influence of spiritualism upon scientific theology, and upon students in theology, we shall offer a word. When it proposes to relieve metaphysical theology of the standing objection, which is sometimes so eloquently urged; that it is unfavorable to spiritual culture, we reply with all due respect to those who bring the charge, that it is the merest humbug. For it is plain, that every theologian must have his metaphysics, and cannot advance an inch without them. He who urges the objection, therefore, can only mean by it, that those who go more deeply into metaphysics than himself, incur this danger. To allow the objection, then, would be to give license to every theologian to speak ill of the piety of his neighbor, who is blessed with a higher capacity than himself, or who has more diligence to use it faithfully.

But did the charge lie against the common metaphysics, it would equally hold against those called transcendental. As far as they are scientific, so far are they metaphysical, and of course, will harden the heart and dry up the soul. As far as they are meditations, and poetry, and praise, so far are they an ill-assorted mixture to the man who would desire with Baxter, that his intellect should "abhor confusion." However splendid and elevating they may be in their place, that place is not upon the page of science.

But they are friendly to theology, as they see mysteries in nature, and of course are not offended at mysteries in religion. And what philosophy does not see mysteries in nature? What science that is true to the reality of things, does not acknowledge truths behind which she cannot go—first truths, which, as they explain other truths, cannot themselves be explained, but must be received? Surely there are mysteries enough in nature without creating new ones to try the faith of the philosopher upon, so that when he comes to theology he may swallow not only mysteries but absurdities. Better at once adopt the sage conclusion of Sir Thomas Brown: "Methinks there be not impossibilities enough in religion for an active faith; the deepest mysteries ours contains, have not only been illustrated, but maintained by syllogism and the rule of reason. I love to lose myself in a mystery, to pursue my reason to an 'O Altitudo!' 'Tis my solitary recreation to pose my apprehension with those involved enigmas and riddles of the trinity, with incarnation and resurrection. I can answer all the objections of Satan and my rebellious reason, with that odd resolution I learned of Tertullian: 'Certum est quia impossibile est.' "

As far as this spiritualism raises expectations which it is sure to disappoint, and carries the mind away from the humbler course of severe and cautious thinking, and intoxicates it with expectations, that some potent mystery is wrapt in its peculiar terminology, which is altogether unlike the truths which the English tongue has ever been able to grasp or to utter, or which the English mind has ever brought within the field of its view,—so far is it certain to prepare the way for a mortifying disappointment, when it has wandered its perplexed rounds—and finished the last of the splendid series of the mysteries of initiation, and as the result finds itself, with time misapplied, with an intellect undisciplined, with principles of philosophizing unhinged, and a science of philosophy which promised every thing, either as yet half compassed, or when gained, no other and no better than what might have been had, without these weary years of confused and vexing toil. To all, over whom we have influence, we would say, read, study, and ponder these writers as much as you will;—used aright, they will reward you well. But let them not lead you captive as partisans, you know not why, blinded and wilful.

As far as this spiritualism prepares the way by its figments and words, which pass for things, for the reveries of pantheism, and either by its modes of reasoning or the factitious influence of its splendid names, imparts a spirit equally foreign to science, to piety and to sense—the desire to astonish the vulgar by dragging from the rotting heap of ancient heresies some transcendental or quietistic vagary—so far will it curse the church, and cause sadly to err and more sadly to suffer its deluded victims. Let those who would put themselves to school to all that passes under the name of spiritualism, even in the evangelical church, mere tyros in science and theology, look well to the spirit which they raise, and see that they forget not the incantation by which he is to be laid.

But it is time we had concluded. Our readers will remember that we proposed to consider the scientific grounds of this philosophy. That promise we hope to redeem at some future opportunity. We dare not now longer trespass on their patience.

[Transcendentalism]

Thomas Carlyle*

Thanks for asking me to write you a word in the *Dial*. Had such a purpose struck me long ago there have been things passing thro' my head,—march-marching as they ever do, in long-drawn scandalous Falstaff-regiments (a man ashamed to be seen passing thro' Coventry with such a set!)[1]—some one of which, snatched out of the ragged rank, and dressed and drilled a little, might perhaps fitly have been saved from Chaos and sent to the *Dial*. In future we shall be on the outlook. I love your Dial, and yet it is with a kind of shudder. You seem to me in danger of dividing yourselves from the Fact of this present universe in which alone ugly as it is can I find any anchorage, and soaring away after Ideas, Beliefs, Revelations and such like,—into perilous altitudes as I think; beyond the curve of perpetual frost, for one thing! I know not how to utter what impression you give me; take the above as some stamping of the fore-hoof. Surely I could wish you *returned* into your own poor nineteenth century, its follies and maladies, its blind or half-blind but gigantic toilings, its laughter and its tears, and trying to evolve in some measure the hidden Godlike that lies in *it*;—that seems to me the kind of feat for literary men. Alas, it is so easy to screw oneself up into high and ever higher altitudes of Transcendentalism, and see nothing under one but the everlasting snows of Himmalayah, the Earth shrinking to a Planet, and the indigo firmament sowing itself with daylight stars; easy for *you*, for me: but whither does it lead? I dread always, to inanity and mere injuring of the lungs! —"Stamp, stamp, stamp!"—Well, I do believe, for one thing, a man has no right to say to his own generation turning quite away from it, "Be damned!" It is the whole Past, and the whole Future, this same

*Letter from Carlyle to Emerson, 29 August 1842. Reprinted from *The Correspondence of Emerson and Carlyle*, ed. Joseph Slater (New York: Columbia University Press, 1964), pp. 328–329.

cotton-spinning, dollar-hunting, canting and shrieking, very wretched generation of ours. Come back into it, I tell you;—and so for the present will "stamp" no more.

Notes

1. Cf. *Henry IV, Part I*, act IV, scene ii, lines 10–50.

A Sermon on Transcendentalism

Simeon Doggett*

Jeremiah v. 30, 31.
"A wonderful and horrible thing is committed in the land—and what will ye do in the end thereof?"

The thing, to which, I fear, our text is too applicable, is not peculiar to our age and country. It appeared, with open face in France, in the days of Voltaire—in England, in the writings of Bolingbroke and Hume; under a more cloaked form in Germany; and in America, an infidel Paine, with his insidious draughts, poisoned with it, many minds.— Though it was quashed by many able pens; I apprehend it has appeared again under a flattering name.[1] Transcendentalism is the lofty style its principles now assume. It will be the object of our discourse, to detail some of its principles, with some remarks, as I proceed; presuming that to reject it, nothing is necessary but a knowledge of what it is. As some of its views have got into the pulpit, it seemed but right, that the pulpit should be guarded against its desecrations. It assumes the aspiring name, Transcendentalism, from two prominent objects—one to exalt the human mind, the other to depress the Bible. That this is a fair statement of its prominent objects, I shall show from a book entitled, "A Discourse of matters pertaining to Religion," recently published. It has long been an object, with unbelievers, to exalt what is styled natural religion. This, I understood, was remarkably the fact with the German Philosophers and Divines before, and at the period of the French revolution. If natural religion, the exercise of our reason, be sufficient to guide men to virtue and happiness, then Christianity is useless. Transcendentalism goes very far in exalting the natural attainments of man. It supposes man in his nature, endowed with a religious element. It supposes, also, that God has stamped upon every soul, an idea of himself. Thus furnished, the developement of his natural powers

*Reprint of A Sermon on Transcendentalism (Taunton, Mass.: J. W. D. Hall, 1843); delivered in response to the publication of Theodore Parker's A Discourse of Matters Pertaining to Religion (1842).

of reason, conscience and love, may carry him to the knowledge of all necessary moral and religious truths. Hence, every person becomes more or less, inspired, as he cultivates and follows the laws of mind—his reason and conscience. In every nation and every age, have been, and still are, manifestations of inspiration. The degree of inspiration depends upon the moral and religious culture of the individual; as the illumination and impulse of the Divine mind are ever in accordance with this culture. The highest degree of this inspiration has given prominence to individuals in different ages, among various nations. Hence, a Confucius of China, Zoroaster of Persia, Socrates of ancient Greece, a Plato of Rome, Mahomet of Turca, Moses of the Hebrews, and Jesus Christ. Their sayings, and fragments of their discourses, either by tradition or writing, have descended to posterity, and carried with them a moral influence. Upon these principles, Christians, Jews, Mahometans, and Heathens differ, only, because they have had a greater or less number, who have cultivated the laws of mind, and hence have enjoyed different measures of Divine inspiration. It also follows, that this transcending light may continue to brighten, and hereafter, produce, as some have hinted, characters more sublime than those that Jews or Christians venerate.

These principles go one step farther, which you may have anticipated, i.e. that there is not, and never was, a miraculous inspiration. The laws of mind, carried to their designed destination, transcend the necessity of any extraordinary inspiration. As there was no need of miraculous inspiration to teach the truth and duties of morality and religion, so, of course, such immediate manifestations of the High invisible, have never been vouchsafed to the world. The Transcendentalist thus viewing the laws of mind, affects to rise above the revealed word, and its believers.

Having stated the starting principles of this heresy, and glanced at its consequent results; I come, in the next place, to notice its view respecting miracles, the foundation of the Christian's faith. Here to dwell a little—it rejects, totally rejects the idea of miracles. Hence, the miracles recorded in the Old and New Testamnt are all deception and fiction. It rejects miracles, because, in the nature of things, impossible—as a miracle violates the laws of nature. But I would ask, who established the laws of nature, and continues their operations? The Omnipresent, invisible mind. Is it probable that God has curtailed his power by his own laws? Surely he, who supports these laws, may interrupt or suspend them, as his wisdom may dictate. If we reject the doctrine of miracles from the Bible, we at once, take away its soul. I would ask, what is the most essential object in a revelation? To teach a knowledge of God and of our duty, and of a future state, are, to be sure, important objects—but not the most important. The most essential object is—*Thus saith the Lord*—i.e. a Divine authority to enforce the truth. Socrates and Cicero have taught many important moral truths and duties, as well as St. Paul. But we want a higher authority than that of man, to enforce the truth—the authority of the great moral Governor of the world. And how is this to be gained? Christ will tell us—"The words I speak unto you, I speak not of myself, but the Father, that dwelleth in me, he doeth the works." Christ uniformly referred to his miracles as the demonstration of his Divine mission, and that his teachings were from God—demonstration surely—since the faithful Creator would not lend his aid to support an impostor. When God raised Christ from the dead, he set the seal of truth, and of Divine authority upon all he taught. Bible truths being founded on miracles, we receive them as the word of God; and hence, as the standard of truth and right, and a full and perfect rule of faith and practice. But Transcendentalism substituting for miraculous inspiration, the spiritual attainments of individuals, more or less perfect, has shorn the sacred volume of its peculiar glory. It is obvious to anticipate what sort of Bible this kind of inspiration would produce. It would comprise a strange mixture of sublime truths, many errors, and much frivolity. This is a fac-simile of the description of the bible, detailed in the Transcendental book, that has, I fear, feasted many an evil heart of unbelief. Lest it should seem that I misrepresent, I will repeat, verbatim, its view of the Bible: "Every book of the Old Testament bears distinct marks of its human origin; some of human folly and sin, all of human weakness and imperfection. And all the writings of the New Testament, as well as the Old, contain marks of their human origin, of human weakness and imperfections." From this general thesis, the result of its details is, that the Bible is little else than the Jewish and Christian mythology, interspersed with legendary tales, and sublime truths. "Mythology means, you know, those fabulous stories, concerning the origin of the world and the objects of worship, which were invented and propagated, by men who lived in the early ages of the world, and transmitted to succeeding generations, either by written records, or oral traditions."[2] The mythology of the different races of the earth, ancient and modern, is peculiar to each, as they worship different Gods.—The Grand Lama is the God of the Tartar race; Foe or Fo, of the Hindoos and Chinese; Odin, of the Northern races; Jubiter, of the Greeks and Romans; Baal, of the Canaanites. These different worshippers and gods, have their peculiar mythologies, or Bibles. So Jews and Christians worship Jehovah, their God, and the Bible contains their mythology. And the only difference that Transcendentalism can see between these different worshippers is, that the latter happened to have a little more mental improvement than the others. And, it would seem, that it places their respective God, nearly on an equality—for animadverting on the repeated wars of Israel and the Canaanites, its literal style is—"Jehovah and Baal could never agree!!"

But I am happy to state, that there is a bright spot, discoverable in this dark and portentous cloud. Out of this book, a strange jumble of wisdom, error, vice and folly, the sharp, transcending, eagle-eye has been able to descry and select the great principles of Religion— love to God and love to man. This reminded me of Æsop—*Dum gallus vertit stercorarium, offendet gemmam.*[3] As though to compensate for the cloud cast over the Divine volume, it makes every thing of this glorious heavenly principle. Exhausts his eminent strength in thought and description, to magnify and impress the perfect religion of this divine contiment. Good, very good; but while we admire, reason remonstrates, the splendid castle is without foundation. But it is difficult to see why it would call this Christianity—that this was the doctrine of Christ, and his miracles stand on the same evidence. If this evidence is insufficient to prove, that he wrought the one, then it is insufficient to prove that he taught the other. If the name be assumed because it is desirable, we will invoke charity. While this doctrine seems to trifle with the mediation of Christ, as resembling the advocacy of an attorney, and with his ordinancies, as the poet's rattle, fit for babes in Christ; how its hope can take hold of immortality, we shall leave to its own inspiration to settle; since it considers the evidence of the gospel insufficient. As to this evidence, I would remark, as I pass some of the most sublime minds, such as Sir Isaac, Monsieur Pascal, Mr. Locke, Dr. Johnson, Mr. Adison, Judge Parsons, William Wirt, Mr. Adams and a host of others, have been as remarkable for their faith in the Divine mission of Jesus Christ, as for their supereminent talents, and have set their seal to the Bible, as containing the "glorious gospel of the blessed God." Thus viewing the holy Scriptures, the benevolent mind must, with peculiar delight, reflect upon the great exertions Christians have made, and are still making, to send this Divine volume to all the heathen nations—that they may be induced to abandon their idol Gods; to worship Jehovah, and to trust in the Saviour, who has brought his will to man. Instead of this, the natural language of Transcendentalism, it seems, must be;—Why send our mythology to the races, we call heathens? They have their mythology as well as we, perhaps as good, and, it may, in some things, be superior.

"This wonderful and horrible thing," that has come into our land, as, I understand, commenced in Germany, under the name of Rationalism; in France, it took the higher name of Illuminism; still aspiring, with us, it is Transcendentalism. But under different names it is the same thing. It is to exalt man above the Bible, and annihilate its Divine authority—it is, to cast upon a boundless ocean, without chart or compass—it is, to erect in every mind the standard of truth and right, and hence for every one to do what is right in his own eyes.

This brings us to the last clause of our text—"And what will ye do in the end thereof!" Cut the ties of restraint, which the community feel from the Divine authority of the Bible, and all the vile passions of man will be let loose. You may as well remonstrate with the falls of Niagara, as with one who knows he is right, let the Bible, or another's reason, say what they may. But the blessed laws of the land will restrain him.— But remember, human laws are a spider's web, if there be not virtue in the community to see them executed. Hence, the lovers of their firesides and their country will cling to their Bibles, as the palladium of their safety and glory. The recent history of France is fraught with instruction on this subject. What was the introductory step that led to their revolution?—a revolution that, for months, kept the streets of Paris flowing with human blood! It is well known, that it was the desecration of the Bible. Illuminism, with a Voltaire at its head, having stripped the word of life of its Divinity, the National Assembly were prepared to vote—that there was no God, and that death was an eternal sleep. This opened upon the nation the flood-gates of iniquity, and the terrors that succeeded, even poetry could not describe! It is, my friends, under Providence, by holding sacred this book of God, that our beloved country must be saved from suicide. It is this, that, this day, prevents us from bowing before our idol Gods, and sacrificing our beloved offspring to Molock. Wives, remember, that it is this holy book that saved you, like the benighted Hindoo, from the funeral pile, to be burnt alive upon the corpses of your husbands. Will you see, as I am told some are rejoiced to see, this Divine volume desecrated by German speculation! Full well may we sanctify a Fast, and pray mightily to the God of nations, that he would allay this moral infection that has lit upon our shores, that its deleterious influence spread no farther— especially, that the breath of wisdom may expel it from the school of the prophets and the pulpit.

APPENDIX.

Extracts from the Age of Reason.

Extracts from a Discourse of matters pertaining to Religion.

1st. Respecting what are called the Five Books of Moses—There is no evidence that he is the author of these books.

1st. Respecting the first Five Books of the Bible, commonly ascribed to Moses, there is no evidence that he wrote a word of them.

2d. The Christian theory is little else than the idolatry of the ancient Mythologists. The Ancient and Christian Mythologists differ very little.

2d. The Jews had a mythology as well as the Greeks. In the Christian documents, there is a mythology as in the Old Testament—mythology and legendary narratives and matter-of-fact are confounded.

3d. In every point of view in which those things called miracles can be placed and considered, the reality of them is improbable, and their existence unnecessary.

3d. If one were to look carefully into the evidence of the Christian miracles, he must come to the conclusion that they cannot be admitted as facts.

4th. There is not the least shadow of evidence who the persons were who wrote the Four Gospels, nor at what time they were written.

4th. The Evangelists, Matthew, Mark, Luke and John, mingle with their story puerile notions and tales, which it is charitable to call absurd.— Their testimony could not be received if offered in a court of justice, where a few dollars were at stake, without great caution.

Notes

1. See Appendix.
2. Encyclopedia.
3. While the Crower turned up the dunghill, he found a Gem.

"Boston Notions"

[J. C. Pennell]*

(These lines were written, on hearing that Mr. Ralph Waldo Emerson, and others, had commenced the publication of a transcendental work called "The Dial," in Boston, the chief city of the old Pilgrim Fathers.)

> Hear! a' ye goodly pilgrim flocks,
> Frae' Kennebec to Plymouth rocks!—
> The market for your wooden clocks,
>   Is well-nigh done!—
> For Boston chields, wi' "Dial" blocks,
>   Now track the sun!
>
> If e'er ye catch an absent wight,
> Gapin' to see what's out o' sight,
> And claimin' to hae' patent-right
>   For this invention;—
> I rede ye!—keep him fast an' tight
>   In your attention!
>
> He has na' lost his mental forces,
> Ye simple ones! when he discourses
> O' "inner light"—which now commences
>   To make us wise,
> By breakin' down the crumblin' fences
>   Of old philosophies!
>
> He's over-grand and sentimental,
> To crush his food by process dental;
> But lives on air, and dainties mental
>   O' purest wit;—
> The foggy—mystic—transcendental!—
>   I think they ca' it.

*Reprinted from *Footprints: or, Fugitive Poems* (Philadelphia: John Penington, 1843), pp. 90–92.

He prates o' "movement" and "unrest;"—
The "nineteenth century" is far the best,
In his opinion, that e'er left the nest
    O' unhatched time,
And Yankee notions richer than the rest
      In true sublime.

Ah! brither Ralph!—pray hae' a care!
My very banes do quake wi' fear,
Lest ye should raise the Pilgrims here,
    Frae out the ground!—
Puir simple folk!—they'd gape, to hear
      Sic' learned sound!

Your "inner light" will never blink,
But frae some tiny little chink,
O' your dark lanthorn;—sae I think,
    'Twad do nae good
To guide my feet, when I would sink
      In moral mud.

And, I would mind ye, one and all,—
That honest men sic' things ne'er handle,
Without the risk to get a fall!—
    Wi' my puir pence,
I'd rather buy the farthin' candle
      O' common sense!

"A Plain Discussion with a Transcendentalist"

[Merrill Richardson]*

Mr. B. Is there any prospect that the community will ever understand your new system of philosophy and faith? For years the inquiry has been "What is Transcendentalism?" and no intelligible answer has been given. The terms you use to express your ideas are new and hard to be understood. If you will drop your strange terminology and give your thoughts in plain, common sense language, you will do me a favor as an honest searcher after truth. If you have new *things* as well as new *words* and *names,* why can not you in a familiar way, communicate them?

Mr. A. You can readily see that a person may have ideas which can not be conveyed with precision to those who have had neither the ideas nor the words by which they are expressed. It is so in all the sciences, and particularly in the science of thought. But the principal reason why we are not understood is, men think so superficially. Most minds skim over the surface of a thousand subjects, but few dive deep into the sea of thought, remain long enough for distinct vision, and seize and bring up the precious pearls. How often do you throw out thoughts which, to your own mind, are great and comprehensive, scarcely a gleam of which enters the brain of one in twenty of your hearers! How little original thinking is there among that numerous class of our citizens who are called educated. Most of them dare not trust themselves with an idea which did not come from their text-books. If the guardian angel, genius, should suggest a new thought to their minds, they would crush it in the birth lest it should grow into an heresy. Look at the books which fly from the press like autumn leaves from the tree, without one new thought. An original mind, a genius, rarely appears, and is as rarely appreciated by his own age. The prophet is not in honor in his own country. This has been true in all time; it always will be true, for to be a genius is to be in advance of one's own age. Human pride and self-sufficiency predispose men to be ungrateful for teachings more inspired than their own. "Dost thou teach us?" is their con-

*Reprinted from *New Englander,* 1 (October 1843), 502–516.

temptuous reply to those who now attempt to open the eyes of the blind; and "they cast them out."

Mr. B. Well, granting that to your mind there is an extent and depth of meaning in the terms of your philosophy which I do not see, yet is it not possible to convey to my mind some true and definite idea of the thing called Transcendentalism? Dropping its scientific terms and all technicalities, can we not talk upon the real thing in plain English?

Mr. A. I trust we may, to some extent at least; for *the thing*, as you call it, is more generally felt than you suppose. It has been said that every one is, in a sense, a poet; no one can read a poem well if not in a poetic mood. So I would say, every one is, in a sense, a transcendentalist; that is, all who allow their minds any latitude of thought, at times have thoughts and feelings which are properly called transcendental. Hence we have aimed to establish schools, that the mind even in childhood, before it becomes cramped by forms, and before the inner light of the soul becomes dimmed or totally extinguished by the senses, may receive a right direction; be made to think for itself, and be led to see—not the forms of things, but things themselves. All men, though in different degrees and varied forms would be transcendentalists if they received a spiritual rather than a sensual culture.

Mr. B. Let us here come directly to the point. I have long suspected myself of transcendentalism, and would gladly gather from you some clear idea of it, that I may know whether I am within or without the pale of discipleship.

Mr. A. But you must remember that this is a very extensive subject. It would lead us a long way back to Kant and even to Plato. The writings of many in Germany, of some in England and France, and a few in our own country, must be discussed, in order to get a clear view of the whole. And then there are all varieties and degrees of transcendentalism. Those in Germany who followed Kant and adopted much of his philosophy, differed from him in many important particulars. Fichte, Schelling, Hegel, had each his own system, though they have been called transcendentalists. What, in loose language, is termed transcendentalism, is variously modified in different countries by different individuals, who have embraced that system of metaphysics which, leaving the field of sensual knowledge, soars into the regions of pure thought. The transcendentalists of our century, influenced to a great extent by the writings of Carlyle, have made great advances upon the Kantean philosophy; we have not only gone farther in our search for spiritual truth, but we have applied our philosophy to different subjects, and made it bear more directly upon the duties and relations of life.

Mr. B. We will leave, as far as possible, names and systems, as well as technicalities, out of view. I wish to talk with you upon *your* transcendentalism, and know whether it is possible for us to understand each other.

Mr. A. I will comply with your request upon one condition. You shall not reproach me with nonsense and fog if you fail to apprehend my meaning. Your sensual school of philosophy—

Mr. B. Stop, lest we raise bad blood in settling the preliminaries. I accept the condition, and propose that we commence with *man.* You claim that your views of man's spiritual nature are altogether truer and nobler than those which generally prevail.

Mr. A. Instead of considering man a mere creature of sense and intellect, but little superior to animal instinct, we view him a free, spiritual existence, of unlimited capacities, possessed of a soul and truly godlike, and in every way qualified for knowing truth and duty. Locke has entirely misled the world in some of the most vital points. Making the soul a blank leaf, upon which, with the pen of the five senses, external objects wrote whatsoever they listed, he left man, like the brute, at the mercy of any thing that chanced to leave upon his brains the deepest impression. He left man no fixed pole-star by which to direct his course, but only the flickering paper of self-interest, in following which, he has been wrecked upon every sand-bar. He granted him reflection, but this was only a kind of ruminating upon the gross food furnished by the senses. This chewing of the cud only aided the digestion; it gave no new spiritual aliment to the system. Man was to ascertain truth and duty, not from listening to the clear response of the divine oracle within him, but from the prompting of the appetite; that was truth which was sweet, that a lie which was bitter to the palate. Duty, virtue, properly speaking, there were none. If a man, by balancing pains and pleasures, present or future, could find which end of the steel-yards would probably preponderate, *there* lay his duty. Such has been the philosophy, for the most part, of the civilized world. In opposition to this sensual system, we maintain that man has other faculties than the bodily senses—a soul distinct from the stomach. He is endowed with reason and strong religious sentiments, which intuitively know and spontaneously feel truth and duty. That is *true,* not because of its greater profit or pleasure, but true because it is in agreement with the eternal nature of things. And God has gifted man with the faculty to discover this truth. Duty rests upon this discovered truth. Man has no arithmetical calculations to make to find his duty; it lies revealed to this faculty. The *right* is to be followed, come pleasure or pain; his obligation to do right is infinite, having all the weight of established and unchangeable truth. We give the soul a faculty which is wanting, or which is certainly overlooked in the common philosophy of the age. And this faculty is the chief quality belonging to man. It is this which, together with conscience, distinguishes him from the brute creation.

This faculty is a divine, truth-seeing reason. Man appears to me in a new light belonging to a higher order of beings, since I have studied him as he is. He is associated in my mind with celestial beings, rather than with creeping things. This view of man affects all his moral relations. It sets aside, or rather rises superior to all that endless calculation and argument about God, conscience, religion, which for centuries have occupied the church.

Mr. B. I can heartily respond to much which you say. And certainly man needs to have his attention turned more to those great facts relating to his spiritual nature. But you will pardon me if I call your attention more particularly to some things which you have stated. This higher faculty of reason which you claim as so great a discovery in mental science, and which you glory in as a distinguishing feature of your system, I believe to be important, but can not see to be new.

Mr. A. It is as old as Plato and Abraham. But for centuries men have lost sight of it. We claim only that we have found what had been lost. Particularly it is a new discovery, though the time was when the great truths which this faculty reveals animated and inspired the greatest minds.

Mr. B. But I can see nothing in this which has not been recognized, and which is not now recognized in some form by those whom you would hesitate to call disciples of your school. You have justly laid more stress upon this faculty, I will admit, than has been usually done; but how can you claim it to be a new discovery, even in the sense you have stated? Has not every enlightened moralist and Christian preacher advocated the idea that truth and falsehood, right and wrong, are, in their very nature, eternally separate? How can this have escaped you, when, for example, you have read the argument in favor of the Christian religion drawn from the *nature of its doctrines?* How repeatedly has it been asserted that the mind is such a thing that it sees and knows many of these doctrines to be true?—that man is compelled, from the nature God has given him, to assent to the rightfulness and the righteousness of the precepts of the gospel? It has ever been claimed that the fundamental precepts of moral conduct are so plain that the fool need not err, and the heathen are without excuse. When the spirit of infidelity, coursing up and down the page of revelation, has sought some weak point at which to commence in sacrilegious work, where has it alighted? Upon the fundamental doctrines and precepts of Christianity? By no means. And why? Because infidelity itself has been forced to acknowledge this citadel impregnable. The leading doctrines of the gospel mankind have felt to be true. They appeal directly to the soul, conscience, reason, the whole inner man, and, except in a strait of desperation, the infidel has not dared to lay his hands upon these truths, but has made his attacks upon some apparent discrepancies in the chronology of Moses, or points alike insignificant, knowing that the common sense and reason of the world would cry out against him, if he assailed the love, the benevolence, the humility, the charity, the forgiveness, the repentance, enjoined in the gospel. When infidelity has denied the validity of the evidence in favor of revelation, and inferred that man is under no obligation to practice the virtues there enjoined, what has been our reply? Why, that proof or no proof on this point, there was still another ground of obligation, one which it could not gainsay, viz. the testimony of man's reason and conscience to the truth-fulness of the practical doctrines contained in the Bible. Hence in various forms and relations we have always held to a truth-seeing and duty-knowing faculty in man.

Mr. A. But you have confounded it with the understanding, which can never see either spiritual or universal truths, but has to do only with the senses. And thus you have subjected all classes of ideas to the scrutiny of the logic of the understanding, which has led to questioning and denying every thing, to throwing religious and sensual truths into the same category, producing endless confusion.

Mr. B. Why not elucidate this matter of the reason and the under-standing thus:—Looking upon the mind as a unit, and not a medley of separate faculties, we say, the mind, when acting in one capacity, judges; in another, remembers; in another, imagines; in another, wills, and so on. It is the whole mind, acting in its various directions and capacities, that gives rise to this distinction of faculties. Now when we speak of the understanding and reason as separate faculties, or as head-ing two different classes of mental operations, we mean no more than that the mind, as one active agent, occupied with one class of objects, or in one capacity, is called the understanding; in another capacity, or acting upon a different class of objects, is called reason. Take an example given by one of your own writers to illustrate this distinction: We draw a triangle, and by examination find its angles equal to two right angles. This is a discovery of the understanding. Now the under-standing would never see that *all* triangles *must* have their angles equal to two right angles; but the *reason* sees this universal truth. Very well. It is the mind, dropping any particular triangle, which grasps a fact common to all such figures. It is the understanding, say you, which is occupied upon the natural sciences, in classifying men, ani-mals, vegetables, minerals, &c. into genera and species; but it is the reason which sees those facts common to all of the same genus or species. But the whole mind is occupied in all this; and those who never heard of the distinction between the understanding and the reason, recognize both these powers of the mind.

Mr. A. But what the reason does here is quite an unimportant part of its official work, compared with what it does in the higher sphere of spiritual truth. The understanding would indeed make blundering work any where, without some aid from the reason. It is only a kind of intellectual hopper, which the senses furnish with grain, and by means of a little grinding power of the reason, it is enabled to furnish flour well bolted, bagged, and ready for use. But while the reason assists the understanding in manufacturing these materials of the senses, its peculiar province is to know God, virtue and religion, and here it receives no aid, but is hindered in its operations by the senses and the understanding. You have tried to make the intellectual mill grind spiritual things as well as material. You have set the senses laboriously to work to fill the hopper with their coarse grains,—arguments for a God, a soul, a Christianity, a religion,—then hoisted the gate, and with deafening screakings and monotonous scrannel pipings, you have produced—meal? the driest unsavory bran, and nothing more, say most, and then you fall to disputing with them whether it is bran or meal. Is it wonderful that none but dyspeptics will partake of such a questionable dish? Not only is there a radical distinction between these two faculties, but it is of the utmost importance to a spiritual religion that it be maintained.

Mr. B. I have no objection to the distinction; I deem it important; but I can not sympathize with your objection to employing the mind, the whole mind, or any one of its faculties, in discussing religious topics. Religion, say you, is not the province of the understanding, but of the reason. Well, if of the reason, then of the mind in the exercise of reason.

Mr. A. Yes! but man has a soul, and you would leave him nothing but a fragment of intellect, to be occupied indifferently, either upon a piece of carpentry, the different methods of cookery, or a system of religion. What faculty, in your metaphysics, is it, by which a man is thrown into raptures by the beauties of nature, the inspirations of the poet, or contemplations of the godlike? You would secularize every thing, and look cool as an icicle, upon the face of beauty, or the wonders of a wonder-working God! Your philosophy has so benumbed your spiritual nature, that you can not even talk upon this subject. You remind me of the clodpole who grunted out—"pshaw! what's the use of those weeds," as he saw a lovely damsel weaving a bouquet. Standing under the roar of Niagara, your only thought would be, whether the position were eligible for a sawmill. You must change your whole method of thinking, and look with a different eye upon the universe, before you can see all that is visible to man's divine reason.

The reason is a faculty quite different from the logical power, by which one gets the better of an opponent in an argument. It directly sees, and at the same time feels the truth, and beauty, and goodness, of all things. True, mind is essentially the same in all men; yet upon almost every subject how varied are men's opinions; and upon no subject do their speculations differ more widely than upon religion. And not their opinions only, but their feelings and whole spiritual nature differ entirely. Of the millions who cultivate the earth, or of the less numerous but more favored class of mere consumers, few, like Burns, are alive to the beauty and infinity of its forms. He saw more in the thistle at his doorstone, than others would see in traversing the whole of leafy India. The soul of one is thrilled with the music of the spheres, while thousands stare at the heavens with the stupidity of the ox. The language of devotion is uttered by every tree, flower, and running brook, but seldom is there an ear to hear, and a heart to feel. Yet the tympanum of all ears is of the same construction; dissect men, and you will find the heart, ventricles, veins, and arteries, the same in all. Why then, you may as well reason, is there such difference in the hearing and feeling of living men? Why this deafness, blindness, insensibility, in some—while others, in the same outward condition, see, hear, and feel sensitively? The only answer is, after abating much for different natural endowments, most men look at every thing through the eye of the understanding, rather than through the eye of reason. I maintain, that all possess the godlike faculty of discerning religious truth, but they neglect to use it. They must argue every point; call councils and diets to weigh evidence, and by a majority of votes, put the matter beyond dispute, decide what is orthodox, and what men shall believe upon due pains and penalties. Hence to-day, *this* is sound doctrine; to-morrow, the mail arrives bringing intelligence from some such ecclesiastical debating club, that if you continue to believe it, you shall be hung, and no mass said for your soul. The fact has been entirely overlooked, that the understanding is not adapted to the discovery of truth in things spiritual. Men have endeavored to settle points in religion, as they settle questions about railroads and banks, and thus the faith of the church has changed with every fresh breeze of ecclesiastical discussion. Notwithstanding the infallibility of popes and prelates, the orthodox and the heterodox have changed places some hundred times. And as long as men disregard or overlook the inner light of reason, and place religion and Christianity among the subjects of debate, so long will these shiftings of belief continue.

Mr. B. Did it belong to the object of our present discussion, I would attempt quite a different solution of this change in religious belief. You seem to grant that reason has been recognized as a mental faculty. I claim, that appeals have ever been made to it in the search for truth, and particularly in the examination of scripture doctrines.

Mr. A. Why then those volumes of arguments, *a priori* and a *posteriori*, to prove that there is a God, a Christianity, even a religion in the universe? Why have not your Christian philosophers pointed men directly to the facts of a religion as they exist, and can be known to exist in the bosom of every man, as they would point them to the existence of any objects of vision, and there leave them, taking it for granted that these facts were *seen?* Instead of this, they have debated all these points as problematical; God's very existence has been left a peradventure, and all truth and duty disputable. So far from turning the mind in upon itself that it might see truth, and feel the infinite weight of duty, you have only led it to question whether they are realities. I am willing to concede that some minds have recognized a reason superior to the understanding. It is too obvious to be overlooked by those who think deeply. Still, this distinction has, to the infinite detriment of truth, been disregarded.

Mr. B. These points have been discussed that the mind might be turned to them. Argument affects the mind in reference to a thousand things concerning which there is really no disbelief. When the sceptic, one starry night, was dealing out his atheistic notions to Napoleon, and Napoleon looked up and asked, "Who made all these then?" there was an argument, virtually the whole argument, for the existence of a God. Now I ask, where was the harm of such a reply? Every thinking mind has reasons of doubting almost every thing which has been considered matter of settled belief. As some of your own philosophers have said, no one has thought sufficiently to be a metaphysician, who has not thought to doubting. Now the mind rights itself at such times by *evidence*, internal or external, of the reason or of the understanding, I care not which, I approve of both.

Mr. A. If men had been rightly educated, taught to look within rather than without, made acquainted with their own powers and the proper method of viewing subjects, they would escape those doubts.

Mr. B. Will you then grant that, under existing circumstances, it is better to continue the discussion?

Mr. A. By no means. Nothing is gained, while much is lost. The man who needs to be convinced of religious truth by the deductions of logic, though his language and outward conduct may be somewhat changed by such conviction, still remains the same at heart. He is no more spiritual. He is still destitute of genuine faith. His religion continues a mere matter of calculation, embodied in outward forms, and not in the rapt emotions of a spiritual life. Much is lost, for while we continue to argue upon those fundamental, intuitive truths, they will continue to be disputed. It is appalling to think to what a depth of spiritual degradation the sensual philosophy of our age has sunk us. We have been led to question whether we have souls even; the being of a God denied; faith, except in things which can be seen and handled, rooted from the heart, and duty reduced to a mere problem in the rule of loss and gain. Let us stop this low and false argumentation at once; for better have no metaphysics, than to continue in this way. Why, only reflect! How have you attempted to convince men that they should be religious? By showing that religion is *useful!* On your system, men are told they had better have religion, for reasons like those which induce them to buy an article of furniture, or a meal of victuals—it will do them good! Really, how such motives can consist with virtue, I can not see. Does not every thief, for the time being, reason that his theft will profit him? And is this same scoundrel a good man, when convinced his gains will be greater, he ceases to steal and begins to pray? The possession of a Spanish galleon laden with Peruvian mines could not offer such rewards to the pirate, as Paley offers him if he will be religious. Strange that any one should have overlooked the self-evident truth, that, properly speaking, there can be no virtue in acting from such motives. Self must be annihilated, denied as the gospel of Christ hath it, and Right, Truth, Goodness, seen, felt, and followed for their own sake, in order that we may be holy. Turn the minds of men in upon themselves, make them see their divine nature and exercise their divine reason, and let them act in a manner *worthy* of happiness.

Mr. B. This is the very thing we endeavor to do. We preach the doctrine—would we could do it in thunder tones, that men should obey the truth, and be virtuous because this is *right*. That duty should be done for duty's sake. "Justitia fiat, ruat cœlum"—let justice be done, though the heavens should fall. No danger, nor suffering, nor glory, nor gain, nor pleasure, should make us swerve a hair from the path of rectitude. And let me say, that a little more candor, or more of that deep thinking which you so highly recommend, would correct your idea of the true happiness-principle, as held by its intelligent advocates.

Mr. A. I never will admit that as a principle in morals. Man, godlike man, is something more, or he is something less, than a mere motive grinder, or, as Carlyle calls it, a mere balance for weighing hay and thistles, pains and pleasures.

Mr. B. Well, permit me to correct your conception of the principles; for I apprehend that if we look at things and not at terms only, we shall not be so wide apart here as you suppose. Follow truth and duty, we both say, without regard to consequences. We both say that the mind is such a thing, that it can see truth—that it does this, either by the faculty you call Reason, or by what some call the Inner Light, or by what others call Reflection—truth, moral, spiritual truth *it can know*. So far we are agreed. Here you stop, and protest "that farther than this we should not go in our inquiry; and can not with safety or advantage." I too am willing to stop here—to leave entirely out of view the *utility* of virtue, and simply inculcate the duty. But I do not believe it hazardous or wrong to take one step more in our reasoning, and inquire—Why do we spontaneously feel that certain truths *are* truths? that *is* right? that *is* duty? Why do we feel, and intuitively see, the truthfulness, the beauty, the righteousness, the goodness of certain actions? You say, "Because we are so made!" Undoubtedly. And do we not find ourselves *so made* that these things would not so appear, were they not adapted to our spiritual nature? And do we not see this adaptation in their tendency so directly and so certainly to ennoble and bless us? Were they *not* thus adapted, did they *not* harmonize with the reality of things—did they tend to *pain*, rather than happiness, I have some doubt whether the happiness-principle would have received such unqualified condemnation by your philosophers. And when, in some connections, you so extol the noble qualities and tendencies of your own system, I have fancied I saw you expose the cloven foot of this same happiness-principle. It would not be a difficult matter to find the very thing in the works of your favorite Carlyle; his French Revolution and his Chartism are full of it, and it is impossible for him or any other man, to write upon such subjects and not tacitly recognize it. In his last work, "Past and Present," p. 25, is the following: "They (quacks) are the one bane of the world. Once clear the world of them, it ceases to be a Devil's-world, in all fibres of it wretched, accursed; and begins to be a God's world, blessed, and working hourly towards blessedness." Also, p. 27, "When a Nation is unhappy, the old Prophet was right and not wrong in saying to it: ye have forgotten God, ye have quitted the ways of God, or ye would not have been unhappy." And the same idea is conveyed more than fifty times in this same book. And if you call this "stomach-happiness," inasmuch as it has reference to governing and feeding men; then let me ask, why will you, night after night, till the oil is gone from your lamp, sit reading with glistening eyes the works of your Carlyle? "O such thoughts, heaven-born, soul-inspired, they rivet a man to his chair!" exclaim you. Will you do yourself the kindness to think a little more deeply upon that answer? If the belief of this principle tends necessarily to selfishness, I have not discovered it. Moses, Paul, Christ himself, alluded to it approvingly. The more a man loves the true, and the good, and is stimulated by this love to pursue them, the better he is. To say of men, they *delight* in iniquity, is to rank them with fallen spirits. To say that they *delight* in holiness, is to rank them with celestial beings. But as you will not listen to any thing in favor of this principle, I propose another topic—your idea of a God. I grant you are peculiar in your views of the Divine existence, and also respecting several important subjects intimately connected with it. Transcendentalism, if I comprehend it, is rather a religion than a philosophy. Your principal oracles often repeat the idea, that religion is the one chief fact in regard to man. And all your writings have a direct bearing upon this point.

Mr. A. It is time some men raised their voice in its favor; for religion, except in what is outward and ceremonial, has well nigh been banished [from] the civilized world. Your sensual systems of faith as well as philosophy, have left little hope, or belief, or spirituality in the soul. You have separated God from his works, seated him upon a throne somewhere in infinite space, at an immeasurable distance from man, and taking it for granted that He had retired from the business of inspiring the heart, working miracles, and controlling all things, you have taken the work of religion into your own hands. And truly you make noise enough about it. God's voice in the soul is hushed; the earnest, rapt spirit is wanting. Your religion is empty and hollow-hearted, a product of the senses and not of the soul. It has not the silent strength of the river, but the rustling noise of the brook rushing over the stony bed. You take a false view of God, and consequently your worship is idolatry.

Mr. B. Do favor me with a clear statement of *your* idea of God.

Mr. A. God is Good, or Goodness; or the animating Principle of goodness, truth, beauty, every where operating in nature and in the soul of man. External nature is but the emblem or garment of the Deity, and serves to body Him forth to the eye. But it is the eye of reason which sees Him, and the soul that feels his presence, while conscience continually whispers his voice in our hearing. God is within us and around us. The truly pious soul feels his presence, hears his voice, and sees him working every moment. Men of genius, of true spiritual insight, have ever taken this view of God. They have seen through the dead matter of the world, and looked directly upon God. Poets, prophets, sages, and all the devout of every age and nation, have viewed all objects which we call material only as the symbol, or visible manifestation of the Eternal Spirit. Some have had a faith which saw every thing as a part of God, the keenness of their spiritual vision scarcely noticing such a thing as matter. Not only was God the *animus mundi*, and

> "All but parts of one stupendous whole,
> Whose body Nature is, and God the soul,"

but all was God, and God was All. Pantheism, a word full of denial and scepticism to superficial minds, is one of the highest products of the devout spirit of man. It has been well said that Spinosa was *God-intoxicated*, transcending time and space, all forms and appearances, God to him was All and in All. Few have sufficiently disentangled themselves from flesh and sense, and from the influence of a wrong education, to rise to such a height in the spiritual world. Some of the ancients, and some at the present time in Germany, and possibly in other countries, have become thus spiritual. But while I admire their spirit, and long for their attainments, I confess I fall short of their faith. While I see God in all things, I do not, strictly speaking, see all things to be God. For example, I can see God in that rose, as the animating principle which gives it its exquisite and esthetic form and tint, yet I can not say, that rose is God. But I do say, God is to be loved and worshiped in the rose. If we have the inner eye to see the beauty of such objects, so far we love, admire, and therefore worship their Maker. Still more clearly do we feel God present in the human soul. Man's conscience is God's voice directly speaking to him. Yielding ourselves up to its clear and truthful notes, we are right. O that all would listen to it, and obey!

Mr. B. As we are upon that feature of transcendentalism which gives coloring to your whole system, I wish you to be more explicit upon one point, viz. In your view, is God, in such a sense separate from men and nature, that, as a distinct being, He controls, governs, rewards and punishes his creatures? You know the prevailing idea of God in enlightened countries—a being distinct from his works; who exercises a providence over them; who takes cognizance of the moral conduct of men, pleased with all right affections and purposes of men, and displeased with their wrong conduct.

Mr. A. If you insist upon a direct answer, I would say, No. The vulgar notion that God, as a person, after creating the world and the universe, and setting causes in operation, or establishing laws for the continuance of all things, retired from his works to watch their operation, and occasionally to interfere, particularly in his moral kingdom, to give a little instruction, or to correct some of the grosser wrongs of men, I do not believe. This view is practical atheism; it virtually excludes God from nature and from the soul. Whereas God,—for he is omnipresent,—is constantly operating every where and in every thing; growing the grass, the tree, the flower; animating and inspiring the soul; producing new forms of beauty; working, as he has eternally worked, works of wonder and goodness. If the sensual philosophy had not so benumbed the soul, men would see this. It is seen by those you call heathen. The wild Indian hears the whisper of the Great Spirit in every breeze; listens to it coming from every dell and cave of his mountains; sees God in the forest, acknowledges his hand in giving him his fishing brooks and hunting grounds. To the earnest Arab soul the star that shines upon his desert path is but the eye of God. As the sun warmed and fertilized the vineyards of the ancient Persian, he worshiped the kindly influence—God. The Ganges fertilizes his rice-fields, and the inhabitant of Hindostan pays to it the homage of the heart. Those eastern people, situated in the garden of the world, have always been a devout people. Not mere dead matter, but the spirit of beauty and goodness, which animated surrounding nature, has always been worshiped by them. In their simple way, with childlike and sincere emotions of wonder, they have bowed before the Eternal in these manifestations of himself.

Mr. B. Really, you must have a transcendental eye, for it is something more than a poet's, to see so much beauty and true piety in those eastern idolaters. You doubtless see the same in the Chinese, in their worship of those half dozen fat hogs kept as gods at Canton. The funeral pile, the hook-swinging, the infanticides, and the thousand disgusting and horrible rites of Bramah, all must come up to your mind with peculiar attractions, in as much as you think them sincere acts of devotion. But it was not my present design to ascertain your views of religious worship. I wished first to understand your idea of God.

Mr. A. I wish to say that I would not be understood to mean that the great mass of those nations are truly spiritual. But there is among them the recognition of an omnipresent Deity, and there are real worshipers. The great body of people in every country are idolaters. They worship the image or form rather than God, the living principle of goodness. But, to come back to the point, I believe God does mark the conduct of men. How can it be otherwise, when He is every where present in his works? And that the obedient are rewarded and the wicked punished, is a matter of consciousness to every one. Not a law of man's nature can be violated without internal discord and misery, while all is harmony and sweet peace when man falls in with the eternal reality of things. The true prophet, poet and philosopher,—for they are the same,—have always represented the soul of man as a divinely constructed instrument, a true Æolian harp, which, rightly tuned, gives forth heavenly music; but, disordered by sin, its sounds are harsh and discordant.

Mr. B. Wherein are your sentiments different from the doctrine that man receives the full punishment of his sins in this life? How often, contrary to all human experience, in the face of what every wicked man knows to be true in his own case, is it assured that, by the remorse of conscience and the evil consequences of sin in this life, men are equitably and fully punished! If I understand your idea of God, you do not consider him a being distinct from man and nature, possessed of personal intelligence, susceptibility and will, but a kind of vivifying principle every where and at all times operating. I do not wonder that you object to producing *evidence* of God's existence, for your God, or rather principle, must be seen intuitively, if seen at all, and this too by a faculty purely transcendental. You complain of the want of faith and of universal prevalence of scepticism. At times you seem clothed in sackcloth, in view of the infidelity of the age. You profess the most ardent desire to revive belief and earnest spiritual life on the earth, and yet if the great mass of people could be made to understand and embrace your views, there would be nothing to restrain them from the worst of crimes. You remove from man the piercing eye of a conscious God; you place him under no government but certain natural laws, and if he will risk (as he most surely will) the natural consequences of vice in this life, there is no more for him to fear. In fact you discard all appeals to fear as a means of moral government, maintaining that man should be so educated that what you call his natural love of truth, beauty and holiness, will be sufficient. If you succeed in making this feature of transcendentalism believed, it needs no prophet to foresee that it will sweep every vestige of pure religion from the world. Not what you call religion, for there will always be minds alive to the beauties of nature and art, and hearts enraptured with the works of God, in which consist your religion and religious worship. But the mass of mankind are never sufficiently refined in their sentiments to appreciate your sentiments, and keep devout on your plan. They will enjoy the beauties of nature, but will never arrive, in their admiration of landscapes and beautiful thoughts, at what you would call earnest spiritual life. It is much to be desired to have the heart softened and ennobled in the contemplation of the works of God. There may be true worship in this; but how many, who, like Byron, feel exquisitely every form of poetic beauty, are hostile to religion, when she lays a restraint upon their passions! Much which you say in this connection is good and important to be said, but it never will be all that man needs. If we stop with mere poetic beauty, with the religion of romance, we shall soon be destitute even of this. There is no man who can not feel in some degree the beauty and grandeur of certain objects. So far you would call him religious: so far he worships your God. We might as well call him so far religious, as he loves a dish of turtle soup or a bottle of Madeira; for while the one may indicate a higher refinement than the other, both are equally involuntary, and both may exist in bad as well as in good men. David, Job and Isaiah, to whom you often refer, all saw God in his works, all "mused on nature with a poet's eye;" but this was not all their religion. They had deep repentance for sin,—for sin committed against God as a being, and not a mere principle. There was faith in those men, but a faith widely differing from your faith. You appropriate the poetic beauty of the Bible and of nature to your system, and leave out of view those truths which are most necessary for man to believe.

Mr. A. You must be aware that, owing to the difference in genius and education of men, we must always have both the exoteric and the esoteric doctrines. The inspired sages of Greece found this to be necessary. There must be a statute religion for the mass, certainly till they are elevated immeasurably above what they have ever been. Hence we never wish to controvert the common notions respecting the Bible, inspiration, religious forms, &c., since these are necessary for a season. But infidelity is chiefly among the educated. During the last century it prevailed in its worst forms in the higher circles of France, and even throughout Europe and America. The sensual philosophy led to this result. We wish to reach this class of men. Let the doctrines of Pythagoras and of the still more divine Plato be expounded and taught, with slight modifications, and we shall arrest the progress of doubt and denial.

Mr. B. Here again I must call for explanation. You apply the epithets *divine, inspired,* and *god-like,* to men unknown to sacred history. But from your idea of God, of worship, of man's reason, I suppose we are to understand that you call Plato, Shakespeare, and certain writers of our day in Europe and America, *inspired,* in the same sense in which Isaiah, David, and Christ were inspired. That is, they have genius, true spiritual insight, and utter what the heart spontaneously responds to as truth.

Mr. A. Exactly so! Yet there are all *degrees* of inspiration. And we consider Christ much more inspired than any other man, and it is owing to this that his religion is superior to all others, and is received in the most enlightened countries. Much of it will doubtless live through all time. When the poet or sage utters true spiritual thoughts, we say he is inspired. His thoughts are the voice of God; they are beyond common ideas, and we know not what else to call them. We read them, they strike us as true, beautiful, good, and we spontaneously exclaim, "Surely this is the voice of God!" Hence we can see by the light of reason, that David had more inspiration than Moses, John far more than the other apostles, and Christ so much more than all others, that they may well call him Master. I trust we have a few in our own day, some even in New England, who listen attentively to the eternal oracle within, and utter divine responses. The Dial is a clear indication that there is still faith, genius and inspiration among us.

Mr. B. I give you credit for clearness and candor, whatever I may think of your common sense. This is no mysticism. To place the Dial and the Bible, as it respects their inspiration, on the same footing, is certainly intelligible, and in all other respects is truly transcendental. Pardon me, Mr. A., but I must ask you if you are serious in this?

Mr. A. You infer too much. I did not design to consider the writers of the Dial on a par with Christ. I only mean that they have uttered the truest things which are uttered among us,—many things truly inspired,— though in their earnest zeal they have said much that I would not say. They do not deserve the contempt in which they are held by many. Every inspired teacher has been deemed by his formal age either a madman, a fool or a knave. It is the fate of genius to be persecuted. The Pharisee, wrapped in his forms, saw nothing true or good in the teachings of the divine Jesus; Socrates was persecuted to death; Kant was sneered at as a deluded dreamer, and Carlyle, after years of true spiritual endeavor, hardly begins to be appreciated at home, though we deem him one of the brightest stars in the constellation of genius. But such men count the cost of their devotion to truth. The world's teachers have had little cause to be pleased with the world, yet they have loved and sought to bless their race. Truth, omnipotent truth, is their support. It is enough for them that they are right. They look to the distant future, when many will rise up and call them blessed.

Mr. B. But you must be aware that your views undermine the foundation of all that is peculiar in Christianity. Here, you profess to be a Christian, and weep strange tears over the unbelief and idolatry of the age. You appear, at times, reverently to worship "God, manifest in the flesh;" but the very next act of your devotion is to kneel at the shrine of a favorite philosopher or poet, pagan or Christian. These you call as truly divine, as really inspired, and in every way as worthy of religious reverence, as Jesus, only in a less degree. You pay no more respect to Christ than a pagan emperor of Rome was willing to pay him,—give him a temple in common with a thousand other deities. Certain parts of the Bible you are ready to pronounce of heavenly origin, in the same sense in which you think the writings of many other men were divinely inspired. The only moral law ever given, your writers assert, is the voice of God in the heart. Your belief is this: Plato had his system of religious philosophy, Mohammed his, Confucius his, Kant his, and Christ his; and all these, so far as we perceive their truth by the light of reason, and no farther, are to us the oracles of God. Some of your sect are willing, but others are not, to give Christianity the preference. You use the language of Christians, with the addition of some buckram phraseology of your own, but with a meaning entirely different from its usual signification. I can not believe this honest. The Universalist, the Unitarian, the infidel, the atheist, frankly state what they believe, in plain terms. I have no desire to class you with them, though it is evident your whole system of religious philosophy may be found in the writings of these various schools. You throw around your transcendentalism such a devotional air, and so much of the language of evangelical piety, that your real meaning is not perceived. The obscurity of your system would vanish instantly if you expressed yourselves in plain language. Not to refer to points already discussed, take the published opinions of your school respecting *miracles*. You are aware that all this has been advanced a thousand times. You only hit the thing differently. You take the same course upon miracles as upon inspiration. As you inspire *all* men rather than deny the inspiration of the sacred penmen, so instead of denying miracles you make every thing *miraculous.*

Mr. A. Carlyle has placed this subject in its true light in the chapter on "Natural Supernaturalism," in his Sartor, which I would commend to your special attention.

Mr. B. I have read it, and will give all the credit you can ask for the genius there displayed. Perhaps we could not take a better illustration of your method of treating subjects connected with religion. Instead of direct denial, backed with the usual arguments, you virtually deny the miracles of the Bible, by making all things so marvelous, and by clothing your expressions in such imagery, that one thing appears to be as miraculous as another. The rising of the sun would be a stupendous miracle to a man who should see it for the *first* time. The rising of a dead man would not appear to be a miracle if we should see dead men rise every day. The chemist could work miracles in the eyes of ignorant heathen. That is, all is miraculous to men which they are not *familiar* with. Had we an eye to see a little farther into the operation of natural laws, every miracle recorded in the Bible or any where else would appear a natural rather than a *super*-natural event. Therefore, whether any thing shall be miraculous or not, depends not upon the thing itself, but upon our degree of insight into the laws of nature. This is the leading idea of Carlyle's chapter on Natural Supernaturalism, and the substance of all your writers have to say upon the subject of miracles. Granting that there is truth in this view of subject, yet the most favorable construction I can put upon the argument is, to call it an evasion of the real point at issue. True, you exhort us with earnestness to think deeper, that we may see more of the miraculous with which we are constantly surrounded. But, believe in a miracle, in any proper sense of the word, you do not.

Mr. A. We are heartily weary of the endless debate upon such questions in the Christian system. It tends only to doubt and denial. The whole forensic discussion from the first century to this, upon the *proofs* of Christianity, have been fruitful in nothing but infidelity. A religion—any part of a religion—which needs the logic of the understanding for its support, is not worth the argument. If men have not an eye to see and a soul to feel religious truth, argument will avail nothing. Religious men should take the high ground that religion is a native germ in the heart of man, and is to be cultivated by other means than disputes about the forms which Christianity has assumed. Let us leave the questions of plenary inspiration, miracles, trinity and unity, the humanity and divinity of the Savior, the sabbath and the church, all which are entirely foreign to religion itself, and retire within ourselves, to listen to God's voice in the soul, and *be* religious.

Mr. B. Ah! but there is a question to be answered—yes or no—upon which very much depends. If at the word of Christ the dead awoke to life, and the eyes of the blind were opened, did he not exercise a power superior to that of the chemist or man of genius; and so much superior that none can doubt it to be supernatural. And you need not be told that if the works attributed to Christ could be shown not to have been wrought by him, instead of being an inspired teacher sent from heaven, as you often term him, he was an impostor. One can hardly give you credit for sincerity, when you eulogize Christ and his religion, and upon the same page say, what, fairly interpreted into intelligible language, stigmatizes him as a deceiver. These inconsistencies need to be explained. You are ready enough to discuss other questions of history; why not those connected with the Christian religion?

Mr. A. It is one of the first lessons of our religion not to use the sensual logic with men, but to turn their attention to the great truths that are written upon the tables of the heart. We expect like the great Master, to be reviled, but we shall not return reviling for reviling. You will yet see, and I hope in this life, that there is enough which is miraculous without going back eighteen hundred years. But at present I must leave you to gaze at God's world, without seeing any thing wonderful in the thousand forms of beauty and goodness which lie in every direction; but only a little chemical matter to be analyzed, explained, and scientifically arranged. But it is painful to see man, standing in the midst of wonders, like the stupid ass, with his whole attention upon food for his stomach; or like an ambitious boy, beating his drum to arrest the eyes of the world, as if he were the only real prodigy to be admired. The secret of the universe is open, but only to those who have an eye to see it. Men must retire into the holy of holies, their own souls, and then the Shekinah will appear, and from the altar of the heart acceptable incense will ascend. Be silent, my brother, as you stand in this star-domed temple of God, and his presence shall overshadow you; and you shall feel that man—all that is in him and around him—is a miracle! Man is the high-priest of Nature beautifully emblemed in the priest of Jewry; he is the eye of the earth which should be turned towards heaven. He is the highest form of the godlike. "Be still and know that I am God," is a text I beg of you to consider.

Mr. B. And I would request you to preach your doctrine from any text in your numerous Bibles, to any uninitiated audience you can find, that you may be convinced of the impracticability of making mankind understand such a sublimated religion. You extol earnest, rapt emotions, whether in the Mussulman at the tomb of his prophet, or in the worshiper of the sun, the river, the star, or any other created object. Try your transcendentalism then, and see if the eye moistens, and the fire of devotion burns in the heart under its influence? You call attention to your new philosophy, and as hearers we have a claim on you to speak in a *known tongue* the very thing you mean. You attack almost every article of our belief, and we have a right to know just what you would have substituted in its place. Our views of God, of Christ, of the Bible, of Christianity, of worship, of man—his nature, his duties, and his destiny—our system of moral science, our literature, and even our civil institutions, are in your opinion defective. You call for a radical change. One of your writers says, "It is not to be denied that the principles of this system are those of reform in church, state, and society, and for this cause they are unpopular." Thus we find ourselves attacked in a new and peculiar manner. We are exhorted in the phraseology of Christianity, to throw off all its present forms of belief and practice, and go on unto perfection! But before we strip naked in this style, we wish to know whether you have better garments for our covering.

"Terpsichore"

Oliver Wendell Holmes*

Once more,—once only,—we must stop so soon,—
What have we here? A GERMAN-SILVER SPOON;
A cheap utensil, which we often see
Used by the dabblers in æsthetic tea;
Of slender fabric, somewhat light and thin,
Made of mixed metal, chiefly lead and tin;
The bowl is shallow, and the handle small
Marked in large letters with the name JEAN PAUL.
Small as it is, its powers are passing strange,
For all who use it show a wondrous change;
And first, a fact to make the barbers stare,
It beats Macassar for the growth of hair;
See those small youngsters whose expansive ears
Maternal kindness grazed with frequent shears;
Each bristling crop a dangling mass becomes,
And all the spoonies turn to Absaloms!
Nor this alone its magic power displays,
It alters strangely all their works and ways;
With uncouth words they tire their tender lungs,
The same bald phrases on their hundred tongues;
"Ever" "The Ages" in their page appear,
"Alway" the bedlamite is called a "Seer";
On every leaf the "earnest" sage may scan,
Portentous bore! their "many-sided" man,—
A weak eclectic, groping vague and dim,
Whose every angle is a half-starved whim,
Blind as a mole and curious as a lynx,
Who rides a beetle, which he calls a "Sphinx."
And O what questions asked in club-foot rhyme
Of Earth the tongueless and the deaf-mute Time!
Here babbling "Insight" shouts in Nature's ears
His last conundrum on the orbs and spheres;

*Reprinted in part from *Graham's Magazine*, 25 (January 1844), 10–11.

There Self-inspection sucks its little thumb,
With "Whence am I?" and "Wherefore did I come?"
Deluded infants! will they ever know
Some doubts must darken o'er the world below,
Though all the Platos of the nursery trail
Their "clouds of glory" at the go-cart's tail?
O might these couplets their attention claim,
That gain their author the Philistine's name;
(A stubborn race, that, spurning foreign law,
Was much belabored with an ass's jaw!)

"What is Transcendentalism?
By a Thinking Man"

J[ames]. K[ennard]., Jr.*

This question has often been asked but seldom answered satisfactorily. Newspaper editors and correspondents have frequently attempted a practical elucidation of the mystery, by quoting from their own brains the rarest piece of absurdity which they could imagine, and entitling it 'Transcendentalism.' One good hit of this kind may be well enough, by way of satire upon the fogginess of certain writers who deem themselves, and are deemed by the multitude, transcendental *par excellence*. COLERIDGE however thought that to parody stupidity by way of ridiculing it, only proves the parodist more stupid than the original blockhead. Still, one such attempt may be tolerated; but when imitators of the parodist arise and fill almost every newspaper in the country with similar witticisms, such efforts become 'flat and unprofitable;' for nothing is easier than to put words together in a form which conveys no meaning to the reader. It is a cheap kind of wit, asinine rather than attic, and can be exercised as well by those who know nothing of the subject as by those best acquainted with it. Indeed, it is greatly to be doubted whether one in a hundred of these witty persons know any thing of the matter; for if they possess sense enough to make them worthy of being ranked among reasonable men, it could be proved to them in five minutes that they are themselves transcendentalists, as all thinking men find themselves compelled to be, whether they know themselves by that name or not.

'Poh!' said a friend, looking over my shoulder; 'you can't prove *me* a transcendentalist; I defy you to do it; I despise the name.'

Why so? Let us know what it is that you despise. Is it the sound of the word? Is it not sufficiently euphonious? Does it not strike your ear as smoothly as Puseyite, or Presbyterian?

'Nonsense!' said he; 'you don't suppose I am to be misled by the sound of a word; it is the meaning to which I object. I despise transcendentalism; therefore I do not wish to be called transcendentalist.'

*Reprinted from *Knickerbocker*, 23 (March 1844), 205–211.

Very well; but we shall never 'get ahead' unless you define transcendentalism according to your understanding of the word.

'That request is easily made, but not easily complied with. Have you Carlyle or Emerson at hand?'

Here I took down a volume of each, and read various sentences and paragraphs therefrom. These passages are full of transcendental ideas; do you object to them?

'No,' said my friend; 'for aught I can perceive, they might have been uttered by any one who was *not* a transcendentalist. Let me see the books.'

After turning over the leaves a long while, he selected and read about a passage from Carlyle, one of his very worst; abrupt, nervous, jerking, and at the same time windy, long-drawn-out, and parenthetical; a period filling a whole page.

'There,' said he, stopping to take breath, 'if that is not enough to disgust one with transcendentalism, then I know nothing of the matter.'

A very sensible conclusion. Bless your soul, that is *Carlyle-ism,* not transcendentalism. You said but now that you were not to be misled by the sound of a word; and yet you are condemning a principle on account of the bad style of a writer who is supposed to be governed by it. Is that right? Would you condemn Christianity because of the weaknesses and sins of one of its professors?

'Of course not,' replied he; 'I wish to be fair. I cannot express my idea of the meaning of transcendentalism without tedious circumlocution, and I begin to despair of proving my position by quotations. It is not on any particular passage that I rest my case. You have read this work, and will understand me when I say that it is to its general intent and spirit that I object, and not merely to the author's style.'

I think I comprehend you. You disregard the mere form in which the author expresses his thoughts; you go beyond and behind that, and judge him by the thoughts themselves; not by one or by two, but by the sum and *substance* of the whole. You strip off the husk to arrive at the kernel, and judge of the goodness of the crop by the latter, not the former.

'Just so,' said he; 'that's my meaning precisely. I always strive to follow that rule in every thing. 'Appearances,' you know, 'are deceitful.' '

That is to say you go beyond or transcend appearances and circumstances, and divine the true meaning, the substance, the spirit of that on which you are about to decide. That is practical transcendentalism and you are a transcendentalist.

'I wish you would suggest another name for it,' said my friend, as he went out of the door; 'I detest the sound of that word.'

I wish we could, said I, but he was out of hearing; I wish we could, for it is an abominably long word to write.

'I wish we could,' mutters the printer, 'for it is an awfully long word to print.'

'I wish we could,' is the sober second thought of all; for people will always condemn transcendentalism until it is called by another name. Such is the force of prejudice.

'I have been thinking over our conversation of yesterday,' said my friend next morning, on entering my room.

'Oh, you have been writing it down, have you? Let me see it.' After looking over the sketch, he remarked:

'You *seem* to have me fast enough, but after all I believe you conquered merely by playing upon a word, and in proving me to be a transcendentalist you only proved me to be a reasonable being; one capable of perceiving, remembering, combining, comparing and deducing; one who, amid the apparent contradictions with which we are surrounded, strives to reconcile appearances and discover principles; and from the outward and visible learn the inward and spiritual; in fine, arrive at truth. Now every reasonable man claims to be all that I have avowed myself to be. If this is to be a transcendentalist, then I am one. When I read that I must hate my father and mother before I can be a disciple of Jesus, I do not understand that passage literally; I call to mind other precepts of Christ; I remember the peculiarities of eastern style; I compare these facts together, and deduce therefrom a very different principle from that apparently embodied in the passage quoted. When I see the Isle of Shoals doubled, and the duplicates reversed in the air above the old familiar rocks, I do not, as I stand on Rye-beach, observing the interesting phenomenon, believe there are two sets of islands there; but recalling facts which I have learned, and philosophical truths which I have acquired and verified, I attribute the appearance to its true cause, refraction of light. When in passing from room to room in the dark, with my arms outspread, I run my nose against the edge of a door, I do not therefrom conclude that my nose is longer than my arms! When I see a man stumble in the street, I do not at once set him down as a drunkard, not considering that to be sufficient evidence, although some of our Washingtonian friends do; but I compare that fact with the state of the streets, and what I know of his previous life, and judge accordingly.'

Well, said I, you are an excellent transcendentalist; one after my own heart, in morals, philosophy and religion. To be a transcendentalist is after all to be *only* a sensible, unprejudiced man, open to conviction at all times, and spiritually-minded. I can well understand that, when you condemn transcendentalism, you object not to the principle, but to the practice, in the superlative degree, of that principle. Transcendentalism is but an abstract mode of considering morals, philosophy, religion; an application of the principles of abstract science to these subjects. All metaphysicians are transcendentalists, and every one is transcendental so far as he is metaphysical. There are as many different modifications of the one as of the other, and probably no two transcendentalists ever thought alike; their creed is not yet written. You certainly do not condemn spiritualism, but ultra spiritualism you seem to abhor.

'Precisely so. I did not yesterday give you the meaning which I attached to transcendentalism; in truth, practically you mean one thing by that term, and I another, though I now see that in principle they are the same. The spiritualism which I like, looks through nature and revelation up to GOD; that which I abhor, condescends hardly to make use of nature at all, but demands direct converse with GOD, and declares that it enjoys it too; a sort of continual and *immediate* revelation. Itself is its own authority. The ultra-spiritualist contains within himself the fulness of the Godhead. He allows of nothing external, unless it be brother spirits like himself. He has abolished nature, and to the uninitiated seems to have abolished GOD himself, although I am charitable enough to believe that he has full faith in GOD, after his own fashion. He claims to be inspired; to be equal to JESUS; nay superior; for one of them lately said: 'Greater is the container than the contained, therefore I am greater than GOD, for I contain God!' The ultra-spiritualist believes only *by* and *through* and *in* his own inward light. Let him take care, as Carlyle says, that his own contemptible tar-link does not, by being held too near his eyes, extinguish to him the sun of the universe. Now the true spiritualist makes use not only of his own moral and religious instincts, but all that can be gathered by the senses from external nature, and all that can be acquired by untiring consultation with the sages who have gone before him; and from these materials in the alembic of his mind, with such power as GOD has given him, he distils truth.'

Truth! Ah, that is the very point in question. 'What is truth?' has been the ardent inquiry of every honest mind from the days of Adam to the present time, and the sneering demand of many an unbeliever. Eve sought it when she tasted the forbidden fruit. But since then, thank GOD! no prohibition has been uttered against the search after truth, and mankind have improved their liberty with great industry for six thousand years; and what is the truth? Is truth discovered? How much? and how much of falsehood is mixed up with what *is* known to be true? These questions are constantly suggesting themselves to thinkers, and to answer them is the labor of their lives. Let them have free scope, ultra-spiritualists and all. Even these latter go through the same operation which you have just claimed to be peculiar to the true spiritualist. All do, whether they will or not, make use of observation, learning, and the inward light. Some arrive at one result, and some at another, because the elements differ in each. If any two could be found whose external observations, learning, intellect and inward light or instincts were precisely equal in volume and proportion, can it be doubted that these two would arrive at precisely similar results? But they are *not* equal; and so one comes to believe in external authority, and the other refers every thing to a standard which he thinks he finds within himself. The latter is deemed by the public to be a representative of pure transcendentalism, and he is condemned accordingly as self-sufficient.

And privately, between you and me, my good friend, I cannot help thinking it rather ungrateful in him, after becoming so deeply indebted to his senses, to books, and the Bible for his spiritual education, to turn round and despise these means of advancement, and declare that they are mere non-essential *circumstances,* and that a man may reach the same end by studying himself *in* himself. It is as if a man should use a ladder to reach a lofty crag, and then kick it over contemptuously, and aver that he could just as well have flown up, and ask the crowd below to break up that miserable ladder and try their wings. Doubtless they *have* wings, if they only knew it. But seriously, I am not inclined to join in the hue-and-cry against even the ultra-transcendentalist. He has truth mixed up with what I esteem objectionable, and some truth to which others have not attained; and as I deem the eclectic the only true mode of philosophy, I am willing to take truth where I can find it, whether in China or Boston, in Confucius or Emerson, Kant or Cousin, the Bible or the Koran; and though I have more reverence for one of these sources than all others, it is only because I think I find there the greatest amount of truth, sanctioned by the highest authority. To put the belief in the Bible on any other ground, is to base it on educational prejudice and superstition; on which principle the Koran should be as binding on the Mahometan as the Bible on us. Do we not all finally resort to *ourselves* in order to decide a difficult question in morals or religion? and is not the decision more or less correct accordingly as we refer it to the better or to the baser portion of our nature?

'Most certainly! I have often said I would not and could not believe in the Bible, if it commanded us to worship Sin and leave our passions unbridled.'

Well said! And in so saying, you acknowledge yourself to be governed by the same principle which actuates the ultra-transcendentalist; the moral sense or instinct, similar to the 'inward light' of the Friends. After all, I apprehend the true point in which men differ is, whether this moral sense is really an instinct, or whether it is evolved and put in operation by education. How much is due to nature? is the true question. But to solve it, is important only theoretically, for practically we all act alike; we cannot, if we would, separate the educational from the natural moral sense; we cannot *uneducate* it, and then judge by it, freed from all circumstantial bias. But whether more or less indebted either to nature or education, it is to this moral and religious sense that the ultra-transcendentalist refers every question, and passes judgment according to its verdict. It is sometimes rather vaguely called the 'Pure Reason;' but that is only a *term*, hardly a 'mouthful of articulate wind.'

'You and I shall agree very well together, I see,' replied my friend. 'If we dispute at all, it will be foolishly about the meaning of a word. All the world have been doing that ever since the confusion of tongues at Babel. That great event prophetically shadowed forth the future; for now, as then, the confusion and disputation is greatest when we are striving most earnestly to reach heaven by our earth-built contrivances. We may draw a lesson therefrom; not to be too aspiring for our means; for our inevitable failure only makes us the more ridiculous, the higher the position we seem to have attained.'

Very true; but we should never arrive at the height of wisdom, which consists in knowing our own ignorance and weakness, unless we made full trial of our powers. The fall of which you speak should give us a modesty not to be otherwise obtained, and make us very careful how we ridicule others, seeing how open to it we ourselves are. Every man may build his tower of Babel, and if he make a right use of his failure, may in the end be nearer heaven than if he had never made the attempt. Ridicule is no argument, and should only be used by way of a *jeu d'esprit*, and never on solemn subjects. It is very hard, I know, for one who has mirthfulness strongly developed, to restrain himself on all occasions; and what is solemn to one may not be so to another; hence we should be very charitable to all; alike to the bigots, the dreamers, and the laughers; to the builders of theoretic Babel-towers, and the grovellers on the low earth.

'There is one kind of transcendentalism,' replied my friend, 'which you have not noticed particularly, which consists in believing in nothing except the spiritual existence of the unbeliever himself, and hardly that. It believes not in the external world at all.'

If you are on *that* ground, I have done. To talk of that, would be wasting our time on nothing; or 'our eternity,' for with that sect time is altogether a delusion. It *may* be true, but the believer, even in the act of declaring his faith, must practically prove himself persuaded of the falsity of his doctrine.

'You wanted a short name for Transcendentalism; if a long one will make *this* modification of it more odious, let us call it *Incomprehensibilityosityivityalityationmentnessism!*'

My friend said this with a face nearly as long as the word, made a low bow, and departed. I took my pen and reduced our conversation to writing. I hope by this time the reader has a very lucid answer to give to the question, *What is Transcendentalism?* It will be a miracle if he can see one inch farther into the fog-bank than before. I should like to take back the boast made in the beginning of this paper, that I could prove in five minutes any reasonable man a transcendentalist. My friend disconcerted my plan of battle, by taking command of the enemy's forces, instead of allowing me to marshal them on paper to suit myself; and so a mere friendly joust ensued, instead of the utter demolition of my adversary, which I had intended.

And this little circumstance has led me to think, what a miserable business controversialists would make of it, if each had his opponent looking over his shoulder, pointing out flaws in his arguments, suggesting untimely truths, and putting every possible impediment in the path of his logic; and if, moreover, he were obliged to mend every flaw, prove every such truth a falsehood, and remove every impediment before he could advance a step. Were such the case, how much less would there be of fine-spun theory and specious argument; how much more of practical truth! Always supposing the logical combatants did not lose their patience and resort to material means and knock-down arguments; of which, judging by the spirit sometimes manifested in theological controversies, there would really seem to be some danger. Oh! it is a v~ry easy thing to sit in one's study and demolish an opponent, who r all is generally no opponent at all, but only a man of straw, dressed u? for the occasion with a few purposely-tattered shreds of the adversary's cast-off garments.

NOTE BY THE 'FRIEND.'—The foregoing is a *correct* sketch of our conversations, especially as the reporter has, like his congressional brother, corrected most of the bad grammar, and left out some of the vulgarisms and colloquialisms, and given me the better side of the argument in the last conversation; it is *very* correct. But it seems to me that the question put at the commencement is as far from being solved as ever. It is as difficult to be answered as the question, What is Christianity? to which every sect will return a different reply, and each prove all the others wrong.

[Transcendentalism]

L[ydia]. Maria Child*

LETTER XIII.

April 24th, 1844.

You ask me what *is* transcendentalism, and what do transcendentalists believe? It is a question difficult, nay, impossible, to answer; for the minds so classified are incongruous individuals, without any creed. The name is in fact applied to everything new, strange, and unaccountable. If a man is non-conformist to established creeds and opinions, and expresses his dissent in a manner ever so slightly peculiar, he is called a transcendentalist. It is indeed amusing to see how easily one may acquire this title. A southern lady lately said to a friend of mine, "I knew you were a transcendentalist the first half hour I heard you talk." "How so?" inquired my friend. "Oh, it is easy enough to be seen by your peculiar phrases." "Indeed! I had thought my language was very plain and natural. Pray what transcendental phrase have I used?" "The first time I ever saw you, you spoke of a person at the North as unusually *gifted;* and I have often since heard you use other transcendental expressions."

If you wish to know the origin of the word transcendentalism, I will explain it, briefly and simply, as I understand it.

All, who know anything of the different schools of metaphysics, are aware that the philosophy of John Locke was based on the proposition that *all* knowledge is received into the soul through the medium of the senses; and thence passes to be judged of and analyzed by the understanding.

The German school of metaphysics, with the celebrated Kant at its head, rejects this proposition as false; it denies that all knowledge is received through the senses, and maintains that the highest, and therefore most universal truths, are revealed within the soul, to a

*Reprinted from *Letters from New-York: Second Series* (New York: C. S. Francis, 1845), pp. 125–130.

faculty *transcending* the understanding. This faculty they call pure Reason; it being peculiar to them to use that word in contradistinction to the Understanding. To this pure Reason, which some of their writers call "The God within," they believe that all perceptions of the Good, the True, and the Beautiful, are revealed, in its unconscious quietude; and that the province of the Understanding, with its five handmaids, the Senses, is confined merely to external things, such as facts, scientific laws, &c.

This idea of an inwardly revealing faculty, *transcending* mere intellectual perception, will naturally remind many of the "inward voice," believed in by the Society of Friends. In fact, the two phrases are different aspects of the same idea. The Quakers saw it through a religious medium, Kant in a light purely philosophic.—Closely connected with this idea is the doctrine of the inspiration of the Scriptures; a doctrine concerning which the most confused and unsettled notions prevail, even among those who would be most shocked at being charged with any doubts upon the subject. It is this idea, which leads some to inquire, "Did Paul mean the same thing as the Transcendentalists, or the Quakers, when he made a distinction between what he wrote of *himself* and what was *given* him to write?"

Unitarianism does not involve transcendentalism: on the contrary, it often cherishes an extreme aversion to it. But generally speaking, minds inclined to transcendentalism are of Unitarian habits of thought. The cause is obvious enough. Both judge the recorded facts of Revelation by the light of Reason; and in no case acknowledge the authority of Revelation over Reason; believing, only when Reason and Revelation seem to them coincident.

The more popular and common forms of theology have a natural affinity with the metaphysics of Locke.—That is, certain things witnessed by the senses, and recorded as miraculous facts are considered sufficient reasons for believing everything uttered by those who performed the miracles. Those who presume to judge of Revelation by Reason may, and generally do, believe the miracles of Christ, as recorded facts; but they could not believe in the doctrines of Christ *because* he worked miracles.

There is slight resemblance between Quakers and Transcendentalists. The former abjure imagination and the Arts, and love to enclose everything within prescribed rules and regulations. The latter luxuriate in the beautiful, and their theories are so expansive and indefinite, that they remind one of the old story of transmigration, in which a philosopher, being asked what form he would like to have his disembodied soul enter, answered, "Form in general; no form in particular."

But the doctrine of perpetual revelation, heard in the quietude of the soul, produces one similar result in both. Neither of them favour the activity of reforms. The Quaker wishes "Israel to remain in his tents;" his cure for evils is to "keep in the quiet." The transcendentalist phrases it otherwise; he advises "to lie still in the spiritual sunshine, and grow." Neither are fond of the maxim, that "action strikes fiery *light* from the rocks it has to hew through."

The style of writing characteristic of Transcendentalists has excited much merriment, and more wonder. That which is *really* uttered has deeper significance, than is usually apprehended by intelligent minds unaccustomed to similar habits of thought; but it has an oracular and mystical sound, because they rather *announce*, than *argue*, what seems to them truth. This comes of their doctrine of intuitive perception. It is the business of the understanding, they say, to analyze, compare, and prove; but reason reveals. Therefore, there is about their writings "a tone and colour *sui generis;* something of the clear and the mysterious, like the sea in a beautiful day in summer. A light, cold and colourless, pierces the liquid mass, giving it a certain transparency that captivates the eye, but which imports that there is always, at the bottom, a mystery unexplained."

Imitations of Transcendentalism are unquestionably the most contemptible form of affectation and sham. Parrots laying claim to Edward Irving's inspired gift of tongues, would be wisdom compared with it. This class of superficial and artificial writers are best described by Daniel O'Connell's witty remark concerning certain public speakers: "They are men who aim at nothing, and hit it."

It is true that some of the profoundest of the transcendentalists are a little too fond of the impersonal abstraction *it*. This *it* often seems to be something "without form and void, and darkness on the face of it." Not long ago, one of this fraternity said to me, "Why do we rummage about with memory in the past, to find out our whereabout and our whatabout? It is because we are not true to ourselves, is it not? If we *were* true to ourselves, we should have no need to rummage about with memory in the past, to find out our whereabout, and our whatabout; for it would be with us, we should be *it*."

However, this obscurity with regard to the "whereabout and whatabout," is not an exclusive peculiarity of the modern school. Old Dr. Bentley, formerly of Salem, Mass., once took for his text, "It is his spirit;" and began his sermon thus: "The sympathy of our loves is the ideal presence; and this with full consent in its best effects."

New-York is in too much of a hurry scurry all the time, to "lie still in the sunshine" and ripen such fruit as either transcendental philosophy, or its poverty-stricken imitations. It never enters into the head of a Wall-street merchant, that he is, as a friend of ours asserts, "personally responsible for the obliquity of the earth's axis."

"Transcendental muslins" I have often seen advertised in the Bowery;

but I have rarely met with transcendentalism in any other form, in this city. I did once, out of pure mischief, send a politician and an active man of business to a house, where I knew they would encounter three or four of these disciples, who occasionally ride a pretty high horse. When they came back, I asked with a sober face, what they had talked about. They said they did not know; but being unmercifully urged to tell something that was said, the politician at last answered: "One of them divided man into three states; the disconscious, the conscious, and the unconscious. The *disconscious* is the state of a pig; the conscious is the baptism by water; and the *unconscious* is the baptism by fire." "How did the conversation impress your mind?" said I, restraining a smile. "Why, after I had heard them talk a few minutes," replied he, "I'll be hanged if I knew whether I *had* any mind."

I then asked the man of business how he had been edified. "My head aches," said he; "they have put my mind and body both in a confounded muss."

You must know that "muss" is a favourite phrase with New-Yorkers, to express everything that is in a state of confusion. Not only mountains, but mole-hills, here bring forth a *"ridiculus mus."*

Being in a tormenting mood, I insisted that my friend should give some account of the conversation.

Thus urged, he at last replied, "Why, one of them seemed to think there *was* some connection between mind and body; but as for the rest, so far as I could understand them, they all seemed to think the body was nothing but a sham."

I am sometimes called a transcendentalist myself, perhaps because I use the phrase "highly gifted." But I acknowledge considerable sympathy with the perplexed politician and man of business. For there are people, very intellectual ones too, who mystify me in the strangest fashion. After talking with them, my spirit always has to bite its finger, to know whether it exists or not; and even then, the question arises whether a sensation *is* a sensation. As for the received axiom that "a thing cannot *be* and *not* be, at the same time," they always set it twirling.

If asked to explain themselves, they answer with Jean Paul, "probably God knows what I meant, but I have forgotten."

[On "the tone transcendental"]

Edgar Allan Poe*

"There are various other tones of equal celebrity, but I shall mention only two more—the tone transcendental[1] and the tone heterogeneous. In the former the merit consists in seeing into the nature of affairs a very great deal farther than anybody else. This second sight is very efficient when properly managed. A little reading of the 'Dial'[2] will carry you a great way.[3] .Eschew, in this case, big words; get them as small as possible, and write them upside down. Look over Channing's poems and quote what he says about a 'fat little man with delusive show of Can.' Put in something about the Supernal Oneness. Don't say a syllable about the Infernal Twoness. Above all, study innuendo. Hint every thing—assert nothing. If you feel inclined to say 'bread and butter' do not by any means say it outright. You may say anything and every thing *approaching* to 'bread and butter.' You may hint at buckwheat cake, or you may even go so far as to insinuate oat-meal porridge, but if bread and butter be your real meaning, be cautious . . . not on any account to say 'bread and butter!' "

Notes

1. This was "the tone metaphysical" in the first three appearances of this story: as "The Psyche Zenobia," Baltimore *American Museum*, 1 (November 1838), 301–317; as "The Signora Zenobia," *Tales of the Grotesque and Arabesque* (Philadelphia: Lea and Blanchard, 1840), I, 213–243; and *Phantasy-Pieces*, Poe's marked and revised copy of *Tales*. This and other textual information is drawn from *Collected Works of Edgar Allan Poe*, ed. Thomas Ollive Mabbott, vol. 2, *Tales and Sketches 1831–1842* (Cambridge: Harvard University Press, 1978).

2. This was " 'The Sorrows of Werther' " in the *American Museum*, and "Coleridge's Table-Talk" in *Tales* and *Phantasy-Pieces*.

*Reprinted in part from "How to Write a Blackwood Article," *Broadway Journal*, 2 (12 July 1845), 1–7.

3. From "Eschew" to the end of the paragraph was added for the *Broadway Journal* printing. Present in the *American Museum* and *Tales* was: "If you know any big words this is your chance for them. Talk of the academy and the lyceum, and say something about the Ionic and Italic schools, or about Bossarion, and Kant, and Schelling, and Fichte, and be sure you abuse a man called Locke, and bring in the words *a priori* and *a posteriori*." Poe's holograph revision in *Phantasy-Pieces* for this section was: "If you know any big words this is your chance for them. Talk of the Ionic and Eleatic Schools—of Archytas, Gorgias, and Alcmaeon. Say something about objects and subjects. Be sure and abuse a man called Locke. Turn up your nose at things in general; and when you let slip anything very unconscionably absurd, you need not be at the trouble of scratching it out, but just put in a foot-note and say you are indebted for the above profound observation to the "Kritik der reinen Vernunft" or to the "Metaphysische Anfangsgrunde der Naturwissenschaft." This will look erudite and at the same time *frank*."

"Bad News for the Transcendental Poets"

[Evert A. Duyckinck]*

Transcendentalism seems to be just now at a discount. It is beginning to be considered a bad card for a young author to play. Those who have embarked in it rather extensively, are losing the dividends of reputation they expected, and begin to be pitied. It is regretted that so much nonsense should have been put up in such very good verses; that so much poetic fervor has been lost upon the moon; that such ardent tributes to chaos, night and nothingness, should have been so entirely unproductive. The public, however, has little feeling in the matter; having never surrendered its judgment to the youthful writers, or fallen so desperately in love with moonshine, it has no reluctance or mortification at the disasters happening to the race. "Served right" will be the popular verdict on the departed authors.

Poor time-crushed martyrs of the "infinite;" sorrowful knife-grinding "friends of humanity;" souls of destiny tripped up by fortune; very "high natures" laid correspondingly low; sublime lovers turned critic-haters; mockers of "the dead corpse of the old king Custom" subdued with laughable retribution by Fashion herself. That it should come to this! But the punishment is deserved. Who does not rejoice in Dickens's story, or the old Roman history of the schoolmaster flogged by his pupils? What do the versifiers deserve better who have perplexed innocent ladies and verdant youths with such mysterious confusions of right, wrong, and English grammar, on Truth, Love, and Eternity?

Honest John Milton, if he could have survived such things, would have added transcendental poetry along with the controversies of theology, to the amusement of the damned.

"I saw," says Nat Lee, in Bedlam, having in prophetic view the young transcendental poets of this generation,—

> "I saw an unscrewed spider spin a thought,
> And walk away upon the wings of angels."

*Reprinted from *Literary World*, 1 (20 February 1847), 53.

But the spider's web is a consistent fabric useful for the destruction of bluebottles, though we know not how the case may be with the web of an unscrewed spider. Probably the comparison will hold, for it may be said safely of the visionary bardlings—"There's a screw loose somewhere." The walking away is peculiarly descriptive of the *musa pedestris* of these poets, who, always boasting of the fine pair of wings they have on, never fly.

The transcendental balloon is rapidly suffering collapse. It received a sword-thrust lately from Mr. Hudson, in his review of "Festus," who, letting the wind out of the mammoth inflation very suddenly, the American parachutes had not time to save themselves. "The public mind," says our resolute champion, "has been fed, or rather starved, with such delightful impressions too long already. Authors, or people calling themselves authors, have thrown off their impressions, until we have a perfect glut of them; we consider them good for nothing; nay, worse than nothing— a nuisance; instead of paying for them, we would rather pay something to get rid of them; for their only effect is to fill the mind with unrest; to starve it into spasms and convulsions, which some people are foolish enough to miscall a hungering and thirsting after knowledge."

Mr. Hudson, it is understood, dates from Boston. We will not be so uncharitable as to suppose that he has any reference to the little volumes of poetry which are issued in smooth covers from the press of that city. But it is a singular circumstance in the connexion that the following remarks should be found in the *Boston Courier*:—

> A large part of the poetry that has recently got into print among us, has belonged to the mystical, if not the misty, school. We have nothing to say in disparagement of the transcendental rhymers. Some of them are men of real poetic genius, and carry in them more than a spark of the divine fire. Even Longfellow often falls into their mood, and walks on the verge of their cloudy kingdom. But others who affect their method, or no-method, who ape their motions, or think to sit on the tripod, give us the contortions without the inspiration. Several of this class, who pretend to be poets, are manifestly no poets at all. And all of them, at the first reading, by a certain illusion of fancy, by a novel construction of verse, or by tricks of composition, pass for rather more than they are really worth. On the whole, the school is an artificial one. *It is essentially imitative; not original. It belongs to Germany, not to America.* Though somewhat fasionable at present, its influence will be transient. Its disciples will generally have a short-lived reputation; and if they survive it, as doubtless many of them will, they will have cause to regret that they did not coin whatever of the real ore was in them into a more substantial and durable currency.

Abroad, in that England where there is generally to be found a little clique ready to support a corresponding cis-Atlantic clique, there are also symptoms of weariness. Says the *Athenæum* on this head—

Doubtless, the introduction of German literature into this country through the labors of Coleridge, Carlyle and others—names which it is hardly necessary to say are individual, not corporate, except as belonging to the chosen guild of master minds—has been on the whole of signal advantage. It shook the tyranny of the positive school,— and weaned us from the superstition of the sensuous to the worship of the spiritual. It is, however, equally certain that these advantages have not been gained without their concomitant evils; namely, the fanaticism that ever follows in the wake of literary revolution—the exaggerated spirit of the reaction. Thus the practical and positive, exposed to the fiery breath of enthusiasts, was not merely softened to its due consistency, but rarefied into the unreal,—until both thought and language evaporated at last into a cloudy incense to the vanity and spiritual pride which transmuted them. *Young men began to see visions, and old men to dream dreams. An extreme contempt of the lucid arose. Common intelligibility was held as backsliding, and perspicuity as filthy rags.* A rhapsodical outpouring of sublime nonsense became the order of the day; and the beggarly elements of sense and purpose were so thoroughly repudiated by these fifth-monarchy men of letters, that their ravings might have been read backwards or forwards, occidentally or orientally, by Anglo-Saxon or by Arab. These fanatics, in fact, conceived that they had nothing to do but string together at random texts taken from Mr. Carlyle's works—and generally the most exceptionable— in order to be themselves Carlyles. They only forgot the one thing needful—the informing spirit of the master. Now this nuisance exists up to the present hour. *It has increased, is increasing, and ought to be diminished.* Were it confined to the zealots alone, it might be laughed at,—or, for that matter, fostered as supplying the compost which manures the field of Hudibrastic satire. But it has created a pestilential atmosphere which occasionally infests even able writers; whilst amongst inferior pens it serves to abet that laxity of construction and careless obscurity which the high-pressure speed of mercenary authorship had already pushed to excess in this our commercial community of letters.

After this the stock may be expected to go down, and that portion of "Young America" which has gone into the operation on time, should hedge as quickly as possible.

What new demonstrations in rhyme, the unfortunate Othellos thus deprived of their occupations may feel themselves compelled to resort to, we know not; we may certainly expect them in a new sphere of action. Modesty has never been their characteristic. We may look for some extraordinary examples of poetical turn-coating, "tergiversations unexampled in the annals of diplomacy," mountebank revolutions from the school of Shelley to the school of Chaucer. The Moon will be treated with irreverence; old Chaos contemned and slighted; the empire of Night surrendered without a scruple or a pang to an unfeeling police. It will be a melancholy sight to witness the ingratitude of poets. Poor Baily Festus, who of the infant brood will first denounce him?

[From *Philo: An Evangeliad*]

[Sylvester Judd]*

The Transcendentalists. In homage, due to
    goodness, Lord, we bend
To thee, who Goodness art. O Wonderful
Of the create, O Miracle of time!
Thou curdled breath of rare divinity,
Thou soul of Virtue, globed in human eyes,
Eternal World on ruddy lips incarne!
Too oft on self we gazed, and less on thee:
To-day the mirror's broken; let it lie,
Since God through thee and us is shining fair.
We would no friend or brother; after us
Thy mother eyes went streaming; flowers the dew,
Harts drink the water-brooks, and we ourselves,
More sweet to us than Jewish muscadine.
Our fount ran dry, alas! good Lord; and now
We bring our empty bowls to thee. We shone,
But inwárd, oven-suns, none blessed our light;
Lord, bless us; we will bless, unsought, unspent.
    Bishops and Clergymen. Repentance, Lord,
      we've urged, how little felt!

*Reprinted from *Philo: An Evangeliad* (Boston: Phillips, Sampson, 1850), p. 232.

[A Conversation with a Transcendentalist]

Orestes A. Brownson*

Mr. Edgerton, a New England Transcendentalist, a thin, spare man, with a large nose, and a cast of Yankee shrewdness in his not unhandsome face, was not favorable to this plan. "I dislike," he said, "associations. They absorb the individual, and establish social despotism. All set plans of world-reform are bad. Every one must have a theory, a plan, a Morrison's pill. No one trusts to nature. None are satisfied with wild flowers or native forests. All seek an artificial garden. They will not hear the robin sing unless it is shut up in a cage. The rich undress of nature is an offence, and she must be decked out in the latest fashion of Paris or London, and copy the grimaces of a French dancing-master, or lisp like an Andalusian beauty, before they will open their hearts to her magic power. Say to all this, Get behind me, Satan. Dare assert yourselves; plant yourselves on your imperishable instincts; sing your own song of joy, your own wail of grief; speak your own word; tell what your own soul seeth, and leave the effect to take care of itself. Eschew the crowd, eschew self-consciousness, form no plan, propose no end, seek no moral, but speak out from your own heart; build as builds the bee her cell, sing as sings the bird, the grasshopper, or the cricket."

"So," said Mr. Merton, a young man, with a fine classic head and face, who seemed to have been drawn hither by mere curiosity, "so you think the nearer men approach to birds and insects the better it will be for the world."

"I never dispute," replied Mr. Edgerton. "I utter the word given me to utter, and leave it as the ostrich leaveth her eggs. Men should be seers, not philosophers; prophets, not reasoners. I never offer proof of what I say. I could not prove it, if asked. If it is true, genuine, the fit word, opportunely spoken, it will prove itself. If it approves not itself to you, it is not for you. You are not prepared to receive it. It is not true for you. Be

*Reprinted from *The Spirit-Rapper: An Autobiography* (Boston: Little, Brown, 1854), pp. 93–96. In Brownson's fictional work, Mr. Edgerton is Ralph Waldo Emerson and "the American Orpheus" is Bronson Alcott.

103

it so. It is true for me, and for those like me. Fash not yourself about it, but leave us to enjoy it in peace."

"But are we to understand," replied Mr. Merton, "that truth varies as vary individual minds?"

"Sir, you will excuse me. I am no logician, and eschew dialectics. Truth is one, it is the Whole, the All, the universal Being. It is a reality in, under, and over all, manifesting itself under an infinite variety of aspects. Every one beholds it under some one of its aspects, no one beholds it under all. Each mind in that it is real, is itself, is a manifestation of it, but no one is it in its integrity and universality, any more than the bubble on its surface is the whole ocean. Under each particular bubble lies, however, the whole ocean, and if it will speak not from its diversity, its bubbleosity, in which sense it is only an apparition, an appearance, a show, an unreality, but from what is real in it, from its real substantial self, it may truly call itself the whole ocean. So, under each individual mind lies all truth, all reality, all being; and hence, in so far as they are real, all minds are one and the same. Men are weak, are puny, differ from one another because they seek to live in their diversity, and to find their truth, their reality, in this individualty. Let them eschew their individuality, which is to their reality, their real self, only what the bubbleosity of the bubble is to the ocean, and fall back on their identity, on the universal truth which underlies them. If they will be men, real men, not make-believes, strong men, thinking men, let them be themselves, sink back into their underlying reality, on the One Man, and suffer the universal Over-Soul to flow into them, and speak through them without let or impediment."

"We must," said another Transcendentalist, sometimes called the American Orpheus, "return to the simplicity of childhood. 'Except ye be converted and become as a little child, ye shall in no wise enter into the kingdom of heaven.' The man who thinks, Rousseau has well said, is already a depraved animal. All learning is a forgetting; science and wisdom are gathered from babes and sucklings. We are not prepared as yet to talk of world-reform. We must 'be before we can do; be men before we can do men's work. All being is in doing; rather all doing is in being. Ideas are the essences, the realities of things. Seek ideas. They will take to themselves hands, build them a temple, and instaurate their worship. Seek not ideas from books; they are lies. Seek them not of the learned and grey-haired; they have lost them. Be docile and child-like; seat yourself by the cradle, at the feet of awful childhood, and look into babies' eyes."

"Unitarianism and Transcendentalism"

George E. Ellis*

Another of the expectations which my critic affirms was entertained by the Orthodox was, that *a portion* of the Unitarians would lapse into the infidelity which I have already referred to as the predicted issue of their views for the mass of those who should receive them. The following paragraph is therefore significant.

There was still another result, not only expected, but expressly predicted. It was predicted by Professor Stuart, and others, thirty years ago, that many Unitarians—the young, the adventurous, the men of impulse and progress—would not long remain where they then were. They would drift farther and farther away from the letter of Scripture and the restraints of the Gospel, until they arrived at the very borders of open infidelity. And neither in this have we been disappointed. We have seen it all verified before our eyes; and Mr. Ellis has seen the same. There are ministers around him, calling themselves Unitarians, with whom he would not exchange pulpits more than we should,—with whom, if I mistake not, the more serious part of his brethren have no longer any Christian fellowship.

The implication conveyed in this paragraph is that the form of scepticism known among us by the misused term *Transcendentalism*, was the natural outgrowth of Unitarianism. This charge has often been boldly made, and more often insinuated. It has no just foundation. Plain facts disprove it. The differences between Orthodoxy and Unitarianism arise from questions of interpretation; questions about the meaning of sacred records whose value and authority are admitted by both parties, and which Unitarians have always shown themselves so zealous to maintain, that they have produced works of acknowledged superiority in defence of revelation and the Scriptures. Transcendentalism, so called, denies a revelation, pronounces its miraculous sanctions to be philosophically im-

*Reprinted from *A Half-Century of the Unitarian Controversy* (Boston: Crosby, Nichols, 1857), pp. 412–414.

possible and absurd, and subverts the authority of Scripture. The relations between the three parties—the Orthodox, the Unitarians, and the Transcendentalists—on the subject-matter of revelation may be illustrated by a reference to the relations of three other parties among us concerning a political question. We have two large parties divided by a very serious issue touching the organic provisions of the Federal Constitution and the functions of Congress on slavery, and all the debates and agitations connected with it. Does or does not the Constitution recognize and legitimate slavery, and implicate all the States in its allowed existence in some of them, and expose free territory to be overrun by it? Has or has not Congress power to discuss the subject, and legislate upon it? On this issue our two prominent parties are divided. They make it a question of the interpretation of an instrument, through its own plain or obscure provisions and through the known views of its authors. Both parties profess to accept and recognize and honor the Constitution. They are willing to receive its fair and decisive meaning, when intelligently expounded, as authoritative, as binding upon them in all their political relations. They will not go behind the Constitution, nor dispute it, nor resist it. In the mean while a third party presents itself, which declares that the Constitution is pro-slavery, that it implicates all our citizens in the iniquity of slavery, and therefore that it must be denounced and subverted. This third party, therefore, plants itself outside of the Constitution. The two former parties, so far as the parallel is designed to illustrate one point of resemblance, may be regarded as representing the Orthodox and the Unitarians, as divided by questions about the interpretation of records and documents whose peculiar authority, value, and sanctions they agree in venerating. Their disputes centre upon and are to be decided by criticism and exposition. The third party, just referred to, represents the Transcendentalists, who insist that the Bible is committed to an unphilosophical, incredible, and impossible theory of miracles, and that they must, therefore, reject it and plant themselves outside of it. Now with what justice can the Orthodox confound Transcendentalists with Unitarians, and condemn the latter for complicity with the former in a theory of unbelief which comes not from methods of criticism and exposition, but from philosophical speculation?

As a matter of fact, too, Transcendentalism, so called, and even New England Transcendentalism, was not the outgrowth of Unitarianism, but an imported product that had been developed from German Lutheranism. A few young New England Unitarians have attracted attention to themselves in connection with their adoption of that form of philosophical scepticism, because of their eminent talents as men of marked endowments. But very many of the undistinguished Orthodox have adopted the same views independently of Unitarianism. It would be an ungracious office to attempt a statistical estimate of the proportionate addition to the ranks of infidelity which has accrued from Unitarianism or Orthodoxy. For myself, I have no doubt on that point. "Secularism," i.e. Atheism, in England numbers millions of adherents. Its leaders came from under the most thorough Orthodox training. Those who compose its ranks were never under the influence of Unitarianism. But Unitarianism is laboring earnestly, and with better promise of success than any other sect has yet realized, to reclaim the Secularists. Professor Stuart's prediction has not been verified among the Unitarians to the extent of its verification among the Orthodox. Justice Story and Dr. Channing both tell us, in their Memoirs, that Unitarianism saved them from the infidelity to which Orthodoxy had exposed them as young men. What saved them has saved thousands.

"Transcendentalism"

C[yrus]. A. Bartol*

The line of a planet is a compromise between two forces, a resultant which students work out on the slate; and social progress has for its factors the old institution and the new idea, from whose struggle the race shoots ahead,—one represented by the prophet, the other administered by the priest. Mankind depends on what it has hived and what it earns. Moral capital is no metaphor. Knowledge and virtue accumulate as well as silver and gold, and are the highest kind of real and personal estate, without which no business in politics or philanthropy could be done. How sad, said a foreigner, to think all the coined money in the United States could not pay the national debt! Yes, answered a Yankee; and to think, if the harvest failed all over the world for a year, all nations would starve! Labor is the only source of wealth, cries the new party. But manual is not the only, hardest, or best labor. If we grew and applied no fresh ideas, all the words of prophets, biographies of saints, and traditions of Palestine would not stay our hunger, more than the granaries of Egypt or last year's load in store and barn. With all respect to those who run the machine, a dearer honor belongs to such as supply the motive-power. Free and wild speculation, as well as custom and ordinance, has its place. Right as Leroux may be in the doctrine of human solidarity, or the advance of the species in column, the particles change in this huge body, as the ranks of an army in the field are depleted and filled up; and civil or ecclesiastical continuity is no mechanical necessity, but that divine order we must put our own heart and will into, and which the boldest thinker or righteous iconoclast is no less part of than any bishop or sheriff,—nay, is leader of the van. *Nature proceeds not by leaps*, was the old Latin phrase. But closer scrutiny shows she does. There is not only expansion, but eruption,—volcano and earthquake; and, in minuter spaces, signs of sudden action, as though the will of God were no figure of speech. Darwin and Spencer have to modify the doctrines of evolution and development to accommodate facts of rapid change into

*Reprinted from *Radical Problems* (Boston: Roberts Brothers, 1872), pp. 61–97.

108

new orders observed by eyes sharp as their own. There is, said my friend, a track we must keep to in grooves of fate. But there is many a place where Nature switches off, and takes a new departure. The free-thinker long ago was said to have come to where was no more road. But his road has no end; and he has advanced ever since, and still keeps on. The traveller in Switzerland, looking from his carriage, beholds his path blocked at a hillside or plunging into a lake, and for the moment imagines in that direction is no further step. But, arriving at the point, he finds the beaten way winding round the the mountain's spur into the rarest beauty of its course; and the mind that goes on without terror comes to the reward of truth. Where will they stop? is the inquiry respecting the critics of established methods; and the answer is, Nowhere. M. Coquerel tells us he was scolded by the French authorities for treating social questions in his paper; and, asking what was meant by social questions, was told, *Things that are!* Yet not a thing but must be unsettled in favor of something better, though the reason of the nickname *Transcendentalist* was, that whoever did this transcended all practical stability. Doubtless he who inhabits the region of pure thought becomes too impatient of existing modes. The air of the church is close and smoky, said one returning from a long sojourn in the country. Yes, I answered: to a person used to the whole atmosphere God makes so big that everybody may have enough, every room, however ventilated, will seem confined. But as we must be content to breathe in houses and temples, and shops and court-rooms, so we must live and morally respire in such establishment of Church and State as the common sense and conscience have been able to secure, enlarging and improving it as we can. The reformer is arraigned as destructive and traitor, accused of breaking the church-windows from the inside, and hewing down the pillars of the pulpit in which he stands. But if the windows are shut too tight to open, or stained with superstitious emblems, and if the sinking pulpit let him down to the level floor where his congregation sits, there may be a blessing from his axe and his stones. There is no church in Christendom where this question, whether some of the keepers are not betrayers of the citadel, does not arise. What free man in any communion is not charged with having broken his pledge, often unawares, as the excellent Deacon Grant with some horror declared *he* had done, with the first mouthful of brandied mince-pie which his hostess had prepared. To think at all is violation of promise, in principle if not in fact, by marring some actual article of faith. How we queried whether those noble English Essayists ought to stay on the theological premises they took such liberty to alter and extend! The papacy in Rome and every bishopric in America are shaken with the same issue of moral casuistry. Universalism and Unitarianism have expelled from their interior offenders they were griped by, with intolerable pain; and what it is to be a true Radical I have heard the banished discuss with each other, as did the Southern seceders from the Union, albeit they have no home from which to drive the disloyal out. The interpreter and originator must quarrel, and organization be at odds with the unorganized or unorganizable: meantime, for benefit as for peace, it is well to have some estimate of the office of the seer, and the value of his addition to the common stock.

The crisis comes unawares. A new vision reforms all our knowledge, as the astronomer catches a planet in the threads on his glass and the solar system is readjusted. The world of shifting opinion hangs on a hair. How little it was thought, forty years ago, that a Boston clergyman's difficulty with his people about the way to administer the Lord's Supper would be the string let into the loose public sentiment to cause a new crystallization. I remember the horror with which a fellow-student announced to me the unbearable criticism of the ancient rite, and my wonder at anybody's being so much moved. But forms hold fast after the ideas have changed which were their source and support, as shells and husks are no less tough and hard when the kernel and substance are gone. So how to eat the bread and drink the wine, or commune without eating or drinking, was another question added to the many which have made the ordinance a very volcano of controversy, ever ready for fresh overflow; though the Oriental custom seemed not much suited to the Western mind. The young minister was told privately to alter the style of the symbol as he judged right, but he doubted his fitness for such reconstruction; and the discussion sufficed to separate sworn friends and unseat a genius soaring like Phaëton, whose freedom with an outward observance was his mishandling the reins of the Sun. It had come to pass that, when men spoke of the elements, not truth or feeling, but the oven and vintage, were meant. In taking up, later, the line of this ceremony between church and congregation, where by no power it could be restored, we felt the force of this prejudice threatening an equally violent result.

The personal distress of all dislocation doubtless attended that severing of the clerical tie. But the portent was of new growth. There are moral pains of birth and struggle for life. The man was not important to the Church till he left to become such a figure as to make his judges the world's benefactors. Now he stood for a thought. His divorce from preaching allowed marriage with an idea, till then coyly courted, for an offspring of the best poetry and philosophy of the age. A shrewd suspicion of German inoculation flung at the movement the word *Transcendental*, for a disgrace, which, as of all names of good and odious things, turned to fame.

In truth, the out-break was nothing new under the sun. The fount of the Nile is discovered, but not of this spiritual Arethusa. Whoever was of that club meeting in Concord and Boston must recall the fellowship so dear, the delight as of another revelation, the Quaker peace, with but a dream of seeds of revolution dropping through the quiet air. Edward

Everett likened the doctrine to Virgil's thunderbolt, three parts empty air. Was it wind the new husbandmen sowed? The whirlwind that was reaped was a boon. Yet most men did not dread, but laughed at the phenomenon as but moonshine or mirage. As well tell Columbus it was no new world he had reached when heaved in view the outlying island, one of a flock which now beat at our windows in the political storm. Previous explorers had sailed into the same latitudes of thought. The startling doctrine of the soul's sufficiency was no upstart or bastard, but a lawful line of ancient origin, in divers branches, Hebrew and Greek,— going back to Plato and Abraham, Lot and Seth, groves of Academus and Garden of Eden, before Bibles were. It was revived in the best words of Jesus and John and Paul. English translators dipped their buckets for it into the wisdom of the East. The Hindoo found himself a Yankee with no questions of caste. The Christian Scriptures were paralleled from books of strange names in other tongues. The spring of wonder burst up in Teutonic soil, the same living water as in Indian bottles or Jewish jars. It filtered into the clear British sense. With astonishing virility the spiritual theory was propagated by Carlyle; and as visionary a mystic as ever wandered on the banks of the Ganges appeared in William Blake. Orthodoxy became ideal with Coleridge's "Aids to Reflection;" Wordsworth put the same meaning into his odes, and Cousin arranged it in philosophic terms. Yet when it was proclaimed in its legitimate conclusions in the sanctuary of Liberal Christianity, it was greeted with a shriek, as though Cudworth or Berkeley or Spinoza had never lived. Religion, under a show of progress, had declined. In too much logic, expression became the ebb of faith, till it reached low-water mark. Sectarian controversy brought down Trinitarian and Unitarian alike to the flats of a dry and barren doctrinality; and the high divine converse with which Puritan and Pilgrim began the Commonwealth gave place to a Babel of words. What splitting of particles, as described by Gibbon in the former age; what ransacking of prophecies, what dispute of the authority of this and that passage, what weighing of jobs and titles in diamond scales; instead of the grand war of ideas, what petty battles of texts! Andover and Cambridge responded to each other with paper pop-guns, not with the noise of His water-spouts. Into this squabble the angel blew his trumpet to summon to the privilege of direct communication with the Infinite; none so much surprised as the trumpeter at the ague-fit of anger and grief that ensued. He felt in order, without break or fault in the natural evolution. He had occasion to avenge his rejected sentiment in an address to the Graduating Class in the Cambridge Divinity School, which, like the last whirl of sticks of the savage's tinder-box, first struck fire. But what a dish to set before the King, that performance! After the short breathings of the gentle prayer, which had in it no pronouns, and one said was no prayer at all, came the textless discourse, preserved for ever in its sweet pungency, while all the replies to it are forgot. It was no hornet or drone lighting on us, but the sting of a honey-bee guarding for us our own luxury. It was the return of the Holy Ghost with voice, not recognized among manifold opposing echoes so long listened to in its stead. But no rude, unwarrantable assault could have begot such fear as that golden-mouthed speech. It meant business, and laid out a stint of work. The dismissed preacher had not been hushed. If he could not have the pulpit's velvet cushion, he would take the Lyceum's pine desk; and what a power he made the Lecture, is it not to be written in our chronicles?

In his farewell sermon, in Hanover Street, he had said there were functions of the ministerial office he should rejoice to discharge wherever he might exist. For these his change of situation was a help. As the painter stands off from the canvas to mark the accuracy of his drawing, this man's absence from his chosen calling gave distance for a true perspective, while he was doubly impressionable to compare another picture with the ecclesiastical. He had the advantage of a smooth temper. Perfect health stood bondsman for his equanimity, and the cool flesh of a child was type of his unfevered mind. He never rested and was never restless; his figure, the rifleman's statue,—not stirring till the fatal shot. He means something in every sketch, it was said of Hunt; and God filled this word-painter with intention, his own or the Spirit's you could not tell. They were the same. But, called to defend what he had said, he could give no account but his order to think. The responsibility was none of his. *So thought Francis Bacon* was authority enough for that philosopher's page; and this man was under command. His thought was not in his hands: he was in the hands of his thought. Like all who wear not their heart in their sleeve, put on no robe of enthusiasm, and warm their audience with no stove of animal heat, he was charged with being cold. The critics did not look close enough. They could not feel the spiritual flame nor appreciate that baptism of fire the Baptist foretold: which to the senses is a cool combustion. A warm temperament would have disqualified him for his task. Temperance was his star. After so much vapor we wanted dry light. Fondness for persons run into idolatry of institutions, and checks audacious words. Only his dispassionate, if not impassioned disposition could deal purely with his theme. It did not occur to him he was going to hurt anybody's feelings: no vision or prophecy had ever hurt his. A full-grown superstition of the past,—as memory, habit, or tradition,—could he throw his whole weight into his axe at the root of the tree? When his friend said, "Here are my facts, I cannot give up them," "Here are my ideas," was his reply. The facts were bad. He wanted them to be better: as Dr. Hedge, being told the facts were against him and were stubborn things, answered, *So much the worse for the facts.* What shall be said to reports of the telescope pointed to sky or sea? We can but repeat them, as the captain below repeats the figures the mate on deck calls out to him from his quadrant lifted to the sun. Here was a finer glass turning to the heaven of truth over the sea of time; and the observer's sentence was translation of his sight. Interrogated, he could but recite what he had already said. When John Marshall's party-friends begged to know why he persisted in refusing to answer Albert Gallatin's speech, he at last said, Because it is unanswerable. So those who complained of and rejected could get no rejoinder to this lesson. He compelled his critics to become his quoters. Out of what root did blossoms of such genuine beauty and fragrance foil the cut-paper flowers of the creeds? The Divine Immediacy with man! One day, before a keen eye, water rising to its own level in a tube made a ruin of the Roman acqueducts. So it was shown the river of God is not confined to Jewish conduits. We must have nearer access to it than that long old file of Hebrew Kings, Judges, and Prophets, magnificent as are their monumental words and refreshing as is the flood they convey.

This seer's originality armed itself with a new style. The surprising fitness of trite terms in his use was a resurrection of the dictionary. The silence of a sage whets our eagerness to hear; and this man's advantage was his superiority to ambition, his willingness to be still, his indifference whether he used his eye or ear, his avoidance of eloquence,—which Dr. Johnson calls exaggeration,—and preference of low to high-sounding words, like the modest artist who gives the whole character of an object in neutral tints or a charcoal sketch. Why be forward or loquacious? Truth will find its own way and organ, and make dumb Moses more persuasive than rhetorical and mellifluous Aaron. It was not the only possible mood, perhaps not the highest manner; but it was his, and apt to the time. There came no prophet's burden or scream, but the voice of one careless of the fate of his person or proposition; trusting truth to the air and allowing it time to sink into the ear, not anxious to multiply himself, but to condense his message. He knew no method could avail but that of his own constitution. Incapable of feeling personal outrage or oppression, in good condition, content with the universe, as well fed as any of the children at the table, delicate in his taste, every pore informing him who was coming, and closing at rude approach, and every nerve an alarm-bell at any catechism,—neither seeking an audience nor itching to hear himself talk, he was quite unfit for an agitator or ecclesiastical demagogue. Yet his individuality kept him out of any class. He stood for humanity, and was one of the people. So his banishment from the Church on a technical ground and punctilio of form was as blessed ostracism as Dante's exile from Florence. Those going without the camp bearing some reproach are always redeemers. Inside the heavens are but half seen. That imagination which is eye and atmosphere is hindered by walls. A fence fences out more than it fences in. I must be free as an Indian, he said; for I want more liberty than that with which Christ has made me free.

These were intrusive allusions but that my topic must be treated with circumstantial illustration. A hero he will not be of his own tale. This story should be told, before all cognizant of the particulars pass from the stage, to vindicate the transcendental position as no affront to history, but protest against a mortgage of the future. It has been described as a transitory affair, like a meteor that shoots and explodes, or a plant without product or healthy root. But, standing guard for progress does not disown the past. Sceptic no more than Orthodox cuts off from his antecedents. Our ancestors had not only their solutions, but their questions too. They had sailed for new discovery, and swung uneasy at their moorings, with doubts suppressed by their situation or unripe for expression,—an inheritance for their sons, and coming to a head in brains born of their own. All our present growth was in their soil. The oak forest, that springs up after the pine is burnt or cleared away, pre-existed as shrubs or germs, for a while overgrown and kept down. Always in generous doubts nobler convictions fasten and thrive. The finest trees on the grounds where I ramble have forced their way through the clefts of the rocks. Paul was all the time in Saul. With his pains to prove his untainted lineage, did it ever occur to him that not the contradiction but cause of his heresy lay in the religious purity of his blood? Gamaliel, be sure, had his queries, however he managed for himself and his pupils, like many a preacher and Sunday-school teacher, to subdue them for the time. Dr. Beecher, accusing some members of the Massachusetts Convention of Congressional Ministers of departing from the faith of the Fathers, was asked by Dr. Lowell if there were any members who adhered to the faith, and could only cough out, Yes, *for substance!* He also in an ordination-sermon hurled Paul's anathema at the Unitarians as preachers of another gospel, and bade them depart and not shoot their poisoned arrows behind. The Unitarians had their pay when Dr. Beecher was arraigned as a heretic before the Presbyterian synod. But were the Unitarians rebellious or degenerate children of their theological sires? No: they maintained the Pilgrim line, were Puritans of the nineteenth century, striking for freedom to worship God.

"Once more unto the breach, dear friends, once more!"

Transcendentalism did not foul its nest, or, as is continually charged, despise its mother; but unfolded the faith implied in every act of the settlers of the land. It cast off naught precious in the old belief; but was a new vessel, a better Mayflower for the Truth's escape from her foes. It set us all afloat but that may be better than to be all ashore. A church once floated off to Nova Scotia from the British in Boston, and still lives. The essence of faith is advance. Like a political constitution, it provides for its own amendment.

In the moving on of mankind, the way-marks differ at each turn of the road. It is the general direction we must look at, like a ship that tacks, or carriage winding round the hill. Would we repeat our Father's case, the items of their life? That were false imitation, mimicry, a poor copy of those great masters. The living likeness is to apply their principles to our condition. One star differs from another, but they all go one way. One boulder has not its neighbor's weight or size, but every scratch on the primitive rock follows the same line of the compass. The icebergs show every sort of shape and similitude, yet all drift to the South. Our reformers square not their theories to those of any former age, yet steadily with every step near the goal of the same millennium. Like the angel that came down to trouble the pool at certain seasons, this visitation of the Spirit is periodical. One said its return was like that of the seventeen-years locust. But it always betokens conflict. Byron describes the cannon-roar that broke in on the ballroom at Belgium's capital as mistaken for thunder or rattling of a car along the stony street; but volley after volley came to prove its nature: and every stroke of religious genius claims kith and kin with prior ones, though fifty generations lie between. At the gates of hell, Sin convicts Satan as her offspring; and all beneficence is born of goodness. The intellectual regenerator is never heady, but calm as he is warm. He is careful as a surveyor of his spirit-level. Of the re-creator none could tell if his temper were flame or phlegm. He struck no attitude, stood on no stage, had looked in no glass, was no oratoric gymnast, never strained nor sweat, rolled neckerchief in his hand, or wiped emotion from his brow, but had laid the robes aside and sang without singing-garlands. He was poet, but not laureate. His leaves were loose: he found them with difficulty; and his only noticeable gesture was an emphatic look, which a famous lawyer, who thought it worth the entrance-fee, said was directed at nothing. But it indicated that the speaker's subject had in his ecstasy become an object of sight. He was of the family of prophets who first are, then see, and then say,—that being the order. In the old controversy, who were the circumcision and Abraham's children, Jesus decides for the patriarch's spirit against his blood; and what bomb-proof occupant of an accredited church could vie with this teacher of Christianity without its name? It signified execution when into the Spirit's hands was put this imaginative tool, polished with courtesy and taking from good humor the finest edge. The least acidity eats into the steel; but the keenness of re-buke is its tenderness.

Yet this genius was too high and subtile for popular effect. A university of education, doing more for scholars than any college, it needed the supplement of talent to spread its inspiration into the common school; and that came in the stalwart figure—like a second Luther—of Theodore Parker. He made no feast for a few of nightingales' tongues, but a board with bread for millions. He was not a seer, but an officer,—the deputy-sheriff of ideas. Never lived man more strong and faithful to execute the writ. Piety and philanthrophy were as the coming and going of his breath. Like an old Hebrew, he turned every piece of paper to see if the name of God were on it; and all his study went into act. He suffered no volume of truth to rest with uncut leaves on the shelf, no scrap of information to be thrown into the waste-basket. There were those well enough pleased to have the new speculations remain mental exercises, and let institutions alone. Parker tore down the partition of esoteric and exoteric as the veil of the temple was rent in twain. He could not conceive of a scholar keeping a bit of his learning from the people to himself. He bitterly denounced the policy of doling out wisdom as the folk were thought able to bear it. All the poetry he undertook to turn into prose, as Wendell Phillips wanted Lincoln's proclamation, in Georgia, in spurs and boots. Whatever could be truly said or sung, with him must be done. Radical doctrine, says my Orthodox friend, is not practical: it goes to pieces in North Street. In Parker's hands every thing the doctrine was opposed to went to pieces,—as Schiller says of the cannon-ball shattering all in its way that it may shatter its mark. Call the new views mist? He condensed them into a thunder-bolt. Call them nebulous? He showed they were world-stuff. Slavery, intemperance, vice, criminal classes, perishing classes, no cause or human condition but he took for his province. Overladen with social work in Boston, he carried his crusade against superstition and iniquity into every corner of the land. Soft-hearted, he made his sensibilities the furnace in which to forge his weapons, beside the transcendental writings which were his Springfield armory. Many friendly ties broke under his heresy. He seemed to have gone to the funeral of his affections, till he lost all bias of sentiment, and dealt justice without extraneous considerations. He disowned the maxim that scorn and anger were instruments unfit to be used. Only bad men had no right to them! Whose contempt should be so great, whose wrath so terrible, as that of the good against the ungodly and all their works? He had no private malice, bore no grudge against the individuals he publicly scored; but he carried his antipathies of principle so far as to be styled an intellectual ruffian. Calling of names in meeting, where the assailed cannot answer, appears to them an unfair advantage, and stirs ill blood. To impeach the motives serves less than to argue the case. But though his sarcasm was resented and complained of, it was the base custom of false doctrine the holders had identified themselves with which felt his severity. In that his arrows stuck. Dr. Channing said the slaveholder was to him an abstraction: it was the system of slavery he discussed. Mr. Garrison answered. Is the slaveholder an abstraction to the slave? To Parker, sin was a man. Living in Luther's time, he would have believed in and thrown his inkstand at the devil. Incarnate evil he condemned, and would make way with that Dragon, planting his shoulders like another Samson at the pillars of

Gaza. "Stick or stone, whatever comes to hand," says Virgil, "the mob will throw." His only choice among means of offence was of the most effective, thinking no such rights of war as Grotius describes belonged to wrong-doers, in the conflict of words. For the tyrant or traitor he had wrath, and freely drew for his portrait a copy of Herod or Iscariot; for the bibliolater, ridicule,—but his anger or irony, like the Indian bullet that cleaves the buffalo and pursues its way, went through the embodiment to the essence of mischief in society and the soul. Had the Calvinist some artificial condition of redemption? He laughed at it as like a red string tied round the little finger for an amulet or charm. He was not revealer, but administrator, of a new testament and Cobden or Cobbett, Webster or Lincoln, did not use a more resistless plainness of speech. He had occasion. Religion had deceased into tenet, like the coral insect into the coral bed. Men were at ease in Zion: liturgy had become lethargy. As the keeper stirs the sleepy lion with his pole, or the electrician passes a spark through the torpid frame, or the guide shakes and rouses the traveller sinking to deathly slumber in the snow, he made no scruple of roughly disturbing the more fatal repose of the elect in their assurance of heaven, while leaving their brethren to perish of oppression on earth. When the fugitive was in his house, this new Templar added cocked pistols on his pillow to his grandfather's rusty gun at the door, and was ready with word or blow. He had a relish for irony and enjoyed the fray. When one said to him, "You have not your ancestor's military bent," "Have I not?" he grimly replied. His brain was a masked battery ever ready to be unlimbered. As public questions degenerate into private disputes, he sometimes descended into personalities and details which he should have looked down on from the sun. But truth took a step forward in his word.

Yet Liberal Christians, already persecuted as extremists, not only refused to follow, but hesitated to own his freedom of thought. They had gone far enough. It was time to stop. Channing was the last result of reason. An inch more was the jumping-off place. Parker had assailed what Channing stoutly defended,—the supernatural; and the miracles of the New if not of the Old Testament were now the citadel whose defence alone prevented the surrender of Christianity. Belief in them was made the test. Norton maintained the miraculous as the essence of religion. Channing was disappointed in Parker because he declared it unessential, if not untrue; but Parker has prevailed, if not in refuting or setting aside, yet in displacing it as the touchstone. Moreover, he questioned any verbal gospel. The leading scholars had with much trouble purged the text. He denied the authority of the text, however pure. He removed every outward landmark, and planted the boundaries in the soul. What we shrank from was the logical conclusion. Yet the basis the Unitarian majority still repose in is the history, the prophet, not the human mind. That is not trusted as a final organ of truth. Channing is leaned on as the pillar of this Scripture position, and it will by many be held sacrilege to doubt his claims as a seer. His writings, however, hold not with thinkers their place. They defy not the tooth of time. His genius was for reflection and sentiment rather than insight. Eloquence was his peculiar mark. Who that was young when he was in his prime can forget the matchless simplicity and fervor of his speech,—that voice of melody so singular, and resonance one could not credit from the slender chest, audible to the vast congregation because of the might of interior whispers it reverberated not a syllable lost because every one was saturated with spirit, and carrying the hearer to heaven on that unique rising inflection which, though a generation has passed, must still ring in every ear on which it once fell? Yet, in the record on the cold page, eloquence takes up too much room. We tire, if we read for information or new direction, of the long climacteric roll. As the world quickens its speed, we dislike preface: we want pith, and praise orators like the English who give us figures of arithmetic rather than rhetoric, and come to the point. Emerson, in the region of intellect, meets this demand. He sees too clearly and too much to dilate with emotion or expand his phrase. If his style for a moment takes on a fine sound, he resists temptation, checks the impulse. Immensity of meaning constrains him to study economy of words. Channing called him poet, but no philosopher. But there is no distinction of poetry from truth. Only verse-wrights deal with the unreal. Shakespeare is as prudent as Bacon, as judicious as Hooker, as metaphysical as Kant. Emerson reaches the supreme height, if not of Mont Blanc, yet one of the *aiguilles*.

As a philanthropist, Channing was sublime; but truth is the highest philanthropy, and whoever describes a circle about yours exceeds you as benefactor. To behold and declare how things stand in the universe,— to widen a man's horizon,—is a greater mercy than to feed or clothe. A good feeling, a humane theory, does not suffice. Conscious benevolence is a lower motive than Christ's martyrdom for the truth. Channing's feeble health and solitary life separated him from the race his ideal goodness would bless. He spoke as an apostle, hardly of the same blood with those who heard, discoursed downward from his desk, distanced the laboring men he talked to, held at arm's length the masses for whom he professed his interest and in whom he felt a serious concern. He was not in direct fellowship. He had views rather than vision. He used a reflecting telescope, not the naked eye. Conversing with him, one felt not so much like a fellow-creature as part of the instrument he was at work with to find and catalogue the celestial facts. He respected another's mind as an explorer does his companion for his help in the expedition. Something not organic, but derivative, characterizes his instructions. "A potted Plato" one called him. Unsurpassably lofty in feeling and aim, his page is so deficient in close reason or imagination one-half the sentences can be omitted with no disturbance of the method or loss of sense. Not for the sake of odious comparison, but of a true leadership, I would lift the standard on which testimony is blazoned in larger letters than any scheme even of charity. To one whose sermons had disturbed his audience it was said, "Why not suit and time your matter better to those in your charge? I suppose you preach to do good?" "No," he answered: "I do not. I preach to testify. Let me be true. God will see to the good, which he alone is and does." The great modern character is the reporter, who keeps the world of society and politics in motion. But he is tool and servant of another head-reporter of thought, of an interviewer of conscience, of a watcher of that sky Coleridge looked at when he said, "Only after celestial observations can terrestrial charts be constructed." *It will make you see stars*, says the coarse worldly proverb, of any sudden shock. But these spiritual stars are no unsubstantial sparkles of a stunned brain. The eye that saw them can turn the other way, and in "English Traits" and "Representative Men" prove as keen in the earthly direction as in the heavenly. *It is all in the eye*, whose lenses no surveyor's theodolite can match. He who has sight need not attack another or defend himself. This ocular or binocular arm makes a new style of warfare, like that introduced into the field. Cæsar led his troops. Napoleon figures in a cocked hat, and Jackson on his horse. In the holy bard's imagery, the Most High is made to copy human warriors, gird his sword on his thigh, and ride prosperously to battle. But here is a war most wonderful in history, fought by an invisible man called Möltke, without musket, spear, or coat of mail,—only map and pencil; and a million of men stand ready to follow where he draws. It is a ghostly conflict, rehearsed on the stage of fancy: the awful engines play harmless as a little model in the secret chambers of the brain, before hosts fall dead and fortresses capitulate, and civil populations, a hundred-fold more than the beleaguering army, surrender and sue for peace, and the old boundaries of nations are changed. Not by unreasoning passion are social victories won. Said Ichabod Nichols, when one talked of using strong words, "Put your strength into your reason." Poisoning of wells, Southern proposals to import plague into the North, assassination, and starvation do not carry the day. The Communist throws petroleum to fire the city, pulls down the Column, tears up coffins and murders priests; but brings not in the free, equal, and fraternal reign. In America or France such methods make the gentler sex the worse. Light is better than lightning; and lightning is the best social and civil help when tamed to run soft and obedient on an errand. The great reformer is the discerner,—

> "Who revolutions works without a murmur,
> Or rustling of a leaf beneath the skies."

Transcendentalism relies on those ideas in the mind which are laws in the life. Pantheism is said to sink man and nature in God, Materialism to sink God and man in nature, and Transcendentalism to sink God and nature in man. But the Transcendentalist, at least, is belied and put in jail by the definition, which is so neat at the expense of truth. He made consciousness, not sense, the ground of truth; and, in the present devotion to physical science and turn of philosophy to build the universe on foundations of matter, we need to vindicate and reassert his premise. Is the soul reared on the primitive rock? or is no rock primitive, but the deposit of spirit, therefore in its lowest form alive, and ever rising into organism to reach the top of the eternal circle again,—as in the well one bucket goes down empty and the other rises full? The mistake is to make the everlasting things subjects of argument instead of sight. No logic can compass them. The more we reason about them in the terms of the understanding, the farther we are away. Wait awhile, says the investigator, and we may tell you if God exists and you are immortal. But God is no conclusion. A Diety deduced from phenomena were finite as they, and nothing worth. God is the commencement, if he be at all; and to expect, by breaking open some atom, to see him come out like the smoke into a giant from the fisherman's box is atheism at the start.

The Transcendentalist sought a basis of knowledge beyond the senses, and of religion beyond ecclesiastical services. His religious feelings were hurt by going to church, and he encountered the odium of going into the woods and fields, or on to the sea instead. He affronted the procession of Sabbath-keepers with the needless insult of secular avocations, or sports in plain sight. Because it was Sunday, in a meeting-house and a pulpit, and with a Scripture text and ordained minister, bigotry and bad scholarship were not sanctified. He heard not only the truckman and porter swear, but the name of God taken in vain in the worst profanity of the lifeless repetition of liturgical forms. In rocky resounding clefts, he could worship better than in the house made with hands. Standing outside the church-door, the music of praise pleased him better that he could not hear the sectarian sermon. On the reeling steamer's deck, with ecstasy through the cabin-windows came to him the anthem accompanied with a part, described in no musical notation, by the winds and waves. He disowned the temple's peculiar claim; and a band of play-actors with the sacrifice of their talent and time to help some poor and aged member, or promote a worthy cause, made the stage a pulpit, and the theatre a church. Holy day or place? There is no such thing. A holy man or woman, and a Holy Spirit, but no holy time or spot save that hallowed by a righteous act. Sacred office or exercise? An innocent child teaches more than a sensual priest, politic cardinal, or bad pope; and we scout the notion that any base officials are in trust with the waters of salvation, or have a lock on the river of life as one commands a valve or faucet with his hand. A face with the beauty of that shadow cast by the first consciousness of a parentage beyond earthly father or mother communicates wisdom which canonical books and apostolic succession cannot match. As in old time some people worshipped in churches and cloisters outside the city walls, these Transcendentalists defied the conventional adoration with a piety of their own.

The Transcendental school must, however, encounter one criticism. Part of it led into the doctrine of Divine Impersonality. Emerson followed Cousin. The objection to Personality was its supposed limitation. It lowered the Infinite. But you say a great deal about God when you say he is *impersonal.* You lower him negatively, and deny his chief attribute, if not his being. The guilt of presumption is not avoided, but incurred. Does piety decline to imprison him in human measures? We had thought humanity not his prison, but his image. What other larger measure of him do you propose? The sky were a prison. Besides, we do not measure God: he measures himself with countless graduations in all his creatures, and without this self-measurement on an endless scale we could not know him at all. We conceive ill of him in outward dimensions like a giant. He can fill the firmament, and dole himself out in the wing of a fly, brain of an ant, or burnish and buzz of a bee. He is spirit; and that we cannot imagine as impersonal. Spirit is intelligence and intent. If you hesitate to ascribe to him purpose, you resist the instinct of mankind in all ages, which from the Hottentot to the Hindoo, the Chinaman to the North-American Indian, the Greek to the Turk, and the Christian to the Mahometan, finds the staple and fundamental article of its devotion in the will of God. In teaching that he is spirit, and that birth from the Spirit is like the *sound* of the wind, Jesus curiously identifies spirit and *person* as synonyms of speech. Spirit or Person: neither implies finiteness more than the other.

The world affirms Personality. Is *world* or *whirled* its proper name? What is it but motion from centres of force, in mighty balls or imponderable particles: in the stone that resolves itself into orbits of atoms, and the drop that is a sea for living things to swim, nor, more than leviathan, lack room? All this action, and no will? Nothing too heavy to lift, or too light and little to get hold of; yet no agent, meaning, energy, or behest? If no divine, then no human personality, which were a causeless effect. In scholastic phrase God is not *personated*, but *personating* Person. If this human quality is no gauge of him, he is lost altogether, as we are lost; for with our personality goes immortality, and we are photograph-plates taking pictures to-day, broken to-morrow; and then no more impressions. A strange way to dignify and exalt the Divinity to make him and his work such a shallow fading surface! To say he is an idea of the human mind, and comes to consciousness, or is conscious of himself in it, does not belittle him. Ideas are substantial and eternal and where or how else he is conscious who shall say? You have several homes,—in city, county, at the Springs, or by the sea. His houses who shall number?

Person signifies the unfathomable. Who shall say where the whisper of the wind begins? A man's voice or sound is from his inmost self, like the character an actor performed through his mask; and what is the material universe but the pipe Omnipotence shapes, as a boy his whistle, to play what tunes he likes. God is the word: what speaks in the beginning was with him and was he. Personality is no degradation. As the sparkle of a dewdrop implies the sun, and that is a spark to the light that feeds it; as a trickling drop balances the sea, and nothing less could be its parent; as the running of the drops together between the shrunken boards of a barn first brought to my mind the mystery of the world; as a pebble dropped in the water or as a blow or gesture of the hand goes to the confines of Nature and is coextensive with gravitation,—so the faintest emotion implies the Most High; and God takes up his abode in the lowly and contrite heart.

Doubtless we bely him, as we do every thing, in our speech. But it is greater untruth to him not to speak. Some word we cannot help. Those most stout like Goethe to say all words are inadequate go on to use them, though every word, used or emphasized alone, cleaves from our thought and breaks down. But if we discard the *Infinite Self* we lose the *Universe*, which is *Version* of One, or Person translated; and what does Person mean but that the world is not senseless surface, but stands for something, was made in earnest, and not by accident for sport? Personality is not part of it, but the whole,—top and bottom of things, sum and substance of philosophy; and the impersonality the sage imputes as an honor is poor, cheap, and finite. We argue what are called the Carlyle and Buckle theories of history. Are events determined by persons, or by laws? If history relates what is done by inspiration or design, the question disappears. Personality is nothing, or it is all. It is not the pound we put God in, but essence of the freedom which is his necessity, and to share which is man's glory. If we are personal, we have a destiny; if impersonal, only a doom. But this personal persistence was by some Transcendentalists treated with slight; and all curiosity about it flouted as impertinent peeping into what we had no business with. Such scorn is affront to the aspiration of mankind. Forceythe Willson, after listening to a lecture that brought immortality into doubt, said, "Philosophy is good; but if philosophy contradicts my instincts, I throw it overboard."

Personality alone vindicates prayer. If Deity be Immeasurable Consciousness in which I have part and lot, then prayer is no gymnastic self-excitation beginning and ending with my own will, but some stir of the Divinity it comes from and goes to. It constrains God so far as his liberty can be constrained; for there is that he cannot help. How can he help seeing and hearing his child whose voice is part of his soliloquy? Can he say, I will not listen or look? He is bound in his own nature to hear and answer prayer; for he is not one Individual and you another, he sitting up there with ready-made laws to apply to you as a foreign substance; but you and he, even as Jesus and he, are One. He cannot get along without you, or avoid blessing you. Your inmost desire is his interpreter. Were prayer an arbitrary whim, across the track of his predestination it were crushed like a pin on the iron rail. But request or answer is foreordained and insured against possible failure or loss.

To one Transcendental philosopher—Mr. Alcott—we are in debt for his vital conception of Personality. A pure mystic, subsisting on the thin sweet grass of the mount of vision, in the full sweep of the pervading theory that blew like a trade-wind against the conception of a conscious and willing Deity, he kept his footing and saw God keeping his. In all his Conversations East and West expounding matters, so singular to charm and hard to penetrate, he has held by selfhood as the sheet-anchor of creation, and rendered a service for which his memory will be honorable and dear. He was true Transcendentalist, teaching that the soul is no ephemeral thing, but lives beyond the momentary impression, in the past, the distant, the future, and in that eternity where time disappears or all times are alike. True philosophy is no peculiarity of dainty speculation, but staple of practical life. It is an idea becoming flesh, or common sense exalted by sentiment. Not only a poet, like Wordsworth, can address his ideal child,—

"Thou whose exterior semblance doth bely
Thy soul's immensity,"

not only Shakspeare can make Lady Macbeth say to her husband,—

"Thy letters have transported me beyond
This ignorant present, and I feel now
The future in the instant,"

but the negro pilot could tell the captain in Charleston harbor, "Wind and tide against you, it is ten miles to the city; but, weather favoring, you are there now." We are not blind to what we see through. The Transcendentalist leaps out of routine, shakes off the weight of custom, most are fettered by and drag as a ball and chain. He detaches every thing from himself, to make it an object of contemplation and enchanting marvel. His own personality he wonders at, and tries half vainly to explore. "I want to know more of myself,—this very Jonathan: I have lived seventy years with him, and he is a great mystery to me." His theory enters into character as well as thought. While dogmatism makes out its exhaustive schemes of the universe, and ambitious conceit and desire to shine babble their presumptuous judgments, he sits and smiles at the depth their lines dangle in; and, when they correct or contradict him, learns not to answer again. He asks nothing for himself but to be allowed still to think, and put his observations in words which passion may reject till reason receives. He takes all injury and wrong, from foes or friends, out of his sensibility and into the alembic of his reflections, whence the crude ore and rough fragments run pure gold. No Caliban or Shylock but enriches the poet's drama; no people so bad and hard the thinker cannot enjoy. Said my friend, I like that "Great Misery" island: it is like so many folks I have seen, barren and unpromising at a distance and first sight; but when you are there, the green fields are all around you. His forecast lights up the darkest hour. Said my friend, walking among the cliffs, Reasoning is like the rock ahead you hope to mount and see further from; and faith has foretaste of paradise.

We shall discover that our glory is not pure passivity, to be the sport of impressions, like feathers in every wandering breeze, but personality. We shall be convinced that conscious selfhood rooted in the self of Nature, and spreading into man or angel, is no selfishness, but the only possible generosity. A certain dissolute sympathy may survive self-reliance; but all genuine love and sacrifice die with it. No earthly good a noble person will not sooner decline or impart than demand. Personality has no measure: it is measure of every thing else. It is the golden rod with which the angel takes the length and breadth of the New Jerusalem. In the present rage of physical science the *particles* are contending with it for victory. But they are its servants, and usurpers when they snatch at its rightful sway. The thinker goes with his thought, which can reach nothing beyond itself. No God is cognizable above my inmost being, which he is. Where my imagination goes, I go; and it goes to him and heaven.

The objection to personality in God is its likening him to man's which is limited. But this objection assumes its own fact. Who has laid down or reported the metes and bounds of *human* personality? It is unlimited. Person in the sense of appearance is finite. The body which the soul is in, or rather which is in the soul, has limits, but not that in which the body is contained. Man's eyes, says Herbert, "dismount the highest star." David's description of trying to leave the Lord by ascending to to heaven, or making his bed in hell, or flying on the wings of the morning to the uttermost parts of the sea, not only shows where God was, but where David was! Is our imagination the compass of Nature? But our imagination is the carriage we sit in. Paul knew a man who was in the seventh heaven. Rise high and float far as the balloon will, the gazer from beleaguered Paris walls, or a Fourth of July muster-field, outstrips it standing on the ground.

> "One morn is in the mighty heaven,
> And one in our desire!"

But the last outshines the first.

> "And those eyes, the break of day,
> Lights that do mislead the morn."

Shakespeare knew space was not the holder, but the accident and servant of the mind. We, like God, possess it; not it us. "I own part of Boston Common," said Father Taylor; "and I will tell nobody which part it is." We cannot tell where our property in Nature ends.

Nor is human personality limited in time more than in space. Doubtless the almanac or family register will tell us when we were born. But our soul is older than our organism. It precedes its clothing. It is the cause, not the consequence, of its material elements; else, as materialists understand, it does not properly exist. Jesus asserted the truth of all men when he said, "Before Abraham was, I am." Who can tell where he began? It is a wise child that knows his own father. Grandparents reappear in the babes they play with. The Jews thought older prophets returned in later ones; and it might be Elias that had come back in Jesus. Naturalism traces man farther than to Eden, and finds his progenitor in some fossil fish or reptile that lived measureless cycles ago. Napoleon said he was the founder of his own family. We were our own ancestors, and shall find it quite impossible to decide our commencement in time, though we point to our cradle in the garret. We all lay in one crib, if we knew where it was; and Plato's doctrine of pre-existence we have laughed at only to see it recur under the flag of the straitest orthodoxy of our day.

Human personality has no intrinsic limitation in itself. It is sometimes said, men or particular races of men, as the Negro or Chinese, stop growing like an animal or plant. But they are only by adverse circumstances or their fellow-creature's oppression tethered for a time. None can predict or set any goal to the progress of science. Yet that is only one of the lines: art, society, government, are others in the progress of man. This shock of conventional horror at supposing any likeness of God with man is as profane as it is inhuman. God and man must rise or fall together. We have been afraid and ashamed to think nobly of ourselves. But he is like us! He made us in his image; and, laugh at it who will, we do and must somehow make him in ours; for were the parent unlike his child, it were absurd to speak of parent or child.

Nothing in us lasts like faith. Richter calls it the night-flower blooming into the hour when sense and memory fade. I learned the fact in an unvoluntary experiment of being thrown to the ground by a train of cars. It was "a vision of sudden death." For a moment it was all of death that can be known, only that in returning consciousness came resurrection to myself and my friends. But in that moment of decease was no fear. Had I been riding above, not with a crushed limb underneath, I could have felt no more sure of the wise regularity, in whose chariot without falling I was borne.

Orthodoxy and Physical Science are considered foes. But they build on the same foundation. In their method they meet. The last asserts we get all knowledge, and the first that we get religious knowledge, through the senses,—the Book, the Prophecy, the Miracle being the foundations of faith, as if there were less piety in Plato than in Locke. Transcendental Thought is the only communion with God, save by some proxy that casts our vote for us, like a master for his slaves, or patron for everybody under the roof of his mill. What wonder the believer should conclude in the scepticism with which the scientist begins, and doubt be the Land's End for them both. With neither is any option. The structures they put up are different, but the site of both alike is the sand; only the believer sees not how he is logically shut up to the scientist's frank expectation that the rain and the wind will beat and blow till the edifice fall, according to the Latin proverb that we owe our possessions and ourselves alike to death. The consistent physicist, like Mill, carries his point to the denial of all necessary truth. The figures of the multiplication-table and the properties of a triangle, all the axioms of the mathematician and geometer, a square, cube, line, or circle, may be such only to us and not in some other world, there being no such thing as ascertainable truth. The contemptuous proverb "He does not know much, and what he does know he does not know for certain," hits the whole race with its vulgar fling. The Christian solace so many millions have hugged to their breast, "What thou knowest not now thou shalt know hereafter," is refused; for death is no solution, but only the last dodge.

So truth is not what is, but what one troweth; a name for everybody's notion and all contradictory beliefs! It is the honor of the Transcendentalist—every great soul from Hebrew Moses to Hebraic John Brown—to affirm truth otherwise as eternal vision of what suffers no change, the consonance of reality in Nature and the mind. Apart from perception truth is not. The Greek tongue excels the English in having a verb for truth corresponding to the noun, and the apostle speaking of "truthing in love." No canonical book has a nobler verse than that in the Apocrypha,—"Wisdom is a loving spirit:" for love is not born of wisdom, but wisdom of love; and neither is born of matter or the flesh. To rest our case in miracle is to rest it in the letter that killeth; for all phenomena, like the letters in the Primer, are but an alphabet making sense only as arranged by some intelligence. It matters not what shape matter may take: it is an unmeaning syllable till adopted by the intellect. If the water became wine, or a few loaves and fishes a ton of food, it was a cipher still of no significance before it was chosen to convey the spirit's despatch. It is not the wire stretching from England to America for which we care; but the messages sent over it beneath the deep, unquenched by all its billows, unsilenced by its mighty roar.

Preoccupied with ideas, God's true mediators, we look upon marvels with an incurious eye. I confess I am not moved when the table tips. The wonder is just as great when it reposes firmly on its legs. Stones thrown through the windows by freakish elfs hold not my reflections like the glass made from the flux of their crumbled grains. All is in discrimination; nothing in the gross fact. The delicate odor of a tea-rose, said one, transports me: but at one smell of the pond-lily I say, No more I thank you! The Divinity gives us facts enough. We cannot manage one of a thousand. I rather ask him to stay his hand than from his horn of plenty continue to pour. He has led me into the Gallery; and I have no fear of his hurrying me out before it is half seen. The Transfiguration by Raphael, or Wedding-feast in Cana by Paul Veronese, or Conception by Corregio, is not a subject that holds or concentres my regards more than any simply human theme,—a ship in port by Turner, landscape by Corot, or the "Sower" by Millet; for God is as near in the field or on the sea as by any mountain, in any marriage or origin of life, with whatever unusual signs. Sinai made no better thunder and lightning than the Jura, or the wood-crowned hill whence in my boyhood flaming cloud made its rush, and the red bolt leaped as a sword from the scabbard. I am grateful to antecedents and ancestors; but why explore the processes by which they earned what I inherit, instead of for my posterity earning more? I value the Bible; but shall I prefer it to what it records? It were to prize the family-register before the domestic joy. The Scriptures are not authority, but notes and memorandum book for experience, which has no Heretofore or Hereafter or Elsewhere, but interminable omnipresent Now.

"Transcendental Wild Oats"

Louisa May Alcott*

A CHAPTER FROM AN UNWRITTEN ROMANCE

On the first day of June, 184–, a large wagon, drawn by a small horse and containing a motley load, went lumbering over certain New England hills, with the pleasing accompaniments of wind, rain, and hail. A serene man with a serene child upon his knee was driving, or rather being driven, for the small horse had it all his own way. A brown boy with a William Penn style of countenance sat beside him, firmly embracing a bust of Socrates. Behind them was an energetic-looking woman, with a benevolent brow, satirical mouth, and eyes brimful of hope and courage. A baby reposed upon her lap, a mirror leaned against her knee, and a basket of provisions danced about at her feet, as she struggled with a large, unruly umbella. Two blue-eyed little girls, with hands full of childish treasures, sat under one old shawl, chatting happily together.

In front of this lively party stalked a tall, sharp-featured man, in a long blue cloak; and a fourth small girl trudged along beside him through the mud as if she rather enjoyed it.

The wind whistled over the bleak hills; the rain fell in a despondent drizzle, and twilight began to fall. But the calm man gazed as tranquilly into the fog as if he beheld a radiant bow of promise spanning the gray sky. The cheery woman tried to cover every one but herself with the big umbrella. The brown boy pillowed his head on the bald pate of Socrates and slumbered peacefully. The little girls sang lullabies to their dolls in soft, maternal murmurs. The sharp-nosed pedestrian marched steadily on, with the blue cloak streaming out behind him like a banner; and the lively infant splashed through the puddles with a duck-like satisfaction pleasant to behold.

*Reprinted from *Independent*, 25 (18 December 1873), 1569–1571. In this satirical portrait of the Fruitlands community, Abel Lamb is Bronson Alcott, Hope Lamb is Mrs. Alcott, and Timon Lion is the English Transcendentalist, Charles Lane.

Thus these modern pilgrims journeyed hopefully out of the old world, to found a new one in the wilderness.

The editors of *The Transcendental Tripod* had received from Messrs. Lion & Lamb (two of the aforesaid pilgrims) a communication from which the following statement is an extract:—

"We have made arrangements with the proprietor of an estate of about a hundred acres which liberates this tract from human ownership. Here we shall prosecute our effort to initiate a Family in harmony with the primitive instincts of man.

"Ordinary secular farming is not our object. Fruit, grain, pulse, herbs, flax, and other vegetable products, receiving assiduous attention, will afford ample manual occupation, and chaste supplies for the bodily needs. It is intended to adorn the pastures with orchards, and to supersede the labor of cattle by the spade and the pruning-knife.

"Consecrated to human freedom, the land awaits the sober culture of devoted men. Beginning with small pecuniary means, this enterprise must be rooted in a reliance on the succors of an ever-bounteous Providence, whose vital affinities being secured by this union with uncorrupted field and unworldly persons, the cares and injuries of a life of gain are avoided.

"The inner nature of each member of the Family is at no time neglected. Our plan contemplates all such disciplines, cultures, and habits as evidently conduce to the purifying of the inmates.

"Pledged to the spirit alone, the founders anticipate no hasty or numerous addition to their numbers. The kingdom of peace is entered only through the gates of self-denial; and felicity is the test and the reward of loyalty to the unswerving law of Love."

This prospective Eden at present consisted of an old red farmhouse, a dilapidated barn, many acres of meadow-land, and a grove. Ten ancient apple-trees were all the "chaste supply" which the place offered as yet; but, in the firm belief that plenteous orchards were soon to be evoked from their inner consciousness, these sanguine founders had christened their domain Fruitlands.

Here Timon Lion intended to found a colony of Latter Day Saints, who, under his patriarchal sway, should regenerate the world and glorify his name for ever. Here Abel Lamb, with the devoutest faith in the high ideal which was to him a living truth, desired to plant a Paradise, where Beauty, Virtue, Justice, and Love might live happily together, without the possibility of a serpent entering in. And here his wife, unconverted but faithful to the end, hoped, and after many wanderings over the face of the earth, to find rest for herself and a home for her children.

"There is our new abode," announced the enthusiast, smiling with a satisfaction quite undampened by the drops dripping from his hat-brim, as they turned at length into a cart-path that wound along a steep hillside into a barren-looking valley.

"A little difficult of access," observed his practical wife, as she endeavored to keep her various household goods from going overboard with every lurch of the laden ark.

"Like all good things. But those who earnestly desire and patiently seek will soon find us," placidly responded the philosopher from the mud, through which he was now endeavoring to pilot the much-enduring horse.

"Truth lies at the bottom of a well, Sister Hope," said Brother Timon, pausing to detach his small comrade from a gate, whereon she was perched for a clearer gaze into futurity.

"That's the reason we so seldom get at it, I suppose," replied Mrs. Hope, making a vain clutch at the mirror, which a sudden jolt sent flying out of her hands.

"We want no false reflections here," said Timon, with a grim smile, as he crunched the fragments under foot in his onward march.

Sister Hope held her peace, and looked wistfully through the mist at her promised home. The old red house with a hospitable glimmer at its windows cheered her eyes; and, considering the weather, was a fitter refuge than the sylvan bowers some of the more ardent souls might have preferred.

The new-comers were welcomed by one of the elect precious,— a regenerate farmer, whose idea of reform consisted chiefly in wearing white cotton raiment and shoes of untanned leather. This costume, with a snowy beard, gave him a venerable, and at the same time a somewhat bridal appearance.

The goods and chattels of the Society not having arrived, the weary family reposed before the fire on blocks of wood, while Brother Moses White regaled them with roasted potatoes, brown bread and water, in two plates, a tin pan, and one mug; his table service being limited. But, having cast the forms and vanities of a depraved world behind them, the elders welcomed hardship with the enthusiasm of new pioneers, and the children heartily enjoyed this foretaste of what they believed was to be a sort of perpetual picnic.

During the progress of this frugal meal, two more brothers appeared. One a dark, melancholy man, clad in homespun, whose peculiar mission was to turn his name hind part before and use as few words as possible. The other was a bland, bearded Englishman, who expected to be saved by eating uncooked food and going without clothes. He had not yet adopted the primitive costume, however; but contented himself with meditatively chewing dry beans out of a basket.

"Every meal should be a sacrament, and the vessels used should be beautiful and symbolical," observed Brother Lamb, mildly, righting the tin pan slipping about on his knees. "I priced a silver service when in town, but it was too costly; so I got some graceful cups and vases of Britannia ware."

"Hardest things in the world to keep bright. Will whiting be allowed in the community?" inquired Sister Hope, with a housewife's interest in labor-saving institutions.

"Such trivial questions will be discussed at a more fitting time," answered Brother Timon, sharply, as he burnt his fingers with a very hot potato. "Neither sugar, molasses, milk, butter, cheese, nor flesh are to be used among us, for nothing is to be admitted which has caused wrong or death to man or beast."

"Our garments are to be linen till we learn to raise our own cotton or some substitute for woolen fabrics," added Brother Abel, blissfully basking in an imaginary future as warm and brilliant as the generous fire before him.

"Haou abaout shoes?" asked Brother Moses, surveying his own with interest.

"We must yield that point till we can manufacture an innocent substitute for leather. Bark, wood, or some durable fabric will be invented in time. Meanwhile, those who desire to carry out our idea to the fullest extent can go barefooted," said Lion, who liked extreme measures.

"I never will, nor let my girls," murmured rebellious Sister Hope, under her breath.

"Haou do you cattle'ate to treat the ten-acre lot? Ef things ain't 'tended to right smart, we shan't hev no crops," observed the practical patriarch in cotton.

"We shall spade it," replied Abel, in such perfect good faith that Moses said no more, though he indulged in a shake of the head as he glanced at hands that had held nothing heavier than a pen for years. He was a paternal old soul and regarded the younger men as promising boys on a new sort of lark.

"What shall we do for lamps, if we cannot use any animal substance? I do hope light of some sort is to be thrown upon the enterprise," said Mrs. Lamb, with anxiety, for in those days kerosene and camphene were not, and gas unknown in the wilderness.

"We shall go without till we have discovered some vegetable oil or wax to serve us," replied Brother Timon, in a decided tone, which caused Sister Hope to resolve that her private lamp should be always trimmed, if not burning.

"Each member is to perform the work for which experience, strength, and taste best fit him," continued Dictator Lion. "Thus drudgery and disorder will be avoided and harmony prevail. We shall rise at dawn, begin the day by bathing, followed by music, and then a chaste repast of fruit and bread. Each one finds congenial occupation till the meridian meal; when some deep-searching conversation gives rest to the body and development to the mind. Healthful labor again engages us till the last meal, when we assemble in social communion, prolonged till sunset, when we retire to sweet repose, ready for the next day's activity."

"What part of the work do you incline to yourself?" asked Sister Hope, with a humorous glimmer in her keen eyes.

"I shall wait till it is made clear to me. Being in preference to doing is the great aim, and this comes to us rather by a resigned willingness than a wilful activity, which is a check to all divine growth," responded Brother Timon.

"I thought so." And Mrs. Lamb sighed audibly, for during the year he had spent in her family Brother Timon had so faithfully carried out his idea of "being, not doing," that she had found his "divine growth" both an expensive and unsatisfactory process.

Here her husband struck into the conversation, his face shining with the light and joy of the splendid dreams and high ideals hovering before him.

"In these steps of reform, we do not rely so much on scientific reasoning or physiological skill as on the spirit's dictates. The greater part of man's duty consists in leaving alone much that he now does. Shall I stimulate with tea, coffee, or wine? No. Shall I consume flesh? Not if I value health. Shall I subjugate cattle? Shall I claim property in any created thing? Shall I trade? Shall I adopt a form of religion? Shall I interest myself in politics? To how many of these questions— could we ask them deeply enough and could they be heard as having relation to our eternal welfare—would the response be 'Abstain'?"

A mild snore seemed to echo the last word of Abel's rhapsody, for Brother Moses had succumbed to mundane slumber and sat nodding like a massive ghost. Forest Absalom, the silent man, and John Pease, the English member, now departed to the barn; and Mrs. Lamb led her flock to a temporary fold, leaving the founders of the "Consociate Family" to build castles in the air till the fire went out and the symposium ended in smoke.

The furniture arrived next day, and was soon bestowed; for the principal property of the community consisted in books. To this rare library was devoted the best room in the house, and the few busts and pictures that still survived many flittings were added to beautify the sanctuary, for here the family was to meet for amusement, instruction, and worship.

Any housewife can imagine the emotions of Sister Hope, when

she took possession of a large, dilapidated kitchen, containing an old stove and the peculiar stores out of which food was to be evolved for her little family of eleven. Cakes of maple sugar, dried peas and beans, barley and hominy, meal of all sorts, potatoes, and dried fruit. No milk, butter, cheese, tea, or meat appeared. Even salt was considered a useless luxury and spice entirely forbidden by these lovers of Spartan simplicity. A ten years' experience of vegetarian vagaries had been good training for this new freak, and her sense of the ludicrous supported her through many trying scenes.

Unleavened bread, porridge, and water for breakfast; bread, vegetables, and water for dinner; bread, fruit, and water for supper was the bill of fare ordained by the elders. No teapot profaned that sacred stove, no gory steak cried aloud for vengeance from her chaste gridiron; and only a brave woman's taste, time, and temper were sacrificed on that domestic altar.

The vexed question of light was settled by buying a quantity of bayberry wax for candles; and, on discovering that no one knew how to make them, pine knots were introduced, to be used when absolutely necessary. Being summer, the evenings were not long, and the weary fraternity found it no great hardship to retire with the birds. The inner light was sufficient for most of them. But Mrs. Lamb rebelled. Evening was the only time she had to herself, and while the tired feet rested the skilful hands mended torn frocks and little stockings, or anxious heart forgot its burden in a book.

So "mother's lamp" burned steadily, while the philosophers built a new heaven and earth by moonlight; and through all the metaphysical mists and philanthropic pyrotechnics of that period Sister Hope played her own little game of "throwing light," and none but the moths were the worse for it.

Such farming probably was never seen before since Adam delved. The band of brothers began by spading garden and field; but a few days of it lessened their ardor amazingly. Blistered hands and aching backs suggested the expediency of permitting the use of cattle till the workers were better fitted for noble toil by a summer of the new life.

Brother Moses brought a yoke of oxen from his farm,—at least, the philosophers thought so till it was discovered that one of the animals was a cow; and Moses confessed that he "must be let down easy, for he couldn't live on garden sarse entirely."

Great was Dictator Lion's indignation at this lapse from virtue. But time pressed, the work must be done; so the meek cow was permitted to wear the yoke and the recreant brother continued to enjoy forbidden draughts in the barn, which dark proceeding caused the children to regard him as one set apart for destruction.

The sowing was equally peculiar, for, owing to some mistake, the three brethren, who devoted themselves to this graceful task, found when about half through the job that each had been sowing a different sort of grain in the same field; a mistake which caused much perplexity; as it could not be remedied; but, after a long consultation and a good deal of laughter, it was decided to say nothing and see what would come of it.

The garden was planted with a generous supply of useful roots and herbs; but, as manure was not allowed to profane the virgin soil, few of these vegetable treasures ever came up. Purslane reigned supreme, and the disappointed planters ate it philosophically, deciding that Nature knew what was best for them, and would generously supply their needs, if they could only learn to digest her "sallets" and wild roots.

The orchard was laid out, a little grafting done, new trees and vines set, regardless of the unfit season and entire ignorance of the husband-men, who honestly believed that in the autumn they would reap a bounteous harvest.

Slowly things got into order, and rapidly rumors of the new experiment went abroad, causing many strange spirits to flock thither, for in those days communities were the fashion and transcendentalism raged wildly. Some came to look on and laugh, some to be supported in poetic idleness, a few to believe sincerely and work heartily. Each member was allowed to mount his favorite hobby and ride it to his heart's content. Very queer were some of the riders, and very rampant some of the hobbies.

One youth, believing that language was of little consequence if the spirit was only right, startled new-comers by blandly greeting them with "Good-morning, damn you," and other remarks of an equally mixed order. A second irresponsible being held that all the emotions of the soul should be freely expressed, and illustrated his theory by antics that would have sent him to a lunatic asylum, if, as an unregenerate wag said, he had not already been in one. When his spirit soared, he climbed trees and shouted; when doubt assailed him, he lay upon the floor and groaned lamentably. At joyful periods, he raced, leaped, and sang; when sad, he wept aloud; and when a great thought burst upon him in the watches of the night, he crowed like a jocund cockerel, to the great delight of the children and the great annoyance of the elders. One musical brother fiddled whenever so moved, sang sentimentally to the four little girls, and put a music-box on the wall when he hoed corn.

Brother Pease ground away at his uncooked food, or browsed over the farm on sorrel, mint, green fruit, and new vegetables. Occasionally he took his walks abroad, airily attired in an unbleached cotton *poncho*, which was the nearest approach to the primeval costume he was allowed to indulge in. At midsummer he retired to the wilderness, to try his plan where the woodchucks were without prejudices and huckleberry-bushes were hospitably full. A sunstroke unfortunately spoilt his plan, and he returned to semi-civilization a sadder and wiser man.

Forest Absalom preserved his Pythagorean silence, cultivated his fine dark locks, and worked like a beaver, setting an excellent example of brotherly love, justice, and fidelity by his upright life. He it was who helped overworked Sister Hope with her heavy washes, kneaded the endless succession of batches of bread, watched over the children, and did the many tasks left undone by the brethren, who were so busy discussing and defining great duties that they forgot to perform the small ones.

Moses White placidly plodded about, "chorin' raound," as he called it, looking like an old-time patriarch, with his silver hair and flowing beard, and saving the community from many a mishap by his thrift and Yankee shrewdness.

Brother Lion domineered over the whole concern; for, having put the most money into the speculation, he was resolved to make it pay,— as if anything founded on an ideal basis could be expected to do so by any but enthusiasts.

Abel Lamb simply revelled in the Newness, firmly believing that his dream was to be beautifully realized and in time not only little Fruitlands, but the whole earth, be turned into a Happy Valley. He worked with every muscle of his body, for *he* was in deadly earnest. He taught with his whole head and heart; planned and sacrificed, preached and prophesied, with a soul full of the purest aspirations, most unselfish purposes, and desires for a life devoted to God and man, too high and tender to bear the rough usage of this world.

It was a little remarkable that only one woman ever joined this community. Mrs. Lamb merely followed wheresoever her husband led,— "as ballast for his balloon," as she said, in her bright way.

Miss Jane Gage was a stout lady of mature years, sentimental, amiable, and lazy. She wrote verses copiously, and had vague yearnings and graspings after the unknown, which led her to believe herself fitted for a higher sphere than any she had yet adorned.

Having been a teacher, she was set to instructing the children in the common branches. Each adult member took a turn at the infants; and, as each taught in his own way, the result was a chronic state of chaos in the minds of these much-afflicted innocents.

Sleep, food, and poetic musings were the desires of dear Jane's life, and she shirked all duties as clogs upon her spirit's wings. Any thought of lending a hand with the domestic drudgery never occurred to her; and when to the question, "Art there any beasts of burden on the place?" Mrs. Lamb answered, with a face that told its own tale, "Only one woman!" the buxom Jane took no shame to herself, but laughed at the joke, and let the stout-hearted sister tug on alone.

Unfortunately, the poor lady hankered after the flesh-pots, and endeavored to stay herself with private sips of milk, crackers, and cheese, and on one dire occasion she partook of fish at a neighbor's table.

One of the children reported this sad lapse from virtue, and poor Jane was publicly reprimanded by Timon.

"I only took a little bit of the tail," sobbed the penitent poetess.

"Yes, but the whole fish had to be tortured and slain that you might tempt your carnal appetite with that one taste of the tail. Know ye not, consumers of flesh meat, that ye are nourishing the wolf and tiger in your bosoms?"

At this awful question and the peal of laughter which arose from some of the younger brethren, tickled by the ludicrous contrast between the stout sinner, the stern judge, and the naughty satisfaction of the young detective, poor Jane fled from the room to pack her trunk and return to a world where fishes' tails were not forbidden fruit.

Transcendental wild oats were sown broadcast that year, and the fame thereof has not yet ceased in the land; for, futile as this crop seemed to outsiders, it bore an invisible harvest, worth much to those who planted in earnest. As none of the members of this particular community have ever recounted their experiences before, a few of them may not be amiss, since the interest in these attempts has never died out and Fruitlands was the most ideal of all these castles in Spain.

A new dress was invented, since cotton, silk, and wool were forbidden as the product of slave-labor, worm-slaughter, and sheep-robbery. Tunics and trowsers of brown linen were the only wear. The women's skirts were longer, and their straw hat-brims wider than the men's, and this was the only difference. Some persecution lent a charm to the costume, and the long-haired, linen-clad reformers quite enjoyed the mild martyrdom they endured when they left home.

Money was abjured, as the root of all evil. The produce of the land was to supply most of their wants, or be exchanged for the few things they could not grow. This idea had its inconveniences; but self-denial was the fashion, and it was surprising how many things one can do without. When they desired to travel, they walked, if possible, begged the loan of a vehicle, or boldly entered car or coach, and, stating their principles to the officials, took the consequences. Usually their dress, their earnest frankness, and gentle resolution won them a passage; but now and then they met with hard usage, and had the satisfaction of suffering for their principles.

On one of these penniless pilgrimages they took passage on a boat, and, when fare was demanded, artlessly offered to talk, instead of pay. As the boat was well under way and they actually had not a cent, there was no help for it. So Brothers Lion and Lamb held forth to the assembled passengers in their most eloquent style. There must have been something effective in this conversation, for the listeners were moved to take up a contribution for these inspired lunatics, who preached peace on earth and good-will to man so earnestly, with empty pockets. A goodly sum was collected; but when the captain presented it the reformers proved that they were consistent even in their madness, for not a penny would they accept, saying, with a look at the group about them, whose indifference or contempt had changed to interest and respect, "You see how well we get on without money"; and so went serenely on their way, with their linen blouses flapping airily in the cold October wind.

They preached vegetarianism everywhere and resisted all temptations of the flesh, contentedly eating apples and bread at well-spread tables, and much afflicting hospitable hostesses by denouncing their food and taking away their appetite, discussing the "horrors of shambles," the "incorporation of the brute in man," and "on elegant abstinence the sign of a pure soul." But, when the perplexed or offended ladies asked what they should eat, they got in reply a bill of fare consisting of "bowls of sunrise for breakfast," "solar seeds of the sphere," "dishes from Plutarch's chaste table," and other viands equally hard to find in any modern market.

Reform conventions of all sorts were haunted by these brethren, who said many wise things and did many foolish ones. Unfortunately, these wanderings interfered with their harvest at home; but the rule was to do what the spirit moved, so they left their crops to Providence and went a-reaping in wider and, let us hope, more fruitful fields than their own.

Luckily, the earthly providence who watched over Abel Lamb was at hand to glean the scanty crop yielded by the "uncorrupted land," which "consecrated to human freedom," had received "the sober culture of devout men."

About the time the grain was ready to house, some call of the Oversoul wafted all the men away. An easterly storm was coming up and the yellow stacks were sure to be ruined. Then Sister Hope gathered her forces. Three little girls, one boy (Timon's son), and herself, harnessed to clothes-baskets and Russia-linen sheets, were the only teams she could command; but with these poor appliances the indomitable woman got in the grain and saved the food for her young, with the instinct and energy of a mother-bird with a brood of hungry nestlings to feed.

This attempt at regeneration had its tragic as well as comic side, though the world only saw the former.

With the first frosts, the butterflies, who had sunned themselves in the new light through the summer, took flight, leaving the few bees to see what honey they had stored for winter use. Precious little appeared beyond the satisfaction of a few months of holy living.

At first it seemed as if a chance to try holy dying also was to be offered them. Timon, much disgusted with the failure of the scheme, decided to retire to the Shakers, who seemed to be the only successful community going.

"What is to become of us?" asked Mrs. Hope, for Abel was heart-broken at the bursting of his lovely bubble.

"You can stay here, if you like, till a tenant is found. No more wood must be cut, however, and no more corn ground. All I have must be sold to pay the debts of the concern, as the responsibility rests with me," was the cheering reply.

"Who is to pay us for what we have lost? I gave all I had,— furniture, time, strength, six months of my children's lives,—and all are wasted. Abel gave himself body and soul, and is almost wrecked by hard work and disappointment. Are we to have no return for this, but leave to starve and freeze in an old house, with winter at hand, no money, and hardly a friend left; for this wild scheme has alienated nearly all we had. You talk much about justice. Let us have a little, since there is nothing else left."

But the woman's appeal met with no reply but the old one: "It was an experiment. We all risked something, and must bear our losses as we can."

With this cold comfort, Timon departed with his son, and was absorbed into the Shaker brotherhood, where he soon found that the order of things was reversed, and it was all work and no play.

Then the tragedy began for the forsaken little family. Desolation and despair fell upon Abel. As his wife said, his new beliefs had alienated many friends. Some thought him mad, some unprincipled. Even the most kindly thought him a visionary, whom it was useless to help till he took more practical views of life. All stood aloof, saying, "Let him work out his own ideas, and see what they are worth."

He had tried, but it was a failure. The world was not ready for Utopia yet, and those who attempted to found it only got laughed at for their pains. In other days, men could sell all and give to the poor, lead lives devoted to holiness and high thought, and, after the persecution was over, find themselves honored as saints or martyrs. But in modern times these things are out of fashion. To live for one's principles, at all costs, is a dangerous speculation; and the failure of an ideal, no matter how humane and noble, is harder for the world to forgive and forget than bank robbery or the grand swindles of corrupt politicians.

Deep waters now for Abel, and for a time there seemed no passage through. Strength and spirits were exhausted by hard work and too much thought. Courage failed when, looking about for help, he saw no sympathizing face, no hand out-stretched to help him, no voice to say cheerily,

"We all make mistakes, and it takes many experiences to shape a life. Try again, and let us help you."

Every door was closed, every eye averted, every heart cold, and no way open whereby he might earn bread for his children. His principles would not permit him to do many things that others did; and in the few fields where conscience would allow him to work, who would employ a man who had flown in the face of society, as he had done?

Then this dreamer, whose dream was the life of his life, resolved to carry out his idea to the bitter end. There seemed no place for him here,—no work, no friend. To go begging conditions was as ignoble as to go begging money. Better perish of want than sell one's soul for the sustenance of his body. Silently he lay down upon his bed, turned his face to the wall, and waited with pathetic patience for death to cut the knot which he could not untie. Days and nights went by, and neither food nor water passed his lips. Soul and body were dumbly struggling together, and no word of complaint betrayed what either suffered.

His wife, when tears and prayers were unavailing, sat down to wait the end with a mysterious awe and submission; for in this entire resignation of all things there was an eloquent significance to her who knew him as no other human being did.

"Leave all to God," was his belief; and in this crisis the loving soul clung to this faith, sure that the Allwise Father would not desert this child who tried to live so near to Him. Gathering her children about her, she waited the issue of the tragedy that was being enacted in that solitary room, while the first snow fell outside, untrodden by the footprints of a single friend.

But the strong angels who sustain and teach perplexed and troubled souls came and went, leaving no trace without, but working miracles within. For, when all other sentiments had faded into dimness, all other hopes died utterly; when the bitterness of death was nearly over, when body was past any pang of hunger or thirst, and soul stood ready to depart, the love that outlives all else refused to die. Head had bowed to defeat, hand had grown weary with too heavy tasks, but heart could not grow cold to those who lived in its tender depths, even when death touched it.

"My faithful wife, my little girls,—they have not forsaken me, they are mine by ties that none can break. What right have I to leave them alone? What right to escape from the burden and the sorrow I have helped to bring? This duty remains to me, and I must do it manfully. For their sakes, the world will forgive me in time; for their sakes, God will sustain me now."

Too feeble to rise, Abel groped for the food that always lay within his reach, and in the darkness and solitude of that memorable night ate and drank what was to him the bread and wine of a new communion, a new dedication of heart and life to the duties that were left him when the dreams fled.

In the early dawn, when that sad wife crept fearfully to see what change had come to the patient face on the pillow, she found it smiling at her, saw a wasted hand outstretched to her, and heard a feeble voice cry bravely, "Hope!"

What passed in that little room is not to be recorded except in the hearts of those who suffered and endured much for love's sake. Enough for us to know that soon the wan shadow of a man came forth, leaning on the arm that never failed him, to be welcomed and cherished by the children, who never forgot the experiences of that time.

"Hope" was the watchword now; and, while the last logs blazed on the hearth, the last bread and apples covered the table, the new commander, with recovered courage, said to her husband,—

"Leave all to God—and me. He has done his part, now I will do mine."

"But we have no money, dear."

"Yes, we have. I sold all we could spare, and have enough to take us away from this snow-bank."

"Where can we go?"

"I have engaged four rooms at our good neighbor, Lovejoy's. There we can live cheaply till spring. Then for new plans and a home of our own, please God."

"But, Hope, your little store won't last long, and we have no friends."

"I can sew and you can chop wood. Lovejoy offers you the same pay as he gives his other men; my old friend, Mrs. Truman, will send me all the work I want; and my blessed brother stands by us to the end. Cheer up, dear heart, for while there is work and love in the world we shall not suffer."

"And while I have my good angel Hope, I shall not despair, even if I wait another thirty years before I step beyond the circle of the sacred little world in which I still have a place to fill."

So one bleak December day, with their few possessions piled on an ox-sled, the rosy children perched atop, and the parents trudging arm in arm behind, the exiles left their Eden and faced the world again.

"Ah me! my happy dream. How much I leave behind that never can be mine again," said Abel, looking back at the lost Paradise, lying white and chill in its shroud of snow.

"Yes, dear, but how much we bring away," answered brave-hearted Hope, glancing from husband to children.

"Poor Fruitlands! The name was as great a failure as the rest!" continued Abel, with a sigh, as a frostbitten apple fell from a leafless bough at his feet.

But the sigh changed to a smile as his wife added, in a half-tender, half-satirical tone,—

"Don't you think Apple Slump would be a better name for it, dear?"

"Transcendentalism"

Samuel Johnson*

"Nothing is easier," said Voltaire, "than for people to read and converse to no purpose. One of the ancients wrote a book to prove that every word was an ambiguity." The epigram of a French diplomat, "Words were invented to conceal meaning," passed into a proverb. This unbelief in the virtue of human speech may have proceeded from deeper unbelief in the virtue of mankind. Our age has a happier view of social relations, and pursues mutual comprehension with boundless faith in the tongue and pen. Yet its speculative and religious terminology does not yield even an alphabet of conversation. Our formulas, piled in the pride of classification, prove but bricks of the ancient Babel after all, and tumble back, ineffectual, upon the heads of the builders. Never was colloquial humanity farther from Plato's all-important preliminary of clear definitions. There is no virtue in "star-eyed science" to dispel these enduring aspects of the truth the idealist sings:—

> "We are spirits clad in veils;
> Heart by heart was never seen:
> All our deep communing fails
> To remove the shadowy screen."

Yet must we have communion on the best terms possible; and so there is deeper interest than ever in bringing speech to judgment, and words to legitimate meanings. We shall hardly prosper in this work till we reform the habit of defining terms of large historical significance by current meanings or associations, ignoring their essential purport in the philosophy of mind. Thus recent materialists, in general, treat with contempt such terms as theism, theology, religion, as concerned with an external personal God; although these terms have always represented, at bottom, the effort to find *unity* and *substance*, as well as providence, in the world. The reason given for this rejection—that unless words are used in their current meaning, they will be misunderstood—is

*Reprinted from *Radical Review*, 1 (November 1877), 447–478.

unfortunate; it being obvious that a material part of the current meaning itself is here rejected, and injustice done to great permanent tendencies of human nature. The term "transcendental" is a notable instance of the same kind.

The popular use of this word to signify the incomprehensible and impracticable is natural enough, since philosophers are the fathers of it, and have applied it to matters that do really lie apart from common observation. We cannot wonder that it was given over to Satan by the Church and the World, among the other dark things,—such as dark glens, dark plans, dark skins, heathen blindness, and "the Black Art,"—to be kept at safe distance, with holy horror by the devout, and off-hand contempt by the wise in their own generation. For the old theology could not help being startled at this Shadow, writing doom on its walls; and to cry "fool and mad" was but natural instinct. Assailed by ignorance and blind authority, the term has been even more contemptuously treated by that current form of system-building which repudiates metaphysics in the name of science. On the other hand, there are metaphysicians who object that it means substitution of sentiment for perception, and assumption for induction. There are Hegelians who sacrifice it to a superficial etymology, and say with Castelar in his eloquent essays on Republicanism in Europe, that "in ancient thought the absolute is transcendental, in Hegel it is inherent:" a distinction for which the proper meaning of the word in question affords no authority. Led in the same way, perhaps, by an etymological inference, not a few would consign "Transcendentalism" to the past as a form of that very Supernaturalism against which it has claimed to be the one thorough and effective protest. Strange, indeed, if a philosophy whose central idea is the immanence of the infinite should mean to affirm that an outside God is working on the world, whether by miracles or in human ways! Transcendentalism is a far stronger reaction against the old theology than scientific induction can be without it; yet there is danger that, in the very impetus of their reaction, scientists shall come to confound that indispensable ally with the foe they would destroy. This will naturally happen in proportion as they accept the explanation of thought, laid down in recent physical text books, as "an impression on the brain derived from the external world through the medium of the senses;" since while the transcendentalist and the supernaturalist are at utter variance on points of utmost moment, this explanation is equally rejected by both. The absorbing question of the hour has here disregarded organic and permanent bearings, and makes one incidental analogy the test of affinity and the measure of worth. A similar illusion confounds the philosophical idea of intuition with the theological idea of inspiration, because both deny the exclusive claim of "experience" to be the source of knowledge, and because both are supposed to affirm certitude in regard to unsolved and open questions, and an ideal basis for what are "pure results of historical derivation." Their common recognition of relations with the Infinite, though under very different meanings of the word, is thought to imply that they agree in denying the universality of law, and their common demand that the less shall be ascribed to a greater than itself, rather than the greater to a less, to indicate that they are alike in tracing the world to supernatural will. Such confusion of ideas increases with the lapse of time during which study has taken an almost exclusively physical direction, until the philosophy which emphasizes principles has come to pass for an ambitious pretence of wisdom beyond what is known as well as what is "written;" so that even the effort to show that it is simply common sense and universal method provokes a new form of contempt, as if much bluster had been made in proclaiming what, after all, is confessed to be but a form of commonplace. The result of all this is an impression that transcendentalism was the opinion of a small and eccentric school, and has already given place to "the scientific method"—the positive gospel of this and all coming time.

As one by whom this philosophy was accepted, not as the opinion of a few thinkers, but as the independent *rationale of human thought,* and who has found its main postulates essentially undisturbed by full acceptance of the results of science, I propose to present that view of its meaning which its history appears to me to warrant, and to state some of its vital relations to the sanity and progress of mind.

That the name "Transcendentalism" was given, a century ago, to a method in philosophy opposed to the theory of Locke—that all knowledge comes from the senses—is more widely known than the fact that what this method affirmed and involved is of profound import for all generations. It emphasized Mind as formative force behind all definable contents or acts of consciousness,—as that which makes it possible to speak of any thing as *known.* It recognized, as primal condition of knowing, the transmutation of sense-impressions by original laws of mind, whose constructive power is not to be explained or measured by the data of sensation: just as they use the eye and ear to tranform unknown spatial motions into the obviously human conceptions which we call color and sound. All this the Lockian system overlooked; a very serious omission, as regards both science and common sense.

Locke was probably somewhat misconstrued. He meant that sense-impressions come first in our conscious experience; his concern being with the apparent process, rather than with the real origin of our knowledge. He was aiming, not only to reduce to plain good sense the medieval metaphysics of his time, but also to combat an enthusiasm of the self-deifying sort, resulting from the spiritual ferment of the

English Revolution. He had seen how easily fanatical ecstasies were glorified as visions and revelation, and how perilous they were to the political and religious liberty which he was building into positive institutions. His famous comparison of the mind to a sheet of blank paper was, I suppose, a vigorous way of repudiating these imaginary inspirations and emphasizing the public and common elements of experience, rather than the startling assertion it would seem to be, that the substance by and through which we think and know is of itself sheer passivity and emptiness. He rejected "innate ideas," considered as distinct conceptions, supernaturally conveyed into the mind, and there preëxisting, ready for use, independent of education and even of growth. His crusade against this antecedence of ready-made ideas as a mass of concrete details prior to experience seems to have drawn away his attention from other and better modes of conceiving the originality and primacy of mind. He posits "experience" as the only source of knowledge; forgetting to inquire how the "blank paper," which could not respond to innate impressions, should be in any degree more competent to report results of "experience" without constructive energies of its own. To pretend that it could do so would have been simply to flee from supernaturalism in one form to fall into it in another. Here is the unconscious incoherence in Locke's account of the matter, as in that of Stuart Mill, the more recent apostle of "experience." Yet Locke's own phraseology shows that his good sense was not unaware of facts wholly incompatible with the "blank paper" theory; as when he says (Book II, chap. i, § 4) that the "operations of the soul (in reflection) do furnish the understanding with another set of ideas which could not be had from things without, we observing them in ourselves."

Every thing depends, if we would fairly interpret a thinker, on recognizing the emphasis given to certain elements of his thought by his special aim, and reading between the lines other elements, which he evidently takes for granted, as not needing statement at all. Locke, though a clear-headed man and liberal politician, was not a metaphysical thinker. The profound meaning involved in the fact that such constant ideas as Substance, Personality, Law, Cause, "could not be had from things without," never interested his practical and concrete mind, which thought it quite sufficient to mass such facts under the vague term "experience," and let them go at that. In this respect, his example is largely followed in days when science, building upon "experience," is to a very great extent absorbed in collecting innumerable physical details. Yet I doubt if Locke would have relished being made the father of the "Sensational School," and put into the limbo of for ever decanting sense-impressions into mental bottles to prove that physical phenomena are the sole authors and finishers of man. Had he inquired into the distinctive origin and significance of what he called "reflection," he might have reached the starting point of Transcendentalism. He was a keen observer of palpable processes; and this habit is very apt to hide those conditions in mental faculty which the processes do not exhibit, but imply; until, as in much modern method which passes for scientific, the mere succession of phenomena is substituted for the substance in which they inhere. Neither the self-consciousness of mind as such, nor the forces that lie behind conscious understanding, attracted Locke's utilitarian temperament. He was, so far, the ancestor of that school of evolutionists which holds itself at war with Transcendentalism. But he could not have anticipated the positive denial of such transcendental conditions in the next century by his enthusiastic disciples, Helvetius, Condillac, and others, who were preparing the French mind to throw aside, in sheer reaction, not only the continuity of human evolution through the past, but that constant, undemonstrable element that makes the prime condition of present certitude.

What we conceive these schools to have misprized is the living substance and function of Mind itself. Conscious of its own energy; productive of its own processes; active even in receiving; giving its own construction to its incomes from the unknown through sense; thus involved in those very contents of time and space which, as historical antecedents, *appear* to create it,—mind is obviously the exponent of forces more spontaneous and original than any special product of its own experience. Behind all these products must be that substance in and through which they are produced. Or are we, as Taine will have it, mere trains of sensation in the void; successions of thoughts without a thinker; incessant flowing, yet no living stream; a process where what proceeds may be neglected or is naught? Can the knower be mere resultant of his own knowledge, call it "experience" or what you will? How should there be any knowing of things at all, except there be first one competent to know, whose nature is father and fount of the act of cognition? When you assert that all is from experience, have you forgotten the experiencer himself? Or, if you reply that he is of course taken for granted, then pray do not immediately consign him over among his products, but consider what your concession involves. Is he not more than all his past processes, and primal condition of all that are to come? If personality be not real, science is at war with human consciousness. If it be real, it involves powers which constantly condition experience and determine its forms and results. Nor can it be regarded as a mere product or transfer of the past experiences of the race, since the transmutation of one conscious personal identity into another is inconceivable; and no transfer of experiences could ever produce an experiencer. To say that this is idealism may remand the statement to the dictionary, but does not refute it.

We affirm, however, that it is actualism also. Processes of phenomena come to us as forms of knowledge; and idea, or conception, inevitably determines form. All we can know is ideas,—yet not as unrealities; 'tis the recognition of them as reporting objective truth that makes them, for us, knowledge. Nor can knowledge ever be any thing else than this. And although in an idea there are two things,—the subject who thinks and the object thought,—the two are one in that common substance of mind which makes them what they are; and this not in the case of secondary qualities only, such as color and sound, which do obviously depend on the mental relations of the organism, but equally for all qualities and even substances, *since these can address us only in the language of mind.* As Goethe says, "to ascribe everything to experience is to forget the half of experience." In other words, no philosophy of human knowledge can be genuine which leaves out man himself, or the unknown, unfathomed continent of active mind of which he is a living portion. Nor can the results of such omission be other than subversive.

> "Were not the eye itself a sun, no sun for it
>   could ever shine:
> By nothing noble could the heart be won,
>   were not the heart divine."

Modern materialism makes much of the supposed distinction between "creating every thing out of the subject (*i.e.,* the thinking mind)" and "letting things speak for themselves."[1] But how are things to speak at all to us, except through the nature of mind? No bridge to reality is possible that does not start from this. And the bridge being granted, why should it carry over our cognitions of sensible particulars, and yet refuse passage to universal conceptions and principles of order, which are the direct and necessary forms of mental action? Does the idea of cause, for instance, depend on mind, individual or general, in any sense which should destroy its objective value, because proceeding from us and not from Nature? By the same logic, the things to which we attach it are under equal uncertainty, since they are knowable only in their relations with our minds; and their succession, which the Lockian would put in place of Cause, is also a form of human conception applied to things. And so we land in a phantom world, out of which the materialist himself who leads us there must be the first to take the back-track. We may add that the doctrine that things can "speak to us for themselves" without regard to mental conditions is not only the metaphysical basis of such dogmas as transubstantiation, but a practical opening for intellectual and spiritual despotism in every form.

But these primal conditions of knowledge are not readily observed.

Inevitably assumed in all mental processes, they are not to be demonstrated; for the very act of demonstration is, itself, as it were, let down from these heavens, and by invisible threads. They are not made palpable, like numbers, sensations, observations, by strict limits of their own. They are as subtle and indefinable as they are universal. That direct conjunction of mind with the real universe by which knowledge is made possible is in fact a natural relation to the infinite, since the universe *is* infinite: and thus there is an unsounded element, a mystic margin, implied in all our thinking,—a something beyond warrant from experience, beyond explanation from induction or observation, whereby our inferences from these data cover indefinitely larger ground than the data themselves. And this inevitable law of mind is the constant guarantee that prompts to progress as endless resource: that sense of moving more or less freely, in open space, which belongs to the activity of reason. On this silent and boundless atmosphere, inviolable, imperturbable, not to be demonstrated or analyzed or defined, but known in our inward necessity of transcending experience; on this universal element, where no brazen firmament shuts down on us, and this unseen, indubitable space, symbolized in the cosmic deep around whose stars but measure an ether traversable by the light of mind; on our senses,—all human aspiration depends, and the more open we are to the sense of it, the larger and more sublime the world of possibility appears. Here float all wings of promise and belief. Its voice haunts us with a rune that was never wholly silent since man began to know: Thou art more than thy limits in any premises, past or present, in any logic of the eye and ear. Thou are not made of senses and experiences: they are of thee, and hint that larger life of Mind which thou sharest as including, transforming, overflowing them,—the greater that must always explain the less.

Locke's system was, with all its merits, a Book of the Understanding. It skipped all mental data which could not be readily utilized and defined, or left them in a state of helpless vagueness.[2] It disparaged whatever is involved in our relations with the Infinite, and could have no philosophy of beauty and sublimity, which depend on these; none of enthusiasm, loyalty, love, and awe. It not only subordinated the universal to the particular, but made the idea of the Infinite the mere product of limited sensuous conditions, at the same time slurring it as incomprehensible.[3] A practical effect of this method appeared in the immense influence of English thought on the French mind of the next century. Whatever phraseology of universal ideas attended it, the social dissolution of France at the close of this epoch showed the practical absence of any philosophy based on the control of egotism by reverent culture of the moral ideal.

Its speculative effect led the same way. All knowledge being granted as coming from the senses, what do you know of these at all except through your consciousness? This was Berkeley's inference of the "non-existence of matter." And then comes Hume's trenchant question: "How do we, whose sense-testimony is so plainly uncertain, know any better that consciousness tells us truth?" What answer could be made to that question by those whose sole test of truth was in sensations, and to whom inherent laws of mind, necessary conditions of all experience and all language, and essential relations of subject to object in all thought, were too impalpable to be studied at all? Here opens a gulf of scepticism as to the very power of seeing truth, which leaves man without root in realities; and it inevitably resulted in that failure of earnestness in ethics, philosophy, and faith, which from this and other causes, characterized literature and life in the latter half of the eighteenth century. That our theories of mind lie very close to the springs of character and conduct is none the less certain in the long run because it would be unjust to infer any special virtues or vices in an individual from his philosophical statements or religious creed. And it is the way in which, consciously or unconsciously, we treat the demand for assurance of that perception of substantial truth which is undemonstrable,— save as being the indispensable condition of earnest thought,—that enables us to contribute to the dignity and progress of mankind. Our philosophy, being the way in which we look at the world, is what we really live by, and goes back of our political or religious relations.

But a philosophic method had commenced which recognized these higher demands; not new in substance, of course, but a fresh inspiration of faith and science to meet them. From Descartes and Spinoza it descended through Leibnitz and Kant, and their later interpreters, Cousin and Jouffroy. It was developed in various forms by Schelling, Hegel, and the higher German metaphysics, and formed an essential part of the English and Scotch philosophies of Cudworth, Reid, and Hamilton, of the idealism of Coleridge and the moral intensity of Carlyle. Its past and present representatives are of no special race, and show, by their great diversity in matters of detail, the endless adaptability of their common method and the wealth of its resources. This method was the psychological, as the other was the "sensational," or experimental. It began at the nearest point; exploring that productive force of mind which constructs the world out of its own laws; itself implied in all terms, processes, explanations, verifications, inductions, as their common substance, which the physicist must presuppose, even when he attempts to find its beginning among the plasmata and cells if plasma and cell themselves are to have any meaning for him; and which thus constructs, so far as they can be known to him, the very germs which he asserts to be its creator. The transcendental method found its first objective point in the universal substance of mind,[4]—that invisible eye and ear implied in all origins conceivable by man; without which preadamitic light and present sounds and colors are alike meaningless and unreal. "Nothing in the mind which was not first in the senses," was the Lockian statement. "Except mind itself," replied Leibnitz.

Analysis of thought as essential and primal leads to the recognition of certain ground-forms of thought as universal, and therefore as I know only by transcending the observation of facts; since no number of observations, or "sensible particulars," could of themselves ever prove a universal principle, but require supplementing by larger forces of mind. Such ideas as Unity, Universe, Law, Cause, Duty, Substance (God), Permanence (Immortality), are thus affirmed to be *intuitively*, or directly, perceived because, while not to be accounted for by any observed and calculated data, they are yet fundamental, and must be referred to organic relations of the mind with truth. And for this sense the term *intuition*, if freed from loose definition, seems to be a very proper one.

Of course the transcendentalist cannot mean by it that at all times and by all persons the truths now specified are seen in the same objective form, nor even that they are always *consciously* recognized in any form. He means that, being involved in the movement of intelligence, they indicate realities, whether well or ill conceived, and are apprehended in proportion as man becomes aware of his own mental processes. They who deny that they perceive these ideas intuitively, mean the more or less questionable forms of them which at the moment prevail. Transcendentalism does not assert that these last are intuitions. It means the enduring substance, not the transient form. What we are to regard as involved in mental movement must surely be, not the special modifications dependent on individual or social opinion, but the universal root-ideas to which all these different branches point. The neglect of this distinction between the necessary conformities of mind and the special inferences that have been built upon them has caused much confused discussion on the subject of intuition.

By intuition of God we do not mean a theological dogma or a devout sentiment; we do not mean belief in "*a* God," Christian or other; but that presumption of the infinite as involved in our perception of the finite, of the whole as implied by the part, of substance behind all phenomena, and of thought as of one nature with its object, which the laws of mind require, and which can be detected, in conscious or unconscious forms, through all epochs and stages of religious belief. The intuition of law does not depend on the opinion that this or that order of events, because oft repeated, must be taken to represent a rule of Nature or mind: it consists in that *sense of invariability*, which no amount of such repetitions can explain, since they only affirm uniformity so far as themselves are concerned. Nor is any particular succession of related events to be taken as measure or test of the intuition of cause; which concerns the universal idea of causality, inexplicable by any amount of successions, and meaning production, not succession at all. Nor is every affirmation of special duties to be laid to the account of intuition; which takes cognizance simply of duty itself, of that which makes duties possible,—the meaning of Ought.

An intuitive perception, however certain, may be of slow growth, though what it recognizes is in fact a necessary part of mental action. In like manner, products of imperfect experience and self-study often claim that certitude of intuition, as such, which they do not really represent. We do not rest the intuition that the world must be known to us through universal principles on the truth of Plato's archetypal ideas as real essences in the hands of a "World-framer," nor on the truth of modern classification by genera and species, which Agassiz called "the thoughts of God." Yet these were forms, however imperfect, in which that intuition was folded. The uncertainty of many common beliefs about immortality has led many to deny that there is such a thing as intuition of immortality. It is not easy to see how we can have intuitive certainty of the continuance of our present form of conscious-ness in a future life; still less, of what awaits it in a future life. But it is certain that knowledge involves not only a sense of union with the nature of that which we know, but a real participation of the knowing faculty therein. When, therefore, I have learned to conceive truths, principles, ideas, or aims, which transcend life-times and own no physical limits to their endurance, the aforesaid law of mind associates me with their immortal nature. And this is the indubitable perception, or intuition, of permanent mind, which no experience of impermanence can nullify and no Nirvana excludes. But this is plainly incompetent to specific knowledge of form or detail. And so we attach less importance to definite conceptions or images of a future life, the stronger our sense of the permanence of ideas, the unities of love, and the continuities of growth. Imagination, too, the open sense of our highest relations, has the same secret of transcending time. The beautiful comes to the poet at once as reminiscence and prophecy, and, lifted in the heavens, he sings:

"I look on the Caucasus, and it seems to me as if it were not the first time that I am here: it seems as if my cradle had been rocked by the torrents below me, and that these winds have lulled me to sleep; as if I had wandered over these mountains in my childhood, and that at that time I was as old as the world of God."

But such foundations as these are not intellectual merely: here is the only firm ground for universal convictions. The grand words, "I ought," refuse to be explained by dissolving the notion of right into individual calculation of consequences, or by expounding the sense of duty as the cumulative product of observed relations of succession. Can you measure by a finite quantity the amount of allegiance involved in that sense? Is not its claim universal and absolute? What would become of it, if it possessed no authority beyond the uncertain foresight of differing minds as to results, a soothsayer whose worth depended on the truth of his special predictions? A criterion in special duties cannot be the basis of the great fact of duty, nor the origin of an absolute and universal allegiance. How explain as a "greatest happiness principle," or an inherited product of observed consequences, that sovereign and eternal law of mind whose imperial edict lifts all calculations and measures into functions of an infinite meaning? And how vain to accredit or ascribe to revelation, institution, or redemption, this necessary allegiance to the law of our own being, which is liberty and loyalty in one! Yet the language of even liberal Christian sects would seem to warrant the inference that it was imported into the human soul by the influence or example of Jesus!

"Two things," said Kant, "command my veneration: the starry universe around me, the law of duty within." Yet neither the infinity of the one nor the authority of the other can be demonstrated by any thing but the fact of sight. They are self-affirmations of mind and for mind. Kant demanded that ethics should not rest primarily on experimental grounds, but on the principle of morality, which is not to be limited or explained by any number of exclusive facts, but stands upon an inherent right to the implicit confidence of men. "Every thing, has either price or dignity. What can be represented by an equivalent has price; what is above all price has dignity."

What Kant did for speculative ethics, Lessing did for theological freedom. It was his working out from this premise of the transcendence of ideal mind, that made Lessing, more truly than any other man, father of our modern liberty to doubt. "Give me, O God, not truth outright, but the joy of striving for truth, even though I never reach that pure light which is thine alone." No grander word was ever uttered. All the free thought of our time is stirring in it. More than any attainment is it to be in earnest to attain: more than any number of special truths is the love of earning truth, the life-task freely taken. Of work and play this is the transcendental ground. For of such rights of mind what demonstration is possible? What induction proves them? 'Tis the open eye itself shining with the very light it sees. Liberty to doubt! If we are products of our sensations, what right or power should we have to doubt? But, if we can doubt all doctrines, so long as we love the earning of truth, what shall explain this but participation in the infinitude of truth? Once more: Spinoza, following this track of transcendent thought to its universal form; assuming, in the serene assurance with which he moves in the pure idea of God, that the perception and participation of the infinite is real, and that philosophy is thus identical with religion; resolving all being into One Substance on the sole authority of thought,— affirms it as man's real life to know, to obey, to love, and, so far, to become, God.

These three leaders of modern thought indicate in their various ways the upward drift of the transcendental method. How indeed should the study of mind in its inherent productive force fail to open those paths of thought which New England transcendentalists used to call man's "inlets to the infinite"? Of such intuition the contents, though not to be proved, are none the less truly knowledge; because they are as- sumed in all processes of verification, and because the infinite is as real as the finite and as really known,—being simply that spatial freedom and undefined possibility which are as essential to our minds as cosmic space to stars.

Our method of intellectual inquiry involves, therefore, the highest interest of ethics, philosophy, and faith. In the unity of these three forces centres the movement of our time. Everywhere it insists on mak- ing this unity real, not only as direct vision of the laws of the world, but as ideal of personal character. This, in short, is its Religion. Thus its "Way to the Blessed Life" is conceived by Fichte as free obedience to immutable laws, discerned by the individual to be at once his own in- most substance and the order of the worlds, with which he becomes at one by escape from selfish individualism into the personal ideal. A system wrongly called egoism; the *ego* being only the starting point of consciousness in our personal sense of the true and the holy, opening the way to universal truths and duties. The intellectual method of our time is rooted in such intuition of the identity of mind with the sub- stance of that world which it perceives. The same principle has given metaphysics its basis for knowledge in the identity of subject and object, and culture its belief that every aspiration is the human side of a divine necessity. It has taught ethics that self-respect is one with the sovereignty of law. It has revealed to sympathy the solidarity of the race, which simply means that humanity without and heart within have one substance and aim. And so it has inspired, in Europe and America, those universalities which we now express by the words People, Labor, Liberty: ideas, in place of traditional conventionalities and vested fictions, as the motive powers of society: a divinity within the life of man, not outside it.

So with our spiritual philosophy. That the soul can give true report of the Universe, as of that which is of the same nature and purport with its own faculties, enters in various forms into all that religious thought which we call "radical." For this word, *root-thought*, there is no other proper meaning than the recognition that human faculty is related to truth, not by secondary adaptation, or artificial conjunction, but by a natural unity. This participation in the substance of what we know abolishes those imagined clefts between God, Nature, and Man, which Christian theology has helplessly tried to bridge over by its equally imaginary mechanism of miracle and incarnation. And, finally, to this self-recognition of the mind in its object is due the fearlessness that now animates science and scatters superstition with a self-confidence that no mere induction can explain. Thus, in Tyndall's fine statement, mind is evolved, not out of mere inorganic matter, but from the universe as a whole. This whole, however, is infinite, and involves inscrutable Substance, which, as recognizable only by mind, is therefore of one nature therewith. The lowest physical beginnings are thus, in virtue of the cosmic force by which they exist, actual mentalities, or mental germs. The crude definition of evolution as production of the highest by inherent force of the lowest, is here supplanted by one which recognizes material parentage as itself involving, even in its lowest stages, the entire cosmic *consensus*, of whose unknown force mind is the highest known exponent. Even when apparent as final fruit of evolution, conscious mind is therefore, we conceive, not a new force in the universe, but the substance of the universe itself under the form of individual relations and growth,—an identity which is seen in its capacity, and even necessity, to open out from individualism into universal truth as its natural home.

We must, then, enter our protest against the treatment of this philosophy as the opinion of a small school of thinkers, or as a transient phase of idealism, in due time supplanted by positive science. It purports to be the rationale of human thinking; its method is as organic as induction or association of ideas. Its postulates are involved in these processes, and make them effective. If true once, it is true for ever. Conscious recognition of the laws of mental method is something else than an *ism*. If we call it transcendentalism, we do not forget that it is also realism, as affirming objective realities and grounds of actual life and work. We believe it to be the organic basis of progress; of every step beyond traditional limits; of all ideal faith and purpose. For these, in their refusal to be judged by the dicta of experience, or by the strict definitions of the understanding, are exponents of an infinite relation in the human ideal. The step beyond experience is the common bond of all upward movements, intellectual, moral, spiritual, æsthetic.

This step is involved in the growth of true personality. Once discern that your experience through the senses is not adequate to account for your conception of the world; once mark how you transform such experience by laws of your own mind and of all mind,— and the free creative function of your being is revealed. And so this perception of a force within us which posits itself over against the limits of experience, as its master, is what delivers individual mind from outward authority into free reason. Ask a dozen men to think of an external object, say a tree: they all turn in one direction, and a supposed common sensation disguises their individuality; but ask them to look at the mental process by which they know the tree, and each finds that the primal source of his perception is internal; and the inference follows that its value must depend on his personal dignity and freedom. I do not mean that personal character is merely an intellectual process. But it is impossible that one should, in any living sense, realize that he is not a mere member of a mass, or product of institutions, but a piece of primal fact and original Nature, unless he is guarded and consecrated by a sense of the law by which he is inwardly related to truth. Then begins high moral culture. Then that earnest dealing with necessity, duty, opportunity, which sets the great tasks, and lifts the life through the aim it serves. Knowing her own solitude and self-dependence, the soul finds at once commandment and freedom in the realities that front her. Self-isolation is the first step to self-consecration. "Gentlemen," began Fichte in his opening lecture on philosophy, "give me your closest attention. Let each of you think this book. Now let each think, not the book, but *himself*." Such his first summons to the noble study of what Kant called the "autonomy of the will," none the less real for the laws of necessity with which it has to deal.

It is by force of the transcendental element in human thought that there was never wanting some measure of healthful reaction from drag-weights of the past, of self-recovery from selfish interests of the present. How could the constant operation of a law of the mind which over-flows all data of experience with ideas whose scope they cannot explain, fail to make prophets in every age,—yea, more or less of a prophet in every thoughtful person? This is the resilient force that throws off effete organized product, supplants waste by repair, adds fresh atoms for an unprecedented life: this the unexplained element, the mystic impulsion, in all growth. The transcendental law becomes impulse and aspiration. Stirred by its ceaseless presence, men listen to the native affirmations of Mind: I am knowledge, and the medium of knowledge; I am inspiration as well as tradition; the instant fire, as well as the inherited fuel, of thought; primal as well as resultant; infinite as well as finite. Hence that eternal dissatisfaction of idealists with the superficial doings around them; with the eager feet and self-waste, the paltry propagandism of book, church, sect; their exacting demand on human nature, which makes them, as Emerson said, "strike work, in order to act freely for something worthy to be done." Whoso scoffs at their refusal to do special things that may seem to him imperative, may well consider whether, after all, the best doing is not *being*. Let him not call it unsocial. What society most wants is criticism by the courage to choose what one respects, and to renounce and reprove what this disdains. We reach civility when men recognize that one in earnest to be doing his proper work is more likely to know what this is than ten thousand other persons who would set him upon theirs. The transcendental impulse accounts not for dissatisfied protest only. It is the basis of interpretations of life and duty by ideal standards: of the spiritual imagination, which for ever confutes, by its far-seeing faith, the gloom and irony in man's actual experience.

A constant in history, it makes "the increasing purpose that through the ages runs." In India, transcendentalism took sensualizing tropic fires for its leverage, and there appeared a philosophy that treated the senses as illusion, and an enthusiasm of brotherhood which gathered a third of mankind into its fold. In Persia and Egypt, it transfigured all great natural forms with inner meaning beyond sensuous traditions and rituals, drawn from the vicissitudes and aspirations of the soul. God, Duty, Immortality—affirmations of the infinite in man, through all special errors,—became the substance of "mysteries" and awe-girded disciplines, wherein the noblest minds of antiquity learned divine philosophies and tasks. In Greece, when the word-play of sensational logic was ·destroying certitude in morals and mind, Socrates affirmed personality the measure of all studies, and brought its intuition of the Good, the True, and the Becoming, to silence noisy pretension and confute moral unbelief. Notwithstanding the sophist's measure of all beliefs by individual opinion, what men really needed in Athens was to be disengaged from the crowd, to front their own consciousness of reality. The Socratic *elenchus*, or confuting process, was no mere bit of argumentation, but, as its author himself described it, "spiritual obstetrics," opening to each mind its own productive force. His "*dæmon*," who was wont to warn him, without giving any reason, against doing this or that thing, was manifestly the self-protective law of a personality that knew its own right to shape circumstances and to reject interference with its ideal. Thence came harvests for all ages in Plato's evolution of his text that the Ideal is the Real; that principles, seen directly by the soul that has found its real self, are the substance of the world. Our chief debt to Greece is summed up in this,—that Socrates and Plato saw the world as outgrowth of mind, mind as its own authority, and personal mind as organically related to universal being.

In Judæa, the reaction against materialism was more intensely moral; authoritative protest of prophet, social exodus of Essene, apocalyptic vision, wilderness cry. Yet the free transcendental philosophy may be read as plainly in writings of the "Apocrypha" dating before the time of Jesus, as in Goethe, or Carlyle, or Emerson, or Parker. In John the Baptist came Hebrew summons to the personal ideal, and Jesus went behind Pharisee ritualism, Sadducee scepticism, and Essene asceticism,—

finalities of Hebrew experience,—to the soul that *makes* experience. To the transcendental impulse the ages owe his resort to self-sovereignty, his rejection of the dominant sources of national hope, his enthusiasm of faith in the unseen, his appeal to humanity and to pure ethics against force and formalism, his assertion of infinte relations. That lofty manhood, though swayed by Hebrew conditions, by supernaturalism, by the monarchical principle of Hebrew piety, by its messianic idea and the traditional habit of claiming special divine commission, by that excessive reaction to despair of the present world which was incident to the times,—was yet so offensive to Jewish experience that martyrdom was the cost of it. But the impulse of humanity that presses beyond experience is greater than any of its own human products, and so it passed the limitations of Jesus to fresh material in other races and times. The democratic movement of that age; the grand Stoic and Epicurean forms of self-respect and faith in Nature; the coalescence of beliefs to higher unities,—did not lose their power of transfusing ages of Christian ecclesiasticism with a redeeming instinct of universality.

Christianity inherited the monarchical idea of a God separate from Man, and a contempt for natural law and human faculty which crippled its faith in the spiritual and moral ideal. It became more and more a materialism of miracle, Bible, Church. Even its essay to realize immanent Deity yielded a more or less exclusive mediatorial God-man; and it treated personality as the mere consequence of one prescriptive historical force, just as philosophical materialism treats it as mere product of sensations. What successions of oppressive creeds and barbarous wars concerning the nature of Christ; what lasting reigns of terror and superstition; what persistent bigotries restrained, not by creed, but only by the political balance of power; what hostility to the steps of science, in crude, perverted forms of ideal desire,—have given way to the patient pressure of an organic necessity behind them all, the transcendental sense of invariable law! Against what reluctant traditions of experience it urges its way! In the Reformation it seemed to thrust its keen edge through the old materialism to the free light. "What makes man's world is not without him, but within: not works then, but faith, not doing, but being, saves." Christianity was broken into individualities. But they proved chips of the papal block. Protestantism swelled with the old leaven of ecclesiasticism. Miracle, Bible, Church, Sabbath, external God, and official Atonement survived in a supernaturalism of which spiritual ideals were regarded as the secretion, just as materialism holds mind to be a function of the bodily organs.

Puritanism was a further protest than Protestantism against institutional experience. It was full of crudities; a pungent mixture of noble insights with gross superstitions, of transcendental day with traditional night; an uncouth Titan, precursor of an intelligence and order hitherto unknown. Superstition so ran in the grain of it that after two centuries and a half of American air and space, its medieval spirit brought ministers together to stop access of the people to free reading on Sunday, "because God has given his Bible for that day, and religion will perish without morality." The real transcendentalists of the seventeenth century were the Mayflower Pilgrims; for America, the Rock of Ages was Plymouth Rock. The moral earnestness of the Pilgrims was a step in conscience, precisely like Kant's in philosophy when he showed the sensationalists the mind-element they had left out of their analysis, and led the way through Atlantic deeps of consciousness which they had not dared explore. Did experience create either of these great unaided ventures upon unknown seas? The Plymouth Pilgrim outstepped the intolerance of the Puritan creed. He followed his undemonstrated vision of a free private judgment out of church, home, and civilization itself. But he carried civilization with him in that step of intuition; he took up the wintry leagues of the Atlantic, and made them shining steps to the People's Throne. Well might the ideality that refused to be the product of traditions transfigure for ever that desert continent and howling sea for which it exchanged them. These spaces were there to show that man makes of his experiences *more than experience* by the lift of his spiritual force. Mark close to this group the imperial man of that day, who refused to persecute for belief in any form, and denounced usurpation in the slayers of a tyrant. "The Lord deliver us from Sir Harry Vane," cried Cromwell, covering his face with his hands, when the clear eyes that never quailed before plot or power searched his own,—eyes of a great conscience conversant with the infinite laws and serenity awaiting martyrdom, that could transfigure with trust the total eclipse of patriot harvests and hopes. Hear that frightened bray of trumpets trying to drown what such a man might dare to say on the scaffold,—a fine expedient, on the theory that mind is the product of things! With what divine irony the transcendental genius of modern liberty meets this pretence of mass-power to abolish men because it is so very easy to abolish the visible shapes of men,—Algernon Sidney and Harry Vane at the beginning of one epoch, John Brown at the threshold of another, dying on scaffolds as fanatics, to ascend as ideal symbols of power! The charter of the Republic is itself an assumption that undemonstrated ideas are masters of the social elements. For ideas were not demonstrated, are not demonstrable. No data of observations can express their universal meaning. The data are their negations; not their cause; and suggest them, as the finite suggests the infinite, by contrast and insufficiency. What else can we say of ideas than they are the wondrous intimacies of the human soul with the infinite and eternal, its contacts with universal forces, its prophetic ventures and master steps beyond any past? Yet Stuart Mill fancied that transcendentalism stands in the way of progress.

Is there offence to science in our dealing with ideas, because ideas are inscrutable to the understanding? Let such science explain any one thing in Nature or man, with which itself claims to deal, and we will lay to heart these complaints against the ideal.

Justice, Humanity, Universal Rights and Duties, on which progress moves, are transcendental. The idea of a unity of races and of religions; the idea of a true State, combining personal with public freedom; the idea of the Abolitionist that went behind parties and fundamental laws, and put a soul into a dead republic; the idea of equal opportunities for race and sex,—are all transcendental. So is philosophy, as a science of independent principles, based on the necessities of thought. What series of actual facts is represented by the philosophy of history, which assumes to judge the steps of the past and interprets them to high uses of which they had no presentiment? Art is transcendental,—realm of refuge from the woes and imperfections of the actual: Art, the infinite hearing of a deaf Beethoven, the celestial vision of a blind Milton, a Michael Angelo's cry for liberty from the stones of the quarry in an age when the tongues of men were forced to be dumb. Morality is transcendental,—turning fate to freedom and limits to liberties by choosing to accept and abide them. Transcendental, too, is a philosophy of life which can offset the limits of the understanding by such entire trust in whatever shall prove to be spiritual law and natural destiny as needs no guarantee from details, and exacts no promises from the wise sovereignty of our own nature. This, which is as truly reason as it is faith, I find to be the best form of religion. "Take philosophy out of life," says Maximus Tyrius, "and you lose the power to pray;" which is certainly true, if there is no real prayer but a free aspiration based on the assumption of ideal good. How indispensable is this wide mystic opening and margin for all thought appears in the life of that chief opponent of intuition in our time, John Stuart Mill. Absorbed from his childhood in habits of logical analysis and utilitarian calculation, which excluded the sense of infinity, he naturally enough fell at last into the dismal conviction that all aims, being logically exhaustible, were therefore worthless, and was saved from despair only by betaking himself, under logical protest, to the transcendental imagination of Wordsworth and the prophetic moral sentiment of Carlyle. Nor was this all. Even against himself, he proves to have been a prince of idealists, not only in his socialist enthusiasm and his zeal for an intellectual liberty never yet achieved, but in his estimates of two persons with whom he was in closest intimacy,—his father and his wife. So the materialism of Harriet Martineau, thorough as it seems, did not prevent her from bearing witness at the awe of infinity sanctified her study and her dream.[5]

And all these things are transcendental for the same reason that the doctine of intuition as held by any school in old or new time is transcendental; namely, as recognition of the inevitable step beyond experience or observation by which man lives and grows. According to the intensity of this recognition the law may work in one as conscious philosophical method, in another as enthusiasm for progress, beauty, or good. The basis is always the same,—an organic element of mind, which may be perverted, neglected, ignored, but which holds in some form while sanity endures. It is assumed in every process of induction, and makes the particular premise justify a general conclusion. It is involved in all deductive reasoning, and makes the fact deduced a mere fresh item under an assumed law that gives it all its value. It is the necessity of the materialist himself, who forsakes his principle of sense-derivation as soon as he reaches the crucial point of his theory of Nature. Thus Lucretius, the representative materialist of the ancient world, explains the order of the universe as one among innumerable arrangements possible to atoms moving without intelligence,—an idea for which there is no more authority in the senses than for any conception ever forced on them by the mind of man. Even Lange, with all his hatred of Platonic Realism and his strong denial of any source of knowledge but the senses, actually allows that "the tendency to the supersensuous helped to open the laws of the world on the path of abstractions," and that "the ideal element stands in closest connection with inventions and discoveries."[6]

If, then, every one is a transcendentalist, whether he knows it or not, what, it will be asked, is the practical worth of the discussion? The same, we reply, which belongs to every question of truth or error. Delusion is not more common than it is harmful. Yet it always consists in mistaking or denying the very laws which are all the while shaping us by their mercies and holding us to their penalties. Papist and radical alike reach their beliefs through acts of choice dependent on their respective mental states: yet ignorance of this inevitable necessity is none the less truly the ground of the vast difference between belief in Freedom and belief in Outward Authority, and of the momentous consequences that result from it. Even if the transcendental method were accepted of all men as the true one, yet, as we have seen, the point of moment is the *emphasis* laid on it, the earnestness and ardor of the acceptance, the force of purpose with which it is applied to life. Its value is in determining our philosophy of culture, as well as in reporting a necessary law of mind.

What, finally, is its relation to science? The idea of law universal and invariable is purely transcendental. No number of experiences could have told us what must of necessity be; no piling of instances could ever have proved that, always and everywhere, like causes must bring like effects. It is a step beyond phenomena, beyond authority from experience; a step of the same significance for philosophy, if not of the same courage, as that of the Plymouth Pilgrim; but taken in the private mind, in the quiet of natural growth; unconsciously, long before it is apprehended. That such steps are but results of the inherited experience of mankind, who have always employed these processes, is therefore untenable, since the transcending of sensation is in every instance a personal act, and implies that the power of mind to perform it is as instant and fresh in the latest man as in the first. What a moment of joy and light, remembered for ever, is that when first the idea of universal law breaks on the consciousness of a youth, and he marks it as the imperishable relation of his mind to knowledge! Well may it move him. With that perception culture begins. It opens the whole past, and the whole future; it participates in the infinite; it revolutionizes belief; it recognizes what must condition and shape all experience. On this intuition the sciences rest; by this they live, and move, and have their being; and every step they take, now in this day of their triumph, this glad tread of man goes to the centre of the world, has a transcendental sanction. Clearer and fuller comes the sense of its meaning through their evolution: till it emancipates religion from exceptional and external masters; substitutes social science for supernaturalism as practical redeemer of man; incessantly reforms tradition and recasts institutions; changes rights of private judgment into universal duties, lifts the spiritual ideal beyond forms and names; and will counteract thing-service in physics, politics, and trade by its reach after the ideal and infinite, after undemonstrated truth and good. This is the undertow that bears all surface-currents along its own masterful way. I fear no scheme of evangelicalism to give over the State to a Church of Miracle in an age so possessed by the vision of universal law. Nor do I fear that scientific criticism will be stayed by all that the arsenals of superstition can bring to bear against Tyndall's prayer gauge or Darwin's evolution. Science can be harmed only by denying its own constant dependence on an unseen ideal principle, authenticated by intuition alone.

A war upon the transcendental method, then, would simply divorce science from that sense of the unlimited and universal which is its own motive force. Science seeks to define, to analyze, to make comprehensible, to show the order and relations of phenomena, to unfold the chain of evolution from lowest matter to highest mind. But, if it finds in these limits and this ascent from the physical the whole truth of derivation, it must either reject such conceptions as God, Duty, Immortality, or else it must so explain and interpret them as to exclude the *infinite* meaning. The greatest things can only be proved outcomes of the least by emptying them of their greatness. An effect cannot be greater than its cause. God, defined as result of evolution from things, is not Infinite Mind, nor can the substance of the cosmos be the result of its phenomena. Duty cannot be a mere generalization of certain observed successions in human experience, and at the same time mean unconditional allegiance to Right. And how can a consciousness of indissoluble relations with being, which, as the real sense of Immortality, underlies all crude notions of a future life, be justified by tests which derive mind wholly from things, or allow for true only what can be strictly defined and historically explained? To deny the intuitive element is, in consistency, to drop all grounds for these conceptions. But more. To carry out the denial is to abolish science itself. It cuts away the idea of law, which is transcendental; it sweeps off all recognized bases of physical order,—atom, ether, vibration, undulation, correlation of forces, unities of evolution,—which are all ideal, and, however reconcilable with observation, were never outwardly seen, nor heard, nor comprehended, and never can be; and therefore, as assumed explanation of the universe, imply powers of intuitive perception, real insight of the imagination. And, although these theoretic forces must be verified by observation, there is no verification needed nor possible for that necessity in the human mind for universal conceptions and transcendent explanations from which they all proceed.

Nor is this philosophy inconsistent with the ascent of evolution from lowest to highest conditions, since every step in this ascent involves concurrence of the whole, and, in some form or other, relations with its Infinite Substance. To hold fast this reality of substance is indispensable to science. Its laborers must not be so absorbed in watching processes as to ignore that enduring fact which the process implies, and in which it inheres. Now, whether mind be regarded as merely the last link in a chain of physical transformations, or resolved into a compound of sensations alone, in either case its substance disappears; it is flow of transmutation and process, involving nothing to be transmuted or to proceed. In such definitions as that of Comte,—that "mind is cerebration,"—or of Hæckel,—that it is "a function of brain and nerve,"—or of Strauss,—that "one's self is his body,"—or of Taine,—that one is "a series of sensations"—mind as personality disappears; substance becomes unreal; and we lose all hold on permanent objective truth. It seems a satire to call this negation of the ground of things positive science. I anticipate from science neither suicide nor usurpation,—neither denial of the ideal basis on which it stands, nor pretence of verifying conditions involved in the constant relations of the mind to truth. None the less must special forms of conceiving these relations be brought through its tests and inquiries to represent their real *universality* as transcendental elements. This obviously requires that God should mean, not the outside monarch of the universe, but its immanent Law and Life; that Duty should be, not the imposed sway of an external will, but loyalty to that moral order of which we are ourselves a part, so that our obedience is our freedom and our growth; and that Immortality should be, not a graft nor gift from without, but participation, under what conditions we know not and probably cannot know, in the permanence of the truth and good we see. Science is freeing these intuitions of our highest relations from false assumptions of definite knowledge and from superstitious prescription, and thus harmonizing their *form* with the real order of the world.

Mill constantly objects to transcendentalism that it is unscientific, because it is of faith rather than reason,—an old distinction, well enough taken when faith meant implicit orthodoxy, and had no recognized basis in the very nature of mental action. The highest act of reason and every breath of common logic rest alike on the vast assumption of faith in the human faculties. Every verification of special belief, by which scientific results are reached, involves this profounder belief; even verification of these faculties has no other organ than the faculties themselves. If "the steps of faith fall on the void to find the rock beneath," not less do the steps of science, the postulates of philosophy, the communications of speech. Will it be claimed that we escape these assumptions when we begin at the senses as the most obvious and trustworthy sources of knowledge? Is there any assumption greater than trusting eye and ear, those mysterious organs, those ether waves that I can neither see nor comprehend? What is all our knowledge but belief? The best physical science swarms with errors. Helmholtz proves the eye an imperfect optical instrument. Proctor takes back his theory of planetary population. Agassiz declares our genera and species the actual thoughts of God, and then Darwin refutes them. The calculus itself is but an approximation. The elements of real knowledge are here, nevertheless. But why do I believe this? Why believe that the world is a whole; that matter and mind, the "me" and the "not-me," are essentially related? I am more certain of this than of any detail of physical science. But as for proof, do I not, in all this, walk by faith, and make that my sight? If I am surer of my ground than an infant or an Australian savage, 'tis none the less true that the experiences which have thus helped me were available only through the constant necessity of the mind to outrun them with universalities which, although thoroughly scientific, were pure ventures of faith.

The transcendentalist emphasizes this basis of faith which science does not outgrow. He will not suffer it to be slighted: and for this reason among others,—that it is the health of the sentiments; of love, hope, aspiration, worship; that it brings to our limitations a sense of relation to a larger serener life, and repose in its adequacy. But it is a caricature of transcendentalism to make it the basis of absolutist and decaying evangelical dogmas like the Atonement, where the ideal is narrowed down to a prescribed, exclusive embodiment in the name of faith. Its intimacy is inward,—oneness of the believer with the believed; so that the sentiments, set free by it, become nobilities of self-respect, spontaneities that bloom into the best sympathies and cultures; into art, prophecy, heroism, sainthood; into the light and sweetness of the world. The manifest dependence of these fruits of sentiment on faith does not make them at variance with science,—that grand corrector of extravagance in feeling and delusion in thought. For all its special errors, the transcendental impulse has generated a cure in the science that flows from its intuition of law. This is its own balance-wheel, its own saving sense of limit, so that with its head in the heavens, teacher of the eternal life of man, it may walk securely, and do practical work under true human conditions. Its science is thus at once the child of its faith and the leader of its culture. And the spirit of our age, well understanding this unity, points more and more plainly to an ideal standard and test of all tendencies in the conception of the Immanent Spirit as world-movement of law and life,—transforming itself, first into the physical order, then into organic form, then into the Person and the State; the equal sexes, the arts, the humanities, the equities of capital and labor, the harmony of races in functions, the unity of the world in liberty and growth. This high accord of intuition and science is the divine espousal of the ideal and the real. The significance of our term "spirit of the age" is none the less positive because it is transcendental; in other words, not adequately given in any list of persons or events, but in somewhat beyond all these, to which they are all referred, not as an idea only, but as reality. And whoso most truly perceives or expresses this spirit is not only the true transcendentalist, but the builder of the future.

If such is the natural development of the transcendental element in human history, it is not a set of opinions, and no school can be the measure of its validity and scope. For one, I do not propose to speak of it as a phase that has had its day, and is giving way to science. It is an organic principle of thought and progress. Naturally unfolding into the grand results we have sketched, it is yet more or less visible in a great variety of beliefs which have little in common but the fact of being reached by a more or less faithful application of its method. Stated philosophically, it means that the self-affirmation of mind, conditioning all experience, and transcending the senses and the understanding with largest and most vital truths, is recognized as the primal source and guarantee of knowledge. It is the application of this principle to philosophy, religion, ethics, life. It points directly to the primacy of personal intuition, conviction, character. Evidently every individual declaration in the name of universal truth involves it, whatever its results, because it is a step beyond the data of experience. But, like all principles, it has its ideal, founded on its conscious culture and higher uses, which tests and judges conduct. He who freely uses the private judgment to measure all outward authority presumes the sufficiency of an inward light. But he is true to the ideal principle of transcendentalism only in so far as he really maintains the primacy of personal mind, instead of so carrying out the right of private judgment as to sink that principle or pervert its meaning. Many a loud protest against traditions and institutions has been been passive obedience to a far more powerful and brutal despotism, a push of sensual tides submerging the soul; not the sanity of intuition, but the insanity of desires. On the other hand, a poetic nature may be disposed to uphold the institutions in which his feelings have found culture, yet be, as Wordsworth was, completely transcendental, because taking these institutions simply as related to a spiritual ideal, which regenerated literature by its appeal to the beautiful and true, as "the soul that rises with us, our life's star."

In their worship of external authority, the Protestant sects have almost seemed to vie in showing how little might be kept of the transcendental principle, while claiming special advocacy of the right of private judgment. And in the great family of appellants to the "Inward Light,"—mystics, rationalists, Quakers, sceptics, ascetics, free religionists, with all unclassified persons of independent and earnest mind,— the intellectual diversities are doubtless not greater than the differences of degree in which their claim of inward light really represents transcendental freedom and progress.

Naturally the main test of fidelity to this principle is one's relation to the moral laws and spiritual forces. Here, again, we must recognize its ideal. The law in his nature, expressed not in articles, rituals, or Bible, not in multitude nor mediator nor specific religious name; this light of his faculties, self-shining with their revelation of the infinity of truth, and the absoluteness of duty, and their participation in that which they know to be eternal; this transcendence to imperfect experience and understanding,—is the consecration of his life; his guarantee of ideal convictions, of broad and beautiful beliefs. And life should seem inestimable, and in this sense at least immortal and divine, through what it is thus proved competent to hold, of enthusiasm for the best cultures, and service of the truth and right that are yet to rule.

In view of this personal ideal, there is a dark side in our social experience. Modern civilization becomes more and more exclusively a life of crowding and concretion. Its solidarity stifles the human atoms, who have been strenuously abolishing space, till the world's immeasurable detail presses directly upon every brain and heart. The intense magnetism of social machinery pushes every demand into unlimited expectation, and gives our vices a force as organic as ever was in State or Church. Corruption wields the resources of recognized method in its management of public and private interests, and has its representative men in every line, who become conspicuous solely because masters in the vulgar arts acknowledged to hold the key to success. An unbounded craving for self-gratification is fostered by the mechanism of our culture, ignoring all differences of material in its training of racers for a common goal. Competition in luxury drives us on in its whirl of dishonest debt and wasteful apery, till you shall barely find a few who dare live with honor, bringing up sons and daughters in just loyalties and simple tastes. Is such demoralization beginning to warn us, in the full tide of organized self-government, of a fatal incapacity of moral freedom and practical self-control?

What shall stay us on such downward tracks? Not, I think, a theory of science, that treats personality as mere run of phenomena, and its claim to be an immediate source of knowledge as a mere fiction of the imagination. This is but an outgrowth of these very degeneracies, and we shall look in vain for healing to the destroyer of our health. Successful trade; gigantic production; school machinery without a germ of individuality or self-reliance in its purpose,—are plainly the forces to be mastered, not the gods to be invoked. Spread of national vanity, grasp of the continent and the isles, are but symptoms of our disease. We want the personal ideal; inward dignities; a self-respect and self-reliance that require new starting points in the philosophy of culture. We want training in principles instead of dissipation on details; conviction that the world reflects the mind, and that the quality of our mind determines the value of our world; respect for the perception of moral order, for the sweep of law that transcends the bounded premise, the insight of prophecy that outruns experience; the freedom of the ideal to judge outward prescriptions, and reshape the concrete world to fresh necessities of growing reason. We need to react from that excessive reaction against unscientific idealism, which ignores all inward conditions of knowledge, and buries itself in the mere external object or sensation as source of all. And the drift of this current materialism towards resolving human personality into a delusion, and defining man and the world as mere run of phenomena, to say nothing of a pessimistic irony, must be met by emphasizing *substance*, and the real conjunction of the conscious mind with what is permanent and universal. In our zeal for teaching every thing, we are forgetting that the learner is more and greater than all he can learn, and that for him the first of all practical needs is a philosophy of culture that shall determine his methods and aims. In fine, to save us from base politics and selfish relations in trade and labor, we need the constant inspiration of ideal public duties, whereof we have hitherto had perhaps only one form; represented by the anti-slavery movement, and its school of moral culture, friendship, self-accountability, and life-long sacrifice. An education we now bitterly miss, and are destined to miss till we have raised to like levels of principle and conviction such transcendental objects as the rights and duties of labor, the union of equal opportunity with difference of function and honor to the best, and full liberty in the conscience to think, to deny, and to believe.

Notes

1. See Lange's *History of Materialism*, p. 213.

2. See, for instance, his self-contradictory discussion of the claims of reason and revelation (Book IV, chap. 18).

3. See Book II, chap. 17.

4. The question of *self-conscious* mind is a different and secondary one. Even in our personal experience some of the noblest instincts and powers seem to have nothing to do with self-consciousness, but to be, rather, escapes from it into a higher quality and realm of mind. What we here emphasize is mind regarded as the universal substance of knowledge.

5. Harriet Martineau, *Autobiography*, ed. Maria Weston Chapman (Boston: James R. Osgood, 1877), 2:91.

6. Lange, *History of Materialism*, pp. 121, 122.

"Transcendentalism in New England"

Joseph Cook*

PRELUDE ON CURRENT EVENTS.

A serious man must rejoice to have Christianity tested philosophically, historically, and in every great way, but not in a certain small, light, and inwardly coarse way, of which the world has had enough, and is tired. Yesterday the most scholarly representative of what calls itself Free Religion told Boston that the Author of Christianity is historically only an idolized memory inwreathed with mystical fictions. Will you allow me to say that the leading universities of Germany, through their greatest specialists in exegetical and historical research, have decisively given up that opinion? Thirty or forty years ago it was proclaimed there in rationalistic lecture-rooms very emphatically: to-day such lecture-rooms are empty, and those of the opposing schools are crowded. On the stately grounds of Sans Souci, where Frederick the Great and Voltaire had called out to the culture of Europe, *"Ecrasez l'infame!"* King William and his queen lately entertained an Evangelical Alliance gathered from the Indus, the Nile, the Danube, the Rhine, the Thames, and the Mississippi. Histories of the rise and progress and decline of German Rationalism, and especially of the power of the Mythical Theory, have been appearing abundantly for the last fifteen years in the most learned portions of the literature of Germany. The incontrovertible fact is, that every prominent German university, except Heidelberg, is now under predominant evangelical influences. Heidelberg is nearly empty of theological students. Lord Bacon said that the best materials for prophecy are the unforced opinions of young men. Against twenty-four theological students at rationalistic Heidelberg there were lately at evangelical Halle two hundred and eighty-two; at evangelical Berlin two hundred and eighty; and at hyper-evangelical Leipzig four hundred and twelve.

*Reprinted from *Transcendentalism, with Preludes on Current Events* (Boston: James R. Osgood, 1878), pp. 29–51; originally delivered in the Boston Monday Lectures series.

168

Before certain recent discussions and discoveries on the field of research into the history of the origin of Christianity, the rationalistic lecture-rooms were crowded, and the evangelical empty. It is notorious that such teachers as Tholuck, Julius Müller, Dorner, Twesten, Ullmann, Lange, Rothe, and Tischendorf, most of whom began their professorships at their universities with great unpopularity, on account of their opposition to rationalistic views, are now particularly honored on that very account. (See article on the "Decline of Rationalism in the German Universities," *Bibliotheca Sacra*, October, 1875.)

We often have offered to us in Boston the crumbs from German philosophical tables; and, although I must not speak harshly, the truth must be told, namely, that the faithful in the uneducated ranks of scepticism—I do not deny that there are vast masses of Orthodoxy uneducated also—are not infrequently fed on cold remnants swept away with derision from the scholarly repasts of the world. If you will open the biography of David Friedrich Strauss, by Zeller, his admiring friend, and a professor at Heidelberg, you will read these unqualified words: "Average theological liberalism pressed forward eagerly to renounce all compromising association with Strauss after he published the last statement of his mythical theory." (See Zeller, Professor Eduard, *"Strauss in his Life and Writings,"* English translation, London, 1874, pp. 135, 141, 143.) It did so under irresistible logical pressure, and especially because recent discoveries have carried back the dates of the New-Testament literature fifty years.

Thirty years ago it used to be thought that the earliest date at which the New-Testament literature can be shown to have been received as of equal authority with the Old was about A.D. 180; but, as all scholars will tell you, even Baur admitted that Paul's chief Epistles were genuine, and were written before the year 60. This admission is fatal to the mythical theory put forth by Strauss when he was a young man, and now for twenty years marked as juvenile by the best scholarship of Germany. These letters of Paul, written at that date, are incontrovertible proof that the leading traits of the character of the Author of Christianity, as given in the so-called mythical Gospels, were familiar to the Christian world within twenty-five years after his death (Thayer, Professor J. Henry, of Andover, *Boston Lectures*, 1871, p. 372). There is now in the hands of scholars incontrovertible evidence that even the Gospels had acquired authority with the earliest churches as early as A.D. 125. Schenkel, Renan, Keim, Weizsäcker, and others widely removed from the traditional views, teach that the Fourth Gospel itself could not have appeared later than a few years after the beginning of the second century. (See Fisher, Professor George P., *Essays on the Supernatural Origin of Christianity,* 1870, *Preface*, p. xxxviii.) These discoveries explain the new attitude of German scholarship. They carry back the indubitable traces of the New-Testament literature more than fifty years. They shut the colossal shears of chronology upon the theories of Baur, Strauss, and Renan. They narrow by so much the previously too narrow room used by these theories to explain the growth of myths and legends. Strauss demands a century after the death of Paul for his imaginative additions to Christianity to grow up in. It is now established that not only not a century, but not a quarter of a century, can be had for this purpose. The upper date of A.D. 34, and the lower date of A.D. 60, as established by exact research, are the two merciless blades of the shears between which the latest and most deftly-woven web of doubt is cut in two. [Applause.] There is no room for that course of mythical development which the Tübingen school describes. As a sect in biblical criticism, this school has perished. Its history has been written in more than one tongue (Thayer, Professor J. Henry, *Criticism Confirmatory of the Gospels, Boston Lectures,* 1871, pp. 363, 364, 371).

Chevalier Bunsen once wrote to Thomas Arnold this incisive exclamation: "The idea of men writing mythic histories between the time of Livy and Tacitus, and Saint Paul mistaking such for realities!" (Arnold's *Life, Letter* cxliv.) Paul had opportunity to know the truth, and was, besides, one of the boldest and acutest spirits of his own or of any age. *Was Paul a dupe?* [Applause.]

But who does not know the history of the defeat of sceptical school after sceptical school on the rationalistic side of the field of exegetical research? The naturalistic theory was swallowed by the mythical theory, and the mythical by the tendency theory, and the tendency by the legendary theory, and each of the four by time. [Applause.] Strauss laughs at Paulus, Baur at Strauss, Renan at Baur, the hourglass at all. [Applause.] "Under his guidance," says Strauss of Paulus (*New Life of Jesus,* English translation, p. 18), "we tumble into the mire; and assuredly dross, not gold, is the issue to which his method of interpretation generally leads." "Up to the present day," says Baur of Strauss (*Krit. Unters. über die canonische Evangel.,* 121, 40–71), "the mythical theory has been rejected by every man of education." And yet New-York lips teach it here in modern Athens! [Applause.] "Insufficient," says Renan of Baur (*Étude d'Hist. Rel.,* 163), "is what he leaves existing of the Gospels to account for the faith of the apostles." He makes the Pauline and Petrine factions account for the religion, and the religion account for the Pauline and Petrine factions. "Criticism has run all to leaves," said Strauss (see Zeller, *Life of Strauss,* p. 143) in his bitter disappointment at the failure of his final volume.

Appropriately was there carried on Richter's coffin to his grave a manuscript of his last work,—a discussion in proof of the immortality of the soul: appropriately might there have been carried on Strauss's coffin to his grave his last work, restating his mythical theory, if only that theory had not, as every scholar knows, died and been buried before its author. [Applause.]

The supreme question concerning the origin of the New-Testament literature is now, whether, in less than thirty years intervening between the death of the Author of Christianity and A.D. 60, in which Paul's Epistles are known to have become authorities, there is room enough in the age of Livy and Tacitus for the growth and inwreathing of mythical fictions around an idolized memory lying in the dim haze of the past. An unscholarly and discredited theory was presented to you yesterday gracefully, but not forcefully.

Let us see what a vigorous and unpartisan mind says on the same topic. "I know men," said Napoleon at St. Helena—the record is authentic; read it in Liddons' Bampton Lectures on the Divinity of Our Lord, the best recent book on that theme,—"I know men, and I tell you that Jesus of Nazareth was not a man." Daniel Webster, on his dying-bed, wrote on the marble of his tombstone "The Sermon on the Mount cannot be a merely human production." Renan was particularly cited to you yesterday; but when I went into the study of Professor Dorner, Schleiermacher's successor, at Berlin, and conversed with him about the greatest sceptics of Europe, I came to the name of Renan, and said, "What are we to think of his 'Life of Jesus'?"

"Das ist Nichts," he answered, and added no more. "That is nothing." [Applause.]

No doubt, in the fume and foam and froth of literary brilliancy serving a lost, bad cause, there may be iridescence, as well as in the enduring opal and pearl; but, while the colors seven flashed from the fragile spray are as beautiful as foam and froth, they are also just as substantial. [Applause.]

THE LECTURE.

Side by side under the lindens in the great cemetery of Berlin lie Fitche and Hegel; and I am transcendentalist enough myself to have walked one lonely day, four miles, from the tombs of Neander and Schleiermacher, on the hill south of the city, to the quiet spot where the great philosophers of transcendentalism lie at rest till the heavens be no more. I treasure among the mementos of travel some broad myrtle-leaves which I plucked from the sods that lie above these giants in philosophy; and, if I to-day cast a little ridicule upon the use some of their disciples have made of the great tenets of the masters, you will not suppose me to be irreverent towards any fountain-head of intuitive, axiomatic, self-evident truth. You wish, and I, too, wish, cool draughts out of the Castalian spring of axioms. You are, and I, too, am, thirsty for certainty; and I find it only in the sure four tests of truth—intuition, instinct, experiment, syllogism,—all agreeing. [Applause.] But of the four tests, of course the first is chief, head and shoulders above all the rest.

Even in Germany the successors of the great transcendentalists have made sport for the ages; and no doubt here in New England it was to have been expected that there should be some sowing of "transcendental wild-oats." [Applause.] That phrase is the incisive language of a daughter of transcendentalism honored by this generation, and likely to be honored by many more. I am asking you to look to-day at the erratic side of a great movement, the right wing and centre of which I respect, but the left wing of which, or that which broke with Christianity, has brought upon itself self-confessed defeat.

What has been the outcome of breaking with Christianity in the name of intuitive truth in Germany? Take up the latest advices, which it is my duty, as an outlook committee for this audience, to keep before you, and you will find that Immanuel Hermann Fichte, the son of this man at whose grave I stood in Berlin, has just passed into the Unseen Holy; and that, as his last legacy, he left to the ages a work entitled "Questions and Considerations concerning the Newest Form of German Speculation." When, one day, the great Fichte heard the drums of Napoleon beat in the streets of Berlin, he closed a lecture by announcing that the next would be given when Prussia had become free; and then enlisted against the conqueror, and kept his word. The son has had a more quiet life than the father; but he has given himself exclusively to philosophy. The second Fichte was the founder of the "Journal of Speculative Philosophy," now conducted by Ulrici and Wirth; and he has lived through much. He knew his father's system presumably well. Has it led to pantheism or materialism with him, as it has with some others? *If Emerson has made pantheism a logical outcome of Fichte's teachings, what has Fichte's son made of them?* The son of the great Fichte has been a professor at Dusseldorf and Bonn, and, since 1842, at Tübingen. He is a specialist in German philosophy if ever there was one; and his latest production was a history of his own philosophical school. He attempted to show that the line of sound philosophy in Germany is represented by three great names,—Leibnitz and Kant and Lotze. You do not care to have from me an outline of his work; and perhaps, therefore, you will allow me to read the summary of it given by your North-American Review, for that certainly ought to be free from partisanship. Thus Fichte loftily writes to Zeller, the biographer of Strauss, and his positions are a sign of the times:—   .

"Ethical theism is now master of the situation. The attempt to lose sight of the personal God in nature, or to subordinate his transcendence over the universe to any power immanent in the universe, and especially the tendency to deny the theology of ethics, and to insist only upon the reign of force, are utterly absurd, and are meeting their just condemnation." [Applause.] (*North-American Review*, January, 1877, p. 147.)

Concord once listened to Germany. Will it continue to listen? Cambridge cannot show at the foot of her text-book pages five English names where she can show ten German. In the footnotes of learned works you will find German authorities a dozen times where you can find English six, or American three. Let us appeal to no temporary swirl of currents, but to a Gulf Stream. Of course, history is apt to be misleading, unless we take it in long ranges. Read Sir William Hamilton's celebrated summary (*Note A, Appendix to* Reid's *works*), if you wish to see the whole gulf current of belief in self-evident truth since Aristotle. But here in Germany is a vast stretch of modern philosophical discussion, beginning with Leibnitz, running on through Kant, and so coming down to Lotze; and it is all on the line of intuitive truth, and it never has broken with Christianity, nor been drawn into either the Charybdis of materialism or the Scylla of pantheism. [Applause.]

The latest and acutest historian of German theology, Schwartz of Gotha, says that Strauss designates not so much a beginning as an end, and that the supreme lack in his system is twofold,—the absence of historical insight and of religious sensibility. Now, I will not deny that rationalism in New England, with eight generations of Puritan culture behind it, has often shown religious sensitiveness. Some transcendentalists who have broken with Christianity I reverence so far forth as they retain here in New England a degree of religious sensibility which is often utterly unknown among rationalists abroad. Heaven cause my tongue to cleave to the roof of my mouth if ever I say aught ironical, or in any way derogatory, of that consciousness of God which underlay the vigor of Theodore Parker, which is the transfiguring thing in Emerson, and which, very much further down in the list of those who are shy of Christianity, is yet the glory of their thinking, and of their reverence for art, and is especially the strength of their philanthropic endeavors! [Applause.] We have no France for a neighbor; wars have not stormed over America as they have over Europe; and it cannot yet be said, even of our erratics, as undoubtedly it can be of many French and German ones, that they have lost the consciousness of God.

What is Transcendentalism?

You will not suspect me of possessing the mood of that acute teacher, who, on the deck of a Mississippi steamer, was asked this question, and replied, "See the holes made in the bank yonder by the swallows. Take away the bank, and leave the apertures, and this is Transcendentalism." The answer to this is the certainty that we are all bank-swallows. The right wing and centre of this social, twittering human race live in these apertures, as well as the left wing; and it would be of little avail to ridicule the self-evident truths on which our own peace depends. I affirm simply that Transcendentalism of the left wing has not been consistent with Transcendentalism itself.

My general proposition is, that rationalistic Transcendentalism in New England is not Transcendentalism, but, at the last analysis, Individualism.

Scholars will find that on this occasion, as on many others, discussion here is purposely very elementary.

1. The plan of the physical organism is not in the food by which the organism is sustained.

2. The mechanism by which the assimilation of food is effected exists before the food is received.

3. But, until the food is received, that mechanism does not come into operation.

4. The plan of the spiritual organism is not in the impressions received through sensation and association.

5. The fundamental laws of thought exist in the plan of the soul anterior to all sensation or association.

6. But they are brought into operation only by experience through sensation and association.

7. It is absurd to say that the plan of the body is produced by its food.

8. It is equally absurd to say that the plan, or fundamental intuitive beliefs of the soul, are produced by sensation and association.

9. Therefore, as the plan of the body does not have its origin in the food of the body, so the plan of the mind does not have its origin in the food of the mind.

You receive food, and a certain plan in your physical organism distributes it after it is received, assimilates it, and you are entirely sure that the mechanism involved in this process exists before the food. It may be that every part of my physical system is made up of food and drink which I have taken, or of air which I have breathed; and yet there is one thing in me that the food did not give me, or the air; and that is the plan of my physical organism. [Applause.] Not in the gases, not in the fluids, not in the solids, was there the plan of these lenses in the eye, or of this harp of three thousand strings in the ear.

Besides all the materials which go to make up a watch, you must have the plan of the watch. If I were to place a book on my right here, and then take another copy of the book and tear it into shreds, and cast these down on the left, it would not be lawful to say that I have on one side the same that I have on the other. In one case the volume is arranged in an intelligible order: in the other it is chaotic. Besides the letters, we must have the coordination of the letters in the finished volume. So in man's organism it is perfectly evident that the food which we eat, and which does, indeed, build every thing in us, is not us; for the plan of us is something existing before that food enters the system, and that plan separates the different elements, and distributes them in such a way as to bring out the peculiarities of each individual organism.

Now, whether or not you admit that there is a spiritual organism behind the physical, whether or not you agree with your Beales and Lotzes and Ulricis in asserting that the scientific method requires that we should suppose that there is in us a spiritual organism which weaves the physical, you will at least admit, that, so far as the individual experience is concerned, we have within us laws, fundamental, organic, and, if not innate, at least connate. They came into the world with us; they are a part of the plan on which we are made. When we touch the external world with the outer senses, and the inner world with the inner senses, no doubt food is coming to our souls; but that plan is the law according to which all our experiences through sensation and association are distributed.

10. The school of sensationalism in philosophy maintains that the soul's laws are only an accumulation of inheritances.

11. To that school, self-evident truths themselves are simply those which result from an unvarying and the largest experience; or those which have been deeply engraved on our physical organisms by the uniform sensations of our whole line of ancestors back to the earliest and simplest form of life.

12. Human experience cannot embrace all space and time.

13. Sensationalism in philosophy, therefore, which holds that all the intuitive or axiomatic truths arise from experience, must deny that we can be sure that these truths are true in all space and time.

14. But we are thus sure; and sensationalism is wrecked on its palpable inability to explain by experience this confessed certainty.

Face to face with this inadequate explanation which evolution offers for the self-evident, necessary, and universal truths of the soul, let us look at the worst.

It matters to me very little how my eyes came into existence, if only they see accurately. You say conscience was once only a bit of sensitive matter in a speck of jelly. You affirm, that, by the law of the survival of the fittest, in the struggle of many jelly-specks with each other for existence, one peculiarly-vigorous jelly-speck obtained the advantage of its brethren, and so became the progenitor of many vigorous jelly-specks. Then these vigorous jelly-specks made new war on each other; and individuals, according to the law of heredity with variation, having now and then fortunate endowments, survived, and transmitted these, to become better and better, until the jelly-specks produce the earliest seaweed. By and by a mollusk appears under the law of the survival of the fittest, and then higher and higher forms, till at last, through infinite chance and mischance, man is produced. Somewhere and somehow the jelly-specks get not only an intellect, not only artistic perception, but conscience and will, and this far-reaching longing for immortality, this sense that there is a Mind superior to ours on which we are dependent. Now, for a moment, admit that this theory of evolution, which Professor Dawson, in an article in the last number of the "International Review," on Huxley in New York, says will be regarded by the next age as one of the most mysterious of illusions, is true, the supreme question yet remains,—whether my conscience is authority.

Take something merely physical, like the eyes. When I was a jelly-speck of the more infirm sort, or at least when I was a fish, I saw something, and what I saw I saw. When I was a lichen, although I was not a sensitive-plant, I felt something, and what I felt I felt. So when, at last, these miraculous lenses began to appear, as the law of the survival of the fittest rough-hewed them age after age, I saw better and better; but what I saw I saw: and to-day I feel very sure that the deliverance of the eyes is accurate. I am not denying here any of the facts as to our gradual acquisition of the knowledge of distance and of dimension; that comes from the operation of all the senses; but we feel certain that what we see we see.

Suppose, then, that, in this grand ascent from the jelly-speck to the archangel, the process of evolution shall at last make our eyes as powerful as the best telescopes of the present day. It will yet plainly be true, will it not, that what we see we see? and as the eyes are now good within their range, so, when they become telescopic, they will be good within their range. Just so, even if we hold to the evolutionary hypothesis in its extremest claims, we must hold, that, if conscience was good for any thing when it was rudimentary, it is good now in its higher stage of development. If by and by it shall become telescopic, what it sees it will see. [Applause.] I will not give up for an instant the authority of *connate*, although you deny all *innate* truth. You may show me that fatalism is the result of your evolutionary hypothesis; you may prove to me that immortality cannot be maintained if your philosophy is true; you may, indeed, assert, as Häckel does, "that there is no God but necessity," if you are an evolutionist of the thorough-going type, that is, not only a Darwinian, but a Häckelian. But let Häckel's consistent atheistic evolutionism, which Germany rejects with scorn, be adopted, and it will yet remain true that there is a plan in man; and that, while there is a plan in man, there will be a best way to live; and that, while there is a best way to live, it will be best to live the best way. [Applause.]

There is, however, no sign of the progress of the Häckelian theory of evolution toward general acceptance. On every side you are told that evolution is more and more the philosophy of science. But which form of the theory of evolution is meant? The Darwinian is *a* theory, the Häckelian is *the* theory, of evolution.

15. Observing our mental operations, we very easily convince ourselves that we are sure of the truth of some propositions, concerning which neither we nor the race have had experience.

16. If it be true that all these certainties that we call self-evident arise simply from experience, it must be shown that our certainties do not reach beyond our experience.

It is very sure, is it not, that the sun might rise to-morrow morning in the west? Neither we nor our ancestors have had any experience of its rising there. Space is a necessary idea, but the rising of the sun in the east is not; and yet our experience of the one is as invariable as that of the other. That blazing mass of suns we call Orion might have its stellar points differently arranged; and yet I never saw Orion in any shape other than that which it now possesses. I am perfectly confident that the gems on the sword-hilt of Orion might be taken away, or never have been in existence; but I never yet saw Orion without seeing there the flashing of the jewels on the hilt of his sword.

John Stuart Mill would say, and so would George Henry Lewes,— whose greatest distinction, by the way, is, that he is the husband of Marian Evans, the authoress of "Daniel Deronda,"—that, although my own experience never has shown to me Orion in any other shape than that which it now possesses, perhaps my ability to give it another shape in thought may arise from some experience in the race behind me. We are told by the school of evolution, that it is not our individual experience that explains our necessary ideas, but the transmitted experience of the race behind us. We have inherited nervous changes, from the whole range, of the development of the species; and so, somewhere and somehow in the past, there must have been an experience which gives you the capacity to say that the sun may rise in the west, and that Orion might have another shape. But is it not tolerably sure that none of my grandfathers or great-grandfathers, back to the jelly-speck, ever saw the sun rise in the west? The human race never saw Orion in any other shape. The truth is, that experience goes altogether too short a distance to account for the wide range of such a certainty, as that every effect, not only here, but everywhere, must have a cause.

17. Experience does not teach what *must* be, but only what *is;* but we know that every change not only *has,* but *must* have, a cause.

I never had any experience in the Sun, or in the Seven Stars. I never paced about the Pole with Ursa Major, across the breadth of one of whose eyelashes my imagination cannot pass without fainting; I know nothing of the thoughts of Saggitarius, as he bends his bow of fire yonder in the southern heavens: but this I do know, that everywhere and in all time every change *must* have a cause. You are certain of the university of every necessary truth. How are you to account for that certainty by any known experience?

18. *We cannot explain by experience a certainty that goes beyond experience.*

John Stuart Mill, perfectly honest and perfectly luminous, comes squarely up to this difficulty, and says in so many words, "There may be worlds in which two and two do not make four, and where a change need not have a cause." (*Examination of* Hamilton's *Philosophy;* see, also Mill's *Logic,* book iii. chap. xxi.) So clearly does he see this objection, that, astounding some of his adherents, he made this very celebrated admission, which has done more to cripple the philosophy of sensationalism, probably, than any other event in its history for the last twenty-five years. Even mathematical axioms may be false. You and I, gentlemen, feel, and must feel, that this conclusion is arbitrary; that it is not true to the constitution of man; that we have within us something which asserts not only the present earthly certainty, that every change must have a cause, but that forever and forever, in all time to come, and backward through all time past, this law holds.

19. Everywhere, all exact science assumes the universal applicability of all true axioms in all time and in all places.

Rejecting in the name of exact science, therefore, Mill's startling paradox, we must conclude that we are not loyal to the indications of our own constitution, unless we say that there is in us a possibility of reaching certainty beyond experience. Now to do that is to reach a transcendental truth.

20. Transcendental truths are simply those necessary, self-evident, axiomatic truths which transcend experience. Transcendentalism is the science of such self-evident, axiomatic, necessary truths.

Kant gave this name to a part of his philosophy, and it is by no means a word of reproach. Of course I am treating Transcendentalism, not with an eye on New England merely, but with due outlook on this form of philosophy throughout the world, especially upon Coleridge and Wordsworth, Mansel and Maurice, and Sir William Hamilton, and Leibnitz and Kant and Lotze. I am not taking Transcendentalism in that narrow meaning in which some opponents of it may have represented it to themselves. That every change, here and everywhere, not only has, but must have, a cause, is a transcendental truth: it transcends experience. So the certainty that here and everywhere things which are equal to the same thing are equal to each other is a transcendental certainty. Our conviction in the moral field that sin can be a quality only of voluntary action is a transcendental fact. This moral axiom we feel is sure in all time and in all space. There are moral intuitions as well as intellectual. There are æsthetic intuitions, I believe; and they will yet produce a science of the beautiful, as those of the intellect and the conscience produce sciences of the true and the good. If man have no freedom of will, he cannot commit sins in the strict sense, for demerit implies free agency; and we feel that this is a moral certainty, and you cannot go behind it.

Coleridge complained much in his time of "that compendious philosophy which contrives a theory for the spirit by nicknaming matter, and in a few hours can qualify its dullest disciples to explain the *omne scibile* by reducing all things to impressions, ideas, and sensations" (*Biograph. Literaria*, chap. xii.). What would he have said to the recent attempt by Tyndall to nickname matter, and call it mind, or a substance with a spiritual and physical side? Only the other day, Lewes endeavored to nickname sensation, and call it both the internal law of the soul and the external sense. Will you please listen to an amazing definition out of the latest, and perhaps the subtlest attempt to justify sensationalism in philosophy? "The sensational hypothesis is acceptable, if by sense we understand *sensibility and its laws of operation.* This obliterates the very distinction insisted on by the other school. It includes all physical phenomena under the rubric of sensibility. It enables psychological analysis to be consistent and exhaustive." (Lewes's *Problems of Life and Mind*, 1874, vol. i. p. 208.)

This passage affirms, that, if you will say food is the body, food will explain the body. If you will take the metal which goes to make the watch as not only the metal, but the plan of the watch too, then your matter and your plan put together will be the watch. He wants sensation to mean sensibility and its laws; that is to say, he would have the very fundamental principles of our soul included in this term, which, thus interpreted, I should say, with Coleridge, is a nickname. Such a definition concedes much by implication; but Lewes concedes in so many words, that, "if by sense is meant simply the five senses, the reduction of all knowledge to a sensuous origin is absurd."

Such is the latest voice, my friends, from the opponents of the Intuitional school in philosophy; and it is substantially a confession, that, unless a new definition be given to sensation, the sensational philosophy must be given up. Stuart Mill affirmed that two and two might make seven in Orion, and that a change possibly might not have a cause in the North Star. He was forced to no greater straits than the husband of George Eliot is, when he says that the only escape from the necessity of adopting the intutional philosophy is to assume its definitions as those of the sensational school itself. Bloody, unjust exploits, are often performed by lawless men on the battle-field of philosophy; but, after all, the ages like to see fair play. We must observe the rules of the game. When Greek wrestlers stood up together, the audience and the judges saw to it that the rules of the game were observed. These were defined rigidly. All religious science asks of scepticism in this age or any other, is, that it will observe the laws of the scientific method. We must adhere to the rules of the game; and when established definitions are nicknamed, as they now are by materialism, suicide is confession. [Applause.]

"The Transcendentalism of New England"

John Orr*

The American mind is intensely practical. Its forte lies in the direction of mechanical invention and the manipulation of the material. It fabricates knives and forks, sewing machines, steam ploughs—also institutions. Its achievements are great in the records of the Patent Office. In the annals of commerce it holds a prominent place. As a last invention, it has just given the phonograph to the world. It is said that a piece of iron worth 75 cents can be converted into table cutlery worth $180; into watch springs worth $2,000, and into hair springs worth $4,000. In effecting such transformations as these the American genius is conspicuous. Given a raw material of indefinite possibilities, such as India rubber or gutta-percha, and before many months go round it is found as an article of convenience on the breakfast table; it is sewn as buttons on our coats; it contributes to the comfort of the traveler in the railway carriage; of the invalid on the sick-bed; of the wounded on the battle field. Inheriting the Roman capacity for organization, the American mind, also, manages corners in Wall street; institutes gigantic undertakings in the West; it invents express systems and mercantile agencies, and its great experiment of national self-government by the people and for the people, it is helping to show the world how to unite liberty with law in administering the affairs of nations.

Thus distinguished in the line of practical interest, the American mind is comparatively weak in the region of ideas. Without undervaluing culture, it has scarcely produced one first-rate thinker. That meditativeness of mind and patient, plodding study, which have produced such results in Germany, seem scarcely in accordance with its genius. On the Mount Blancs or Mount Hookers of spiritual contemplation, the air is rather thin for its robust organization. Engaged so much with the measurable and the ponderable, and developing the material resources of the country, its interest is not great in that which cannot be seen and handled. The sensible, rather than the rational,

*Reprinted from *International Review*, 13 (October 1882), 381–398.

horizon bounds its vision. Even in education, as Emerson says, the aim is less culture than equipment, less development of faculty than the furnishment of the individual for some special work in life.

And yet, some forty years ago, there uprose in New England about the most remarkable manifestation of Idealism that modern history can show. Into this region Transcendentalism imported its bit of Oriental sky, and called men to admire the constellations it contained. And the peculiarity of this movement lay in the fact that, instead of offering ingenuities of speculation addressed to the few, it was a powerful, practical influence, operating on the minds of the many. Its auroral lights of splendid promise awoke something of enthusiasm, especially among the young. It exercised a powerful moral influence, calling to manliness and high aims, and to its call many responded. It colored the religion of the day; to many it was in itself a religion.

Before attempting to describe the characteristics of this Transcendentalism, it may be well for us to take a glance at circumstances and influences tending to its production. It is said that when a fire occurs out in the forest the winds immediately carry in abundant germs of life, and cover the earth with vegetation till then partly unknown in the district. And among the causes of Transcendentalism, some may be compared with the burning of the forest, some with the incoming germs of life; some are the remoter occasions, preparing the way; others may more properly be denominated causes. Among the former we would give a prominent place to the following:

The decadence of the Puritan spirit. The stern Calvinism of New England, with its gloomy views of life and its severe intolerance, had in a great measure passed away, or experienced changes that amounted almost to a transformation. The severity was toned down; the knobs and angularities rubbed off. The moral earnestness still remained—the conception that righteousness is highest of all things—but it had largely gone over and become Unitarianism. The rigid views of parental authority, with which Puritanism was identified, disappeared entirely, and a greater place was given to sunshine, joy and liberty. Thus the shadows were lifted, and as Puritanism lost ground and no longer solved to the public satisfaction the great problems of life, a vacant place was made which Transcendentalism aimed to fill. A new religious philosophy seemed to be wanting, and this philosophy the new movement aimed to supply.

A second cause ministering at least negatively to Transcendentalism was the proven insufficiency of the old sensational philosophy. This philosophy, whose great apostles in England were Locke and Hartley, held the place of honor throughout the whole eighteenth century, and did more to explain the characteristics of that century—its superficiality, its scepticism, its materialism, its barrenness—than any other influence whatsoever. Proceeding on the principle that all knowledge comes through sensation, it proved inadequate to the treatment of the deeper questions, as the will, emotion, conscience, the religious nature; and in its attempts at their explanation it simply degraded or denied that which it undertook to explain. Especially when it spoke of conscience, and tried to account for it as an elaboration from experiences of pleasure and pain; when it went beyond the question, "What is the right?" to the further question, "Why should its mandates be obeyed?" it betrayed unmistakable incompetency by appealing to mere selfish considerations. This philosophy has always gone, more or less distinctly, in the direction of materialism and low aims; of selfishness in morals and scepticism in religion. As summed up in its worst representatives, it boldly taught that the aim of life is happiness, and that happiness is to be largely identified with mere physical enjoyment. And when the "Moral Philosophy" of Paley, with its well-known definition of virtue—"Virtue is the doing good to mankind in obedience to the will of God and for the sake of everlasting happiness"—when this work became an accepted text-book in the great universities of England and received the approbation of high-church dignitaries, it was time to show that there was something higher than any balancing of selfish considerations; that, in fact, it is only when selfish considerations are trampled on that true virtue can be said to begin. As early as 1829 Emerson says, speaking of a sermon he was writing, "I am striving to-day to establish the sovereignty and self-existing excellence of the moral law in popular argument, and slay the *utility swine*." Within certain limitations the philosophy of utility is valuable, but the sensational system, with which it is generally connected, takes the sunlight of the soul and reduces to something poor and paltry the highest sentiments and purposes possible to man. Like Epicureanism, its influence went to paralyze conscience.

In the decline of the Puritan movement, and the decadence of this sensational philosophy, the encumbering forest of the past was cut down, allowing opportunity for new growths, and, among these growths, was Transcendentalism. The period we are referring to—that of the first quarter of this century—was, as Emerson has shown, one of great unrest and agitation. "No one can converse much," says he, "with different classes of society in New England without remarking the progress of revolution. . . . This spirit of the time is felt by every individual with some difference—to each one casting its light upon the objects nearest to his temper and habits of thought; to one coming in the form of special reforms in the state; to another, in modifications of the various callings of men, and the custom of business; to a third, opening a new scope for literature and art; to a fourth, in philosophic insight; to a fifth, in vast solitudes of prayer. In all its movements it is peaceable, and in the very lowest marked with a triumphant success. . . . It has the step of fate, and goes on existing like an oak or a river—because it must." And among the movements urged on by the temper of the times, not the least remarkable or prolific of results was that one we are now attempting to portray.

The temper of mind out which Transcendentalism directly came is called the mystical—the contemplative—whose organ is intuition, and whose aim is immediate union with God. Sometimes this union is sought through emotion, and then mysticism issues in some form of the pietistic or meditative life—in the ecstasy of the Neoplatonists, and the quietism of Madame Guyon. Then the union is sought through the intellect and the possession of divine ideas, and under the pressure of this tendency, mysticism, produces a philosophy more or less pantheistical, or what is generally called a theosophy. The mystic of both these types, the Indian Yogi, dwelling in contemplation, the Persian Sufi, Saadi, Plotinus, Erckhart, Bohme, Schelling, Lord Herbert of Cherbury, all accept a theory of knowing and being that is substantially of the transcendental type, and without their previous existence probably Transcendentalism could not have been. The dominant conception of all is that of an omnipresent spirit, overflowing into every nook and cranny of creation, and in communication with the mind of man, offering inspiration and the indubitable in truth.

Transcendentalism grew into a movement principally through the writings of three men, Coleridge, Carlyle, and Emerson. Coleridge, the earliest in time, was rather a psychological curiosity. A remarkable poet, a profound or a muddy philosopher, a passionate devotee of high-church orthodoxy, which he held on the ground that it was the perfection of reason, he accomplished much; and yet, considering his genius and the works he was always projecting, he seems to have accomplished nothing. He was always preparing to do something great, but the great thing was never done. With laborious perseverance preparing the apparatus that he might look out for the new star, the new star was never seen. And yet, with his mystic utterances, his occasional flashing of light into the heart of deep questions, he was a powerful influence on the religion of his age. His special signification to us lies in the fact that, importing into England the results of German metaphysics, he taught that men possessed a faculty for apprehending truth superior to the intellect by which they have direct cognizance of supersensible things. This reason, as he names it, lying behind all processes of reasoning, corresponded very much with the intuition of the German philosophers and gives us knowledge of basal, indubitable truth. Thus Coleridge made a departure in the direction of a profounder and more spiritual philosophy, and by his varied utterance of the one principle, and his stimulating conversations and writings, did much to produce the belief that the views he taught contained in themselves great possibilities of reconcilement and, illumination.

Carlyle was a more powerful personality, and in his early enthusiasm, a certain fascination he threw over life, and his wonderful appeals to the manliness in man, became a teacher and an inspiration of no small importance. He did for German literature generally what Coleridge did or attempted for German philosophy, and made its poets and thinkers—Novalis meditating under the starlight, Richter with his exuberant imagination, Herder, Goethe the many-sided—known to England and the English-speaking nations. A preacher, too, on his own account, he taught the nearness of God, the supremacy of the divine laws, religion as a present communion with the Infinite and Eternal. He belongs to the company of the idealist; he emphasizes intuition; oscillating between the two great schools of mysticism, he taught now that self-development, and again that self-renunciation, is the realization of the divine. With withering scorn he branded the materialism of the age, the selfish spirit of the old philosophers and moralities, and in a living religiousness, and a brave assertion of the immutable moral law, recognized the divine meaning of life.

But the leader of the Transcendental movement was undoubtedly Emerson. Born in Boston in 1803, of a good New England stock, his ancestors to the sixth generation being clergymen, Emerson was brought up under good influences intellectually and morally. At Harvard he is remembered as a shy, gentlemanly young man, attentive to classical study, and with some faculty in the way of elocution. Educated for the ministry, and for a term settled in Boston, his qualities in the pulpit were a certain grace of style, a most musical voice and a simple directness of teaching that were charming. Through his college and ministerial days, however, he is learning something that seems to disqualify him for the work of the Christian ministry. He is studying Plato, Plotinus and other representatives of that school; the works of Marcus Antoninus are found often in his pocket during his college course; the good Saadi "who dwells alone" has for him a strange fascination; he delights in the writers of the Elizabethan era—in Swedenborg and Bohme; in the English latitudinarians. After a time he leaves the pulpit and retires to the home of his family in Concord; and there, in the companionship of books, enjoying country life, learning of solitude, writing, lecturing, he spent his life. Whether his idealism came from natural proclivity or from the influence of books, or both, it were not, perhaps, easy to say. Vaughan, in his "Hours with the Mystics," says of mysticism that it has no genealogy; instead of being transmitted by teaching, it grows spontaneously in a certain temperament of mind. Be this as it may, Emerson leaves behind him considerably the religion in which he was educated, and among the contemplatists of the world, the theosophists, the trismegisti, the illuminati, he finds his religious home.

Transcendentalism as a visible movement began in 1836, with the publication in America of Carlyle's "Sartor Resartus." In this volume Emerson prefixed a recommendatory notice, in which he says that "the philosophy and the purity of moral sentiment which inspires the work will find their way to the heart of every lover of virtue." Previous to this time, no doubt, the new philosophy found individual supporters here and there. Dr. Channing went deeper than experience for the foundation of his faith, and believed in real communion, with a present God. Dr. Hedge and President Walker, of Harvard, found avenues to truth not recognized in old systems, and accepting the revelations thus obtained, went on their way rejoicing. But only in 1836 did Transcendentalism attain to the dignity of a movement. Then it first came to attract much attention and to dictate a characteristic method of thinking and speaking. Then men began to talk Carlyle; they were at home in the infinities and eternities; a new valuation, in theory at least, was placed on silence; there was a prevailing disposition to use plain language, and call a spade a spade. In the universities the spasmodic English of the students disturbed the equanimity of the professors of rhetoric. Among the young generally a conviction began to grow that a new era was coming on. C. T. Congdon says of the movement that, while expressing itself in eccentricities and absurdities of various kinds, it amounted to a kind of hobbledehoy aspiration after manliness. When Emerson then came out of his seclusion in Concord to assume command of the movement it had made considerable progress. Some, no doubt, laughed; some denounced. John Quincy Adams said that the transcendental message simply amounted to this—that the old doctrines are superannuated and worn out, and that the revelations to supersede them are coming. But the young generally responded with enthusiasm. J. R. Lowell says that the course of lectures delivered by Emerson in the Masonic Hall in Boston, in 1836, constituted an era in the life of many a young man. The Harvard students came in almost in a body to hear the new teacher, and went home, under the starlight, on foot. After hearing one of these lectures Dr. Channing's daughter, Mary, exclaimed: "After hearing Mr. Emerson I think I can sin no more." The elevation of the tone and the novelty of the teaching, and the trumpet-call uttered to a noble life, even the enigmatic language that awakened curiosity, translated many into a new region, in which they found much to wonder at and much to inspire. J. F. Clark says two things came out, stimulating in the teaching—self-reliance and God-reliance.

Before glancing at the future and the fortunes of Transcendentalism, we may look closer at it to see what it means. Not a very easy task.

Some things admit of a ready definition. They are a simple substance, or an easily identified fact. Others comprehend in their totality a miscellaneous variety of attributes, or constituents, and can only be defined by description. Any one could define a spade; but could he with the same facility tell the essential element in civilization? And as many-sided as civilization, as capable of reflecting a different look from a variety of angles, is Transcendentalism. Goethe was once asked what was the central idea in "Faust," and he replied, "It has none;" and then he added: "I am of opinion that the more incommensurable and incomprehensible to the understanding a poetical production is, the better it is." And a certain incommensurableness belongs to Transcendentalism. What Emerson said of the mountain may be said of it— instead of being one thing it is a hundred things, according to the position and temperament of the observer. In virtue of this multifariousness, the first Transcendentalists were satirically called the "Like-minded"; and when Emerson defines the new philosophy, he is taken to task by Frothingham, the historian of Transcendentalism, and the definition given by Frothingham in its turn is disputed by Dr. Osgood, his critic, in the "International Review." Yet the mountain is still a particular thing, independent of the observer, and can definitely be measured and mapped out. So is the phenomenon we are now endeavoring to describe.

As to the name "Transcendentalism," how it came to be applied to the New England idealism no one knows. At any rate, in a certain sense it is appropriate, though in some ways it is unfortunate. The word had a certain meaning in the philosophy of the Middle Ages, describing classes of things not comprehended in the categories of Aristotle, yet it is not from the Middle Ages, but from the philosophy of Kant, in which is described one department, that it obtained its signification and use as a recognized English word. With Kant the transcendental department concerned itself with those fundamental beliefs and ideas that are independent of observation, and come to us guaranteed by the very constitution of the human mind. And the mingled appropriateness, and yet unfortunateness, of the term lies in the fact that it carries with it a fine flavor of German metaphysics, and suggests a traveling out into regions bounding at least on the mystical and unintelligible.

The definition of Emerson, referred to as criticised by Frothingham, is the following: "This mode of thinking (the ideal), falling on Roman times, made stoic philosophers; falling on despotic times, made Catoes and Brutuses; falling on superstitious times, made prophets and apostles; on popish times, made Protestants and ascetic monks preachers of faith against preachers of works; on prelatic times, made Puritans and Quakers, and falling on Unitarian and commercial times, made the peculiar shades of idealism that we know." This description, unsatisfactory, perhaps, because not descending sufficiently to particulars, brings forward two characteristics we believe important in Transcendentalism—the essential element, *idealism;* the specific difference, an idealism suited to practical, commercial and reformatory times. To each of these we call attention.

This idealism, however varied in form, is well known in essential features. It recognizes in the human mind a certain capacity of apprehending directly supersensible truth, and of communicating directly with the spiritual world. Instead of the roundabout and precarious method of observation, it takes the high *a priori* road to truth presented by intuition. Whilst materialism would depress everything into matter, and in the action of the moral sense see only a disturbance in the molecular constituents of the brain, it believes only in spirit and in the spiritual aspects of things. Conscience is to it no elaboration from experience, but a light kindled by the spirit of God, and in its announcements it gives revelations from the empyrean. The soul is the crown lily, the edelweisse of creation; it is a microcosm, containing a small universe in itself, not without its constellations, and in communication with the oversoul it finds its life. Eternity, instead of being looked forward to in hope, is a present reality; we live in the centre of eternity now. And, throughout, the tendency of idealism is in the direction of aspiration and enthusiasm; it believes in mystery and miracle; it sees in all things a contribution to the solution of the great problems of existence; it speaks in the superlative degree. Private fancy it may mistake for revelation, and many an interest unquestionably important it may despise, yet its aim and spirit are high. It proclaims the value of ideas; it throws a splendor over duty; it announces the categorical imperative; it awakens an enthusiasm for the beautiful and true and good, identifying all these with God.

This, we reckon, is Transcendentalism generally; the specific difference lies in the fact that the idealism it comprehends is not Oriental, taking the soul away into solitudes of profitless contemplation; not sentimental, finding in emotion the point of union with God; nor speculative in any sense, but essentially practical and reformatory. It may go into solitude and deal with the deepest questions that could occupy the mind, but the aim is to confer additional grace and nobleness on life. George Gilfillan says, rather funnily, of Emerson that he prefers "to stray to and fro along the crooked serpent of eternity," but his business at the same time was very intelligibly with the things of time. The "news he brought from the Empyrean" bore on the meaning of life, and had a lesson for the common weekday world. As Emerson himself says in one of his most beautiful poems:

Think me not unkind and rude,
    That I walk alone in grove and glen;
I go to the god of the wood
    To fetch his word to men.

Tax not my sloth that I
    Fold my arms beside the brook,
Each cloud that floated in the sky
    Writes a letter in my book.

Chide me not, laboring band,
    For the idle flowers I brought,
Every aster in my hand
    Goes home laden with a thought.

Wherever the head of the poet might be—in the clouds, if you choose—his feet ever stood on the solid earth. And among his followers we find the same interest in human culture and improvement. In those memorable conversations of hers delivered in Boston, Margaret Fuller might discourse on art and Grecian mythology, but the real topics never lost sight of were culture and the ennoblement of character. Mr. A. B. Alcott not unfrequently runs his head against a post, and is often found in depths which he cannot fathom, but in all his wanderings he is gathering simples for the cure of human ills. Lowell says of Thoreau, that only when a thing became useless did it present any attraction to him, yet the desire to reach higher than ordinary levels dictated his love of the simplicity of rural life. What Carlyle called the "potato philosophy" of Alcott, the shanty building of Thoreau, the experiment of Brook Farm, and the interest of the Transcendentalists in the question of slavery and the emancipation of women, all attest the practical character of the idealism which we are describing.

Nay, it is more than practical—it is a stern reaction against prevailing maxims and ways, against materialism, formalism and utilitarianism in its lower aspects, and therefore reformatory. With almost a Calvin preference for dark shades, Emerson pictures the comprehensive, almost total, depravity of existing manners and institutions. Men were immersed in sense; accumulating the materials of life, they forgot to live; they garnished the tombs of the fathers and neglected the living calls of to-day. "'Tis the day of chattel, web to weave and corn to grind; things are in the saddle, and ride mankind." As in the days of Sir Walter Raleigh, the soul's errand to man was one not of compliment, but of condemnation.

Go, soul, the body's guest,
    Upon a thankless errand;
Fear not to touch the best,

> The truth shall be thy warrant;
> Go, since I needs must die,
> And give them all the lie.

And as an antidote to this comprehensiveness of evil, what is presented? Not the favorite nostrums of religion—revivalistic enthusiasm,
or faith, or prayer—but culture generally, the revelations that come to
the soul from the present spirit of God, and especially solitude and a
return to the simplicity of arcadian life. An exaggerated importance is
attached to the influence of scenery. "All my hurts," as Emerson says,

> My garden spade can heal.   A woodland walk,
> A quest of wild grapes, a mocking thrush,
> A wild rose or rock-loving columbine,
> Salve my worst wounds.

Fresh air and simple living and innocent surroundings were to
bring round again the era when angels were morning and evening
visitors, and the gods communed familiarly with men. Alcott seemed
to think that the devil might be exorcised by well-regulated diet. Altogether, it was on the principle of lessening the denominator rather
than increasing the numerator that the contented, ideal life was to be
sought. But, through all exaggerations of unimportant moral remedies,
there ran a high spirit and purpose, and many persuasive invitations to
the nobler life.

The special form which Transcendentalism took is largely due to
Emerson. That epigrammatic brilliancy, the presentation of truth in
compact parcels containing essences and extracts, the serene equipoise
in the region of ideas, the retreat from the artificiality of towns, the
contempt of argument, the association of things remote by the filmiest
of relations, and the wondrous elevation of tone, all these are his. That
God speaks inwardly to the soul, and in that gives stimulus, strength
and peace, is the essential transcendental teaching; but in many of the
messages delivered, the optimism that scarcely sees evil anywhere, the
conception that the meaning of any one thing contains the meaning
of all creation, his circular philosophy, the union of high vision with
devotion to practical realities, we have contributions from Emerson.
Much of the substance, and the form generally, came from him.

Quite a breeze has lately risen on the subject of the imputed pantheism of Transcendentalism. Mr. Alcott has gone about announcing
to orthodox coteries, and elsewhere, that he was authorized to say that
Emerson is a theist and a Christian theist, and "if you leave out the
word *Christian* you leave out everything." The inference generally drawn
from this has been that the Sage of Concord is another example of

the interesting convert, and from avowed pantheism he has passed on
to avowed theism. This assumption has, however, been denied on
authority by a member of Mr. Emerson's family, and by Mr. Alcott
himself, in a letter to the present writer, and we only glance at the
subject for the purpose of signalizing what we consider a defect and
indeed a contradiction in the ethical teaching of Transcendentalism.
Pantheism teaches that there is one agent in all creation—in the movement of the star, in the blowing of a flower, in every noble and every
depraved act of man. It abolishes human responsibility when logically
carried out. "Whatever is" to it "is right." And tried by this standard
how does Transcendentalism appear? Is it pantheistic? Certainly not, in
general terms. Emerson again and again lays the emphasis on human
freedom and consequent responsibility, and in the alliance existing
between virtue and nature he found almost everything around—winter
and summer, the stars, the river, the wood—teaching the ten command-
ments. He calls the liberation of the will from certain sheaths and clogs
the very "end and aim of the world." Yet in reading the works of Emerson
we stumble with some dismay upon such sayings as these: "And thus,
O circular philosopher, I hear some reader exclaim, you have arrived
at a fine pyrrhonism, at an equivalency and indifference of all actions,
and would fain teach if we are true, forsooth, our crimes may be lively
stones out of which we shall construct the temple of the true God."
To this remonstrance no reply repudiating the imputation it conveyed
is given. And in poetry the same ethereal doctrine is taught:

> Yet speaks yon purple mountain,
>   Yet said yon ancient wood,
> That day or night, that love or crime,
>   Leads all things to the good.

Surely this is remarkable teaching, and not easily reconciled with any
decent respect for the commands of the moral. If there is a splendor
in the noble life, there is a corresponding degradation in the contrary.
Without attempting to explain the paradox, or endeavoring to reconcile
what appears contradictory, we would name as one of the two capital
errors of Transcendentalism as a moral system, that it betrays a
deficient apprehension of the sinfulness of sin. Its optimism recognizes
no shadows. The "saccharine element" is so universal in nature that it
is considered to be equally universal in human life. The doctrine, in
fact, so often found connected with mystic religionism, that evil is
a mere negation, is accepted, or the doctrine that evil is good in the
making and to be characterized at the worst as only an impediment
to our progress. The other deficiency of the system lies in its want of
sympathy. Developed far away from the world, in the serene heights

of contemplation, it scarcely recognized the facts of human suffering and infirmity. Sickness is to it merely an inconvenient fact, to be got rid of as soon as possible; in no sense was it to be considered a moral teacher. Nor are the experiences that draw men to one another in the fellowship of weakness, and thereby soften and humanize, pronounced of any value in the disciplining of human character.

The propagandism of Transcendentalism was carried out by various instrumentalities. Emerson lectured over the country on Reading, and Art and Poetry, and Natural Aristocracy and Society, and kindred subjects. He published three or four series of essays, and "Nature," that wonderful prose poem. The Transcendentalists of Concord and the neighborhood—Alcott, Thoreau, Hawthorne and, not unfrequently, Margaret Fuller—held converse on high subjects every Monday afternoon in Emerson's parlor. The Transcendental Club was instituted, and, meeting in various houses, especially in Boston, discussed Mysticism as an element in Christianity, Pantheism and the American genius. These efforts to promote the new views culminated in a magazine, to which at the suggestion of Alcott, the name "The Dial" was given, and which commenced its career in 1840. Of this publication Margaret Fuller was at first the principal editor, but after a time the responsibility of its supervision fell on Emerson, and its principal contributors were the members of the Transcendental Club. Emerson wrote the introductory article, and sent to it some well-known essays and poems of strange mystic beauty, such as "The Sphynx," "The Problems." Alcott entered on a congenial field by the publication of a series of what he called "Orphic Sayings." Whether these fragmentary utterances are to be considered commonplaces of thought invested in an enigmatic garb, or paradoxes more or less effectively disguised, or a genuine upspringing of waters from the deep well of truth, may reasonably be questioned. At any rate, they furnished the reader such information as the following: "God is instant but never extant in his works; nature does not contain but is contained by him; she is the memoir of his life." "Action is composition, thought is decomposition." "Opinions are life in foliage, deeds in fruitage; always is the fruitless tree accursed." Theodore Parker published in the "Dial" some of his finest papers, as his essay on Dörner's Christology and the powerful satire called "The Pharisees of Modern Times." W. H. Channing gave expression, in his characteristic enthusiasm for the ideal in life and institutions, in a kind of philosophical romance called "Earnest the Seeker." Among the occasional contributors were James Freeman Clarke; Dr. Hedge, who sent a fine poem called "Questionings;" Thoreau, who earned his first laurels as a poet in these pages, and Ripley, who furnished the monthly review. The most voluminous of all the writers was Margaret Fuller, who contributed discussions and biographies, more remarkable for length than brilliancy. Her most notable paper discussed the question of woman's rights in an article called "The Great Lawsuit—Man versus Man, Woman versus Woman." The paper was afterwards enlarged and published as a volume under the title "Woman in the Nineteenth Century." The poetry of the "Dial" was remarkably good. Some departments of philosophic speculation go downwards in search for foundations; with others the tendency is to soar aloft, and through the kindling of enthusiasm to blossom into poetry. To the latter class belonged Transcendentalism, which stimulates more than it informs. In the "Dial," therefore, we find some remarkable poetry, of rather unusual type, wierd, mystical, full of blue skies and green fields; now and then careless of measure, but full of musical thought, and that thought conveying the poetic aspects of Transcendentalism itself. The principal writers in this department were, in addition to Emerson and Thoreau, C. P. Cranch and William Ellery Channing, nephew of the more famous Dr. W. E. Channing.

One outcome, partly of the hopes kindled by Transcendentalism, and partly of the reformatory enthusiasm of the time, was the curious socialistic experiment of Brook Farm. The age fairly teemed with new ideas and philosophic schemes for the reorganization of society. Robert Owen had been trying his plan for the regeneration of the working classes at New Lanark, Scotland; Saint Simonism, in France, and the plan of Fourier, of superseding the home by the phylanstery, had not yet demonstrated their incapacity for the purposes intended; societies are formed to carry out the principle of non-resistance; Garrison is commencing to thunder against slavery; the temperance question comes forward for discussion, and Rev. John Pierpont is compelled to leave Hollis Street Church, Boston, for what was called his injudicious zeal against the rum-seller. Great expectations were entertained of what phrenology and mesmerism and homœopathy were about to accomplish. The prevailing idea of the time, in fact, is that by the adoption of certain social panaceas the evils and sins and diseases under which men groan might be effectually encountered and the millennium that enthusiasts are all looking for might be ushered in. And out of this agitation and expectancy, assisted, perhaps, by a certain impetus given by Transcendentalism, the retreat into primal simplicity, attempted in the Brook Farm scheme, was made.

In this experiment Mr. Ripley, a Unitarian minister of Boston, was the moving spirit. Impressed with the vanity of mere preaching, and desirous of attempting something practical, he sold off his library, and organizing a company of chosen spirits, purchased a farm in the neighborhood of Boston. They wished, by conducting the whole work of the farm, to give a new illustration of the dignity of labor, and offer an emphatic protest against the artificiality of modern life. With the new movement some of the Transcendentalists were in full sympathy, notably Alcott, who for twenty years had been trying the moral effect of vegetarianism; but not so Emerson. Whilst recognizing the excellent intentions that led to the experiment, he still held to the idea that all true reform must come from the uprising of the individual. Parker felt the incongruity of the whole proceeding, but, notwithstanding, spent an occasional happy day among the philosophers turned plowmen, and the poets who did not disdain the wash-tub. Hawthorne actually went through the drudgery of the farm for a number of days, and retired with the conviction that if the soul can be buried in money, the soul, also, can be buried in manure. The movement could only have one end. Financially, it ended in disaster; morally, it was a disappointment. After a trial of the new plan of social regeneration for four years, its promoters turned back to the familiar ways of life somewhat saddened, but convinced that the Arcadian methods they had adopted—sowing and reaping—did not necessarily promote the higher life of man.

Transcendentalism as a living movement is largely a thing of the past. It is said of the projectors of the "Dial," forty years ago, that they were all young men; it may be said of the Transcendentalists now that they are all octogenarians. The impulse of the movement has died. If the old bitter antipathies have changed to something of tolerance, the expectations once entertained have proved mostly dreams. The glories of that brilliant morning have faded into the gray lights of common day; and the world goes round on its axis, and day succeeds night, and men sleep and awake, and suffer and do very much as if Transcendentalism never had been. But have no permanent results been left; have no contributions been made to the world's higher wealth, by all that Emerson and Margaret Fuller and Thoreau and Alcott thought and did? We think there have.

Not that at this time Transcendentalism is very much of a power in the field of philosophy. The leading ideas in this department are now the doctrine of evolution as formulated by Darwin; the idea of Spencer that experience deposits results in the texture of the brain, which are transmitted from generation to generation in the form of aptitudes, instincts and intuitions. Whatever the fluctuations in speculation, these principles stand unmoved, and by the light they cast into many dark regions are only increasing in importance. But Transcendentalism furnished no such commanding ideas. If it contained in itself the materials of a philosophy, it was a philosophy never intelligently rendered to the understanding. Brilliant but fragmentary, offering many an individual truth but no concatenated thinking, a series of scattered stars without the firmament that converts them into a whole, it was to a certain extent one-sided, and to the thinker unsatisfactory. Unable, too, in its devotion to ideal methods to discriminate between the fancy of the individual and a general revelation from the deep nature within or behind, it said strange things, and was compromised by the fantastic utterances of its friends. It ran over into exaggerations and extravagances. And at this time any influence it exercises as a philosophic system it exercises through the writings of Emerson, and by the lectures delivered through the short summer course of study instituted by what is called the Concord School of Philosophy. The school, however, is scarcely transcendental. Inaugurated at St. Louis by two or three persons—Lieutenant-Governor Brockmeyer and William T. Harris in particular—who had organized themselves into a club for the study of German metaphysics, it became transferred to the East, and it is now only transcendental because the place where its lectures are delivered is the Orchard House of Concord, and that the great questions of philosophy are treated by it prevailingly from the ideal point of view. Its leaders are Platonists, Hegelians, or mystics, and in its spiritual aim and method it meets Emerson at many points.

But Transcendentalism was par excellence a *stimulus*, and to some extent a revelation, morally and religiously. It purified the air and amplified the horizon. It invited men to bravery and aspiration; and in some way, not easily explained perhaps, cast auroral lights around life. Speaking of Emerson in the early days of his career as a lecturer, J. R. Lowell says: "There is no man living to whom, as a writer, so many of us feel and thankfully acknowledge so great a debt for ennobling impulses." "It is the sound of the trumpet that the young soul longs for, careless what breath may fill it. Sidney heard it in the battle of Chevy Chase, and we heard it in Emerson. Nor did it blow retreat, but called to us with assurance of victory. If asked what was left—what we carried home? we should not have been careful for an answer. It would have been enough if we had said that something beautiful had passed that way. Or we might have asked, in return, what one brought away from a symphony of Beethoven. Enough that he had set that ferment of wholesome discontent at work in us."

In religion Transcendentalism was more than an inspiration; to a certain extent it transformed leading men to look at essentials, it broadened out sympathy, it gave emphasis to the spiritual aspects. Especially, it dismissed the Divinity of the last century, who was represented as having returned after creation into the remoteness of eternity, and to have been a non-resident, as far as the world is concerned, ever since; and it taught a living God, present in every changing day and season, and in the heart of man, and giving immediate revelations intended for you and me. The nearness of God, the authority of the spiritual laws that went on in their course with the relentlessness of fate, and at the same time with the beneficence of Providence—inspiration, not mechanical or miraculous, but natural as the sunlight, were its themes. Emerson was neither Unitarian nor Trinitarian, exclusively—thanking God for what was good in both.

Margaret Fuller says she was cheated out of a Sunday by hearing Mr. A. "He refused to deny mysteries, to deny the second birth, to deny influx, to renounce the sovereign gift of insight, for the safe of what he called a 'rational' exercise of will." This Mr. A., we believe, was a Unitarian, and fifty years ago scarcely a Unitarian minister could be found who did not sympathize in the opinions he held, and at this day there is scarcely a Unitarian minister who has not, in the matter of insight and communion with God, gone over to Margaret Fuller and the Transcendentalists. A present living God, addressing communications to men in this day, is now the theme of all the churches. And if this is so, and if men care less for the formal and more for the spiritual in religion, and in every good and beautiful act recognize something that is well-pleasing to God—if the sympathies of the churches are broadening, and their influence on life less marred with harsh and disfiguring accompaniments—the result is largely due to Transcendentalism and the causes that made Transcendentalism what it was.

"Some Phases of Idealism
in New England"

O[ctavius]. B[rooks]. Frothingham*

Among the papers of the late George Ripley is the following list of names under the head of "Transcendentalism," plainly intended to convey his notion of the phases through which idealism in New England passed during the several passages of its career. No hint is given of the rule adopted by the author in making this enumeration. It was evidently not the order of development in time, for in that case W. E. Channing, R. W. Emerson, James Walker, F. H. Hedge, would claim mention among the first. It was not the order of speculative rank; for in that case some who are placed at the beginning would be omitted entirely. The author probably followed a classification suggested by some conception of his own in regard to the unfolding of ideas and their sequence from one stage to another. It will be observed that a few important names are passed by altogether, as, for instance, that of O. A. Brownson, who made idealism the basis of his speculative position, first as a reformer, and afterwards as a Roman Catholic; and also that of Henry James, an exceedingly able, eloquent, and uncompromising writer, who applied the Transcendental postulate to society in a manner to terrify cautious men. Why these were omitted does not appear; perhaps Mr. Ripley did not take the trouble to complete his list; perhaps he had in view only the philosophical aspects of the Transcendental movement, and did not care to follow it beyond the line of recognized ideas, either in reform or theology. Here is the list, as existing in his manuscript: N. L. Frothingham (1820), Convers Francis, John Pierpont, George Ripley (1830), F. H. Hedge, James Walker, Thomas T. Stone, W. E. Channing, J. F. Clarke, R. W. Emerson, W. H. Channing, Theodore Parker. Such a grouping of itself implies that idealism took its hue from the temperament of those professing it; that it was no definite or fixed system, but rather a mode of speculative thought which each believer pursued according to the bent of his mind. The first two names suggest the literary tendency of the new faith; the third, its application to specific reform; the next four, its bearing on the principles

*Reprinted from *Atlantic Monthly Magazine*, 52 (July 1883), 13–23.

of philosophy; the two Channings, J. F. Clarke, and Theodore Parker illustrate its bearing on points of religious opinion, while Mr. Emerson represents idealism pure and simple, apart from all philosophical or sectarian
beliefs, from all critical or speculative dogmas.

Only by virtue of some such general classification can N. L. Frothingham be ranked among Transcendentalists. He was not a philosopher,
not a man interested in abstruse speculation, not a reformer of society
as a whole or in part, not an innovator on established ways of thinking
or living. He was a man of letters, an enthusiastic admirer of literary
form, of eloquent language, of ingenious, elegant thought. His large
library contained none of the great masterpieces of speculation, little of
Plato, less of Aristotle, next to nothing of Spinoza or Kant, nothing of
Schelling or Hegel, but much of Heine, Schiller, Rückert, and poets in
either prose or verse, whether English, French, or German. Writers of
opposite schools interested him if they wrote brilliantly, but to profound
spiritual differences he was insensible. He enjoyed Macaulay and Ruskin,
Walter Scott and Dickens, Cicero and Shakespeare. Novelties he disliked
and repelled. Wordsworth he did not read, or Byron; Keats he never
spoke of; Shelley he abhorred; the Victorian bards he could not relish.
In the Transcendental reform of his time he took no part, had little
sympathy with Dr. Channing, and, though personally intimate with R. W.
Emerson, F. H. Hedge, George Ripley, Theodore Parker, and other
leaders in the new movement, could not be persuaded to concern himself with it, even in its initiatory stages. When invited to conferences, he
courteously declined, as one might do who did not feel called to leave
his wonted round of pursuits. But his interest in theological and Biblical
literature was very keen, as the books on his shelves and his translations
of Herder's Briefe abundantly attest. It is on the strength of these translations, and of an article in the Christian Examiner on The Beginning and
Perfection of Christianity, evidently prepared for the pulpit, that Mr.
Ripley assigns to him a place among the friends of Transcendentalism.
This place he undoubtedly deserved, for, although averse to public demonstration, and unoccupied with speculative issues, topics, or discussions,
his mind lived in the spirit of the new ideas. He was at heart an idealist.
His sermons were free from dogma, from doctrinal bias, from controversial animosity, almost from debatable opinion on the theological
ground. He was a friend of knowledge. With him, refined reason was the
test of truth. He loved air and light, liberty combined with law. Views
that exhilarated, books that cheered, intercourse with expansive, joyous
intellects, charmed him especially. If hard-pushed by antagonists, he
might have called himself an idealist, but he never was hard-pushed. The
smooth and even tenor of his life fell in with his scholarly disposition,
and allowed him to pursue his favorite studies undisturbed by polemical
aggressions. He had all the liberty he wanted. Emerson called him an

Erasmus, and he had some warrant for his definition. But it must be remembered that Mr. Frothingham belonged to an older generation, and consequently was less open than young men are to new emotions. Had he been Luther's contemporary he would have been more open to criticism than he was. The only ones of his generation who took an active part in the new protest were Convers Francis and Caleb Stetson. Dr. Channing was in sympathy with the movement, but did not join it. The rest were new men. Belonging to the most liberal sect of Christians, while others broached new doctrines or contended for larger spiritual freedom, his gentle, peace-loving spirit was contented with the permission to read and think without embarrassment. Neither Dr. Channing's earnest pleading for the dignity of human nature, nor George Ripley's calm exposition of the powers of the soul, nor James Walker's vindication of the spiritual philosophy, nor Theodore Parker's vehement denunciation of formalism in religion, nor William Lloyd Garrison's arraignment of the United States Constitution stirred his enthusiasm. The numerous projects for regenerating society which hurtled in the air offended him. He was not of the crowd which followed Mr. Emerson. He never visited Brook Farm. Like Longfellow, he hated violence, delighting in the still air of his books, and lacking faith in the transforming efficacy of insurgent ideas. His was a poetic mind,—delicate, fastidious, disinclined to entertain depressing views, averse to contention on any field. The evils of the world did not shroud him in gloom, or summon him to the combat with either error or sin. Very far from being self-indulgent,—on the contrary, being generous, affectionate, disinterested,—he was wanting in the vigor of conviction which makes the champion, the reformer, or the martyr. His conscience was overlaid by the peradventures of critical thought. He detested Calvinism, for in his nostrils it smelt of blood. He had no liking for the ordinary Unitarianism, which, in his view, was prosaic. Idealism fascinated him by its poetic beauty rather than by its philosophical truth, and drew him towards the teachers whose steps he could follow. This position was fully recognized by his friends, who read his books, enjoyed his converation, profited by his counsel, and were inspired by his enthusiasm for generous thoughts, but soon ceased to expect partisan sympathy or coöperation from him. Such a man may be called a pioneer in the Transcendental movement, for he was in the spirit of it, and such force as he threw was cast in that direction; but in no other sense was he a leader.

The service rendered by men of his cast was nevertheless very great at a time when literature was so closely associated with theology as to be quite unemancipated. In fact, there was no such thing as a literary spirit in America before Transcendentalism created one, by overthrowing dogma and transferring the tribunal of judgment to the human mind. A literary taste, correct, fastidious, refined, and firm, first became possible

when all literary productions were placed on the same level and submitted to the same laws of criticism; and idealism of this type supplied
the necessary conditions. One must have been through and through pervaded by the Transcendental principle before he could have cast a free,
bold regard on the beauties of the pagan classics, or on the deformities
of books hitherto looked on as above human estimate. The services of
those scholars who first ventured to do this, who did it without hesitation, who encouraged others to do it, has never been appraised at its full
value. The influence of Transcendentalism on literature has been lasting
and deep, and that influence is shown in nothing more signally than in
this liberation of the human mind from theological prejudice. Writers felt
it who would not call themselves Transcendentalists, but who read books
which had been sealed to them before. In Germany the literary spirit was
illustrated by minds like Goethe, Schiller, Herder, to mention only three
of many names. In France authors famed for brilliancy made it attractive.
In England Coleridge, among others, made it honorable. In New England
Emerson, Margaret Fuller, Hedge, the writers in the Dial, took up the
tradition. For pure literary enthusiasm, N. L. Frothingham was distinguished among his compeers. On his library shelves all books stood side
by side. His sermons were marked by exquisite felicity of expression and
by admirable literary proportion. The appeal was always made to the
hearer's reason; the argument was in all cases addressed to his understanding; and the assumption was that the human heart was the final
tribunal. Many things were doubted that were not disproved. Some things
were questioned in private that were not doubted in public, the evidence
not being esteemed conclusive, and official responsibility forbidding
hasty utterances.

It has been conjectured that Theodore Parker had Dr. Frothingham
in mind in the famous discourse on the Transient and Permanent, where
he vehemently rebukes the preacher who said one thing in his study and
another in his pulpit. But this could hardly have been the case, for Mr.
Parker was a man of scrupulous honor, and Dr. Frothingham was his
personal friend. Besides, it was not true that Dr. Frothingham said one
thing in his study and another in his pulpit. He simply did not say everything in his pulpit that he said in his study. He was a scholar and a
critic; he was, too, a singularly frank, conversable, outspoken man among
his friends and intimates. But he was likewise a preacher, a man addressing from week to week an assembly of people who were neither scholars
nor critics, but plain men and women looking to him for rational instruction in religion. There is no reason to think that he ever pushed outside
of cardinal beliefs, or ever felt the ground giving way beneath his Unitarian feet. In his own mind he may have entertained speculations which,
if carried out in all their bearings, would have been destructive of the
usual conventionalities of faith. But he never did carry them out in all

their bearings. In his pulpit he was a thoughtful man, mindful of his accountabilities to the truth. It never occurred to him to utter all the misgivings that came into his head. In this he was not alone. James Walker, a more pronounced Transcendentalist than he, and a far more impressive preacher,—an authority on matters of belief; looked up to, quoted, followed; a wise, deeply-inquiring man,—said in private things more searching than Dr. Frothingham, while his public addresses were more conservative; he felt that his personal lucubrations, however interesting they might be to him, would be quite out of place in sermons which aimed at inculcating broad truths and urging universal sentiments.

In a word, temperament is one thing, philosophy is another. There was a temporary coolness—there could not be a long one, with two such men—between Theodore Parker and his old friend and benefactor, Convers Francis, because the latter declined to compromise the Divinity School at Cambridge by preaching for him. But Mr. Francis, however much he admired Mr. Parker, and however warm his personal sympathy with his position may have been, felt the pressure of organized responsibilities, and postponed his private predilections to his public duty. He belonged to the first generation of New England Transcendentalists. He was a man of deep emotions, strong feelings of personal affection, a true friend, an ardent humanitarian, an anti-slavery man of pronounced opinions, a dear lover of intellectual liberty, as all Transcendentalists were. But he had none of the gifts of the popular orator; his voice was unmusical, his action unimpassioned, his style of address scholastic. An enthusiast in his love of natural beauty, the melodies of creation, the singing of birds, the rustling of leaves, the murmur of brooks did not get into his discourse. There was dryness in his tone and in his manner. A quality of bookishness seemed a part of the man. He was an enormous reader of all sorts of books, old and new, conservative and liberal; but his delight was in books that emancipated the mind, whether theological, philosophical, critical, poetical, or simply literary. He was too universal a reader to be a partisan of reform. He saw the strong features of both sides, and while holding very decided opinions of his own, was respectful towards the honest opinions of others. Mr. Francis was a devoted member of "The Transcendental Club;" an attendant at its initial meeting at the house of George Ripley; an intimate friend of Mr. Emerson; in close, sympathetic intercourse with all the men who favored what were known as "advanced opinions." There is no doubt whatever that he belonged to the party of progress. He himself never concealed or disguised the fact that he did. Nevertheless, such was the literary attitude of his mind that he was asked by the party which was not that of progress to leave his parish in Watertown for a professorship in the Divinity School at Cambridge.

His teaching there, on pulpit eloquence, the pastoral office, with all that it implied of history, doctrine, Biblical criticism, was characterized by the same temperate, impartial, truthful spirit. Such, in fact, was his fidelity to the unprejudiced view that it often seemed as if he had no view of his own. The students tried, usually in vain, to drive him into a corner, and extract from him an avowal of private belief; until at last it was the current opinion that he had no belief of his own. Never was there a greater mistake. Out of the class-room he could be explicit enough. Nobody who conversed with him on books, men, and doctrines could for a moment doubt where his personal convictions were. As one who was in the Divinity School during his service there, I can bear witness to the singular candor of his instruction, and to the pleasure he took in imparting knowledge, in stimulating inquiry, in extending the intellectual horizon of young men. His library, his erudition, his thought, were open and free to all. He was even grateful when a scholar wanted anything he had. As I look back over the long course of years that has elapsed since those university days, I can trace distinctly to him liberating and gladdening influences, which, at the time, were not acknowledged as they should have been.

Mr. Francis was an early friend of Theodore Parker, then a youth, teaching school at Watertown. He lent him books, gave him suggestions, encouraged his pursuits, sympathized with his aims, poured out his own stores of learning, put the ambitious scholar in the way of mental advance. And though the pupil presently took a stand which the teacher could not altogether applaud, the feeling of affectionate interest never was diminished, nor at the last was the cordial regard less than it was at the first. The two men, so unlike, yet understood and loved one another.

The philosophical phase of Boston Transcendentalism was also represented by two men,—James Walker and George Ripley. The former has already been spoken of. He was a thinker, calm, profound, silent; a student of opinions, a reader of books, a friendly, warm-hearted man, candid and generous, but in no way demonstrative or oracular. His was a judicial mind, slow in coming to conclusions, but clear, close, firm, reticent; never impatient or forward, outspoken only when fully and finally convinced. His tastes were not especially literary; his reading was severe; he did not much concern himself with political or social reform; was neither leader nor orator. He pondered over Cudworth, Butler, Reid, in England; over Kant, Jacobi, Schleiermacher, in Germany; over Cousin, Jouffroy, Degerando, in France. He occupied himself with problems. In 1834, in a discourse printed later as a tract, on the Philosophy of Man's Spiritual Nature in Regard to the Foundations of Faith, he said, "Let us hope that a better philosophy than the degrading sensualism out of which most forms of infidelity have grown will prevail, and that the minds of the rising generation will be thoroughly imbued with it. Let it be a philosophy which recognizes the higher nature of man, and aims, in a chastened and reverential spirit, to unfold the mysteries of his higher life. Let it be a philosophy which continually reminds us of our intimate relations to the spiritual world," etc. The philosophy thus commended was, it is quite unnecessary to say, Transcendentalism. In 1840, the same teacher, discoursing to the alumni of the Cambridge Divinity School, declared that the return to a higher order of ideas had been promoted by such men as Schleiermacher and De Wette, and gave his opinion that the religious community had reason to look with distrust and dread on a philosophy which limited the ideas of the human mind to information imparted by the senses, and denied the existence of spiritual elements in the nature of man. This was two years after the delivery of Mr. Emerson's famous "Address" which brought on the controversy between Mr. Norton and Mr. Ripley. Mr. Walker's statement was cautious, inasmuch as orthodox theologians might maintain the existence of a spiritual susceptibility which revelation would develop; but at that epoch of time, and from Unitarian lips, the declaration was construed as a confession of faith in the "intuitive" doctrine. There is no evidence that Mr. Walker went beyond the opinion given above, unless an expression used in a sermon be taken as evidence. "The drunkard and the sensualist," he said, "are the monsters;" implying that depravity was not of nature, but a *violation* of nature, which was holy and divine. This, however, may have been only another way of saying that evil was a deprivation, and that goodness was the normal condition of man,—a very innocent proposition. Mr. Walker was in no sense a naturalist, a believer in instinct, an advocate of passion, a patron of organic temperament or constitutional bias. He was a devout Christian in every practical respect, humble, submissive, obedient. Infidelity he ascribed to the opposite school of speculation, and looked to the system he espoused for a restoration of faith. For his own part, he held fast to divine inspiration, Christ, Bible, Church, the established means of grace, simply transferring the sanctions of authority from outward to inward, from external testimony to immediate consciousness, from the senses to the soul, as the deepest thinkers in all ages had done. It was not in his thought to erect a new tribunal, merely to remove an old one from an exposed and precarious position to one of absolute safety. Beyond that he seems not to have gone. In other words, he attributed to the soul a *receptive* but not a *creative* power; an ability to take what was given, but not to *originate* ideas. Dr. Walker had great influence over the young men of his generation, and imparted to them an impulse toward spiritual belief; made them self-respecting, high-principled, noble of purpose, pure, and God-fearing, but he made no skeptics. His last asseveration was of a personal faith in prayer.

The same, essentially, was the position of George Ripley, though the more ardent, impulsive temperament of the man pushed him nearer to the social confines of liberalism. Ripley was not a slow, silent, recluse thinker, not an original creative mind; but a great reader, a student of German, a lover of philosophy, a master of elegant English, a careful writer, a singularly clear expositor. Only in an ideal sense, however, and as democratic ideas were involved in the Transcendental premises, was he a social reformer. He took on himself the most opprobrious names, the more heroically as he was not distinguished as a worker in any of the causes which those names represented. He made heavy sacrifices for Brook Farm, but his was rather a Utopian view of the possibilities of such an institution. There seems to have been a gulf between his conception and his execution. He raised his hand, but could not strike the blow. He was convinced, yet cautious; frank in his persuasions, but reserved in his expressions; his feelings were warm, but he kept them very much to himself. A Transcendentalist he certainly was, an outspoken one; but his chief interest was in the speculative aspects of the faith. He perceived whither the faith tended in times like his, and was not sorry to see others—Parker, for instance—push it to its conclusion, but he could not do so himself. The philosophy alone would not necessarily have led to rationalism. Ripley stood midway between the philosophy and the rationalism to which it readily lent itself, and while standing apart welcomed all earnest scholars in the new field. Materialism he detested; animalism he feared; criticism he never pursued. The French school, as represented by Cousin, Jouffroy, and Constant, was his favorite before the German, which he sought rather for literary stimulus, Goethe being his model writer. It was evident that the Transcendental system, which was but a literal form of idealism, was running into sentimentalism, the deification of human nature, but in 1836 that was merely a tendency. Its real influence was conservative of established institutions and ideas. So it was in James Walker, so it was in George Ripley, the two men who stood for the philosophical truth of idealism. From thought to feeling, however, the step was short and quickly taken, as we shall see.

The ethical element in Transcendentalism followed closely on the intellectual. This, also, had two representatives,—John Pierpont and Theodore Parker. Why John Pierpont? He is the third named on Mr. Ripley's list, and is a good example of the indirect force of philosophical ideas. Forty years ago he was conspicuous as a champion of temperance in Boston, as the hero, in fact, of an ecclesiastical council held to determine his relations to his parish in Hollis Street. He was not a philosopher, not a man of letters, though he wrote verses. "Poetry is not my vocation," he said, in the preface to his published volume. It evidently was not. With a few exceptions, his verses were reform manifestoes, rhymed sermons, exhortations in metrical form. He published sermons and letters, but they were more remarkable as specimens of dialectics than as examples of philosophical acuteness. Apparently he was not greatly concerned with speculative questions, not abstract, introspective, ethereal, but tremendously concrete. In the ranks of the idealists he was never conspicuous. The lists of attendants on the discussions of the newest phases of thought do not contain his name. He was a reformer of an extreme description,—an abolitionist, a temperance man, a general iconoclast. But all this he seems to have been by virtue of that faith in the natural man which was characteristic of the Transcendentalism of the period. His views of Christianity as a religion of humanity; of the gospel as a proclamation of universal good will; of the Christ as an elder brother, saving by unfolding men and women; of God as a loving Father,—all pointed in the direction of social reconstruction. He believed in remodeling circumstances, in obtaining liberty, in securing better conditions of life for the unprivileged. The agitators loved him, the teetotalers, the come-outers, the spiritualists, because he hit hard the lucrative, organized evils of the time, but he was a thorn in the flesh of moderate people who hated such inspiration.

The air of the period was agitated by furious winds. Naturalism in every shape was abroad. Meetings were held, newspapers were printed, and "organs" were established in advocacy of new ideas in every direction. Temperance, anti-slavery, non-resistance, mesmerism, phrenology, Swedenborgianism, spiritualism, antimonianism [sic], materialism, had all their prophets. There was a general outbreak of protest against received dogmas and institutions. In the heat of this turmoil appeared the Luther of the time,—Theodore Parker. He was a man of prodigious intellectual voracity united with a corresponding moral earnestness; no mystic or seraphic enthusiast, no idealist by native temperament, but a stout reformer in the sphere of practical ethics, honest, faithful, courageous, uncompromising. His first direction was theological. Convers Francis stimulated his appetite for reading of a religious character. The Divinity School at Cambridge threw him into a whirl of questioning, which involved him in argument, and resulted in doubt. The spirit of the age added fuel to the flame. N. L. Frothingham lent him books. George Ripley gave him the guidance of a clear mind, of capacious knowledge and firm convictions, not to speak of the quickening sympathy of a hopeful, bright spirit. The new theology found him an easy convert, especially as led by men like Herder, Schleiermacher, De Wette, in Germany; like Channing, Walker, Ripley, at home. Emerson fascinated him, excited in him the passion for liberty, animated his courage, awoke his confidence in the soul. But after all he did not come rapidly to his final convictions. To be a Unitarian, making reason a critic of dogmas, was something. To be a *liberal* Unitarian, setting reason to judge certain records of the Bible, as well as certain dogmas of the creed, was the next step. To exalt reason as the final judge of revelation was the final conclusion. He was critical rather than speculative, concrete rather than abstract. He became an idealist from reading and personal association, but he was not one by constitution. He preferred Aristotle to Plato, Fichte and Jacobi to Kant and Schelling, was more akin to Paley than to Cudworth. His Transcendentalism had a basis in common-sense. Instead of serenity withdrawing, like Emerson, from a profession he could not follow, instead of plunging heroically into some humane enterprise, like Brook Farm, as his friend Ripley did, leaving the pulpit he could not occupy with hearty conviction, he maintained his attitude, threw down the glove of defiance, and took the profession to task for its shortcomings, waging a war that lasted for years. He was not a seer or a regenerator, but a prophet and a warrior, "the Orson of parsons," as Lowell called him. He used idealism as a safe territory to lodge cardinal truths in while criticism was ravaging the country of historical Christianity. His very idealism took practical form. Not satisfied with the sublime indefiniteness of Emerson, or the silent stoicism of Ripley, he put his transcendental postulates into portable packages, doing for them what he did for Webster's philosophy of a republic: "The people's government, made for the people, made by the people, and answerable to the people." Parker turned the formula over in his mind as the sea turns over rough stones, until finally it became smooth and round, as thus: "Democracy, that is, a government *of* all the people, *by* all the people, *for* all the people." So, unable to hold idealism pure and simple, he condensed its aroma into the three ultimate facts of consciousness: The Existence of God; The Immortality of the Individual Soul; The Moral Law. When Ripley was content, in the controversy with Andrews Norton, to illustrate and maintain the excellence of the spiritual philosophy, Parker, as "Levi Blodgett," contended that man had a spiritual eye by which he could look directly on specific ideas, and obtain an immediate knowledge of truths. Emerson knew Parker incidentally only, and, while admiring his brave independence, was too far removed from him by the method of arriving at convictions, as well as by the convictions themselves, to be intimate with him.

In a word, Parker was a reformer. Yet, even as a reformer, he was a critic. He saw the weak points in the argument of the total abstinence men; he detected the vulnerable places in the armor of the champions for a secular Sunday; and he shot deadly arrows at phrenology. Though a close personal friend of Ripley, a minister at West Roxbury, a frequent visitor at Brook Farm, he would not join the community; once, being asked what he thought of it, he replied: "Ripley, there, seems like a highly finished engine drawing a train of mud-cars." The anti-slavery reform seems to have been the only one to which he gave himself without reserve, and to this he devoted his energies with singular constancy and extraordinary power. It summoned his whole force to combat,—his religious zeal, his moral earnestness, his scorn, his pity, his faith in God,

his confidence in man, his trust in Providence, his belief in democratic
institutions, his passon for statistical proof, his love of conflict, his eloquence, his sarcasm. Here was genuine, unadulterated humanity in its
most practical shape. It is hardly doubtful that multitudes were attracted
to him by this alone,—multitudes who did not comprehend or sympathize
with his religious views, but were fascinated by his manliness, and by the
undercurrent of faith which sustained it. Finally he became an ethical
idealist. Had he lived longer, he would probably have thrown himself
into one of the social causes that have come up since the war. The much
meditated book on Theism which was to have embodied his spiritual
ideas would have been interrupted by the battle-cry that summoned him
to arms. The music of the spheres would have been drowned in the din
of conflict.

To Dr. Channing really belongs the credit of transferring the evidence of Christianity to the field of human nature. He was a Christian,
but a spiritual one. He believed in Christ as "Mediator, Intercessor, Lord
and Saviour, ever living, and ever active for mankind; through all time,
now as well as formerly, the active and efficient friend of the human
race." He was persuaded that all spiritual wisdom and influence came
from above. From this persuasion he never was separated. At the same
time he had faith in the human soul as the organ through which the
divine communications were made. "We have, each of us, the spiritual
eye to see, the mind to know, the heart to love, the will to obey God."
"A spiritual light, brighter than that of noon, pervades our daily life.
The cause of our not seeing it is in ourselves." "They who assert the
greatness of human nature see as much of guilt as the man of worldly
wisdom. But amid the passions and the selfishness of men, they see another element,—a divine element,—a spiritual principle." He was not
afraid of philosophy or criticism; in fact, he listened to them patiently,
hopefully, as long as they promised a nearer access of the human soul
to the divine, as long, that is, as they tended to remove obstructions
of ignorance; beyond that he had no interest in them. To him the panic
about Emerson's famous Divinity School address seemed uncalled for.
Parker's positions gave him no uneasiness. But he did not think that
science or philosophy or criticism were likely to solve the problems of
being, and when he perceived that their energies were expended in a
mundane direction, his expectation from them was at an end. "I see
and feel the harm done by this crude speculation," he wrote in a letter,
"whilst I also see much nobleness to bind me to its advocates. In its
opinions generally I see nothing to give me hope. I am somewhat disappointed that this new movement is to do so little for the spiritual
regeneration of society."

Dr. Channing's faith in human nature led him to take a deep concern
in all reforms that contained the germ of a new life for the future of

humanity,—temperance, the education of the working classes, anti-slavery. He was one of the inspirers of Brook Farm. To use the language of his biographer,—"His soul was illuminated with the idea of the absolute, immutable glory of the Moral Good; and reverence for conscience is the key to his whole doctrine of human destiny and duty." But Channing thought as well as felt, considered as well as burned. Hence the restraining limitations of his zeal. He desired the elevation of the race, not of any single class. His very idealism, therefore, in proportion to its earnestness and breadth, made him pause. He was in communication, chiefly through letters and conversation, with the current ideas of the time, but no thought fairly engaged him that had not an ideal aspect; no reform enlisted his support which did not hold out the prospect of a large future for mankind. He was a Unitarian, primarily because Unitarianism seemed to him the more spiritual form of the Christian faith. His whole view of Unitarianism was spiritual, and except for that had little attraction for his mind. The dogmatic side of it had no charm for him; he was not a formalist in any degree, and it is not probable that he would have advocated any system of mere opinions which promised nothing for the well-being of the race.

Mr. Emerson was a man of different stamp from any of those mentioned. An artist in the construction of sentences and the choice of words, he was not a man of letters, for he ever put substance before form. A student of Plato, he was not a philosopher, for the intellectual method was foreign to his genius. Though foremost in every movement of radical reform,—the antislavery cause, the claims of woman, the stand for freedom in religion, a bold speaker for human rights, a eulogist of John Brown, of Theodore Parker, of Henry Thoreau, he was not a reformer, for he avoided conventions, eluded associations, and perceived the limitations of all applied ethics. He was not, in any recognized sense of the term, a Christian. He would call no man Master. He knew of no such thing as authority over the soul. He would acknowledge no mediator between finite and infinite. He had no belief in Satan; evil, in his view, was a shadow; the sense of sin was a disease; Jesus was a myth. "There are no such men as we fable; no Jesus, nor Pericles, nor Cæsar, nor Angelo, nor Washington, such as we have made. We consecrate a great deal of nonsense because it was allowed by great men." "A personal influence is an *ignis fatuus.*" All his life he resisted interference with the spiritual laws. One might call him Buddhist as easily as Christian. He was the precise opposite of that,—the purest idealist we have ever known.

But no diligent reader of his books will doubt that Emerson was a theist of a most earnest description; so earnest that he would not accept any definition of deity. From this faith came his passion for wild, uncultivated nature, for rude, unsophisticated men, as most likely to be informed with the immanent Spirit. From this came his invincible optimism; his boundless anticipation of good; his brave attitude of expectancy; his sympathy with whatever promised emancipation, light, the bursting of spiritual bonds; his love of health, beauty, simplicity; his serene confidence that the best would ultimately befall in spite of grief and loss. He was disappointed in individuals, in groups of individuals, in causes and movements; but although the looked-for Spirit did not come down, his assurance of the justness of his method kept him on tiptoe with expectation. He would not call himself a Transcendentalist. "There is no such thing as a Transcendental party; there is no pure Transcendentalist; we know of none but prophets and heralds of such a philosophy; all who by strong bias of nature have leaned to the spiritual side in doctrine, have stopped short of their goal. We have had many harbingers and forerunners; but of a purely spiritual life, history has afforded no example." Transcendentalism, he said was but a form of idealism, a name bestowed on it in these latter days; but the fact was as old as thinking. The notion that the soul of man could *create* truth, or do anything but meekly receive it from the divine mind, probably never occurred to Emerson. No virtue was more characteristic of him than humility.

Shortly after the History of Transcendentalism in New England was published, Mr. Emerson said to the author, that in his view, Transcendentalism, as it was called, was simply a protest against formalism and dogmatism in religion; not a philosophical, but a spiritual movement, looking toward a spiritual faith. And so it was in great part, undoubtedly, though it may be questioned if it would have seized on minds like Walker, Ripley, Hedge, and many besides, but for Kant, Fichte, Jacobi, Shelling [*sic*], Schleiermacher, De Wette in Germany, Cousin in France, Coleridge and Carlyle in England. Unitarianism had lapsed into a thin, barren conventionality, a poor mixture of Arianism, Arminianism, Priestleyism. Consciously or unconsciously, an arid version of Locke's empirical philosophy was accepted by the leaders of the sect. Materialism was avowed and proclaimed. The lectures of Dr. Spurzheim created a rage for phrenology throughout New England, and many a Socinian fell a prey to what Emerson then called a doctrine of "mud and blood." Transcendentalism was a reaction from this earthward tendency, and Emerson was one of its leaders. The young men principally felt the new afflatus. Hedge, who was educated in Germany, and brought the German atmosphere home with him; Parker and Ripley, who read German; Bartol, Bartlett, Dwight, Alcott, Margaret Fuller, Elizabeth Peabody, W. H. Channing, Orestes Brownson, added their genius and fiery zeal.

Thus philosophy and faith, thought and feeling, literary and poetic fervor, united to produce that singular outburst of idealism which has left so deep an impression on the New England intellect. The circumstances of the time determined the particular form it assumed. As those circumstances passed away, the fashion of speculation altered, but the old original idealism remained, and will remain when Channing and Emerson are forgotten except as its interpreters. The local and incidental phases that have been noticed are of the remote past. Literature has come into possession of all its rights. Philosophy sits serenely on its throne, unvexed by its old-fashioned controversy with materialism. Reform is no longer obliged to be one-sided, or extreme, or anarchical, but is taken up by reasonable men and women. Religion is released from dogmatism, at least in a measure, the championship of it being left to scholars of whatever denomination. And all this has been, in great degree, accomplished by men who were once called heretics.

"Transcendentalism: The New England Renaissance"

Francis Tiffany*

The subject given me for my brief hour in this course of lectures reads simply "Transcendentalism." I propose to enlarge the title into "Transcendentalism; or, The New England Renaissance." The especial designation, Renaissance, or Re-birth, I would emphasize from the outset, as starting in the mind a distinct class of conceptions, without the aid of which the New England movement cannot be treated with due sense of historical continuity.

This term, "The Renaissance,"—the New or the Second Birth of the world,—is one we are all familiar with nowadays. In its broadest, its only scientifically historical sense, it denotes what Symonds, who has written the history of the movement in Italy, summarizes as "the whole transition from the conceptions of the Middle Ages to the conceptions of the Modern World." Its two grand achievements were, as Michelet puts it, "the discovery of the world and the discovery of man." High-sounding terms these,—"the discovery of the world and the discovery of man"; but in how vast a sense are they literally true! Go back in imagination to the Middle Ages, and ask yourselves, Did man then know, did he so much as dream of, this majestic universe which has finally become revealed to the modern mind? Question, again, man's actual knowledge in those days of the character and scope of his own indwelling powers. Did he so much as dream of the triumphs reason was to achieve, of the intellectual systems thought was to build, of the world of beauty art and literature were to create, of the order and stability law was to inaugurate, of the conquests of disease and misery medicine was to usher in, of the richness, variety, and charm all these were to impart to human life? No: as such potential miracle-worker he never suspected himself. He would have thought you were talking of wizards or demons, and have shrunk back in horror. Thus, in a thousand higher aspects of his being, man had not yet been discovered by himself.

*Reprinted from *Unitarian Review*, 31 (February 1889), 97–117; originally prepared for the Channing Hall Course of Lectures.

And how was brought to pass this double discovery of the inner and the outer world? In the one only possible way,—of the foremost intellectuals and characters of Europe beginning to trust in and use their natural powers, thus finding out experimentally alike what these powers were made for, what they could hope to achieve, and to what marvels of marvels they were externally related. The compass, first heard of in 1302, gave the world later on the discovery of America, the rounding of the Cape of Good Hope, the circumnavigation of the globe. The telescope enabled Copernicus and Galileo to prove the revolution of the earth and the true theory of the planetary system. Printing began its marvellous career, and made accessible to thousands the works of the mighty spirits of Greece and Rome. Gunpowder revolutionized the art of war. Men of genius in sculpture and painting revealed the grace and glory of the human form. To France, to Germany, to Holland, to England, the movement spread, to break out in original shapes in Shakespeares and Bacons, in Erasmuses, in Luthers, in Descartes, in Spinozas. Was not all this in truth, then, what Michelet so accurately calls it, "the discovery of man and the discovery of the world"? Did it not inaugurate a new human consciousness, and bring to the lips the ecstatic cry: "What a piece of work is a man! How noble in reason! how infinite in faculties! in form and moving, how express and admirable! in action, how like an angel! in apprehension, how like a god!" How Transcendental, by the way, this last quotation sounds!

Meantime, however, while all this was going forward, there was another and a vastly larger class of people, who looked on with anything but eyes of favor. Nor is it to be wondered at. The smug citizen, who has been accustomed all his days to walk on level ground and with his head up in the air,—no wonder he has a vindictive word to say of the impious physicist, who makes his brain spin by telling him that, in the course of the next twelve hours, he will be where he will have to stand with his feet turned up to the bottom of the globe and his head hanging down into a frightful abyss. The Mediterranean sailor, with a love in every port, whom Columbus drags off to cross the boundless ocean; the routine student, who is contemptuously told to learn to think for himself, when he naturally supposed that others had done all that for him; the comfortable priest, whose whole needful stock in trade had been a string of beads and the mumbling of a few unintelligible Latin prayers; the splendid prelate, with stipends and dignities entirely dependent on the continued ignorance and superstition of the masses; nay, too, the earnest, self-consecrated, saintly man,—the Saint Bernard perhaps,—who does not care an iota whether the world is round or square, beautiful or ugly, learned or ignorant, so that it can only be saved from the leprosy of sin, and who feels that all possible hope of salvation is supernaturally bound up in the dogmas of the Church,—

why should not from all of these break forth a fierce and infuriated protest against the advancing movement? "This blasphemous prying into what God meant to keep secret must be put down." So the infuriated Franciscans cried to Roger Bacon. Mobs, papal anathemas, inquisitions, were in the very air.

We are now getting on to ground upon which it behooves us to tread very carefully, in order to be at once appreciative and just. These two great classes of the human race, which we now see confronted face to face, and glaring at one another with angry eyes, persist in every age,—the champions of the new, the champions of the old; the believers in the future and the believers in the past; the men who trust in reason and think all things possible to it, and the men who distrust it, dread it, in certain fields abhor it. Each party has something to say for itself which it is well to heed. And so, first, a word for this latter party.

Not unlikely, quite a number of persons here present, addicted to pedestrianism, and yet short of stature, may—in the White Mountains, say—have noticed a certain tendency on the part of men six feet in their stockings to exaggerate the statement of the number of miles that may be reeled off per hour with positive comfort and without calling a halt. Laboriously accompanying one of these nine-league booters through a long day's march, does not the man of shorter stride and scantier breath feel, toward the contemplative hour of nightfall, irresistibly impelled to raise the question, "Is not my six-foot friend somewhat exposed to the danger of becoming the victim of what philosophers call 'his own subjectivity'? Does he not, in fine, take a somewhat too transcendental view of average legs,—a view too much lifted into the realm of the absolute and unconditioned, and freed from all impertinences of time and space?" Now here is a simple reactionary feeling, which, duly extended from mere pedicular to intellectual and moral considerations, will serve to interpret vast conservative and even retrograde movements in human history.

We can easily see, then, why a whole range of such sublime sentiments as that "Truth is its own evidence," "Beauty its own witness," "Virtue its own reward," should commend themselves very rapturously to a class of highly spiritual minds, and seem very perplexing and irritating to a denser and opaquer. Oh, yes: only give us a picture, these last poor fellows pathetically cry, in which, as in the earliest human efforts at art, it was plainly written over every animal in the landscape, "This is a cow," or "This is a horse," and then we will freely admit that a cow or a horse is its own intrinsic evidence. Now, for one, I cannot but feel a certain tender and loving sympathy with this particular mental condition. The first awkward, fumbling attempts of the human reason, like the first awkward and fumbling attempts at art, produce rather indiscriminate results. We all perfectly recall the bygone school-days, in which, after four times adding up a column of figures, and getting four entirely distinct answers, we felt a not unnatural uncertainty as to which one of the four might be in strictest accordance with immutable truth. But there was one infallible authority we regarded with as awful reverence as do devout Catholics the symbol of Saint Peter,—the Key to the arithmetic. One glance at this, and we could proudly say of the correct answer, "This is the cow," "This is the horse," and rejoice that truth now shone in its own light and had become its own intrinsic evidence.

But we are seemingly keeping too long away from New England, unless possibly it be on the principle that "the longest way round is often the shortest way home."

The New England colonies were settled by a class of men and women who were a salient illustration of one aspect of the grand uprising of the Renaissance, considered from the point of view of the "whole transition from the conceptions of the Middle Ages to the conceptions of the modern world." In flagrant defiance of the doctrine of the long-assumed divine rights of kings, here was a class of men on the high road to the discovery that kings had a "lith" in their necks. In many directions, their faith in the powers of human reason was emphatically pronounced. That men had abundant capacity for founding States, and that a town-meeting of ministers, lawyers, traders, and farmers was as august a body as a House of Parliament,—of this they rapidly became entirely convinced. In other directions, however, these self-same men were an equally salient instance of a distinct retrogression from the on-setting tide of the Renaissance,—a band of reactionary protesters against what they regarded as its inherent vice.

Every river has its current and its eddy, and so flows two ways at once. Look at its current, and you say it flows north. Look at its eddy, and you say, "No: south." Like flint had the Puritans of England—spite of a few exceptions—set their faces against the joyous, the poetical, the beautiful, the scientific, the speculative and critical aspects of the Renaissance. They would have put a very different estimate on Shakespeare and "all his works" than do you and I, and would have thought his chances in the world to come far more promising if Mr. Ignatius Donelly should only succeed in proving himself to be in the right.

Settled down on the hard soil of New England, with Indians to fight, forests to fell, communities to found, churches to build, forced more or less to become jack-of-all-trades,—in farming, trading, legislation, law, medicine, and, erelong, even divinity,—a literally unexampled growth took place in practical confidence in the power of reason to deal with all kinds of emergencies. The Yankee habit of asking questions, and of always replying by asking another question, now made rapid headway. But, at one point, all this inquisitiveness, all this desire of

learning something new, stopped short. The same man who would question with the most radical audacity the whole political tradition of past
history would recoil in horror at the idea of questioning either the
physical ability or the devout willingness of a foreordained whale to
swallow Jonah. Here the mental arrest was absolute, here the paralysis
of human reason entire.

Time will not serve me to enlarge on the logical consequences of
a mental attitude like this, so radical and defiant in one direction, so
conservative and submissive in another. You can readily see that it
meant two distinct tribunals of judgment,—the tribunal of free reason,
the tribunal of the written Scripture. Neither, farther, will time serve
me to dwell—as I would much like to—on the retarding effect exercised
on the development of many sides of the New England mind by the
almost utter isolation in which it so long found itself, cut off, as it was,
from the great circulating currents of European life,—from its refine-
ments, its science, its art, its philosophy, its literature,—and shut up to a
monotonous diet of politics and technical theology. Enough that all this
necessitated a very narrow and starved mental condition, and left whole
sides of human nature unsolaced and uninspired by any stimulating
environment.

Now, unfortunately for any long-continued success in the establishment of a rigid and inflexible theocracy in New England, the very
worst book in the world had been chosen to found it on,—the Bible.
Strive as you may to overlay it and load it down with a whole Ætna
of burnt-out dogmatic slag scoriæ, and ashes, the Titans within are ever
rending the mountain flanks and pouring out their indomitable insurgent hearts in fresh streams of fiery lava. And so New England had its
perpetual, even though sporadic, witnesses to the inextinguishable
hunger and thirst of the spirit after a fresh, spontaneous, originally
creative, eye to eye, soul to soul, religious life of its own. The first Transcendentalist in New England, Emerson was always fond of saying,
was Jonathan Edwards. A grim, cast-iron specimen of the breed! you
will be tempted to say. Not at all. There are beautiful passages in his
so generally lurid and terrific sermons, which I would agree—could I
only make a private arrangement with Emerson's publishers—to insert
in his essays, and which would be read by his most ardent devotees
without a suspicion that they had not flowed straight out of the mind
and heart of the Concord seer. Of course Jonathan Edwards would have
put in his proviso. "Yes, this glorious power to see God eye to eye,
'to glorify him and enjoy him forever,' is all true. God is his own divine
witness, his own clear interpreter,—but to *the elect alone.*" Of the Quakers,
too, the same might have been said, and in an even broader sense. Their
doctrine of the Inner Light, of the Spirit that judges all things, even
the deep things of God,—what was this but a still bolder assertion of the

indwelling power of the soul to rise above book, priest, formulated creed, and cry to the Eternal, "In thy Light I see light!"

Spite, however, of these not infrequent incursions of a freer and more subjective spirit,—among which I would certainly rank certain aspects of the personal experience doctrine of Methodism, under the lead of its fiery apostle, Whitefield,—it will have to be confessed, I feel sure, that the tendency alike of thought and emotion in New England set steadily on towards a lower, a more literal, a more prosaic and commonplace level. For Calvinism in full eruption we must all feel, I think, the same half-sublime, half-terrific sense of glory and dread with which ₁we look on Vesuvius or Ætna in fiery outbreak. For Calvinism, its craters dead, and its flanks one desert of monstrously contorted rocks and dreary, barren ashes, we must equally feel as we do when toiling up the sun-scorched heights of an extinct volcano of to-day. Such Calvinism in due time became,—a literal burnt-out volcano. Indeed, it would historically look as though the very capacity for deep and strong emotion had been annihilated in the New England heart, so long, so monotonously, and so remorselessly had the soil been religiously overcropped, so frightfully had it been seared and baked by revival fires. It must be suffered to lie fallow a generation or two, to recover heart.

Man shall not live by volcanoes alone. This thousands on thousands were now beginning to feel. Parishes began negatively to express their sense of fatigue by seeking relief in *not* settling "men of strong doctrine." Life had grown to be far more comfortable. Material wealth had witnessed a great increase. A smug, unheroic, average-citizen temperament had been generated. The sensation philosophy of John Locke had won a numerous following. Reason—that is to say, reason within reasonable limits—had gained increased respect. Arminianism began to creep in, and gradually to work on towards Unitarianism. And never, perhaps, —as Rev. O. B. Frothingham so clearly points out in his invaluable *History of Transcendentalism*, a book I would earnestly commend to your reading as the only full and adequate account of this important movement,—never, perhaps, had what I have ventured to call "reason within reasonable limits" so admirable a quarry to disport itself with as was now furnished to Unitarian polemics in the dried and desicated mummy of Calvinism.

For a time "reason within reasonable limits" held high carnival. Now came the days of its young espousals. So delightful was the sense of the privilege of exercising reason on what had hitherto been forbidden fruit, such a fresh and unwonted sensation did it communicate, that no wonder it drew so many able men to embrace the profession of the ministry. The moral argument against Calvinism,—what a glory in heroically calling (and it was heroism then) right, right, and cruelty, cruelty, and tyranny, tyranny, in their own intrinsic nature! The contradictions and absurdities of the received doctrine of the Trinity,—what a fine intellectual invigoration in subjecting these to the canons of a rational logic! Then, too, the rehabilitation of a pure and good life, the loyal championship of it as above all creeds and professions, the stripping off from the dethroned and beggared heir of God the "rags of filthy righteousness," and throwing over his shoulders the royal purple,—who shall tell what a discovery of a new world, of a new man, this was to thousands! Perpetual honor to the early leaders of this movement,—the Worcesters, Channings, Nortons, Noyeses, Deweys, Greenwoods, Ephraim Peabodys, and a host of others. Without the solid foundations of sanity, character, and piety they laid, the more ebullient movement that was to succeed would have run great dangers of eventuating in license and excess.

As time went by, however, the original impulse of Unitarianism began to lose its first vitality. You cannot call a new thing new forever. There is a first cry of "Land! land!" which not even a Columbus can raise a second time. People became accustomed to the exercise of "reason within reasonable limits," and to feel the stirrings of a call to "fresh hills and pastures new,"—that is, a limited number did. As for the bulk of the body, it began to manifest a strong disposition to settle down in a traditional way. Channing, with his high-wrought prophetic sense of the new glory that was to break forth, expressed the keenest disappointment over this state of arrested development, and declared he felt less and less interest in Unitarianism. "Reason within reasonable limits" had grown highly respectable; its adherents were the prosperous and honored; it had its scholars, whose conclusions were to be insisted on as impregnable and final; it had established noble charities and entered energetically on the work of a more rational education and of wiser and better institutions for the pauper, the felon, the insane,—what more could reasonably be asked of it? Why could it not be suffered to enjoy its laurels?

Ah, friends, laurels wither, when long since plucked from the living tree. As a momentary symbol, and while green and glistening, how beautiful! when dry, sere, and rattling, what a mockery! Unitarianism had always had carried with it one serious limitation and drawback. It had the note of provincialism; it was cut off from the grand circulating currents of the world's larger life; it lacked alike the prophetic sense of its own fuller mission and the spiritual imagination to build its inspiring ideal. It was abandoned to no infinite principle. It was to be the leaven of Orthodoxy, its work accomplished when it had taught Orthodoxy to make the same kind of bread with itself. This bread had come to be a certain regulation loaf with whose size, weight, and easy digestibility the majority were entirely satisfied. Its Channing, whom it never half comprehended, and in many ways hampered and distressed, was to it the utmost limit of the horizon, if not a suspicious degree beyond. Its look was turned backwards. And so it began to ossify. Angry recriminations were now to be heard against any proposal of innovation; and, while no hands were more munificent in subscriptions for building the tombs of its past prophets, none were handier with a brick or an egg for the reception of new prophets. The mercantile influence, the mercantile standard of spiritual values, was paralyzing it. I beg everybody's pardon, but one more generation of the like, and Unitarianism would have degenerated into a simple gospel for the Philistines. Transcendentalism, we now see clearly enough, saved it by breathing into it the spirit of a newer and larger life.

Who are the Philistines?—peace to the shade of Matthew Arnold after all his effort to define them! They are an eminently respectable body of half-vitalized men and women, good fathers, good mothers, good citizens, exposed to the perpetual danger of perishing of dry rot through the prosaic, commonplace, and utterly unimaginative character of their constitutional temperament and actual environment. Woe to the world that does not possess solid masses of them! and woe equally to themselves, if, for their own best good, their Canaan is not every now and then invaded, conquered, and reconstructed by the children of light!

Who, again, are the children of light? They are the mobile, impressionable, and impassioned temperaments of every age, the diviners of the signs of the oncoming future, the cordial welcomers of every promise of a fuller, richer, more spiritually imaginative life, the believers in the things eye hath not yet seen nor ear heard. And such were the early leaders of Transcendentalism in New England. I need but to enumerate such names as those of Emerson, Alcott, Margaret Fuller, Elizabeth Peabody, Mrs. Ripley, Dr. Hedge, Dr. Furness, George Ripley, Dwight, Cranch, Caleb Stetson, Clarke, Bartol,—almost all Unitarians by nurture. Faithful to the best that had come down to them from their inheritance in the past, they yet turned eager, anticipating eyes toward a diviner future, and from their heart of hearts prayed the prayer,—

> "Let knowledge grow from more to more,
> But more of reverence in us dwell;
> That mind and soul, according well,
> May make one music as before,
> But *vaster*."

Now we have already taken notice of certain signs in the past of what Emerson recognized as having the note of genuine Transcendentalism,—the confidence, namely, of the spirit in itself. But it was only in a very restricted way that this confidence of the spirit in itself held true. The Quakers, with their emphasized doctrine of the function of the

Inner Light, made the nearest approach to it. These Quakers as a body were, however, spite of a few very beautiful exceptions, a narrow, ignorant, and fanatical class of men and women, who most unhappily thought that the more completely they cut themselves off from nature, literature, beauty, art, science, and philosophy, the brighter would be the shining of the Inner Light. Indeed, in the Quaker horror of such profanities as music and dancing, there could hardly have sprung up among them, and been told of one of their prophets and one of their prophetesses, such a myth as that which records the story of how, on witnessing together the exquisite aërial evolutions of the Viennese *danseuse*, Ellsler, as she came down tiptoe, with "a station like the herald Mercury, new lighted on a heaven-kissing hill," Mr. Emerson bent over with effusion to Miss Fuller, and exclaimed, "Margaret, this is poetry!" while she, in turn, breathlessly ejaculated, "Ralph, it is religion!"

This, of course, is simple travesty. And yet what an ill historical student would he be, who did not reckon alike with the travesties and with the broadest comic caricatures of any period he studies! seeing how, under exaggerated and laughable aspects, these are so many illustrations of the popular feeling of the day. What is really hit at, in this especial one I have cited, is the entirely novel and unrestricted ranges of experience on which, in contrast with the sober earlier New England habit of mind, the Transcendentalists began to insist as sources of light and inspiration. In point of fact, we are here directly led to what must be emphasized as the *most characteristic feature* of the Transcendental Movement in New England; namely, that it took its rise among a class of men and women at once *highly impressionable* and *broadly cultivated*. Their Bible had to be a very large one, and with very little line of distinction between its canonical and apocryphal books.

Now, for all the clearly enunciated belief of the votaries of the new movement in their own eyes and ears, just as significant a fact was it that they believed equally in the eyes and ears of a vast range of other authoritative teachers. Their attitude was quite as much docile and reverential as it was self-assertive. Communications were beginning to be re-established between isolated, provincial New England and the grand circulating currents of European literature, art, philosophy, and science. Through the writings of Coleridge—especially that epoch-making book of his, the *Biographia Literaria*—aspiring young minds in New England were beginning to get hints, and more or less satisfying outlines, of a grand order of thinking, inaugurated in Germany by men of the stamp of Kant, Fichte, and Schelling. Such shorter pamphlets of Fichte as "The Vocation of the Scholar" and "The Destination of Man" rang like the battle-call of the bugle in their ears. The volcanic mind of Carlyle had, moreover, broken out in full eruption; and, in the lurid clouds of fuliginous smoke with which he seemed to fill the whole canopy,—clouds lighted up with the fiery glare of the crater burning in his own breast,—sensitive spirits seemed to read once more the revelation of a world sublime and awful as that of Calvinism, but with its symbols plucked out of the fiery heart of the nineteenth century instead of out of the heart of the Middle Ages.

He professed to have made an Alpine, a Himalayan discovery. A new mind had come into the world, an original creation fresh from the hand of God,—a mind towering to the zenith, continental in the base of its foundations, its flanks all glorious with forests and gorges and fertile valleys, teeming with corn and wine. This Mount Blanc, this Mount Everest, he named by the name of Goethe, and cried to the world "Lo! the man who has experienced everything, suffered everything, closed in Jacob wrestle with everything, only to triumph at last in clear, loving, utterly reconciled Olympian serenity over them all!" There was in those days a note in the voice of Carlyle as of some Titanic Promethean sufferer, long-riveted to the bleak rocks of Caucasus, to whom has at last come the glorious prophecy of deliverance; and mightily it stirred the hearts of others.

Still not alone in the way of indirect importation, through the medium of the English intellect were the influences coming in that were to throw the more susceptible minds of New England into ferment. Aspiring young scholars, like George Bancroft were beginning to cross the ocean to learn the tongue of Germany, and to come into direct contact with its masters in theology, philosophy, and historical criticism. It may seem out of place to name Mr. Bancroft as a force in the development of the Transcendental movement; but such a force he indirectly was through the broader style of thinking, the more ideal philosophy, and the fresher and more vital views of the right interpretation of history he brought back with him from Germany. But along with him went, in a boy of thirteen, to be placed at school there, a boy who had got ready for college at so irrationally early an age that his father was at his wits' ends to know what to do with him till he should be old enough to enter,—one who was destined to exert a still more direct and profound influence on the New England movement. I speak, of course, of Dr. Frederic H. Hedge. There, on its native soil, he laid the foundations of that thorough and idiomatic acquaintance with the German language which, later in life, when he came to be settled as a minister in what is now Arlington, Mass., enabled him to deal at first hand, and as one "to the manner born," with the treasures of German criticism, philosophy, and literature. Still another example in the same way I might instance in Mr. John S. Dwight, who, crossing the ocean and coming under the spell of Bach, Mozart, and Beethoven, did such invaluable work through a long life-time in helping on the grand march of the Musical Renaissance, from the day of "Old Hundred" and "Coronation" to the day of the St. Matthew Passion Music and of the Fifth and Seventh Symphonies.

A most serious mistake, however, would it be to regard the Transcendental movement as a simple importation from abroad, a servile imitation of English, French, or German ideas. It was at the last remove from this, and was full of the sap of a spontaneity and freshness all its own. Vasari's old story, of how one sight of a gloriously sculptured Greek sarcophagus in the Campo Santo of Pisa so wrought on the susceptible soul of Niccolò Pisano that, from the hour, all Italian sculpture was revolutionized, was simply repeated on New England soil. Nine-tenths of the early Transcendentalists rubbed but lightly against Plato, Plotinus, Saadi, Firdusi, Kant, Fichte, Goethe, Schleiermacher, Schelling; but it was fructifying pollen they bore away from the contact, and by it their own minds were vitally impregnated. And so it was a genuine Columbus cry of, "The New World! the New World!" even though later voyagers were to discover that it was raised only over San Salvador and not over the whole new continent. For better or worse, then, I repeat it, Mr. Alcott had got hold of Plotinus, Margaret Fuller of Plato and the Greek legends, Dr. Hedge of Kant and Fichte, Emerson of the Hindu and Persian mystics, Mr. Dwight of Goethe and Beethoven, Mr. Ripley of Schleiermacher and, later on, of the works of great French socialistic leaders, Theodore Parker of De Wette, James Freeman Clarke and others of the ethics of Jouffroy and the writings of Cousin. From all alike came the cry, "Oh, brave new world that hath such spirits in it!" Simply impossible was it that such men should not begin to see visions and dream dreams of a new and better order of things,—some of them confining themselves to trying to knead the new leaven into the old lump; others demanding, as in the Brook Farm experiment, the outright inauguration of a new social era.

It will be the pleasant task of other lecturers to speak to you in detail of the bearing on Unitarianism of the various special directions into which the new movement soon branched, and on their domain I must not trespass. Enough for me, if I can make vivid to you the essential spirit and inevitable trend of New England Transcendentalism. First and foremost, it can only be rightly conceived as an intellectual, æsthetic, and spiritual *ferment*, not a *strictly reasoned doctrine*. It was a Renaissance of conscious, living faith in the power of reason, in the reality of spiritual insight, in the privilege, beauty, and glory of life. Perhaps, when Emerson described it as the "very Saturnalia of faith," he touched the centre, alike in the characteristics of its ecstasy and of its excesses. To understand its full significance, therefore, it is absolutely necessary that we summon clearly before the imagination alike what it reacted against in the past and what it sprang eagerly forward to greet in the future. And the readiest and most picturesque way to do this is to call to our aid the presence of two powerful personalities,—the Achilles and the Hector of the war of two distinct intellectual civilizations that had now joined in the issue of battle. They must unhesitatingly be Ralph Waldo Emerson and Professor Andrews Norton.

When, in the summer of 1838, Mr. Emerson gave before the Cambridge Divinity School that marvellous address, whose perennial beauty and perfume are as entrancing today as though exhaled from a fresh-plucked rose or lily, it wrought on a limited class of highly susceptible minds with a sensation only to be paralleled with that of an escape from the crowds, heat, and dust of the stifling city to the scent of the pines and balsams of the forest or the stimulating iodine and boundless horizon of the seashore. "Behold, new heavens and a new earth!" was their literally ecstatic cry. It had given them back, they said, nature, life, Jesus, God. Here was one, they declared, who saw these ineffable presences and shining ones with his own eyes, interpreted them from his own heart, and adored them in the sanctity of his own conscience.

Far differently, however, did this address act on the minds of others, notably on that of their most stalwart champion, Professor Andrews Norton. To him Emerson's utterance stood for a wild, visionary, and utterly reckless assault on the very foundations of religious faith. Peremptorily did he challenge and deny its every premise. "Nothing is left," he declared, "that can be called Christianity, if its miraculous character be denied. Its essence is gone: its evidence is annihilated. . . . There can be no intuition, no direct perception of the truth of Christianity, no metaphysical certainty. . . . No proof of his [Christ's] divine commission could be afforded but through miraculous displays of God's power."

Now, of Professor Andrews Norton no competent man will ever speak but in terms of the highest intellectual and moral respect. His piety, moreover, was of a deep, tender, and inward stamp, as is witnessed by some of his hymns, so uplifting to the devout heart. But here, nevertheless, he stood; and this was his philosophy, or reasoned account of his ground of faith. It was the old Lockian doctrine. Man gets all his ideas through the medium of the senses. These bear witness to the reality of the Now and Here. There must, then, be a direct outward sensation from another realm, to introduce into the world trustworthy confidence in a commissioned revealer of the Elsewhere. A miracle is such outward sensation. The suspension, or outright infraction of, the order of nature is a sense-impression introduced from another realm. The teacher who can do what no other man can—turn water into wine, rebuke the tempest, raise the dead—has hereby produced his credentials from on high, and to him must all hearken.

I do not raise this issue here as a preliminary towards a discussion of the question of miracles, but simply in the way of the elucidation of my own subject,—that of "Transcendentalism,"—whose essential root-

principle is here involved. A conversion by miracle? Why, it is a profanation of the soul! It is outright denial of the whole foundation of religion
in the reason, heart, conscience, spiritual yearning of men. Such was
Emerson's high-wrought and passionate feeling on the subject. And it
was, I think,—in its broad implications,—the fundamental issue of Transcendentalism.

Ah! this whole question of external authority and inward recognition, how infinitely wider a one is it than men suspect! what endless practical issues does it raise in life! How often I used to meditate its full
import in the picture-galleries of Europe, where, in a fresh shape, it was
forced on my attention! There hanging on the walls are the masterpieces
of Raphael, Titian, Correggio, Rembrandt, Rubens, along with no end
of inferior works. What shall the poor, unaided mind do, turned loose
in such a labyrinth? What assurance that the soul shall not "dilate with
the wrong emotion" before an inferior work mistaken for a superior, before a Palma Giovane mistaken for a Titian? Ah! is there not a commissioned and duly authenticated Baedeker, guide-book, philosopher,
and friend? Open his pages, and lo! before every picture marked with
one star you can feel peacefully assured that you are in the presence of
something great, and before every one marked with *two stars* of something superlative. No fear, then, of abandoning yourself to an unjustifi-
able emotion. Yes; and, duly subordinated to the spirit, it is an admirable
contrivance for saving time and for reserving one's vitality for what is
presumably excellent. And yet—and yet—it must never be forgotten what
inherent evils there are in having one's work thus done beforehand for
him. The pictures one finds out for himself through vital elective-affinity,
—those are the ones that make the fructifying impression. Only look at
those poor mortals in the gallery who have yielded themselves uncon-
ditionally to the courses of the stars. What a lack-lustre in their eyes!
What a barren conventionality in their tones!

Sometimes, indeed, this absolute subjection to accredited authority
works utterly paralyzing results. There is, for example, in the Accademia
of Venice, a picture by Carpaccio, about which Ruskin fulminates in his
Mount Sinai way,—fulminates in substance, for I quote him from memory, and confess to far less proficiency in the use of thunder and lightning than he: "Whoever places himself before this picture will be judged
by it forever. If he does not see at a glance that here painting reaches
its highest culminating apex, let him lay it down as adamantine truth
that he is by nature totally destitute of any and every capacity for ever
hoping to cherish one true feeling for art." I have given only feebly what
is expressed by Ruskin himself with all the vigor of the damnatory
clauses of the Athanasian Creed. Well, we know how the Athanasian
Creed has always worked on the free development of private sentiment
in the Church. Now for the way in which its imitation works on the free

development of genuine feeling for beauty. Here come along the gallery, for example, four or five sweet, peach-bloom, demure-looking English girls, each with her Ruskin devoutly in her hands. They have manifestly read their Athanasius; for *Dies iræ, dies illa*—"The Day of Wrath, that Dreadful Day,"—is visibly written on every face. And no wonder! "To be or not to be" in the glorious kingdom of beauty is now the question; and there hangs the painting, and over it the flaming sentence of the infallible Judge. They take their seats in awful silence, and hardly dare to lift their eyes. Do they really like the picture? It is hard to tell; for under such stupendous conditions the fledgling maiden mind does not work spontaneously. Anyhow, like it they must, or else, "without doubt, perish everlastingly." And so they think they do, and go away so relieved.

"Oh! you dear, sweet, silly girls," I was often impelled to cry over such a group, "it is all right that you should be under authority, but why not under the authority of some one who has an inkling at least of the law of the natural development of the human mind? Why, instead of this annihilating Ruskin, should you not have some sensible father, uncle, or elder brother, who would merely turn you loose here, and say: 'Now, girls, fearlessly and honestly, try for yourselves what you really enjoy and what you do not enjoy; no matter whether it be only the simplest face or the simplest figure, so long as it is your own genuine impression. From one genuine impression, you may go on to another, and another, and still another; and who knows at what height you may arrive at last in your enjoyment of the beauty, pathos, and sublimity of these masterpieces? But this simple travesty of education, why, it is falsifying, it is paralyzing your natural capacities from the very start.'"

And now, in conclusion, let me say that I do not know of any better way of illustrating what seems to me the root-idea of New England Transcendentalism than through just this picture-gallery experience of my own in Europe. It is an illustration which gives to the discussion the real breadth I would like to impart to it. In truth, it was no simple theological issue these eager men and women were debating in the question of miracles or in the question of any external authority like that insisted on for the Bible. Many of them had no objection to the admission of miracles, so long as they were not made tests of truth. It was a far wider reaching question, and one that affects our attitude to all that is beautiful, noble, and divine in life,—namely, that of the competency of mind to spontaneously recognize it. At this point, Transcendentalism took resolute and final stand. With your own eyes must you see. If color-blind, then in vain for you arches the prismatic glory of the rainbow, even though Iris herself should glide down to assure you it is beautiful. Now, in what way this differs from the absolute imperative of the Beatitudes of the Sermon on the Mount I confess myself constitutionally incapable of perceiving. But it was the crowning glory of the Transcendentalists that they made this principle co-terminous with the universe, prophetically anticipating in the spirit those later material revelations of the spectroscope, which proclaim how precisely the same elements that are burning and shining in our own little planet are burning and shining in Sirius and the Sun. What! shall we ban and bar a rose because it originated in Persia, or a lotus because it first floated on the bosom of the Nile? was their instinctive thought. Why, then, ban and bar any beautiful flower of the spirit, because first unfolding its petals and breathing forth its perfume in a Hindu, Parsee, or Sufi garden of the soul? Theirs as Transcendentalists to justify their name by simply transcending all those arbitrary boundaries of creed, race, nationality, local self-conceit, which narrow, harden, and poison the human mind, till it becomes constitutionally incapable of truly knowing and loving Him of whom, through whom, and to whom are all things, to whom be glory forever. And so, in this direction, the service of Transcendentalism to the future development of Unitarianism was priceless; and for one I most heartily concur in the words with which Rev. Joseph Henry Allen sums up his own conviction on the subject. "Transcendentalism," he says, "melted quite thoroughly the crust that was beginning to form on the somewhat chilly current of liberal theology...." Indeed, "it is the great felicity of free religious thought in this country, in its later unfolding, that it had its birth in a sentiment so poetic, so generous, so devout, so open to all the humanities as well as to the widest sympathies of philosophy and the higher literature."

Am I not right, then, in characterizing Transcendentalism as the New England Renaissance?

[Transcendentalism]

Octavius Brooks Frothingham*

That transcendentalism was mainly speculative may be doubted, but if it was so this may be accounted an incidental circumstance to be explained by the prevailing theological temper of the age, and the duty imposed on it of transferring the body of doctrine to an ideal realm; a task which demands an intellectual effort of no common magnitude. And when with this task was joined the endeavor to sift out the purely spiritual ideas from the mass of dogmatical and ecclesiastical error, it is no wonder that it should have been speculative in its tendency. Certainly, Brook Farm was concrete enough, and the transcendentalists were, as a rule, interested in social reconstruction, though not in a way to touch popular emotion. One cannot, even at this distance, think of the quickening radiance shed by the transcendentalists over the whole region of religious belief and duty, without gratitude. The hymns, the sermons, the music, the Sunday-schools, the prayers, the charities, the social ministrations, breathed forth a fresh spirit. If there were fewer tears of woe, there was more weeping for joy. There was too much gladness for crying. Life was made sunny. Human nature was interpreted cheerfully. There was an unlimited future for misery, ignorance, turpitude. Sin was remanded to the position of crudity, and was banished from the heavenly courts. Violence was protested against in laws, customs, manners, speech. Harsh doctrines were criticised. Austere views were discarded. Intellectual barriers were removed. Spiritual channels were deepened and widened. Light was let into dark places. The brightest aspects of divinity were presented. Immortality was rendered native to the soul. The life below was regarded as the portal to the life above.

In my own case, whatever of enthusiasm I may have had, whatever transports of feelings, whatever glow of hope for mankind, whatever ardor of anticipation for the future, whatever exhilaration of mind to-

*Reprinted from *Recollections and Impressions 1822–1890* (New York: G. P. Putnam's Sons, 1891), pp. 136–137.

wards God, whatever elation in the presence of disbelief in the popular theology, may be fairly ascribed to this form of the ideal philosophy. It was like a revelation of glory. Every good thought was encouraged. Every noble impulse was heightened. It was balm and elixir to me. If transcendentalism did not appear as a sun illuminating the entire mental universe it was the fault of my exposition alone. Absolute faith in that form of philosophy grew weak and passed away many years since, and the assurance it gave was shaken; but the sunset flush continued a long time after the orb of day had disappeared and lighted up the earth. Gradually the splendor faded, to be succeeded by a softer and more tranquil gleam, less stimulating but not less beautiful or glorious.

Transcendentalism in New England

Caroline H. Dall*

Transcendentalism, then, is idealism made practical as it appeared in 1842. "Amid the downward tendency of things," wrote Emerson, "when every voice is raised for a new house, a new dress, or larger business, will you not tolerate one or two solitary voices in the land speaking for thoughts and principles which shall be neither marketable nor perishable?"—words suggested perhaps by those of Archbishop Leighton, who, when his Westminster catechisers demanded, "Do you preach to the times?" answered, "May not one man preach to eternity?" "The senses," said its votaries, "give us representations of things, but what the things are they cannot tell." Every materialist may become an idealist, but an idealist cannot become a materialist. Mind is the only real thing. Is it not the power which makes tools of things actual?

The Transcendentalist made an extravagant demand on human nature,—that of lofty living. He quarrelled with every man he met. There was not enough of him! "So many promising youths," said Emerson, "and never a finished man!"

The anthropologists may find in this movement the origin of nearly every one of their multiform lines of inquiry. "It is a misfortune," said one, "to have been born when children were nothing, and to have lived until men have become nothing!" New voices began to be heard in the air. Channing had prepared the way by his magnificent vindication of the dignity of human nature. New principles in philosophy, new methods of criticism, began to stir. The origin and contents of the Scriptures were carefully scrutinized. The mind of New England was leavened by the thought of Emerson and the scholarship of Hedge. The "Transient and Permanent" were examined and contrasted by a fearless iconoclast. The title "humanitarian" began to be applied to theologians. God is not outside the world, a mere lawgiver: he is in the world; he is the world; man's relation to him is immediate. God is the Over Soul; above all,

*Reprinted from *Transcendentalism in New England: A Lecture* (Boston: Roberts Brothers, 1897), pp. 23–26, 31–33.

228

through all, *under* all, as well. The spirit must speak to spirit. Jesus was but a man, therefore a child of God who had attained to his proper heritage. He was the ideal man, type of mankind, become so through entering into perfect harmony with the Divine. If he wrought miracles, they must have been manifestations of normal law not yet perceived by undeveloped souls. Conceptions like these inspired the best spiritual life of the time, and modified the sentiments of many who were still unwilling to break the bonds of their training.

The characteristics of the Transcendental movement were shown in the temper of its agitation for the rights of woman and the enlargement of her duties. Like Dryden, every Transcendentalist was ready, and indeed had good reason, to assert that there was "no sex in souls." The editors of "The Dial," which was first issued in July, 1840, and lasted hardly four years, were Margaret Fuller and Ralph Waldo Emerson. In this, besides exquisite poems which, dropped from their original setting, have since travelled all over the world, the "Great Lawsuit" of Margaret Fuller, seven wonderful chapters on the "Ethnical Scriptures," a remarkable paper of Theodore Parker's, and the absurd "Orphic Sayings" of Alcott were first given to the world.

Transcendentalism had now come to be a distinct system, and, practically, to be the assertion of the inalienable worth of man, and of the immanence of the Divine in the Human. Its votaries were now the most strenuous workers of their day—not only that, but the most successful. Men and women are healthier in their bodies, happier in their domestic and social relations, more ambitious to enlarge their opportunities, more kind and humane in sympathy, as well as more reasonable in expectation, than they would have been if Margaret and Emerson had never lived. Under the influence of transcendental thought and hope, the mind of universal man leaped forward with a bound. The Transcendentalist of that day was always on the wing. A new hymn-book, issued by Samuel Johnson and Samuel Longfellow,—for which reason it was called by Theodore Parker the "Sam Book,"—was not only one of the manifestations of clerical sympathy, but had much to do with securing popular attention to the new ideas.

The Transcendentalists did not write about immortality. Theodore Parker called it a fact of consciousness, and in all their conferences faith in it was assumed. No belief was more characteristic of them than this. Emerson's life and walk and literary utterance were full of this faith. His power lay in his pure idealism, his absolute faith in thought, his supreme confidence in spiritual law. He lived in the region of serene ideas: "he did not visit the mount now and then, but set up his tabernacle and passed the night among the stars, ready for the eternal sunrise." He was the descendant of eight generations of Puritan clergymen,—some of whom had persecuted, some of whom had cherished, the "exaltation" of Anne Hutchinson. He inherited their thoughtfulness and their spirit of inward communion. The dogmatism fell away, the peaceful fruits of discipline remained. He bore with him the atmosphere of eternal youth. For what he says or what he does he makes no apology. He never explains. He trusts to affirmation pure and simple. I appealed to him once, when a wholly unncessary misunderstanding had put me in a painful position: "What should I do?" "Do?" he answered, with the look of a bewildered child; "if understanding were possible, misunderstanding would not have occurred!" I have never tried to explain myself since; but many a time has that serene dogma comforted my soul.

❉ ❉

The true Transcendentalist did not wrap a glimmering idea in miles and miles of tortuous vocabulary to remind us of the daughter of Genghis Khan, who, when her father reproached her with being but half clad, replied, "Sire, I wear forty thicknesses of the royal Dacca muslin." Who wrote more lucid words than Emerson? Whence come phrases of "solid impact" if not from the pages of Hedge? When are we lifted into the clear empyrean if not on the wings of Cyrus Bartol's fancy? The true disciple walked erect, with uplifted eyes, clear purpose, and clear sight. If he stumbled, he knew that walking comes by a succession of falls. He neither claimed nor expected happiness for himself. What he sought and gloried in was the development and happiness of all men: "He lived," wrote Emerson, "but to gather the Edelweiss" (a flower which grows only on the heights), which let us translate as "noble purity."

The man of science should know that to human eyes fulness of light does not insure perfection of vision. Man must shade his eyes a little from the noonday sun if he would see clearly the world of beauty and use that it illumines. The almost invisible midge that floats in the sunbeam which crosses the shuttered room finds there something that it needs; but it is not the fulness of light, that, like man in his present condition, the insect has not the power to appropriate.

For myself, I am a Transcendentalist of the old New England sort. I believe myself to be a child of God; and if a child, then an heir,—a very condensed way of saying that the spirit within me is the breath of the creative spirit, and therefore infinite in its reach, in its possibilities, and its final destiny. The Over Soul is the Under Soul as well. Matter is immortal. No agency, human or divine, has so far been able to destroy one particle of it; and yet, the world over, we see matter not only plastic in the grasp of mind, but subordinate to the uses of the race or the individual solely through the spirit's power. Is the spirit less, then, than the flesh which it masters? If matter cannot be destroyed, it can be transformed. So can spirit. I remember to have heard James Freeman

Clarke say of another whose virtue was in question: "Do not dwell on his transgressions. *His face is set the right way.* He keeps his heel firmly on every tempting thought. If it slip now and then, what matter? The purpose is the thing!" This, I suppose, is rank antinomianism, capable of great abuse; but is it not the doctrine we all accept to-day? Life is a glorious thing, whether it is the life that now is or the life that is to come. To be born immortal; to pass through life in the consciousness of an immortal destiny; to try steadfastly to be worthy of this,—what grander atmosphere could encompass a man? There is only one thing sweeter and more desirable,—to trust one's self wholly to the love of the informing Spirit. There is only one clew which it is safe to hold as we pass through the mysteries of this life to the confines of the next. It is a *Surrendered Will.*

The body, to be healthy, must be constructed and sustained in harmony with psychical and physiological law. No less must the soul be held to the conditions of that spiritual law which underlies both. I wish I could make my statement such that it would satisfy my agnostic friends. I have many who call themselves such, but I do not put faith in their nomenclature. Sometime they will understand themselves better, and the mists which hide their mortal goal will float and vanish on the beams of the eternal sunrise. *Language* may then be transformed as well as matter and spirit.

> "It matters not how strait the gate,
>   How charged with punishments the scroll:
> I am the Master of my fate,
>   The Captain of my soul!"

"Thoughts on the Transcendental Movement in New England"

Louis James Block*

The condition of our literature seventy years ago was not such as to inspire the patriotic American to enthusiastic expression. The names upon whose high sound we now depend to carry our literary renown beyond the limits of our shores had not then begun to be musical and impressive. What was to be expected from names so unpromising as Cooper, and Longfellow, and Poe, and Whittier? The mediocrity and middle-class flavor of a country which built its commonweal upon the supposed equality of every one of its members rested upon them all, to the alien mind. Here were no class distinctions, no aristocracies to speak of, whether of rank or wealth or learning. The young aspirant for literary honors was indeed born into traditions and scholastic habits to which he was expected to pay a certain homage; but the example of his forefathers in making light of similar bondages and prescriptions, more sacred, time-honored and obligatory, filled him with a sense of his own importance and a determination to accept of the old as much as commended itself to his needs and permit the remainder to find its way to the limbo of forgetfulness. It may not be undesirable, however, to inquire what those traditions and habits were, as a sort of analysis of the soil from which the later and more luxuriant literary growth sprang, dissipating the mists which overhung the new nation and obscured us from the understanding of nations not prone to look with favorable eyes upon a political attempt which, if successful, would leave them the representatives of a polity outlived and doomed to dissolution.

Such literary activity as America had during her colonial period was perforce a reflection of the literary activity of the mother country; yet there were some differences and peculiarities. The traditions of an elder period remained longer with the colonists; and a certain Elizabethan savor was perceptible here when all traces of that great age had vanished from the polished periods of the wits and essayists who succeeded the great poets and dramatists in England. The so-called quaint-

Reprinted from *New England Magazine*, 15 (January 1897), 564–570.

232

nesses of New England speech are directly derived from the speech then in vogue in the parent land, and one often has only to turn to the pages of Hooker, or Beaumont, or Fletcher, to discover there in classic usage what has been thrown up to us as a reproach. The absence of established organs of criticism and a generally cultivated auditory gave rein to individual caprice in expression; the fantastical element, a heritage of the Middle Ages, subjected to artistic control by Shakespeare and his contemporaries, burst all fetters and revelled in the productions of weaker men. Grave theological writings masqueraded under such titles as "Nails Fastened or Proposals of Piety Complied With," or "Ornaments for the Daughters of Zion, a Discourse which directs the Female Sex how to express the Fear of God and obtain Temporal and Eternal Blessedness." With the French influence in English literature, the clearness and directness of prose took the place of the splendors of poetry. English prose, aware for the first time of her important separate existence, achieved the most vivacious steps of her progress. Clearness, simplicity, and manly expression of emotion took the place of obscure and far-fetched allusion, and the often ludicrous intrusion of the lofty extravagance admissible only to poetry. The language of the time was full of vigor, alive in all its syllables. These qualities were repeated in such essays in literature as our forefathers made. Moreover, the conquest of a virgin wilderness and the reclamation of a continent for civilized needs heightened these qualities and imparted to them a novel intensity. The circle of ideas within which these writings moved was a narrow one, although divided into several segments. The gloomy Puritanic theology brightened into a more genial spirit in the middle colonies, and abandoned the field, beaten, before the joyousness and elegances which the warmer gales of Virginia inspired. The poetry which enlivened the leisure and adorned the lighter moments of our forefathers was of a sufficiently ponderous and utilitarian kind, little obnoxious to charges of seducing the spirit into flowery paths or forgetfulness of the responsibility of this existence in its perilous suspension between condign darkness and monotonous blessedness. Mrs. Anne Bradstreet, the tenth muse, rarely condescended to those elemental emotions out of which the texture of our daily lives is woven; that was altogether too familiar, too much involved in the darkness of naturalness, too interesting to our human affection, to receive the irradiation of her muse; nothing short of the conflicting potencies of the four primary elements, Earth, Air, Fire and Water, or the doings of men in ancient Babylon or Assyria, were worthy of her efforts. As Professor Tyler says, such poetry could be read "without any twinges of self-reproach; it was not too pleasant; it was not trivial or antic or amusing; men were in no danger of losing their souls by being borne away on the vain and airy enticements of frivolous words."

But the effect of all this activity was to lay the foundations of a style divergent far enough from that of the mother country to give it a character of its own, a style combining the lucidity of prose with an imaginative coloring that was a heritage of earlier and Elizabethan times. Literature in the true sense did not exist, but the preparation for it was strenuously going on. The mixture of nationalities, each embodying aims and aspirations of its own, began to modify the seething mass; a new type of character and a new form of expression were rapidly coming to the surface; the solidity of English manners and English expression were in process of transformation to something more gracious and adapted to airier and lighter conceptions. The liquor of a new inspiration was fermenting in the hearts of men, and a new literary product was on the way to make its claims upon human attention. New climatic influences furthered the creation of a new physical type; and the effervescence promised something rich and strange.

But there was yet needed a national sentiment which should furnish a background and support for all such new literary endeavors. The successful revolt of the colonies and the magnificent spectacle of a nation forming itself into a genuine political unity supplied this desideratum. The elements were mixed in something like due proportion; the times were propitious, and the result was at hand. Moreover, a whole phase of national existence had passed away into a remoteness which gave it the romance needed for successful application to artistic purposes. Modern scientific realism was a thing yet undreamed of; the immediate fight with the wilderness was over; wealth and leisure were beginning, and the higher nature of man demanded sustenance. The heroism of the men who had abandoned ease and comfort and happiness for the sake of a freedom which they could not find at home, the vigor which had converted a barren waste into a smiling expanse of field and village, the courage which had inspired a cause apparently hopeless and forlorn and led it to victory, evoked an answering response in souls alive to nobility of purpose and greatness of execution. The poet Clough wonders in one of his lyrics

> "How in heaven's name Columbus got over,—
> Cabot and Raleigh too, that well-read rover,
> Frobisher, Dampier, Drake and the rest,"

who came after. But the passage had been made, through greater difficulties than the weltering waste of ocean; through hunger and poverty, through religious and political strife, through bloodshed and battle, the way had been followed,—and the wonder of it all was plainly to be seen. Then the great future which loomed in the opening heavens of achievement, the promise of a destiny vast and mysterious, exercised a controlling fascination. The rise of the colleges, the spread of the newspaper and periodical literature, furnished incentives, and promoted common sympathy and feeling. The morning red hovered upon the horizon, and the voices of song birds awoke to greet the increasing glory.

Here then was a public unanimous for a time and ready to listen, a vehicle of expression plastic, fine and gracious, a stock of ideas ranging from the gloomy religious musings of Puritanism to the impulses inherent in the effort to establish freedom for every man, something very like a legendary lore to draw upon for materials of story, and above all the determination to subject all the achievement of the past to re-investigation before the bar of the individual judgment. Freedom in the state found its counterpart in freedom in the use of man's reason. Besides all this, there was the red man, about whom it was so easy to weave a halo of story and mystery, and who had a whole treasure house of legends and marvels of his own to explore and draw from.

But the new literature yet worshiped at the old shrines; it made pilgrimages to Europe, and sought satisfaction in the old splendors, but with a freedom which savored of newer realities. If Irving lingered in the shadows of Westminster Abbey, and laid the tribute of his gentle humor and fine literary workmanship at the feet of Addison, other writers deserted the shores of England for pilgrimages through sunny France, or wanderings up and down the byways of legend-haunted Germany, or amid the heroic imaginings of Spain. Plainly the old seriousness was giving way to a lighter touch, and even to a levity which made mirth at what had been held in soberest reverence. Men took to story writing, an amusement not to be contemplated without many misgivings, and to be pursued under many reservations. Brockden Brown published his weird and melodramatic romances. The poetry became marvelously sentimental; there were mysterious invocations of the muse and flutterings of nameless bliss at the sight of golden sunsets. But one deeper and more genuine result of poetic striving soon began to manifest itself, a profound sympathy with Nature in the novel aspects in which she presented herself to the western eye and heart.

The effects of all these influences on young and ardent minds in New England were magical. An era of the greatest import to mankind seemed opening, and the efforts of those taking part in it were of the largest scope and grandest intention. That the country needed a literature which should express what it had already accomplished and what the future promised was clear to the bold spirits who were prepared to plunge into any speculations. This literature should bear upon it the impress of genuine originality, should be the result of lonely ponderings and novel discoveries, should robe itself in draperies not woven in any looms of the old world. The whole past should be called to the witness stand, and divulge before a new tribunal what it had of permanent value and eternal worth. The conditions upon which society depends were to be investigated anew, and if possible a nobler order of things was to be inaugurated. The skepticism which assailed the loftiest convictions of man was to be met in daring wrestle and floored forever. Religious faith, no longer dependent upon outer and mere historic authority, was to be built upon the indestructible foundation of the transcendental vision of God. What vistas of achievement unfolded themselves to young and ardent spirits!

The beginning of such movements who shall discover? The influence is in the air; the seed has been sown in the soil; and the plant and flowerage spring up at once everywhere. The Unitarians of New England had broken away in a greater or less degree from the bonds of authority and had accustomed the minds of men to a freer discussion of questions ordinarily supposed beyond the pale of question. But in 1832 Ralph Waldo Emerson preached the "epoch making" sermon which made him no longer the mouth-piece of a creed or doctrine, but the voice of a new effort at self expression. The revolt against the merely traditional was fairly inaugurated. It was a renaissance of the Protestant movement. The earlier one had not gone far enough. What was humane and rational proclaimed itself as identical with the divine in life and thought. In the sermon of 1832, Emerson laid down his priesthood and raised issues to whose settlement on the free platform of thought he devoted the remainder of his life. In 1836 appeared "Nature," in which the whole system of Emersonian thought received exposition as systematic and complete as in anything to be found in his later writings. In 1838 came the wonderful address before the Harvard Divinity School, which aroused all the latent enthusiasm of young hearts and made the older ones aware that their opinions were to be assailed in a hand-to-hand conflict. James Walker welcomed the new philosophy. The wrath of the conservative was aroused, and the sensationalism of the time, the sense-thought, felt itself tottering in its hitherto seemingly unassailable preëminence. Andrews Norton and the rest arose in defense of the assailed positions, but the attack went bravely on. George Ripley and Theodore Parker joined the ranks of the new school, and both showed the skill and learning of practiced thinkers and fearless controversialists. In 1840 appeared the first series of essays by Emerson, containing the characteristic and incomparable essays on "Self-Reliance," the "Over-Soul," and "Circles."

But there were other adherents of the new faith. It would be a great mistake to consider the transcendental movement as solely a theological one. It had by this time swung loose from all theological moorings and was sailing on the free ocean of rational investigation, bound for such ports as the freest of speculations would lead the reason to rest and abide in. Orestes Brownson started the Boston Quarterly Re-

view in 1838. That restless and audacious intelligence swept from sphere to sphere of thought, and planted itself wherever its changeful experiences led it. He studied whatever came in his way, and believed with all his strength whatever he had come to see. But no doctrine satisfied him long, and it is not strange that he reverted at last to a more dogmatic point of view than the one from which he originally revolted. He is a significant figure, and illustrates some inevitable tendencies of all intellectual movements, as well as of those in New England sixty years ago.

The organ of the New England transcendental movement was the *Dial*, begun in July, 1840, and ending in April, 1844. Its chief editors were Margaret Fuller and Emerson. Its contributors constituted a band of scholars and thinkers whose superiors the country had not seen, and it may be questioned whether the country has seen since. George Ripley, James Freeman Clarke, Henry Thoreau, John S. Dwight, Bronson Alcott and many others filled its pages with papers which are not likely to lose their freshness. Of course it was received with a chorus of abuse, and a condescension which now appears to us more comical than the most mystical utterance of its own pages. The critics were quite unable to take the measure of the strange phenomenon.

The conversations of Margaret Fuller must not be omitted from an enumeration of the channels in which transcendentalism addressed the public and moulded opinion. Their influence was not less than that of all her published productions.

The effect of all these strivings on young and ardent minds it is easy to conceive. Amelioration of the unhappy condition of mankind, the righting of wrongs festering for ages, the establishment of the era of good-will and peace on earth, at last seemed conclusions ready to descend from the heavens. The deepest problems of the mind and heart, the mysteries which environ the destinies of the race, seemed about to be solved. Nature was answering her interrogators as she had not done before; her high-priest, Thoreau, offered his prayers at her altar, and from under the shadows of the pine forest at Walden came responses whose music ravished the sense even if their purport was often as dark as that of other oracles. Literature felt the thrill of an awakening impulse. A new day of spiritual achievement was building itself up in resplendence before the eyes of men, and the first genuine literary epoch of America, uniting influences from so many sources, produced a flora characteristically differenced from that of all other climes and times. The golden breath of the early morning filled all endeavor with its freshness and glory, and achievement seemed easy. It was the beginning of America and of things American in art and literature.

The thought of the period swiftly thrust itself into action. The claims made for the individual were to be seen in institutions which put no fetters upon the free march of his development but were only the indispensable instruments of lofty attainments. The revolt against institutions assumed various forms. In Thoreau the spirit asserted its strongest claims to be enfranchised from external forms with whose creation it asserted that it had nothing to do. The spectacle of his imprisonment for refusing to pay taxes wears unquestionably a comic aspect, and the Walden experiment to live at no charge to any one and be as independently related to Mother Nature as the primitive man, has the humorous element in it; but the undertaking had the noblest of origins, and its result is the bequeathal to us of an inalienable heritage. The mystical Alcott carried his reforms into his daily food and drink. The effort for the emancipation of woman need not be ashamed of its maternity in Margaret Fuller; her paper on the Great Lawsuit remains in the best literature of the movement contributed by America.

The Brook Farm experiment confronts us. The speculations of Fourier and Saint Simon had reached this country, and, with the minds to whom they commended themselves, to believe in them was to put them into practice. Not that the transcendentalists accepted these speculations in their entirety: they could accept no doctrines which infringed the individual rights of the individual man; but the establishment of an ideal society, a community in which brotherhood should be a real thing and not a glittering generality, a commonweal which should definitely accomplish the best culture of each member, was an ideal fascinating and irresistible to the fraternity that adventured upon the Brook Farm endeavor. We know how Hawthorne in his diary threw over it the play of his delicate humor; and although he disavows the application of the "Blithedale Romance" to what he observed at Brook Farm, we cannot doubt that his last words upon such attempted ameliorations of social conditions are to be found in that book. We can see that such efforts are dependent for what success they secure on the very conditions which they impugn; the society from which they flee is the constant source of the blessing which they most prize and enjoy. Thoreau at Walden communes with the great writers of the Orient and wanders with delight through translations of Hindoo books which were made by help of that wicked wealth he would have no lot or share in. We are all at last obliged to confess our allegiance to that universal spirit of history which has through the ages built the institutions through which we attain the best that has been attained, and which are in truth the beneficent supporters of all we do; yet we cannot on that account withhold our sympathy from undertakings whose inspiration was to hasten the time when that which is now the appanage of the few shall be the daily bread and drink of all.

But the intellectual tendencies and developments of the movement are the most interesting and permanent. The influences emanating from the ardor of speculation and the resolute pursuit of ideas to their ultimate consequences, which were part and parcel of the transcendentalist's equipment, spread far beyond the confines of New England; and club after club, coterie after coterie, in larger cities, in villages and hamlets all over the land, owe their inspiration and continuity to Emerson and his compeers, so that his tours, and those of Alcott, seemed like the progress of some person possessed of reverence that belongs to power exercised for what is noblest and most elevating. Many a man, no matter how far his present opinions may diverge, looks back to his first acquaintance with these names as the first splendor which arose on the night of his intellectual wanderings.

The life and spirit of the intellectual ferment of the time was liberty. Nothing accepted or generally believed was too sacred for demonstration of the grounds on which it rested; religion, art, philosophy, science, were passed in review, and each must listen to a verdict upon its claims. Boundless freedom and horizon,—that was the demand of the scholar, and every outward authority seemed almost an impertinence. This freedom was accompanied by boldness in the pursuit of ideas. There were no doubts expressed as to the power of the human soul; discussions of the limitations belonging to man's faculties were little to the taste of the fearless navigator to marvelous and novel spiritual realms; there were no problems placed beyond the pale of human investigation; indeed it was impossible that there should be, for with the postulate of absolute freedom comes another: this freedom is itself the deepest essence of the universe, and its own creations are the only realities. This freedom is no personal possession; it is the being and life of all men. To allow its unimpeded action, controlled only by the laws it frames for itself, is to conduct into all that is permanent and eternal. This has been the claim of idealism in all ages, and the New England idealists were not slow in making it. God, immortality, life, fate, substance, reality, were the themes most interesting and most discussed.

This method when applied to the study of nature was as fruitful and significant in its results. Nature was all alive; she was a symbol of the eternal mind that was mirrored in her. Every new fact, every new theory, every discovery—the more marvelous the better—was precisely what the transcendentalist wanted. To him nature was throughout her expanse the manifestation of spiritual potencies,—mind infinitely divided, as Schiller says in his Philosophical Letters; every new law, every systematic procedure therein discovered, makes all the movements and periodicities of nature the more consonant to the movements and periodicities of mind.

The atmosphere in which the transcendentalists lived was tonic and inspiring. To them it would have seemed vain and impertinent to engage in speculations on the most profound subjects, if they had no relation to practice. The conduct of life was the subject above all other subjects. The Puritan remained in them in the steadfast regard to noble living and right doing. Morality has never had loftier teachers or more inspired prophets; but morality was not isolated from the beliefs which underprop it and alone make it possible. The universal and eternal law of right, as Kant had demonstrated, presupposes freedom as the basis of all responsibility, immortality as a field for its ultimate and perfect exercise, and a Lawgiver to afford it sanction and invest it with authority. Emerson in the wide range of his thought endeavors to do justice to its varied demands. In the Essays, the "Over-Soul" and "Circles" stand side by side with "Self-Reliance" and "Love"; the latter are based upon the former; action requires nothing less than the universal to give it spring and impetus; the merely expedient, the trivial, the transitory, cannot hold the fixed regard of mankind.

The charge of mysticism made against these writings is largely due to the expression. Yet we have no reason to quarrel with this expression. Every new literature is strange to the generation which bears it. If we take up the *Dial* now, we wonder that any one found difficulty with what seems so natural to us. Yet the delving in literary quarries disused for many years, the working in mines which had been long abandoned, gave to the diggers a somewhat uncanny aspect. A man who gave his days and nights to enthusiasm and the gorgeous Neo-Platonism of Thomas Taylor might be expected to have something unusual about his modes of talking and thinking; devotion to Cudworth and Henry More might give the devotee a physiognomy somewhat unlike the ordinary. Still the strangeness is no greater than one will find in the most flourishing poetry of to-day. The writers were averse to systematic exposition; the logical method appeared to them not a means for attaining truth, but an attempt to put it into a straight-jacket and divest it of life and health. Philosophy when it drops out system and travels away from dogmatism cannot be otherwise than mysticism; it is the having of insights, glimpses of verity all the more dazzling for their isolation. Such writings have inconsecutiveness, but are like a succession of gems strung upon a golden thread. The objection has often been made against Emerson that you can read him backwards as well as forwards; but if we reach his plane of thought, we shall not find ourselves disturbed by the mysticism.

Thus the great men and women struggled and toiled. They attempted to fathom those problems of life and destiny whose depths no plummet has ever sounded, and which will forever remain abysses into which speculation will plunge and bring thence newer and nobler treasures. The fine enthusiasm which pervaded their circle may have led them into strange and difficult thickets of thought. They expected too much, perhaps, and hoped to ameliorate the world more rapidly than can be done with the good dame, used to the slow process of the centuries. But the spectacle of such single devotion to truth, of such inspiring hopefulness, of such vigorous thinking, stands supreme in the history of the land. When making up the record of what we have done in our brief experiment of establishing free institutions, we must not fail to award the proper place to what was done by these pioneers in the continent of free thought.

"The Genteel Tradition in American Philosophy"

George Santayana[*]

Ladies and Gentlemen,—The privilege of addressing you to-day
is very welcome to me, not merely for the honour of it, which is great,
nor for the pleasures of travel, which are many, when it is California that
one is visiting for the first time, but also because there is something I
have long wanted to say which this occasion seems particularly favourable for saying. America is still a young country, and this part of it is
especially so; and it would have been nothing extraordinary if, in this
young country, material preoccupations had altogether absorbed people's
minds, and they had been too much engrossed in living to reflect upon
life, or to have any philosophy. The opposite, however, is the case. Not
only have you already found time to philosophize in California, as your
society proves, but the eastern colonists from the very beginning were
a sophisticated race. As much as in clearing the land and fighting the
Indians, they were occupied, as they expressed it, in wrestling with the
Lord. The country was new, but the race was tried, chastened, and full
of solemn memories. It was an old wine in new bottles; and America
did not have to wait for its present universities, with their departments
of academic philosophy, in order to possess a living philosophy—to have
a distinct vision of the universe and definite convictions about human
destiny.

Now this situation is a singular and remarkable one, and has many
consequences, not all of which are equally fortunate. America is a young
country with an old mentality: it has enjoyed the advantages of a child
carefully brought up and thoroughly indoctrinated; it has been a wise
child. But a wise child, an old head on young shoulders, always has a
comic and unpromising side. The wisdom is a little thin and verbal,

[*]Reprinted from *University of California Chronicle*, 13 (October 1911), 357–380;
present text from *Selected Critical Writings of George Santayana*, ed. Norman Hen-
frey (Cambridge, Engl.: University Press, 1968), II, 85–107. This was first given as
an address before the Philosophical Union of the University of California on 25
August 1911.

not aware of its full meaning and grounds; and physical and emotional growth may be stunted by it, or even deranged. Or when the child is too vigorous for that, he will develop a fresh mentality of his own, out of his observations and actual instincts; and this fresh mentality will interfere with the traditional mentality, and tend to reduce it to something perfunctory, conventional, and perhaps secretly despised. A philosophy is not genuine unless it inspires and expresses the life of those who cherish it. I do not think the hereditary philosophy of America has done much to atrophy the natural activities of the inhabitants; the wise child has not missed the joys of youth or of manhood; but what has happened is that the hereditary philosophy has grown stale, and that the academic philosophy afterwards developed has caught the stale odour from it. America is not simply, as I said a moment ago, a young country with an old mentality: it is a country with two mentalities, one a survival of the beliefs and standards of the fathers, the other an expression of the instincts, practice, and discoveries of the younger generations. In all the higher things of the mind—in religion, in literature, in the moral emotions—it is the hereditary spirit that still prevails, so much so that Mr. Bernard Shaw finds that America is a hundred years behind the times. The truth is that one half of the American mind, that not occupied intensely in practical affairs, has remained, I will not say high and dry, but slightly becalmed; it has floated gently in the backwater, while, along-side, in invention and industry and social organization, the other half of the mind was leaping down a sort of Niagara Rapids. This division may be found symbolized in American architecture: a neat reproduction of the colonial mansion—with some modern comforts introduced surreptitiously—stands beside the skyscraper. The American Will inhabits the skyscraper; the American Intellect inhabits the colonial mansion. The one is the sphere of the American man; the other, at least predominantly, of the American woman. The one is all aggressive enterprise; the other is all genteel tradition.

Now, with your permission, I should like to analyse more fully how this interesting situation has arisen, how it is qualified, and whither it tends. And in the first place we should remember what, precisely, that philosophy was which the first settlers brought with them into the country. In strictness there was more than one; but we may confine our attention to what I will call Calvinism, since it is on this that the current academic philosophy has been grafted. I do not mean exactly the Calvinism of Calvin, or even of Jonathan Edwards; for in their systems there was much that was not pure philosophy, but rather faith in the externals and history of revelation. Jewish and Christian revelation was interpreted by these men, however, in the spirit of a particular philosophy, which might have arisen under any sky, and been associated with any other religion as well as with Protestant Christianity. In fact, the philosophical principle of Calvinism appears also in the Koran, in Spinoza, and in Cardinal Newman; and persons with no very distinctive Christian belief, like Carlyle or like Professor Royce, may be nevertheless, philosophically, perfect Calvinists. Calvinism, taken in this sense, is an expression of the agonized conscience. It is a view of the world which an agonized conscience readily embraces, if it takes itself seriously, as, being agonized, of course it must. Calvinism, essentially, asserts three things: that sin exists, that sin is punished, and that it is beautiful that sin should exist to be punished. The heart of the Calvinist is therefore divided between tragic concern at his own miserable condition, and tragic exultation about the universe at large. He oscillates between a profound abasement and a paradoxical elation of the spirit. To be a Calvinist philosophically is to feel a fierce pleasure in the existence of misery, especially of one's own, in that this misery seems to manifest the fact that the Absolute is irresponsible or infinite or holy. Human nature, it feels, is totally depraved: to have the instincts and motives that we necessarily have is a great scandal, and we must suffer for it; but that scandal is requisite, since otherwise the serious importance of being as we ought to be would not have been vindicated.

To those of us who have not an agonized conscience this system may seem fantastic and even unintelligible; yet it is logically and intently thought out from its emotional premises. It can take permanent possession of a deep mind here and there, and under certain conditions it can become epidemic. Imagine, for instance, a small nation with an intense vitality, but on the verge of ruin, ecstatic and distressful, having a strict and minute code of laws, that paints life in sharp and violent chiaroscuro, all pure righteousness and black abominations, and exaggerating the consequences of both perhaps to infinity. Such a people were the Jews after the exile, and again the early Protestants. If such a people is philosophical at all, it will not improbably be Calvinistic. Even in the early American communities many of these conditions were fulfilled. The nation was small and isolated; it lived under pressure and constant trial; it was acquainted with but a small range of goods and evils. Vigilance over conduct and an absolute demand for personal integrity were not merely traditional things, but things that practical sages, like Franklin and Washington, recommended to their countrymen, because they were virtues that justified themselves visibly by their fruits. But soon these happy results themselves helped to relax the pressure of external circumstances, and indirectly the pressure of the agonized conscience within. The nation became numerous; it ceased to be either ecstatic or distressful; the high social morality which on the whole it preserved took another colour; people remained honest and helpful out of good sense and good will rather than out of scrupulous adherence to any fixed principles. They retained their instinct for order, and often created order with surprising quickness; but the sanctity of law, to be obeyed for its own sake, began to escape them; it seemed too unpractical a notion, and not quite serious. In fact, the second and native-born American mentality began to take shape. The sense of sin totally evaporated. Nature, in the words of Emerson, was all beauty and commodity; and while operating on it laboriously, and drawing quick returns, the American began to drink in inspiration from it aesthetically. At the same time, in so broad a continent, he had elbow-room. His neighbours helped more than they hindered him; he wished their number to increase. Goodwill became the great American virtue; and a passion arose for counting heads, and square miles, and cubic feet, and minutes saved—as if there had been anything to save them for. How strange to the American now that saying of Jonathan Edwards, that men are naturally God's enemies! Yet that is an axiom to any intelligent Calvinist, though the words he uses may be different. If you told the modern American that he is totally depraved, he would think you were joking, as he himself usually is. He is convinced that he always has been, and always will be, victorious and blameless.

Calvinism thus lost its basis in American life. Some emotional natures, indeed, reverted in their religious revivals or private searchings of heart to the sources of the tradition; for any of the radical points of view in philosophy may cease to be prevalent, but none can cease to be possible. Other natures, more sensitive to the moral and literary influences of the world, preferred to abandon parts of their philosophy, hoping thus to reduce the distance which should separate the remainder from real life.

Meantime, if anybody arose with a special sensibility or a technical genius, he was in great straits; not being fed sufficiently by the world, he was driven in upon his own resources. The three American writers whose personal endowment was perhaps the finest—Poe, Hawthorne, and Emerson—had all a certain starved and abstract quality. They could not retail the genteel tradition; they were too keen, too perceptive, and too independent for that. But life offered them little digestible material, nor were they naturally voracious. They were fastidious, and under the circumstances they were starved. Emerson, to be sure, fed on books. There was a great catholicity in his reading; and he showed a fine tact in his comments, and in his way of appropriating what he read. But he read transcendentally, not historically, to learn what he himself felt, not what others might have felt before him. And to feed on books, for a philosopher or a poet, is still to starve. Books can help him to acquire form, or to avoid pitfalls; they cannot supply him with substance, if he is to have any. Therefore the genius of Poe and Hawthorne, and even of Emerson, was employed on a sort of inner play, or digestion of vacancy. It was a refined labour, but it was in danger of being morbid, or tinkling, or self-indulgent. It was a play of intra-mental rhymes. Their mind was like an old music-box, full of tender echoes and quaint fancies. These fancies expressed their personal genius sincerely, as dreams may; but they were arbitrary fancies in comparison with what a real observer would have said in the premises. Their manner, in a word, was subjective. In their own persons they escaped the mediocrity of the genteel tradition, but they supplied nothing to supplant it in other minds.

The churches, likewise, although they modified their spirit, had no philosophy to offer save a new emphasis on parts of what Calvinism contained. The theology of Calvin, we must remember, had much in it besides philosophical Calvinism. A Christian tenderness, and a hope of grace for the individual, came to mitigate its sardonic optimism; and it was these evangelical elements that the Calvinistic churches now emphasized, seldom and with blushes referring to hell fire or infant damnation. Yet philosophic Calvinism, with a theory of life that would perfectly justify hell fire and. infant damnation if they happened to exist, still dominates the traditional metaphysics. It is an ingredient, and the decisive ingredient, in what calls itself idealism. But in order to see just what part Calvinism plays in current idealism, it will be necessary to distinguish the other chief element in that complex system, namely, transcendentalism.

Transcendentalism is the philosophy which the romantic era produced in Germany, and independently, I believe, in America also. Transcendentalism proper, like romanticism, is not any particular set of dogmas about what things exist; it is not a system of the universe regarded as a fact, or as a collection of facts. It is a method, a point of view, from which any world, no matter what it might contain, could be approached by a self-conscious observer. Transcendentalism is systematic subjectivism. It studies the perspectives of knowledge as they radiate from the self; it is a plan of those avenues of inference by which our ideas of things must be reached, if they are to afford any systematic or distant vistas. In other words, transcendentalism is the critical logic of science. Knowledge, it says, has a station, as in a watch-tower; it is always seated here and now, in the self of the moment. The past and the future, things inferred and things conceived, lie around it, painted as upon a panorama. They cannot be lighted up save by some centrifugal ray of attention and present interest, by some active operation of the mind.

This is hardly the occasion for developing or explaining this delicate insight; suffice it to say, lest you should think later that I disparage transcendentalism, that as a method I regard it as correct and, when once suggested, unforgettable. I regard it as the chief contribution made in modern times to speculation. But it is a method only, an attitude we may always assume if we like and that will always be legitimate. It is no answer, and involves no particular answer, to the question: What exists; in what order is what exists produced; what is to exist in the future? This question must be answered by observing the object, and tracing humbly the movement of the object. It cannot be answered at all by harping on the fact that this object, if discovered, must be discovered by somebody, and by somebody who has an interest in discovering it. Yet the Germans who first gained the full transcendental insight were romantic people; they were more or less frankly poets; they were colossal egotists, and wished to make not only their own knowledge but the whole universe centre about themselves. And full as they were of their romantic isolation and romantic liberty, it occurred to them to imagine that all reality might be a transcendental self and a romantic dreamer like themselves; nay, that it might be just their own transcendental self and their own romantic dreams extended indefinitely. Transcendental logic, the method of discovery for the mind, was to become also the method of evolution in nature and history. Transcendental method, so abused, produced transcendental myth. A conscientious critique of knowledge was turned into a sham system of nature. We must therefore distinguish sharply the transcendental grammar of the intellect, which is significant and potentially correct, from the various transcendental systems of the universe, which are chimeras.

In both its parts, however, transcendentalism had much to recommend it to American philosophers, for the transcendental method appealed to the individualistic and revolutionary temper of their youth, while transcendental myths enabled them to find a new status for their inherited theology, and to give what parts of it they cared to preserve some semblance of philosophical backing. This last was the use to which the transcendental method was put by Kant himself, who first brought it into vogue, before the terrible weapon had got out of hand, and become the instrument of pure romanticism. Kant came, he himself said, to remove knowledge in order to make room for faith, which in his case meant faith in Calvinism. In other words, he applied the transcendental method to matters of fact, reducing them thereby to human ideas, in order to give to the Calvinistic postulates of conscience a metaphysical validity. For Kant had a genteel tradition of his own, which he wished to remove to a place of safety, feeling that the empirical world had become too hot for it; and this place of safety was the region of transcendental myth. I need hardly say how perfectly this expedient suited the needs of philosophers in America, and it is no accident if the influence of Kant soon became dominant here. To embrace this philosophy was regarded as a sign of profound metaphysical insight, although the most mediocre minds found no difficulty in embracing it. In truth it was a sign of having been brought up in the genteel tradition, of feeling it weak, and of wishing to save it.

But the transcendental method, in its way, was also sympathetic to the American mind. It embodied, in a radical form, the spirit of Protestantism as distinguished from its inherited doctrines; it was autonomous, undismayed, calmly revolutionary; it felt that Will was deeper than Intellect; it focused everything here and now, and asked all things to show their credentials at the bar of the young self, and to prove their value for this latest born moment. These things are truly American; they would be characteristic of any young society with a keen and discursive intelligence, and they are strikingly exemplified in the thought and in the person of Emerson. They constitute what he called self-trust. Self-trust, like other transcendental attitudes, may be expressed in metaphysical fables. The romantic spirit may imagine itself to be an absolute force, evoking and moulding the plastic world to express its varying moods. But for a pioneer who is actually a world-builder this metaphysical illusion has a partial warrant in historical fact; far more warrant than it could boast of in the fixed and articulated society of Europe, among the moon-struck rebels and sulking poets of the romantic era. Emerson was a shrewd Yankee, by instinct on the winning side; he was a cheery, child-like soul, impervious to the evidence of evil, as of everything that it did not suit his transcendental individuality to appreciate or to notice. More, perhaps, than anybody that has ever lived, he practised the transcendental method in all its purity. He had no system. He opened his eyes on the world every morning with a fresh sincerity, marking how things seemed to him then, or what they suggested to his spontaneous fancy. This fancy, for being spontaneous, was not always novel; it was guided by the habits and training of his mind, which were those of a preacher. Yet he never insisted on his notions so as to turn them into settled dogmas; he felt in his bones that they were myths. Sometimes, indeed, the bad example of other transcendentalists, less true than he to their method, or the pressing questions of unintelligent people, or the instinct we all have to think our ideas final, led him to the very verge of system-making; but he stopped short. Had he made a system out of his notion of Compensation, or the Over-Soul, or Spiritual Laws, the result would have been as thin and forced as it is in other transcendental systems. But he coveted truth; and he returned to experience, to history, to poetry, to the natural science of his day, for new starting-points and hints toward fresh transcendental musings.

To covet truth is a very distinguished passion. Every philosopher says he is pursuing the truth, but this is seldom the case. As Mr Bertrand Russell has observed, one reason why philosophers often fail to reach the truth is that often they do not desire to reach it. Those who are genuinely concerned in discovering what happens to be true are rather the men of science, the naturalists, the historians; and ordinarily they discover it, according to their lights. The truths they find are never complete, and are not always important; but they are integral parts of the truth, facts and circumstances that help to fill in the picture, and that no later interpretation can invalidate or afford to contradict. But professional philosophers are usually only apologists: that is, they are absorbed in defending some vested illusion or some eloquent idea. Like lawyers or detectives, they study the case for which they are retained, to see how much evidence or semblance of evidence they can gather for the defence, and how much prejudice they can raise against the witnesses for the prosecution; for they know they are defending prisoners suspected by the world, and perhaps by their own good sense, of falsification. They do not covet truth, but victory and the dispelling of their own doubts. What they defend is some system, that is, some view about the totality of things, of which men are actually ignorant. No system would have ever been framed if people had been simply interested in knowing what is true, whatever it may be. What produces systems is the interest in maintaining against all comers that some favourite or inherited idea of ours is sufficient and right. A system may contain an account of many things which, in detail, are true enough; but as a system, covering infinite possibilities that neither our experience nor our logic can prejudge, it must be a work of imagination and a piece of human soliloquy. It may be expressive of human experience, it may be poetical; but how should anyone who really coveted truth suppose that it was true?

Emerson had no system; and his coveting truth had another exceptional consequence: he was detached, unworldly, contemplative. When he came out of the conventicle or the reform meeting, or out of the rapturous close atmosphere of the lecture-room, he heard nature whispering to him: 'Why so hot, little sir?' No doubt the spirit or energy of the world is what is acting in us, as the sea is what rises in every little wave; but it passes through us, and cry out as we may, it will move on. Our privilege is to have perceived it as it moves. Our dignity is not in what we do, but in what we understand. The whole world is doing things. We are turning in that vortex; yet within us is silent observation, the speculative eye before which all passes, which bridges the distances and compares the combatants. On this side of his genius Emerson broke away from all conditions of age or country and represented nothing except intelligence itself.

There was another element in Emerson, curiously combined with transcendentalism, namely, his love and respect for nature. Nature, for the transcendentalist, is precious because it is his own work, a mirror in which he looks at himself and says (like a poet relishing his own verses), 'What a genius I am! Who would have thought there was such stuff in me?' And the philosophical egotist finds in his doctrine a ready explanation of whatever beauty and commodity nature actually has. No wonder, he says to himself, that nature is sympathetic, since I made it.

And such a view, one-sided and even fatuous as it may be, undoubtedly sharpens the vision of a poet and a moralist to all that is inspiriting and symbolic in the natural world. Emerson was particularly ingenious and clear-sighted in feeling the spiritual uses of fellowship with the elements. This is something in which all Teutonic poetry is rich and which forms, I think, the most genuine and spontaneous part of modern taste, and especially of American taste. Just as some people are naturally enthralled and refreshed by music, so others are by landscape. Music and landscape make up the spiritual resources of those who cannot or dare not express their unfulfilled ideals in words. Serious poetry, profound religion (Calvinism, for instance), are the joys of an unhappiness that confesses itself; but when a genteel tradition forbids people to confess that they are unhappy, serious poetry and profound religion are closed by that; and since human life, in its depths, cannot then express itself openly, imagination is driven for comfort into abstract arts, where human circumstances are lost sight of, and human problems dissolve in a purer medium. The pressure of care is thus relieved, without its quietus being found in intelligence. To understand oneself is the classic form of consolation; to elude oneself is the romantic. In the presence of music or landscape human experience eludes itself; and thus romanticism is the bond between transcendental and naturalistic sentiment. The winds and clouds come to minister to the solitary ego.

Have there been, we may ask, any successful efforts to escape from the genteel tradition, and to express something worth expressing behind its back? This might well not have occurred as yet; but America is so precocious, it has been trained by the genteel tradition to be so wise for its years, that some indications of a truly native philosophy and poetry are already to be found. I might mention the humorists, of whom you here in California have had your share. The humorists, however, only half escape the genteel tradition; their humour would lose its savour if they had wholly escaped it. They point to what contradicts it in the facts; but not in order to abandon the genteel tradition, for they have nothing solid to put in its place. When they point out how ill many facts fit into it, they do not clearly conceive that this militates against the standard, but think it a funny perversity in the facts. Of course, did they earnestly respect the genteel tradition, such an incongruity would seem to them sad, rather than ludicrous. Perhaps the prevalence of humour in America, in and out of season, may be taken as one more evidence that the genteel tradition is present pervasively, but everywhere weak. Similarly in Italy, during the Renaissance, the Catholic tradition could not be banished from the intellect, since there was nothing articulate to take its place; yet its hold on the heart was singularly relaxed. The consequence was that humorists could regale themselves with the foibles of monks and of cardinals, with the credulity of fools, and the bogus miracles of the saints; not intending to deny the theory of the Church, but caring for it so little at heart that they could find it infinitely amusing that it should be contradicted in men's lives and that no harm should come of it. So when Mark Twain says, 'I was born of poor but dishonest parents', the humour depends on the parody of the genteel Anglo-Saxon convention that it is disreputable to be poor; but to hint at the hollowness of it would not be amusing if it did not remain at bottom one's habitual conviction.

The one American writer who has left the genteel tradition entirely behind is perhaps Walt Whitman. For this reason educated Americans find him rather an unpalatable person, who they sincerely protest ought not to be taken for a representative of their culture; and he certainly should not, because their culture is so genteel and traditional. But the foreigner may sometimes think otherwise, since he is looking for what may have arisen in America to express, not the polite and conventional American mind, but the spirit and the inarticulate principles that animate the community, on which its own genteel mentality seems to sit rather lightly. When the foreigner opens the pages of Walt Whitman, he thinks that he has come at last upon something representative and original. In Walt Whitman democracy is carried into psychology and morals. The various sights, moods, and emotions are given each one vote; they are declared to be all free and equal, and the innumerable commonplace moments of life are suffered to speak like the others. Those moments formerly reputed great are not excluded, but they are made to march in the ranks with their companions—plain foot-soldiers and servants of the hour. Nor does the refusal to discriminate stop there; we must carry our principle further down, to the animals, to inanimate nature, to the cosmos as a whole. Whitman became a pantheist; but his pantheism, unlike that of the Stoics and of Spinoza, was unintellectual, lazy, and self-indulgent; for he simply felt jovially that everything real was good enough, and that he was good enough himself. In him Bohemia rebelled against the genteel tradition; but the reconstruction that alone can justify revolution did not ensue. His attitude, in principle, was utterly disintegrating; his poetic genius fell back to the lowest level, perhaps, to which it is possible for poetic genius to fall. He reduced his imagination to a passive sensorium for the registering of impressions. No element of construction remained in it, and therefore no element of penetration. But his scope was wide; and his lazy, desultory apprehension was poetical. His work, for the very reason that it is so rudimentary, contains a beginning, or rather many beginnings, that might possibly grow into a noble moral imagination, a worthy filling for the human mind. An American in the nineteenth century who completely disregarded the genteel tradition could hardly have done more.

But there is another distinguished man, lately lost to this country, who has given some rude shocks to this tradition and who, as much as Whitman, may be regarded as representing the genuine, the long silent American mind—I mean William James. He and his brother Henry were as tightly swaddled in the genteel tradition as any infant geniuses could be, for they were born before 1850, and in a Swedenborgian household. Yet they burst those bands almost entirely. The ways in which the two brothers freed themselves, however, are interestingly different. Mr Henry James has done it by adopting the point of view of the outer world, and by turning the genteel American tradition, as he turns everything else, into a subject-matter for analysis. For him it is a curious habit of mind, intimately comprehended, to be compared with other habits of mind, also well known to him. Thus he has overcome the genteel tradition in the classic way, by understanding it. With William James too this infusion of worldly insight and European sympathies was a potent influence, especially in his earlier days; but the chief source of his liberty was another. It was his personal spontaneity, similar to that of Emerson, and his personal vitality, similar to that of nobody else. Convictions and ideas came to him, so to speak, from the subsoil. He had a prophetic sympathy with dawning sentiments of the age, with the moods of the dumb majority. His scattered words caught fire in many parts of the world. His way of thinking and feeling represented the true America, and represented in a measure the whole ultra-modern, radical world. Thus he eluded the genteel tradition in the romantic way, by continuing it into its opposite. The romantic mind, glorified in Hegel's dialectic (which is not dialectic at all, but a sort of tragi-comic history of experience), is always rendering its thoughts unrecognizable through the infusion of new insights, and through the insensible transformation of the moral feeling that accompanies them, till at last it has completely reversed its old judgments under cover of expanding them. Thus the genteel tradition was led a merry dance when it fell again into the hands of a genuine and vigorous romanticist like William James. He restored their revolutionary force to its neutralized elements, by picking them out afresh, and emphasizing them separately, according to his personal predilections.

For one thing, William James kept his mind and heart wide open to all that might seem, to polite minds, odd, personal, or visionary in religion and philosophy. He gave a sincerely respectful hearing to sentimentalists, mystics, spiritualists, wizards, cranks, quacks, and impostors —for it is hard to draw the line, and James was not willing to draw it prematurely. He thought, with his usual modesty, that any of these might have something to teach him. The lame, the halt, the blind, and those speaking with tongues could come to him with the certainty of finding sympathy; and if they were not healed, at least they were comforted, that a famous professor should take them so seriously; and they began to feel that after all to have only one leg, or one hand, or one eye, or to have three, might be in itself no less beauteous than to have just two, like the stolid majority. Thus William James became the friend and helper of those groping, nervous, half-educated, spiritually disinherited, passionately hungry individuals of which America is full. He became, at the same time, their spokesman and representative before the learned world; and he made it a chief part of his vocation to recast what the learned world has to offer, so that as far as possible it might serve the needs and interests of these people.

Yet the normal practical masculine American, too, had a friend in William James. There is a feeling abroad now, to which biology and Darwinism lend some colour, that theory is simply an instrument for practice, and intelligence merely a help toward material survival. Bears, it is said, have fur and claws, but poor naked man is condemned to be intelligent, or he will perish. This feeling William James embodied in that theory of thought and of truth which he called pragmatism. Intelligence, he thought, is no miraculous, idle faculty, by which we mirror passively any or everything that happens to be true, reduplicating the real world to no purpose. Intelligence has its roots and its issue in the context of events; it is one kind of practical adjustment, an experimental act, a form of vital tension. It does not essentially serve to picture other parts of reality, but to connect them. This view was not worked out by William James in its psychological and historical details; unfortunately he developed it chiefly in controversy against its opposite, which he called intellectualism, and which he hated with all the hatred of which his kind heart was capable. Intellectualism, as he conceived it, was pure pedantry; it impoverished and verbalized everything, and tied up nature in red tape. Ideas and rules that may have been occasionally useful it put in the place of the full-blooded irrational movement of life which had called them into being; and these abstractions, so soon obsolete, it strove to fix and to worship for ever. Thus all creeds and theories and all formal precepts sink in the estimation of the pragmatist to a local and temporary grammar of action; a grammar that must be changed slowly by time, and may be changed quickly by genius. To know things as a whole, or as they are eternally, if there is anything eternal in them, is not only beyond our powers, but would prove worthless, and perhaps even fatal to our lives. Ideas are not mirrors, they are weapons; their function is to prepare us to meet events, as future experience may unroll them. Those ideas that disappoint us are false ideas; those to which events are true are true themselves.

This may seem a very utilitarian view of the mind; and I confess I think it a partial one, since the logical force of beliefs and ideas, their truth or falsehood as assertions, has been overlooked altogether, or confused with the vital force of the material processes which these ideas express. It is an external view only, which marks the place and conditions of the mind in nature, but neglects its specific essence; as if a jewel were defined as a round hole in a ring. Nevertheless, the more materialistic the pragmatist's theory of the mind is, the more vitalistic his theory of nature will have to become. If the intellect is a device produced in organic bodies to expedite their processes, these organic bodies must have interests and a chosen direction in their life; otherwise their life could not be expedited, nor could anything be useful to it. In other words—and this is a third point at which the philosophy of William James has played havoc with the genteel tradition, while ostensibly defending it—nature must be conceived anthropomorphically and in psychological terms. Its purposes are not to be static harmonies, self-unfolding destinies, the logic of spirit, the spirit of logic, or any other formal method and abstract law; its purposes are to be concrete endeavours, finite efforts of souls living in an environment which they transform and by which they, too, are affected. A spirit, the divine spirit as much as the human, as this new animism conceives it, is a romantic adventurer. Its future is undetermined. Its scope, its duration, and the quality of its life are all contingent. This spirit grows; it buds and sends forth feelers, sounding the depths around for such other centres of force or life as may exist there. It has a vital momentum, but no predetermined goal. It uses its past as a stepping-stone, or rather as a diving-board, but has an absolutely fresh will at each moment to plunge this way or that into the unknown. The universe is an experiment; it is unfinished. It has no ultimate or total nature, because it has no end. It embodies no formula or statable law; any formula is at best a poor abstraction, describing what, in some region and for some time, may be the most striking characteristic of existence; the law is a description *a posteriori* of the habit things have chosen to acquire, and which they may possibly throw off altogether. What a day may bring forth is uncertain; uncertain even to God. Omniscience is impossible; time is real; what had been omniscience hitherto might discover something more today. 'There shall be news,' William James was fond of saying with rapture, quoting from the unpublished poem of an obscure friend, 'there shall be news in heaven!' There is almost certainly, he thought, a God now; there may be several gods, who might exist together, or one after the other. We might, by our conspiring sympathies, help to make a new one. Much in us is doubtless immortal; we survive death for some time in a recognizable form; but what our career and transformations may be in the sequel we cannot tell, although we may help to determine them by our daily choices. Observation must be continual if our ideas are to remain true. Eternal vigilance is the price of knowledge; perpetual hazard, perpetual experiment keep quick the edge of life.

This is, so far as I know, a new philosophical vista; it is a conception never before presented, although implied, perhaps, in various quarters, as in Norse and even Greek mythology. It is a vision radically empirical and radically romantic; and as William James himself used to say, the visions and not the arguments of a philosopher are the interesting and influential things about him. William James, rather too generously, attributed this vision to M. Bergson, and regarded him in consequence as a philosopher of the first rank, whose thought was to be one of the turning-points in history. M. Bergson had killed intellectualism. It was his book on creative evolution, said James with humorous emphasis, that had come at last to '*écraser l'infâme*'. We may suspect, notwithstanding, that intellectualism, infamous and crushed, will survive the blow; and if the author of the Book of Ecclesiastes were now alive, and heard that there shall be news in heaven, he would doubtless say that there may possibly be news there, but that under the sun there is nothing new—not even radical empiricism or radical romanticism, which from the beginning of the world has been the philosophy of those who as yet had had little experience; for to the blinking little child it is not merely something in the world that is new daily, but everything is new all day.

I am not concerned with the rights and wrongs of that controversy; my point is only that William James, in this genial evolutionary view of the world, has given a rude shock to the genteel tradition. What! The world a gradual improvisation? Creation unpremeditated? God a sort of young poet or struggling artist? William James is an advocate of theism; pragmatism adds one to the evidences of religion; that is excellent. But is not the cool abstract piety of the genteel getting more than it asks for? This empirical naturalistic God is too crude and positive a force; he will work miracles, he will answer prayers, he may inhabit distinct places, and have distinct conditions under which alone he can operate; he is a neighbouring being, whom we can act upon, and rely upon for specific aids, as upon a personal friend, or a physician, or an insurance company. How disconcerting! Is not this new theology a little like superstition? And yet how interesting, how exciting, if it should happen to be true! I am far from wishing to suggest that such a view seems to me more probable than conventional idealism or than Christian orthodoxy. All three are in the region of dramatic system-making and myth to which probabilities are irrelevant. If one man says the moon is sister to the sun, and another that she is his daughter, the question is not which notion is more probable, but whether either of them is at all expressive. The so-called evidences are devised afterwards, when faith and imagination have prejudged the issue. The force of William James's new theology, or romantic cosmology, lies only in this: that it has broken the spell of the genteel tradition, and enticed faith in a new direction, which on second thoughts may prove no less alluring than the old. The important fact is not that the new fancy might possibly be true—who shall know that?—but that it has entered the heart of a leading American to conceive and to cherish it. The genteel tradition cannot be dislodged by these insurrections; there are circles to which it is still congenial, and where it will be preserved. But it has been challenged and (what is perhaps more insidious) it has been discovered. No one need be browbeaten any longer into accepting it. No one need be afraid, for instance, that his fate is sealed because some young prig may call him a dualist; the pint would call the quart a dualist, if you tried to pour the quart into him. We need not be afraid of being less profound, for being direct and sincere. The intellectual world may be traversed in many directions; the whole has not been surveyed; there is a great career in it open to talent. That is a sort of knell, that tolls the passing of the genteel tradition. Something else is now in the field; something else can appeal to the imagination, and be a thousand times more idealistic than academic idealism, which is often simply a way of white-washing and adoring things as they are. The illegitimate monopoly which the genteel tradition had established over what ought to be assumed and what ought to be hoped for has been broken down by the first-born of the family, by the genius of the race. Henceforth there can hardly be the same peace and the same pleasure in hugging the old proprieties. Hegel will be to the next generation what Sir William Hamilton was to the last. Nothing will have been disproved, but everything will have been abandoned. An honest man has spoken, and the cant of the genteel tradition has become harder for young lips to repeat.

With this I have finished such a sketch as I am here able to offer you of the genteel tradition in American philosophy. The subject is complex, and calls for many an excursus and qualifying footnote; yet I think the main outlines are clear enough. The chief fountains of this tradition were Calvinism and transcendentalism. Both were living fountains; but to keep them alive they required, one an agonized conscience, and the other a radical subjective criticism of knowledge. When these rare metaphysical preoccupations disappeared—and the American atmosphere is not favourable to either of them—the two systems ceased to be inwardly understood; they subsisted as sacred mysteries only; and the combination of the two in some transcendental system of the universe (a contradiction in principle) was doubly artificial. Besides, it could hardly be held with a single mind. Natural science, history, the beliefs implied in labour and invention, could not be disregarded altogether so that the transcendental philosopher was condemned to a double allegiance, and to not letting his left hand know the bluff that his right hand was making. Nevertheless, the difficulty in bringing practical inarticulate convictions to expression is very great, and the genteel tradition has subsisted in the academic mind for want of anything equally academic to take its place.

The academic mind, however, has had its flanks turned. On the one side came the revolt of the Bohemian temperament, with its poetry of crude naturalism; on the other side came an impassioned empiricism, welcoming popular religious witnesses to the unseen, reducing science to an instrument of success in action, and declaring the universe to be wild and young, and not to be harnessed by the logic of any school.

This revolution, I should think, might well find an echo among you, who live in a thriving society, and in the presence of a virgin and prodigious world. When you transform nature to your uses, when you experiment with her forces, and reduce them to industrial agents, you cannot feel that nature was made by you or for you, for then these adjustments would have been pre-established. Much less can you feel it when she destroys your labour of years in a momentary spasm. You must feel, rather, that you are an offshoot of her life; one brave little force among her immense forces. When you escape, as you love to do, to your forests and your sierras, I am sure again that you do not feel you made them, or that they were made for you. They have grown, as you have grown, only more massively and more slowly. In their non-human beauty and peace they stir the subhuman depths and the super-human possibilities of your own spirit. It is no transcendental logic that they teach; and they give no sign of any deliberate morality seated in the world. It is rather the vanity and superficiality of all logic, the need-lessness of argument, the relativity of morals, the strength of time, the fertility of matter, the variety, the unspeakable variety, of possible life. Everything is measurable and conditioned, indefinitely repeated, yet, in repetition, twisted somewhat from its old form. Everywhere is beauty and nowhere permanence, everywhere an incipient harmony, nowhere an intention, nor a responsibility, nor a plan. It is the irresistible suasion of this daily spectacle, it is the daily discipline of contact with things, so different from the verbal discipline of the schools, that will, I trust, inspire the philosophy of your children. A Californian whom I had recently the pleasure of meeting observed that, if the philosophers had lived among your mountains, their systems would have been different from what they are. Certainly, I should say, very different from what those systems are which the European genteel tradition has handed down since Socrates; for these systems are egotistical; directly or indirectly they are anthropocentric, and inspired by the conceited notion that man, or human reason, or the human distinction between good and evil, is the centre and pivot of the universe. That is what the mountains and the woods should make you at last ashamed to assert. From what, indeed, does the society of nature liberate you, that you find it so sweet? It is hardly (is it?) that you wish to forget your past, or your friends, or that you have any secret contempt for your present ambitions. You respect these, you respect them perhaps too much; you are not suffered by the genteel tradition to criticize or to reform them at all radically. No; it is the yoke of this genteel tradition itself that these primeval solitudes lift from your shoulders. They suspend your forced sense of your own importance not merely as individuals, but even as men. They allow you, in one happy moment, at once to play and to worship, to take yourselves simply, humbly, for what you are, and to salute the wild, indifferent, noncensorious infinity of nature. You are admonished that what you can do avails little materially, and in the end nothing. At the same time, through wonder and pleasure, you are taught speculation. You learn what you are really fitted to do, and where lie your natural dignity and joy, namely, in representing many things, without being them, and in letting your imagination, through sympathy, celebrate and echo their life. Because the peculiarity of man is that his machinery for reaction on external things has involved an imaginative transcript of these things, which is preserved and suspended in his fancy; and the interest and beauty of this inward landscape, rather than any fortunes that may await his body in the outer world, constitute his proper happiness. By their mind, its scope, quality, and temper, we estimate men, for by the mind only do we exist as men, and are more than so many storage-batteries for material energy. Let us therefore be frankly human. Let us be content to live in the mind.

"Two Types of Transcendentalism in America"

Woodbridge Riley*

I. FRANCO-AMERICAN TYPE

There is a tradition that New England transcendentalism was "made in Germany."[1] This tradition has been allowed to grow by a double default, both through the supineness of American scholars, and through the positive propaganda of German *Kultur*. It has remained for a Franco-American to dispose of the matter, by showing that the American transcendental movement, with its idealism and individualism, was but part of the greater movement of European romanticism. This was not pan-Germanic, but had its roots in the very characters of Emerson and Channing, of Ripley and Brownson; in the speculations of Coleridge and Carlyle; and especially in the eclecticism of Cousin, Jouffroy, and Constant. Common opinion, again may assert that these groups—American, English, French—had their source and inspiration from beyond the Rhine, but that remains to be proved. M. Girard, to put it tersely, contends that there was an epidemic of emotionalism breaking out in the republic of letters, a kind of metaphysical measles—but not necessarily German measles. The endemic character of this movement is portrayed under a truly transcendental postulate, namely, a national soul belonging to each country.

The New England leaders had many points of agreement with the great German idealists, but if we add to the list Theodore Parker and Henry David Thoreau, Amos Bronson Alcott and Margaret Fuller, there is suggested a native strain, a peculiar virtue in the soil which fed the tree of transcendentalism. From this kind of speculative soil-analysis, then, one might learn what to expect in the way of a metaphysical crop. So Girard fitly begins his monograph with an introductory study of philosophic thought in America prior to the appearance of transcendentalism. The immigration into New England is called *"des hommes d'action et*

*Reprinted from *Journal of Philosophy*, 15 (23 May 1918), 281–292. The part of the essay reviewing Wenley's biography of Morris (pp. 287–292) has been omitted.

des hommes de Dieu." The Colonial college is described—and quite
properly—as interested more in the evidences of design than the body-
mind controversy; in the spiritual relations between man and God, than
in the material explanations of man as a machine. But while the process
of rationalizing was one-sided, that process led to a marked reaction
against Puritan orthodoxy. The very preference for purposiveness was
a sign of revolt against an inscrutable ruler, working in a mysterious
way his wonders to perform. The deists, then, as rationalists, were veritable forerunners of the reasonable Emerson, yet it can hardly be held
that the emotional element, which was so strong in the sage of Concord, was supplied before the day of triumphant deism with its cut and
dried arguments. To intimate—as does the author—that the lacking
element of sentiment was furnished as early as 1738 by the arrival of
George Whitefield, the "revivalist," is going too far. The English evangelist influenced the subsoil of society rather than the upper strata.
Read Charles Chauncy's *Seasonable Thoughts on the State of Religion in New England* and see how unseasonable that cool thinker considered the arguments and actions of the "hot" men.[2]

Girard misses the mark in intimating that there was anything
"romantic" in the early eighteenth-century revivalism; he nevertheless
offers a suggestive explanation for the later opposition to the French
revolutionary romanticism. The wars of the great Emperor—diplomatic
conflicts, the embargo against Napoleon—here is a new line of evidence
for the Yankee dislike of a "Frenchified" philosophy. Another good point
is made in showing how the Scottish philosophy of Dugald Stewart
and Thomas Brown failed to satisfy the romantic impulses of the heart.
So the generation which bridged the period between the eighteenth and
nineteenth centuries, unable to return to the traditional Calvinistic dogma,
disillumined as to the utopias promised by the French revolutionaries,
apprehensive of the skeptical *cul-de-sac* of materialism—this generation
was ready and eager for another and better philosophy. This was offered
by the rising transcendentalism. By this is not meant the religious spiritualism of the Unitarians, which tended to grow more and more vague
as time went on, but the real transcendentalism which, accurately speaking, had a new and fresh aspect supplied on the religious side by the
writings of Madame de Staël, of Benjamin Constant, of Theodore Jouffroy, and on the philosophic by Coleridge, Cousin, and Carlyle, rather
than by Kant, Fichte, and Schelling (p. 387).

The author at this juncture brings forward his first critical contention,
namely, that the failure to distinguish between the religious and philosophic phases of the New England movement has led the historians of
transcendentalism to attribute to the Germans an exaggerated influence
(p. 383, note 2). H. C. Goddard and the reviewer are here mentioned,
but both of these, curiously enough, had meanwhile made his answer.

Goddard's new account of Transcendentalism has just appeared in the *Cambridge History of American Literature*. My own account in the summary volume, *American Thought*, was evidently overlooked by the author.[3] In this were presented grounds for thinking that New England transcendentalism, as represented by Emerson, had other sources than Teutonic. Girard objects to making Emerson the soul and standard bearer of transcendentalism. If I have done that it is because Emerson's *Nature*, published in 1836, presented in the most compact form "the very soul of the machine." I confess, in that brief study, to having failed to appreciate the French contribution to the movement. This has been well supplied by the present author, who shows that the Gallic eclecticism was a prime incentive to the transcendental belief that, in the human soul, there exist certain intuitions, certain first causes of the entire religious and moral life, independent of all sensible experience and prior to all reason (p. 385). Channing and Ripley and Theodore Parker held these views, so did de Staël, Constant, and Cousin. The similarity between the two groups may be granted, but the crux of the problem is the priority of the *a priori*. When Channing is charged by Brownson with being "answerable for no small portion of the soul-worship which was for a time the fashionable doctrine of the metropolis," the question still remains, at what original fane was Channing first inspired with this worship? Was it German or French, or possibly that of the Scottish intuitional school? As to the first alternative, Girard offers new evidence. Such is the statement from *The Memorial History of Boston* that "long after French became a matter of course, the great German writers remained practically unknown on these shores."[4] This *History* has been too little consulted by the critics. It contains a mine of information as to the New England conscience and the rise of transcendentalism, and its evidence is further confirmed by such contemporary reviewers as that of the *Christian Examiner* of 1831, who complains that in neglecting the literature of Germany, the Americans have followed the bad example of the English—"treasures of philosophy, history, poetry, and critic, speculative for the most part, having been sealed up from foreign eyes."[5] The proof from the periodicals is important and goes to push the date of borrowings from across the Rhine to a time after, not before, the Nov-Anglian cult of "the innate knowledge." Germany, it seems—and the evidence is cumulative—did not directly affect leaders like Channing and Emerson. With characteristic Yankee independence—when it came later to their reading the Teutonic originals—they claimed that Fichte and Schelling merely served to confirm what they already had in mind. Such conceit to the Germans may seem "*colossal*," but Girard has cleverly suggested that these very leaders had other sources for their thought, sources of which they were, in a measure, unconscious. A generation before a German dictionary could be bought in Boston, the market was flooded with the works of the Scots and the colleges from Cambridge to South Carolina were filled with the text-books of Stewart and Brown, of Reid and Beattie. But this argument cuts two ways. To prove his central point—the preponderance of French over German influence—Girard is at pains to show how largely the scholars of Paris were indebted to their predecessors of Glasgow, Aberdeen, and Edinburg, Cousin being said to have adopted from Francis Hutcheson his conception of "the moral sense," and from Reid and Stewart his experimental method.

Intuition plus introspection—that which was once Gaelic soon became Gallic—such appears the argument of the author, an argument which seems to detract from his case rather than strengthen it. Now all this valuable material might have been used to a different issue, for it can be shown that the New England transcendentalism was "set" in its local mold before the advent of either French or German craftsmen. The French merely put the *ormolu* about the original vessel; the vessel itself was not made in France, nor in Germany, but was of British-American manufacture. In their historic order the materials were in part derived from Berkeley and his spiritual realism, from the Cambridge Platonists and their archetypes, and from the Lake School with its "spirit far more deeply interfused." Further proofs that the French finish came late is shown in Emerson's rather unfavorable opinion of Cousin—a mere eclectic method, he asserts, being too mechanical to catch such "a fly-away" as truth. Then, too, W. E. Channing, despite his admiration for Rousseau, expressed a certain hesitation as to the tendencies of Gallic thought. Yet this by no means implies that, in fear of the French, the New Englanders went over to the Germans. Girard has collected some very illuminating quotations on this point. According to Margaret Fuller, "Kant was thought by evangelical divines to be more dangerous than any French novelist." According to Brownson no works of Goethe "are exempt from the charge of immoral tendency" (p. 404, note 26).

And the discounting of foreign influences may be carried further. While the attitude toward the Continentals was rather provincial, towards the British it was decidedly independent. As the author intimates, Coleridge loosened up the orthodox Calvinists, but had little influence on the transcendentalists, because they were already liberal. In fact they went much further than the transcendental talker of Highgate. At this turn an interesting point is made that Coleridge's obscurity of style could not obscure a certain attachment of his to the traditional Calvinistic doctrines. Indeed, as we take it, the contrast between the vague Coleridge and the precise Channing is typical. When the English rhapsodist concealed his real beliefs, the American rationalist exactly stated his points of disagreement with the old beliefs.

A like argument holds true in regard to German influences. In their attitude toward the early eighteenth-century system, Channing, Ripley, and Theodore Parker manifested the same critical spirit as did Kant toward the cold formalism of Wolff. Around their philosophies were drawn the black lines of dissent; these lines were bitten in like that of the etcher; they were not the indefinite pastel effects of the mere romanticist. This critical attitude is also exemplified in regard to Carlyle. Here Girard supplies the deficiencies of previous historians of transcendentalism by showing that the individualism of Emerson and Thoreau was not due to a blind hero-worship of the author of *Sartor Resartus*. Nor did the New Englanders get their idealism through the diffracting lenses of the Scotchman, and for three several reasons: Kant's system was declared "an absurdity" by Carlyle; Carlyle in turn was declared unintelligible by the Americans; while the latter, earlier in the century, had already received a diluted form of idealism through Cousin (pp. 410–411).

The problem of priority we shall take up subsequently, but the last contention as to the transcendentalist's kinship to the French rather than the German idealism is ingeniously upheld by another line of evidence. This is to the effect that, while the German metaphysics was counted too radical, the French furnished arguments to reconcile faith and reason, religion and science, the gospel and life (p. 470). The problem of the respective weights of foreign influences is not a simple one. New England transcendentalism was evidently not made in Germany, nor France, nor Britain. As is so commonly thought, it was not a mere mechanical assembling of imported parts, but rather an organic growth, a native plant, fertilized indeed from abroad, but nevertheless rooted in the local soil. Yet even such considerations are not wholly correct. Our philosophic flora can not be divided into two classes, the imported and the indigenous. The problem is like one in comparative botany, where the plants of two divided continents possess resemblances due to the common ancestry of a remote age. So if Emerson appears akin to the Cambridge Platonists, it is because both hark back to the groves of the Academy; and if Channing be called the Fénelon of America, it is because the thinkers of Boston and of Cambrai were alike grounded in the ancient mysticism. Girard has performed a distinct service in pointing out these affinities. The influence, especially, of the French mystics, Fénelon, Pascal, and Madame Guyon, has been but slightly noticed outside of Quaker circles,[6] so at this point the part played by Madame de Staël is properly introduced. *De l'Allemagne* was almost a family text-book in America and its author an advance agent of the notion that there exists in man a special faculty, primitive, innate, by virtue of which, and without the aid of reason or sensible experience, one gains a knowledge of religious truth (p. 418).

The stage was set in America, yet the actors said their lines but haltingly, before French masters instructed them. Thus it is reported of

Channing the elder that he made acquaintance with the master minds of Germany through the medium, first of Madame de Staël, and afterwards of Coleridge. The importance of the rôle of Gallic influence is further argued from the fact that de Staël obtained from Rousseau the notion of a special intuitive religious faculty, while, subsequently, Constant deduced from this the two kindred corollaries that the religious sentiment is universal, and that this sentiment goes through various progressive forms (p. 420). This tracing of the New England romanticism through various intermediances to its sources is of great significance. It may, however, be overdone, unless one keeps in mind that the reason the New Englanders were so sympathetic was because they themselves had been through the same experiences, and had undergone the same reactions. Like causes brought like effects. Rousseau was what he was because of Voltaire and the Encyclopædists, and Channing, because of the skepticism of Hume and the dry rationalism of Thomas Paine.

The comparative study of sources discounts the Teutonic influences on transcendentalism; so does comparative chronology. The problem of priority I have undertaken elsewhere in a comparison of Emerson's *Nature* of 1836 with his early *Journals*, in order to show that he was but slightly affected by German thought in his main tenets.[7] Girard does the same thing for Channing through an examination of the current magazines. Such is a statement from the *Christian Examiner* of 1827 that Schiller and Goethe "are still unfamiliar in America . . . more exciting are the books of Constant and Jouffroy." And what holds for the poets of Germany holds the more for the philosophers. As a matter of fact, New England knew almost nothing of Kant, Fichte, and Schelling until the 60's. In the 30's its knowledge came by a double refractive process through English translations of French treatises. Thus the translations of Cousin by Lindberg in 1832 and by Caleb Henry in 1834 led Orestes Brownson to assert that "Germany reaches us only through France." This statement was made in 1837. The following year came Ripley's important *Specimens of Foreign Standard Literature*, consisting of translations of Cousin, Jouffroy, and Constant. And yet in spite of all this, French eclecticism, though it contained fragments of the high German idealism, was not accepted as a whole by the independent Yankees. As Ripley remarked, that which the transcendentalists borrowed from Cousin were the arguments rather than the system, for "the reign of authoritative dogmatic systems has never been firmly established over the mind of this nation: every exclusive faith has called forth a host of dissent."[8]

Notes

1. William Girard, *Du transcendentalisme considéré essentiellement dans sa définition et ses origines française*, University of California Publications in Modern Philology, vol. 4, no. 3 (Berkeley: University of California, 1916), pp. 351–498; R. M. Wenley, *The Life and Works of George Sylvester Morris, A Chapter in the History of American Thought in the Nineteenth Century* (New York: Macmillan, 1917).

2. Cf. my chapter on "Early American Philosophers and Divines" in the *Cambridge History of American Literature* (New York: Macmillan, 1917), vol. I.

3. A similar misadventure has just befallen me regarding Girard. My article on "French Philosophy in America" was printed in the *Revue Philosophique* (November 1917) only a short time before I discovered Girard's valuable contribution to the subject. And since writing this review there have appeared two more pertinent discussions: Henry David Gray, *Emerson, A Statement of New England Transcendentalism* (Stanford: Stanford University, 1917), and Albert Schurz, "French Origins of American Transcendentalism," *American Journal of Psychology*, 29 (January 1918), 50–65.

4. *The Memorial History of Boston*, ed. Justin Winsor (Boston: James R. Osgood, 1881), III, 653.

5. *Christian Examiner*, 8 (March 1831), 75.

6. Cf. Rufus Jones, *Studies in Mystical Religion* (London: Macmillan, 1909).

7. "The Sources of Transcendentalism," *American Thought* (New York: Henry Holt, 1915).

8. *Philosophical Miscellanies, Translated from the French of Cousin, Jouffroy, and B. Constant*, trans. George Ripley (Boston: Hilliard, Gray, 1838), pp. 29, 30.

"The Background of the Unitarian Opposition to Transcendentalism"

C. H. Faust*

In the opening years of the nineteenth century, New England Calvinists—theological heirs, as they were fond of pointing out, of the founders of New England—were disquieted by indications, such as the appointment of Henry Ware to the Hollis chair of divinity at Harvard College, that the heresies of Socinus were making inroads upon American Congregationalism. The publication in 1815 of Thomas Belsham's *American Unitarianism*, which contained the announcement on no less authority than that of a Boston publisher, William Wells, that "most of our Boston Clergy and respectable laymen (of whom we have many enlightened theologians) are Unitarian,"[1] seemed to confirm their direct forebodings and roused them to battle. The controversy thus precipitated racked New England Congregationalism for three decades.

In 1827 there was added to the host of books, pamphlets, and articles which had appeared in the course of this controversy an anonymous review of a sermon entitled "Unitarian Christianity most favorable to piety," which had been delivered by William Ellery Channing at the dedication of the Second Unitarian Church of New York City in the preceding year. The reviewer, a staunch Calvinist, prefaced his criticisms of Channing's discourse by an illuminating survey of the conflict. In his view, it had moved through two phases and had entered a third. In the first of these, he wrote,

> The weapons of attack and defense .... were chiefly derived from *Biblical literature*. Erroneous readings, mistranslations, and wrong interpretations, were the charges perpetually preferred against the doctrines of the Orthodox, and the scriptural arguments by which they were maintained.

In the second, "the trial of Orthodoxy was," he said, "transferred to another tribunal, that of philosophy. Its doctrines were declared to be irrational and absurd, wholly inconsistent with the perfections of God,

---

*Reprinted from *Modern Philology*, 35 (February 1938), 297–324.

and the freedom and accountability of man." Finally, the opposing creeds were "brought to another test, that of *tendency*," the "main question" being "which of the two systems, the Unitarian or the Orthodox, is of superior tendency to form an elevated religious character." The author thereupon presented a list of Unitarian publications in which the claim that the Unitarian doctrines were more likely than Calvinistic beliefs to promote piety and virtue had been strongly urged: Jared Sparks's *An inquiry into the comparative moral tendency of Trinitarian and Unitarian doctrines* (originally published in the *Unitarian Miscellany* in 1822); Channing's sermon at the ordination of his colleague Ezra Gannett (1824); a discourse by the Boston Unitarian, John Palfrey, in 1824; and a half-dozen articles and reviews in the *Christian Examiner, Christian Register*, and *Christian Inquirer*.[2]

He might easily have expanded this catalogue by including such publications as Henry Ware's *The faith once delivered to the saints* (1825), in which the author contended that the claims of Unitarianism were supported by its being "peculiarly favorable" to virtue; Channing's "Unitarian Christianity" (1819), in which that acknowledged leader and spokesman of the "liberal" party declared that Calvinism "tends strongly to pervert the moral faculty"; and his "Objections to Unitarian Christianity considered" (1819), a large part of which was a reply to the charges that Unitarianism was not conducive to religious zeal and that it was "'a half-way house to infidelity.'"[3] The reviewer might, indeed, have observed that the most notable defense of Calvinism on philosophic grounds, the *Letters to Unitarians* published in 1820 by Leonard Woods, professor of Christian theology at Andover, was concluded by an elaborate discussion of the comparative tendencies of the two systems to "promote particular parts of Christian virtue and duty"; and that the most thoroughgoing defense of Calvinism on biblical grounds, the *Letters to Dr. Channing on the doctrine of the trinity*, published a year earlier by Woods's colleague, Moses Stuart, was climaxed with a stern warning that Unitarian principles of biblical interpretation were likely to induce infidelity.[4]

The Calvinistic charge thus formulated by Stuart that Unitarianism encouraged infidelity, that is, a rejection of the final authority of the Scriptures,[5] was a particularly important aspect of the debate over the "tendencies" of the two opposing creeds; for, in the course of the controversy over this question, Unitarians assumed a position which they found peculiarly embarrassing when, late in the thirties of the century, Transcendentalism emerged in their midst. During the twenty years before Emerson delivered his divinity-school address at Harvard in 1838, they had been harassed by predictions, shrewdly particularized and vigorously supported, that their system of belief would carry them inevitably to the position with respect to the Christian Scriptures announced in that lecture and proclaimed by Theodore Parker in the years immediately after it. They had in defense committed themselves to principles that made it well-nigh impossible for them to dissociate themselves from the new heresy. A survey of this aspect of the controversy will, I believe, contribute to our understanding of the Unitarian opposition to Transcendentalism and to its leading exponents—will, perhaps, make it easier to understand why Emerson was stigmatized as the purveyor of "the latest form of infidelity," and for many years denied further hearing at Harvard; why Parker was denounced as a "deist," "unbeliever," "atheist," and was invited to withdraw from the Boston Unitarian Association.

I

The Calvinistic opponents of Unitarianism, or, as they preferred to be called, "the Orthodox," had not been content simply to reiterate the warning that Unitarianism was "a half-way house to infidelity." They had supported this charge, which since the days of Tom Paine had been in New England a particularly grave one, by arguments based upon the nature of Unitarian belief, had strengthened it by comparisons with the course of similar movements abroad, and had rendered it ominous by arousing distrust for the character of the Unitarian leaders.

They asserted, for one thing, that Unitarianism was a merely negative system. "It is evident," wrote Samuel Miller, professor of theology at Princeton, in 1823, "that Unitarianism, according to the statement of one of its most zealous friends in the *United States*, consists 'rather in NOT BELIEVING.' "[6] The zealous friend referred to by Miller was the Boston publisher William Wells, and the phrase quoted had been taken from a letter to the English Unitarian, Thomas Belsham, which had been published in the latter's *American Unitarianism*. A reviewer for the Calvinistic *Panoplist*, Jedidiah Morse, had put his finger on Wells's statement and had suggested its implications with respect to the religious influence of Harvard, which had long been regarded with sharp suspicion by Calvinists. It is clear, he wrote, that at Harvard college

> the religion, which consists in *not* believing, is taught by a well concerted and uniformly executed plan of negatives. All systems but Unitarianism are openly, or secretly, impugned or ridiculed, while the "*not* believing" religion is dexterously substituted in their place.[7]

By 1834 Channing's colleague at the Federal Street Church in Boston, Ezra Gannett, was complaining, in a sermon called "Christian Unitarianism not a negative system," that this charge had been "reiterated in one form or another from north to south."[8]

Not infrequently Calvinists represented Unitarianism as merely a stage in the decline from orthodoxy to general skepticism. Having renounced one creed, said Lyman Beecher in "The faith once delivered to the saints" (1823), Unitarians relinquish one doctrine after another until they have no clear convictions left:

> Unitarians, who have been educated in Orthodoxy, abandon what they call one error, and adopt what afterwards they call another, and abandon this and adopt a third error, and abandon this and adopt a fourth, and are ever learning their past errors, and are confident of nothing but that in all their opinions, except the last, they have been wrong; while even these, as it is meet they should after such reiterated admonition of their frailty, they hold with such magnanimous uncertainty as renders confidence arrogant.[9]

The point was sometimes framed in more prophetic terms: Unitarianism, it was said, being by nature opposed to belief, and having abandoned one theological position after another, would eventually lapse into open infidelity. "The fire of unbelief has been the ruling spirit in your system," wrote George Cheever, for instance, in an article addressed to Unitarians through the columns of that militantly Calvinistic journal *The Spirit of the Pilgrims* in 1833:

> It is a system, as shifting as the sands, having no stability, no permanent creed, no grounds of certainty, nothing fixed but a mortal aversion to the evangelical scheme. It is a system, from beginning to end, designed, such as Hall said the infidels, whom he found rejoicing at the progress of Unitarianism, undoubtedly considered it, "as a natural opening, through which men may escape from the restraints of revealed religion." . . . . It is a system, indeed, in which doubt and darkness are thrown over every subject involving the eternal destiny of man and therefore over the whole Bible.

Cheever devoted a section of his article to a consideration of the doctrines which Unitarians had already abandoned: the doctrines of human depravity, of the atonement, of the existence of Satan, of eternal punishment, and so forth. "Nor can you hope," he pressed on to say, "to keep the actual nature and tendencies of your system much longer concealed. They will not be repressed. Your system is displaying itself, and you need not expect to restrain its freaks and sallies of infidelity." In particular he expressed alarm over the rapid progress of "liberal Christianity" toward a rejection of revelation:

> At present we must bend our efforts to the preserving of the Scriptures themselves from the grasp and sweep of your reckless infidelity. Were we to let you go on, we should very soon have no Bible whatever to appeal to.

In more ways than one you have shown your jealousy and dislike of the sacred volume. The publications that have emanated from the presses and institutions of your system, both in this country and in Europe, contain either an effective rejection of revelation or principles that lead to it.[10]

What the Unitarian principles were which would lead to a rejection of revelation the author of this statement did not say; he contented himself with quoting passages from Unitarian writings which contained what he regarded as demonstrations of a tendency to infidelity or as covert embracings of it. Other Calvinists had, however, explored the subject in some detail. Moses Stuart, for instance, undertook in 1819 an analysis of Channing's statement of the Unitarian principles of exegesis. He agreed with Channing, he said, that the meaning of the Bible was "to be sought in the same manner as that of other books," that grammatical analysis of the biblical texts was the only justifiable method of interpretation.

We both concede, that the principles by which all books are to be interpreted, are those which apply to the interpretation of the Bible; for the very plain reason which you have given, that when God condescends to speak and write for men, it is according to the established rules of human language . . . .

From this great and fundamental principle of all interpretation, it results that the grammatical analysis of the words of any passage, i.e., an investigation of their meaning in general, of their syntactical connection, of their idiom, of their relation to the context, and of course of their *local* meaning; must be the essential process, in determining the sense of any text or part of Scripture. On this fundamental process depends the interpretation of all the classics, and of all other books; from this result laws which are uniform, and which cannot be violated, without at once plunging into the dark and boundless field of conjectural exegesis.[11]

Having stated this basic agreement with his opponent, Stuart took exception to Channing's position with respect to the relationship of reason and revelation. Channing had said,

The Bible treats of subjects on which we receive ideas from other sources besides itself; such subjects as the nature, passions, relations, and duties of man; and it expects us to restrain and modify its language by the known truths which observation and experience furnish on these topics.[12]

This principle Stuart felt obliged to reject, on the ground that it involved the ascription of final authority to reason rather than to revelation. He argued that once the claims of the Bible as a divine revelation had been allowed, as Channing professed to allow them, the only proper question was: What did the Bible teach? That question had to be answered, he said, by a careful, grammatical interpretation of the text. Once the meaning of the text had been ascertained, reason had performed its function. It had no authority to modify propositions thus derived from revelation so as to bring them into accord with conclusions arrived at independently:

> My simple inquiry must be, what sentiment does the language of this or that passage convey, without violence or perversion of rule? When this question is settled, *philologically* (not philosophically), then I either believe what is taught, or else reject the claim of divine authority. What can my own theories and reasonings about the absurdity or reasonableness of any particular doctrine, avail in determining whether a writer of the New Testament *has taught* this doctrine or not? My investigation must be conducted independently of my *philosophy*, by my philology. And when I have obtained his meaning, by the simple and universal rules of expounding language, I must choose the course I will take; I must either believe his assertion, or reject his authority.[13]

Quoting Channing's statement that Unitarians "do not hesitate to modify, and restrain, and turn from their most obvious sense" certain difficult passages of Scripture in which human beings are called gods, because the sense of these passages "is opposed to the known properties of the beings to whom they relate," Stuart wrote: "I must *hesitate* however to adopt this principle, without examining its nature and tendency." His investigation of its tendency led him to predict that those who applied it would end in infidelity:

> I am well satisfied, that the course of reasoning in which you have embarked, [and the principles by which you explain away the divinity of the Saviour,] must eventually lead most men who approve of them to the conclusion, that the Bible is not of divine origin, and does not oblige us to belief or obedience. I do not aver, that they will certainly lead *you* [Channing] there. The remains of your former education and belief may still serve to guard you against the bolder conclusions of some of your brethren, who have not been placed under instruction such as you enjoyed in early life. You have more serious views of the importance of religion, than many, perhaps than most, of those who speculate with you. *Consistency*, too, will afford strong inducement not to give up the divine authority of the Scriptures. Yet many of your younger brethren have no inconsistency to fear, by adopting such views. . . . . Feeling the inconsistency (as I am certain some of them will and do feel it); of

violating the fundamental rules of interpretation, in order to make the apostles speak, as in their apprehension they ought to speak; and unable to reconcile what the apostles say with their own views; they will throw off the restraints which the old ideas of inspiration and infallibility of the Scriptures impose upon them, and receive them simply on the ground, on which they place any other writings of a moral and religious nature.[14]

Some Calvinists were confident that they could chart exactly the course which this subordination of revelation to reason would lead Unitarians to take. It was the road which German rationalism had traveled before their eyes. Again and again they pointed out that American Unitarians were treading in the steps of German heretics. It is true, wrote Samuel Miller of Princeton, in 1823, that the Germans, less restrained by public opinion, have gone a little farther; but Unitarians "will probably soon overtake them."[15] Moses Stuart, watching the new movement from Andover, was very sure that they would "at last, go full length with the most liberal of them all." Reasoning as they did, he asserted, they "must necessarily . . . . come to the same conclusions with Eichhorn, and Paulus, and Henke, and Eckermann, and Herder, and other distinguished men of the new German school." "I shall be ready to confess my apprehensions are quite erroneous," he wrote, "if the lapse of a few years more does not produce the undisguised avowal of the German divinity, in all its latitude."[16] In 1829 Stuart's colleague at Andover, Leonard Woods, in his *Lectures on the inspiration of the Scriptures* likewise pointed in warning to the decline of prominent German theologians into infidelity. Commenting on this section of the book, a Unitarian reviewer referred impatiently to those "who have rung all the changes of argument, warning, and sarcasm" upon the parallels between Unitarianism and German rationalism "till we should think it could scarcely yield another note." "Is the learning of Germany, with its hasty, though monstrous growth, to deter all the world from inquiry?" he asked.[17]

Irritating these comparisons and prophecies must have been to Unitarians in the years before the appearance of Transcendentalism. They were made even more galling by an accusation which often accompanied them, namely, that Unitarians habitually and as a matter of policy concealed their subversive opinions.

This charge had gained its impetus from the circumstances under which the Unitarian controversy proper had begun in America. The provocative power of Behlsam's *American Unitarianism*, which had been the signal for that controversy, lay largely in a half-dozen letters from American to English Unitarians reproduced in it, reporting the gratifying progress of the movement in this country. Calvinists had professed to be shocked by the disclosure in these letters of the fashion in which

Unitarianism had "silently and covertly extended itself." The author of a widely read review of the work for the Orthodox *Panoplist* seems, indeed, to have represented the general feeling of his party when he wrote that the book had done good service to true Christianity by exposing the Unitarian program of stealthy penetration. The "work of error," he wrote, "was carried on for the most part in secret." Unitarians "have not dared to be open. They have clandestinely crept into orthodox churches, by forebearing to contradict their faith, and then have gradually moulded them, by their negative preaching, to the shape which they would wish."[18] This review was the starting-point for a pamphlet skirmish, and the charge of "concealment" thus brought into prominence reappeared often in Orthodox journals and books.[19] Linked with the assertion that Unitarianism induced infidelity, it made a formidable controversial weapon. The editor of the *Spirit of the Pilgrims* used it in 1829, for example:

> The discussions and disclosures of a twenty years' controversy have brought them [Unitarian sentiments] out on several points; but over others of equal importance there is still thrown a covering of disguise. For instance; expressions are frequently dropped, which shew that Unitarians regard the *Bible*, as not altogether to be depended on, in questions of a religious nature. "The sacred documents of our faith" are represented "as prepared for *temporary use*, and filled with subjects of local interest or popular accommodation." . . . . "The reasoning of St. Paul *will not always bear a philosophical scrutiny*." Yet these writers talk of believing the inspiration of the Scriptures, and regard themselves as greatly misrepresented, and grossly slandered, if they are charged with any approaches to infidelity.

"Let them throw off the cloak which they have so long worn," the writer urged, "and, like Unitarians in England and on the continent of Europe, let them no longer be afraid or ashamed to make a full disclosure of their sentiments."[20]

Until such disclosure should be made, said the author of a series of "Letters on the introduction and progress of Unitarianism in New England" which appeared in the same journal during the following year, friends of Orthodoxy cannot but be apprehensive concerning the growth of the movement. The success of Unitarianism, he wrote, has been "greatly promoted by concealment. . . . . The poison would in this way be taken without alarm, and the infection spread through the religious community, before apprehension should be excited, or the friends of truth were apprised of their danger." He warned his readers that, although the extent of the Unitarian defection from Orthodoxy had been in part exposed, the Unitarian practice of concealment made it impossible to determine how much farther it had "in private proceeded."[21]

II

It is not to be imagined, of course, that Unitarians endured in silence the reiteration of these charges that they had adopted a system of negations which must inevitably bring them, as it had the German rationalists, to open infidelity, and that they had deliberately fixed upon a policy of concealment which would lead unsuspecting folk into following them.

In countering these accusations, they insisted, for one thing, that instead of leading to infidelity, Unitarianism was a safeguard against it—a better safeguard, indeed, than Orthodoxy. Channing in 1819 laid down the main points in this line of defense. He admitted that one who had given up the doctrines peculiar to Calvinism might be expected to go on relinquishing one portion of his faith after another until he reached infidelity. Having found one part of his creed untenable, he would be inclined to distrust the whole of it. For this tendency Unitarians could not, however, be held responsible. The odium of it must be borne by their opponents, who had preached "false and absurd doctrines." "None are so likely to believe too little as those who have begun with believing too much; and hence we charge upon Trinitarianism whatever tendency may exist in those who forsake it, to sink gradually into infidelity." Unitarianism, on the other hand, fortified faith, because, having cast off the corruptions which through the centuries had fastened themselves upon Christianity, it did not, like the current Orthodoxy, bewilder and disgust thoughtful, morally sensitive souls:

> Unitarianism is Christianity stripped of those corrupt additions which shock reason and our moral feelings. It is a rational and amiable system, against which no man's understanding, or conscience, or charity, or piety revolts. Can the same be said of that system which teaches the doctrines of three equal persons in one God, of natural and total depravity, of infinite atonement, of special and electing grace, and of the everlasting misery of the non-elected part of mankind?

Unless Christianity freed itself of these perversions, Channing pressed on to say, intelligent men would soon abandon it. Only a more "rational and amiable" system could save them. He was certain, then, that "Unitarianism does not lead to infidelity. On the contrary, its excellence is that it fortifies faith."[22]

Unitarians often proclaimed this conviction in the years that followed Channing's sermon, and often repeated the arguments which he had employed to support it. They insisted that the time had come when "with men of intelligence and reflection the only question likely to arise" was whether they should have a "more rational religion or none"; and they published widely their certainty that the principles they had embraced, far from inducing infidelity, were the one sure protection against it. Their position was stated succinctly by the *Unitarian Miscellany* in 1823:

> Unitarianism has been stigmatized as the half way road to infidelity. Let it be seen, in coming time, whether it is not rather the only barrier against a wild, unprofitable enthusiasm on the one hand, and a deadening unbelief on the other.[23]

Calvinists had argued that the "new theology" tended to undermine faith in revelation because it was a negative system; Unitarians insisted, by way of objection to this conclusion, that their creed was favorable to faith because it was rational. But they went farther: they attacked the premise of the argument, denying repeatedly that Unitarianism was merely negative. Thus, in 1834 Ezra Gannett preached a sermon, later published for distribution as a Unitarian tract with the title *Christian Unitarianism not a negative system.* According to Gannett, those who asserted that "liberal Christianity" consisted in not believing did so on the ground that it rejected certain Calvinistic doctrines. With equal reason Calvinism might be said to consist in not believing, he contented [*sic*], since the disciples of Calvin rejected certain "peculiar dogmas of still larger divisions of the Christian Church." How, he inquired, could they reply to the Roman Catholic who declared that the discarding of the doctrines of transubstantiation and of purgatory made their system a negative one? In short, Gannett argued that the Calvinistic slur upon Unitarianism as a system of negations bound to end in infidelity, reduced itself upon examination simply to a narrow insistence that one must swallow the whole of Calvinism.[24]

Against such arbitrary marking of the boundary between faith and unbelief Unitarians stoutly protested. They objected to the assumption that the denial of certain tenets of Calvinism, which they regarded as corruptions of Christianity, involved a complete abandonment of faith. Thus, a reviewer for the *Christian Examiner*, leading organ of the new party, wrote in 1830:

> Because it [Unitarianism] comes out and denies the truth of certain doctrines which for centuries have been generally received as fundamental and essential doctrines of Christianity, it is charged with the denial of Christianity itself. . . . . One fact is confirmed to us by this state of things, which is, that the doctrines to which we just now alluded, and which we regard as the corruptions of our religion, such as the imputation of Adam's sin, the trinity, and the popular

scheme of the atonement, have been intertwined and incorporated with the Christian system, that they have been esteemed, in almost universal opinion, as one and the same thing with that system. . . . . It is in perfect accordance, therefore, with this prevalent, though extremely erroneous notion, that we, who have discarded those doctrines, which we conceive to be gross misconceptions of Christianity, have been accused of an utter want of faith, and suspected of a corresponding laxity of principle. And it is in reference to this notion principally, as the root of a rank growth of error, prejudice, and abuse, that we now propose to set forth, in a few pages, the real seriousness of the Liberal and Unitarian system of belief, and to show that it denies not a single doctrine of revelation.[25]

Unitarians accordingly protested against the refusal of orthodox Congregationalists to recognize as Christians those who could not accept the Genevan system. The *Unitarian Miscellany* of 1821 addressed Calvinists as follows:

You have defined Christianity in your own way; you have made its essence to consist in doctrines of your own choosing, and then declared, that whoever does not receive your definition, and believe the doctrines you have selected, is "no Christian."[26]

In 1815 Channing censured this practice sharply in a sermon entitled "The system of exclusion and denunciation in religion considered."[27] And in 1832 the American Unitarian Association published as a tract James Walker's *On the exclusive system*, in which Calvinists were denounced for denying "Christian fellowship, the Christian name, and all Christian privileges to such as differ from them beyond a certain mark; which they assume the right to fix for themselves and alter at pleasure."[28] The principle here implied, it may be suggested at this point, was to cause Unitarians no little worry when, later on, they grappled with the problem of how to treat Emerson and Parker.

Unitarians prided themselves on being free from the fault of exclusiveness. At the annual meeting in 1830 of the Society for Promoting Theological Education at Harvard College, for instance, F. W. P. Greenwood, in an address often quoted, made a great point of the liberality of the Cambridge Divinity School. Unitarianism, he said, was not committed to "a timid creed-bound theology." It had, to be sure, its own peculiar doctrinal position; "but above the doctrinal opinions there is seated the high spirit of freedom." Again, "*Exclusiveness is its utter aversion.*" Greenwood was plainly in harmony with the traditions of his party; indeed, Unitarians often assumed the title "Liberal Christians."[29]

They prided themselves, furthermore, on recognizing the claims of unhampered inquiry in religious matters, particularly in biblical studies. "Free inquiry is a fundamental principle with Unitarians," wrote a reviewer for the *Unitarian Miscellany* in 1822.[30] While urging the necessity of freedom in the study and interpretation of the Bible, they declared repeatedly, however, their confidence in its supernatural authority. At this point they met squarely the Calvinistic criticism that their system tended to produce infidelity. "Whatever doctrines seem to us to be clearly taught in the Scriptures," said Channing in 1819, "we receive without reserve or exception."[31] His associates and followers were fond of asserting their allegiance to this Protestant principle. A writer for the *Christian Examiner*, discussing the "Misapprehensions of Unitarianism" in 1830, thought it not too much to say that Unitarians "recognize the divine authority of the Scriptures as completely as do our most Orthodox brethren."[32] Not infrequently Unitarians declared themselves ready to support this assertion by submitting the doctrinal differences between themselves and Calvinists to the test of the Bible. The American editor of James Yates's *Vindication of Unitarianism* wrote in 1816 that his fellow-believers

> would esteem themselves but too happy, if the determination of the question, whether there is *one* Supreme Object of worship, or *three* Supreme Objects of worship, should be left to the clear and simple language of the Bible, explained by *any* consistent laws of interpretation.[33]

Indeed, Unitarians commonly remarked that if they could discover Calvinism in the Bible they would accept it. Wrote William Peabody in 1823:

> We bring every doctrine and every duty to the test of Scripture; the reason of our rejecting certain doctrines, is, that we cannot find them taught in the Bible; if we did, we should embrace and avow them, as readily as we now disown and cast them away. No man can point to any sentiments which we have rejected because they are opposed to our reason merely; if we reject them, it is because we think they are not taught of God.[34]

Since they were ready to submit their creed to the test of the Bible, Unitarians professed to be surprised at being accused of having an inadequate faith in revelation and of nurturing infidelity. The infidel rejects revelation, said a reviewer for the *Christian Examiner* in 1830, but the Unitarian confesses the "divine supernatural, miraculous origin of that system of interpositions and instructions, that is recorded in the Bible." And he added dramatically: "Was anything ever heard of, in all the annals of theological extravagance, more monstrous, than to charge men,

who devoutly and gratefully profess to receive the Bible in this supernatural character, with being Infidels?"[35]

III

By 1835 the chief points in the Orthodox attack on Unitarianism
had often been stated and elaborated; they had, too, often been answered.
There the matter apparently rested for a few years; and it might, in the
fashion of such controversies, have gradually subsided had it not been
for Ralph Waldo Emerson and Theodore Parker. In the decade beginning
in 1838, these two young men embarrassed the leaders of the Unitarian
movement, with which they had been identified, by assuming positions
that seemed to Calvinists to justify their predictions concerning the tendency of the liberal theology toward infidelity.

In the summer of 1838, Emerson, addressing the graduating class
of the Harvard Divinity School, urged candidates for Unitarian pulpits
to forswear dependence upon the "Hebrew and Greek Scriptures." He
frowned upon the "assumption that the age of inspiration is past, that
the Bible is closed." He complained that "men have come to speak of
revelation as somewhat long ago given and done, as if God were dead."
Each of you, he assured his hearers, is "a newborn bard of the Holy
Ghost."[36]

Here was infidelity—an open rejection of the final and supernatural
authority of the Bible. Unitarians, themselves, were among the first to
point it out. Among the attacks on Emerson's address was one generally
ascribed to Andrews Norton, professor of theology at Harvard. It contained the assertion that it was sufficient to say of Emerson that he "professes to reject all belief in Christianity as a revelation."[37] For a later,
more carefully considered statement of objections to the doctrine of
Emerson's address, he chose the title, "The latest form of infidelity."

Not all of Emerson's hearers, however, agreed with Norton. The
young minister of the Unitarian congregation at West Roxbury, Theodore
Parker, was delighted and stirred. "This week," he determined after
listening to the address, "I shall write the long-meditated sermons on
the state of the Church and the duties of these times."[38]

The sermons which Parker, under the inspiration of Emerson's
words, resolved to preach seem not to have disturbed his parishioners,
countryfolk apparently unfamiliar with the nice aspects of the controversy. It was otherwise, however, when he spoke his mind in Boston
before fellow Unitarian ministers. In May of 1841 he delivered the ordination sermon of Charles Shackford at the Hawes Place Church in that
city on the subject, "The permanent and transient in Christianity." Less
lofty than Emerson's address, his attack on the supernatural authority
of the Bible was much more pointed and particular. Among the tran-

sitory elements in current Christianity, he placed the "doctrine respecting the origin and authority of the Old Testament." "It has been assumed at the outset, with no shadow of evidence," he said, "that those writers held a miraculous communication with God, such as he granted to no other man. What was originally a presumption of bigoted Jews became an article of faith, which Christians were burned for not believing." Surely, he continued, the belief that the Old Testament was miraculously inspired and infallibly true could not long endure. It was, in fact, already crumbling. Nor was the case for the infallibility of the New Testament any sounder. "Men have been bid to close their eyes at the obvious differences between Luke and John, the serious disagreements between Paul and Peter; to believe, on the smallest evidence, accounts which shock the moral sense and revolt the reason." Against this reverence for the Bible Parker protested. "An idolatrous regard for the imperfect scripture of God's word is the apple of Atalanta," he declared, "which defeats theologians running for the hand of divine truth." He dared to hope that it was passing away.[39]

Such assertions did not, of course, remain unchallenged; Boston ministers refused to open their pulpits to this infidel. But a group of Boston laymen, interested in hearing him further, persuaded him to deliver a series of lectures in the city during the winter of 1841–42. In these discourses he elaborated his views of revelation, coming to the conclusion that

> laying aside all prejudices, if we look into the Bible in a general way, as into other books, we find facts which force the conclusion upon us, that the Bible is a human work, as much as the Principia of Newton or Descartes, or the Vedas and Koran.[40]

When Calvinists read these pronouncements and those of Emerson, they felt justified in announcing that their predictions concerning the eventual decline of Unitarianism into infidelity had been fulfilled. They pointed to Transcendentalism as the end of the road along which "liberal Christianity," despite their warnings, had been traveling. From the strongholds of Orthodoxy at Princeton, New Haven, and Andover came such announcements. The *Biblical Repository and Princeton Review* noted Emerson's attitude toward revelation, and minced no words in characterizing him as an infidel:

> There is not a single truth or sentiment in this whole Address that is borrowed from the Scriptures. And why should there be? Mr. Emerson, and all men, are as truly inspired as the penmen of the sacred volume. Indeed he expressly warns the candidates for the ministry, whom he was addressing, to look only into their own souls for the truth. He has himself succeeded thus in discovering many

truths that are not to be found in the Bible. . . . . In a word, Mr. Emerson is an infidel and an atheist.[41]

A review of the first series of Emerson's *Essays* two years later contained a blistering analysis of his "pantheism" and of his "characteristic profanation of scripture." This, said the reviewer, is what Unitarianism has come to. He found it a shocking, but not a surprising, development—one that had, in fact, been forseen:

> And this it is, which, if we are rightly informed, is to take the place of Unitarian Rationalism. The change is certainly great, but not surprising. Step by step the Unitarian theology has come down from the true position as to the inspiration of the scriptures, and thus having abandoned the only sure footing, those who are foremost in the descent have found themselves among the ooze and quicksands of atheistic philosophy.[42]

In New Haven the *New Englander* likewise announced that the Transcendental infidelity was a logical outgrowth of Unitarianism. In the first of two articles on Theodore Parker in 1844, Parker's opinions were described as "the infidelity of the age";[43] and in the second the question was raised: "What is the process by which he was led to these results?" The author, Noah Porter, recently elected professor of metaphysics and moral philosophy at Yale College, felt sure that it was Parker's Unitarian training. He knew that Mr. Norton placed the blame for Parker's defection upon German metaphysics, but he was prepared to reject this defense.

> Where learned Mr. Parker his philosophical system? Where did he discover that man himself might be so inspired, that his God could give him no added inspiration? . . . . Mr. Norton will start up with his accustomed promptness, and reply: "Not from me—not from me. I have always taught as I do now, that man could not know God, or a future state, or his own moral nature, except as truths concerning these points are attested and confirmed by miracles. . . . . But it is all German metaphysics, the adoption of the last importation from the dominion of tobacco smoke, and the taking up of the last extravagance that has come from the addled head of some German professor, that has done the mischief." Thus much might Prof. Norton say. But we are not quite certain that this is a complete and satisfactory account of the matter. We have some of us heard of Dr. Channing, and have known of his influence in shaping the principles and in forming the spirit of the liberal school. . . . . We all know the relation in which he was accustomed to place man in respect to the Scriptures, and the office which he made the Bible fulfill to his wants. These views of Channing have pervaded, if indeed they have

not constituted, the atmosphere of liberal Christianity. They have been as the unseen and impalpable particles which are diffused through the fluid, as the elements of future crystals. There was only wanting the fragment of some German system to serve as a nucleus, and behold they are gathered and shoot out from it at once, and we have them polished and hardened in all the beauty and symmetry of a perfect philosophic system.

After making a detailed analysis of "the principles and modes of thinking peculiar to liberal Christians," Porter concluded that Parker "is a consistent and logical thinker, and has carried them to no unnatural conclusions."[44] A year later, writing about Parker's difficulties with the Boston Unitarian Association, he argued that Parker's strongest claim to recognition as a Unitarian in good standing was "that his opinions are the legitimate and logical consequence of the liberal theology."[45]

At Andover, where every move among Boston Unitarians was keenly scrutinized, the doctrines of Emerson and Parker provoked a similar response. In 1846 Moses Stuart republished his letters to Channing of 1819, in which he had predicted the decline of Unitarianism into infidelity. He now added a long "postscript," pointing, not without pride, to the fulfilment of his prophecy. "A false prophet I was not, as it seems from the present state of *facts*," he wrote, "when I penned those remarks in my letters, twenty-six years ago." The opinions of Parker, he asserted, had derived lineally from those of older Unitarians, and must, if Unitarians remain consistent, eventually be shared by all of them. In the meantime, he was willing to credit Parker with superior consistency, frankness, and courage:

> The fruits, in our own country, of beginnings like those in Germany during the years 1770–1800, are now plain and evident to all attentive observers. Had Dr. Channing lived until the present time, it is difficult to say what position he would have taken. But we know what position many of his friends and followers have taken. . . . . But above all, the Rev. Theodore Parker, in his book *Of Religion*, and other publications, has fully and openly taken the ultimate ground to which the principles in question naturally and even necessarily lead, in the mind of the bold and consistent men. . . . . In my view, he has greatly the advantage, in respect to consistency and frankness and courage, over those Unitarians who are at variance with him, and who still cherish principles that must, at least if *logic* has any part to act, inevitably end in bringing them to the same views as those of Mr. Parker.[46]

In the face of these and similar reproaches, many Unitarians felt it necessary to cut the ties that bound Transcendentalists to them. Those who took this view, however, encountered a serious hindrance—their repeated declamations against the "exclusive system." With what grace, they were asked, can you, who have long inveighed against such a system, now exclude men like Parker and Emerson from your fellowship? This objection was first raised during the furore that followed Emerson's Divinity School Address. At that time the *Christian Examiner* had proposed that hereafter the faculty of the Divinity School exercise a power of veto over student choices of lecturers.[47] The proposal was vigorously denounced by James Freeman Clarke in the *Western Messenger*. He quoted at length from Greenwood's eulogy of the liberality of the Cambridge school[48] and recalled how as a student there he had been warned against exclusiveness in religion and had been urged to independent pursuit of truth. Referring to the suggestion for faculty control of invitations to lectures, he said: "This is indeed a 'New View.'" "At this late date," he asked, "is a new system to be introduced? Is that school really to become a college of propagandists? Is censorship to be established there?" Sadly he predicted the decline of the institution if this "novel policy" of "*religious exclusiveness*" should be adopted.[49] A year later there appeared in the same journal a review of Norton's "The latest form of infidelity," in which Emerson's critic was reminded that in denying the Christian title to Transcendentalists he was employing the very tactics which he had formerly condemned.[50] Much the same tone was adopted by George Ripley, who in his reply to Norton's pamphlet observed that the author's "Application of the exclusive principle is the more remarkable when we consider the vehemence with which he had opposed it in reference to his opinions."[51]

Objections of the same character arose when Unitarians proposed expelling Parker from the Boston Association. The problem presented to "Liberal Christians" by the infidelity of Parker was far more acute than that raised by Emerson's doctrines, for, while Emerson had voluntarily stepped out of a Unitarian pulpit, Parker chose to remain in it. To the suggestion from the Boston Unitarian Association that, since he "hurt their usefulness, compromised their position," he ought to offer his resignation to the Association, he replied: "So long as the world standeth, I will not withdraw voluntarily while I consider rights of conscience at issue." When in January of 1843 the Boston Association debated in his presence his eviction from the society on the ground of his disbelief in the biblical miracles, he reminded them that no statement of belief had been required of him when he entered the society, and that Unitarians, unlike other sects, had never set up creedal shibboleths—"had no symbolical books."[52] When, a year later, he had been barred from "the great and Thursday lecture," Parker complained in a letter to the members of the Association that he was being made to suffer by their violation of their own principle that no man should be excluded from Christian fellowship on the basis of his theology. "Now, gentlemen," he said, "it seems to me that some of you are pursuing the same course you once complained of."[53] One of the members of the Association to which this letter was addressed, Joseph Henry Allen, said, in reporting the difference between Parker and the Association: "Old memories of protest against 'the exclusive system' made a return to it impossible."[54]

Thorny was the dilemma that was thus presented to Unitarians. To continue association with Parker was to lend color to the old charge of the Orthodox that Unitarianism was a halfway house to infidelity. To expel him was to abandon a principle that they had long fought for and earnestly cherished. Their predicament was shrewdly analyzed by Joseph Thompson in the *New Englander* for October of 1846. Thompson was reviewing George Putnam's sermon at the ordination of David Fosdick as minister of the Hollis Street Church in Boston.[55] He found in the addresses delivered on that occasion evidence of "the difficulties that encompass the Unitarian body," in which "there is a great and portentous commotion." He discovered, too, the admission that Unitarianism "is a system of mere negations," and waxed facetious over Putnam's difficulty in framing a satisfactory definition of the movement, asking finally: "Is a Unitarian one who rejects miracles and the inspiration of the Scriptures? This appears to be the latest style of this indefinite character." This led him to an analysis of the infidelity of Theodore Parker, and to the dilemma that Parker's views had forced upon Unitarians:

> What now shall be done? For those who have made it their boast that they stood upon the elevated platform of the Bible, to retain in their fellowship one whom they accuse of reducing the Bible to a level with mere human productions, would be to forfeit the respect and confidence of the serious-minded and substantial members of their communion; while to disclaim him, yet professing to believe in Christ, would be to outrage all consistency and self-respect, and to set up one of those very standards so long denounced as arbitrary and popish,—which would bear upon the accused with the injustice of an *ex post facto* law.... It is impossible to disown Mr. Parker without sacrificing their own consistency; it is impossible to retain him in their fellowship without giving up all pretence of being a Christian denomination. Yet one or the other of these things they must do. They must bring to light that unwritten creed; give it shape and expression; make it definite and stringent; make a new sect of orthodox Unitarians;—or they must evade all responsibility for such doctrines or their advocates, by disorganizing themselves completely; otherwise this new Rationalism must be regarded as the legitimate offspring, or the familiar associate of Unitarianism.[56]

Unitarians were not at one concerning the solution of this uncomfortable problem. A few favored expelling Parker.[57] Others suggested dissolving their Association to escape the odium of his attachment to it.[58] The majority took a less strenuous, if less logical, course. Parker was not expelled, but he was vigorously denounced. He was allowed to remain in the Association, but he was shunned by most of its members. The *Christian Examiner* was at pains to make perfectly clear the general disapproval of him in Unitarian circles,[59] and most of his colleagues refused to participate in the customary pulpit exchanges with him. His own account of his troubles, while bitter, seems amply justified:

> At length, on the 19th of May, 1841, at the ordination of Mr. Shack-ford, a thoughtful and promising young man, at South Boston, I preached a "Discourse of the Transient and Permanent in Christian-ity". . . . a great outcry was raised against the sermon and its author. . . . . I printed the sermon, but no bookseller in Boston would put his name to the title-page—Unitarian ministers had been busy with their advice. . . . Most of my clerical friends fell off; some would not speak to me in the street, and refused to take me by the hand; in their public meetings they left the sofas or benches when I sat down, and withdrew from me as Jews from contact with a leper. In a few months most of my former ministerial coadjutors forsook me, and there were only six who would allow me to enter their pulpits. . . . . The controlling men of the denomination de-termined, "This young man must be silenced!" The Unitarian per-iodicals were shut against me and my friends—the public must not read what I wrote. Attempts were secretly made to alienate my little congregation, and expel me from my obscure station at West Roxbury.[60]

Such intense antagonism and detestation Parker was to encounter from many Unitarians throughout his life. In 1857, for instance, the faculty of the Cambridge Divinity School canceled the invitation extended to him by the Senior class to be its graduation lecturer; and at a meeting of Cambridge alumni two years later, when he was seriously ill, a resolution of sympathy for him was voted down.[61]

The feeling which underlay actions of this sort is revealed in the *Reminiscences* of Samuel Lathrop, minister of the Brattle Street Uni-tarian congregation in Boston during the perturbation over Parker's beliefs. He is discussing the effects of Parker's discourse, "The transient and permanent in Christianity":

> This outbreak, if I may call it so, of Mr. Parker disintegrated the clergy and the whole body of Unitarians, and dealt a blow from which Unitarianism has not, and probably as a religious denomination never will recover. The trouble caused ten years before by Mr. Emerson, when he preached against the Lord's supper and proposed to discontinue its administration, was slight and limited, because he

resigned his charge and left the ministry; and, like an honest man, did not wish to make or hold the religious body to which he belonged and in which he had been educated responsible for his opinions. Mr. Parker insisted on retaining in all the ways that he could his connection with the Unitarians, and maintained that his views, opinions, and doctrines were not imported—not the result of his study of German theologians and philosophers,—but the logical result of the New England Unitarian theology. This made his influence damaging to Unitarianism, excited afresh the prejudice of the ortho-dox against it, and obtained for him sympathy and a large follow-ing, both of clergy and laity, among Unitarians themselves.[62]

The resentment exhibited toward Emerson, who had left the Uni-tarian ministry before announcing his heresies, was, as is suggested by Lathrop's account, less harsh. Even so, Emerson observed that the Cambridge address had "given plentiful offense," and, writing in his journal concerning what he described to Carlyle as "the storm in our wash bowl," modestly reminded himself that "a few sour faces,—a few biting paragraphs,—is but a cheap expiation for all these shortcomings of mine."[63] The *Christian Examiner* announced with respect to the doc-trines of Emerson's address that "so far as they are intelligible, [they] are utterly distasteful to the instructors of the School, and to Unitarian ministers generally, by whom they are esteemed to be neither good divinity nor good sense."[64] Andrews Norton of the Divinity School attacked them as "The latest form of infidelity," and was generally be-lieved to be the author of an article in the Boston *Daily Advertiser* (Au-gust 27, 1838) in which the point was made that the officers of the Divinity School were in no wise responsible for Emerson's subversive discourse.[65] His colleague, Henry Ware, published a sermon which the *Christian Examiner* hoped would "tend to disabuse the minds of many respecting the true character and tendency of a set of newly broached fancies, which, deceived by the high sounding pretensions of their proclaimers, they may have thought were about to quicken and reform the world."[66] The sharpest words were written, perhaps, by Professor Felton, who found Emerson's discourse "full of extravagance and over-weening self-confidence, ancient errors disguised in misty rhetoric, and theories which would overturn society and resolve the world into chaos."[67] Unitarians, said the *Western Messenger* in 1838, "have already fully vindicated themselves from the charge of agreeing with him [Emerson] in opinion. He has certainly been very soundly rated by them, in some instances we think with too much harshness and dogmatism."[68]

Between the beliefs of the older group of Unitarians, to which men like Felton, Norton, and Ware belonged, and those of the new Tran-scendental school which sprang up among them, a wide chasm opened up. The opposition thus naturally engendered accounts in large part, of course, for the Unitarian dislike of Transcendentalism, even when full allowance is made for the amicable way in which men with differing theological views had co-operated in furthering the liberal movement. Its intensity, I am suggesting, can be fully understood only by considering the perplexing problems arising both from the character of the earlier Calvinistic attack upon Unitarianism and from the nature of the defense Unitarians had chosen to make. Squirming on the horns of a dilemma, many of them very naturally exhibited a bitter resentment toward those who, they felt, had forced them into their uncomfortable position.

Notes

1. *American Unitarianism; or a "Brief History of the Progress and Present State of the Unitarian Churches in America." Compiled from Documents and Information Communicated by the Rev. James Freeman, D. D. and William Wells, Jun. Esq. of Boston, and from other Gentlemen in this Country. By the Rev. Thomas Belsham, Essex Street, London. Extracted from his "Memoirs of the Life of Theophilus Lindsay." Printed in London, 1812, and Now Published for the Benefit of Christian Churches in this Country, without Note or Alteration* (Boston: Nathaniel Willis, 1815). The passage cited was quoted in a review of the work which appeared in the Calvinistic *Panoplist*, 11 (1815), 253.

2. *A Review of the Rev. Dr. Channing's Discourse, Preached at the Dedication of the Second Congregational Unitarian Church, New York, December 7, 1826* (Boston: Isaac R. Butts, 1827), pp. 3–13.

3. *Works of Henry Ware, Jr., D. D.* (Boston: James Munroe, 1846), II, 245–246; *Works of William E. Channing* (Boston: American Unitarian Association, 1895), pp. 377, 405–408. The *Christian Disciple* carried in 1823 an article, "On the Practical Tendency of Trinitarianism" (5, 112–121), and the subject was discussed in a refutation of Lyman Beecher's "The Faith Once Delivered to the Saints," in the *Christian Examiner*, 1 (1824), 71–81. For statements of the Calvinistic position on these points, see Lyman Beecher, "The Faith Once Delivered to the Saints" (1823), *Works* (Boston: J. P. Jewett, 1852), II, 259ff, and "Reply to a Review," *Works*, II, 382–413; Samuel Miller, *Letters on Unitarianism* (Lexington, Ky.: T. T. Skillman, 1823), pp. 235–278; [Lewis Tappan], *Letter from a Gentleman in Boston to a Unitarian Clergyman of that City* (3d ed.; Boston: T. R. Marvin, 1828), p. 19; "Unitarianism in New England," *The Spirit of the Pilgrims*, 3 (1830), 399–400; Nehemiah Adams, *Remarks on the Unitarian Belief* (Boston: Peirce and Parker, 1832), p. 18.

4. *Works of Leonard Woods* (Boston: J. P. Jewett, 1851), IV, 99–121; Moses Stuart, *Miscellanies* (Andover, Mass.: Allen, Morrill, and Wardwell, 1846), pp. 167–192. The important place occupied by the argument from "tendency" in the Unitarian controversy has, I believe, never been properly recognized. George Ellis in his *A Half-Century of the Unitarian Controversy* (Boston: Crosby, Nichols, 1857) deals almost exclusively with the doctrinal differences of the two parties, although he does, in an appendix, undertake to defend Unitarianism against the accusation that it tended to promote infidelity. Joseph Henry Allen in *Our Liberal Movement in*

Theology (Boston: Roberts Brothers, 1892), *Sequel to "Our Liberal Movement"* (Boston: Roberts Brothers, 1897), and *Historical Sketch of the Unitarian Movement Since the Reformation* (in Allen and Richard Eddy, *A History of the Unitarians and the Universalists in the United States* [New York: Christian Literature Co., 1894]) neglects the point, as does George Willis Cooke in his *Unitarianism in America* (Boston: American Unitarian Association, 1902). These writers may have shared the feeling of Frank Hugh Foster who, in *A Genetic History of the New England Theology* (Chicago: University of Chicago Press, 1907), says of Leonard Woods's use of the argument from tendency in the *Letters to Unitarians* (1820) that it was "an argument essentially invidious and therefore improper in such a discussion" (p. 306). Nor is the importance of this aspect of the Unitarian controversy given appropriate recognition in the biographies of Emerson and Parker.

5. With rare exceptions, the term "infidelity" has, in the controversial writing of the period, the meaning indicated. See "What Constitutes Infidelity?" *Spirit of the Pilgrims*, 3 (1830), 1–17, 447–458.

6. *Letters on Unitarianism*, pp. 30, 232, 243.

7. 1 (1815), 261. Lowell seems to be repeating a well-worn charge when, in the "Fable for Critics" (1848), he writes concerning Unitarians:

> "They believed—faith, I'm puzzled—I think I may call
> Their belief a believing in nothing at all,
> Or something of that sort; I know they all went
> For a general union of total dissent."

(*The Complete Poetical Works of James Russell Lowell* [Boston: Houghton, Mifflin, n.d.], p. 130).

8. A.U.A. tract (1st ser.), No. 94, p. 3.

9. *Works*, II, 368; see also *Works*, II, 271. A review of this sermon in the *Christian Examiner* including the remark apropos of this passage that "this charge has been so often alleged and repeated, exposed and refuted, that it is weariness to mention it" (1 [1824], 75).

10. 6, 703–726. See, further, Miller, *Letters to Unitarians*, pp. 233–234, 272, 276, 307; review of *American Unitarianism*, in *Panoplist*, 1 (1815), 269; *Review of the Unitarian Controversy* (n.d.), p. 20.

11. *Letters to Dr. Channing on the Trinity*, in *Miscellanies*, pp. 76–77.

12. In Channing's view, reason exerted itself by "comparison and inference" ("Christianity a Rational Religion" and "Unitarian Christianity" [1819], *Works*, pp. 368, 234–235). Revelation "rests on the authority of reason" (1) because reason "furnishes the ideas or materials of which revelation consists," (2) because it is to reason that revelation "submits the evidences of its truth, and nothing but the approving sentence of reason binds us to receive and obey it," and (3) because revelation "needs and expects this faculty [reason] to be its interpreter, and without this aid would be worse than useless" (pp. 237–237).

13. *Letters to Dr. Channing on the Trinity*, in *Miscellanies*, p. 79.

14. Pp. 167, 175–176. See, too, Leonard Woods, "Letters to Unitarians" (1820), *Works*, IV, 111–114; John C. Green, *The Doctrine of the Trinity Proved and Established; or the Doctrines and Errors of the Unitarians Exposed and Refuted* (Wincester, Pa.: Samuel H. Davis, 1822), pp. 24–26; Samuel Miller, *Letters on Unitarianism*, pp. 191–234, 275; Lyman Beecher, "Reply to a Review" (1825), *Works*, II, 331–343; *A Review of the Rev. Dr. Channing's Discourse* (1827), pp. 88–89. In the following articles and reviews in the *Spirit of the Pilgrims* this aspect of the orthodox attack on Unitarianism is fully exhibited: "Review of a Review of

Professor Stuart's Commentary," 2 (1829), 540–550; "Review of an Article in the *Christian Examiner*," 3 (1830), 95–101; "Review of the *Christian Examiner* on Inspiration," 3 (1830), 423–436; "What Constitutes Infidelity?" 3 (1830), 8ff and 447ff; "Review of Norton on the Trinity," 6 (1833), 686–702.

15. *Letters on Unitarianism*, pp. 205–206, 94–95.

16. "Letters to Dr. Channing on the Trinity" (1819), in *Miscellanies*, pp. 182–188. See also Lyman Beecher, "The Faith Once Delivered to the Saints," *Works*, II, 271; *A Review of the Rev. Dr. Channing's Discourse*, pp. 60–66. The warning appeared often in the *Spirit of the Pilgrims*: "Review of the Evangelical Church Journal," 1 (1828), 34–36; "Stuart's Commentary on the Epistle to the Hebrews," 2 (1829), 102; "Review of a Review of Professor Stuart's Commentary," 2 (1829), 546; "What Constitutes Infidelity?" 3 (1830), 16.

17. *Christian Examiner*, 8 (1830), 372.

18. 11 (1815), 241–250.

19. The "charge of concealment" was carefully elaborated by Samuel Worcester of Salem in his *Letter to the Rev. William E. Channing on the Subject of his Letter to the Rev. Samuel C. Thatcher, Relating to the Review in the Panoplist of American Unitarianism* (Boston: Samuel T. Armstrong, 1815), pp. 14–25. See also Miller's *Letters on Unitarianism*, pp. 237–246. The charge was often reiterated in the *Spirit of the Pilgrims*: "Services of the *Panoplist*," 1 (1828), 3; "*Unitarian Advocate*," 1 (1828), 325–327; "Why do you not Exchange with Unitarian Ministers?" 1 (1828), 459–460; "*Unitarian Advocate*" 1 (1828), 559–560; "Introduction and Progress of Unitarianism in New England," 2 (1829), 183–184, 289, 293–294; "Review of Pamphlets on the Cambridge Controversy," 2 (1829), 560; editorial, 2 (1829), 4–8; "More Evidence of Concealment," 3 (1830), 443–444; "Notice of the *Unitarian Advocate*," 3 (1830), 549–551; "Review of Publications on the State of Unitarianism in New England," 4 (1831), 92–93.

20. 2, 7–8. For other texts in which the accusation that the Unitarians practiced concealment was linked to the charge that their views tended toward infidelity see the *Spirit of the Pilgrims*: "Review of Stuart's Commentary on the Hebrews," 2, 97–101; "Reviews of Letters of Canonicus on Fallen Spirits," 2, 496–497; "Review of a Review of Professor Stuart's Commentary," 2, 540ff; "Review of an Article in the *Christian Examiner*," 3 (1830), 101; "Review of the *Christian Examiner* on Inspiration," 3, 436; "What Constitutes Infidelity?" 3, 455–456; "Letter to the Conductors of the *Christian Examiner*," 6 (1833), 704.

21. *Spirit of the Pilgrims*, 3 (1830), 113, 125.

22. "Objections to Unitarian Christianity Considered," *Works*, pp. 406–408. The sermon was published in the *Christian Disciple*, 7 (1819), 436–449.

23. "The Prospects of Unitarianism," 15, 250. Among the more important statements of the Unitarian position on this point are the address of the Hon. Stephen C. Phillips, of Salem, at the first annual meeting of the American Unitarian Association in 1830, published as a Unitarian tract (1st ser., No. 47); *A Dialogue on Some of the Causes of Infidelity* (A. U. A. tract, 1st ser., No. 21), in which the parents of a young man who had avowed the beliefs of Tom Paine come to the conclusion that the lad's loss of faith in revelation was the result of his having lived for some time with an aunt and uncle of Calvinistic persuasion, where he had conceived a "disgust to all religion, by being harassed with inexplicable doctrines"; and *A Young Man's Account of his Conversion from Calvinism, a Statement of Facts* (A. U. A. tract, 1st ser., No. 128), in which a youth confessed that, when on the verge of plunging into skepticism, as a result of the revolting character of his Calvinistic training, he had found "in Unitarianism the amplest support against infidel

tendencies." Other texts bearing on the point: "On the Safety of Believing too Much," *Christian Disciple*, 7 (1819), 433–436; Henry Ware, *Letters Addressed to Trinitarians and Calvinists* (Cambridge, Mass.: Hilliard and Metcalf, 1820), p. 149; Andrews Norton, *Statement of Reasons for Not Believing the Doctrines of Trinitarians* (Boston: Wells and Lilly, 1819), preface; "Infidelity Among the European Clergy," *Unitarian Miscellany and Christian Monitor*, 6 (1824), 318–320, and an editorial in the same journal, 1 (1821), 272; Henry Ware, "An Address Before the York County Unitarian Association," *Works*, II, 166–167; "The Scriptures not a Revelation but the Record of a Revelation," *Christian Examiner*, 7 (1829), 353–354; Lant Carpenter, *The Beneficial Tendency of Unitarianism* (A. U. A. tract, 1st ser., No. 4), p. 17; "Misapprehensions of Unitarianism," *Christian Examiner*, 8 (1830), 135; "Unitarianism Vindicated Against the Charge of Skeptical Tendencies," *Christian Examiner*, 11 (1831), 192; Orville Dewey, "On the Nature and Extent of Inspiration," *Works* (Boston: American Unitarian Association, 1883), pp. 464ff (published in the *Christian Examiner*, 8 [1830], 364ff); sermon by Ezra Gannett quoted in William C. Gannett, *Ezra Stiles Gannett, Unitarian Minister in Boston, 1824–1871* (Boston: Roberts Brothers, 1875), p. 125; "Communion Between Trinitarians and Unitarians," *Western Messenger*, 6 (1838), 76.

24. A. U. A. tract, 1st ser., No. 94, pp. 3, 4, 14. A reviewer for the *Christian Examiner* made the same point apropos a dedication sermon preached by Moses Stuart at the Hanover Street Church in Boston in 1826 (3 [1826], 235–236).

25. 8, 135.

26. 1, 268.

27. *Works*, pp. 475–486. Moses Stuart replied to this charge in *A Letter to William E. Channing on the Subject of Religious Liberty* (Boston: Perkins and Marvin, 1830).

28. A. U. A. tract, 1st ser., No. 39, p. 3. See also Joseph Hutton, *Unitarians Entitled to the Name of Christians* (A. U. A. tract, 1st ser., No. 64); "On the Attempt to Deprive Unitarians of the Name of Christians," *Christian Disciple*, 4 (1822), 313, 325; "The Folly of Classing Unitarians with Unbelievers," *Unitarian Miscellany*, 4 (1823), 212–213; "Believing and not Believing," *Unitarian Miscellany*, 4 (1823), 178–182; Henry Ware, "Address Before the York County Unitarian Association" (1827), *Works*, II, 149, and "Three Important Questions Answered, Relating to the Christian Name, Character, and Hopes," *Works*, II, 255; James Walker, *Unitarianism Vindicated Against the Charge of not Going Far Enough* (A. U. A. tract, 1st ser., No. 11), pp. 16–17; and the following articles in the *Christian Examiner*: "Catholic Emancipation," 7 (1829), 302–303; "Obstacles to the Progress of Knowledge," 8 (1830), 107–114; "Misapprehensions of Unitarianism," 8 (1830), 135; "Nature and Extent of Inspiration," 8 (1830), 372–373.

29. *The Theology of the Cambridge Divinity School* (A. U. A. tract, 1st ser., No. 32), pp. 7–10 (Greenwood was quoted in 1838 by the *Western Messenger* as representing the spirit of early Unitarians [6, 120–121]). For other texts in which a point is made of the liberality of Unitarians see William Ellery Channing ,"Letters on Creeds," *Works*, pp. 486–489; *Remarks on Creeds, Intolerance, and Exclusion* (A. U. A. tract, 1st ser., No. 122); Henry Ware, "'The Christian Conjunction," and "Sober Thoughts on the State of the Times (1835)," *Works*, III, 215 and 115–120; "Power Less Likely to be Abused by Unitarians than the Orthodox," *Christian Examiner*, 7 (1829), 229–240; "On the State of the Question Between the Orthodox and Liberal Parties in this Country," *Christian Examiner*, 5 (1828), 12; "Memoirs of Dr. Doddridge," *Christian Examiner*, 8 (1830), 81; "A Dialogue

on Salvation," *Christian Disciple*, 1 (1819), 34; "The Unitarian Reform," *Western Messenger*, 6 (1838), 5.

30. "Mr. Little's Discourse on Religious Liberty and Unitarianism," 3, 77. See also Channing, "The System of Exclusion and Denunciation," *Works*, p. 482; Henry Ware, "Sober Thoughts on the State of the Times," *Works*, II, 116; John G. Palfrey, "An Address Delivered Before the Society for Promoting Theological Education," *Christian Examiner*, 11 (1831), 91; "Stability in the Christian Faith," *Christian Examiner*, 11 (1831), 280–281.

31. "Unitarian Christianity," *Works*, p. 367.

32. 8, 143.

33. (Boston: Wells and Lilly, 1816), pp. 29–30n.

34. *"Come and See" or the Duty of Those who Dread the Sentiments of Other Christians* (A. U. A. tract, 1st ser., No. 71), pp. 5–6. For other expressions of Unitarian belief in revelation see: "Sabine's Sermon and the *Panoplist*," *Christian Disciple*, 1 (1819), 139; [John Lowell], *Are You a Christian or a Calvinist?* (Boston: Wells and Lilly, 1815), pp. 3–4; Andrews Norton, *Statement of Reasons for not Believing the Doctrines of Trinitarians* (Boston: Wells and Lilly, 1819), pp. 16–17; Henry Ware, "An Address Before the York County Unitarian Association" (*Works*, II, 149ff), "The Faith Once Delivered to the Saints" (*Works*, II, 237–238), and "Two Letters, on the Geniuneness of the Verse 1 John v. 7, and on the Scriptural Argument for Unitarianism" (*Works*, II, 318–323); "Review of Stuart's Letter to Channing," *Christian Disciple*, 1 (1819), 398; "Review of Woods's *Letters to Unitarians* and Ware's *Letters Addressed to Trinitarians*," *Christian Disciple*, 2 (1820), 396; Orville Dewey, "The Unitarian Belief," *Works*, p. 342; James D. Green, *Unitarianism not a New Doctrine but Genuine Christianity* (A. U. A. tract, 1st ser., No. 186), p. 7; James Walker, *A Discourse on the Deference Paid to the Scriptures by Unitarians* (A. U. A. tract, 1st ser., No. 121); Ezra Gannett, *Christian Unitarianism not a Negative System* (A. U. A. tract, 1st ser., No. 94), p. 6; E. Peabody, *Charges Against Unitarianism* (A. U. A. tract, 1st ser., No. 123), pp. 4–5; and the following articles in the *Christian Examiner*: "Beecher's Sermon at Worcester," 1 (1824), 53–60; "Editor's Address," 2 (1826), 2; "The Scriptures not a Revelation but the Record of a Revelation," 7 (1829), 346; "Obstacles to the Progress of Knowledge," 8 (1830), 110; "Misapprehensions of Unitarianism," 8 (1830), 138ff; "Female Writers on Unitarianism," 11 (1831), 139–140; "Unitarianism Vindicated Against the Charge of Skeptical Tendencies," 11 (1831), 183.

35. "Nature and Extent of Inspiration," 8, 373. A year later the author of an article in the *Christian Examiner* entitled "Unitarianism Vindicated Against the Charge of Skeptical and Infidel Tendencies" wrote in much the same vein: "And here we cannot but express our surprise and regret at the ignorance, or want of candor, or profligacy of those, who take every opportunity to affirm or insinuate that Unitarians do not believe in inspiration, or in the Bible as containing the Christian revelation" (11, 188). See also the review of Samuel Gilman's "Unitarian Christianity Free from Objectionable Extremes," *Christian Examiner*, 5 (1828), 84–85; "Misapprehensions of Unitarianism," *Christian Examiner*, 8 (1830), 138; "Who are Christians?" *Unitarian Advocate*, 1 (1830), 221–223.

36. *The Complete Works of Ralph Waldo Emerson*, ed. Edward Waldo Emerson (Boston: Houghton, Mifflin, 1903–1904), I, 134, 144, 146.

37. *Boston Daily Advertiser*, 27 August 1838, quoted by James Elliot Cabot, *A Memoir of Ralph Waldo Emerson* (Boston: Houghton, Mifflin, 1887), I, 335.

38. Quoted by Octavius Brooks Frothingham, *Theodore Parker: A Biography* (New York: G. P. Putnam's Sons, 1886), p. 106.

39. *Views of Religion* (Boston: American Unitarian Association, 1885), pp. 301–306.

40. *A Discourse of Matters Pertaining to Religion* (Boston: American Unitarian Association, 1907), p. 295.

41. "Transcendentalism," 11 (1839), 97.

42. 13, 544. In 1840 Andrews Norton's attack on Emerson was made the excuse for reading him a lesson on the tendency of Unitarianism to infidelity (see "The Latest Form of Infidelity," *Biblical Repertory and Princeton Review*, 12, 67–68). See also in the same journal, "The Connection Between Philosophy and Revelation," 17 (1845), 395–396; "Review of Robert Baird's *Religion in America*," 17, 35.

43. "Theodore Parker," *New Englander*, 2 (1844), 374.

44. "Theodore Parker and Liberal Christianity," *New Englander*, 2 (1844), 553–556.

45. "Theodore Parker and the Boston Association," *New Englander*, 3 (1845), 462. See also "Orthodox Unitarians," *New Englander*, 5 (1847), 576–585.

46. *Miscellanies*, pp. 192–193, 196. Stuart ascribed a decline which he believed he saw in Unitarianism to the negative character of the movement: "A religion, the prominent feature of which is NOT TO BELIEVE, can never deeply interest any community, for any great length of time" (p. 195). The *Christian Examiner*, in reviewing Stuart's book, observed concerning the postscripts that they "contain rambling remarks on almost all sorts of subjects connected with theology and theological parties. . . . will add nothing to the author's posthumous reputation. . . . portions of them bear marks of his once vigorous intellect, others show a senile garrulousness, occasionally something worse" (41 [1846], 293). Other expressions of the belief that Transcendentalism was a logical outgrowth of Unitarianism may be found in "Mr. Parker's Discourse," *Christian Review*, 7 (1842), 161ff, and *Christian Observer*, 2 (1848), 139; 3 (1849), 4.

47. 25 (1838), 266–267.

48. See note 29 above.

49. "The *Christian Examiner* for November," 6 (1838), 188ff.

50. 7, 435. See also "The Unitarian Reform," *Western Messenger*, 6 (1838), 5ff; "Emerson and the New School," *Western Messenger*, 6, 38–39.

51. *A Letter to Mr. Andrews Norton, Occasioned by His "Discourse Before the Association of the Alumni of the Cambridge Theological School," on the 19th of July 1838* (Boston: James Munroe, 1839), pp. 6, 23, 27–28. Cf. Norton's "Defense of Liberal Christianity," *General Repository*, 1 (1812), 11, 24.

52. John Weiss, *Life and Correspondence of Theodore Parker* (New York: Appleton, 1864), I, 190–195.

53. "A Letter to the Boston Association of Congregational Ministers Touching Certain Matters of Their Theology," *Saint Bernard and Other Papers* (Boston: American Unitarian Association, 1911), p. 103.

54. *Historical Sketch of the Unitarian Movement Since the Reformation*, p. 214. See also James Freeman Clarke, "Ezra Stiles Gannett," *Memorial and Biographical Sketches* (Boston: Houghton, Osgood, 1878), p. 194: "And the other day, looking over some old letters, I found one relating to the time when Parker was most offensive to the conservatives, and it was proposed to put him out of the Boston Association. . . . He [Gannett] disliked and feared Parker's views, but he would not consent to the spirit of exclusion or persecution . . . and it was so resisted by him and by others that every such attempt was defeated."

55. Parker's article in the *Dial* over the dismissal of the former pastor, John

Pierpont, had given great offense to Boston Unitarians. See Frothingham, *Theodore Parker*, p. 164.

56. "The Dilemma of Unitarianism," *New Englander*, 4 (1846), 498.

57. Allen, *Historical Sketch of the Unitarian Movement Since the Reformation*, p. 214. Allen was a member of the Boston Association at the time.

58. George Putnam, *A Discourse Delivered at the Installation of the Rev. David Fosdick* (Boston: William Crosby and H. P. Nichols, 1846).

59. See reviews of Parker's "Permanent and Transient in Christianity," 31 (1841), 98ff; review of *A Discourse of Matters Pertaining to Religion*, 32 (1842), 337ff; "Mr. Parker and His Views," 38 (1845), 251ff.

60. "Experience as a Minister," *Autobiography, Poems and Prayers* (Boston: American Unitarian Association, 1911), pp. 324–325.

61. Note by Rufus Leighton, editor of the volume (p. 483). "The opposition and unfriendliness of the Unitarian clergy to Mr. Parker, with a few notable exceptions, continued to the end of his life" (Leighton's note, p. 482). Edward Everett Hale made the observation that when Parker refused to resign from the Boston Unitarian Association, "Unitarian leaders of that day in Boston tried the poor experiment of making him uncomfortable" (James Freeman Clarke, *Autobiography, Diary, and Correspondence*, ed. Edward Everett Hale [Boston: Houghton, Mifflin, 1891], p. 152). Accounts of Parker's conflict with Boston Unitarians may be found in Weiss, *Life and Correspondence of Parker*; Peter Dean, *Life and Teachings of Theodore Parker* (London: Williams and Norgate, 1877), pp. 61–90, 106–118; John White Chadwick, *Theodore Parker, Preacher and Reformer* (Boston: Houghton, Mifflin, 1901), pp. 102ff; Frothingham, *Theodore Parker*, pp. 147–182, 210–240; Henry Steele Commager, *Theodore Parker* (Boston: Little, Brown, 1936), pp. 61–100.

62. *Some Reminiscences of the Life of Samuel Kirkland Lathrop* (Cambridge, Mass.: privately printed, 1888), p. 202.

63. *Journals of Ralph Waldo Emerson*, ed. Edward Waldo Emerson and Waldo Emerson Forbes (Boston: Houghton Mifflin, 1909–1914), V, 123.

64. 25 (1838), 266.

65. Cabot, *Memoir of Emerson*, I, 335.

66. 25 (1838), 267.

67. Quoted by Edwin D. Mead, *The Influence of Emerson* (Boston: American Unitarian Association, 1903), p. 98.

68. 6, 41–42.

"The Genteel Tradition: A Re-Interpretation"

Frederic I. Carpenter*

Some thirty years ago, George Santayana first named and described "The Genteel Tradition."[1] Since then many men have repeated his words:

> America is not simply a young country with an old mentality: it is a country with two mentalities, one a survival of the beliefs and standards of the fathers, the other an expression of the instincts, practices and discoveries of the younger generations. . . . The one is all aggressive enterprise; the other is all genteel tradition.[2]

The persistent popularity of his description suggests that it is essentially true. But the partisan violence which it has engendered suggests that its meaning is confused. Santayana described truly the general conflict between aristocratic tradition and democratic practice in American life and thought. But he misunderstood the historic origins of this conflict, and he misinterpreted its modern manifestations. During the last generation, the terms of the dualism have become clearer.

In naming the genteel tradition, Santayana fathered two major confusions. First, he identified this tradition with Puritanism, and traced the genteel mentality to Calvinistic theology. This accentuated the confusion in general usage between "puritanism" as a state of mind, and Puritanism as a historical movement. Second, Santayana denied that the ideal opposite of the genteel tradition was really a "mentality" at all. "Instincts, practices, and discoveries," he called it, and added that, "in all the higher things of the mind—in religion, in literature, in the moral emotions—it is the hereditary spirit that prevails."[3] Specifically he charged that Walt Whitman possessed nothing more than "sensations,"[4] and that William James possessed no consistent philosophy.[5] Identifying the genteel tradition with Puritan theology, he also denied that popular democracy had any clear ideal basis.

These two opinions may be disproved. The genteel tradition which

*Reprinted from *New England Quarterly*, 15 (September 1942), 427–443.

Santayana named was something less—and something more—than Puritanism in America. Historically, it derived only from the conservative half of the Puritan religion. And beyond Puritanism, it derived from the traditionally aristocratic culture of the Central and Southern States, as well.[6] It may be defined broadly as the traditionalist mentality in America, as that has been influenced by Puritan morality and aristocratic culture.

Historically, the genteel tradition sprang from Puritanism, but only from one half of that religion. For the Puritanism of early New England had included a liberal, and even radical, element. The most conservative theocrat recognized that "the unknown God" did not always follow customs of traditional morality. "Moral living" was good, but "divine grace" was infinitely better. The stern realism that recognized this unpalatable truth, and the intense "piety"[7] which positively gloried in it, gave greatness to the old faith. But the narrow traditionalism and intolerant moralism which we often call puritan, resulted in its later decadence.

In opposition to the genteel tradition, this radical element of the earlier Puritanism developed into the Transcendentalism of later New England: the Transcendental idealists worshipped the unknown God with intense piety. Although Santayana called them genteel, these transcendentalists were neither traditional nor moralistic. Emerson prophesied a new America, and Whitman continued his prophecy. Even the later pragmatists stemmed from this root.[8] The worst confusion of American thought is that which seeks to divorce the idealism of the early Puritans and the Transcendentalists from the idealism of the later democrats and pragmatists. Not only Santayana but many popular critics have furthered this interpretation. Yet Emerson did more than any other single writer to discredit the genteel tradition of orthodox morality: in him Transcendentalism became "the philosophy of democracy,"[9] and the arch enemy of conservatism. It stemmed from Puritan piety, but repudiated the authoritarian moralism of the past.

Neither the intense piety of the old Puritanism, nor the enthusiasm of the later Transcendental idealists was traditional, or "genteel." But from this point of view, the anti-transcendental morality of Hawthorne *was*; and the tragic vision of Melville also described the futility of the transcendental ideal. In *The Scarlet Letter* Hawthorne recognized a certain heroism in self-reliance, but emphasized its greater evil. And in *Moby Dick*, Melville described the heroism of Ahab, but also his fanatical delusion. In their later novels, both authors denounced the libertarian heresy and returned to traditional orthodoxy; although they borrowed the new techniques to describe the liberal emotions, their moral philosophy remained traditional. Therefore they illustrate the genteel tradition at its best, recognizing the beauty and the heroism of the Transcendental ideal but denouncing its romantic extravagances.

Through three centuries of American life, this genteel tradition has developed and changed. From the early Puritans to the new humanists, its champions have denounced as utopian all dreams of a new world. But from the early Puritans to the modern pragmatists, the democratic dreamers have opposed, or "transcended" this tradition.

I

Like most Americans, the early Puritans really worshiped two Gods: they worshiped an absolute and unknown God, whose will was secret and whose face was hidden;[10] but also they worshiped the God of revelation or tradition, whose will was declared in the Bible, and whose face was turned toward man. Between the great "I Am" of piety and the revealed "I Ought" of morality, they admitted no discrepancy, in theory. The few sought the grace of the hidden God, while the many obeyed literally the laws laid down. The Bible, and after the Bible, literature, revealed this God to the populace.

The narrow puritanism against which the modern mind has revolted is that traditional half of historic Puritanism which deduced inflexible moral law from Biblical revelation. What we call the genteel tradition has elevated past precept into omnipotence, and conversely, has minimized the difficult truth which Calvin taught: that divine grace may supersede traditional precept. Looking back, the modern historian can see that "the space between the revealed will and the secret will . . . was the portal through which ran the highway of intellectual development."[11] But although the greater Puritans gloried in the unknown God and kept the portal open, their gentler descendants institutionalized revelation and sought to close the gate.

Moralistic "Puritanism" and secular "humanism," therefore, both sought to interpret and to apply God's will as revealed in the Bible and the classics. They disagreed only in the supreme authority which Puritanism granted to the Bible. They agreed that "the Revival of *Letters* . . . prepared the World for the Reformation of *Religion*."[12] They both appealed to logic and human reason to interpret the Bible and the classics. They both applied their interpretations primarily to the fields of morality and human conduct. And they agreed that art (in its broadest sense) was all-important: "Perhaps we have laid bare the innermost essence of the Puritan mind when we find that its highest philosophical reach was a systematic delineation of the liberal arts."[13] The arts direct conduct, and therefore man should imitate art. "Nature is inchoate art; art is nature consummated."[14] The nature of God may never be understood, but the Book of man may be.

This all-too-human half of Puritanism reached its nadir in eighteenth-century New England when the old piety became mere complacency, and the old morality, ritual:

> Our churches turn genteel:
> Our parsons grow trim and trig,
> With wealth, wine and wig
> And their heads are covered with meal.[15]

Of the old religion, only the moral and churchly forms remained. But these forms were, and always had been, important: the new "gentility" was no "reversal" of the Puritan philosophy, as has been asserted,[16] but rather a distortion of it, through exaggeration of the formal element. The old revelation had merely become absolutely systematized.

˙ This moralistic puritanism, on the other hand, reached its most mature development in the proverbial wisdom of Benjamin Franklin. Wholly "emancipated" from the old Puritan piety, Franklin reasserted the Puritan morality in its simplest terms: "Revelation had indeed no weight with me, as such; but I entertained an opinion, that, though certain actions might not be bad, *because* they were forbidden by it . . . ; yet probably these actions might be forbidden *because* they were bad for us."[17] Having freed himself, that is, from the dead hand of the past, he nevertheless returned to the past for wisdom.

This was valid. Tradition is good. As Stuart Sherman has pointed out,[18] "tradition" also includes the tradition of revolt, of progress, and of change. It is good, therefore, as long as it includes all the wisdom of the past, and not merely the prudential part. But when tradition excludes novelty and freedom, it becomes genteel. It denies the unknown God in the name of the God of Moses.

Franklin himself escaped this narrow traditionalism by virtue of his broad tolerance, his instinctive democracy, and his scientific spirit. But his wisdom remained partial. He emphasized the traditional morality so exclusively that he seemed to deny the religious idealism. In his phrase, "health, wealth, and wisdom" became the ideal ends of life. And this fairly translated one-half of the Puritan gospel. But the other half—"the Covenant of Grace" and the practice of piety—he omitted. The intense devotion to the unknown God which motivated Jonathan Edwards would have to wait for the advent of Transcendentalism. Then the religious ideals of "God, freedom, and immortality" would compete anew with the moralistic ideals of "health, wealth, and wisdom" for the devotion of the descendants of the Puritans. Then the mind of America would revolt against the too-narrow Puritan morality with a violence fathered by the almost forgotten Puritan piety.

II

Considered politically, of course, Transcendentalism was not necessarily a liberal philosophy. It might result either in revolt or in reaction, for "God, freedom, and immortality" were not partisan ideals. The thought of Kant, developing through Hegel, resulted eventually in a justification of the totalitarian state. Only in America did the alliance of Transcendentalism with the antislavery movement and with Western democracy produce complete liberalism.

But considered intellectually, Transcendentalism was liberalism itself. It was "the newness." It was the revolt of the younger generation against the forces of conservative tradition. It was the deification of the undiscovered. It was the worship of the unknown God.

Therefore Transcendentalism stood opposed to all forms of traditionalism. As Santayana recognized, it "embodied, in a radical form, the spirit of Protestantism as distinguished from its inherited doctrines; it was autonomous, undismayed, calmly revolutionary."[19] But this historic Transcendentalism had no new system to offer, specifically, in place of the old. Therefore it often resulted in "the dilemma of the liberated." By reaction, it sometimes caused a blind return to tradition. "Similarly in Italy, during the Renaissance, the Catholic tradition could not be banished from the intellect, since there was nothing articulate to take its place."[20] Therefore Santayana considered Transcendentalism a failure. And modern American humanists have sought to escape this frustration by a return to tradition—to religion—to authority—even to Catholicism.[21]

It is true that the negative or anti-authoritarian element of Transcendentalism gave grounds for this negative, or anti-liberal, reaction against it. If the old idealism had resulted only in emptiness and denial, the reaction of the traditional humanists would have been wholly justified. But even the hostile Santayana recognized that Walt Whitman had developed an inarticulate democracy in place of the old moralism, and that William James had developed a more articulate pragmatism. These developments were positive and progressive. But the reactions of nineteenth-century traditionalists against "the newness" were more obvious.

By far the greatest of the latter-day puritans were two who escaped the smugness of gentility through their intense sympathy with the followers of the unknown God. Having been tempted, like Faust, with the desire for freedom, they did not imagine all apostates from traditional morality to be absolute sinners—rather they described them as the dupes of a romantic idealism. In *The Scarlet Letter* Hawthorne recognized the integrity of his transcendental heroine, even though he condemned her. And in *Moby Dick* Melville realized the magnificence of Ahab, even while describing the inevitable destruction of his romantic ideal. Although these two writers went beyond the genteel tradition to pay homage to the unknown God, they returned to tradition, arguing that men should follow a known god rather than seek a fancied perfection.

Perhaps Hawthorne was the most typical, as well as one of the greatest, writers of the genteel tradition. Born in puritan Salem, in an atmosphere of genteel poverty, he learned to revere as well as to hate his heritage. If he accepted for himself the curse of Maule, which he described in *The House of the Seven Gables*, he did not accept it blindly. In *The Scarlet Letter* he followed in imagination the alternative of individual freedom to its end, and concluded that, like Dimmesdale, it was not for him. In *The Blithedale Romance* he rejected the alternative of social liberalism. And finally, in *The Marble Faun*, his imagination sought refuge in Rome, the source of all orthodox tradition. Through the character of Hilda, who worshiped at the shrine of the Virgin Mary and became "almost a Catholic," he prophesied the return of modern Americans such as T. S. Eliot to the Catholic faith. But Hawthorne remained true to his own tradition, and ended his days in ancestral New England. Rejecting the two living religions of militant liberalism and of Roman Catholicism, he resigned himself, without hope, to his own puritan traditionalism.

Less genteel and less puritan than Hawthorne, Melville followed a less familiar path to the same end. Where Hawthorne experimented with freedom at Brook Farm and in imagination, Melville actually pursued this ideal over the seven seas. But in *Mardi* he concluded that ideal freedom was empty, and in *Pierre* that it was immoral. In *Clarel* he recorded his pilgrimage to the traditional Holy Land. And in *Billy Budd* he reaffirmed the justice of the established morality, even when it condemned a righteous man to death. With the sad eyes of a reformed romantic, he accepted as inevitable the defeat of human freedom. And like Hawthorne, he too resigned himself to fate.

Thus Transcendental liberty caused reaction: to escape the apparent emptiness following the new revolt from tradition, Hawthorne returned to the Puritan past and Melville to the stern old morality. Hawthorne even suggested that the vacuum might be filled by the Roman Catholic faith. But meanwhile other descendants of the Puritans sought to fill it instead with the rich culture of a humanistic past. If the religion of liberty seemed empty, if the religion of Puritanism was out-moded, and the religion of Rome alien, there remained the religion of human culture. This was more credible than Calvinism, and more universal than

Catholicism. The immense popularity of the writings of Longfellow and Lowell bears witness to the genuine spiritual need which their gentility satisfied. If the narrow Puritan humanism had failed, the broad classical humanism might succeed.

To be exact, Puritan humanism now expanded to become classical humanism: the religion of the Bible became the religion of Books. Lowell felt this continuity when he prophesied, with characteristically heavy humor, that "the broad foreheads and the long heads will win the day at last..., and it will be enough if we feel as keenly as our Puritan founders did that those organs of empire may be broadened and lengthened by culture."[22] Although it is significant that he described culture as a means to empire, it is even more significant that he traced it to the Puritan past and that he made it a continuing means to salvation: "It will be enough."

As a religion, genteel humanism had two aspects, the first moralistic, the second pious (in the more modern sense of the word). The first found expression in Longfellow's famous "Psalm of Life," and second in his "The Day is Done." Although the first bore a certain resemblance to the Transcendental faith, it preached a morality not of self-reliance but of dutiful acceptance: "With a heart for any fate...Learn to labor and to wait." And the second preached the religion of culture, that literature has power to make life acceptable:

> ... songs have power to quiet
> The restless pulse of care
>   And come like the benediction
> That follows after prayer.

But the purpose of both poems was religious, like the purpose of Puritan humanism. Either poetry inspires, like a psalm, or else it consoles, like a prayer. To take the place of the Puritan faith which had faded, Longfellow substituted a more humanistic piety.

For this reason, perhaps, Longfellow was greater than Lowell: where the critic merely preached the culture of the classical past, the poet made it live. He filled the spiritual emptiness which the Transcendental revolt from tradition had caused. He invoked the gods of Olympus and of Valhalla to reinforce the old Puritan God. And in a twilight realm of poetry, his fabulous heroes kept the faith. Lowell was to make clear the implications of that faith.

Like Hawthorne and Melville, Lowell had shared in the Transcendental dream. His essay on Thoreau describes this enthusiasm from the mature perspective of *My Study Windows*. There was something good in it, of course: "the Puritanism that cannot die" had produced Emerson. But there was more that was bad in it; Thoreau reflected its selfishness, its moral emptiness, and its morbid escape to nature.

Instead of this naturalism with its worship of newness, Lowell sought to substitute the solid wisdom of the human past: "What a sense of security in an old book that Time has criticised for us!" From the confusion of modern thought, he turned to the "sane and balanced" writers before Rousseau. More liberal than his follower, Irving Babbitt. he agreed that Rousseau "is as consistent as a man who admits new ideas can ever be." But his conclusion is clear: what is new cannot be consistent, and what is traditional is good. "Democracy" is good, he said, because "properly understood, it is a conservative force." And America, the child of Great Britain, is "a democracy with conservative instincts." To strengthen this hereditary conservatism the genteel descendant of the Puritans preached a religion of humanistic culture: *Among My Books*.

III

Following Lowell, a host of minor gentlemen refined the old tradition still further. Thomas Bailey. Aldrich, E. C. Stedman, E. P. Whipple, and Charles Eliot Norton became so exclusively "genteel," indeed, that they hardly remained human. Were it not for their far-reaching influence—first, on the thought of the new humanists, and secondly, on popular taste—they might now be forgotten. But they helped carry the old ideas to their logical conclusions.

While this gentility was developing, the meaning of words was changing, and narrowing. For instance, "puritanism" was slowly coming to mean an exclusive, moral traditionalism. And "humanism" was coming to mean an equally exclusive cultural traditionalism. The content of "puritanism" and of "humanism" was being divided in half. Reacting against the Transcendental enthusiasm, gentility was supplanting the old gods with half-gods; soon, only the cultured would be human.

The exclusive aspect of this "new humanism" found its clearest expression in the first book of Irving Babbitt, in which the young author specifically avowed his debt to the gentle Charles Eliot Norton. In *Literature and the American College*, Babbitt outlined all his major ideas. The Renaissance humanists, he said, had taken for their motto Terence's "*humani nihil a me alienum puto*," and had embraced everything human. But they had missed true (*i.e.*, classical) humanism because they had denied "the idea of selection," which Aristotle had first established. "Very few of the early humanists were really humane . . . Rabelais, for instance, is neither decorous or select."[23] So the new humanist emphasized selection rather than humanity—classical culture rather than human sympathy. Rejecting the indecorous elements of the broadly humanistic past, he sought to establish a strict cultural tradition, just as the latter-day puritans had rejected the unknown God to establish a strict moral tradition.

As Santayana was to point out, this was really not humanism at all, but supernaturalism.[24] It was the degradation of one half of humanity and the deification of the other half, an attempt "to sacrifice ruthlessly one set of passions merely in order to intensify another set." That the virtuous set of passions were called "human," and were even denied the name of "passions" made little difference. Essentially this new humanism sought to reinforce a passionate conservatism by an appeal to the quasi-religious authority of classical literature. It made cultural absolutism the cloak for moral absolutism. "The new humanism" was really the old Puritan moralism in new clothes.

The virtue of this new humanism was that it recaptured some of the religious enthusiasm and logical rigor of the old Puritan theology. Unlike the urbane Lowell and the genteel Norton, Babbitt fought for his convictions against all comers, using all the weapons of the intellect. Let an opponent once admit his premises, and his conclusions were inescapable. The only way to conquer him (besides ignoring him, as many critics did) was to attack his first principles (as Santayana did). His logic was powerful.

The weakness of Babbitt's "humanism" was partly the narrowness of his moral principles, but even more the rigidity with which he applied them to literature. If his moral philosophy was authoritarian, it was nevertheless based upon a classical tradition. But his literary applications of this moral philosophy were wholly negative: he damned every important modern writer since Rousseau. Where others had been content to describe the failure of the romantic enthusiasm, he sought utterly to eradicate it. Where Hawthorne, Melville, and even Lowell, had sympathized while they condemned, Babbitt denied all human value to Romance. He insisted not only that literature should inculcate strict morality, but also that it should refrain from treating the romantic passions with sympathy. *Moby Dick* seemed to him bad because the character of Ahab lacked all self-restraint, or "decorum": that it described the self-destruction of the monomaniac hero was not enough.

Clearly, this narrow "humanism" implied "puritanism," and even a genteel censorship: it would not merely condemn all unrestrained emotion in literature but would wholly exclude it. Against this narrowness, therefore, other "humanists" objected. Paul Elmer More sought to apply Babbitt's standards with greater tolerance, although with less precision. Yvor Winters showed how even the romantic heroism of Melville's Ahab and of Hawthorne's Hester implied a traditional morality. And a recent humanist has suggested that, although Babbitt's ethical or moral criticism was usually excellent, his literary criticism was merely negative.[25]

Thus the genteel tradition which began as Puritan moralism, has returned to orthodox morality as the source of all judgment and the end of all argument. It has rejected, therefore, the Puritan piety which admitted the omnipotence of a hidden God. It has rejected the Transcendental enthusiasm which sought to discover the hidden God, even in defiance of established morality. It has rejected the naturalistic science which has called all revealed truth into question. It has rejected even that part of the humanistic tradition which gloried in the natural instincts of man. Although it has recognized the strength, and even the beauty, of the human instinct of liberty and desire for newness, it has opposed this liberalism in the name of morality and of law.

IV

If the genteel tradition is narrow, illiberal, and opposed to everything modern, why is it so strong? Santayana prophesied its death, but lived to describe its renaissance. A Marxian critic has attacked it as "fantastic," but has approved T. S. Eliot's statement that only this tradition and Marxian socialism offer living faiths to modern man.[26] In American universities, even in the untraditional West, the tradition continues to flourish. And it continues to govern popular taste, as evidenced by the best-seller lists and by the frequent outbursts of "moral" censorship by elected authorities. The genteel tradition is not dead, nor is it dying.

The reason for this vitality is suggested by the words of a hostile critic: "In the plainest, least evasive of words, gentility is conservatism. It is the moral and social orthodoxy of the bourgeois who has, so to speak, been 'refined.' "[27] But if the genteel tradition is conservatism, a fair majority of Americans are genteel; a recent poll of public opinion showed that fifty-three per cent of all American citizens consider themselves "conservative," rather than "liberal." And if the genteel tradition is "bourgeois," a majority of Americans believe that they belong to the middle class. Finally, most middle-class Americans still desire to become "refined," as well: the old cultural ideal remains popular in our political democracy.

Actually, the genteel tradition has developed from historic American beginnings, and remains widely popular today. But beyond these clear facts, the tradition also includes permanent values. It reaffirms the truth of those humanistic ideals which were preliminary, and therefore remain necessary, even to the naturalistic philosophy of a scientific age. And it reaffirms the eternal necessity of ideals, or "standards" of some sort, to every age: it challenges democratic naturalism to define its own new standards.

The old Puritan and humanistic virtues of hard work, discipline, moderation, and the rest (which Franklin formulated and which Irving Babbitt reaffirmed) can never be discarded. Emerson and Whitman did not deny them, but rather relegated them to the realm of unconscious habit, and then went on to emphasize that imagination, invention, and artistic creation are greater virtues than these. But in the process of revolt from the extreme discipline of the old morality, Transcendental self-reliance and equalitarian democracy often neglected, and often still neglect, the preliminary needs of discipline and routine. The old Puritans and the new humanists have wisely emphasized the evil consequences of this neglect.

The genteel tradition has recently found imaginative embodiment in the character of Henry Pulham, Esquire, hero of John Marquand's novel. As the personnel director of a New York advertising firm says of him: "There is something basic there."[28] Among the "idea-men" and high-pressure salesmen of the modern metropolis, this genteel and conscientious routineer remains indispensable. And the solid strength of his character emphasizes the unstable weakness of his associates.

But when this typical Henry Pulham, Esquire, returns to his ancestral Boston to fill the niche which his father has occupied in the mahogany offices of a securities investment firm, he becomes merely genteel. He cuts himself off from the struggle of modern life to take refuge in a decadent security. He denies the potentialities of growth which have always lain dormant in his character, until what was "basic" becomes merely solid. The fundamentals of human morality which he has embodied become fundamentalism. And in him, "the great tradition" of American life forgets the principle of growth and change, and becomes merely "the genteel tradition."

To summarize: this genteel tradition of American humanism has become reactionary only when it has divorced itself from the forces of change and renewal; just as the old Puritan moralism became decadent only when divorced from the old Puritan piety. When gentlemen have sought to impose a rigidly classical culture upon a growing, democratic society; when conservatives have sought to impede the process of democratic change; when "puritans" have denied the possibility of a more liberal morality than the old, and when "humanists" have taken refuge from the unknown God of high religion and of science in the revealed literature of the past—then the great tradition has become decadent and partial. Too often has this been so. But when the old tradition has married the new idealism and merged itself in the larger life of the country, it has contributed "something basic" and indispensable, and has ceased to be "genteel."

Notes

1. George Santayana, "The Genteel Tradition in American Philosophy," *Winds of Doctrine* (New York: Scribners, 1912), pp. 186–215.
2. "The Genteel Tradition," pp. 187–188.
3. "The Genteel Tradition," p. 188.
4. In *Interpretations in Poetry and Religion* (New York: Scribners, 1900), p. 180. See also H. A. Myers, "Whitman's Conception of the Spiritual Democracy," *American Literature*, 6 (November 1934), 241; and F. I. Carpenter, "Walt Whitman's Eidolon," *College English*, 3 (March 1942), 534–545.
5. In *Character and Opinion in the United States* (New York: Scribners, 1920), pp. 64–97.
6. If this essay emphasizes the Puritanism of New England to the partial exclusion of the culture of the Central and Southern States, it is partly because the Puritanism of New England was more articulate than the religious culture of other regions, and partly because Santayana so emphasized it.
7. See Joseph Haroutunian, *Piety Versus Moralism* (New York: Henry Holt, 1932); and Perry Miller, *The New England Mind* (New York: Macmillan, 1939).
8. See F. I. Carpenter, "William James and Emerson," *American Literature*, 11 (March 1939), 39–57; and Carpenter, "Charles Sanders Peirce: Pragmatic Transcendentalist," *New England Quarterly*, 14 (March 1941), 34–48.
9. John Dewey, "Emerson: The Philosopher of Democracy," *Characters and Events* (New York: Henry Holt, 1929), pp. 69–77.
10. See Miller, *New England Mind*, p. 20.
11. Miller, *New England Mind*, p. 21.
12. Miller, *New England Mind*, p. 97.
13. Miller, *New England Mind*, p. 161.
14. Miller, *New England Mind*, p. 166.
15. Quoted in Herbert Schneider, *The Puritan Mind* (New York: Henry Holt, 1930), p. 90.
16. See Schneider, *The Puritan Mind*, p. 97.
17. *The Autobiography* in *The Complete Works of Benjamin Franklin*, ed. John Bigelow (New York: Putnams, 1887–1888), I, 139.
18. S. P. Sherman, "Tradition," *Americans* (New York: Scribners, 1924), pp. 13–27.
19. "The Genteel Tradition," p. 196.
20. "The Genteel Tradition," p. 201.
21. See Yvor Winters, *Maule's Curse* (Norfolk, Conn.: New Directions, 1938).
22. From "New England Two Centuries Ago," *Among My Books* (Boston: Fields, Osgood, 1871), p. 244.
23. *Literature and the American College* (Boston: Houghton, Mifflin, 1908), p. 20.
24. *The Genteel Tradition at Bay* (New York: Scribners, 1931), p. 28.
25. Wylie Sypher, "Irving Babbitt," *New England Quarterly*, 14 (March 1941), 64.
26. Bernard Smith, *Forces in American Criticism* (New York: Harcourt, Brace, 1939), p. 384.
27. *Forces in American Criticism*, p. 40.
28. John P. Marquand, *H. M. Pulham, Esquire* (Boston: Little, Brown, 1941), p. 131.

"The Minor Transcendentalists and German Philosophy"

René Wellek*

The relations between New England Transcendentalism and German philosophy have never been studied in any detail. Most discussions are content to assume the influence of German philosophy, referring in general terms to Kant, Schelling, and Fichte, or try to dismiss the influences altogether.[1] There are many suggestive remarks in books and articles, but we have no systematic study which would examine this relationship in the light of all the evidence, on the background of a thorough knowledge of the German philosophers. In this paper little more can be attempted than the first outlines of such an investigation. As an excuse for presenting it, I shall only plead that I have not met such a survey elsewhere and that possibly my earlier studies in Kant and his influence in England[2] have given me a starting point and some initial scheme of reference.

In approaching the question of the relations between New England Transcendentalism and German philosophy, it will be necessary to touch first on a subordinate question: the exact beginnings of this influence and the way in which German thought was imported into this country. I touch on it only because there are two widely held views on this point which seem to me mistaken. One theory ascribes the importation of German thought to the return of American students such as Ticknor and Bancroft from Germany; the other assumes that German philosophy reached America first and only through Coleridge and Carlyle.

It has been shown convincingly that intellectual relations between America and Germany were by no means nonexistent even in the seventeenth century, and that the general lack of German books or of the knowledge of the German language in America has been exaggerated.[3] Especially toward the end of the eighteenth century there was considerable interest in German *belles lettres*: John Quincy Adams, for instance, translated Wieland's *Oberon* into good verse, and the Reverend William Bentley, pastor at Salem, collected German books which included the

*Reprinted from *New England Quarterly*, 15 (December 1942), 652–680.

works of Klopstock and Schiller and many others. In the periodical literature there appear even scattered mentions of the recent German
philosophers. An issue of the Philadelphia *Monthly Magazine* for 1798
included a note on Kant based on a German source, which speaks of the
Criterion [*sic*] *of Pure Reason*; and the *Boston Register* of 1801 contains
quotations from Fichte refuting the charges of atheism.[4] In Samuel
Miller's interesting *Retrospect of the Eighteenth Century* (1803) there
is a hostile account of Kant which reproduces a review by William
Taylor of Willich's *Elements of Critical Philosophy* (1798) from the
London *Monthly Review* of January, 1799.[5] Obviously not much can be
made out of such scattered notices except to suggest that the names
of Kant and Fichte had begun to reach America.

   An actual motive for the study of German thought was supplied only
by the New England theologians, who became interested in German
Biblical scholarship long before the earliest migration of American students to German universities, after the end of the Napoleonic wars.
As early as 1806, the Reverend Joseph Stevens Buckminster, later pastor
of the Brattle Street Church at Cambridge, brought a library of some
three thousand German books from Europe and started to lecture on
Biblical criticism at Harvard College. Buckminster died young and
apparently left few traces of his interests.[6] But Moses Stuart, Professor
of Sacred Literature at Andover Theological Seminary, must have
been a far more influential figure. In 1812 he encouraged his young
friend Edward Everett to translate Herder's *Letters on Theology*; and in
1814, when Everett went on a trip to New York, Stuart asked him to
buy German books. He wanted him especially to get a "copy of Kant's
philosophy," whatever that may mean, which "would be a great curiosity."[7] He used Rosenmüller and De Wette in his classroom and translated from the Latin a book called *The Elements of Interpretation* by
the German J. A. Ernesti, in 1822. In 1825 he underwent investigation
for his views by the trustees of his college. The Committee reported that
"the unrestrained cultivation of German studies has evidently tended to
chill the ardor of piety, to impair belief in the fundamentals of revealed
religion, and even to induce, for the time, an approach to universal skepticism."[8] But Stuart continued with his work, and as late as 1841 sent
a spirited defense of German Biblical scholarship to the *Christian
Review*. Other figures, such as Dr. Convers Francis and James Walker,
both students of German theology, still need exploring.

   The strongest argument for the role of Coleridge in transmitting
German thought is furnished by the work of James Marsh, President of
the University of Vermont from 1826 to 1833. He edited *Aids to Reflection* in 1829, with a long preliminary discourse which expounds the distinctions of German philosophers, such as that between Reason and
Understanding, in the interpretation of Coleridge. In a letter to Coler-

idge, Marsh acknowledged his debt on this point quite specifically: "The German philosophers," he wrote,

> Kant and his followers are very little known in this country; and our young men who have visited Germany have paid little attention to that department of study while there. I cannot boast of being wiser than others in this respect; for though I have read a part of the works of Kant, it was under many disadvantages, so that I am indebted to your own writings for the ability to understand what I have read of his works, and am waiting with some impatience for that part of your works which will aid more directly in the study of those subjects of which he treats.[9]

But Marsh certainly extended his interest in German thought beyond a secondhand knowledge derived from Coleridge. He read also the anthropological and scientific writings of Kant and planned a book on logic designed to follow the textbook of Johann Jacob Fries, who had given an extreme objectivist interpretation to Kant. Nor could Marsh have needed Coleridge's stimulus to translate Herder's *Spirit of Hebrew Poetry* in 1833, or two scholarly German books, the *Geography of the Scriptures* and the *Historical Chronology*. Marsh can be described as a belated Cambridge Platonist, whose interests were primarily theological and educational.[10] Thus clergymen who studied German Biblical scholarship and Kant appear to have made the first contact with modern German thought.

The role of the American students who returned from Germany has been, it seems to me, extremely overrated, at least for our question. Edward Everett, who was to procure that copy of Kant's philosophy for Moses Stuart, studied classical philology in Göttingen. Everett was President of Harvard from 1846 to 1849, but no interest in German philosophy is recorded in his life except an abortive plan to give an address on "the influence of German thought on the contemporary literature of England and America," in 1837.[11] George Ticknor came as early as 1816 to the conclusion that the present "barrenness" of German literature was to be charged to the philosophy of Kant, which "absorbed and perverted all the talents of the land." It was a vast "'Serbonian bog where armies whole have sunk.'"[12] After his return to Harvard, Ticknor lectured on French and Spanish literature. George Bancroft, who kept up an interest in German *belles lettres* and later wrote several valuable studies, went to hear Hegel in Berlin, but thought the lectures merely a "display of unintelligible words." He admired Schleiermacher, however, whom he heard lecture on education, largely because "he has never suffered himself to be moved by any one of the many systems which have been gaining admirers and losing them successively for thirty years past."[13]

Neither Motley nor Longfellow showed any interest in German

philosophy.[14] The one exception among these students was Frederick Henry Hedge, who was, however, in Germany as a boy and developed interest in German philosophy only much later. In 1833 he wrote a review of Coleridge for the *Christian Examiner* which gives a fairly detailed account of German philosophy.[15] Hedge there deplores the meager information on German philosophy in Coleridge and proceeds to explain his own views. They show a knowledge which is quite independent of Coleridge and a first-hand acquaintance with Fichte's *Wissenschaftslehre* and Schelling's *System des transzendentalen Idealismus.* Kant, according to Hedge, "did not himself create a system, but furnished the hints and materials from which all the systems of his followers have been framed." The transcendental point of view is described as that of "interior consciousness."

> In the language of the school, it is a free intuition, and can only be attained by a vigorous effort of the will. The object is to discover in every form of finite existence, an infinite and unconditioned as the ground of its existence, or rather the ground of our knowledge of its existence, to refer all phenomena to certain *noumena,* or laws of cognition. It is not a *ratio essendi,* but a *ratio cognoscendi.*

This sounds like a description of Kant's procedure. Hedge, however, elaborates the point that the method is "synthetical, proceeding from a given point, the lowest that can be found in our consciousness, and deducing from that point 'the whole world of intelligences, with the whole system of their representations.'" Immediately afterwards this description, which might apply to Schelling, is modified, and an explanation of the "alternation of synthesis and antithesis" in Fichte is followed by a quite technical and literal reproduction of the beginnings of the *Wissenschaftslehre.* But Fichte is criticized as leaning toward skepticism and as "altogether too subjective." Schelling seems to Hedge the most satisfactory of all the Germans. "In him intellectual philosophy is more ripe, more substantial, more promising, and, if we may apply such a term to such speculations, more practical than in any of the others." Hedge describes briefly the main principle of Schelling's natural philosophy as an endeavor to show that "the outward world is of the same essence with the thinking mind, both being different manifestations of the same divine principle." Hedge alludes to Oken's development of Schelling's system and mentions him with Hegel and Fries, apologizing that "our information would not enable us to say much, and our limits forbid us to say anything" about them. Unfortunately Hedge never followed up the promise held out by these few competent pages. He collaborated in the *Dial,* to which he contributed a translation of Schelling's inaugural lecture at Berlin, and published an anthology of the

Prose Writers of Germany (1848) which contained nothing philosophic except Fichte's *Destiny of Man*. Late in his life Hedge became Professor of German at Harvard and wrote also papers on Liebniz and Schopenhauer.[16] Hedge was no original mind, but he had a really good knowledge of German from the time of his schooldays. He could talk on German philosophy with his elders and friends, Emerson and Alcott, and may serve as an indication that America was not confined to secondhand information on German philosophy through either Coleridge or the French eclectics.

The influence of the German immigrants belongs mostly to a later time. Charles Follen, the first instructor and later professor of German at Harvard, is the most important figure among these. He was an enthusiastic German *Corpsstudent*, an admirer of Jahn, the nationalistic gymnastics teacher, and of Theodor Körner, the poet of the Napoleonic wars. But he also studied theology under Channing, and in 1830 gave a course on moral philosophy which shows firsthand knowledge of Kant.[17] In the course of a brief history of ethics which discusses the Greeks, the New Testament, and Spinoza, we get a fairly full exposition of Kant's philosophy. The description of the *Critique of Pure Reason* is elementary and vitiated by Follen's repeated reference to time, space, and categories as "innate ideas": he suspects Kant's system of leading to subjective idealism and skepticism, but then gives an exposition of the moral philosophy which shows far better insight and even critical acumen. Kant is criticized for his mistake of considering man "sometimes entirely as a rational and moral, and sometimes entirely as a sensual or phenomenal being," and some good points are scored against the categorical imperative, which to Follen appears vague and general and merely an advice to search the nature, particularly the rational and moral nature, of man. Kant's religion of reason seems to him "nothing less than an avowal of atheism." His attitude toward Kant is extremely unsympathetic: he criticizes him not from the point of view of later German idealism (which he apparently did not know though he alludes to Fichte), but with empirical arguments which he manages to combine with a philosophy of faith. Nevertheless, in the following year, Follen, in his inaugural discourse as professor of German at Harvard, included a defense of German philosophy. He argued that its "records, from Liebniz to Kant and his disciples, Fichte, Schelling, Jacobi, and Fries do not exhibit the name of a single materialist or absolute skeptic."[18] Though Follen, in spite of his premature death, did something to foster interest in things German, he can scarcely be described as a propagandist for German idealist philosophy.

The other Germans who wrote on philosophy came later and could not have been of decisive importance. Frederick A. Rauch became President of Marshall College in Pennsylvania and wrote a Hegelian *Psy-*

chology: or a View of the Human Soul (1841). Johann Bernhard Stallo
settled in Cincinnati and wrote *General Principles of the Philosophy of
Nature* (1848), a book which attracted Emerson's interest sufficiently to
warrant long extracts in his *Journals*.[19] The editor of the *Journals* printed
so few quotations from Emerson's transcript that it is impossible to judge
the nature of his interest in Stallo, but the book may very well have
been a source of Emerson's knowledge of Schelling, Oken, and Hegel.
Since Stallo does little more than give abstracts, it is difficult to lay one's
hand on any indebtedness which Emerson might not have incurred from
the original texts or from other secondhand accounts.[20] Another German,
Emmanuel Vitalis Scherb, tried to instruct Emerson on Hegel in 1849
and 1851, but since the *Journals* do not tell us of what precisely this instruction consisted, we might as well not even begin to guess.[21]

II

All this is strictly preliminary, by way of clearing the path to a
direct examination of the main figures in the Transcendentalist group.
But I cannot suppress a few reflections on the general problem presented
by the contact of two great intellectual movements. I avoid the term
"influence," which needs some closer definition to be used safely. In
discussing such a relation, we must, I think, distinguish carefully several
questions which are frequently not kept clearly apart by investigators.
First, we must see what was the reputation of German philosophy, the
vague secondhand or tenth-hand information which was floating about,
and distinguish it from actual knowledge of German philosophy, either
in more detailed descriptive accounts by English or French writers or in
a real firsthand acquaintance with the texts themselves, in translation
or in the original. Only when this first problem of the actual knowledge
has been settled can we profitably inquire what precisely was the attitude and the opinion that American writers had of the German philosophers. Only after this can we raise the question of actual influence.
Even then we have to distinguish between the use of isolated quotations
or ideas and a really basic similarity in philosophical outlook or mental
evolution. Isolated parallels merely establish the fact of the relation; of
real influence one can only speak if we compare the whole system of one
man with the whole system of another. ("System," of course, need not
imply any systematic exposition in any technical sense, but merely means
a personal view of the world.) Even then we ought to know exactly
the original features, or at least the peculiar combinations of ideas in the
two systems we are comparing, before we can maintain with absolute
certainty that we have not merely uncovered a spiritual kinship, possibly explainable by similar intellectual antecedents, but have defined
a shaping and determining influence. In the case of American Transcen-

dentalism, this problem becomes extremely complex, since the ancestry of Transcendentalism includes almost the whole intellectual history of mankind: Plato; the pre-Socratic philosophers known to Emerson and Alcott in fairly detailed accounts; Neo-Platonism, partly available in the recent translations of Thomas Taylor; the English Neo-Platonists of the seventeenth and eighteenth centuries; the great tradition of mysticism represented especially by Jacob Böhme and Swedenborg, not to speak of Swedenborg's disciples in America (Sampson Reed) and France (Oegger); the native tradition of Calvinist and Unitarian theology; the British "moral sense" philosophy of the eighteenth century, represented by Bishop Butler, Price, and others; Coleridge, Carlyle, and a few other interpreters of Kant, writing in English; and the French eclectic philosophers and the early Utopian socialists, including Mme. de Staël, Cousin, Jouffroy, Benjamin Constant, Pierre Leroux, and Fourier. At a later period Oriental philosophies must be added, and finally, before we mention the actual German philosophers, the many German poets and novelists who, in one or another form, assimilated and transmitted the philosophical thought of the technical philosophers: Goethe, of course, Schiller, Jean Paul, the Schlegels, and Novalis. Who has ever clearly defined which idea comes from where? The historian of ideas would almost need a dictionary similar to the *Oxford Dictionary* which would list the first occurrence (subject to correction) of thoughts, giving author and date. And even this would not solve our difficulties, since the history of thought is the history not merely of unit-ideas but of systems and interrelations, new combinations and syntheses. When we look at German philosophy itself, we are also confronted with a difficult problem of distinctions, trends, and conflicts within the fold itself. There is Leibniz looming in the background; Kant, still steeped in eighteenth-century rationalism, open to at least three or four widely divergent interpretations, not to speak of the hundred misinterpretations; then Herder, Jacobi, and Schleiermacher, who sought the intuitive evidence of religion; then the dialectical philosophy growing out of Kant: Fichte, the early Schelling, and later Hegel, all three distinct in their approach and intellectual background—Fichte, a moralist and dualist; Schelling primarily a philosopher of nature with mystical leanings; Hegel a logician and philosopher of history. Lorenz Oken and Henrik Steffens, a Norwegian, are speculative scientists nearest to Schelling; Novalis and Friedrich Schlegel have the closest links with Fichte, Jean Paul with Jacobi, Schiller with Kant, Goethe with Herder and Neo-Platonism. The Transcendentalists knew them all, more or less intimately, without, of course, necessarily understanding their relationships but instinctively looking for congenial ideas in kindred minds. Here is, at least, the suggestion of a convenient and feasible approach. We may take up each important figure in the Transcendental movement and ask several questions. What did he know about German philosophy: what from hearsay and what secondhand and what from actual texts? What did he think of the German philosophers? Which of the German thinkers did he treat with greatest sympathy and understanding? Thus, by empirical methods, we may place every American thinker in the scheme of the much-studied and carefully analyzed development of German philosophy and determine his approximate historical position. We may then make distinctions and lay out at least the ground for a discussion of direct influences.

We may begin with Bronson Alcott, who not only was the oldest in the group, but in his mental makeup represented also the oldest tradition of thought among them. Alcott knew scarcely any German (though he bought books in German when he was in London in 1842, including the mysterious volume called Vernunft by Fichte),[22] but early found his way to what appealed to him in German thought, namely, Jacob Böhme, the seventeenth-century cobbler from Silesia who evolved an elaborate system of mystical theosophy that was widely read in English translations during both the seventeenth and the eighteenth centuries. In 1833, when Alcott was in Philadelphia, he read Okely's Life of Behmen, and he read and re-read much of Böhme at different times. As late as 1882 he founded a small Mystic Club for the express purpose of discussing and reading Böhme.[23] The few published writings of Alcott contain a little essay on Böhme, (first published in The Radical, 1870; reprinted in Concord Days, 1872). In this Alcott praises his "teeming genius, the genuine mother of numberless theories since delivered."[24] Law, Leibniz, Oken, Schelling, Goethe, and Baader seem all derived from him. Alcott thinks of Böhme as "the subtilest thinker on Genesis since Moses,"[25] though he disagrees with him on the fall of man and the symbolism of the serpent, as mystics are apt to disagree on the details of their allegories and symbols.

In 1849, Alcott read Lorenz Oken, the speculative scientist, whose Elements of Physiophilosophy had been translated in England in 1847.[26] Soon afterwards Alcott had his second "illumination," in which he saw the universe as "one vast spinal column";[27] and all his following speculations on Genesis and the meaning of nature seem to be full of Oken's ideas and terminology, though obviously Alcott drew also from many other sources in the same tradition. To illustrate this, I like to point out a passage in Emerson's essay on Swedenborg,[28] in which he speaks of "a poetic anatomist of our day," obviously referring to Alcott, and then proceeds to reproduce his ideas. These ideas represent a combination of two different authors from whom Alcott seems to have drawn. He speaks first of the mystical quadrant of man (the vertical) and the serpent (the horizontal), an idea derived from Oegger's True Messiah, which Emerson had copied in his Journals more than twenty years before;[29] and then he paraphrases Oken's curious fancy that the skull is another spine, and that the hands have been transformed into the upper jaw, the feet into the lower.[30] Alcott's precise relations to the German scientists like Oken and von Schubert, and possibly to the theosophist Baader, are quite unexplored and cannot be solved definitely without access to the fifty manuscript volumes of his journals. For our purpose it is sufficient to say that he was strongly attracted by the speculations of the Schellingian philosophy of nature and combined it with Neo-Platonic and generally mystical elements.

But Alcott knew also something of the main German idealistic philosophers. As early as 1833, in Philadelphia, before he had met Emerson or settled at Boston, Alcott read two expositions of Kant written in English by Germans, late in the eighteenth century.[31] One was Willich's *Elements of Critical Philosophy* (1798), in Odell Shepard's life of Alcott ascribed to Wellick. From the other, Friedrich August Nitsch's *View of Kant's Principles* (1796), Alcott copied out some fifty-seven pages, a proof, by the way, that he did not need the mediation of either Coleridge or the French to learn something about Kant. But Alcott's own view of Kant was soon decidedly unfavorable: he classed him with Aristotle and Bacon and Locke, and thought that all had "narrowed the range of the human faculties, retarded the progress of discovery by insisting on the supremacy of the senses, and shut the soul up in the cave of the Understanding."[32] Alcott here, then, interprets Kant as a skeptic, as a critic of all metaphysics, and uses Kant's own distinction between Reason and Understanding in a Coleridgean sense to condemn Kant's philosophy as pedestrian and sensual.

Later in his life, Alcott was brought into personal contact with the St. Louis Hegelians. He visited them in 1859 and again in 1866, and became the nominal head of the Concord School of Philosophy, where for years Hegelians like William Torrey Harris expounded their doctrines under Alcott's patronage.[33] At first he was flattered by their admiration and overwhelmed and puzzled by Hegel's *Philosophy of History* and James Hutchinson Stirling's *Secret of Hegel*, which his daughter Louisa had brought from Europe as a present.[34] In the *Tablets* (1868) and the *Concord Days* (1882) there are quotations from Harris and two little essays on speculative philosophy and dialectics.[35] For a time, at least, Alcott expected a new philosophy in New England, "to which the German Hegel shall give impulse and furtherance."[36] But he soon decided that Hegel is not only "dry and crabbed," "strange and unintelligible," but that his own thinking is "ideal, his method analogical rather than logical" and thus "of a subtler and more salient type" than Hegel's, since it "implies an active and sprightly imagination inflaming the reason and divining the truths it seeks."[37] Thus Alcott defines his own position clearly as an adherent of an imaginative, "analogical" mysticism which rejects as irrelevant the epistemological and logical methods of both Kant and Hegel.

George Ripley and Theodore Parker present a striking contrast to Alcott in their attitude towards German philosophy. Both were Unitarian clergymen who found in German thought additional support for their liberal religious convictions. Ripley was the more timid and also the more othodox of the two. His early writings praise Herder and Schleiermacher[38]—"the greatest thinker who ever undertook to fathom the philosophy of religion,"[39]—and his own thought seems to agree in every way with this professed sympathy. But Ripley knew also something of Kant. As early as 1832 he defended him as a "writer and reasoner from whom the great questions . . . have received more light than from any uninspired person, since the brightest days of Grecian philosophy." He contrasts him sharply with Coleridge, describing Kant's "cool, far-reaching, and austere habits of thought," "the severe logic, the imperturbable patience, the mathematical precision, and the passionless exhibition of the results of pure reason."[40] But soon, in a detailed account of Herder's conflict with Kant, Ripley sides with Herder, praising him for having made the system "lower its pretensions, and assume a more modest rank," though he recognizes Herder's incompetence to "do justice to the great merits" of the Kantian system "as an analytical exposition of the grounds of human knowledge."[41] In a later article on Fichte (1846) Ripley criticizes him as having failed to solve "the mighty problems of Divine Providence and Human Destiny" and tries to find in him merely negative virtues. According to Ripley, Fichte has shown the fruitlessness of speculation and thrown man back into "the world of moral emotions," "the instinctive sense of justice," "the interior vice,"[42]—that is, precisely the teachings of Herder and Schleiermacher, with whom the historical Fichte had only scant sympathy. Ripley even sees in the study of Fichte a preparation for the acceptance of the doctrines of Fourier, possibly because of Fichte's strong collectivist outlook on social questions.

Later Ripley's attitude towards German philosophy became more and more hostile. Reviewing Hedge's *Prose Writers*, he asks "to what does [German philosophy] amount";[43] and a review of Stallo's book *Philosophy of Nature* is completely negative. Ripley thinks that its thoughts "offer no points of contact with the American mind." To him now, the study of German philosophy has only historical interest, as "studying the remains of the Later Platonists or the Oriental philosophers" would have. The German thinkers produce only "wonderful specimens of intellectual gymnastics." They try to "explain the universe or the human soul by the mere force of thought, without the scientific analysis of facts," which is "as absurd as the attempt to leap over one's own head."[44] Later Ripley also attacked Strauss and Feuerbach and the mid-nineteenth-century materialists like Büchner, and he showed some interest in Eduard Hartmann's *Philosophy of the Unconscious*.[45] But evidence enough has been presented to show that Ripley stands with Herder and Schleiermacher as a philosopher of faith, that he welcomed the German idealists only as far as they seemed, in his interpretation, to make room for such a philosophy, and that later he roundly condemned what he considered their mistaken intellectualism and *a priori* ways of thinking. It would be difficult to say which ideas Ripley could have derived from Germany, because the idea of a "religious sense" could have been found in British and French philosophy too.

Theodore Parker was both a bolder mind and man and a greater scholar than Ripley; but in our context he is nearest to Ripley, though he broke away from the moorings of the church much further. Parker early studied German Biblical criticism and theology and translated a two-volume *Introduction to the New Testament* by De Wette, a liberal German theologian who was a follower of Fries and thus remotely of Kant. Parker's learning in German scholarship, theological, historical, and literary, was really imposing, though the long strings of indiscriminately jumbled names in an article in defense of the German literature in the *Dial*[46] arouse some suspicions whether his knowledge, at least at that time, was always so thorough and firsthand as it seems. In this long and able article, which is ostensibly a review of Menzel's *History of German Literature*, little is said of German philosophy, though Parker calls Menzel's view on Kant "exceedingly unjust" and recognizes the political bias of his attacks on Hegel.[47] The next year, 1843, Parker went to Germany, called on De Wette and other theologians, and heard Werder, a Hegelian, lecture on logic in Berlin. The performance seemed to him merely ridiculous, and so also appeared Schelling lecturing on the philosophy of revelation.[48] After his return, Parker became immersed in German theology, jurisprudence, ecclesiastical history, and later, of course, the cause of abolitionism. He thus never returned to German philosophy proper. But in the fine confession of faith which he wrote to his parishioners from Santa Cruz when on his last voyage to Italy in 1859, he confessed his debt to Kant, "one of the profoundest thinkers in the world, though one of the worst writers, even of Germany."

> He gave me the true method, and put me on the right road. I found certain primal institutions of human nature, which depend on no logical process of demonstration, but are rather facts of consciousness given by the instinctive action of human nature itself: the instinctive intuition of the divine, the instinctive intuition of the just and right, the instinctive intuition of the immortal. Here, then, was the foundation of religion, laid in human nature itself.[49]

There is little point in stressing that this is a false interpretation of Kant. It is more interesting to note that this interpretation is in perfect harmony with the intuitive philosophy of Jacobi or Schleiermacher, of the French eclectics, and even of the Scottish common-sense school. Parker stands with Ripley, but succeeds in interpreting the *Critique of Practical Reason* as support for a philosophy of faith as an instinctive intuition of the human mind.

Orestes Brownson, or rather the early Brownson before his conversion to Roman Catholicism in 1844, who alone can be called a Transcendentalist, is related in outlook and starting point to both Ripley and Parker. He also became early an intuitionist, who read, admired, and propagated Cousin and the other French eclectics. But Brownson had a stronger philosophical bent than his friends and associates, and a genuine gift for speculation as well as an altogether unusual grasp, in his time and place, of philosophical technicalities. He alone of all the Transcendentalists seems to have been seriously disturbed by the problems of knowledge and truth, and he alone made a close examination of Kant's actual text. This was written down shortly after his conversion, but the point of view there expounded can be found already in the scattered and unsympathetic pronouncements of his pre-conversion writings. The remarkable consistency and uniformity of his criticism of Kant and Hegel, which extends over a period of some thirty-five years of indefatigable writing, seems to point to a greater coherence and consistency in Brownson's philosophical outlook than is usually allowed by those who see only the shiftings and changes of his religious associations.

As to German philosophy, there is only one marked change of attitude. Brownson had learned to read German in 1834; and in a little book, *New Views of Christianity* (1836), he recommended the German theological movement starting with Herder and culminating in Schleiermacher. Brownson commended the "meeting of inspiration and philosophy" in Schleiermacher and praised him as a man for "remarkable warmth of feeling and coolness of thought," hinting at the similarity between him and Saint-Simon.[50] After the conversion, Brownson condemned Schleiermacher's views, since he makes religion purely objective and "resolves the church into general society." He even went out of his way to brand Schleiermacher's "pantheistic spiritualism" as worse than rationalism, deism, and even the atheism of D'Holbach.[51]

But no such marked change can be discerned in his relations to Kant, Fichte, Schelling, and Hegel. His attitude towards Kant seems to have been defined very early. Brownson had a great admiration precisely for the technical side of Kant's analysis of judgment and categories. In all his writings he was again and again to repeat the view that "Kant has with masterly skill and wonderful exactness, drawn up a complete list of the categories of Reason. His analysis of Reason may be regarded as complete and final."[52] This analysis, Brownson thought, was purely empirical and correct as far as it went. Very early he defended Kant against the charge of transcendentalism. Kant's method, he argued, "was as truly experimental as Bacon's or Locke's." Even when Kant professed to describe *a priori* knowledge, he did so "by experience, by experiment, by a careful analysis of the facts of consciousness, as they actually present themselves to the eye of the psychological observer." If Kant is to be criticized, he should not be charged with leaving the "path of experience" or "rushing off into speculation." Rather, Brownson suggested, Kant fails in a thoroughgoing application of his method because he conceives of experience too narrowly as merely experience of the senses.[53]

But in spite of these frequent acknowledgments of Kant's power as an analyst of thought, Brownson seems never to have been in doubt as to his objections to the main epistemological position of Kant. In a review dating from 1842, Brownson rejected philosophical idealism as clearly and forcefully as he was to reject it for the rest of his life.

> The refutation of Kant and Fichte, and therefore of all idealism, egoism, and skepticism, whether atheistic or pantheistic, is in a simple fact . . . that the objective element of thought is always *not me*. The error of Kant, and the error which led astray his whole school and all others, is the assumption that the *me* does or may develop as pure subject, or, in other words, be its own object, and therefore at once subject and object. Kant assumes that the *me* develops itself, without a foreign object, in cognition; hence he infers that all knowledge is purely subjective, and asserts the impotency of reason to carry us out of the sphere of the *me*.

In a note, Brownson recognizes that this was not all of Kant's teaching.

> We know very well that this was not the real doctrine of Kant, that it was only demonstrated by him to be the result, to which all philosophy must come, that *is based on pure reason*. He himself relied on practical reason, that is to say, on plain common sense, and his purpose of writing critiques of pure reason, was to demonstrate the unsatisfactory character of all purely metaphysical speculations. A wise man, after all, was that same Emanuel Kant.[54]

But this partial retraction, which seems to point to some knowledge of the *Critique of Practical Reason*, did not remain in Brownson's mind. He dismissed Kant's practical reason as nothing else than the common sense of Hume[55] and later was to write his criticisms of Kant without regard to other books than the *Critique of Pure Reason*.

When Brownson, immediately after the conversion, in the "Introduction" to *Brownson's Quarterly*, surveyed his own intellectual development, he could, it seems to me, with reason minimize the importance of German philosophy for his own development and define his attitude towards Kant in terms substantially in agreement with the earlier pronouncements. "The German philosophers," he says,

> have afforded me very little satisfaction. It is true, that I have made no profound study of them; but, so far as I know them, I claim no affinity with them. I feel and own, the eminent analytic ability of Kant, but I am forced to regard his philosophy as fundamentally false and mischievous. His *Critic der reinen Vernunft*, if taken in any other light than that of a protest, under the most rigid forms of analysis, against all modern philosophy, is sure to mislead, and to involve the reader in an inextricable maze of error.[56]

Strangely enough, Brownson thought it worth while to make a careful study of the *Critique of Pure Reason*, apparently in the original, shortly afterwards and to write three closely reasoned essays on it for the first volume of his new quarterly.[57] There we find his fullest discussion of Kant, which is, however, in its approach and conclusion, completely identical with the pre-conversion pronouncements. Brownson criticizes Kant's fundamental question. It is "absurd to ask if the human mind be capable of science; for we have only the human mind with which to answer the question." Kant's phenomenalism is completely mistaken. One cannot find the object in the subject. "This simple truism, which is nothing but saying what *is*, is, completely refutes the whole critical philosophy." Brownson drives home this main point with considerable dialectical power. Kant is thus interpreted as the arch-skeptic, who denied the very possibility of knowledge, as the "most masterly defender of Hume." With a flourish of Carlylean rhetoric Brownson depicts the dire consequences of this supposed universal skepticism. "So all science vanishes, all certainty disappears, the sun goes out, the bright stars are extinguished, and we are afloat in the darkness, on the wild and tempest-roused ocean of Universal Doubt and Nescience."[58] Kant, according to Brownson, turned out to be fundamentally a "sensist" and a "materialist." Brownson dismisses Kant's own development of his teachings in the other *Critiques* far too lightly;[59] but he has come, at least, to actual grips with the text of Kant, with his dialectics and logic, as no contemporary in America did. All the many later pronouncements of Brownson on Kant are merely variations on this point of view. He reiterates again and again his admiration for Kant's analysis of mind, his table of the categories, and his negative conclusion which seems to Brownson to have established that "man's own subjective reason alone does not suffice for science."[60] But he also condemns his subjectivism, the views that the categories are mere forms of our mind, the denial of the objectivity of knowledge, and hence the skepticism which seems to him the "hardly disguised" result of Kant's philosophy. Kant thus was a philosopher who asked questions and who gave acute technical discussion of logical and epistemological questions; but his main position was entirely repugnant to Brownson, who early in his life had become an objectivist, an enemy of Cartesianism and all its forms.[61]

It is almost needless to expound Brownson's attitude toward Fichte. He appeared to him early as the *reductio ad absurdum* of idealism. Fichte, he says in an article written before the conversion,

> asserted the power of the *me* to be his own object and sought the proof of it in the fact of volition. Hence he fell into the absurdity of representing all ideas as the products of the *me*, and even went so far as to tell his disciples how it is that man makes God.

But again, as in the case of Kant, Brownson was aware of the existence of Fichte's later views, which corrected some of his speculative errors.[62] Later Brownson was to repeat several times that the "egoistic philosophy, so energetically asserted by Fichte, that God and the external world are only the soul projecting itself, is only a logical deduction from the Kantian premises," and that Cartesianism leads to Fichtean egoism.[63]

Towards Schelling and his disciples Brownson had at first, during the Emersonian stage of his development, shown some vague though cautious sympathy. He thought that "they give us a magnificent poem, which we believe to be mainly true, but which nevertheless is no philosophy and can in no degree solve the difficulty stated by Hume."[64] But later Schelling was neglected or put down as an atheist and Spinozist. He "maintains the identity of subject and object, and thus asserts, from the subjective point of view, the Egoism of Fichte and, under the objective point of view, the Pantheism of Spinoza, while under both he denies intuition and even the possibility of science."[65]

From these pronouncements, we can already guess at Brownson's attitude towards Hegel. It was again defined long before the conversion. Brownson first rejects the whole deductive method. He cannot believe that "the system of the universe is only a system of logic," that the "ideal and essential, idea and being," are identical. Hegel's method "claims for man confessedly finite, absolute knowledge, which would imply that he himself is absolute and therefore not finite, but infinite." But "the boast is also in vain, for in the order of knowledge we are obliged to reverse the order of existence. We rise through nature up to nature's God, instead of descending from God through man to nature. None but God himself can know according to the order of existence, for none but he can know being in itself, and from the absolute knowledge of the cause, have a perfect *a priori* knowledge of the effect." While rejecting the pretensions of Hegel's philosophy to absolute knowledge, the American democrat Brownson can not help smiling at Hegel's view that "the infinite God and all his works through all the past have been engaged expressly in preparing and founding the Prussian monarchy" and that "his gracious majesty Frederick William" could be "the last word of creation and progress."[66] After the conversion the tone of the objections against Hegel become more strident. Hegel's system appears to him, under other forms, "nothing but a reproduction of old French Atheism," his principles appear "unreal and worthless," and his philosophy "really less genuine, less profound, and infinitely less worthy of confidence" than that of Reid.[67] In detail, Brownson pays some attention to Hegel's first triad, in which he sees a false attempt to derive the real from the possible, existence from nothing.[68] He does not admit that Hegel is an ontologist. To Brownson he is a pure psychologist, who only ostensibly attempts to identify the psychological process with the ontological. Hegel is a subjective idealist who ends in pantheism and atheism, like all the other followers of Kant.[69]

Brownson's criticisms of German philosophy cannot always be justified: he surely overstressed the purely negative critical side of Kant and misunderstood the Hegelian dialectics, but within limits he presented the case against German philosophy forcefully and consistently from the point of view of an objective intuitivism which deplored the whole turn modern philosophy had taken since Descartes. He could even write that "Germany has produced no philosophical system not already exploded and no philosophers to compare with Vico, Galluppi, Rosmini, Gioberti and Balmes."[70] Thus, from his own point of view, Brownson rightly thought Leibniz to have been the "greatest of all modern philosophers" not in the Catholic communion. He could praise his refutation of the Cartesian doctrine that the essence of substance is extension and his rejection of the atomic in favor of the dynamic theory of matter. But even Leibniz is criticized as "the veritable father of German rationalism," and as a believer in the ontological argument and the priority of the possible before the real.[71] Brownson's lifelong sympathies were with an intuitivism and realism which managed finally to reconcile Reid and Gioberti, Catholicism and Common Sense philosophy. In spite of his interest in some of the arguments of Kant, German philosophy stood for everything Brownson rejected all his life: subjectivism and pantheism, skepticism and atheism.[72]

Margaret Fuller stands apart from the other Transcendentalists. Her interests were obviously not primarily philosophical and theological, but rather aesthetic and later political. Her study of German led her to

Goethe, Jean Paul, and, rather incongruously, the sentimental Theodor Körner and the spiritualist Justinus Kerner. Her direct contacts with German philosophy seem rare and not too happy. In Cambridge (presumably some time before 1833) she obtained books by Fichte and Jacobi, and she tells us: "I was much interrupted, but some time and earnest thought I devoted. Fichte I could not understand at all; though the treatise which I read was intended to be popular, and which he says must compel (*bezwingen*) to conviction."[73] She must refer to Fichte's *Sonnenklarer Bericht* (1801), which in its subtitle is called "Ein Versuch, die Leser zum Verstehen zu zwingen."[74] "Jacobi," she continues, "I could understand in details, but not in system. It seemed to me that his mind must have been moulded by some other mind, with which I ought to be acquainted, in order to know him well—perhaps Spinoza's." Later, in the *Dial*, when she wrote a review criticizing Menzel's view of Goethe, she referred to Jacobi as having written "the heart into philosophy as well as he could."[75] Reading the life of Sir James Macintosh, she was pleased, "after my late chagrin, to find Sir James, with all his metaphysical turn, and ardent desire to penetrate it, puzzling so over the German philosophy, and particularly what I was myself troubled about, at Cambridge,—Jacobi's *Letters to Fichte*."[76] In Groton, when she was planning her abortive "Life of Goethe," she came to the conclusion that she ought to get "some idea of the history of philosophical opinion in Germany" in order to understand its influence on Goethe. She consulted Buhle's and Tennemann's *Histories of Philosophy* and dipped into Brown, Stewart, and "that class of books."[77] In the winter 1836–1837 she went one evening every week to Dr. Channing and translated for him German theological writings, mainly De Wette and Herder.[78] In 1841, apparently in connection with her "conversations," she translated Schelling's famous lecture "Über das Verhältniss der bildenden Künste zur Natur," a labor she might have saved had she noticed that Coleridge had paraphrased the very same oration very closely.[79] The translation by Margaret Fuller has remained in manuscript. Later, after her arrival in New York, she drifted more and more away from Transcendental contacts and interests. In the last year of her reviewing for the New York *Daily Tribune* (1846), she wrote a report on William Smith's *Memoirs of J. G. Fichte*, which have mainly biographical interest;[80] and once, in a review of Charles Brockden Brown's *Ormond* and *Wieland*, she interestingly reveals her (and the Transcendentalist) conception of Hegelianism. She calls Brown and Godwin "born Hegelians, without the pretensions of science" as "they sought God in their consciousness and found him. The heart, because it saw itself so fearfully and wonderfully made, did not disown its Maker."[81] Sometimes she protests against all analytical philosophy, alluding particularly to Fichte. "I do not wish to *reflect* always, if reflecting must be always about one's identity, whether '*ich*' am the true '*ich*' etc. I wish to arrive at that point where I can trust myself."[82] On the whole, if one can combine these meager and scattered statements, they seem to show that Margaret Fuller cared nothing for what she thought were German technicalities and had only vaguely understood that German philosophy from Jacobi to Hegel justified the religion of the heart. Her point of view thus seemed to be nearest to Ripley's.

Thus the minor Transcendentalists show only slight contacts with German philosophy proper. Alcott neglected the great German philosophers and found solace and support in the fanciful speculation of Jacob Böhme and Lorenz Oken. Ripley and Parker looked for a religion of the heart, a justification of intuitive faith, and found it either in Schleiermacher or in a misinterpreted Kant. Margaret Fuller faintly echoes this view in her writings. In Brownson, the Germans had a formidable critic of their subjectivism and pantheism. But only a full discussion of Emerson's relations to German philosophy will make these distinctions stand out more clearly and allow us to draw general conclusions.

Notes

1. There are no discussions of the relations of Alcott, Parker, Brownson, Miss Fuller, Follen, or Hedge to the German thinkers, except references in biographies and general studies of Transcendentalism (Frothingham, Goddard, Riley, Girard, Muirhead, Townsend). There is, however, a recent paper, "George Ripley: Unitarian, Transcendentalist, or Infidel?" by Arthur R. Schultz and Henry A. Pochmann in *American Literature*, 14 (March 1942), 1–19, which discusses Ripley's relations to German philosophy.

2. *Kant in England, 1793–1838* (Princeton: Princeton University Press, 1931).

3. Harold S. Jantz, "German Thought and Literature in New England, 1620–1820," *Journal of English and Germanic Philology*, 41 (January 1942), 1–45.

4. I. W. Riley, *American Thought from Puritanism to Pragmatism and Beyond* (New York: Henry Holt, 1932), pp. 232–235; Jantz, "German Thought and Literature in New England," p. 41.

5. Cf. *Kant in England*, pp. 13, 268. Harold S. Jantz, "Samuel Miller's Survey of German Literature, 1803," *Germanic Review*, 16 (December 1941), 267–277, notes that Miller owes this section to a "British literary journal," but does not identify the source.

6. *The Dictionary of American Biography.*

7. O. W. Long, *Literary Pioneers* (Cambridge: Harvard University Press, 1935), p. 237n6.

8. Daniel Day Williams, *The Andover Liberals* (New York: King's Crown Press, 1941), p. 17.

9. Marjorie H. Nicholson, "James Marsh and the Vermont Transcendentalists," *Philosophical Review*, 34 (January 1925), 33.

10. Nicholson, "James Marsh," p. 49. Cf. also John Dewey, "James Marsh and American Philosophy," *Journal of the History of Ideas*, 2 (April 1941), 131–150.

11. Long, *Literary Pioneers*, p. 75.

12. Letter of 29 February 1816, Long, *Literary Pioneers*, p. 16.

13. Letters of 28 December 1820 and 13 November 1820, Long, *Literary Pioneers*, pp. 248n53, 133.

14. Long on Motley. On Longfellow, see James Taft Hatfield, *New Light on Longfellow* (Boston: Houghton, Mifflin, 1933). In 1844 Longfellow read Fichte's *Nature of the Scholar* (Hatfield, p. 110) and in 1848 he read Schelling's essay on Dante, which he translated for *Graham's Magazine* (Hatfield, p. 118).

15. *Christian Examiner*, n.s. 9 (1833), 108–129.

16. O. W. Long, *Frederic Henry Hedge: A Cosmopolitan Scholar* (Portland, Me.: Southworth-Anthoensen Press, 1940).

17. In Follen's *Works* (5 vols.; Boston: Hilliard, Gray, 1841), vol. 3. The "Life" by his widow in volume 1 gives date of delivery of the lectures (p. 290).

18. "Inaugural Discourse" (3 September 1831) in Follen's *Works*, V, especially 136.

19. December 1849, *Journals of Ralph Waldo Emerson*, ed. Edward Waldo Emerson and Waldo Emerson Forbes (Boston: Houghton Mifflin, 1909–1914), VIII, 77.

20. Two possibilities will be suggested in the ensuing paper on Emerson. [See Wellek, "Emerson and German Philosophy," *New England Quarterly*, 16 (March 1943), 41–62 (Ed. Note).]

21. Emerson, *Journals*, VIII, 69. See also VIII, 246.

22. Odell Shepard, *Pedlar's Progress: The Life of Bronson Alcott* (Boston: Little, Brown, 1937), p. 341.

23. Shepard, *Pedlar's Progress*, pp. 160, 341, 350, 416; see also *The Journals of Bronson Alcott*, ed. Odell Shepard (Boston: Little, Brown, 1938), pp. 34, 109, 332, 530.

24. *Concord Days* (Boston: Roberts Brothers, 1872), p. 238.

25. *Tablets* (Boston: Roberts Brothers, 1868), p. 189.

26. Translated by Alfred Tulk, member of the Royal College of Surgeons of England; printed for the Ray Society (London, 1847). Cf. Alcott, *Journals*, pp. 211, 212.

27. Shepard, *Pedlar's Progress*, p. 439.

28. Emerson, *Representative Men, The Complete Works of Ralph Waldo Emerson*, ed. Edward Waldo Emerson (Boston: Houghton, Mifflin, 1903–1904), IV, 107–108.

29. Emerson, *Journals*, III, 515, from Oegger, *Le Vrai Messie* (Paris, 1829). A partial translation by Elizabeth Peabody was published in Boston in 1835.

30. Oken, *Elements of Physiophilosophy* (London, 1847): "The Mouth is the stomach in the head, the nose the lung, the jaws the arms and feet" (p. 564).

31. Shepard, *Pedlar's Progress*, p. 160. Willich and Nitsch are discussed in *Kant in England*, pp. 7–15.

32. Alcott, *Journals*, pp. 38–39.

33. Shepard, *Pedlar's Progress*, pp. 474–476, 480–484, 507ff. Cf. Austin Warren, "The Concord School of Philosophy," *New England Quarterly*, 2 (April 1929), 199–233.

34. August 1861 and July 1866, Alcott, *Journals*, pp. 340, 383.

35. Alcott, *Tablets*, pp. 164–165; *Concord Days*, pp. 73–74; "Speculative Philosophy," pp. 143ff; and "The Dialectic," pp. 156ff.

36. *Concord Days*, p. 145.

37. July 1879 and August 1882, *Journals*, pp. 497, 536.

38. Review of James Marsh's translation of Herder's *Spirit of Hebrew Poetry,* in the *Christian Examiner,* 18 (1835), 167–221; "Herder's Theological Opinions and Services," *Christian Examiner,* 19 (1835), 172–204; and "Schleiermacher as a Theologian," *Christian Examiner,* 20 (1836), 1–46. Also Ripley's "Letters to a Theological Student" (written in December 1836) in the *Dial,* 1 (1840), recommends Herder highly (p. 187).

39. O. B. Frothingham, *George Ripley* (Boston: Houghton, Mifflin, 1882), p. 229.

40. Review of Carl Follen's "Inaugural Discourse," *Christian Examiner,* 11 (1832), 375.

41. Review of Marsh's *Spirit of Hebrew Poetry,* p. 209.

42. *Harbinger,* 2 (1846), 297ff.

43. *Harbinger,* 6 (1848), 107.

44. *Harbinger,* 6 (1848), 110.

45. Frothingham, *George Ripley,* pp. 230, 286.

46. *Dial,* 1 (1841), 315–339. Reprinted in Parker's *Critical and Miscellaneous Writings,* 2d ed. (New York: Appleton, 1864), pp. 28–60.

47. *Dial,* 1 (1841), 335–336; reprinted in *Critical and Miscellaneous Writings,* pp. 54–55.

48. H. S. Commager, *Theodore Parker* (Boston: Little, Brown, 1936), pp. 95–96.

49. J. Weiss, *Life and Correspondence of Theodore Parker* (New York: Appleton, 1864), II, 454–455.

50. *Collected Works,* ed. H. F. Brownson (Detroit: Nourse and Henry F. Brownson, 1882–1907), IV, 44–45.

51. *Collected Works,* III, 45; IV, 519; VIII, 424; X, 480: quotations from 1850, 1844, 1872, and 1873, respectively.

52. "Synthetic Philosophy," *Democratic Review* (1842), reprinted in *Works,* I, 165; see also I, 222; II, 299; V, 507; and IX, 263.

53. "Eclectic Philosophy," *Boston Quarterly Review* (1839), reprinted in *Works,* II, 536–538.

54. "Charles Elwood Reviewed," *Boston Quarterly Review* (1842), reprinted in *Works,* IV, 355.

55. "The Philosophy of History," *Democratic Review* (1843), reprinted in *Works,* IV, 391.

56. "Introduction," *Brownson's Quarterly Review,* 1 (1844), 8.

57. "Kant's Critic of Pure Reason" (1844), 137–174, 181–309, 417–499; also in *Works,* I, 130–213.

58. "Kant's Critic of Pure Reason," pp. 282, 284, 308, 309; reprinted in *Works,* I, 162, 163, 184, 185.

59. "Kant's Critic of Pure Reason," p. 309; reprinted in *Works,* I, 185–186. Here Brownson quotes Heine, in the French translation, ridiculing the *Critique of Practical Reason* as prompted by "fear of the police."

60. "An Old Quarrel," *Catholic World* (1867), reprinted in *Works,* II, 299.

61. Later passages on Kant, in *Works,* I, 222, 244–245; II, 47, 295, 520; V, 507; VI, 106; X, 263; XIX, 384.

62. "Charles Elwood Reviewed," *Works,* IV, 355.

63. "The Giobertian Philosophy," *Brownson's Quarterly Review* (1864), reprinted in *Works,* II, 250; and "The Cartesian Doubt," *Catholic World* (1867), reprinted in *Works,* II, 373.

64. *Christian Examiner,* 21 (1836), 46.

65. "The Giobertian Philosophy," *Works*, II, 251.

66. "The Philosophy of History," *Works*, IV, 369, 384.

67. "Introduction," *Brownson's Quarterly Review*, 1 (1844), 8. See also a passage containing the astonishing assertion that Hegel reproduces Holbach's *Système de la Nature* in "Transcendentalism," *Brownson's Quarterly Review* (1873), reprinted in *Works*, II, 76; and "The Giobertian Philosophy," *Works*, II, 251.

68. Repeated frequently, e.g., *Works*, I, 401; II, 38, 71, 268; VI, 97; VIII, 384; IX, 273; XI, 229. Brownson refers several times to Hegel's *das Ideen*, a mistake for *Das Ideelle*, which does not inspire confidence in his reading of Hegel or close knowledge of German (cf. *Works*, VIII, 384; III, 502).

69. *Works*, I, 401; II, 268; III, 502, 504; XI, 229.

70. "Spiritual Despotism," *Brownson's Quarterly Review* (1857), reprinted in *Works*, VII, 486.

71. "Catholicity and Naturalism" (1865), *Works*, VIII, 352; "Holy Communion —Transubstantiation," *Brownson's Quarterly Review* (1874), reprinted in *Works*, VIII, 268; and "Refutation of Atheism," *Brownson's Quarterly Review* (1873), reprinted in *Works*, II, 38.

72. A fuller discussion of Brownson's intellectual development, with stress on social and political questions, is given in Arthur M. Schlesinger, Jr., *Orestes A. Brownson: A Pilgrim's Progress* (Boston: Little, Brown, 1939).

73. *Memoirs of Margaret Fuller Ossoli*, ed. Ralph Waldo Emerson, William Henry Channing, and James Freeman Clarke (Boston: Phillips, Sampson, 1852), I, 127.

74. J. G. Fichte, *Werke* (Berlin, 1843), II, 323. "Bezwingen" in the text of the *Memoirs* is certainly an error, either of the transcriber or printer, for "zu zwingen."

75. *Life Without and Life Within* (Boston: Brown, Taggard and Chase, 1860), p. 15. First appeared in the *Dial*, 1 (1841), 342.

76. *Memoirs*, I, 165.

77. See note 73.

78. *Memoirs*, I, 175.

79. Coleridge's lecture "On Poesy or Art" was first printed in *Literary Remains* (vol. 1, 1836). Sara Coleridge's edition in *Notes and Lectures* (1849) gives a list of the parallels to Schelling's lecture.

80. *New York Daily Tribune*, 9 July 1846. Inaccessible. Listed in Mason Wade's bibliography, *The Writings of Margaret Fuller* (New York: Viking, 1941), p. 600.

81. *Art, Literature and the Drama* (Boston: Roberts Brothers, 1875), p. 323; originally appeared in the *New York Daily Tribune* of 25 July 1846.

82. *Memoirs*, I, 123.

"Victor Cousin and American Transcendentalism"

Georges J. Joyaux*

In the intellectual history of France, Victor Cousin (1792–1867) marks the idealistic reaction of the nineteenth century against the materialism of the eighteenth. His Eclecticism attempted to synthetize into a new unity all that was best in the various philosophical systems. Though Cousin never presented a complete *exposé* of his theory in a single work, his philosophical speculations achieved wide popularity in the first half of the nineteenth century, first through his well-attended lectures—at the Sorbonne and later at the Ecole Normale Supérieure—and through his numerous publications.

The material for this paper was gathered in a study of American periodicals published in the first half of the nineteenth century.[1] Its objective is to examine the reception of Victor Cousin and his Eclecticism by the contemporary American periodical press, and to throw some light on the much-debated question of the relations between American Transcendentalism and French Eclecticism.

Transcendentalism and Eclecticism are the two chief philosophical systems which colored American and French intellectual history respectively during the first half of the nineteenth century. Since the high point of Eclecticism preceded that of American Transcendentalism by about a decade, the question of the latter's debt to the former has long elicited discussion. The answers tend to fall into two categories. Some, as William Girard, "would like to depreciate the whole German influence and substitute in first place that of Cousin, Maine de Biran, Jouffroy and Madame de Staël." Others, such as Walter Leighton or Octavius Frothingham, feel that "the influence of French philosophy was not particularly predominant" on American transcendentalism and that "the German idealists apparently appealed more strongly to the young idealistic philosophers of New England, than did the more rational, urbane, compromise philosophy of the French Eclectics."[2]

Certainly, a clear and definite answer to the question of Eclectic-

*Reprinted from *French Review*, 29 (December 1955), 117–130.

Transcendentalist influences is hard to give when one keeps in mind that the two systems are both philosophically eclectic in nature, and that, furthermore, both represented a phase of idealistic reaction. Idealism was in the air, and what the two systems have in common might not necessarily be the result of the influence of one on the other, but might rather be the reflection of the climate of opinion of the epoch.

The statistics found in this study are eloquent: in the first half of the nineteenth century there appeared eighty references to French philosophy in the files of American magazines. Only fourteen of them appeared during the first twenty-five years, while the rest, sixty-six, were published from 1828 to 1848, coinciding with the years of Cousin's success and the triumph of Eclecticism in France. Of these sixty-six references, all but fifteen deal with Eclecticism and its leader.[3]

The first reference to Cousin appeared in 1829, in the *North American Review*. In the fifty-six pages devoted to a review of four of Cousin's earlier works, the reviewer shows a very high opinion of Cousin and his works:

> Mr. Cousin unites, in a superior degree, most of the qualifications necessary for complete success in his writings . . . He combines the vivacity and fine taste that are in some degree natural to his countrymen, with the indefatigable industry, the wide research and patient meditation which, in these degenerate days, have been considered as almost peculiar to the Germans.

As to Eclecticism, the reviewer was rather cautious:

> We have already taken the liberty to express our doubts of the correctness of the peculiar theories of this writer; but we would not be understood to speak with confidence on the subject because we have not yet the means of ascertaining with precision what his views really are . . .[4]

The books reviewed were Cousin's first writings, some preceding Cousin's trip to Germany where he studied German philosophy at first hand. Also, it should be noted that the review came only a year after the publication—in French—of many of the books reviewed. A firm stand on the part of the reviewer would have been surprising, and it was to be expected that this first contact with French eclecticism would be cautious. At any rate, this first article clearly showed America's interest in France's intellectual life. This is confirmed by the comments made by Charles J. Ingersoll, in his 1823 oration before the American Philosophical Society, and reprinted in the *Christian Examiner*; Ingersoll, speaking in favor of a national literature, and for a greater intellectual independence from England declared:

We fear that at the present moment English books want much which we need .... In England there is a great want of philosophy in the true sense of the word ..., and although we have little respect for the rash generalizations of the bold and eloquent Cousin, yet, the interest which his metaphysics awaken in Paris is, in our estimation a better presage than the lethargy which prevails on such topics in England.[5]

More important is the informative essay published in the *American Quarterly Review* (December, 1831), in which the writer gives a very detailed outline of Cousin's philosophical system, displaying throughout a thorough acquaintance with the subject. "Cousin," the reviewer remarks, ". . . is no disciple of any of the schools which are commonly thought to include all philosophies . . . Indeed, he is so original that it is not easy to convey within reasonable limits any just idea of the character, origin and aim of his philosophy."

After a lengthy presentation of Eclecticism, the reviewer denies the rightness of Cousin's method of synthesis, agreeing that while "the various truths or various parts of truth can be gathered and purified from all admixture, and freed from undue limitation and aptly arranged and moulded into a new unity," the philosopher omits one condition, that "the new truth which is to grow out of the operation shall itself create and direct the operation and give to it vitality, order and certainty . . ."[6]

Though not in complete agreement with Cousin's doctrine, the author praises him for "the novelty and comprehensiveness of his views and for the energy and eloquence with which he urges them upon his hearers and upon the rest of the world." "His influence is great and growing" the reviewer believes, "and recently his name has passed the Atlantic and is beginning to be heard here, widely if not loudly."

In conclusion the reviewer declares: "We have no doubt that his lectures will be of great and wide use in imparting to thinking minds a sympathetic activity and freedom." However, the reviewer did not show much enthusiasm for the system itself, adding that the lectures were not ". . . in any way positively instructive."[7]

The impetus given by Cousin to philosophical speculation in America formed the main topic of the next reference to Cousin in the *North American Review*. "Cousin's genius," the reviewer wrote, "alike brilliant and profound, has given an attraction to the subject of metaphysics, altogether unprecedented in the annals of philosophy." He concluded that though Cousin's system could not be regarded as the ultimatum of intellectual philosophy, "yet the Science [was] deeply indebted to him for the new light bestowed by his genius, and the attraction with which he has clothed a subject often unjustly and ignorantly depreciated."[8]

In 1834 Caleb Sprague Henry, professor of philosophy at New York University, and a Christian Transcendentalist,[9] published his translation of Cousin's *Elements of Psychology*. The same year the first reviewer of Henry's translation took advantage of the occasion to praise Cousin for his stylistic facility, in contrast to that "dry and frigid abstractness which [one] expects in metaphysical writers." On the whole, the reviewer felt that Cousin's work was "particularly adapted to the taste of the English world," because there was in it "less of that misty vagueness of conception, and repulsive technicality of style, which have been complained of in the philosophers of the ideal school."[10]

After the publication of Henry's translation, references in the journals to Cousin and Eclecticism increased considerably, and no reviewer of Henry's *Elements of Psychology* failed to devote a large part of his comments to a discussion of Eclecticism.

In 1835, in a review of Cousin's works on education—he wrote reports on the educational systems in Prussia and Holland—we find the following remarks:

> The name and character of Mr. Cousin are already familiar to our readers. We have, on more than one occasion, been led to notice his labors in the great field of intellectual philosophy, and if we have not been able to give our unqualified concurrence to all his theories upon that subject, we have never risen from the perusal of any of his works without fresh admiration of his learning, eloquence and indefatigable industry.

Here again, the founder of Eclecticism is compared to the German philosophers, and he is praised for the clarity of his expression as opposed to the abstruseness of German philosophical writings. Furthermore, the reviewer added, Cousin combines "the vivacity and brilliancy of the French school of Literature, with the immense erudition and dogged perseverance in study [of the German scholars]."[11]

In 1836 there appeared an interesting review of three of Cousin's works—two in their American editions—by Orestes A. Brownson, an early member of the transcendentalist group. In his introduction Brownson wrote: "These works have attracted already considerable attention among us, and are beginning to exert no little influence on our philosophical speculations." Surprisingly enough, Brownson felt that Cousin's works would afford "important aid in rescuing the church and religious matters in general from their present lamentable condition." Though later, on religious grounds, he reversed his attitude and he attacked both Eclecticism and Cousin, here he reviewed Eclecticism as a reaction against the skepticism and materialism of the eighteenth century. Therefore, he welcomed it as a possible way to end the war between Religion and Philosophy:

Everybody knows that our Religion and our Philosophy are at war. Instead of quarreling . . . , we should re-examine our philosophy and inquire if there be not a philosophy true to human nature, and able to explain and verify instead of destroying the religious beliefs of mankind . . . We evidently need such a philosophy; such a philosophy we believe there is and we know of no works so well fitted to assist us in finding it as those of Mr. Cousin.

On the whole Brownson felt that not only had Cousin brought about the downfall of materialism, but also he had broken ground for a new philosophy, "which shall include them all, and yet be itself unlike any of them."[12]

The next year, in a review of Theodore Jouffroy's *Cours de Droit Naturel,* Brownson devoted several pages to Cousin, Jouffroy's master.[13] For the first time, in many reviews, Eclecticism and Transcendentalism were joined. Comparing French Eclecticism with German and American Transcendentalism, Brownson distinguished between those men "who deem themselves competent to construct a new philosophy of man and universe by means of speculation alone," and those "who will attach no scientific value to any metaphysical system which is not a legitimate induction from facts patiently collected, scrupulously analyzed, and accurately classed." Turning on the critics of French Eclecticism, he added:

If it be meant that the French Eclectics are transcendental in the sense these last are, we have no objection . . . , but this is not the case. They who call them Transcendentalists with the feeling that Transcendentalism is an accusation, mean to identify them with the other class, the speculators, the systematizers . . . But in this sense, the Eclectics are not transcendentalist. Cousin, their acknowledged chief, bases his whole system on psychology.

Brownson then endeavors to demonstrate that French Eclecticism is strictly scientific and experimental. To quote Cousin, adds Brownson, "there is and there can be no sound philosophy which does not begin with the observation or analysis of the facts of consciousness . . . ," and Cousin "does not begin with what ought to be in the consciousness . . . , [but] what is." The observation of facts is then completed by the inductive method: "We cannot remain in the observation of facts, we are compelled to add facts together and find their sum total . . . These two methods of activity of the Reason, observation and induction, constitute Cousin's method." In conclusion, Brownson again emphasizes that French Electicism is not of German origin: "It received its impulse, its method, and its direction from Royer-Collard, who was, as everybody knows, the founder of the Scotch school."[14]

In 1838, George Ripley, an important member of the Transcendentalist group and the founder of Brook Farm, included large excerpts from the philosophical writings of Cousin, Constant and Jouffroy, in the first volumes of his new *Specimens of Foreign Standard Literature.* As Gohdes points out, "some significance may be attached to the fact that Ripley chose, as the first of his *Specimens,* not German idealism, but the spiritual philosophy of France."[15] These volumes were very well received. An article published in the *Boston Quarterly Review* praised Ripley for his project, since the reviewer felt that Americans had "much to learn in the department of philosophy, theology and history, from the literatures of France and Germany." French writings in general, and in particular the philosophical writings of the Eclectics were praised for their underlying democratic ideals: "(Their) writings breathe altogether more of a democratic spirit than do those of the English. Those of the French are altogether more democratic than the writings of American scholars themselves." In conclusion the reviewer declared that Cousin, Constant, Jouffroy were three authors who are an honor to France and mankind, while Cousin, "the chief of the new French school," was "if not the first, at least one of the first philosophers of the age."[16]

The *Christian Examiner* raised a dissenting voice, giving forty pages to a well documented discussion of Eclecticism. The attitude of the author of the article was summed up in his conclusion:

> Eclecticism cannot, strictly speaking, be applied to mental philosophy. It may be employed in matters of taste or utility, but in an affair of argument it is entirely inapplicable . . . He that carries in his own hand the measuring rod by which the truth of the system can be tested, must have first constructed a true system of his own. Eclecticism, therefore, is below the dignity of a true philosopher; and if we trace its history, we shall find that it has always originated from ignorance of the true method of philosophysing, from the darkness and perplexity of the human race with reference to difficult subjects, or from a timid disposition to sacrifice truth, in order to tranquillize the minds of heated partisans.[17]

Again in 1838 Rufus Dawes hurled another blast at Cousin in *The Hesperian.* Comparing Swedenborg to Cousin, the author declared: "The writings of that illustrious man [Swedenborg] contain all that is valuable in the French philosophy of the day, and infinitely more, in which the severest analysis and the closest logic cannot detect a fault."[18]

The second edition of Henry's translation from Cousin (1838), also received very favorable reviews. In the words of a contributor to *The Biblical Repository,* a conservative Presbyterian journal, the work "was a splendid production." Quoting from other magazines, he called it "the most important work on Locke since the *Nouveaux Essais* of Leibnitz," and "perhaps the greatest masterpiece of philosophical criticism ever exhibited to the public." In the reviewer's opinion, Cousin's American reputation was growing rapidly, and Henry's translation "had been introduced into a number of our most respectable universities and colleges."[19]

Likewise in the *Boston Quarterly Review* there appeared another essay in defense of Cousin:

> [He] is thought by many in this country to be merely a philosophical dreamer, a fanciful framer of hypotheses, a bold generalizer without solid judgment or true science . . . But nothing is more unjust than this impression. Mr. Cousin is the farthest in the world from being a mere theorizer, or from founding his philosophy, as some allege, on mere "a priori" reasoning.

The author, Brownson perhaps, insisted that "Cousin has very little in common with those [we] are in the habit of calling Transcendentalists." The latter, the reviewer felt, were of German origin; as to Cousin, "he cannot be classed with Kant, nor with any of the Germans. He has all that Germany can give, which is worth having, and much that Germany cannot give." Though Cousin had much in common with the Scotch school, the reviewer continued, "he leaves that school at an immeasurable distance behind him." And, after quoting at great length from the work reviewed, he concluded: "Cousin's method is the experimental method of modern philosophy itself, the only method philosophy has been permitted to follow since Bacon and Descartes."[20]

The same year, 1839, Ripley's *Specimens of Foreign Standard Literature*—the translations from Cousin, Constant and Jouffroy—again received laudatory reviews. A short notice published in the *Knickerbocker* declared that the three authors selected ". . . are the brightest stars in the philosophical constellation of France." Though mindful that Cousin "had been censured as an eclectic and as advocating a characterless philosophy," the reviewer expressed his gratitude "to him, who has by turns, interpreted ancient and modern doctrines, and revealed to us the sublimity of Plato, the casuistry of Descartes, and juxtaposition with the sensualism and transcendentalism of Locke and Kant."[21]

Quite different, however, was the judgment of a contributer to the *Princeton Review* who devoted seventy pages to a discussion of Cousin's Eclecticism and German Transcendentalism. America's need for a "new and American-born philosophy," the writer felt, will not be fulfilled "so long as we received our philosophemata by a double transportation, from Germany via France, in parcels to suit the importers." In an attempt to create an American philosophy, some young philosophers were busily learning French and German, while those who could not were striving ". . . to gather into one the Sibylline oracles and abortive scraps of the gifted but indolent Coleridge, and his gaping imitators, or in default of this sit at the urn of dilute wisdom, and sip the thrice-drawn infusion of English from French and French from German."[22]

To the author of this article, Cousin's Eclecticism was "a conduit from the stream of German transcendentalism at the most corrupt part of its current," and the writer expressed hope that the progress made by "this system of abomination among us,"[23] could be checked.

The irreconcilable opposition which he saw between Eclecticism and Christianity was the basis for the *Princeton Review's* bitter assault on Cousin's speculations. Likewise German transcendentalism came in for rebuke: "In the French imitation, no less than in the German original, there is a perpetual self-delusion practised by the philosopher who plays with words as a child with lettered cards, and combines what ought to be the symbols of thought into expressions unmeaning and self-contradictory."[24]

Naturally, American transcendentalism itself was tarred with the same brush, and the reviewer singled out Ralph Waldo Emerson, the flag-bearer of the movement, as the chief American legatee of Cousin. In Emerson's Famous Divinity Address at Harvard he saw "an alarming symptom of the progress among us of [Cousin's] system," and after reading the address he "wanted words with which to express [his] sense of the nonsense and impiety which pervade it."[25]

The following year, 1840, a contributor to the *Boston Quarterly Review* undertook to answer these and similar charges against American transcendentalism. In defense of the movement, he wrote:

> It is really of American origin, and the prominent actors in it were carried away by it even before they formed an acquaintance with French or German metaphysics; and their attachment to the literatures of France and Germany is not the effect of their connexion with the movement, but the cause.[26]

Also, in 1840 William Henry Channing, one of the earliest advocates of socialism in the United States, published his translation of Jouffroy's *Introduction to Ethics* as the volumes V and VI of Ripley's *Specimens.* This naturally increased the number of references to Cousin, as the commentators of Jouffroy—Cousin's most important disciple—could not avoid referring to his master. In a review of these volumes in the *Christian Examiner*, Samuel Osgood expressed what seems to be a fair view of the part played by Cousin in the intellectual development of America: "German and English philosophers are indebted to the French for the clearest exhibitions of their various systems. . . . We are indebted to Cousin for our clearest idea of German philosophy." Altogether this seems to have been Cousin's greatest contribution to the transcendentalist movement, for as the reviewer puts its, German philosophical thought "must first pass through the French mint, [to] take the form and beauty that fit it for practical purposes."[27]

In the next few years nothing of importance is added to the list of references to Cousin, except for several laudatory reviews which emphasized his importance as the link between America and Germany. Thus, in the *American Eclectic*, a reprint of Cousin's article on "Kant and his Philosophy" was introduced with these words:

> It is now sixty years since the Critical Philosophy was first submitted to the judgment of a restless and inquiring age. Its merits are still undetermined, but its success has been much less complete than the sanguine author anticipated. In Germany, indeed, the new system gained the ascendancy, but elsewhere its progress was slow . . . [28]

Explaining this partial failure, the writer added: "The deep thinking German [Kant] has been seldom understood except by his reflective and speculative countrymen." Cousin's labors, the reviewer felt, "will contribute something to the removal of these doubts," and help in making Kant and his philosophy better understood in America. Indeed, the reviewer concluded, "we can think of no living writer . . . better qualified to become the faithful interpreter of the *Critical Philosophy*," adding furthermore, that "if he [Cousin] shall fail to render Kant intelligible, we may well conclude that the cause is hopeless."[29]

Even such a magazine as *The Ladies' Repository* urged its most intelligent female readers to skip the next popular novel, and read instead the *Philosophical Miscellanies* of Cousin, Constant and Jouffroy. However, a few paragraphs later the reviewer tempered his enthusiasm with a warning against Cousin's errors in religion: "We do not, of course, recommend the theological opinions of these men to the approval of our readers. They are often far enough from the true light."[30]

The same year, a contributor to the *Methodist Quarterly* declared that Cousin's great success was caused by "the boldness and originality of his ideas, (and) the eloquence and effectiveness with which they are urged upon his immense auditory." Though writing in a conservative magazine, the reviewer was evidently not aware of the theological implications of Cousin's philosophy. Unlike his colleague of *The Ladies' Repository*, he declared: "Though [Cousin] is a most absolute free-thinker in philosophy, he is also a Christian, a believer in religion and revolution; and his philosophy, instead of being infidel in its character or tendency is essentially Christian throughout."[31]

In 1841 the *North American Review* published a forty page essay on Eclecticism. In the subtitle, the reviewer, who later explained that

Cousin's doctrine must be pieced together from prefaces, lectures, and scraps of criticism, listed three of Cousin's works in translation. In the reviewer's words, "Cousin's success in this country is well attested by the appearance of these three translations . . . , one of which has passed on to a second edition and has been prepared as a text-book for use in some of our principal colleges." This reviewer, too, contrasted Cousin's clarity with the abstrusities of German metaphysicians, feeling that Cousin's great success resulted from his ability to express doctrines admittedly borrowed from the Scotch and Germans "with greater force and clearness . . . freed from objectionable peculiarities, and thus brought within the reach of a wider circle of readers."[32]

In 1842 Cousin's *An Epitome of the History of Philosophy*, in Henry's translation, was published in Boston. The work was hailed immediately as excellent and a contributor to *The Ladies' Repository* advocated its "immediate introduction as a text-book in all our schools."[33] The same year, the *Methodist Quarterly Review* devoted a long essay to Cousin's philosophy. The "tardy" acceptance of Eclecticism in America, the writer declared, was not surprising when one reflected "with what suspicion every metaphysical system, originating in France, is received on this side of the Atlantic," a suspicion normally extended by Americans to any kind of writing coming from France. Concluding his study, the author declared: "The works of Cousin, we have no doubt, will have a tendency to excite a spirit of philosophical inquiry in this country."[34]

By 1842, Cousin had reached the peak of his success in America. In the following years, the number of references to his philosophy and favorable reactions to it decreased considerably. In 1844, Orestes Brownson, who so far had contributed many interesting articles on Cousin and his Eclecticism, launched his own *Quarterly Review* on its brief career. Introducing the first issue, he declared:

> [In] the Boston Quarterly Review in 1839, I was still under the influence of the French school of philosophy founded by Mr. Cousin. That school took fast hold of me—completely subjecting me. It was long before I could master it and recover the free action and development of my own mind. I think I have finally mastered it; but I must not be understood as having rejected it. I am still a disciple of that school, though a free disciple, not a slave . . . I have obtained a clear, consistent, well-defined system of philosophy, satisfactory to my own mind; but, in obtaining it, I have assimilated no small share of the teachings of that school, and I cannot but feel myself largely its debtor.

But though he still held a high opinion of the Eclectic school and ranked its founder "along-side Abelard, Descartes, Locke, Leibnitz, and Schelling,"[35] Brownson's conversion to Catholicism brought a complete change in its attitude. Reviewing Jouffroy's *Cours de Droit Naturel*, he firmly stated that he had repudiated his former allegiance to Eclecticism, and undertook to "assign some of the reasons which have finally operated to change [his] views, and to induce [him] to reject its principal doctrines as insufficient, false or mischevious." In essence, Brownson felt that the Eclectics committed "one fatal error—that of assuming that religion and philosophy do not differ as to their matter, but only as to their form." This was true not only of Eclecticism, but of contemporary philosophy as a whole, which was at war with religion:

> The Eclectic school, the modern German school, and even our liberal Christians . . . , really reject all supernatural revelation in believing themselves able to explain its mysteries. To explain, in the sense these understand it, is to make intrinsically evident to natural reason. A supernatural revelation must necessarily contain some mysteries. A mystery is something whose intrinsic truth is inevident to natural reason. The pretended explanation of a real mystery is never its explanation, but always its rejection.[36]

By the late forties Cousin's influence in American thinking was fast disappearing. Eclecticism in its turn was overthrown by the Positivism of Auguste Comte (the first reference to Comte dates from 1846), and references to Cousin and his school gradually disappear.

The last important reference to Cousin appeared in 1848, when *De Bow's Review* published five articles dealing with the Eclectic school. Feeling that much of the opposition to Eclecticism arose from its name, the critic endeavored to give a better presentation of the doctrine:

> Eclecticism does not attempt to admit as both true, such opposites as sensualism and spiritualism. After each has developed in its own way, Eclecticism sets about to reunite them . . . In Eclecticism, sensualism and spiritualism meet to reconcile their differences, to explain, illustrate and verify each other.[37]

Tracing the development of philosophical ideas in France during the last century, he concluded: "Cousin and Eclecticism may be said to be the last word, the last grand product and the highest and most perfect expression, not only of the philosophy of the eighteenth and nineteenth centuries, but also of all the antecedent times." Also, he regretted that not all of Cousin's works were translated into English, for "he is undoubtedly the greatest dialectician, the ablest master of his language, and the most erudite scholar that has lived in modern times."[38]

From this survey of American reception of Cousin and French Eclecticism, it appears that Cousin's doctrine was widely known in America and generally well received, lending support to Howard Mumford Jones's assertion that "no French thinker in the nineteenth century was more vigorously debated and discussed in the United States in our epoch (1750–1848)."[39] Much of the interest devoted to Cousin originated in the transcendentalist *milieu*, most of it paralleled closely the rise and development of transcendentalism.[40]

It would be wrong, of course, to assign a single source to American transcendentalism, and still more incorrect to find it in Eclecticism. However, if as Jones says, "Cousin was not the European foster-father of Transcendentalism—and he was not—"[41] it seems only fair to add that he was nevertheless an important contributor to the philosophical evolution of America, and certainly a collateral contribution to the development of American transcendentalism. Acting as a catalyst, Cousin assisted Americans in assimilation of German thought: "If Germany is known as the land of speculators, scholars, philosophers, France seems to have been appointed to state the results of German speculation in clear, distinct propositions and practical rules."[42] Finally and not the least, Cousin had a significant role in stimulating metaphysical speculations among young American philosophers.

Notes

1. "French Thought in American Magazines, 1800–1848" (Ph.D. diss., Michigan State College, 1951).

2. Howard Mumford Jones, *America and French Culture 1750–1848* (Chapel Hill: University of North Carolina Press, 1927), pp. 461–462.

3. These figures confirm Clarence Gohdes's opinion that "the influence of French Eclecticism upon the development of American transcendentalism deserves a special study" (see *The Periodicals of American Transcendentalism* [Durham: Duke University Press, 1931], p. 54).

4. *North American Review*, 20 (July 1829), 67–69. The four works reviewed were: *Œuvres de Platon* (1822–1828), *Fragments philosophiques* (1826), *Cours de philosophie* (1828), and *Nouveaux Fragments philosophiques* (1828). It is interesting to notice that here, as in many other cases, Cousin's works were reviewed in their French dress, which speaks highly of American intellectual leaders' acquaintance with the French language.

5. *Christian Examiner*, 7 (January 1830), 292.

6. *American Quarterly Review*, 10 (December 1831), 291–293.

7. *American Quarterly Review* (December 1831), pp. 301–304.

8. *North American Review*, 35 (July 1832), 19, 23.

9. Ronald Vale Wells, *Three Christian Transcendentalists: James Marsh, Caleb Sprague Henry, Frederic Henry Hedge* (New York: Columbia University Press, 1943).

10. *Literary and Theological Review*, 1 (December 1834), 691–692.

11. *North American Review*, 11 (April 1835), 512.

12. *Christian Examiner*, 21 (September 1836), 34–38.

13. Again Brownson expressed his faith in the new paths of investigation

opened by Cousin's speculations: ". . . We believe an acquaintance with the researches [of the French Eclectics] . . . , a very important acquisition in the work of elaborating a better philosophy than any which has hitherto prevailed among us" (see *Christian Examiner*, 22 [May 1837], 185).

14. *Christian Examiner* (May 1837), pp. 187–193.
15. Gohdes, *Periodicals*, p. 54.
16. *Boston Quarterly Review*, 1 (October 1838), 438–443.
17. *Christian Examiner*, 4 (March 1839), 35.
18. *Hesperian*, 2 (April 1839), 482.
19. *Biblical Repository*, 1 (January 1839), 247.
20. *Boston Quarterly Review*, 3 (January 1839), 27, 35.
21. *Knickerbocker Magazine*, 13 (March 1839), 353.
22. *Princeton Review*, 11 (January 1839), 42–43.
23. *Princeton Review* (January 1839), pp. 56, 92.
24. *Princeton Review* (January 1839), p. 88.
25. *Princeton Review* (January 1839), pp. 92, 95.

26. *Boston Quarterly Review*, 3 (July 1840), 271. On the whole, this position is not unlike that reached by more recent students of the transcendental revolution. See Professor René Wellek's study of "Emerson and German Transcendentalism," *New England Quarterly*, 16 (March 1943), 41–62.

27. *Christian Examiner*, 28 (March 1840), 137–138.

28. *American Eclectic*, 1 (March 1841), 276. This article originally appeared in *La Revue des Deux Mondes*.

29. *American Eclectic* (March 1841), pp. 277–278.
30. *Ladies' Repository*, 1 (March 1841), 159.
31. *Methodist Quarterly Review*, 1 (July 1841), 336–337.
32. *North American Review*, 3 (July 1841), 1, 3.
33. *Ladies' Repository*, 2 (April 1842), 127.
34. *Methodist Quarterly Review*, 2 (April 1842), 165, 192.
35. *Brownson's Quarterly Review*, 1 (January 1844), 6–7.

36. *Brownson's Quarterly Review*, 2 (January 1845), 54–57. It is clear, however, that despite this reversal of opinion during the later years of the movement, Brownson, who was influential in spreading the gospel of transcendentalism, had a large share in introducing and popularizing Cousin's theories in America. For the past ten years Brownson had been an "avowed disciple of the foreign master [Cousin]," and many of the latter's ideas found their way into transcendental circles through Brownson's articles in leading New England magazines (see Gohdes, *Periodicals*, p. 54).

37. *De Bow's Review*, 5 (January 1848), 62–63.
38. *De Bow's Review*, 5 (March 1848), 216.

39. Jones, *America and French Culture*, p. 463. His works, in translation, went through several American editions during his life time, and were even chosen as text books for use in colleges.

40. Though most of the material discussed in this paper originated in New England, we should point out that Cousin's influence spread as well throughout the country. Thus, Henry P. Tappan, President of the University of Michigan, had an almost complete collection of Cousin's works—most of them in the original—and "offered a course in the History of Philosophy which included as one of three topics 'Cousin and Eclecticism'" (*Michigan History*, 36 [September 1952], 301).

41. Jones, *America and French Culture*, p. 471.
42. *United States Magazine and Democratic Review*, 15 (July 1844), 22.

"Transcendentalism and the Beginnings of Church Reform"

William R. Hutchison*

The late eminent historian James G. Randall once remarked that "there are times when the avoidance of a readable formula of broad interpretation requires downright force of character." Everyone likes brief definitions which are not only readable but recallable, and most writers feel under a certain obligation to provide them if possible. But many significant historical movements defy reduction to rough-and-ready formulae; and the Transcendental Movement clearly is one of that class. Almost any concise definition of the methods and aims of this group will either be theoretically broad enough to include all philosophical idealists from Plato through Bradley or else so narrowly technical as to exclude persons who were consciously and actively a part of what is called American Transcendentalism.

The very name "Transcendentalism," unfortunately, suggests a more extensive agreement in technical philosophy than actually existed in the group; and its members, fully aware of this, did all they could to avoid having that name attached to their movement. If there had to be a party designation, this, they thought, was an improper one, and they tried to bring other names into currency. "Disciples of the Newness" or simply the "New School" were favorite and sufficiently vague terms; "The Symposium" was Alcott's preferred name for their Club; Orestes Brownson tried for years to popularize the term "Eclecticism"; and the designation "Hedge's Club" did make some headway with the public. When they finally began answering to the name "Transcendentalists," it was not because they had come to terms with a set of philosophical principles that all could accept but because the public, delighted with the term, had refused to accept any other.

The name was deplored not as an entire misrepresentation of the spirit and aims of the group, for that it certainly was not, but rather as an ambiguous term which had several popular and several technical

*Reprinted from *The Transcendentalist Ministers: Church Reform in the New England Renaissance* (New Haven: Yale University Press, 1959), pp. 22–51.

definitions, no one of which was suitable for what the American group had in common.

Popularly, the adjective "transcendental" was affixed to any philosophy thought to be "enthusiastic, mystical, extravagant, impractical, ethereal, supernatural, vague, abstruse, [or] lacking in common sense."[1] Sir William Schwenck Gilbert's parody, in *Patience*, of transcendental aestheticism reflected both the common man's disdain for such nonsense and his tendency to confuse Transcendentalism with such distantly related groups as the medievalist Pre-Raphaelite Brotherhood:

> If you're anxious for to shine in the high aesthetic
>   line, as a man of culture rare,
> You must get up all the germs of the Transcendental
>   terms, and plant them everywhere.
> You must lie among the daisies and discourse in
>   novel phrases of your complicated state of mind
> (The meaning doesn't matter if it's only idle
>   chatter of a transcendental kind)...
> Though the Philistines may jostle, you will rank
>   as an apostle in the high aesthetic band,
> If you walk down Piccadilly with a poppy or a
>   lily in your medieval hand...

The technical definitions were usually, though not invariably, more rigorous than the popular ones. Perhaps the most specific meaning the term was ever to enjoy was given to it by Immanuel Kant, who first coined the term for the kind of application it was to have in nineteenth-century usage. The "transcendental philosophy" which Kant proposed, and for which he provided the "architectonic plan" in his *Critique of Pure Reason*, was to be a systematic exposition of the nature and conditions of a priori knowledge. This philosophy would concern itself, he said, "not so much with objects as with the mode of our knowledge of objects in so far as this mode of knowledge is to be possible *a priori*."[2]

According to Kant, the contribution of Pure Reason is its provision of the "forms" of sensibility and the "categories" of understanding which are imposed upon sensory material by the perceiving mind. Concepts such as space, time, and causality belong to the nature of the human mind, and thus are logically prior to experience, even though in a chronological sense "all our knowledge begins with experience." The mind is furnished with pure concepts and forms of intuition which it could not obtain through induction but which are necessary conditions for a reliable knowledge of the world of phenomena.[3]

Kant set definite limits to the area within which Pure Reason can function. He made a distinction between the "transcendental" concepts which relate to the substructure of experience and those "transcendent" concepts which have to do with a sphere of reality that is beyond experience. Such objects of thought as God, freedom, and immortality, he argued, are "transcendent" (rather than transcendental) and are known by Practical Reason, not by Pure Reason. These two spheres of knowledge, he explained, must not be confused, for the objects in each are not equally knowable. Practical Reason does make possible a knowledge of "transcendent" things which is sufficient to guide moral action, but it cannot provide the scientifically accurate account which is gained in the experiential realm by the interworkings of Pure Reason and the faculties of sense perception.[4]

The post-Kantian idealists of Europe accepted the spirit and many of the hints of Kant's system without always observing this distinction between the two types of Reason and the proper functions of each. German idealists, for example, far from agreeing with Kant that the conclusions of the Practical Reason could not be the basis for reliable scientific knowledge, sought to "unify" his system by removing or blurring the distinction between Pure and Practical Reason, and by making a single "self-determining spiritual principle"—a unified "Reason"—the common basis for their variously articulated systems of knowledge. The most important of these revisers of Kant were Fichte, Schelling, and Hegel, but such lesser figures as Jacobi, Schiller, Richter, Novalis, Schlegel, and Baader each contributed in his own way to the same development.[5]

Still another turn was given to the definition of the transcendental method by the French Eclectic School dominated by Victor Cousin and Theodore Jouffroy. The name given this school suggests accurately what they thought the true philosophy would be, namely an extraction and recombining of the best from all other systems; but an epistemological method of determining what is "best" in any philosophy had also to be selected, and their insistence upon "psychological introspection" as "the supreme criterion of philosophical truth" is the primary justification for linking them to the German post-Kantian idealists, and particularly to Schelling. What differentiates them, however, from the Germans is their insistence upon objective validation, through both psychological and historical analysis, for the truths given in intuition.[6]

Coleridge and Carlyle, whose transmission of German idealism was especially important in the early stages of the American Transcendental Movement, provided no systematic redefinition of transcendentalism, but in the manner of the Eclectics brought some of its elements into bold relief. Coleridge, drawing most heavily on Schelling's philosophy, stressed the introspective method, the distinction between Reason and Understanding, and an evolutionary theory of natural-spiritual "correspondences" derived from Schelling's *Naturphilosophie*. Carlyle made pronounced use of Fichte's assertive "transcendental ego."[7]

The American school of idealists, who followed Coleridge in a vast oversimplification of the relations between Reason and Understanding, sometimes invoked the name of Kant in their pursuit of speculations which Kant would have regarded as unsound, and attached the term "transcendental" to concepts which he had labeled "transcendent." As Francis Bowen of Harvard wrote in 1877:

> Kant's influence was but indirect, and his opinions were imperfectly known. . . . Hence it was, that, misled by the term Transcendentalism, applied to his philosophy as a whole, and by his doctrine of the subjective character of space and time, the opinion became general, that his system was rather Platonic than Aristotelian, placing the essence of things and the characteristics of true knowledge in the realm of pure ideas and supersensual intuitions of the truth,— the very region, according to his philosophy, of necessary illusions and abortive attempts of the intellect to overstep its natural boundaries.[8]

Thus any claim on the part of the Concord group to be thoroughgoing disciples of Kant would have been unjustified. But in fact their misapprehensions of the Kantian system did not result in any such claim. They acknowledged varying degrees of indebtedness to the critics and reinterpreters of Kant. And they knew the extent to which they had drawn upon Plato, Neoplatonism, Swedenborg, and Oriental religions, together with the concepts of universal order in Newton and Paley, the mystical elements in American Puritanism, and the moral theories of the Scottish philosophy.[9] They resisted the "Transcendentalist" tag, then, not only because its popular connotations were insulting and its technical meaning uncertain, but also because they knew the name would mislead others into expecting from them a concerted adherence to one or another of the systems going by that name.

The Transcendentalists' fears in this respect were only too well borne out in later assessments of their movement. Although most writers have recognized that their essential agreements were not in technical philosophy, a few have devised "readable formulas" which exclude one or more of the most active participants. Orestes Brownson, Theodore Parker, Bronson Alcott, and even Ralph Waldo Emerson have all been told by one writer or another that they do not deserve to be called Transcendentalists.[10]

The wide-eyed sense of discovery which has sometimes been manifested by such revisionists would no doubt have caused innocent merriment at the meetings of Hedge's Club, for the Transcendentalists were fully aware of their disagreements and were rather prone to take pride in them. James Freeman Clarke once remarked that their group was called "the Club of the Like-Minded," and added that he supposed this was "because no two of us thought alike." All were agreed, as Emerson said, on the value of the "spiritual principle," but they did not always concur on the question of how it should be articulated and applied to contemporary problems. In epistemology, Parker, Brownson, and several others modified their faith in intuition by a Cousinian emphasis upon historical and scientific verifications. Despite general agreement on a symbolic theory of the universe, Thoreau's writings (his later ones in particular) showed an intense interest in recording natural facts for their own sake; and the tendencies toward Pantheism in the writings of Emerson were scrupulously avoided in the work of most of the others. In their attitudes toward religious institutions, most Transcendentalists dissented from the extreme iconoclasm of Parker and Emerson. In social theory, despite a common aim of protesting against commercial materialism, the spectrum of divergence extended from Thoreau's intense individualism, through the Utopian collectivism of George Ripley and W. H. Channing, to the radical reformism of Brownson. Only in the field of aesthetic theory—that is, in their advocacy of organic expression of the intuitions instead of classical regularity—does the group appear to have been free from significant internal disagreement.[11]

Their similarities of basic philosophy, of background, and of temperament, however, were more marked than these differences, and produced a unity of purpose which was as apparent to their amused contemporaries as it was to the Transcendentalists themselves. Most conspicuous among the unifying factors were their common tendency toward an intuitive philosophical method, their generally romantic approach to the universe, their almost invariable optimism about human nature, and their common feeling of participation in a movement of awakening and protest. Solutions differed, and so did the philosophical rationales for those solutions, but they agreed in placing "intuition" above all traditions and conformities, all sacred books and special revelations. They were fundamentally united in condemning formalism in religion and literature, Lockean "sensationalism" in philosophy, and all that was inhuman or materialistic in the popular social morality. Between such ways of thinking and the accepted attitudes of their time and place there was a gulf much wider than any of the divergences within Transcendentalist ranks.[12]

On September 19, 1836, Bronson Alcott recorded in his diary that the "Symposeum" (as he preferred to spell it) had had its first meeting that evening at George Ripley's home.[13] In attendance, besides Alcott and Ripley, had been Emerson, Brownson, Clarke, Convers Francis, and Frederic Henry Hedge. The main topic of conversation had been the organization and membership of the group, and though a high degree of informality had been agreed upon, it had been decided that membership should be by invitation. Hedge, who had made the original proposal of a Club in a letter to Emerson during the preceding summer, had suggested it be limited to ministers, but Emerson had demurred, insisting that Alcott, "a God-made priest," must not be excluded. The rule decided upon at the first meeting was "that no man should be admitted whose presence excluded any one topic," and with this criterion in mind the charter members agreed to invite four of the elder statesmen of Unitarianism—James Walker, Nathaniel Frothingham, Dr. Channing, and the free-thinking layman Jonathan Phillips. They also voted to include three young ministers—John Dwight, Cyrus Bartol, and W. H. Channing.[14]

Of the twenty-six persons who became closely associated with the Club and its activities, seventeen were Unitarian ministers—all but four, that is, of the male members. The story of Transcendental church reform centers around seven of them: Emerson and Ripley, who first announced and argued the program of reform; Parker, who carried forward and expanded that program in its later stages; Hedge, who above all others saw the reform of Unitarianism within the context of universal Christianity; and finally Clarke, Brownson, and W. H. Channing, founders, along with Parker, of experimental religious societies in which the Transcendentalist principles were applied. In addition, Convers Francis and William H. Furness were of importance in the earliest phase of the movement, while Bartol, Charles Brooks, Christopher Cranch, John Dwight, Sylvester Judd, Samuel Osgood, Caleb Stetson, and Jones Very made less tangible contributions during ministerial careers of varying length.[15]

To a remarkable degree the program of the Transcendentalists, and especially its application to formal religion, was set forth within a few months of the year 1836. Hedge understated the case when he recalled later that there had been, in that summer, "a promise in the air of a new era of intellectual life."[16] Among the Transcendentalist writings published in 1836 were Alcott's *Conversations on the Gospels*; Brownson's *New Views of Christianity, Society, and the Church*; Emerson's *Nature*; a highly controversial review by George Ripley of James Martineau's *Rationale of Religious Inquiry*; Furness' *Remarks on the Four Gospels*; a tract, *Christianity as a Purely Internal Principle*, from the pen of Francis; and a semitranscendental work by Charles Follen, *Religion and the Church*.[17] "The spiritualists," as Francis remarked at the time, appeared suddenly to be "taking the field in force."[18]

Alcott's *Conversations on the Gospels*, though not directly concerned with church reform, had an important part in the general excitement. This extraordinary man, who was largely self-educated and who for several years had been a peddler in Virginia, had already attracted notice as an educational innovator. During short-lived experiments in Boston, Philadelphia, and several Connecticut towns over the previous decade, he had pleased many by his ability and warmth, and frightened others with his strange methods and heterodox religious philosophy. In the Temple School, which he had established in Boston in 1834, the children were taught not by the usual devices of exposition and recitation but by the "conversational" method, which presupposed in the young an intuitive knowledge of religion and morality, and assumed that true teaching consists in "drawing them out" on these and other subjects.[19]

Bronson Alcott drew the children out on some subjects—childbirth, for example—which Bostonians thought unfit for childish lips, however plainly the underlying truths might be written on their hearts. When the Transcendentalists began their meetings in the fall of 1836, the storm of public criticism was still several months in the future but Alcott's record of the pedagogical conversations was about to be published, and Elizabeth Peabody, his collaborator, had already informed Alcott that she could not share responsibility for publishing those passages which, as she correctly foresaw, the public would consider indecent.[20] Until March of 1837, however, when the bitter attacks upon Alcott began, the Temple School was to the other Transcendentalists an inspiring example of successful reform activity.

Emerson's *Nature*, the most significant expression of Transcendentalist philosophical ideas to appear in this early period and one of the several great manifestoes of the movement, had been published in early September 1836 and was already being discussed among the *illuminati* when they first met on the nineteenth. Within a month, moreover, five hundred copies had been sold, and the first Unitarian reaction, in the *Register*, had been highly favorable, if somewhat puzzled.[21]

For the Transcendentalists the importance of *Nature* was its teaching of the correspondences between natural facts and spiritual truths, and its insistence upon the primacy of "spirit," whose laws nature both obeys and teaches. For Emerson himself, the book, and the warmth of its reception in some quarters, also had an importance in deciding the course of his career.

Thirty-three years of age in 1836, Emerson had spent the preceding decade in search of his vocation; and the story of that search reveals much about his relation to the Transcendentalist efforts of reform. After graduation from Harvard College in 1825 he had entered the Divinity School, where all efforts to apply himself steadily had been vitiated by the necessity of teaching, by bouts with rheumatism, and by an eye ailment which prevented him from writing or taking part in recitations. None of this was conducive to a very thorough theological indoctrination. But Emerson even in normal circumstances would not have been one to indulge in doctrinal certainties. His religious and vocational ideas were constantly in flux. Like his brother William, who had doubted himself out of the ministerial profession, Waldo was accustomed to harboring unorthodox ideas; and his preoccupation with the art of eloquent self-expression made him especially impatient with theological systems and parish details.

Settlement as a regular minister in 1829, while quieting some of his vocational doubts, had raised new ones. In March of that year he had been elected colleague of Henry Ware, Jr., at the Hanover Street Church, and he had assumed full charge of the pastorate shortly afterward. He had immediately discovered that he disliked leading public prayers, and his earlier doubts about institutional Christianity had been intensified when he was obliged to administer rites in which he did not wholly believe. Since he cared still less for visiting and similar parish duties, there had been little but preaching to make the young Emerson glad in his calling.[22]

The accumulation of doubts expressed itself in his sermons, in which he began to complain about what he called "historical Christianity." Too many pious people, he told his parishioners, "see God in Judea and in Egypt, in Moses and in Jesus, but not around them."[23] In February of 1832 he addressed a letter to the church members in which he suggested revisions in the service of Holy Communion. He wished, he said, to give that rite a more exclusively commemorative character and to diminish the role of the pastor in administering it.

Emerson, though he may have been aware from the beginning that separation from his pastorate could follow if he persevered in this protest, was undoubtedly sincere in thinking that his parishioners might agree to his proposals. "I had hoped," he said later, "to carry them with me." He had chosen the Communion as target of his protest not only because it seemed to him an especially noxious example of religious formalism, but also because the New England churches had had a long history of changing ideas on the subject. If the innovator sought an entering wedge, this was not an illogical one.[24]

The extent to which Emerson was acting as a "reformer" in this episode must nonetheless be stated cautiously. After a summer of negotiations, during which his proposals were rejected first by a special committee and then by the church membership, the young pastor concluded that he could not "go habitually to an institution which they esteem holiest [i.e. Communion] with indifference and dislike,"[25] and he accordingly submitted his resignation, which was accepted by the church in October. Charles Emerson thought that his brother's actions bore the stamp of the true reformer, and predicted that Waldo would found a new society conforming to his own ideals. But their aunt, the astute Mary Moody Emerson, scouted any such expectation. "You talk of his being a *reformer*," she protested to Charles:

A reformer! and beginn at the wrong end? annuling a simple rite
w'h has bound the followers of Jesus together for ages & announced
his resurrection! A reformer—who on earth with his genius is less
able to cope with opposition? Who with his good sense less *force*
of mind—and while it invents new universes is lost in the surrounding
halo ... No, he never loved his holy offices—and it is well he has left
them.[26]

What Mary Emerson saw more clearly than others was that while
Waldo might speak out in favor of sweeping changes, he would never
make himself responsible for carrying them through. He had placed
himself accurately among reformers when he said, in the sermon announcing his final refusal to administer the traditional Communion:
"That is the end of my opposition, that I am not interested in it." He
was content, as he told his parishioners in perfect sincerity, that the
rite should "stand to the end of the world."[27]

From the point of view of the intensely spiritual individualist, seeking to give vent to all positive intuitions of his own mind, lack of interest
was indeed a decisive objection against any human activity. But the
thoroughgoing reformer is likely to make lack of interest the beginning
rather than the end of his protest. From the latter perspective Emerson's
position could be thought a supine and even an irresponsible one.

During a nine-months' tour of Europe in 1833, Emerson apparently
did entertain thoughts of gathering "a parish of his own" on his return
to the United States; but subsequently he made no definite moves in this
direction. His nearest approach to the role of reformer in the next few
years was a suggestion to the church in New Bedford that he might
become their pastor if they would relieve him of the duties of administering Communion and leading prayers. Members of the New Bedford
pastoral committee were so shocked that they suppressed the letter in
which these proposals were made, and negotiations appear not to have
been resumed.[28]

If Emerson shrank from assuming the place of an active reformer,
however, he did not cease to be a Unitarian preacher. His break with
the ministerial profession had not been so complete as has sometimes
been imagined.[29] From 1834 through 1837 he occupied an average of
forty-one Sundays each year with ministerial duties, acting as regular
supply preacher for several extended periods at New Bedford and East
Lexington. At East Lexington his commitment ran from mid-1835 until
February 1838—nearly as long a period as he had served in the Second
Church. He did not preach for the last time until January 20, 1839.[30]

It does seem clear, however, that Emerson continued to preach
in this period mainly because his income was as yet only partially sustained by lecturing and writing. His attachment to the ministry declined
as those other ventures succeeded. The ending of negotiations with the

New Bedford church occurred shortly after his first season (winter 1833–34) as a public lecturer, and though he made a three-year arrangement at East Lexington in 1835, he was doing his best to get out of that responsibility by late 1837, after the public had responded favorably to *Nature* and to his "American Scholar" address of the summer of 1837.[31] The fact that he wrote his last new sermon in July of 1836, and that the frequency of his preaching declined from fifty Sundays in 1836 to thirty-four in 1837[32] would in fact give grounds to argue that the publication of *Nature* was at least as much a turning point in Emerson's career as was the resignation of 1832.

Another of the Transcendentalist group who eventually left the ministry was George Ripley.[33] In the fall of 1836 his resignation was four years in the future, and Ripley at this time was an active and highly respected member of the Boston clergy. Though still in his early thirties, he was, as O. B. Frothingham later recalled, "formal, punctilious, a trifle forbidding" in manner. Gold-rimmed spectacles betokened the scholar, but the intense black eyes behind them betrayed the reformer. He had been graduated at the head of his Harvard class in 1823 and then had taught mathematics in Harvard College while attending the Divinity School. His pastorate at Purchase Street Church, in Boston, had begun in 1826 under the most favorable auspices, the church having been organized expressly for him in what was then a fashionable quarter of the city.[34]

Ripley's high expectations for the success of this society were, however, not realized. The church did not become large or prosperous; and though this was partly because of a sudden movement of wealth and respectability from the Purchase Street area, the young preacher tended to berate himself and to doubt his qualifications as a parish minister.[35]

Another development which influenced Ripley's eventual decision to quit the ministry was the increasing liberalism of his theology as he became better acquainted with German speculations. His fondness for the new "transcendental" themes was evidenced throughout the 1830's in articles written for the *Christian Examiner;*[36] and his preaching began to show the effects of these investigations.

Ripley's sermon entitled "Jesus Christ, the Same Yesterday, Today, and Forever," first preached in 1834, anticipated not only his own later heresies but also Theodore Parker's celebrated discourse of 1841, *The Transient and Permanent in Christianity*. Ripley's sermon contained little of Parker's severe denunciation of the "transient" elements in the popular faith, but there was a similar conception of what constitutes permanence. "Religion," he said, drawing upon the theology of Schleiermacher, "has always existed, and in its essential elements is always the same. Its ideas are inseparable from man." When it is said that Christ is "the same yesterday, today, and forever," he explained, the true meaning is not the eternal existence of the person of Christ, but "the Immutability of the religious truths which he taught." Thus, parting from the standard Unitarian belief, Ripley portrayed Jesus as merely the enunciator, albeit the clearest and best enunciator, of principles which the human race has always known. The implication was that all religious systems, Christianity included, are based upon "natural" human sentiments and ideas, rather than upon supernatural occurrences.[37]

This interpretation was not likely to cause widespread alarm so long as it was merely preached to a congregation unschooled in theological niceties, and so long as Ripley and the other Transcendentalists did not attack specific doctrines of supernaturalism. An *Examiner* article by Ripley in November 1836, however, did adopt this more negative tack, arguing that Christian truths can be made plain to the human mind without the aid of miraculous confirmation. Since this article was "the opening gun in a long battle" between Transcendentalists and conservative Unitarians, fuller discussion of it is reserved for the chapters dealing with that controversy. Here it is enough to say that Ripley's turning of long-pondered "spiritualistic" ideas to an attack on Unitarian doctrines was one symptom of the increasing self-assurance of the younger intellectuals in the period when they first came together.

A volume somewhat ambitiously titled *New Views of Christianity, Society, and the Church* was published in December 1836 by Ripley's close friend, Orestes Brownson. It brought to public notice an emphasis in Transcendentalist thought which differed from either Emerson's or Ripley's. Though broadly critical of both Catholic and Protestant theology, the book's radicalism was far more social than doctrinal. It was the work of a man whose chief interest was to make Christianity a more suitable vehicle for social amelioration, and who after much searching believed he had found, in Unitarianism, the most promising starting-point for this endeavor.

Orestes Augustus Brownson was easily the most colorful of the Transcendentalists—as a speaker, writer, and disputant as well as in appearance. Well over six feet in height and powerfully built, he accented the strange complexities of his nature by wearing a black swallow-tail coat that fluttered behind him, a kerchief tied at the neck, books on each arm, a quid of tobacco in the mouth. In the pulpit he was a fiery and convincing orator, on the printed page a relentless logician.

Brownson had had the most turbulent personal religious history of all the Transcendentalists. As a Vermont farm lad he had been exposed to a variety of sectarian influences, most notably to the mild Congregationalism of an elderly couple who had become his foster parents. At the age of nineteen, when living at Ballston Spa in upstate New York, he had joined the Presbyterian church; but shortly thereafter, finding himself unable to accept Calvinist doctrine, he had gone over to the Universalists. In his twenty-third year, prepared by wide reading which served in the place of formal education, he had been ordained as a Universalist minister. While serving as a preacher and newspaper editor for that sect, he had found himself gradually losing confidence in the internal consistency of Universalist doctrine, and colleagues had begun to complain of his wavering in the faith. By 1830, at age 27, he had entered upon a brief agnostic period, during which he had aided in the formation of the abortive Workingmen's party in New York City and had become an editor of their newspaper, the *Free Inquirer.*

In 1832 Brownson had exercised his acute analytic powers on the premises of skepticism and discovered that that system, too, was wanting in consistency. Strongly influenced by the theological and social writings of W. E. Channing, he had rejected both the agnostic position and the Owenites' environmental approach to social reform. He had come to believe, with Channing, that social salvation would be achieved not by the uprooting of institutions, but through individual regeneration, and that the Christian religion provided the only hope for such regeneration. He had resumed his ministerial career by accepting the Unitarian pastorate in Walpole, New Hampshire, where he remained until 1834.

It was during this stay in Walpole that Brownson had begun to attract the attention of the Boston Unitarians. In 1834 he had contributed a series of "Letters to an Unbeliever" to the *Christian Register,* and these had been widely praised as a convincing refutation of the rationalistic skepticism with which one Abner Kneeland was then making a successful appeal to the working class. Brownson, with his argumentative skill and his first-hand knowledge of the by-ways of infidelity, had seemed especially fitted to lead a Christian counteroffensive against Kneeland. George Ripley and Channing had encouraged him to come to Boston, and Bernard Whitman, editor of the *Unitarian,* had assured Brownson that his newspaper writings on infidelity had gained wide reading and hearty acceptance among the liberal clergy.

Brownson's first response to these solicitations had been to take a church nearer to Boston, in Canton, Massachusetts. Then, in the spring of 1836, he had moved into the metropolis to initiate the work which was to give him a major place as a religious reformer. On May 29 he formally inaugurated an experimental church, called the "Society for Christian Union and Progress," and in July obtained a literary vehicle by securing appointment as editor of the weekly *Boston Reformer. New Views,* his volume of December 1836, was the manifesto of this experimental ministry to the working class, laying out its theological rationale and expressing the reformer's confidence that a transcendentalized Unitarianism would bring the Kingdom of God in the not-too-distant future.[38]

It is an additional commentary on the unusual potency of the transcendentalizing atmosphere of 1836 that the least outspoken of the Club members published, in the summer of that year, his first and only defense of the new religious ideas. Convers Francis, the mildest and at age 41 the most venerable of the transcendental group, produced a brief tract called *Christianity as a Purely Internal Principle*. In this he argued that the Christian religion is unique precisely because of its entire independence of "forms." Insofar as the churches set credal standards or demand adherence to particular rituals, Francis said, they revert to pagan practices which Christ himself abhorred. True Christianity judges men by their personal virtue and not by their stated beliefs.

In thus exalting morality over creed, Francis was no doubt following a well-beaten Unitarian path, but the sharp distinction which he made between the internal and external in religion showed his participation in the Transcendentalist movement of thought.

Despite his general lack of assertiveness, Francis had given other earnests of his sympathy with the new school, most notably in his championing of German philosophy. During the early years of his long pastorate at Watertown, Massachusetts (1819–42), he had begun to acquaint himself with scholarly works of every description. One year's authors included Henry More, Cicero, Plato, Tacitus, Sophocles, Coleridge, Herder, DeWette, Eckermann, Lardner, Baur, and Constant.[39] Owner of a considerable library, and of an infinitely receptive if not acutely discriminating mind, he gained a reputation for "all-sidedness" which was to be confirmed all too well for his Transcendentalist friends when he appeared in the 1840's to be suppressing his liberal principles for the sake of his Harvard professorship. In the early years, however, Francis was the revered elder statesman of the Club and the moderator— probably in more than one sense—of their discussions.

William Henry Furness, a close friend and former school-mate of Emerson, was pastor of the Unitarian society which Joseph Priestly had founded in Philadelphia in 1796. Although he was rarely in Boston to meet with the Transcendental Club, he was considered a leading spirit of their movement.

Furness' *Remarks on the Four Gospels*, published in late 1836, showed the marked coincidence of his biblical views with those which Ripley and others were putting forward. Like the others, Furness had no intention of denying that the miracles recorded in Scripture had actually occurred. On the contrary, he argued that the substantial agreement and uniform ingenuousness of the Gospel writers makes it impossible to suppose that their accounts are unreliable. But turning to a refutation of common attitudes about the miracles, he took the position, similar to Ripley's, that the miracles were not performed for the purpose of convincing men of the truths of Christianity. It is true, he acknowledged, that Christ's resurrection and wonderful acts provide added confirmation of Christian teachings; but the human mind, which has direct intuitions of religious truths, needs no such confirmations, and would have received the Gospel with equal assurance had the miracles never been recorded.[40]

Furness' special contribution to the Transcendentalist discussion of miracles, besides his intense insistence upon their validity, was a naturalistic theory which links him to David Friederich Strauss and the Tübingen School on the one hand, and the theology of the American Horace Bushnell on the other. Rejecting the standard Unitarian and Orthodox interpretation of the miraculous as constituting an "interruption" of the natural order, he held that such manifestations belong to a "spiritual" realm which indeed is beyond the sphere of ordinary human activities, but still is a part of the natural world. To deny that the miraculous can occur within the natural realm, he said, is to make the presumptuous assertion that we know all there is to know about our universe.

The place of Jesus in this scheme was that of a man uniquely endowed and enabled to draw upon the resources of the "spiritual" stratum of nature, and to make real the power that would otherwise have remained merely potential in this higher realm. Such a singular endowment, Furness thought, makes Jesus "divine" in a sense that other men are not, and constitutes his special claim to veneration.[41]

By the time Furness had finished insisting upon the moral grandeur of Jesus and the authenticity of the Gospel narratives, his rejection of the word "supernatural" rested on little more than semantic hair-splitting, and the book caused a minimum of discomfort in conservative circles. What allied him most clearly with the Transcendentalists was his assertion of the dispensability of miracles as Christian proofs, together with his championing of a naturalism which could easily be carried to conclusions more startling than his own.

Frederic Henry Hedge, although he contributed nothing of first importance to the spate of New School writings in 1836, had played a major part throughout the 1830's in bringing transcendental doctrines to the fore. Hedge at age thirty had already acquired a wide reputation for scholarship, and particularly for erudition in the field of German metaphysics. Since 1832 he had contributed major articles to the *Examiner* on Coleridge, Swedenborg, and Schiller, and on phrenology. Although he had been outspoken for transcendental philosophy in these writings, such criticisms as he had made of prevailing Unitarian ideas had as yet caused no serious reaction, and in fact had been praised highly by so conservative a Unitarian as Henry Ware, Jr.[42]

Hedge was the only member of the immediate Transcendentalist circle who had been educated in Germany. His father, professor of logic at Harvard, had sent him abroad in the company of George Bancroft in 1819, and young Hedge had spent three years there before entering Harvard College. By 1829 he had completed his theological studies and had been ordained in the church at West Cambridge. Six years later he had accepted a call to the Unitarian society in Bangor, Maine. Although he was a regular attendant at meetings of the Club—which acquired one of its names because it met when he came to Boston—this timely removal from the hotbed of religious radicalism may have helped to determine his eventual position in the more conservative wing of the Transcendentalist Movement.[43]

The optimism of the Transcendentalists as they took the field in force during 1836 was increased by their belief that some older Unitarians would come to their aid. Channing, James Walker, and Charles Follen were the leaders upon whom they placed most reliance. All of these men, and Channing in particular, had given constant emphasis to the free search for truth, and to the need for expanding and developing Unitarian doctrine.[44]

Walker, as editor of the *Examiner*, had seemed to show a friendly disposition toward the younger intellectuals by welcoming their writings for that periodical in the early 1830's.[45] What seemed even more conclusive, however, were his frequent protests against the Lockean philosophy. Walker's lecture of 1834 called "The Foundations of Faith" had stated the good transcendental principle that the "rightly constituted" soul receives the truths of religion "with a degree of intuitive clearness, and certainty, equal at least to that of the objects of sense." He had called for "a better philosophy than the degrading sensualism out of which most forms of modern infidelity have grown."[46]

Walker's "better philosophy" was Scottish, not German, and he wished less extreme innovations in theology and the Church than those which the Transcendentalists were adumbrating. But the younger group expected tolerance if not active support from Walker, and in this, at least, they were not to be disappointed.

Charles Follen, a theological and political liberal who had escaped from Germany to the United States in 1824, had expressed sympathy for transcendental reform ideas in a work entitled *Religion and the Church*, which he brought out during the summer of 1836.[47] In this treatise he had drawn heavily upon the work of Friederich Schleiermacher and Benjamin Constant, making particular use of Constant's belief that religious institutions must undergo constant modification as society itself advances.[48] In the volume which appeared in 1836, Follen had made the human "religious sentiment" the starting-point of the theological system he intended to elaborate. The intuitions of the mind, he said, rather than "those records, which, by different portions of mankind, are considered as of divine origin," must form the basis for reforms in religion; and the new theology, when completed, must contain not simply the best insights of the Christian religion, but an historical synthesis of the true elements in all earlier faiths.[49]

Follen has generally been excluded from listings of the Transcendentalists, or at most has been considered a transitional figure. He was preaching in New York and the West during the early years of the Transcendental Club, and he died when returning to Boston in 1840; so it is difficult to say precisely what his position would have been in the controversy of the 1840's. It is plain, however, that in certain respects—notably in his emphasis on the intuitional basis of religion and in the syncretism of his theological method—he contributed to the structure of Transcendentalist reforming thought.[50]

In view of the prodigious output of the younger intellectuals in the latter part of 1836, it is easy to see why that year has been called the annus mirabilis of their movement. In the field of religious reform alone, nearly all the characteristic Transcendentalist themes had been introduced, with Alcott and Emerson advocating reliance on the intuitions and moral awareness of the individual, Ripley and Furness initiating a critique of accepted canons of authority, and Brownson, Francis, and Follen interpreting the Christian Church as a mutable expression of man's evolving religious conceptions.

The strong note of reforming optimism which pervades these writings makes the terms "ferment" and "enthusiasm," so often used to describe Transcendentalism, seem especially applicable to this early period. The Transcendentalists were never so united as in the fall of 1836, when they had just begun to find each other out, and had not yet elaborated the varied schemes of action and revolt which were later to cause divergence among them. It was this "enthusiasm"—a common resolution that society could be changed for the better if reliance were placed upon human intuitions—which provided the center and integrating force for their movement.

The probability of disagreement was inherent in the very form of this common enthusiasm. Clarke's witticism meets the case almost exactly; they were perhaps most like-minded in their unabashed eclecticism, in a determination that beyond a certain point no two of them should think alike. This is why technical philosophical definitions of American Transcendentalism are so unsatisfactory, and always tend to exclude persons who considered themselves part of the movement. Such "readable formulae" trace circles which cut across the area in question but are not concentric with it. The reach and variety of this group's accomplishments stemmed not from a philosophy, or even a set of related philosophies, but from a complex interaction of ideas, of the men who held them, and of the times in which they lived.

Notes

1. *The Dictionary of Philosophy*, ed. Dagobert D. Runes (New York: Philosophical Library, 1942).

2. *Critique of Pure Reason*, trans. Norman Kemp Smith (London: Macmillan, 1929), pp. 59–61.

3. *Critique of Pure Reason*, pp. 41–42, 65–119. Sterling P. Lamprecht, *Our Philosophical Traditions: A Brief History of Philosophy in Western Civilization* (New York: Appleton-Century-Crofts, 1955), pp. 363–370.

4. *Critique of Pure Reason*, pp. 299, 380–381, 483–484; *Critique of Practical Reason*, trans. Lewis W. Beck (Chicago: University of Chicago Press, 1949), pp. 118–120.

5. Frank Thilly, *A History of Philosophy*, rev. Ledger Wood (New York: Henry Holt, 1951), pp. 451–453; Harald Høffding, *A History of Modern Philosophy . . . from the Close of the Renaissance to Our Own Day*, trans. B. E. Meyer (London: Macmillan, 1900), II, 110–192.

6. William Turner, *History of Philosophy* (Boston: Ginn, 1903), pp. 606–608; "Cousin," Runes, *Dictionary of Philosophy*.

7. Alexander Kern, "The Rise of Transcendentalism," *Transitions in American Literary History*, ed. Harry Hayden Clark (Durham: Duke University Press, 1953), pp. 274–275.

8. *Modern Philosophy from Descartes to Schopenhauer and Hartmann* (New York: Scribner, Armstrong, 1877), p. 160. For a recent appraisal of the interpretation and frequent misapprehension of Kantian ideas by New England writers see Henry A. Pochmann, *German Culture in America: Philosophical and Literary Influences, 1600–1900* (Madison: University of Wisconsin Press, 1957), pp. 119, and 79–242 passim.

9. Stanley M. Vogel, *German Literary Influences on the American Transcendentalists* (New Haven: Yale University Press, 1955); René Wellek, "Emerson and German Philosophy," *New England Quarterly*, 16 (March 1943), 41–62; Wellek, "The Minor Transcendentalists and German Philosophy," *New England Quarterly*, 15 (December 1942), 652–680; Harold Clarke Goddard, *Studies in New England Transcendentalism* (New York: Columbia University Press, 1908), chap. 2; Kern, "Transcendentalism," pp. 270–275.

10. Parker is read out of the movement by John Edward Dirks, *The Critical Theology of Theodore Parker* (New York: Columbia University Press, 1948), p. 136; Parker and Brownson by Herbert W. Schneider, *A History of American Philosophy* (New York: Columbia University Press, 1956), pp. 262–268; and Alcott by Caroline H. Dall, *Transcendentalism in New England: A Lecture* (Boston: Roberts Brothers, 1897), pp. 22–23. O. B. Frothingham, who does not at all deny Emerson's central place in the American movement, nonetheless illustrates the confusion of definitions. "A Transcendentalist," Frothingham writes, "in the technical sense of the term, it cannot be clearly affirmed that he was. Certainly he cannot be reckoned a disciple of Kant, or Jacobi, or Fichte, or Schelling" (*Transcendentalism in New England* [New York: Putnams, 1876], p. 226).

11. Kern, "Transcendentalism," pp. 252–309 passim.

12. Kern has compiled a list of twenty specific matters in which there was significant agreement among the Transcendentalists ("Transcendentalism," pp. 250–251).

13. For accounts of the early meetings, see *The Journals of Bronson Alcott*, ed. Odell Shepard (Boston: Little, Brown, 1938), pp. 78–79; *Journals of Ralph Waldo*

Emerson, ed. Edward Waldo Emerson and Waldo Emerson Forbes (Boston: Houghton Mifflin, 1909–1914), IV, 85–87. The number of years during which the Club was in existence is hard to determine. Estimates have ranged from "three or four years" (Alcott, quoted in George Willis Cooke, *An Historical and Biographical Introduction to Accompany* The Dial [Cleveland: Rowfant Club, 1902], I, 51) to "a dozen years" (Cooke, *Introduction*, I, 55). The longer estimate undoubtedly includes later informal meetings, such as the "conversations" at Miss Peabody's bookshop in the 1840s, which were attended by some of the same persons. As for the frequency of the meetings, Alcott later remembered it as "probably" four or five times a year (Cooke, *Introduction*, I, 51).

14. None of the older men became a regular member. Convers Francis, forty-one years of age in 1836, remained the senior member of the Club throughout its existence.

15. The roster of the Club is completed with the names of Bronson Alcott, Ellery Channing, Margaret Fuller, Ellen Hooper, Elizabeth Peabody, Sophia Ripley, Caroline Sturgis Tappan, Henry Thoreau, and Charles Wheeler. Dr. Channing, James Marsh, and Sampson Reed are frequently and justly mentioned as precursors of the movement. Moncure Conway, O. B. Frothingham, Thomas Wentworth Higginson, Samuel Johnson, Samuel Longfellow, Charles Newcomb, Franklin B. Sanborn, David Wasson, and John Weiss were later converts to Transcendentalism. George Bancroft and Caleb Sprague Henry were significant as philosophical adherents to transcendentalism but were not closely associated with the Concord group. See Kern, "Transcendentalism," p. 249.

16. Quoted in James Elliot Cabot, *A Memoir of Ralph Waldo Emerson* (Boston: Houghton, Mifflin, 1887), I, 245.

17. A. Bronson Alcott, *Conversations with Children on the Gospels*, 2 vols. (Boston: James Munroe, 1836–1837); *The Works of Orestes A. Brownson*, ed. Henry F. Brownson (Detroit: Nourse and Henry F. Brownson, 1882–1888), IV, 1–56; William H. Furness, *Remarks on the Four Gospels* (Philadelphia: Carey, Lea, and Blanchard, 1836); Convers Francis, *Christianity as a Purely Internal Principle* (American Unitarian Association Tract Series, 105; Boston: American Unitarian Association, 1836); *The Works of Charles Follen, with a Memoir by His Wife*, 5 vols. (Boston: Hilliard and Gray, 1841–1842), V, 254–313; George Ripley, "Martineau's *Rationale of Religious Inquiry*," *Christian Examiner*, 21 (1836), 225–254.

18. Quoted in Clarence L. F. Gohdes, *The Periodicals of American Transcendentalism* (Durham: Duke University Press, 1931), p. 40.

19. Odell Shepard, *Pedlar's Progress: The Life of Bronson Alcott* (Boston: Little, Brown, 1937), pp. 112–184.

20. Alcott, typically, exercised the best intentions and the worst practical judgment by segregating the offensive passages in appendices, where the guardians of public morals could and did peruse them out of context (Shepard, *Pedlar's Progress*, pp. 187–191).

21. Ralph L. Rusk, *The Life of Ralph Waldo Emerson* (New York: Scribners, 1949), pp. 242–243. For other reactions, see Alcott, *Journals*, p. 78; *The Letters of Ralph Waldo Emerson*, ed. Ralph L. Rusk (New York: Columbia University Press, 1939), II, 36.

22. Rusk, *Emerson*, pp. 76–81, 110–119, 139.

23. *Young Emerson Speaks: Unpublished Discourses on Many Subjects*, ed. Arthur C. McGiffert, Jr. (Boston: Houghton Mifflin, 1938), p. xxxv.

24. Rusk, *Emerson*, pp. 160–164.

25. Emerson, *Journals*, II, 497.

26. Emerson, *Letters*, I, 355; Rusk, *Emerson*, pp. 165–167.

27. Quoted in Frothingham, *Transcendentalism*, p. 380.

28. Rusk, *Emerson*, pp. 186, 199–200.

29. Frothingham called the events of 1832 "his resignation of the Christian ministry" (*Transcendentalism*, p. 120).

30. "Preaching Record," Emerson Papers, Harvard University Library. The agreement with the East Lexington Church called for Emerson to preach until May 1838, but he arranged for John Dwight to take most of the services in the last few months (George Willis Cooke, *John Sullivan Dwight* [Boston: Small, Maynard, 1898], pp. 17–18; *Young Emerson Speaks*, p. xxxvii). A pulpit appearance at Nantucket in 1847, sometimes cited as Emerson's last sermon, was differently interpreted by the speaker himself: Cabot, *Emerson*, II, 498.

31. For public response to the "American Scholar" see Rusk, *Emerson*, p. 266.

32. "Preaching Record."

33. Of the seventeen Transcendentalist ministers, eleven remained permanently in that calling, and ten of the latter continued as Unitarians. Samuel Osgood became an Episcopalian minister. Emerson, Ripley, Brownson, Cranch, Dwight, and Very left the profession altogether.

34. Octavius Brooks Frothingham, *George Ripley* (Boston: Houghton, Mifflin, 1882), pp. 36–37, 45. The church building stood at the corner of Purchase and Pearl streets (near present-day South Station) (Frothingham, *George Ripley*, p. 36).

35. Frothingham, *George Ripley*, p. 61.

36. For Ripley's articles of the 1830s see William Cushing, *Index to the Christian Examiner* (Boston: J. S. Cushing, 1879). Ripley also had been acting editor of the *Christian Register* for a brief period in 1833 (Frothingham, *George Ripley*, p. 94) and had established his own newspaper, the *Boston Observer and Religious Intelligencer*, in January 1835. The *Observer* was merged with the *Register* in June of the same year. For an excellent study of Ripley's relation to foreign thought see Arthur R. Schultz and Henry A. Pochmann, "George Ripley: Unitarian, Transcendentalist, or Infidel?" *American Literature*, 14 (March 1942), 1–8, 18–19.

37. George Ripley, "Jesus Christ, the Same Yesterday, Today and Forever," *The Transcendentalists: An Anthology*, ed. Perry Miller (Cambridge: Harvard University Press, 1950), pp. 284–293.

38. Arthur M. Schlesinger, Jr., *Orestes A. Brownson: A Pilgrim's Progress* (Boston: Little, Brown, 1939), pp. 8–27, 64; Henry F. Brownson, *Orestes A. Brownson's Early Life, Middle Life, Later Life* (Detroit: H. F. Brownson, 1898–1900), I, 85–110, 140.

39. William Newell, "Memoir of the Rev. Convers Francis, D.D.," *Proceedings of the Massachusetts Historical Society*, 8 (March 1865), 233–253.

40. Furness, *Remarks on the Four Gospels*, pp. ix–x, 252–253, 310–312. His lengthy argument for the accuracy of the Gospel narratives is contained in chaps. 2–7.

41. Furness, *Remarks on the Four Gospels*, pp. 145–188, 217–218.

42. Hedge's article on Coleridge, despite its air of profundity and a few supercilious remarks about the mental qualities requisite to an understanding of transcendental philosophy, apparently did not "infuriate the opponents," as Perry Miller suggests (*The Transcendentalists*, p. 67). Ware thanked Hedge for "the pleasure I have received and which I hear expressed in every quarter" (Roland Vale Wells, *Three Christian Transcendentalists* [New York: Columbia University Press, 1943], p. 97). For Hedge's articles of the 1830s see Cushing, *Index to the Christian Examiner*.

43. *Heralds of a Liberal Faith,* ed. Samuel A. Eliot (Boston: American Unitarian Association, 1910–1952), III, 162.

44. See, for example, his letters to Sismondi and Martineau, in Charles T. Brooks, *William Ellery Channing: A Centennial Memory* (Boston: Roberts Brothers, 1880), pp. 155, 159; and in W. H. Channing, *The Life of William Ellery Channing, D.D.* (Boston: American Unitarian Association, 1880), p. 435. Henry A. Pochmann has assailed "the common impression that Unitarians consistently and implacably opposed German ideas" in his *German Culture in America,* pp. 148–151.

45. But cf., for Walker's warnings about excessive radicalism, Brownson, *Orestes A. Brownson,* I, 120–121.

46. *Christian Examiner,* 17 (1834), 13, 14.

47. This was intended as the first installment in a major study of religious institutions, but Follen's death by shipwreck in 1840 prevented completion of the work. One additional chapter was published posthumously in Follen, *Works,* V, 293–313.

48. Constant's theory of religious institutions had its fullest expression in his *De la Religion, considerée dans sa source, ses formes, et ses developpements,* 5 vols. (Paris, 1824–1831).

49. *Works,* V, 256–257, 287–290.

50. *Heralds of a Liberal Faith,* II 286–288. For Follen's influence upon Brownson, see Brownson, *Works,* IV, 2; for his connection with Dwight, see Cooke, *Dwight,* pp. 39–40.

" 'This Unnatural Union of Phalansteries and Transcendentalists' "

Charles R. Crowe*

One of the most ideological and social experiments in nineteenth-century America was the attempt by leaders of the Brook Farm community to reconcile Transcendentalism and Fourierist socialism. The New England Transcendentalists who came to intellectual maturity between 1834 and 1838, emphasized individualism, non-conformity, and spontaneous living. Yet even before the movement had fully matured, the Jacksonian drive for equality, the coming of the industrial revolution, and the hardships brought about by the panic of 1837, combined to lead George Ripley, John S. Dwight, and other Transcendentalists away from ultra-individualism and toward the advocacy of collectivistic reform ideas.[1] In 1841 Ripley led a small group to West Roxbury, Massachusetts and began his celebrated socialist experiment. The conversion of Brook Farm leaders to the doctrines of Charles Fourier in January 1844[2] resulted in an even more intense collectivism, and made the community a powerful influence in the New England labor movement; it constituted the heart and mind of American Fourierism. Neither the early plans for Brook Farm nor the later commitment to Fourierism were made from any conscious desire to abandon Emersonian individualism. On the contrary, the Brook Farmers hoped to apply Transcendentalist ideas in a socialist context.[3]

Many Transcendentalists and some Fourierists thought that the two ideologies were incompatible. Emerson, Margaret Fuller, Bronson Alcott, and other Transcendentalists were basically sympathetic toward Brook Farm but refused to join the community, largely because of its collectivism. After the coming of Fourierism, the suspicion that Brook Farm was an exchange of Emersonian individualism for communal solace became a certainty.[4] G. W. Curtis, a young Emersonian, who had spent several years at Brook Farm, expressed a common response in his rejection of all collective approaches to reform:

*Reprinted from *Journal of the History of Ideas*, 20 (October–December 1959), 495–502.

> What we call union seems to me only a phrase of individual action.
> I live only for myself; and in proportion to my growth, so I benefit
> others. . . . Besides I feel that our evils are entirely individual. What
> is society but the shadow of the single men behind it?[5]

Hawthorne, sceptical from the beginning, left the community partly
for practical reasons and partly because he felt that the artist was buried
in the mass at Brook Farm.[6] Other Transcendentalists thought that
spontaneity, the community's greatest asset, had been destroyed by
Fourierist organization.[7] Even before the coming of Fourierism, Ripley
began to place a greater emphasis on socialist ideology, and as a result
some of the Transcendentalists who had not made a total commitment
to reform left the community.[8]

By 1845 several Fourierists had added their criticisms to those of
the Transcendentalists in protest against the effort to combine ideologies
so diverse. When Brook Farm was on the verge of collapse in 1846,
James Kay, Jr., the President of the Philadelphia Fourierist Union, argued
vehemently that "the Jonathan Butterfields and the John Orvises" (i.e.,
the Transcendentalists) should "stay in the classroom where they belong," and not meddle in "practical" affairs. Kay insisted that the "indolent" and the "ethereal" no longer be defended by "this unnatural
union of Phalansteries and (I dare not say Transcendentalists) the
Spiritualists." Kay's implied meaning was clear enough: since Transcendentalism and Fourierism were contradictory, the Transcendentalists
should resign positions of leadership in favor of the "practical" socialists.[9]

Even Ripley sometimes spoke as if the two ideologies could not be
reconciled and individualism had to be abandoned:

> Much was said of the suffering . . . and Mr. Ripley said we had best
> own it, meet it strongly and care nothing about it,—our individualities
> must be forgotten; or rather, as unity itself without individualism
> would be tame, we must put up with the evil and suffering atten-
> dant upon this transition state and keep alive our faith, and hope that
> it will be temporary.[10]

This pessimistic thought, however, was the product of a despairing
moment in which Ripley spoke carelessly about ideals that seemed to
be slipping away. As a matter of fact, his entire life was committed to
the belief that the two ideologies were compatible, and Brook Farm was
essentially an attempt to demonstrate the practicality of this belief.

Emerson and Thoreau often complained about the fragmentation
of the whole man by the specialized requirements of modern society,
but it was Ripley who proposed to do something about this problem. At
Brook Farm he wished to combine the thinker and the worker because

he believed that the separation of manual labor and intellectual activity cheated the worker of a natural right to cultural goods and deprived the literate classes of work which was needed to give their lives unity and completeness.[11] When perfected, the Brook Farm Phalanx would provide hundreds of different occupations and each man might engage in as many of them as the complexity of his nature demanded. Thus, all aspects of the modern divided personality would be combined in the context of a society which would always make work, play, and education intrinsically satisfying.[12]

Socialist society, Ripley promised, would bring the freedom and the fulfillment that had always been Transcendental goals. The Emersonians thought of liberty as the freedom to develop creatively, and Fourier provided the blueprint for a society which would make possible the fullest self-development of all men. Most of the Transcendentalists had long believed that under optimum circumstances society might breed a race of Miltons and Shakespeares. When Ripley first came to Brook Farm he defined his ultimate goal as an attempt to substitute "a race of free, noble, and holy men and women" for the existing "dwarfish and mutilated specimens," and Fourierist ideology assured the Brook Farmers that "science" demonstrated the feasibility of this project. Poverty, vice, crime, aesthetic indifference, and lack of intellectual development, were the products of disorganized social relations. In socialist society, human nature was infinitely perfectible.[13]

According to Fourier, every human "passion" (instinct, emotion, or interest) was given by God for a specific reason. Ripley confidently asserted that "the desires of man" were "the promises of God," and insisted that if every passion were gratified, the end result would be harmonious personalities and the good society rather than crime and chaos. Evil acts were the result of conflicting passions arising from the stresses of competitive society.[14] Emerson had declared that "If I am the devil's child, then I shall live from the devil," but neither Fourier nor Ripley was willing to make this admission, and Ripley believed that a Phalanx would inevitably create a Transcendentalist paradise with social relations

> which are in perfect unison with the nature of man; to which every chord in his sensitive and finely vibrated frame will respond; which will call forth, as from a well tuned instrument, all those exquisite modulations of feeling and intellect, which were aptly termed by Plato, the 'music of his being.'[15]

Harmony with nature, God, and man as well as inner harmony was the product of self-development. According to Fourier, man was the only exception to the otherwise universal harmony that God had created. The universe was very much like a musical composition dominated and unified by a single thematic thread. From stellar nebulae to the surface of the globe, everything fell into series resembling measures of music with constituent parts similar to musical notes. When all men lived in socialist society, the universal harmony would be perfectly realized. Until the time when the harmonious personality was universal, freedom, as the irresponsible individualist imagined it, was impossible.

Accepting Fourier completely on this point, Ripley argued that those who accused the Brook Farmers of sacrificing individual freedom, did not realize the multitudinous ways in which competitive society enslaved men.[16] For example, "civilizees" were in bondage to class hatred. Ripley could point with pride to the harmony and ease of freely mingling mechanics and intellectuals at Brook Farm as evidence of "genuine" social freedom. When conflicts did arise, Ripley argued that Brook Farm was only a limited attempt to achieve socialism. Presumably these conflicts would disappear in a Phalanx of two thousand persons and a full schedule of occupations.

In competitive society, men were also in bondage to exploitative emotions toward nature and the feelings of guilt which were created. Again Brook Farm could be produced as evidence of another kind of freedom—that of forming harmonious relations with nature, and here the evidence is impressive. In spite of bitter struggles with sandy soil, Brook Farmers displayed an unusual gentleness toward physical nature. No hunting was ever permitted on community grounds. Wild animals came boldly to the Hive door, and not even the birds who pillaged the newly planted grain were begrudged the seeds they took. When the Brook Farmers discovered that the birds were apt to eat as much as three or four rows of grain in each field, they planted extra rows and good humoredly dismissed the problem.

Capitalist society, Ripley believed, also enslaved man by making of him a thing rather than a person, an instrument of work and ends alien to his nature. Nowhere did human slavery seem more complete to Brook Farmers than in the case of the screw turner, the lever puller, or the clerk who spent his days in recording meaningless figures. Awareness of these problems brought Ripley all the more enthusiastically to Fourier's doctrine of attractive labor. If men were given a sense of participation, ownership, and fruitful labor; if they were assigned the proper quality, quantity, and variety of labor in correspondence with human nature and the individual personality, then harmony and freedom rather than "passional" frustration and soul-destroying, mechanical drudgery would be the end products of modern society.

The Brook Farmers ardently believed that socialist organization was the key to freedom. How could a man be free when he was at war with himself; when he had strong drives toward both brotherly co-operation and unscrupulous competition? In moderate quantities neither emotion was evil, and both would be recognized in socialist society where all human passions would be harmonized and balanced.

Moreover, social unity did not necessarily mean rigid conformity. The Fourierist structure of authority, Ripley asserted, demonstrated that freedom and regulation, variety and unity, could be reconciled. Brook Farm supported Ripley's beliefs in many respects.[17] An amazing variety of men and women lived in the community and each one chose his leader as well as his occupation. A group leader was elected every week and the series chiefs were chosen by the workers with the advice and consent of the community council, itself an elective body. Never was an individual compelled to perform a task against his will. There was absolute freedom to join any group and a worker might change groups as often as he liked. In the course of a single day, a man might change not only from hoeing to a milking group, but even from the agricultural to the industrial or the educational series. The most disagreeable tasks were performed by a special group, the "Sacred Legion," which had a high morale and more volunteers than it could use. Apparently a sense of self-sacrifice and high community prestige more than compensated for the unpleasant nature of many tasks.[18]

If, in spite of all this freedom, individualists still chose to complain about regimentation, Ripley was prepared to reply that when sufficient financial and human materials were available for a Phalanx, very few rules and regulations would be needed. In Ripley's mind the perfected Phalanx was an anarchistic society in which "everything would be regulated with spontaneous precision by the pervading common sense of the Phalanx, and the law written on the heart, the great and holy law of attraction, would supersede all others."[19] Marx was not the first to suggest that the establishment of socialism would be followed by a withering away of the state.

Thus, if the protestations of Ripley, Dwight, and others can be believed, there was no conflict between Transcendentalism and Fourierism. The Transcendentalists who came to Brook Farm had always defined freedom as the right to be one's self, to develop into a mature and distinctive personality, and this, they now believed, was possible only in a socialist society which would guarantee self-development for all men. To preach the salvation of isolated individuals was to mock both man and God. Communal values and individual liberty were combined in the Phalanx, which would secure and increase human variety rather than destroy it. Through the meditation of Fourier's law of universal harmony, distinctive personalities could become members of a vast organic body without losing their individuality. The Brook Farmers insisted that the maximum self-development led to a soul motivated by love, an emotion which was the very essence of the human personality. John S. Dwight carried the collectivist spirit to an apex by insisting that the truest way for a man to realize himself was to blend his individual love into the universal love, to merge his life with the life of humanity:

> No man is himself, *alone*. Part of me is in you, in every fellow being. We "live and move and have our being" in one another, as well as in God. An individual is nothing in himself. . . . We are real *persons* only entering into true relations with all other beings; we enter into our lives and find ourselves just in proportion as we realize and make good those relations. Only so far as the electric chain of sympathies which God threw around us all, in sign that we are one . . . is kept entire and unobstructed . . . can we be said to live; and most men live, like old trees that are dying, only in a few branches, an incoherent, fragmentary, partial life; nothing continuous, fresh, and whole about it. It takes the life of all mankind to make our single life happy. . . . there is one life, one destiny in all humanity; . . . all men make up the one perfect man, and . . . only all men sharing each other's life, co-operating with and completing one another, can ever realize and bring out the full meaning of the idea of man. So far as each lives not in the whole, does he lack life; so far as he is indifferent to any, does he miss a portion of himself.[20]

Dwight's near mystical approach to the problem of the individual and the community helped to sustain the Brook Farmers, and most of them would have accepted his ideological position. In the actual life of the community, however, there were some conflicts between those who had been recruited as Transcendentalists and those who had come to the community because of Fourierist convictions. A few of the working-class members regarded the education group as an "aristocratic" element, even though all of the teachers worked in industrial and agricultural groups. Some craftsmen, led by the carpenter W. H. Cheswell, repeatedly expressed resentment and caused several stormy debates over the expansion of the school in 1844 and 1845. Their hostility was repaid by a little middle-class snobbery from some of the bluestockings in the community. From time to time there were also complaints that cliques had been formed on the basis of common residence in the same building. "Cabalism" was one of the twelve basic passions in Fourier's psychology, but the community leaders felt that these cliques represented an over-emphasis on a single emotion. Several reports were also made of discord within the work groups. In 1845 Christopher List and William Reynolds were expelled by the carpenter's group as "discordant elements."[21] On the whole, however, middle-class intellectuals and workers got along very well and supported Ripley's attempt to combine the two ideologies and apply the synthesis concretely to community life.

Brook Farm as an attempt to embody Transcendentalist ideas in a socialist context cannot be labeled either a total success or a total failure. Criticism enough can be made. Apparently some individual personalities found communal life stifling. There was some social conflict, and Ripley's glib explanation that all of this would completely vanish in a "true Phalanx" is no more satisfactory than similar statements from modern Russia explaining away the shortcomings of "socialist" society. Moreover, there is reason to believe that even the perfectly organized Phalanx might breed non-conformists for whom the society had no place. The sterile completeness of Fourier's system and the naïveté of Ripley's beliefs about human nature and social organization may also be criticized.

If Ripley does not convince us that the one and the many can be reconciled so easily and if Fourier does not persuade us that the socialist millennium will literally transform the seas into lemonade, we must still admit that Brook Farm was an interesting and significant attempt to retain some of the virtues of individualism in a collectivist society, and that Fourier had enough social realism to grapple with urgent human problems which Marx overlooked. Ripley and his followers were successful in combining co-operative living with much color, variety, and individualism. For all of their shortcomings, the Brook Farmers made an important effort to solve some of the most pressing cultural problems of the nineteenth century: how shall industrial labor be made "attractive"; how shall the problem of personality alienation among those in routine industrial and clerical occupations be overcome; how can the social isolation of so many in an impersonal industrial society be alleviated; how shall men and women be given a sense of participation, ownership, and interest in their occupations, communities and nations; how can a social climate be created which makes it possible for individualists to thrive in a mass society? These problems persist and the Brook Farm effort to reconcile Transcendentalism and Fourierism has as much significance for the twentieth century as it had for the nineteenth century.[22]

Notes

1. The emergence of Transcendentalism is skillfully presented by Perry Miller in *The Transcendentalists: An Anthology* (Cambridge: Harvard University Press, 1950). Professor Miller's anthology contains a brief general bibliography which lists many of the relevant sources and secondary accounts and which is useful to both the general reader and the student of the period. Octavius Brooks Frothingham's *Transcendentalism in New England* (New York: Putnams, 1876), with all its obvious flaws, is still the only book which gives a detailed and systematic account of Transcendentalist ideologies. F. O. Matthiessen's *American Renaissance* (New York: Oxford University Press, 1941) contains many valuable insights. The drift of Ripley's group toward political radicalism is discussed more fully in Charles R. Crowe, "George Ripley: Transcendentalist and Utopian Socialist" (Ph.D. dissertation,

Brown University, 1955) [since published, with the same title, by the University of Georgia Press in 1967 (Ed. Note)]. The writer is aware of the complexity of this intellectual movement and realizes that in a very true sense there were almost as many Transcendentalisms as there were transcendentalists. However, some beliefs were held by all who accepted the label. No serious student of the movement would deny that all of those who called themselves Transcendentalists believed in personal liberty, spontaneous and creative living, and intuitive knowledge. Only those aspects of the movement will be dealt with here.

2. On this conversion to Fourierism see the *Present*, 1 (15 January 1844), and the *Phalanx*, 1 (5 February 1844).

3. See Ripley to Emerson, 6 November 1840, Octavius Brooks Frothingham, *George Ripley* (Boston: Houghton, Mifflin, 1882), pp. 306–310.

4. Emerson's changing attitudes, which were fairly representative of the most ardent individualists among the Transcendentalists, can be followed in *Journals of Ralph Waldo Emerson*, ed. Edward Waldo Emerson and Waldo Emerson Forbes (Boston: Houghton Mifflin, 1909–1914).

5. *Early Letters of George Wm. Curtis to John S. Dwight*, ed. George Willis Cooke (New York: Harpers, 1898), p. 96.

6. Hawthorne, *The American Notebooks*, ed. Randall Stewart (New Haven: Yale University Press, 1932), pp. 75–89.

7. For examples, see Amelia Russell, *Home Life of the Brook Farm Association* (Boston: Little, Brown, 1900), p. 85.

8. Although he was most worried about community morals, George P. Bradford was in most respects a good example of this group. On Bradford's leaving Brook Farm see Emerson's *Journals*, VI, 391.

9. James Kay to J. S. Dwight, Philadelphia, 12 March 1846, Dwight Papers, Boston Public Library.

10. Marianne Dwight, *Letters from Brook Farm, 1844–1847*, ed. Amy L. Reed (Poughkeepsie, N. Y.: Vassar College, 1928), p. 91.

11. See Ripley's letter to Emerson, Frothingham, *George Ripley*, pp. 306–310.

12. Ripley, "Tendencies of Modern. Civilization," *Harbinger*, 1 (1845), 33; "Association," *Harbinger*, 1 (1845), 48.

13. Frothingham, *George Ripley*, p. 308. Also see "Association in This Country," *Harbinger*, 1 (1846), 189–190.

14. Fourier's significant writings are in *Oeuvres Complètes*, 6 vols. (Paris, 1841–1848), but Albert Brisbane's *The Social Destiny of Man* (Philadelphia: C. F. Stollmeyer, 1840) is the key work for the movement in America.

15. Ripley, "Association," *Harbinger*, 5 (1847), 137.

16. This "discussion" has been synthesized by the writer from numerous articles and letters. See, for example, Editor's Statement, *Harbinger*, 1 (1845), 16; "Signs of Progress," *Harbinger*, 1 (1845), 47–48; and Ripley's letters from 1843 to 1848 in the Boston Public Library and the Massachusetts Historical Society.

17. *Constitution of the Brook Farm Phalanx* (Boston: n.p., 1845); and the Brook Farm Minutes and Resolutions Book, Massachusetts Historical Society.

18. For the best accounts of Brook Farm during the Fourierist phase, see Marianne Dwight, *Letters*, the *Harbinger*, and John Thomas Codman, *Brook Farm: Historic and Personal Memoirs* (Boston: Arena, 1894). The letters of George and Sophia Ripley, John S. Dwight, Albert Brisbane, John Allen, and W. H. Channing in the Boston Public Library and the Massachusetts Historical Society are also useful.

19. Ripley, "Association," *Harbinger*, 1 (1845), 160.

20. J. S. Dwight, "Association," *Harbinger*, 6 (1848), 170. Also see "Individuality in Association," *Harbinger*, 1 (1845), 264–265.

21. On social conflicts at Brook Farm, see Marianne Dwight's *Letters*, pp. 38–40, 40–42, 61–63, 159–166.

22. On the relevance of utopian socialism to twentieth-century life, see Erich Fromm, *The Sane Society* (New York: Rinehart, 1955).

"John Locke and New England Transcendentalism"

Cameron Thompson*

I

The Great Mr. Locke, America's Philosopher. (Merle Curti)

The pivotal role of John Locke in the philosophical development of Transcendentalism has not been asserted with sufficient emphasis. Some years ago, Odell Shepard remarked that "We may yet come to realize that the entire Transcendental Movement was a revolt against Locke and rediscovery of his predecessors."[1] Since then, much has been written to correct the second half of this indictment, but equal justice has not been paid to the essential first half—nor to the additional fact that the "men of Locke" responded with vigor and point to the "revolt."

The revolt was against the philosophy dominant in academic and clerical institutions. This philosophy was empiricism, and its father was Locke. It was commonly—and not necessarily with depreciatory intention —called Sensationalism,[2] and it included not only Locke, but also the Scottish "Common Sense" philosophers: notably (in New England), Reid, Stewart and Brown. So typically cavalier an identification of the Scottish school with Locke prompted some contemporary indignation, and modern scholarship has given support to the protest. An evaluation of this peripheral controversy, however, is not part of the present essay. It will be enough to show that the Transcendentalists themselves considered the Scottish philosophy to be a mere "modification" of Locke— especially of his epistemology—designed to make the founder more palatable to current tastes.

The Transcendentalists were accurate in their appraisal of the prevalence of Sensationalism in influential quarters during the early part of the century. With respect to its esteem in education circles, the Reverend James Murdock, writing in 1842, is explicit: "Until within about twenty years, the empirical philosophy as taught by Locke and the Scotch writers

*Reprinted from *New England Quarterly*, 35 (December 1962), 435–457.

. . . had dominion in all our colleges and schools and was regarded everywhere as the only true philosophy."[3] This relatively early judgment was to be corroborated by later studies. Indeed, with respect to Locke these studies reveal a reign for the celebrated *Essay* which in duration, as well as in extent, is astonishing. Noah Porter was to remember that "Locke's Essay on the Human Understanding [*sic*] was for a long time the well-studied text-book in the instruction of the youth at the most important of the American colleges,"[4] and a few years later C. Emory Aldrich supplied impressive additional testimony. Aldrich addressed "letters of inquiry . . . to gentlemen connected with ten of our oldest and best known colleges," and although in certain instances the replies were of little help because of incomplete records, taken together they constitute effective evidence on the sustained popularity of "Locke's Essay." Thus, it was used as a textbook at Yale from 1717 to 1825, when Stewart was introduced; at Dartmouth it appears to have been studied from 1769 to 1838 and to have been assigned as a text from 1822 to 1838, when it was replaced by Stewart; at Brown it was a text from 1783 to 1825, when Stewart was substituted. Harvard and Williams (in addition to colleges outside of New England, such as Princeton, Columbia, William and Mary) also furnished Aldrich with reports which, if more sketchy, support the conclusion that Locke's appeal was widespread and long continued.[5] Moreover, in the instance of Harvard, where the philosophical traditions are especially pertinent to this study, we are fortunate in having excellent confirmation of Aldrich's informal investigations; for Benjamin Rand has shown that the *Essay* was introduced in 1742 and held its own even after the weight of the Scottish influence began to be felt, some seventy-five years later, and he is led to assert that "No other text-book of modern philosophy has been used in this University for such an extended period of time."[6]

Finally, it is significant that when Locke began to lose his individual pre-eminence in the classroom, it was the Scottish philosophers who inherited the mantle of authority.[7] James Marsh, writing to Coleridge in 1829, notes the new emphasis: "The works of Locke were formerly much read and used as text books in our colleges, but of late have very generally given place to the Scottish writers; and Stewart, Campbell and Brown are now almost universally read as the standard authors on the subjects of which they treat."[8] These men, if they sought to combat the skepticism implicit in Locke, if they attempted to find a place for the "intuitions of common sense," were avowed empiricists in their presuppositions and in their methodology. In short, they offered what Noah Porter was later to describe as "the newly modified philosophy of Locke," and they therefore found a ready welcome in academic environments which had been long nurtured on Locke but were happy to have the oracle[9] brought up to date by the "realistic" interpretation.[10]

Turning to the correlative prestige of Sensationalism within the church, a reminder is necessary. While it will be shown that the clergy of New England (and we have, of course, particular reference to the Unitarian clergy) embraced Locke or the Scots so far as it rested its religious convictions on any philosophy at all, it should not be thought that this acceptance is indicative of any developed philosophical interests. On the contrary, Alexis de Tocqueville's observation, "I think that in no country in the civilized world is less attention paid to philosophy than in the United States,"[11] applies with particular force to the customary attitude of the ministry both toward philosophy and toward any expressed philosophical basis for religion. The explanation of this intellectual lethargy is not hard to find. Formalized religion—even so loosely formalized a one as Unitarianism—has often considered philosophical buttresses to be of dubious value, since these buttresses, erected as "the rational security of faith," have been known to develop an alarming independence. Behind this dubiety has commonly lain the suspicion that philosophy and religion ("reason" and "faith") are innately hostile to one another, and that in a marriage of the two the latter is all too likely to be relegated to a progressively uxorious position. That some such apprehension existed among the New England clergy, thereby discouraging philosophical inquiries of a more searching nature, is the charge of Marsh in his Introductory Essay to Coleridge's *Aids to Reflection*:

> No one, who has had occasion to observe the general feelings and views of our religious community... can be ignorant that a strong prejudice exists against the introduction of philosophy ... in the discussion of theological subjects. The terms philosophy and metaphysics, even reason and rational, seem in the minds of those most devoted to the support of religious truth, to have forfeited their original, and to have acquired a new import, especially in their relation to matters of faith. By a philosophical view of religious truth would generally be understood a view, not only varying from the religion of the Bible ... but at war with it; and a rational religion is supposed to be, of course, something diverse from revealed religion.[12]

There was, then, an inherent suspicion of philosophy as an ally of religion (a suspicion which predictably would be confirmed by any "philosophy," such as Transcendentalism, which emphasized the free play of "reason").[13] If we remember, in addition, that America had produced no philosophical literature of importance (always with the exception of Edwards'), it is readily understandable that the pedestrian New England clergyman of the day accepted, uncritically, the philosophy which he had imbibed at the colleges and the innocuousness of which was attested by the fact that it was taught at all in institutions administered, in large part, for and by the ministry.[14]

His confidence would be heightened by the evident compatibility of Sensationalism with conventional Unitarianism. At first blush, it may seem paradoxical that a religious movement which had had its stimulus and earlier momentum in dissatisfaction with the diminishing role to which orthodox Congregationalism (heavily Calvinistic in temper) had consigned the capacity of the individual for direct religious insight should have grown to marriage with a philosophy identified with the limitation of human knowledge to sense experience—and the potential skepticism of which had been demonstrated in the "infidelity" of deism.[15] But the seeming incongruity, although it was to be seized upon and exploited by the Transcendentalists, was pronounced illusory by Unitarians, and the very circumscription of the mind's capacities became for them warrant for a church, since by 1830—or thereabouts—Unitarianism had lost much of its previous character as a reaffirmation of the unmediated relationship with religious truths and was becoming increasingly doctrinal. The invigorating protests of its adolescent years were already becoming watered down to what Emerson was disdainfully to call "the pale negations of Boston Unitarianism" as age brought to the movement the sclerotic symptoms of an established sect. In short, Unitarianism was becoming "respectable,"[16] and in its respectability it found Sensationalism a congenial philosophy, for by its insistence that empirical knowledge was dependent on experience derived through the senses. Sensationalism encouraged the inference that the only source of supra-empirical knowledge must be revelation. The question here is not the correctness of this interpretation of Locke's writings; it is enough to have established how so accommodating a reading cut the ground beneath the apparent anomaly of a union between religion and Sensationalism—a union which (it must be repeated) could be satisfying only to a Unitarianism which had drifted toward a traditional caste view of the functions of the clergy.[17]

So it was that " . . . in the Unitarian body . . . the philosophy of Locke had been accepted in its extremest form. . . ."[18] George Ripley's measured exposition of Andrews Norton's views affords a succinct description of the "correct" stance resulting from this acceptance:

> Adopting the cardinal positions of Locke and Hume in regard to the origin of knowledge and the foundation of belief, he pursued them with strict logical sequence to their natural conclusions. In his view there could be but two sources of ideas—experience and testimony,—which in the final analysis were resolved into one. We have the teachings of experience in regard to the facts of the material universe; and concerning the realm of spiritualities, we are dependent

on the authority of divine revelations. The human mind has no inherent faculty of perception in the sphere of facts which transcends the cognizance of the senses. We cannot rely upon the intuitions of reason as the ground of faith in the suggestions of the soul. The veracity of the human spirit as the condition of truth formed no part of his scheme of philosophy. . . . Intuition can inform us of nothing but what exists in our own minds . . . ; it is therefore a mere absurdity to maintain that we have an intuitive knowledge of the truths of religion.[19]

The declarations of a Unitarian clergyman, quoted by Frothingham as a typical example of the "Unitarian of a conservative stamp," are contributive here, as indicating that the platform of the formidable Norton was not unrepresentative of that adopted by the less conspicuous members of his persuasion:

The Christian minister is to preach the declarations and principles of the Gospel. In his view, religion is identified with Christianity, and he values Christianity because it gives him assurance of certain Truths which he regards as of infinite importance. These truths constitute his religion. . . . All our knowledge of Christ and Christianity is derived, not from consciousness or intuition, but from outward revelation. It is not innate, spontaneous and original with us, but extrinsic, derived, super-induced. . . . Once admit that the New Testament does not contain all the principles of spiritual Truth . . . and you open the door to all sorts of loose and crude speculations . . . the heathen sages, it is true, stumbled on some fortunate conjectures, but they could assert nothing with assurance; they could not speak with certainty and authority.[20]

II

Locke's mind will not always be the standard for metaphysics. (Sampson Reed)

For a questing younger generation which had become increasingly disenchanted with the blandness of the established culture, the confident lucidities of the Andrews Nortons and the echoings of anonymous clergymen were sufficient irritants to incite repudiation. To a degree, the ground had been prepared for the Transcendentalists. Themselves Unitarians, so far as they retained ties to any church, they were members of a sect which had had its American birth in distaste for the "obnoxious" tenets of Calvinistic theology and which had reaffirmed the essentially Protestant principle of the worth, dignity, and capacity of the individual.[21] Moreover, if in its intellectual rationale Unitarianism seemed to have reached a sorry pass, there remained its heritage of tolerance and the encouragement of free enquiry to fortify those who would urge a philosophy more consonant with its intrinsic religious idealism.

Yet the past was at best preparatory. If there had been much in earlier expressions of Unitarian faith, notably in the sermons of Channing,[22] which voiced aspirations that the Transcendentalists were to reassert and augment, the present stimulus was first to come from the outside, for it was a Congregationalist, Marsh, who provided the Transcendentalists with their Old Testament.[23] In his Introductory Essay, the earlier (1821) prophetic opinion of Sampson Reed[24] on the future of Locke's influence is expanded, and the uncritical acceptance of Sensational philosophy is indicted as the principal cause of the deficiency of spiritual content evident in contemporary religion. Marsh named the enemy, exposed his baneful effects, and presented (in Coleridge) a new leader with an invigorating platform. His challenge was unequivocal: ". . . I do not hesitate to express my conviction, that the natural tendency of some of the leading principles of our prevailing system of metaphysics, and those which must unavoidably have more or less influence on our theoretical views of religion, are of an injurious and dangerous tendency. . . . Let it be understood . . . without farther preface, that by the prevailing system of metaphysics, I mean the system of which in modern times Locke is the reputed author, and the leading principles of which, with various modifications, more or less important, but not altering its essential character, have been almost universally received in this country. . . . If the spirit of the Gospel still exerts its influence; if a truly spiritual religion be maintained, it is in opposition to our philosophy, and not at all by its aid." Finally, in the concluding words of the Essay, Marsh anticipates the crux of the whole of Transcendentalism's religious-philosophical protest: "It may at length be discovered, that a system of religion essentially spiritual, and a system of philosophy which excludes the very idea of all spiritual power and agency, in their only distinctive and proper character, cannot be consistently associated together."[25]

It was as if Marsh's Essay, well timed as it was in its articulation of existing undercurrents of discontent, had sounded a clarion call for the young Unitarian liberals, and henceforth their identification of Locke (and, of course, the "derived" Scots) with all that they considered objectionable in contemporary Unitarianism is ubiquitous.[26] Remembering the initial meeting of the Transcendental Club in September, 1836, Cabot quotes a letter from F. H. Hedge recalling that "Mr. Emerson, George Ripley, with one another, chanced to confer together on the state of current opinion in theology and philosophy, which we agreed in thinking very unsatisfactory. Could anything be done in the way of protest and introduction of deeper and broader views? What precisely we wanted would have been difficult for any of us to state. What was strongly felt was dissatisfaction with the reigning sensuous philosophy, dating from Locke, on which our Unitarian theology was based."[27] Nor were the individual members of the Club, and those associated with them, less preoccupied with the iniquities of Locke, especially his guilt in the "materialization" of religion. Emerson speaks slightingly of "philosophers like Locke, Paley, Mackintosh and Stewart . . . men of the world who are reckoned accomplished talkers,"[28] of "the skeptical philosophy of Locke";[29] Alcott is released from "the Philosophy of Sense,"[30] from being "a disciple of Experience," from those philosophers, including Locke, who "narrowed the range of the human faculties, retarded the progress of discovery by insisting on the supremacy of the Senses, and shut the soul up in the cave of the Understanding";[31] Brownson finds Locke's philosophy "altogether unfriendly to religion" and doubts if Harvard will ever contribute much to society "so long as Locke is her text-book in Philosophy";[32] James Freeman Clarke is rescued from the "wooden philosophy" of Locke by the "higher" thought of Coleridge;[33] George Ripley scores "the sensuous philosophy of Locke" as the cause for the divorce between religion and philosophy,[34] and elsewhere singles out the men of religion "who were led by the philosophy of Locke to attach an extravagant value to external evidence";[35] Theodore Parker ironically compliments the Unitarians on being "consistent Sensationalists,"[36] while he strenuously advances the claims of a more spiritual theology. Finally, it is F. H. Hedge who has given us one of the best summary statements of Transcendentalism's objection to Locke, for in the following comments, although as editor of an American edition of English writings he is directing his attention to theological developments in England, he clearly reflects the judgment of his fellow Transcendentalists on the essential danger to religion implicit in Sensationalism:

> The problem which mainly occupied the theological mind of the time (c. 1800) was the attempt to prove the Gospel by demonstrating the *external* relation between it and God. Christianity, whose fundamental postulate is the inner light by which it manifests itself as the Truth of God, was advocated on the ground of certain facts, which, if true, would prove God to be its Author. . . . The student of the history of opinions might trace here a legitimate result of the then prevailing philosophy of Locke. A germ of mischief lurked in the immortal "Essay," whose fructification had so infected the intellectual atmosphere of the time, so vitiated its conceptions, so dimmed and confused the consciousness of God, that instead of the divine Inpresence and informing Word of the old theologians, a prodigy in nature was held to be the only possible

mediator between God and man, the only possible voucher and
vehicle of revelation. Christianity was to be received on account
of its miracles, not the miracles on account of the more commend-
ing Truth of Christianity . . . the very being of God was no longer a
self-evident truth, but a question of logic, to be tried and settled by
the understanding.[37]

Here, in words fully applicable to New England Unitarianism, we have
the Transcendental development of those seeds of insurrection first firmly
planted by the popularity of Marsh's edition of the *Aids*.

But the Transcendentalists were far too emotionally involved to
remain content in mere renunciation of their immediate past. If Sensationalism was permanently to be dethroned, a philosophy—particularly
an epistemology—more contributive to their religious conviction must be
convincingly adduced. Marsh had given them assurance that no satisfaction could be salvaged from the empirical tradition of Locke. They must,
ironically, be Separatists, not Puritans. To them, dependence upon Locke
as a starting point sanctioned but two eventualities: the "crass materialism" which his French followers had evolved, or, at best, the deceptive
compromise of Scottish Realism. No, the epistemological implications of
Locke could not be acceptably mitigated; the only promise of success
lay in a bold challenge of the premises from which they flowed. If, in the
final analysis, the unpardonable deficiency of Locke and his fellow Sensationalists was the limitation which they put upon the extent of human
knowledge, this limitation of *extent* issued, irrevocably, from a limitation
of *origin*. In short, once grant Locke's presuppositions, all the rest—including, it seemed, Boston Unitarianism—followed. This conclusion was
to be given explicit (if naïve) statement in the *Dial*:

> Every system of theology grows out of and is shaped by the
> philosophical system of those by whom it is first digested, and scien-
> tifically taught . . . all systems of philosophy may be divided into
> two classes—those which recognize innate ideas and those which do
> not. . . . For those who do not accept innate ideas there is but one
> system of theology logically possible, and that is Unitarianism . . .
> which is the result of an attempt to explain Christianity by the
> sensual philosophy instigated by a desire to get rid of mystery and
> make everything clear and simple. If this philosophy is not true to
> psychology, then its interpretations of Christianity are wrong, and
> the soul is against them, and will finally triumph.[38]

"The soul is against them." Here, surely, is the very pulse of the
Transcendental protest, and by the time the words were spoken, the
movement had already contrived to bolster its certitude by means of a
sympathetic philosophy of mind. The substantive concepts of this phi-

losophy are too familiar to require exposition. The happy distinction between Reason and Understanding, which Emerson was once unabashed enough to call "philosophy itself"[39] (and which constituted the epistemological tenet most commonly identified with Transcendentalism in its early stages), the concepts of Spontaneous Reason, of Intuition, of Instinct—all were affirmations of the inadequacy of the Sensationalistic psychology. If each Transcendentalist seemed, at times, to be wedded to his private phraseology, and if some (notably Emerson)[40] seemed capable of oscillating between one vocabulary and another with an exasperating disregard for helpful definition, it was perfectly clear to Transcendentalists (and also to their critics) that running through all the differences of designation was a unifying agreement in maintaining a capacity within the mind to *transcend* "experience" and thereby luxuriate in direct and irrefutable contact with Truths whose very nature precluded discovery by way of sensuous channels. Given this confidence, it followed that the poverty of Understanding was not merely the limitation of its epistemological reach: a more pernicious deficiency was that its inescapable preoccupation with empirical experience acted as an inhibiting factor on the free play of Reason, encouraging men toward contentment with the half-truths of the sensory world while obfuscating the light of those verities which only Reason (unfettered from the "iron lids" of the Understanding) could companionably grasp. The import of these contentions for Transcendentalism's expressed religious goals was evident: broadly speaking, it rendered the "necessary mediator" justification of the church baseless and proclaimed instead, if only by implication, that each man found his Church within his own soul, his Revelation within the voice of Reason itself.[41]

III

...a philosopher of some repute in his day. (Francis Bowen)

It could not be expected that the "men of Locke"—entrenched spokesmen for established Unitarianism—would be found weaponless against the sound and fury of such intransigency. They were powerfully numerous; they represented the ingrained acceptance of New England's current thinking; they were intellectually equipped to defend themselves with pungent vitality. Philosophically speaking, much of their defense was one by implication. The Transcendental "controversy" was, after all, in the first instance a religious contention, and such tiltings as those between George Ripley and Andrews Norton are sufficient witness of the extent to which it was the specifically religious issues which engaged the concern and resources of the interested parties, the extent to which the fate of rival philosophies rested upon the outcome of theological tussles. Nevertheless, even here the awareness that antagonistic philosophies were also involved was never far from the surface. Ripley was careful to note that the "radical defect" of Norton's theology ". . . proceeds from the influence of the material philosophy on which it is founded. The error with which it starts, that there is no faculty in human nature for perceiving spiritual truth, must needs give rise to the other errors which I have formerly pointed out";[42] and Norton, as has been shown, felt constrained to reassert the Sensationalistic principles which he embraced.

However, while the many excommunications of the "latest form of infidelity," along with the consistently caustic reviews of Transcendental writings (and the writings of such foreign "inspirers" as Coleridge and Cousin)[43] constituted cogent, if tacit, expressions of continued loyalty to the tradition of Locke, more explicit defenses were also at hand. As early as 1829, Edward Everett had published two articles in the *North American Review* on the history of philosophy. In the course of surveying the modern schools, he deals in terms of surprising moderation with the Transcendental philosophy in Germany; yet he feels compelled to score the alleged obscurity of this Idealism and its "unintelligible nomenclature," and in the end he emerges a "man of Locke," denying that Locke encourages the materialistic position to which his French followers had progressed and giving his appreciation of the *Essay* in no uncertain terms: "This great work is, and will probably always remain, the textbook of the noblest branch of human learning. What higher honor could mortal ambition attain or aspire to, than that of achieving it?"[44] In such unstinted eulogy, as in his attack on Idealism's "unintelligible nomenclature," Everett foreshadows much of the character of the opposition which Transcendentalism was to face. It is a character suggested again, two years later, by an unidentified contributor to the same periodical when, in answer to an *Edinburgh Review* article in which Locke's epistemology is dismissed as merely "mechanical," he asserts, "Give us Locke's Mechanisms and we will envy no man's Mysticism. Give us to know the 'origin of our ideas,' to comprehend the phenomena 'which we see in the mind' and we will leave the question of the mind's essence to Transcendental speculation."[45]

These judgments were harbingers of more pointed rebuttals soon forthcoming. An article by the Reverend Leonard Withington in the *Quarterly Christian Review*, entitled "The Present State of Metaphysics,"[46] deprecates the value of philosophy in general, but at the same time appears to have been the first favorably to contrast Locke's views with those of a native Transcendentalism still in its germinal stage. It is note-worthy that Withington concentrates on the "psychological issue" involved. Charitably allowing that "Coleridge and his followers" really meant something by their "celebrated distinction" between Reason and Understanding, Withington proceeds to ask, "But what do they mean and how would an Englishman express the same thing?" Consideration leads him to the decision that ". . . . The whole mystery seems to be this: the mind sometimes turns its eye on the material world, surveys its operation, learns its laws, and makes its powers subservient to its purposes; and sometimes it looks inward on itself, learns its own powers, and surveys the agreement or discrepancy among its own ideas . . . ," but to consider these two operations evidence of a distinction in mental faculties has as little propriety ". . . as a one-eyed man would call his eye two faculties, because it was sometimes turned towards the heavens and sometimes toward the earth." Again, "Either this 'reason,' this Transcendental and supersensuous faculty, is something so sublime as to be above our reach . . . or it means what has been far better seen, and more clearly expressed, by every sober writer since the days of Locke." Suggested here is an apologia for Locke's epistemology that was to become standard among the critics of Transcendentalism: namely, the contention that a correct reading of Locke would show him to have recognized the two *operations* of the mind which the Transcendentalists professed to have discovered and distinguished by the terms "Reason" and "Understanding," and that if the Transcendentalists meant to accomplish more than merely the elevation of acknowledged operations by bestowing resounding titles—if, in short, they were bent on transforming the twofold capacity of the mind into a dichotomy of faculties—they were talking arrant nonsense. Withington himself is unable to find Coleridge's Reason a contributive concept since Locke had long ago pointed out "two sources of our ideas—sensation and reflexion," and he questions whether Reason "is anything more than a reflexive mind, conscious of its own operations." His conclusion is uncompromisingly severe: ". . . we do not remember in the whole history of human delusions a more pompous profession ending in a more contemptible nothingism."[47]

More consequential than Withington's article were two by Francis Bowen. Bowen's objections to Transcendentalism are to be read as complementary to the rejoinders of Andrews Norton in his dialogue with George Ripley, since taken together they comprise the gist of the Sensationalist-Unitarian answer to the challenge of Transcendentalism. For our purposes, the Bowen articles alone contain, at least in nucleus, all the pertinent arguments which were to be recurrently leveled against Transcendentalism—arguments which in reducing the foe constituted implied reaffirmation of allegiance to conventional Unitarianism and its associated philosophy. The occasion of Bowen's first article[48] was the publication of Emerson's *Nature*. In reviewing it, he finds it representative of a class of writings and is led to observe that "Within a short period, a new school of philosophy has arisen. . . . It rejects the aid of observation, and will not trust to experiment. . . . General truths are to be attained without the previous examination of particulars, and by the aid of a higher power than the understanding. . . . The sphere of intuition is enlarged and made to comprehend the most abstruse and elevated propositions respecting the being and destiny of man." He notes that the adoption of such a novel philosophy entails the forging of a special vocabulary, a practice which must encourage an unwarranted obscurity of language: "It would avail but little, perhaps, with some Transcendentalists to assert that the deepest minds have ever been the clearest, and to quote the example of Locke and Bacon, as men who could treat the most abstruse subjects in the most familiar and unintelligible terms." To his mind, one is well within one's right to "infer vagueness and incompleteness of thought from obscurity in language," and in support of this judgment he quotes with approval "a few homely remarks from the writings of a philosopher who enjoyed some repute in his day." The ironic allusion is, of course, to Locke.

Bowen's second article, coming shortly afterwards,[49] is a more sweeping censure of Transcendentalism. For purposes of summary, its content can be broken down into seven charges:

1. "There is *prima facie* evidence against it . . . for . . . it is abstruse in its dogmas, fantastic in its dress, and foreign in its origin."

2. Its passion for phraseological innovations leads not only to the "depravation of English style," but to a highly suspicious obscurity of thought.

3. As a necessary result of 1 and 2, it has "deepened the gulf between speculative and practical men," since clarity of philosophical language is "the only bridge which spans the chasm."[50]

4. It appeals from the authority of argument to that of "passion and feeling."

5. Its advocates include men familiar with the "sublimated atheism" of Fichte and the "downright pantheism" of Schelling. (Bowen merely hints these charges of atheism and pantheism; others are destined to make them familiar.)[51]

6. It does not recognize that ". . . there are mysteries in nature which human nature cannot penetrate; there are problems which the philosopher cannot solve."

7. Its touted distinction between Reason and Understanding either solely directs attention to two *aspects* of the mind's capacity, in which case it says nothing new; or it proclaims two *kinds* of mental faculties, in which case it is false. (This criticism is, of course, essentially the same as Withington's.)

The articles in the *Princeton Review* were still to be published, the formidable Norton was still to be heard from, innumerable random passages of hostile references were still to be penned, but the future indictments of Transcendentalism had been sharply prefigured by Bowen. Prescient, too (as well as timely), was the title Bowen chose for his second article, "Locke and the Transcendentalists," for although disputation over Transcendentalism was to rage for many years, integral to its philosophical history was to remain the name of John Locke, symbol of commitments too diverse and too profoundly rooted to permit facile compromise.

Notes

1. *The Journals of Bronson Alcott*, ed. Odell Shepard (Boston: Little, Brown, 1938), p. 24. An abbreviated account of Locke's relationship to Transcendentalism is contained in Merle Curti's "The Great Mr. Locke, America's Philosopher (1783–1861)," *Huntington Library Bulletin*, 11 (April 1937), 107–151.

2. The mere pejorative designation "Sensualism" is also common in contemporary literature. Thus, in an article ascribed to Charles Mayo Ellis: "The old Philosophy is sensual; that is, it affirms that all knowledge . . . may be shown to have come into the body through the senses . . . the new is spiritual" (*An Essay on Transcendentalism* (1842; rpt. Gainesville, Fla.: Scholars' Facsimiles & Reprints, 1954), pp. 22–23. Andrews Norton protested the application of "Sensualism" to Locke's philosophy and cited the "barbarism" as an example of the importation of Germanic usages, incompletely understood and inaccurately translated (*Remarks on a Pamphlet Entitled " 'The Latest Form of Infidelity' Examined"* [Cambridge, Mass.: John Owen, 1839], p. 58).

3. *Sketches of Modern Philosophy* (Hartford, Conn.: John C. Wells, 1842), p. 34.

4. Friedrich Ueberweg, *A History of Philosophy*, trans. G. S. Morris, with additions by Noah Porter (New York: Scribner, 1872), p. 451.

5. The Aldrich material is in "Report to the Council," *Proceedings of the American Antiquarian Association*, April 1879, pp. 22–39.

6. "Philosophical Instruction in Harvard University (1636–1906)," *Harvard Graduates' Magazine*, 37 (1928–1929), 36.

7. But not without protest from the more devout. As early as 1822, the Rev. Frederick Beasley, in the Dedication to his *A Search of Truth in the Science of the Human Mind* (Philadelphia: S. Potter, 1822), had maintained that Locke had been grossly misinterpreted by the Scottish philosophers, to whose claims of impressive innovations the bulk of his work is an energetic rebuttal. Edward Everett expressed his trust that Brown would not long be permitted to "usurp" the place "once occupied by the great master of intellectual science" (*North American Review*, 29 [1829]), and the *Christian Register* ([September 1834], 97) expressed its satisfaction that Giles has reintroduced the *Essay* as a textbook at Harvard.

8. *Memoir and Remains of the Rev. James Marsh*, ed. J. Torrey (Burlington, Vt.: C. Goodrich, 1852), p. 136. There is abundant evidence of the Scottish authority at the time of the Transcendental revolt. E. W. Todd provides especially

valuable information in his "Philosophy at Harvard College," *New England Quarterly*, 16 (March 1943), 63–90.

9. ". . . that justly celebrated oracle . . ." The accolade is Benjamin Rush's.

10. As Channing put it in answer to the surprise expressed by Miss Peabody that Brown had been adopted to the Andover curriculum: "I think I understand it. It denotes a change of tone at Andover, that will not reach the depth of their error, but make it a less noxious error" (Elizabeth Palmer Peabody, *Reminiscences of Reverend Wm. Ellery Channing* [Boston: Roberts Brothers, 1880], p. 140). From a very different quarter comes more specific assertion of the derived character of Scottish philosophy: "Locke is the proper father of Reid and Stewart with their school who, we must say, have rendered him but scanty justice" (Francis Bowen, *North American Review*, 53 [1841], 40). Bowen had maintained this position from the first: in 1837 he used the word "additive" ("Here everything is additive") to describe the relationship between the Scots and Locke ("Locke and the Transcendentalists," *Christian Examiner*, 23 [1837], 188).

11. *Democracy in America*, rev. and ed. Francis Bowen (Cambridge, Mass.: Sever and Francis, 1864). G. Stanley Hall has also noted the common indifference toward philosophical subjects and he reminds us of a half-forgotten simile once applied to nineteenth-century American thought: "philosophers in America are as rare as snakes in Norway" ("Philosophy in the United States," *Mind*, 4 [1894], 89–105).

12. First American edition, edited by James Marsh (Burlington, Vt.: Chauncy Goodrich, 1829). That this distrust of philosophical speculation was not limited to the ministry of New England is made clear by one of John McVicker's professed reasons for issuing his own edition of Coleridge's *Aids*, in 1839, without Marsh's *Essay*. McVicker, an Episcopalian theologian at Columbia, states of the *Essay* that ". . . it circulates what is deemed false and dangerous principles, *viz.*, that some system of metaphysical philosophy is essential to soundness in Christian doctrine." (An account of the rivalry between Marsh and McVicker will be found in "American Comments on Coleridge a Century Ago," by Alice D. Snyder, in *Coleridge: Studies by Several Hands on the Hundredth Anniversary of His Death* [London: Constable, 1934].) Presbyterian conviction that the encouragement of philosophy endangers orthodox dependence on revelation is found in an article by Samuel Tyler in the *Princeton Review*, 15 (1843), 249–250.

It may be observed that the alleged divorce between religion and philosophy constituted a strong incentive for the attacks of the Transcendentalists, so we are not surprised to find numerous references to the effect that "the bans of wedlock have been forbidden to religion and philosophy" (*Dial*, 1 [1840], 1; see also 1 [1840], 2, and 2 [1841], 1). Nine years after Marsh's remarks, George Ripley was to notice that "the wedded union of philosophy and religion . . . has not yet been consummated in the sanctuary of our holiest thoughts. This is the true cause of the ominous fact that an open dread of philosophy, and a secret doubt of religion, are not unfrequent in the midst of us" (*Specimens of Foreign Standard Literature* [Boston: Hilliard, Gray, 1838], I, 15). Fourteen years later, at least one Transcendentalist suggests that the movement, now past its first great challenge, had failed to effect the marriage: "You know the actual condition of the American church, that it has a theology which cannot stand the test of reason; and accordingly it very wisely resolved to throw reason overboard before it began its voyage" (Theodore Parker, "Some Account of My Ministry," November 1852); whereas it was Parker's conviction that ". . . a true method in theology marries the religious instinct to philosophical reflection and they will increase and multiply, replenishing the earth and subduing it; toil and thought shall dwell in their household, and desire and duty go hand in hand therein" ("A Sermon on True and False Theology," February 1858).

13. Representative are the sentiments of the elder Frothingham, spoken in 1834, in the midst of the furor over Transcendentalism, and quoted by his son: "The present era seems to be that of the apotheosis of human nature . . . give me back the simple form of a child's credulity, rather than mislead me into any philosophical refinement, that instructs me to presume, and leaves me to perish" (Octavius Brooks Frothingham, *Boston Unitarianism: 1820–1850* [New York: Putnams, 1890], p. 44).

14. G. Stanley Hall ("Philosophy in the United States," pp. 89–105) considers the extent and the effect of the control exercised over philosophical instruction by the nineteenth-century clergyman-professor. A. C. Armstrong states flatly that at the time in question ". . . the trend of philosophical instruction was controlled by dogmatic conviction" ("Philosophy in the United States," *Education Review*, 10 [1895], 11).

15. Curti comments on Locke and American deism. He also says of Locke's *Essay* that ". . . its plea for reliance on sensory experience and reflection rather than on innate ideas and the 'mysterious' tended to undermine the traditional sanctions of orthodoxy. Locke's position was, in many respects, anticipatory of that maintained a hundred years later by the early Unitarians" ("The Great Mr. Locke," p. 115). It should be pointed out, however, that by the time with which we are dealing Unitarianism had itself become comparatively "orthodox"; yet by emphasizing the restrictive aspect of Locke's epistemology in order to further the claim for revelation, it was able to continue, with happy consistency, its acceptance of the *Essay*.

16. As the *Dial* was to put it, "Religion had become chiefly and with the well-clad class of men, a matter of conviction, and they write Christian with their name as they write 'Mr.' because it is respectable" (1 [1840], 2).

17. This "caste" view was to be singled out for assault in the theological objections of the Transcendentalists, to whom it was a cardinal betrayal of the Protestant liberal tradition. Thus, in his controversy with Andrews Norton, George Ripley inveighs against his opponent's adoption and defense of "the exclusive principle"; that is, "the assumption of the right for an individual, or any body of individuals, to make their own private opinions the measure of what is fundamental in the Christian faith" (*The Latest Form of Infidelity Examined* [Boston: James Munroe, 1839]).

In concluding this sketch of Unitarian acceptance of Locke's philosophy, it is interesting to note the understandable prevalence of contemporary writings claiming Locke himself to be a Unitarian: e.g., the *Christian Examiner*, 11 (1831), and an American Unitarian Association reprint (Series 1, no. 77, 1833) of an English pamphlet, *Religious Opinions and Example of Milton, Locke and Newton*, by the Rev. Henry Acton of Exeter.

18. Noah Porter in Friedrich Ueberweg, *A History of Philosophy*, p. 454. Octavius Brooks Frothingham agrees: "The Unitarians as a class belonged to the school of Locke . . ." (*Transcendentalism in New England* [Boston: American Unitarian Association, 1903 [1876], p. 109).

19. Quoted in *The Memorial History of Boston*, ed. Justin Winsor (Boston: James R. Osgood, 1881), IV, 300. Ripley has here been scrupulously accurate (except, of course, in his lumping together "the cardinal positions of Locke and Hume") in reproducing Norton's view; e.g., one compares the last sentence of his summation with the following: "There can be no intuition, no direct perception of the truths of Christianity . . ." (*A Discourse on the Latest Form of Infidelity* [Cambridge,

Mass.: John Owen 1839], p. 32). Indeed, all of Ripley's sentences seem to have been suggested by passages in the pamphlets which Norton issued during his controversy with Ripley. For a chronology of the Norton-Ripley altercation, see Clarence L. F. Gohdes, *The Periodicals of American Transcendentalism* (Durham: Duke University Press, 1931), pp. 59–60.

20. *Boston Unitarianism*, p. 169.

21. The "radical" inheritance of Transcendentalism is the subject of Perry Miller's "From Edwards to Emerson," *New England Quarterly*, 13 (December 1940), 589–617.

22. Schneider calls Channing's sermon, "Likeness to God" (1828), "one of the first American formulations of transcendentalism" (Herbert W. Schneider, *A History of American Philosophy* [New York: Columbia University Press, 1946], p. 65).

23. The designation is Odell Shepard's in *Pedlar's Progress* (Boston: Little, Brown, 1937), p. 159; Emerson's *Nature* was, of course, their New Testament.

24. "Oration on Genius"; it is reprinted in Kenneth Walter Cameron, *Emerson the Essayist* (Raleigh, N.C.: Thistle Press, 1945), II, 9–12.

25. Marsh, Introductory Essay in his edition of Coleridge's *Aids to Reflection*.

26. Marjorie Nicolson has presented some of the considerable evidence of the popularity enjoyed by Marsh's edition of the *Aids* ("James Marsh and the Vermont Transcendentalists," *Philosophical Review*, 34 [January 1925], 28–50). It was probably this enthusiastic reception which prompted Marsh, in his Preface to Coleridge's *The Friend* (Burlington, Vt.: Chauncy Goodrich), two years later, to express the premature confidence that "It is no longer hazardous to one's reputation to call in question the authority of those philosophers who have been most popular among us."

27. James Elliot Cabot, *A Memoir of Ralph Waldo Emerson* (Boston: Houghton, Mifflin, 1887), I, 244.

28. *The Complete Works of Ralph Waldo Emerson*, ed. Edward Waldo Emerson (Boston: Houghton, Mifflin, 1903–1904), II, 287.

29. *Works*, I, 340.

30. Alcott, *Journals*, p. 66.

31. Alcott, *Journals*, p. 39.

32. *Boston Quarterly Review*, 2 (January 1839), 105–112. However, the unpredictable Brownson, always an unreliable ally of the Transcendentalists, was to contribute (only three years later) a recantation of his many barbed criticisms of Locke: ". . . we are not ashamed to own that our respect for Locke is every day increasing and we would not repeat the severe things which the indiscreet zeal of admirers has, on some former occasions, induced us to say of him. . . . The philosophy which commends itself by detracting from the imperishable glory of such a man as John Locke can be in vogue only for a day and must soon take its place with the things which are as if they had not been" (*Boston Quarterly Review*, 5 [April 1842], 181).

33. James Freeman Clarke, *Autobiography, Diary and Correspondence*, ed. Edward Everett Hale (Boston: Houghton, Mifflin, 1891), pp. 39, 89–90.

34. Introductory Notice, *Specimens of Foreign Standard Literature*.

35. *The Latest Form of Infidelity Examined*.

36. "A Sermon on the Moral Condition of Boston," February 1849.

37. *Essays and Reviews by Eminent English Churchmen* (New York, 1874). The volume reproduces Hedge's prefatory remarks of 1860 to the first American edition. For more on Hedge's background and opinion, see Ronald Vale Wells, *Three Christian Transcendentalists* (New York: Columbia University Press, 1943).

In quoting the evaluations of Locke by the rebellious younger men, one should not overlook the judgment of the less engaged Channing: "Locke's philosophy has quenched spirituality in modern thought, and so brings men to enthrone logical abstraction above the spirit . . ." (Peabody, *Reminiscences of Channing*, p. 140).

38. 1 (1841), 4.

39. *The Letters of Ralph Waldo Emerson*, ed. Ralph L. Rusk (New York: Columbia University Press, 1939), I, 412.

40. The most satisfactory single volume on Emerson's "formal" position remains Henry David Gray's *Emerson: A Statement of New England Transcendentalism as Expressed in the Philosophy of its Chief Exponent* (Palo Alto: Stanford University, 1917).

41. "Revelation is the disclosure of the Soul" (Emerson, *Works*, II, 282). "Each of us is a new born Bard of the Holy Ghost" (*Works*, I, 146). ". . . experience of the soul is a revelation of God" (Alcott, *Dial*, 1 (1841), 3).

42. *A Third Letter to Mr. Andrews Norton* (Boston: James Munroe, 1840).

43. Cousin's most specific contribution to the Transcendental controversy was his *Lectures on Locke*, presented to America under the title of *Elements of Psychology* (translated and introduced by C. S. Henry, 1834). Of the book, which by 1855 had achieved a fourth edition, so qualified a commentator as Noah Porter has said, "This work openly raised the standard of revolt against the fundamental principles and methods of Locke" (Ueberweg, *A History of Philosophy*, p. 453). In the light of the evidence attesting to the impact of Marsh's edition of the *Aids*, which preceded the *Elements* by five years, and the marked lack of evidence which would confirm any comparable influence asserted for Cousin's work (except on Brownson, who at the time was a combative disciple of Cousin and who, it should be recalled, disassociated his Cousinism from Transcendentalism), we can say that Porter was in error if his evaluation is meant to claim *American* priority of significance for the *Elements*. The truth is that Cousin's "professional" analysis of Locke's deficiencies could only corroborate the already established objections of the Transcendentalists; in contrast, the chief reason for the greater effect of Marsh's Introductory Essay, aside from its precedence in time, was that Marsh articulated their highly emotional repugnance towards Locke's role in the spiritual life of New England.

This suggested weight of Cousin on Transcendentalism is a reminder that non-American sources of basic influence on the movement have been commonly over-emphasized. Many such sources have indisputable claim for recognition, but it is always necessary to remember that to a considerable extent the Transcendentalists borrowed those European (and Asian) concepts and emphases which most satisfactorily expressed the core of their rebellion. The core itself had a strong indigenous history (as, of course, had American Unitarianism as well). With respect to German philosophy, this view is supported by Wellek: "What attracted the American thinkers was . . . the fact that the German philosophy shared with them a common enmity to the methods and results of eighteenth century British empiricism and to the tradition of skepticism and materialism in general. . . . The Transcendentalists were merely looking for corroboration of their faith. They found it in Germany, but ultimately they did not need the confirmation. Their faith was deeply rooted in their minds and their own spiritual ancestry" (René Wellek, "Emerson and German Philosophy," *New England Quarterly*, 16 [March 1943], 61–62).

44. The Everett articles are in 18 (1824) and 19 (1829). The quotations are from the second article.

45. "Defence of Mechanical Philosophy," 33 (1831), 122.

46. December 1834.

47. That the Transcendentalists' reading of Locke could find in his "reflexion" nothing that would justify Withington's reduction of Reason to an idiosyncratic "translation" of Locke's concept is evident from the following passage: "It seems obvious at first sight that, in denying the mind any primary principles, and reflection being, by definition, only the notice which the mind, this blank piece of paper, takes of its own operations, reflection can add nothing to the stock of ideas furnished by sensation. It is a mere spectator; its office merely to note impressions" (*Dial*, 2 [1841], 1).

In addition to the reference to be made to Francis Bowen's stand, warm agreement with Withington on the speciousness of the Reason-Understanding distinction may be found in an article by James W. Alexander and Albert Dod entitled "Transcendentalism" (*Princeton Review*, January 1839). This piece and one by Charles Hodge, entitled "The School of Hegel" (*Princeton Review*, January 1840), were subsequently to be published together by Andrews Norton under the title *Two Articles from the Princeton Review, Concerning the Transcendental Philosophy of the Germans and of Cousin and Its Influence on Opinion in this Country* (Cambridge, Mass.: John Owen, 1840). Brownson is also critical of the distinction (*Boston Quarterly Review*, April 1842). Withington's article comes in for high praise in a pamphlet attributed to William Mitchell and entitled *Coleridge and the Moral Tendency of his Writings*, a vitriolic attack on the alleged moral and religious implications of Coleridge's thought.

48. *Christian Examiner*, 11 (1836), 371. Wells gives us the following statement on Bowen's own position: "Basically . . . Bowen's interest lay in demonstrating the validity of the principles of natural religion, whereas Marsh, Hedge, and Henry sought to re-establish Christian principles by means of a marriage of philosophy to religion. This union Bowen considered the source of all evil both to religion and to philosophy" (*Three Christian Transcendentalists*, p. 8).

Wells's summary calls for two comments. The first is that Bowen's interest in establishing the validity of natural religion is harmonious with Locke's own concern: e.g., "Locke believed that he had established, philosophically, the existence of God and 'natural' religion" (*Encyclopaedia Brittanica*, 14th ed., XIV, 272). The second is that, read out of context, the judgment that ". . . Marsh . . . sought to re-establish Christian principles by means of a marriage of philosophy to religion" could suggest a closer affinity of Marsh to the Transcendentalists of the Boston-Cambridge-Concord stamp than in point of fact existed. In truth, although Marsh's goal (". . . a marriage of philosophy to religion") was the same as that of the Young Turks his edition of the *Aids* had awakened, his Andover Congregational training, his convictions (and, no doubt, his personality) could not permit him to be sympathetic with their perspective of this goal—or with their intemperate rhetoric. Thus: "There are, I am persuaded, but two thoroughly consistent [and] complete systems [and] these are, *the evangelical system*, which places the ultimate views of truth and grounds of conviction beyond the sphere of the speculative understanding [it is significant that Marsh is here using 'understanding' with the Kantian, not the Coleridge-Transcendental connotation] in the voice of conscience [and] the perishing *need* of a spirit fully awakened to a sense of what it needs; [and] for the other a system, that, confiding in speculative conclusions, explains away in the last resort the authority of conscience [and] terminates in a *consistent pantheism*. I very much fear that those, who talk of spiritual philosophy among you, mean nothing more than the opposite of sensualism, [and] still have a wide space between them [and] the spiritualism of St. Paul" (Marsh to Richard Henry Dana, Burlington, 21 August 1832, Wells, *Three Christian Transcendentalists*, p.

161). Again: "The whole of Boston Transcendentalism I take to be rather a superficial affair; and there is some force in the remark of a friend of mine that the 'Dial' indicates rather the place of the moon than of the sun. . . . They pretend to no system or unity, but each utters, it seems, the inspiration of the moment, assuming that it all comes from the universal heart, when ten to one it comes only from the stomach of the individual" (Marsh to Henry J. Raymond, Burlington, 1 March 1841, Wells, *Three Christian Transcendentalists*, p. 161).

49. *Christian Examiner*, 23 (1837), 371.

50. It was this arraignment which Brownson took as the springboard for a rejoinder in the *Boston Quarterly Review* (January 1838): "Philosophy and Common Sense."

51. Notably, Andrews Norton, *A Discourse on the Latest Form of Infidelity*, and the *Princeton Review*: 11 (January 1839); 12 (January 1840); 20 (April 1848); 28 (April 1856). One must also remember the judgment of Marsh.

The alleged "infidelity" of the "new school" became an increasingly awkward issue in the internecine conflict between Unitarianism and Transcendentalism and was intimately related to the eventual resignation of Emerson from the ministry and the "excommunication" of Parker. The stridency and extravagance of expression of the more vocal Transcendentalists placed Unitarianism in an embarrassing position. Calvinism had long since labeled an early Unitarianism "a half-way house" to infidelity and had predicted that by the dropping of one orthodox doctrine after another the infidelity would become complete. Stung by this reminder, Unitarianism might have been expected to have dealt with conscionable severity with its refractory minority. However, not only did its tradition of liberalism make such chastisement distasteful, but also its past remonstrances against Calvinism's "exclusive system" would emphasize the inconsistency of any attempt to discipline its own protestants. The subject is covered in C. H. Faust's "The Background of the Unitarian Opposition to Transcendentalism," *Modern Philology*, 35 (February 1938), 297–324.

"New England's Transcendentalism: Native or Imported?"

Perry Miller*

Transcendentalism, a fairly parochial disturbance in and around Boston in the 1830's and 1840's, may be of interest to all serious students of American culture, wherever they reside, because it is at least an instructive episode in the history of the American intellect. Its intrinsic importance must not be exaggerated, but the issues it presents invest it with a fascination.

Perhaps a good way of attempting to place New England's Transcendentalism in a proper perspective is to review briefly the fortunes of Emerson's reputation in literary discourse of the last century. Indeed, the critical estimation of all the group around him has followed the same fluctuations—with, as we shall see, one exception. As Emerson repeatedly insisted, this was no organized band. They were simply a number of young people who around 1830 found themselves sharing a set of new ideas of which their elders disapproved. They were steadily ridiculed and finally attacked, especially after 1838 when Emerson delivered "The Divinity School Address" at Harvard. The graduate students had invited him; thereafter the faculty took away from the students the right to invite anybody.

Emerson was denounced by the greatest pundit of the Divinity School, Andrews Norton—who had been Emerson's mentor and was popularly known as "the Unitarian Pope"—for purveying "the Latest Form of Infidelity." What did Norton mean by infidelity? He made clear that the essence of Emerson's heresy was a trust in intuition, in direct perception of truth. Confident as was the Unitarian reliance on the powers of the human reason, Norton was certain that men have never by unassisted reason been able to attain assurance concerning fundamentals. But Emerson blandly asserted,

*Reprinted from *Literary Views: Critical and Historical Essays*, ed. Carroll Camden (Chicago: University of Chicago Press for William Marsh Rice University, 1964), pp. 115–129.

> The intuition of the moral sentiment is an insight of the perfection of the laws of the soul. These laws execute themselves. They are out of time, out of space, and not subject to circumstance.

It is not difficult to see wherein this notion would outrage the clergy, or indeed the faculty of Harvard College, or anybody who holds forth to an audience in time and space in an effort to instruct them on something which they are presumed not to know of themselves.

Emerson added insult to injury in a once famous passage which his Unitarian colleagues felt was a rude caricature of their pulpit manner:

> I once heard a preacher who sorely tempted me to say I would go to church no more. Men go, thought I, where they are wont to go, else had no soul entered the temple in the afternoon. A snow-storm was falling around us. The snow-storm was real, the preacher merely spectral, and the eye felt the sad contrast in looking at him, and then out of the window behind him into the beautiful meteor of the snow. He had lived in vain. He had no one word intimating that he had laughed or wept, was married or in love, had been commended, or cheated, or chagrined.

After all, we should not be too hard put to it to understand why dignified gentlemen of the stature of Andrews Norton would snort with rage when not only did they have to hear nonsense of this nature delivered from the pulpit of Divinity Hall but also to behold their students greeting it as wisdom. What minister then or now (or for that matter what professor in his classroom) who, instead of expounding doctrine or sticking to his subject matter, should talk to his audience on how often he had been in love, how many times married, and how frequently he had been chagrined and cheated, could expect to hold their attention for more than one relation?

Emerson himself never, of course, made such a ludicrous parade of his inward life on the lecture platform as this passage, had he taken it literally, would have obliged him to exhibit. But many of those who gathered around him—who in public opinion were known as his followers—invited the derision of proper Boston by conduct which, according to the standards of the day, was manifestly absurd. Jones Very, we can now perceive, was veritably insane. Margaret Fuller, possessed by her "mountainous me," indulged in extravagances of costume, rhetoric, and eventually of sexual daring which could bring only the most severe reprobation upon the ideas which she was supposed to have taken from the saintly Mr. Emerson. And indeed, in the considered opinion of respectable Boston and likewise of all solid New England, the supreme example of the pernicious consequences of Emerson's bland tuition was Henry

Thoreau. Here was a youth who resolved not to be spectral as against the snowstorm. So he fled from all civic responsibilities, did not marry, begot no children, never held a steady job, paid no taxes, and lived alone as a hermit. No wonder that many then feared Transcendentalism to be, as Emerson ironically remarked, a "conspiracy against State Street."

The revolution in popular esteem was somehow wrought along with the Civil War. For thirty years after the "Divinity School Address" Emerson was officially ostracized from Harvard Yard, never officially asked to speak. But at long last, coincident with the election of Harvard's revolutionary President William Eliot, Emerson was chosen an overseer— on which board his first vote was for the retention of compulsory chapel! Harvard has long since done public penance for this neglect of one of its most distinguished children by naming its hall of philosophy for Emerson. In the lobby is a statue made by Daniel French; if you look at it carefully, especially when there are no other people about, you will see that it frequently lights up with an amused grin. By the end of the century, Oliver Wendell Holmes can write a biography of Emerson; Barrett Wendell considers him a pillar of the orthodox New England mentality, along with Longfellow and Lowell. Indeed, as early as 1876 O. B. Frothingham, in what was generally taken to be the definitive treatise, *Transcendentalism in New England*, presented the whole business as an American counterpart of the great German philosophical assertion of idealism. The once outcasts of Unitarian New England were now saluted as worthy equivalents of Kant, Fichte, and Schelling. So Frothingham could enthrone Emerson and surround him with his courtiers— Parker, Ripley, Hedge. Interestingly enough, however, in this work of canonization, Henry Thoreau is left out. Emerson and even the firebrand Parker might be made respectable, but not Thoreau.

Yet in the most complacent days of Emerson's elevation there were a few dissenting murmurs. Both Henry Adams and Charles Eliot Norton could be irritated by the dogmatic blindness of Emerson's resolute optimism. Their affectionate objections were, as the event proved, only mild prefigurations of the revolt which in the 1920's became a savage condemnation of what Santayana indelibly smeared as the "genteel tradition." Oddly enough the incendiary of 1838 now appeared the symbol of all that was most repulsive, evasive, emasculated in this blanket of gentility. He was now denounced not because he had preached a trust in intuition but because he was pale, sexless, and an imitator. He was demoted from the eminence he had so painfully acquired, on the grounds that he was entirely derivative. And by this time, the attitude of rejection of his optimism was an orthodoxy beyond any that Unitarianism ever dreamed of. Yet the fascination and complexity of the story increase as we note that in the 1920's the surge of Thoreau's reputation really gathered momentum.

I think it fair to say that the period when the favorite sport of commentators on American letters was making fun of Mr. Emerson came to an end with the passing of the vogue of H. L. Mencken. There has lately been considerable sane discussion of Emerson; while there is no need to reassert some of the extravagances of late nineteenth-century New England patriotism, still we can see him looming large precisely because, however great was his debt to Wordsworth or Coleridge, he was *not* derivative. His sanity, clear perception, and intermittent wit become the more highly prized the less we have to lament his emotional limitations. At the same time, we may welcome a similar steadying of the critical estimate of the group as a whole. Christopher Cranch, for example, has been receiving mature treatment, let alone Theodore Parker and George Ripley, for whom it is long overdue; Margaret Fuller is being rescued from the folds of adoring feminists who did their best to smother all evidences of her intellect. We are attaining a new, and I am sure a salutary, sense that though they were a small band and had little or no effect upon American politics and economy, their real importance is that they were the first (and in many respects most eloquent) protest of the American sensibility against what in their day was rapidly becoming and in ours has implacably remained a "business" civilization.

Inevitably the Transcendentalists' wails about the pressures of making a living or making money seem quaint to us. Their world was as yet so little industrialized or financialized, was still so close to the agrarian pastoralism of the eighteenth century, that we who know Pittsburgh and Wall Street may pardonably wonder what they had to complain about. But precisely here their prescience becomes remarkable. Emerson, with serenity and precision, became their spokesman, as for instance in "Man the Reformer," read before the Mechanics' Apprentices' Library Association in Boston on 25 January 1841:

> It cannot be wondered at that this general inquest into abuses should arise in the bosom of society, when one considers the practical impediments that stand in the way of virtuous young men. The young man, on entering life, finds the way to lucrative employments blocked with abuses. The ways of trade are grown selfish to the borders of theft, and supple to the borders (if not beyond the borders) of fraud. The employments of commerce are not intrinsically unfit for a man, or less genial to his faculties; but these are now in their general course so vitiated by derelictions and abuses at which all connive, that it requires more vigor and resources than can be expected of every young man, to right himself in them; he is lost in them; he cannot move hand or foot in them. Has he genius and virtue? the less does he find them fit for him to grow in, and if he would thrive in

them, he must sacrifice all the brilliant dreams of boyhood and youth as dreams; he must forget the prayers of his childhood and must take on him the harness of routine and obsequiousness.

One could easily compose an *explication* on this passage longer than this whole paper, simply on the connotations and even the unconscious implications of the superb vocabulary—"inquest," "supple," "intrinsically," "dreams of boyhood." The whole history of the impact of an evolving society upon an intellect utterly unprepared for what it was working upon itself is contained within this passage. But surely the most striking, and the most significant, phrases are in the concluding clauses, where the dreams of boyhood become "prayers," now harnessed to "routine and obsequiousness." Henry Thoreau would put the anguish more memorably: "Everywhere I go, men pursue me and paw me with their dirty institutions." Those of us today who annually on 15 April are pawed by the dirtiest of institutions can barely comprehend what Henry was talking about. Nevertheless, he conceived that the American order, even in that easy period, had already come to be one which pawed men into conforming, into obsequiousness, and above all into routine. And we suspect that the threat of the latter was to him and to Emerson the most repulsive—as it was to prove in the twentieth century to those more humiliatingly subjected to it.

Thus we are obliged to ask the central question: if these Transcendental children of a (to our way of thinking) relatively idyllic America were propelled to express so vehement a revolt against their society, from whence did the vehemence spring? Why a revolt at all? Here is the issue for historical and for critical appreciation.

One factor, a factor that must never be underestimated, was the impact of Europe. But is this to be rated, in the manner of O. B. Frothingham, the sole one, or even the chief one? Margaret Fuller no doubt received early in her tempestuous life the inspiration of Madame de Staël's *Corinne*, and it drove her through the rest of her career. The young men who issued during the early 1830's the various articles that became statements and manifestoes produced writings which are replete with invocations of names which meant nothing to Andrews Norton—strange, weird creatures like Herder, Coleridge, Benjamin Constant, John Paul Richter. The youths who pushed these reviews into the pages of the Unitarian *Christian Examiner*—until at last the editors put a stop to the nonsense—made an elaborate and generally awkward effort to speak the names with nonchalance, as though of course all cultivated persons knew who these authors were. For example, Frederic Hedge in an 1833 article on Coleridge (which years later he modestly claimed was the first in America to ask for a respectful recognition of Transcendentalism) declared with affected casualness, "In a review of Mr. Coleridge's literary life, we must not omit to notice that marked fondness for metaphysics, and particularly for German metaphysics, which has exercised so decisive an influence over all his writings." This innocent observation may seem to us merely Hedge's sharp recognition of historical contiguity, but to his elders in New England it was a flag of revolt, doubly unfurled.

When the faculty of the Harvard Divinity School—and along with them the professors at Harvard College—bestirred themselves to ask who were these foreign people, they discovered that Madame de Staël had had many lovers and that George Sand was still having them. For these reasons, even if not for a variety of more intellectual worries, men like Andrews Norton might justifiably have striven to relegate Emerson, Parker, and Ripley to a side show named the latest form of infidelity—and so of no pertinence to the life of any American mind. These heretics were none of our breeding; they were merely a few (as indeed they were) infatuated appropriators of obscure European notions. If this was all they had to say for themselves—and despite their volubility they seemed to have no more to say—they were a pale imitation of a pretentious and mystagogical German silliness. If this were what they were, then in America they were exotics. They were justifiably excluded from any effect, or even indirect influence, upon the development of American thought.

The exoticism of the Transcendentalists' figure in American life— if I may so use the term—has long figured as a hindrance to our comprehending their historical role. Nothing, I suppose, can more linger in the fantasy of tourists as a symbol of futility than the "Concord School of Philosophy," so assiduously visited by those who enter with reverence the house sanctified to the memory of Louisa May Alcott. Yet when Louisa May becomes the favorite of posterity above her ineffectual father, what is happening for the moment is a triumph of Andrews Norton over "infidelity." It is an insubstantial victory. If the American hostility to what Norton and his colleagues called the "German disease" was a vindication of their conception of Americanism, then they had yet to reckon with—in fact never did reckon with—the respects in which Transcendentalism was only in part an importation.

I am the last historian in America—I hope—who would endeavor to treat Transcendentalism as wholly, or even primarily, a native phenomenon. There is no gainsaying that as an intellectual perturbation it was as much stimulated from abroad as was the assiduous campaign, then fully in progress, for the appropriation to American circumstances of the English Common Law and of portions of the Continental Civil Law.

New England Transcendentalism will always signify the effect upon an American provinciality of a European sophistication with which it was not entirely competent to deal—despite the swaggering assurances of such would-be pundits of the *Examiner* as Hedge, Ripley, Brownson, and Parker. But we have always this reflection to disturb us: from this influx— this lesson of discontent against routine, against "sensualism," against externalism in all its forms—came (to an America which by all proprie- ties should have been the ultimate in content) the message of discontent. And among the most sensitive of Americans, those who could easily have had no cause for discontent, the response was immediate. They instinctively, or intuitively, rebelled against the "sensualism" of a society which had barely begun to exhibit the enormity of its potential.

Once we can perceive the galvanizing effect of European ideas—of those we glibly term "romantic"—upon the domestic situation, we are tempted to suggest that "galvanic" is the wrong adjective:—they were catalytic. They did not so much arouse by imparting new viewpoints as they stirred latent propensities. They inspired these youths to reject all forms of what they called sensualism—and often these were quite indis- criminate in their application of the term. They gave the greatest offense by equating the sensational psychology of John Locke and the Scottish philosophers with profane sensualism. Since the Unitarian liberation from Calvinism had been achieved under the aegis of such thinkers, and since Unitarians were eminently men of probity and self-discipline, they could not help seeing in every invocation of the Germans a nasty aspersion on themselves. The young men never accused their elders of profligacy, but they were becoming so distressed by a society wherein things had leaped into the saddle that in order to object to being ridden they struck at the very foundation of the system they hated. Only when we appreciate fully both the spiritual and social gulf that the "German disease" (as most normal Americans called it) created can we compre- hend how divisive was, for example, Hedge's advertising of the German virtues in his 1834 essay of Schiller:

> The class of writings, to which this work [a biography of Schiller] belongs, is peculiar, we believe, to modern times. It is characterized by a spirit of fierce disquietude, a dissatisfaction with the whole mechanism of society, and a presumptuous questioning of all that God or man has ordained. It represents a state of being which no word or combination of words can exactly express; a disease peculiar to ardent natures, in early life:
>
> > "The flash and outbreak of a fiery mind;
> > A savageness of unreclaimed blood;"

a keen sensibility to all that is absurd and oppressive in social life, a scorning of authority and custom, a feeling that all the uses of this world are weary and unprofitable, together with the consciousness of high powers, bright visions of ideal excellence, and a restless yearning after things not granted to man.

Assuredly this was not a frame of mind that Harvard College or the Divinity School wanted in the least to cultivate! And even more assuredly, it was no mood in which to get ahead on State Street!

To students aware of the violence of the several European forms of Romantic tumult the words Emerson employed in his aged recollection of the 1830's in New England may seem melodramatic and ludicrously exaggerated. Yet they attest the accuracy of his failing memory, because they recapture what the "ardent natures" of the period deeply felt. "The key to the period," he wrote, "appeared to be that the mind had become aware of itself. Men grew reflective and intellectual." Previously the standard belief had been that "a shining social prosperity was the beatitude of man," but suddenly the conviction arose that the nation existed for the individual. In one of his finest sentences Emerson continues: "The young men were born with knives in their brain, a tendency to introversion, self-dissection, anatomizing of motives." Hence this new race hated "tolls, taxes, turnpikes, banks, hierarchies, governors, yea, almost laws." They rebelled against both theological and political dogmas, against saints "or any nobility in the unseen." If all this was not sedition and subversion, what was it? No wonder the ancient and the honorable of the earth heard here the crack of doom!

Thus our question becomes all the more pressing: why foment such a rebellion in America? We can readily understand how the contagion of the French Revolution excited young Germans to arise against the decrepit and fossilized system of petty principalities. We can comprehend why in France itself the populace were goaded into storming the prisons, burning chateaus, and cutting off the head of King Louis. We can also understand the rage of a Hazlitt or a Byron against the reactionary regime of King George. But in the United States we had no king to execute and no nobility to proscribe. We had got rid of all those encumbrances. America was prosperous, expanding, and there was abundant opportunity for all. From our point of view we may indeed ask where in all the history of the world were careers more open to talent, let alone genius, than in the nation of Andrew Jackson? What could the terms "conservative" or "reactionary" mean in that community? Emerson's motto of "self-reliance," though it may have seemed infidelity to Andrews Norton, now appears to us the banner of the whole age, not just of a few eccentric Transcendentalists. What epoch was ever more self-reliant than that of Fulton and Morse, of steamboats and railroads, of the moving frontier, of the sewing machine and the Hoe press? Where could the individual more unhamperedly express himself? Emerson might sound terribly radical when he declared, "Whosoever would be a man must be a non-conformist," but even in his lifetime the sentence could be inscribed on plaques in the offices of vice-presidents of banks. And why then were there so many efforts to escape the relation to even so loose a society as this, why Brook Farm and the myriad other would-be ideal communities? Henry Thoreau denounced the social order in the time of his Walden sojourn as a "joint stock company." Certainly compared with the regulations imposed upon our living today, our economy of giant corporations and foundations, the America of Thoreau's day was a joyful chaos, a marvelous realm of rugged individualism and free competition which some of our presently styled "conservative" politicians dream can be revived.

The problem of properly evaluating Transcendentalism as a movement of protest in America is further complicated by the fact that in New England, because of local historical circumstances, it was enmeshed in the controversy over the historicity of the miracles related in the New Testament. Norton and the Unitarian critics were not half so much enraged with Emerson for saying that truth is intuitive as they were for his concluding therefrom that in the name of intuitive truth mankind no longer needed the external (and sensual!) support of recorded exceptions to the laws of nature in order to be truly religious. To make the miracles a test of the spiritual mission of Christ was indeed to manacle the conception of a divine teacher to a sensual notion of history; it was to prostitute the possible meaning of the Gospel to exactly the same materiality of the commercial society against which the ardent natures were objecting. A "joint stock company" which pretended to be Christian and then could conceive of Christianity in only this way had already so lost the idea of spirituality as to call for a savageness of unreclaimed blood from those with knives in their brain.

Now a similar attack upon a literal acceptance of the biblical miracles was being levied in Europe. The historian of ideas may rightly see in it one among many manifestations of the new sense of historical process that everywhere was a symptom of the Romantic revolt against the age of static reason. Some of these European expessions exerted an influence in America or at least in New England, particularly Strauss's *Life of Jesus* in 1835. Yet actually these New Englanders were not so much inspired by the German "higher criticism," about which most of them (with the exception of Theodore Parker) knew very little, as they were by a disgust with the dogmatic way the Unitarianism in which they were raised had fastened upon the miracles as the sole attestation of spiritual reality. In Europe the debate over the historicity of the miracles and the quest for a historical Jesus is indeed an intense intellectual affair, but it is not central to the life of the mind. Nobody imagined that society would be toppled or morality destroyed because Strauss or Renan sought to put the Messiah into a historical context. But in Cambridge and Boston the Transcendentalists' reduction of the miracles to the plane of "nature" seemed infinitely more dangerous even than their denunciations of the joint stock company of society. Consequently a vast amount of the literature in the decade or so after Emerson's "Address," and a disproportionate amount of youthful energy, were expended in the sterile argument. In the larger perspective of American intellectual history this is not one of the major issues of the century—compared, let us say, with those of geology and then of evolution in relation to Christian belief. Because New England Transcendentalism could never rid itself of the incubus thus early fastened upon it, it always presents itself to a critical world as lamed by a provincial accident. It was parochial enough to begin with, but its effort to achieve at least an affectation of cosmopolitanism was sadly hindered by the fanatical demand of its enemies that it fight on the ground of their choosing.

And then we have a still more annoying puzzle in our endeavor to place the Transcendentalists both in time and space. They were undoubtedly stirred, even aroused by their importation of the intoxicating literature of European Romanticism. But the Europeans were intoxicating because, primarily, they were conducting a violent reaction against the eighteenth century. They universally denounced the previous age as one of sterility and frivolity, of the heroic couplet, of the rules, of the artificial vocabulary, as well as of political oppression. Especially in Germany was the regime of the petty courts identified with the corruption of French manners. We may find the image of those principalities given in *The Marriage of Figaro* charming (the scene is of course Germany and not the pretended Spain), but such antics were not so charming to the actual peasants and not at all to the intellectuals. Therefore the young Americans were avidly reading writers who burned with anger against the Enlightenment. Yet as Professor Alfred North Whitehead once remarked, in that casual profundity of which only he was capable, "the secret of understanding America is that it never had an eighteenth century." Many have objected against him that the Declaration of Independence is thoroughly of the century, Benjamin Franklin incarnates it, the Constitution is a product of it. Well, in a sense yes, but these manifestations are relatively few. We do not have an eighteenth-century experience in the way in which Voltaire is of the age, or Diderot is, or the German courts were. The American eighteenth century is squeezed in between Jonathan Edwards and the Second Awakening of 1800. It is fortunate for us that our great state papers and our War for Independence could be enacted in this interval, but even then the Enlightenment did not bite deeply into the Protestant, or if you will Puritan, heritage of the seventeenth century. We jump fairly abruptly from the rural, pious, hard-working world of the colonies into the nineteenth-century era of expansion, exploitation, movement, and romantic unrest.

In New England the Enlightenment can be said to have produced Unitarianism, or rather imparted to the provinces an atmosphere in which this could painlessly evolve out of Puritan intellectualism. But New England Unitarianism as compared with Continental Deism—with for example Helvetius—is very, very mild indeed. When therefore these young men with knives in their brain were becoming excited by books and articles denouncing the eighteenth century and they looked about them for something to denounce in their region, about all they could find for a target was this inoffensive Unitarianism. They had no need for resisting traditional Christianity. They were kept from fighting Calvinism because their Unitarian fathers and teachers stood between them and the orthodoxy of the back-country. It was not the Awakening or the Methodists who were oppressing them; it was this liberal Unitarianism that was crushing them in the vise of routine and obsequiousness. They aspired to be rebellious in terms comparable to those of their European heroes and heroines—Novalis, Herder, Madame De Staël, Carlyle—but they could not muster up a really profound revulsion against the past. The best they could manufacture was a revulsion against the very recent past, actually the present. They might suppose that they were being American Byrons but they had no way to get out of the moral patterns that ruled New England from the Puritan foundation and had never been shattered by any eighteenth-century cynicism. Their quarrel with their past was no satanic rebellion but only a shame that America had so little to show in the life of the mind. As Emerson beautifully summed up the American predicament in the opening paragraph of "The American Scholar" in 1837, our festivals so far have been simply a friendly sign of the persistence of a love of letters among a people too busy to produce any. The American task thus was not to reject the eighteenth century and the rule of reason, but to contend with the present: "Perhaps the time is already come when it ought to be, and will be, something else; when the sluggard intellect of this continent will look from under its iron lids and fill the postponed expectation of the world with something better than the exertions of mechanical skill." In this spirit he announced that the day of our dependence on the learning of other lands was drawing to a close—just in the very day that he and his contemporaries were finding a resolution to achieve independence in a voluminous absorption of the new learning of Romantic Europe!

New England Transcendentalism thus is, after all, a peculiarly American phenomenon: while New England did have a past, and sentient young persons like Emerson, Thoreau, and Margaret Fuller were entirely conscious of it, yet in a very real sense they were without a past. Or a more precise way of putting it is simply that they had no experience of the French Revolution and all its woes, no share in the disillusionment which came from committing oneself to the wild hope of the Revolution and then being broken by the Terror. They could read of these matters, and often talk fluently about them, but they did not actually *know*. One need only compare the heartbreaking account in Wordsworth's *The Prelude* with the lighthearted treatment of it in Emerson, particularly in the "Napoleon" chapter of *Representative Men*. Furthermore, in America there were no unrepentant revolutionaries who had to stand with their backs against the wall and maintain the radical stance against the tides of black reaction. We never had a Hazlitt. Perhaps the only American of the era who had at least some awareness of what the agony of keeping his head high amid defeat could be was Herman Melville, but his suffering was as remote from Transcendental comprehension as Hazlitt's.

The Transcendentalists are a part of the international movement historians call Romanticism. Their devotion to the Germans, to Wordsworth, to Victor Cousin, demonstrate their participation in it. Still, we have to say of them that an essential chapter in the biography of Romanticism is entirely missing in the lives of these Americans. It is as though, having barely passed the age of puberty, and become adolescents at the age of eighteen, they awoke the next morning to find themselves aged thirty or so, having missed all those turbulent and charming perturbations of age twenty. Wherefore the peculiar pathos of their attempts to appropriate the delirium of a Romanticism they could not experience. There is something gallant and at the same time poignant in their efforts to play the role of men and women of the world. In this contradiction we may find—or at least I fancy we may— the compulsion behind their special veneration of *Nature*, behind Emerson's book so entitled in 1836, which is the heart of all their thinking and feeling. They go to Nature not for solace against the betrayals worked upon them by civilization and by reason, as in the last books of *The Prelude*, but for a source of the resistance which they must begin to put up against the iron lids of American mechanism. It is all they have to save them from routine obsequiousness. In this respect the supreme statement—even more than Emerson's *Nature*—is, as time has now made clear, Thoreau's *Walden*.

Among the little band there is perhaps only one exception—Margaret Fuller. In 1846, after devouring more of the literature of Romanticism than any of her colleagues, and contributing to the American image of Europe, she at last went there and encountered the reality. She took part in a real revolution, the Roman one of 1848. She nursed

wounded and dying men in the hospitals while her husband stood guard
on the ramparts. She and he went down in defeat before the soldiers
of reaction, and so she learned what Europe meant. One is moved
to tears to find that she received from, as she called them, "the clean
white hands" of Mr. Emerson, in the midst of the ordeal, a letter saying
that Italy needs a great man. She shot back in cold anger, "Mazzini is
a great man." But in Concord nobody could understand that. Nobody
there could understand that she had bitten deep into the bitter fruit,
and all were dismayed at the prospect of having to cope with her upon
her return, complete with a husband (at least putative) and a child.
Her cruel extinction in 1850 saved them the necessity.

They could therefore rest content with their original formulation
of the American problem as an opposition or confrontation between
nature and civilization. Out of this arose a happy version of the American genius. He stands amid Nature, and with it to assist him, to guide
his steps aright, he will not be sucked into commerce or trade. He can
ransom himself, Emerson told the mechanics, from the duties of economy
by the rigor and privation of his habits:

> For privileges so rare and grand, let him not stint to pay a great tax.
> Let him be a caenobite, a pauper, and if need be, celibate also. Let
> him learn to eat his meals standing, and to relish the taste of fair
> water and black bread. He may leave to others the costly conveniences
> of housekeeping, and large hospitality, and the possession of works
> of art. Let him feel that genius is a hospitality, and that he who can
> create works of art needs not collect them. He must live in a cham-
> ber, and postpone his self-indulgence, forewarned and forearmed
> against that frequent misfortune of men of genius—the taste for
> luxury.

This taste for luxury—and Emerson clearly implies the luxuries of
emotion and the senses as well as those of housekeeping—is the tragedy
of genius. But there are many forms of tragedy. In *Walden*—which in
part is the record of Henry's endeavor to act out the progam Waldo
outlined to the mechanics—Thoreau cried in unmistakably oratorical
tones, "Simplify, simplify, simplify." The American genius thus stands
amid Nature, either literally as did Thoreau or in dreams of it within
the city as did Bryant in New York. He does not go to the left bank of
Paris and live in a garret. He does not loll in splendor as did Goethe in
Weimar. He does not even flee to the Alps of Switzerland, for they are
rife with hotels. He stands for the concept of Nature against the iron
lids, for Walden against State Street, for Concord against New York.

All this is to say that the Transcendentalists really stand for the
moral innocence which they identify with Nature, against the corruptions of civilization. They might read Madame de Staël on Germany

or Wordsworth's *Prelude*, but they could not understand why these writers were so up in arms against the eighteenth century. But they could understand that these found in Nature a defense against the wiles of artificiality, and this they could adopt as their defense against what in America was the threat to their innocence. And by this device they did not need to attribute a positive evil to that which they were opposing, as Carlyle would cheerfully behold nothing but depravity in the *ancien régime*. They would not have to say that Unitarians were wicked men, but merely that they had severed their hearts from Nature and so had become corpse-cold.

This maneuver has provided, as I noted to begin with, opportunities for uncomprehending readers to accuse the whole group, but especially Emerson, of having been morally obtuse. But a bit more exercise of a sympathetic insight into the historical situation may find in this characterization not an indictment but an evidence of the reaction of a supple intellect to a situation in which any proclamation of an evil American eighteenth century would make no sense. It was not a contradiction in terms for Emerson to announce that our long day of dependence upon the learning of other lands was drawing to a close and in the same oration make an incantation of the great names the young Americans were still reverently studying.

> Meek young men grow up in libraries, believing it their duty to accept the views which Cicero, which Locke, which Bacon have given; forgetful that Cicero, Locke, and Bacon were only young men in libraries when they wrote these books.

The peculiar use of the word "scholar" by the Transcendentalists derives its special flavor from this background. They did not mean the professional scholar, delving for forgotten facts amid manuscripts and ancient tomes. The American scholar is a student but all the while a rebel against study. The point was—and still is—that the American independence had to be achieved *through* dependence. This is how America perforce stands in relation to the past. It is not going to achieve independence through violent assertions of the uniquely American quality of our experience or through discounting the influence of Byron on Herman Melville in order to set up some mythological native impetus as the true informing spirit of *Moby-Dick*. Emerson and the Transcendentalists were fully aware of this double pressure, this inner tension. Out of their consciousness comes their curious mingling of sophistication and innocence. This is a quality they variously exhibit, but it is pre-eminently displayed by Emerson and Thoreau. In the final analysis this Americanism is their indestructible virtue. It is their splendid ambiguity. On the one hand they talk of independence and on the other make clear their dependence.

This very ambiguity—or possibly antinomy is a better word—is the reason for their growth in stature, despite the fluctuations of critical fashions. In this respect they stand firm, quite apart from the student's personal opinion of the concept of the "Over-Soul" or his liking or disliking the chapter on higher laws in *Walden*. They are spokesmen not merely for a tiny intellectual tempest in the New England teapot, but as representatives of a persistent problem in American culture, compounded of our dread and our joy. Is our culture entirely a satellite of the European or do we have a culture of our own? If our culture is both at once, how do we reconcile the two? Or rather, not reconcile—for that would be the death of us—but how hold them in suspension in order to conduct an active life of the mind by alternating pole to pole? If this conclusion has any validity, it may throw some light on the respects in which these New England writers are not merely local peculiarities but are indeed eminently national and profound expressions of the American spirit.

"The Theological Response of the Transcendentalists to the Civil War"

Robert C. Albrecht*

Although the movement of Transcendentalism ended some time before the firing on Fort Sumter, most of the people identified with it were still active in 1861. Since the 1840's many of them had changed their beliefs but most continued to be idealists, and for them the war was a time of crisis. The Transcendentalists had been preaching in their lectures and sermons the divinity of man, man's potential, the good society to come. The year 1861 brought man at war, man in hate, man destroying. Accustomed to finding meaning in Nature and Man, what meaning would they find in bloodshed? What rhetoric would they use? Could they provide a new rhetoric as they had tried to provide a new religion beyond Unitarianism? For most Transcendentalists the answer to these questions was their concept of the war as "a remission by blood."

Before the war many Transcendentalists had been leaders toward a more liberal religion. Though many of them had begun their lives in Calvinist homes, they moved into the Unitarian church in which many became ministers; some went beyond that to establish nondenominational churches of their own or to leave organized religion entirely. During the Civil War, however, most of the Transcendentalists reverted to the religious concepts they had apparently rejected years before. Sin and salvation, the doctrines preached in Congregational and other orthodox churches, became their themes. They became religious nationalists in formulating their response to the crisis, preaching that the war was a remission by blood for the salvation of man and nation.

Rather than becoming an intellectual elite which could lead the nation around war or through the war on a rationalistic or humanistic basis, they reverted to earlier, perhaps more primitive, ideas which demanded blood sacrifice for the remission of sins. Intellect turned back upon emotion. To the Transcendentalists the war was not a legal controversy, a mere war for union, a sectional struggle, not even a war

*Reprinted from *New England Quarterly*, 38 (March 1965), 21–34.

to end slavery. It was a cosmic battle which could be talked about only in the rhetoric of orthodoxy. While to the modern historian the Civil War is a concurrence of battles, generals, armies, and politics, for the Transcendentalists it took place on quite a different level of reality. The meaning of the war was theological, its significance, moral.

A typical theme of the Transcendentalists' response to the war was that of the millennium. Though it was not typical of their thought in the 1850's or the 1870's, this theme, so strong in conservative Protestant thought, appeared continually in their writings during the war. At that time the Transcendentalists put history in the hands of Providence and mitigated man's efforts to achieve salvation. Free will became less important. The movement towards the millennium was in God's hands. The Transcendentalists no longer believed in man's ability to construct a utopia.

The pattern of response was not universal among the Transcendentalists. For instance, Emerson's conception of the war, as evidenced by his rhetoric, was not the same as that of James Freeman Clarke or Cyrus A. Bartol. But the responses of most Transcendentalists whether they were Unitarians or religious radicals—the two groups whose writings I shall later discuss—were quite similar. Before an examination of the writings of the Transcendentalists, however, a brief look at doctrines preached by an orthodox clergyman may establish a basis for comparison.

George B. Cheever, an outspoken abolitionist, was a Congregational minister who had severely attacked the Unitarians in the 1830's. Just before the Civil War he published *The Guilt of Slavery* in which he warned, "If God's judgment is really revealed against slavery as sin, then we, as a people, are condemned and guilty beyond any other nation under heaven."[1] Having perceived this guilt of the whole nation, he was ready to say during the war, "The opportunity is granted to us of God, of saving ourselves by doing a commanded work of justice, mercy, deliverance for others." Though it was God's decision, and not man's, to bring the war upon the nation, the salvation of the nation depended upon its actions in the crisis. The meaning of the war was theological when Cheever described it: "It is God's judgment, and it calls us to repentance; and the work of giving freedom and salvation to four millions of human beings held as slaves, in a work of immediate benevolence, the opportunity of which, if we avail ourselves of it, converts the war itself into the greatest of our blessings, drawing from it indeed the salvation of our country, as well as the redemption of the enslaved."[2]

This interpretation of the war, one which emphasized the place of God's will, the nation as an instrument of God, the theological realities of sin and salvation, belonged no less to the Transcendentalists than to the orthodox. Though the Transcendentalists emphasized the place of atonement and sacrifice, the basic view of the reality of the war most of them shared with men like Cheever. This assertion can most clearly be substantiated by examining the writings of the conservative–Unitarian–Transcendentalists. However, if we then turn to the more liberal ministers, we will find their interpretation of the war to be along the same lines. Only in Emerson's writings can there be found the breath of a new rhetoric which comprehends the cataclysm of the war.

Four clergymen who represent the conservative Transcendentalists are Thomas Starr King, James Freeman Clarke, William Henry Channing, and Cyrus A. Bartol. All were Unitarian ministers during the war, though Clarke's Boston church, the Church of the Disciples, resembled a free church. These men—closer to Cheever's orthodoxy than the others discussed here—more often and more clearly expressed their ideas in the rhetoric to which most of the Transcendentalists reverted. It was in the concepts and language of orthodoxy that they were able to find and express the meaningful reality of the war.

Unlike his friends in the East, Thomas Starr King often spoke of the war as one for union rather than against slavery. But the imagery and metaphors in his sermons and letters reveal that his basic view was similar to theirs. In a letter of May 1, 1861, King wrote, ". . . I assure you, in these times of moral separation,—the political judgment-day in America,—that California is *true to the cause of civilization.*"[3] King did present the North's cause as that of civilization carried forward by democracy. But the use of the term "judgment-day" indicates that he thought of the conflict as primarily a religious one which would lead to salvation and millennium. The combination of the two types of rhetoric was not unusual among the Transcendentalists, and the use of both reveals at once an attempt to find a new rhetoric and a failure to do so.

Calling the war a trial, King prophesied in his sermons that in a hundred years historians would say, "Then God sat by the furnace, and smelted America till her crime was purged, and she became pure gold." (King's notion of the written history of 1960 is indicative of what he thought, or hoped, the nation would be.) The concept of purification is similar to the Transcendentalists' common themes of testing and atonement, as well as George Cheever's view of the war as an opportunity for salvation. King's conception of "pure gold" was that the nation would be "homogeneous,—sounder in its system of labor, nobler and more symmetrical in its civilization. . . ."[4] On the one hand, his interpretations transcend the concepts of orthodoxy; on the other, they remain firmly anchored in that faith. History, for example, was a moral tale. In "Secession in Palestine and Its Results," King said, "He [God, in the Bible] reveals to us the principles which we are to set as lights behind the moving panorama of events in all kingdoms, so that history may be translucent with Divine radiance, and preach to us always the moral rule of a Holy God."[5] History was a moral lesson to be read for man's instruction.

Since history was a moral tale to King, he readily linked patriotism and religion. In 1862 he delivered to college students a lecture called, "Intellectual Duties of Students in Their Academic Years." Two books he urged that all must read were the New Testament and a history of their country. "Religion and patriotism must stream into every fibre of his [the student's] brain, into every duct of his blood." The conjunction of ideas that King presented in that passage is a key to an idea held by many Transcendentalists, that of religious nationalism. The nation itself was an object of religious concern. King said, "If there had been a deeper study of the history of America in the last twenty years in the rebellion districts, and a baptism in the spirit which that study liberates, this war would not have been."[6] A study of history would have had a religious effect. Religion and patriotism were inseparable. For King, the war was part of the drama of religion and history, of religion in history.

Though King may have tried to employ a new rhetoric, other conservatives did not make this attempt. James Freeman Clarke, for example, employed the orthodox language and concepts to understand, interpret, and explain the war. He saw it as a remission by blood. The national sins of money-love and slaveholding required expiation—suffering by the sinner to expiate the sin—and atonement—suffering by innocent people which, when borne willingly, reconciles the sinner to God. When he reviewed Cyrus A. Bartol's sermon, *The Remission By Blood*, he assented to the doctrine "that suffering and death are necessary to expiate sin, and that this suffering may often fall on the innocent . . . and this truth is fully illustrated in the present war."[7] In a funeral sermon he used the following imagery to explain the doctrine: "Our Massachusetts mothers . . . bring their spotless lambs to the altar, expiatory victims for a nation's sins."[8] The symbols were those of orthodoxy, though the congregation to which he preached was nondenominational, a "free" church.

At the end of the war Clarke told his congregation that the North won by its ideas and its faith in God and human rights, while the South continued to sin and did not have God's support.[9] Expressing the optimistic faith which had led him on, he said in a letter to a friend, "Abolition of slavery, fall of Charleston, fall of Richmond,—when they arrive they are like things foreordained from the foundation of the world."[10] On the same day he asked in a sermon, "But who has not seen through all these glorious and terrible days, the visible arm of God's providence leading our nation on?"[11] These statements evidence more than a belief in the Christian interpretation of history; they suggest he believed in foreordination, if not predestination.

Another member of this group who asserted his beliefs in these doctrines was William Henry Channing. A Transcendentalist minister who had been a member of several utopian communities in the 1840's, Channing related the visions of the millennium he had in the earlier period to those he had in the 1860's. Writing to a friend in December, 1860, he said, ". . . all the glowing hopes which after the night of reaction in 1848–49 fell into a trance and were reverently laid in the tomb amid sweet spices, with an ever-burning lamp at head and foot, are now putting off their cerements, pushing aside the heavy stones, and rising glorified on this Easter morn of the Republic." In the central metaphor here the resurrection of the nation—the utopian dreams of heaven on earth—are substituted for the familiar resurrection of Christ, the very kernel of orthodoxy. Channing felt that he and his fellow Christian socialists had planted the seeds of the future in the 1840's. The fault, the delay, was not in their vision but in that of the people. "True, inasmuch as the nation would not choose the better way of peaceful transformation, God, in his infinite grace, compelled us to enter this flinty, trying way of destruction."[12] Since the nation would not follow the right path twenty years before, God was forcing it to move towards the millennium in this fashion. Channing had joined the utopian dreams to the promise of the result of the war. The war was an instrument of purification, an impetus to salvation, a bridge to the millennium, and it was a direction not chosen by men but by God. Cheever, the Congregationalist, agreed.

In 1861, before the fighting had begun, Channing proclaimed the war as the "Providential method of National redemption." (It was, he said, "a HOLY WAR.") He explained, "Monstrous has been the Nation's crime; total let the repentance be, and costly the sacrifice of atonement; it is the martyr spirit calling for its suffering. By May of 1864 asked for widespread death and destruction. It is a prayer for punishment; it is the martyr spirit calling for its suffering. By May of 1864 he was to cry, "Enough!" In a letter to James Freeman Clarke, he asked, "Ah! loving Heavenly Father, must there be all this hideous butchery ere our sins be washed white as wool?"[14] Working in the hospitals around Washington, Channing saw the butchery he could but imagine in his prayer of 1861. Yet this was the fire he thought God was leading the nation through to reach the utopia Channing expected. Here was no constitutional view of the war, no legal interpretation, no economic analysis; here was a theological view.

Though Clarke and Channing did preach the concept of the war as atonement, neither of them preached it as often or as long as Cyrus A. Bartol. During the war he emphasized sacrifice. In 1861 he told his Boston congregation, "It is the law of our life, that all earthly progress in every good cause starts in sacrifice, lives on sacrifice, and without ever-new sacrifice would faint and die."[15] Sacrifice was part of history and history was a theological drama. Like Channing, he was sure of the results to come. In his sermon, *The Nation's Hour*, Bartol said, ". . . God is using our action with that of our rulers, the citizens, leaders, soldiers . . . as elements in the great result to come."[16] Bartol saw the theological-historical process as soon reaching a termination, a millennium.

The war which had come from God he welcomed as a penalty, since neither North nor South was "very good or holy anywhere." The war was from God, a "summons to a struggle against our own sins." But North and South were not equal foes, for ". . . the terrible North, as the fate and finger of God, moves to meet the tropical South." Bartol pointed out in this sermon that while the interference of gods in the affairs of mortals in Homer was often called "a fine fancy," it was but another example "that celestial strength is always pledged to righteous enterprise."[17] That the North was both agent and victim is not a theological paradox, only a secular one. Bartol, like Clarke and Channing, thought and said that God acted directly in the history of men.

It was in his sermon, *The Remission By Blood*, that Bartol set forth his central explanation of the war. He presented the death of Christ on the cross, that sacrifice of blood, as the "supreme token of the moral endurance by which atonement must be made for all transgression." But that was not enough; there was not enough blood shed. All who bore sacrifice for the sake of others completed that act. "Every martyr to the cause of truth and duty in the world mingles his blood . . . with that of the great Redeemer of mankind." He continued, "For the sins of our country there was no remission but by the shedding of blood."[18] Bartol had voiced the view held by most of the Transcendentalists. His language was not that of a freethinker, a rationalist, but of an orthodox clergyman, because in that he could best express his concepts. The war in this interpretation was not merely a civil war of the nineteenth century but a sacrificial battle in the theological drama of history.

Though it is not altogether surprising to find Bartol and other Unitarian Transcendentalists viewing the war in this way, it is more unexpected to find this view held by Transcendentalists who were leading religious radicals before and especially after the war. Three representatives of this group are Moncure Conway, Samuel Johnson, and David A. Wasson. Conway decided to stay in England in 1863 to become minister at the South Place Chapel, preaching a faith of "humanized theism," as he called it. Johnson was a contributor to the *Radical*, a supporter of the Free Religious Association, and a minister at the Free Church at Lynn, Massachusetts, for almost twenty years. Wasson was an essayist, poet, and minister who, in 1865, was asked to take Theodore Parker's old congregation, the Twenty-Eighth Congregational Society in Boston. None of these men could accurately be described as a Unitarian, since each had left that faith sometime before the war. The war, however, caused them to preach on themes of atonement for, or expiation of, sins, judgment and salvation. While seeing the issues of union and slavery, and responding to the personalities who led the nation, they preferred to find the reality of the war on a theological level.

In *The Rejected Stone*, his first book published during the war, Conway expressed his conceptions of the war in the rhetoric of orthodoxy. There he wrote, "The shame of repelling the fugitive from her [Liberty's] door has nerved her to the atonement she is now ready to make by shedding of blood. . . ."[19] The same sort of rhetoric he employed in *The Golden Hour*. "America is to-day in the wilderness of temptation, and beside her is the Tempter."[20] Similar examples can be found in his third book of the period, *Testimonies Concerning Slavery*, where he called the war, "the Day of judgment for our guilty land. . . ."[21] This was a common metaphor in the Transcendentalists' writings, since many of them believed the war would be followed by national salvation. In his *Autobiography* Conway wrote that he was happy in England where he had moved in 1863, "to have no further need to preach about slavery and dogma."[22] Had the American situation forced him to use a rhetoric from which he wished to escape?

Statements concerning the Day of Judgment and salvation can also be found in the writings of another minister who was to become a radical after the war, Samuel Johnson, minister of the Free Church at Lynn. Writing to George L. Stearns, the industrialist who had been a financial supporter of John Brown and a recruiter of Negro troops during the war, Johnson said, "We are borne on the saving tide towards issues which the whole nation, North and South . . . has resisted and still resists. A terrible Nemesis, a stern atonement, and then, the 'IRRESISTIBLE *Grace* OF GOD!'" Six months later he commented on the war as "this magnificent *sweep of purification*."[23] He found the war most impressive in its theological aspect and could only express its significance in the rhetoric most meaningful to him.

The purification about which these Transcendentalists spoke was to be accomplished through atonement, the doctrine of the suffering of the innocent for the redemption of all. Wasson, social conservative and theological radical, wrote in 1863 that the bloodshed of the war was the price the nation was paying for its vice and for its virtue.[24] In his installation sermon in 1865, Wasson discussed the meaning of atonement, "that monstrous doctrine of vicarious atonement." Referring, perhaps, to Lincoln's death less than a month before, he said, "He who stands for the divine in humanity is most tasked at its dead weight, and to stretch a little wider its limitations." It was particularly "the noblest hearts," the "greatest," "the representative soul" who suffered for others.[25] The "monstrous doctrine" helped to explain not only Lincoln's death, but the deaths of all those virtuous men who died to atone for the sins of the nation.

Wasson's statement about "the representative soul" can be better understood with reference to the Transcendentalists' continual search for a hero during the war. Throughout the conflict many of them lamented the absence of a leader to take the nation through the crisis. They did not find a hero until 1865 and Lincoln's death. The comments on Lincoln at the time of his death as well as many of the complaints concerning the lack of a leader were made in language suggesting the orthodox conceptions of Christ or Moses, the chosen redeemer or leader. The notions of deliverance and salvation are not humanistic or deistic, but beliefs accepted by orthodox Protestants in the nineteenth century. The lamentations over the lack of a political leader in the 1850's became, during the war, faint prayers for a deliverer.

While most of the Transcendentalists employed a rhetoric which seemed more appropriate to the orthodoxy of men like Cheever, one man did manage to use a new rhetoric in describing and interpreting the war. Emerson himself seldom reverted to orthodox language and concepts as did other Transcendentalists. Only he was able to express an interpretation of the war in a contextual rhetoric which removed it from the realm of orthodox theology to the new level of religion which he had so long been advocating in his lectures. Only Emerson interpreted the war in the rhetoric which one might have expected from all of the Transcendentalists.

Although in 1861 he wrote, "If the abundance of heaven only sends us a fair share of light and conscience, we shall redeem America for all its sinful years since the century began," such rhetoric was not typical of Emerson.[26] Far more often he spoke of the moral problem: "We must get ourselves morally right. Nobody can help us."[27] While others spoke of religious salvation, Emerson spoke of moral triumph. He was certain of the increased importance of morals; "Certain it is that never before since I read newspapers, have the morals played so large a part in them as now."[28]

Emerson's employment of a rhetoric quite distinguishable from that of other Transcendentalists can easily be seen in statements such as this of 1863: "The war is an exceptional struggle, in which the first combatants are met,—the highest principles against the worst. What a teacher! what a field! what results!"[29] Other Transcendentalists would fall back upon the terminology of sin and righteousness to express a similar concept, but Emerson had gone beyond this. While he could describe the war to Carlyle as "the battle for Humanity," others would call it a battle for salvation.[30] While others could say the war saved the nation, Emerson wrote that the war had "*moralized* cities and states."[31] The

Congregationalist, Cheever, would not employ such a term. Emerson had found a rhetoric in which to express a conception of the war not characterized by "a remission by blood." His view, like those of other Transcendentalists, was a religious one, but his rhetoric demonstrated radicalism in religion.

In the wartime writings of some of these Transcendentalists, especially the more radical, are the barest beginnings of a new religious rhetoric. But it is never primary, it is never whole, it is never developed. But even when the rhetoric is somehow new, it is still theological. Emerson's statement, "The evolution of a highly destined society must be moral; it must run in the grooves of the celestial wheels," is an excellent example. The key phrases—highly destined, moral, celestial wheels—all suggest a religion beyond orthodoxy but a religion, nevertheless.

The significance of the reversion to orthodoxy which commonly occurred among most Transcendentalists is primarily what is revealed about that group. Transcendentalism was primarily a religion. The reversion to orthodoxy suggests that most of the Transcendentalists were unsuccessful in their attempt to form a new body of religious thought signified by a new rhetoric distinguishable from that of an orthodox Congregationalist like Cheever. That they were driven back to orthodoxy and found there the rhetoric appropriate to explain the war indicates also the impress of the war upon them. They could treat it only as cataclysm, as Armageddon, as Judgment Day.

To the Transcendentalists the American Civil War was not a series of battles between armies over union, slaves, economic theories or the Constitution. It was a struggle of theological importance and meaning. They justified the bloodshed by raising the stakes: men died not only for ground or law or loyalty; they died for the salvation not only of themselves but of the nation. The war had driven these idealists back to the bedrock of their ideas and their ideals. They asserted not the divinity in man, not his natural goodness, not the shallow optimism of which they have so often been accused; they asserted the justice of God and the essential optimism of that faith. This view of reality allowed them to accept the defeats and the carnage. It allowed them to hate not the South but the evil it represented. It allowed them to continue to ignore the political realities they had always overlooked. They need not concern themselves with elections, executives, and legislatures for these were not the instruments of bringing war or ending it. The war did not change the Transcendentalists; their theological response was not an escape to a refuge. Rather, it was the essence of that path they had always trod. They revealed themselves to be what they had always been—religious nationalists searching for the meaning of the existence of themselves and their nation and finding it in the traditional Christianity which they sought to interpret but never discard.

Notes

1. *The Guilt of Slavery* (Boston: J. P. Jewett, 1860), p. 21.

2. *The Salvation of the Country Secured by Immediate Emancipation* (New York: John A. Gray, 1861), pp. 4, 24.

3. *Monthly Journal*, 2 (June 1861), 263.

4. *Christianity and Humanity* ..., ed. Edwin P. Whipple, 3d ed. (Boston: J. R. Osgood, 1878), p. 354.

5. Manuscript sermon, 2, Boston Public Library; by courtesy of the Trustees of the Boston Public Library.

6. *Substance and Show, and Other Lectures*, ed. Edwin P. Whipple (Boston: Houghton, Mifflin, 1881), pp. 428, 431.

7. "The Remission by Blood," *Monthly Journal*, 3 (August 1862), 369.

8. "From 'Lieut. William Lowell Putnam . . . ," *The Fallen Brave*, ed. John Gilmary Shea (New York, 1861), p. 195.

9. Original quotation in Arthur S. Bolster, Jr., *James Freeman Clarke: Disciple to Advancing Truth* (Boston: Beacon, 1954), p. 284.

10. *Autobiography, Diary and Correspondence*, ed. Edward Everett Hale (Boston: Houghton, Mifflin, 1891), p. 290.

11. *Sermon preached before the delegates to the National Unitarian Convention* (Boston: Walker, Fuller, 1865), p. 29.

12. Octavius Brooks Frothingham, *Memoir of William Henry Channing* (Boston: Houghton, Mifflin, 1886), p. 333.

13. *The Civil War in America . . .* (Liverpool: W. Vaughan, 1861), pp. 90–91, 93.

14. Frothingham, *Channing*, p. 326.

15. *Our Sacrifices* (Boston: Ticknor and Fields, 1861), p. 3.

16. *The Nation's Hour* (Boston: Walker, Wise, 1862), p. 5.

17. *The Duty of the Time* (Boston: Walker, Wise, 1861), pp. 6, 11–12.

18. *The Remission by Blood* (Boston: Walker, Wise, 1862), p. 5.

19. *The Rejected Stone* (Boston: Walker, Wise, 1861), p. 22.

20. *The Golden Hour* (Boston: Ticknor and Fields, 1862), p. 110.

21. *Testimonies Concerning Slavery* (London: Chapman and Hall, 1865), p. 113.

22. *Autobiography, Memories and Experiences* (Boston; Houghton, Mifflin, 1904), I, 290.

23. *Lectures, Essays, and Sermons*, ed. Samuel May (Boston: Houghton, Mifflin, 1883), p. 93.

24. "The Law of Costs," *Atlantic Monthly Magazine*, 11 (February 1863), 241.

25. *The Radical Creed* (Boston: Walker, Fuller, 1865), p. 23.

26. *The Letters of Ralph Waldo Emerson*, ed. Ralph L. Rusk (New York: Columbia University Press, 1939), V, 253.

27. *The Correspondence of Thomas Carlyle and Ralph Waldo Emerson, 1834–1872*, ed. Charles Eliot Norton (Boston: James R. Osgood, 1883), II, 281.

28. *Journals of Ralph Waldo Emerson*, ed. Edward Waldo Emerson and Waldo Emerson Forbes (Boston: Houghton Mifflin, 1909–1914), IX, 492.

29. Emerson, *Journals*, IX, 576–577.

30. Emerson, *Carlyle Correspondence*, II, 285.

31. Emerson, *Journals*, X, 105.

"Transcendentalist Catalogue Rhetoric: Vision Versus Form"

Lawrence Buell*

Whitman's catalogues are a most salient feature of his poetry, and certainly the most neglected. It is tempting to skip over them as we read. "The pure contralto sings in the organ loft," etc.—why bother with the rest? After all, we can predict what the next sixty lines will say. And so we pass quickly by the redundant images to follow the "movement" of the poem, whatever that is, so as to be able to come up with a theory of structure which will satisfy our struggling students, and our own rage for order. Dawdling among the catalogues only slows us down.

Still, when we allow ourselves to "loafe" awhile, we may be struck by Whitman's art in such passages, which at first seem the very antithesis of art. Sensitive discussions of Whitman, like Randall Jarrell's, show that other readers have felt the same way;[1] and the impact of catalogue rhetoric upon poets is certainly attested to by the tradition in American poetry which, following Whitman, employs it, not to mention the long antecedent tradition of prophetic poetry from the Bible to Blake. But not only can Whitman's catalogues be regarded as prominent examples of a pedigreed technique; in his case the device has special significance because it is the exact stylistic counterpart of an important article of transcendentalist philosophy, as advanced by himself, Thoreau, and especially Emerson, whose essays make use of the catalogue almost as frequently as Whitman's verse, and for similar reasons. In reading Emerson, indeed, we are apt to experience just the same sort of alternation of impatience and fascination as our mental mood switches from analysis to receptivity and back again. Such responses to Emerson may be less keen than to Whitman, because Emerson is writing in prose and his appeal is intellectual rather than sensuous; but by the same token, he writes oftener and more articulately about the aesthetic theory behind the catalogue, and it is to him we must frequently turn in order to understand Whitman's use of the technique.

In this essay, then, I shall want to consider the catalogue, in Whit-

*Reprinted from *American Literature*, 40 (November 1968), 325–339.

man's verse and Emerson's essays, both as an aesthetic device and as the expression of transcendentalist thought, relying on Whitman for most of the examples and Emerson for most of the theory. In particular, I hope to defend the catalogue against the charge of formlessness which has frequently been made against it.

I

To see how a good Whitman catalogue works, let us examine the following lyric from "Calamus":[2]

> Roots and leaves themselves alone are these,
> Scents brought to me[n] and women from the
> > wild woods and pond-side,[3]
> Breast-sorrel and pinks of love, fingers that wind
> > around tighter than vines,
> Gushes from the throats of birds hid in the foliage
> > of trees as the sun is risen,
> Breezes of land and love sent from living shores
> > to you on the living sea, to you O sailors!
> Frost-mellow'd berries and Third-month twigs offer'd
> > fresh to young persons wandering out in the fields
> > when the winter breaks up,
> Love-buds put before you and within you
> > whoever you are,
> Buds to be unfolded on the old terms,
> If you bring the warmth of the sun to them they will
> > open and bring form, color, perfume, to you,
> If you become the aliment and the wet they will
> > become flowers, fruits, tall branches and trees.

Upon first reading, the poem appears to be little more than it says it is: a cluster of images, placed in loose apposition, with a bit of moralizing at the end. The casual bouquet is presented to the reader as if unsorted and not yet even in bloom. "Roots and leaves themselves alone are *these*"—these lines, in other words, which are to the finished poem what buds are to flowers. These buds of language are "to be unfolded on the old terms": we must "bring the warmth of the sun to them" and supply the nourishment ourselves if the cluster is to blossom for us. In plain language, Whitman seems to be saying that his poem, more than most, depends for its meaningfulness upon our participation. This is true, and not merely of this one lyric, but of all of Whitman's poetry. It requires us to take part in two main ways.

First, the reader must respond sensuously: smell the scents; feel the fingers tighter than vines, and the breezes; hear the gushes from the throats of birds; taste the frost-mellowed berries; and behold all. This is not as easy to do as it may seem. The sensuous appeal of poetry is made via the intellect and is too often weakened in the process; it is one thing to recognize the technique of synesthesia used here, another thing to participate in it. The odors in the poem, for instance, are much more apt to come across as "perfume" in the abstract than as the particular scents of "breast-sorrel and pinks of love." After all, most readers do not know what sorrel and pinks smell like, and the mixture of floral and human odors here implied may seem droll or repulsive (though only to the mind, not to the lover actually experiencing the sensation), so that the degree to which even the most sensitive reader can unfold such buds as these is bound to be limited. Nevertheless, a greater opening of the senses than is usually made in reading poetry is possible here, and if we can so respond, the buds *will* open and bring color and perfume to us. And in the same manner, all of Whitman's good catalogues will be felt as far richer than most poems.

But, one might argue, not only must the buds blossom; they must also be arranged, in order to be fully satisfying as art. As will soon become evident, I think this proposition is debatable, but since Whitman does promise that his buds can take "form" for us, we may assume that a second demand a Whitman catalogue makes upon us is the perception of some sort of design. So, too, does most poetry; but in Whitman's case, the demand is more difficult, because it is made so faintly. To find structure in Whitman's catalogues, beyond the obvious and rudimentary prosodic controls, is much harder than responding to them sensuously. In the "Calamus" poem quoted above, one immediately feels that some of the images could be repositioned with almost equal effect; that in places words, phrases, and even lines could be excised or added without doing great violence to the poem. Still, like a surprising number of Whitman's catalogues and catalogue poems, it has a definite organization, as subtle in its own way as a good lyric by that modern master of plethora, Dylan Thomas.

To begin with, the very miscellaneousness of the poem is a kind of unity. "A great disorder is an order," as Stevens's Connoisseur of Chaos says. Roots, leaves, scents, vine-like fingers, breast-sorrel, pinks, and all the rest come tumbling out of Whitman's horn of plenty, creating the impression of all nature (here a metaphor for the poet's words) burgeoning to unfold itself to the lover-reader. Through the piling up of images in every line Whitman conveys the sense of plentitude which is also his message.

Indeed throughout Whitman a main purpose of the catalogue seems to be to express the boundless fecundity of nature and human life, and thereby his own "leaves" also. The tone varies, of course. In "Roots and

Leaves" it is loving and intimate. Elsewhere the poet may be filled with
a religious awe, as in "limitless are leaves stiff or drooping in the fields ..."
And sometimes the catalogue has a comic aspect:

> I find I incorporate gneiss, coal, long-threaded
>   moss, fruits, grains, esculent roots,
> And am stucco'd with quadrupeds and birds
>   all over . . . .
>
>   ("Song of Myself," ll. 670–671)

These lines are of special interest, because they show in miniature how,
in the midst of apparent randomness, Whitman may structure his lists
in a second and more subtle way, so as to express something more than
mere plenitude. At first, we probably feel a kind of bemused amazement:
gneiss, coal, long-threaded moss, fruits, grains, esculent roots—how in
the world did all these diverse things get thrown together in one
package? The speaker seems just as surprised as the reader: "I find I
incorporate" so many different things, he exclaims. The heterogeneity
of the list is positively droll, especially the zoological collage in the
second line. But despite this initial response, and the fact that it depends
partly upon the sense that the items in the passage are as unrelated as
the items in a garbage can, we can find a careful and significant arrangement of parts. Word sounds help to paste them together, subliminally,
as it were. Gneiss-moss, fruits-roots, stucco-quadrupeds—these are some
examples of coherence by means of alliteration and assonance. But in
addition to this, Whitman has listed the items in an almost-evolutionary
order, beginning with gneiss, which is inanimate, and moving up the
scale of being to quadrupeds and birds. The lines which follow give the
key to the progression:

> And have distanced what is behind me for
>   good reasons,
> But call any thing back again when I desire it.
>
>   (ll. 672–673)

The "I" of the passage, that is, personifies the evolutionary process, which
has just unscrolled itself in the previous catalogue.

In "Roots and Leaves" as well, the sheer proliferation of images is
like an ornate screen which hides as much of Whitman's artistry as it
exhibits. Other devices lie behind it, implicit. One, already noted, is the
appeal to *all five* senses. Parallelism, too, shapes and gives emphasis:
in lines 7–8, which point to the moral, and 9–10, which draw the conclusion, for example. More subtle is the alternation earlier in the poem of
lines which merely list (1, 3, 4) with lines that connect the images to a

subject (2, 5, 6) and are constructed around the pattern noun-past-participle-to-subject-(from-place). One wonders if this pattern was consciously formulated, but its existence shows, in any case, a sense of order on Whitman's part. There is even a visual pattern in the lines, a little like the floral arrangement of Thoreau's "*Sic Vita*." The first six lines are progressively longer; then two short lines make the assertion which ties together what precedes, while the implications dangle like the stems in a bouquet in the two longer lines at the end of the poem.

In order to show that Whitman's catalogues *can* be as rich in unity as they are in diversity, I have deliberately chosen good examples. Often, it is true, the structure of his catalogues consists almost wholly in their plenitude, in the parallelism of piled-up, end-stopped lines, producing, at its worst, rudimentary paeans or chants like litanies from the *Book of Common Prayer*. But often enough both tone and structure are more complex, creating tapestries of imagery and rhetoric which are fine by any standard, like the eighth section of "Song of Myself," section three of "Brooklyn Ferry," and the two shorter examples analyzed here. We tend not to acknowledge the art of such passages, partly because we read Whitman's good catalogues with his bad ones in mind, but partly because Whitman's art is so implicit. His verbal pyrotechnics are meant to seem spontaneous, but that does not mean they are.

And yet because Whitman's art *is* so implicit it is dangerous to analyze it too persistently in the way I have just done, stressing the instances of sophisticated design in his catalogues. It is necessary to realize that such design can be found, but wrong to attach too much significance to it. In so doing we are liable to rest in a too simple evaluation of Whitman's poetry: to divide his catalogues into a small group which have design and are therefore "good," and a large group which are relatively amorphous and therefore "flawed." Such a polarization ignores the fact that the element of structure in a Whitman catalogue—indeed in any Whitman poem—even where refined, is relatively unstressed. The order of importance is the order in which we have proceeded: the individual sensuous and emotional responses are paramount, then the sense of plenitude, and lastly, when it exists, the design. Nor is this order of priority mainly the result of sloppiness or incapacity on Whitman's part, though these doubtless contributed. Rather it reflects Whitman's conscious aesthetic purpose, which will become more clear as we define, in the next section, the sense of values which underlies the catalogue technique.

II

It has been noted that among his contemporaries Whitman was by no means the sole maker of literary catalogues. Emerson, Thoreau, and even Melville also used the device; indeed, the paratactic and reiterative qualities of Emerson's and Thoreau's prose are so strong that in places they are indistinguishable from Whitman's verse.

What was responsible for this affinity? Partly, no doubt, the stylistic influence of Emerson and/or Carlyle. But a more basic reason is that the catalogue expresses a particular way of looking at the world, one which has its roots in transcendentalist idealism but was shared with Emerson and Thoreau by Whitman and, to a lesser extent, Melville.

A look at a representative Emerson catalogue, from "Compensation," will help show the connection:

> The world globes itself in a drop of dew. The microscope cannot find the animalcule which is less perfect for being little. Eyes, ears, taste, smell, motion, resistance, appetite, and organs of reproduction that take hold on eternity,—all find room to consist in the small creature. So do we put our life into every act. The true doctrine of omnipresence is that God reappears with all his parts in every moss and cobweb. The value of the universe contrives to throw itself into every point. If the good is there, so is the evil; if the affinity, so the repulsion; if the force, so the limitation.[4]

Stylistically, this paragraph differs from Whitman's catalogues only in the irregular length of its items and their predominantly intellectual appeal. In Whitmanian fashion, each sentence repeats the first assertion in a fresh context. The doctrine of the microcosm is justified in turn by microbiology, human action, theology, metaphysics, and the laws of morality and physics. Like the separate lines of Whitman's catalogues, Emerson's sentences give the appearance of being self-contained and interchangeable; transitions are at a minimum; and it seems as if sentences could be added or deleted without cost. But again like Whitman, closer inspection shows that rhythm and Emerson's tactic of moving from the elementary (dew-drop, animalcule) to the more significant (human action, doctrine of omnipresence) do give the order of the paragraph a certain amount of inevitability. And again, this twofold impression the passage makes is well suited to what seems to be Emerson's purpose—to overwhelm us with the multiplicity of instances but at the same time impress us with the design inherent in these. The sentences are the dewdrops, and the paragraph is the world.

But more noteworthy than the parallels between Emerson's lists and Whitman's is the fact that this paragraph reveals the basis for those affinities, the principle of microcosm itself. In both writers, this principle underlies and, to a great extent, determines the use of the catalogue. Elsewhere Emerson's criticism makes this quite plain. Because every particular nature is a symbol of spirit, all natures, he argues, are related to each other by analogy: "each creature is only a modification of the other" (I, 44). And just as symbol and analogy are the bases of natural law, so they are the chief methods of literary style, for a work of art is properly "an abstract or epitome of the world. . . . the result or expression of nature, in miniature" (I, 23). In the process of composition (another term which Emerson characteristically uses with double reference to rhetoric and nature, to denote the arrangement of parts both in a landscape and in a discourse), analogy is of special importance. For the order of nature is a unity of endless variety, in a constant state of flux, with all objects blending together on the one hand, and melting into spirit on the other—"as the bird alights on the bough, then plunges into the air again, so the thoughts of God pause but for a moment in any form" (VIII, 15). Therefore "the quality of the imagination" must likewise be "to flow, and not to freeze" (III, 34). The "essential mark" of good poetry "is that it betrays in every word instant activity of mind, shown in new uses of every fact and image, in preternatural quickness or perception of relations" (VIII, 17).[5]

The rapidity of metamorphosis which Emerson perceives in nature and demands of literature is precisely the outstanding feature of his own dazzling batteries of aphorisms in such passages as the one from "Compensation" quoted above. For many readers, this quality has seemed the hallmark of his style and thought, as distinctive to him as the verse catalogue is to Whitman. "The whole fascination of life" for Emerson, O. W. Firkins once wrote, without much exaggeration, "lay in the disclosure of identity in variety, that is in the concurrence, the *running together*, of several distinct images or ideas."[6]

A similar sense of nature's unity in diversity, we have seen, underlies the plenitude of images in the Whitman catalogues discussed earlier. But Whitman, less concerned with man's relation to nature than with his relation to other men, characteristically expressed the principle in a way slightly different from Emerson. He accentuated its democratic side, so to speak. Whitman's fundamental purpose in *Leaves of Grass*, as he often said, was "to articulate and faithfully express in literary or poetic form, and uncompromisingly, my own physical, emotional, moral, intellectual, and aesthetic Personality, in the midst of, and tallying, the momentous spirit and facts of its immediate days, and of current America."[7] This plan, however, had much the same implications for style as Emerson's theory of nature, because Whitman shared Emerson's basic assumption of divine immanence. For this reason, the persona—the "I"—in Whitman's poetry is, like the "self" described in "Self-Reliance," not merely individual but cosmic, and as such can participate in the experiences of all men in the same way that Emerson's Oversoul inheres in all men and all parts of nature. For rendering this collective conception of the self poetically, the catalogue is a most appropriate technique. Through it, the self can be sung in such a way as to incorporate, or seem to incorporate, all particular selves. "Of these one and all I weave the song of myself," Whitman says at the end of one long catalogue. "These" are the disparate images of human life which the poet has just listed, to the end of showing how, "one and all," they are united in "myself." The method of the song mirrors the complex unity of the singer.

We must be careful, of course, not to apply the principle of unity in diversity to the analysis of catalogue rhetoric in a too mechanical way, to reduce every catalogue to an illustration of the principle. Nobody writes great poetry on principle, at least not very often. On the contrary, it is likely that the flatness of Whitman's later poetry, for example, was caused at least in part by writing from principle, by imitating himself, as it were. And yet the connection between paratactic style and microcosmic universe was undeniably felt by him and by Emerson; it was not merely a matter of principle but of perception. Thoreau's sensitivity to it was equally keen (see the conclusion to his description of the thawing Walden hillside in "Spring") and so, almost, was Melville's. Melville is an especially interesting case because he was writing out of doubt instead of affirmation and yet adapted the catalogue brilliantly to those ends in the rhetoric of such passages as "The Whiteness of the Whale." Unlike the other three writers, he exploited the ironic possibilities of the technique: the variety of instances Ishmael cites may or may not have unity; the appearances may or may not be significant. But the habit of conveying ideas by means of a barrage of linked analogies is distinctly transcendental. It is the end product of transcendentalism's cardinal tenet: that the Oversoul is immanent in all persons and things, which are all thereby symbols of spirit and conjoined by analogy in an organic universe.

III

The fact that the transcendental catalogue is based upon the sense of the universe's spiritual unity in diversity makes it unique in Western literature. Though the catalogue as a literary device is as old as Homer, and the principle of plenitude is almost as hoary, in no other period, so far as I know, are the technique and the Weltanschauung fused so closely as they are in the American renaissance.

This fusion, to my mind, accounts for a good deal of the richness and fascination of transcendentalist literature. It has not, however, tended to arouse much enthusiasm in other readers. An important reason for this seems to be that it also goes far in explaining why, in the style of the catalogue, structure plays a subordinate role and why, in general, transcendentalist literature is often rather formless. For Emerson, Whitman, and Thoreau all regarded art pragmatically, that is, as properly the expression of something beyond itself—call it vision, truth, or what you will; they were, in short, not trying to write poems but nature; and they were therefore convinced that the secret of design in art rested rather in the ability to perceive the natural order than in imposing an aesthetic order upon their perceptions. Thus Thoreau structured his major works around the days of the week or the course of the seasons or the sequence of a journey; Whitman, for his controlling motifs in "Lilacs" to "Passage to India," relied on personal experience and contemporary history; and Emerson arranged his first book and many subsequent essays in what he considered were natural orders, hierarchical and dialectical patterns chiefly. Clearly all three believed that there was design in nature and likewise valued design in art; but they did not believe in making the latter an end in itself. And so we find Emerson exclaiming in one place: "It is much to write sentences; it is more to add method, and write out the spirit of your life symmetrically . . . to arrange many general reflections in their natural order so that I shall have one homogeneous piece"—but affirming elsewhere that "the truth-speaker may dismiss all solicitude as to the proportion and congruency of the aggregate of his thoughts, so long as he is a faithful reporter of particular impressions."[8]

Recent criticism, setting a high valuation upon structure, has often been nettled by this second attitude and blamed transcendentalist art for insufficient attention to form and transcendentalist criticism for making art the handmaiden of its nebulous doctrines. Such criticisms invariably hold up the catalogue as the epitome of these deficiencies. Charles Feidelson, for example, has argued in the case of Emerson that the principle of unity in diversity inhibits him as a symbolist because when applied as a concept of structure it provides "no brake on the transmutation of form" and thus easily degenerates into a mere multiplication of instances.[9]

Up to a point, this line of reasoning is persuasive. Plenitude, both as a theory of nature and as a theory of structure is, in itself, a quite elementary conception. In fact, from remarks like Emerson's last, one suspects that the transcendentalists used it partly just as a substitute for something better: that they seized upon it as a formula for order partly because it was such a convenient way of accounting for the prevailing *dis*order. The principle was specific enough to give them a sense of design, yet vague enough to relieve them of the need to order their thoughts more rigorously—a difficult problem to begin with for diarists like Emerson and Thoreau or an imagist like Whitman. As a result, their catalogues, like the thought which produced them, seem fitted as structures for the short run only. In the more elementary units of composition —the short lyric, the paragraph, the passage: in other words, the kinds of examples analyzed above—they were able to do impressive things with plenitude as an ordering principle, but when they extended themselves further they lapsed into sheer itemization. Perhaps Whitman had this problem in mind when he made the decision to divide his longer poems into sections or when, in his old age, he stated his agreement with Poe's dictum that there is no such thing as a long poem.[10]

But is "Roots and Leaves" really a better poem than "Song of Myself," or even a better catalogue than the longest section of the "Song," section 33, which is much less tightly knit than many of Whitman's shorter lists? State the issue this way and at once we sense that it is risky to disparage the catalogue for formlessness, even where it is clearly amorphous, and riskier still to chastise the transcendentalist world view, however simple, for cramping its style. Where the lines are good, who cares about the structure? Where the philosophy makes good poetry, why cut off the stream at its source?

The passage just referred to begins with a beautiful eighty-line list of places visited by the singer, now "afoot with my vision" more ecstatically than at any other place in the poem. The voyager sees, for example:

> Where herds of buffalo make a crawling spread
>   of the square miles far and near,
> Where the humming-bird shimmers, where the neck of
>   the long-lived swan is curving, and winding,
> Where the laughing-gull scoots by the shore, where
>   she laughs her near-human laugh,
> Where bee-hives range on a gray bench in the garden
>   half hid by the high weeds,
> Where band-neck'd partridges roost in a ring on the
>   ground with their heads out . . . . (ll. 761–765)

The list could be, and is meant to seem, endless. It is the longest and loosest catalogue in a long, loose poem. Even in these five lines, the connection among the images is tenuous. All are pictures of wildlife, and one could say something about interplay between motion and rest or near and distant perspective, but the true impact of these lines does not really depend upon such relations, any more than it depends elsewhere in Whitman upon almost-evolutionary orders or the tailoring of a poem's shape to look like a bouquet of flowers. The contribution of rhythm excepted, it consists in the language ("crawling spread of the square miles," "humming-bird shimmers," "scoots by the shore," "range on a gray bench in the garden half hid," "roost in a ring on the ground with their heads out," etc.) and the tremendous sense of vitality conveyed by running these and many more epiphanies together—a vitality made more intense by those phrases within individual lines whose sounds slide and bounce into one another, as in the five phrases just quoted. Texture and vision: these, in short, are what make the passage beautiful. We cannot share as doctrine the Emersonian idea that every creature is only a modification of every other, but we can experience it by allowing ourselves to drift with the speaker through these images.

Indeed we have to experience it, even accept it, if we are to read the passage, since the visionary element is inextricable from the best "poetic" qualities of these and other Whitman catalogues. In its ascendency, this element forces structure and aesthetic considerations generally to play second fiddle, but at the same time produces great poetry. Our recognition of this fact needs to be less grudging. We tend to separate inspiration from craftsmanship as naïvely as the transcendentalists confused them, and so are deprived of the critical habits and terminology needed to appreciate works which are committed to the use of style as a vehicle for vision. The distinction, to be sure, is important, but when taken as inherent rather than provisional it prevents us from reading a catalogue for anything more than the pictures. The poet and the prophet are not so easily divorced; and we may even find that it is the second which makes the first worthwhile, if we will permit ourselves to think like Old Critics for a moment. In much good literature, I should venture to say, and certainly in literature so vatic as the transcendentalists', the literary expression is only the beginning, albeit an indispensable beginning, of its appeal, just as it was only the result or end product of the forces which produced it.

Such, at any rate, was the opinion of the transcendentalists. The basic message they had to offer, if one may generalize so sweepingly about a field so wide and hazy, was power. Books, as Emerson wrote in "The American Scholar," "are for nothing but to inspire" (I, 89). This purpose finds impetus and justification in the principle of plenitude, the idea of microcosm underlying it, and the belief in divine immanence which is at the heart of both. All of these are essentially doctrines of open-endedness, promising limitless possibilities for adumbration, refinement, and growth. To the end of expressing these conceptions, and above all the sense of power from which they spring, the catalogue is ideally suited. Even where formless—indeed, we could say, *especially* where formless—the catalogue has the potential for power. Its very rawness makes it all the more vigorous and striking.

The structural limitations of the catalogue, then, are finally irrelevant. It is meant to be wild; the inspired poet, as Emerson put it, "knows that he speaks adequately . . . only when he speaks somewhat wildly"

(III, 27). If there is a limit to the length a catalogue can be sustained, it is not so much in the number as the quality of the items. We could easily dispense with a "Salut au Monde," but that does not mean that another catalogue poem of the same length cannot succeed. Naturally, just as the mixture of short and long sentences in a paragraph makes for a pleasing variety, so in a poem of sizable proportions or a prose work as long as an Emerson essay, discursive passages are most effective if punctuated by terse ones. The same rule of variety applies in miniature to rhythm and line-length, as Emerson's less inspired efforts in iambic tetrameter couplets attest. But both expansion and concentration can be equally effective; and so long as there are freshness and variety in the images, and a minimum amount of modulation from one item to the next in addition to mere juxtaposing, the catalogue can be prolonged almost indefinitely.

What the reader most needs to bring to the catalogue, perhaps, is a sense of abandonment. This does not mean the complete denial of the critical faculty, but only its suspension, for as long as it takes to get caught up, or at least to give the piece a fair trial. One feels that whatever intricate design a catalogue may later be seen to have, it is essentially an outpouring, intended to stir up, not to settle. Maybe this is partly why Whitman, in so many poems like "Roots and Leaves," explicitly beckons to the reader and invites him to participate. An Emerson paragraph makes the same demand, in its own way. It is not merely a bag of duckshot, as Carlyle suggested, speaking like a structural critic;[11] it is a bag of snakes. And the fact that so often critics, even as they deplore the lack of discipline in Emerson's prose, line their own paragraphs with his aphorisms, shows that they are still hissing.

Notes

1. See Jarrell's, "Some Lines from Whitman," in *Poetry and the Age* (New York: Vintage Books, 1955), pp. 101–120. Several more scholarly though less sensitive studies of Whitman's catalogues have been made. Mattie Swayne, "Whitman's Catalogue Rhetoric," *University of Texas Studies in English*, 21 (July 1941), 162–178, is illuminating on the underlying purpose of the catalogue but confines its discussion of the style itself mainly to the characteristic grammatical patterns used by Whitman. Detlev W. Schumann, "Enumerative Style and Its Significance in Whitman, Rilke, Werfel," *Modern Language Quarterly*, 3 (June 1942), 171–204, is chiefly valuable for general comparisons and contrasts among the three writers. Stanley K. Coffman, Jr., " 'Crossing Brooklyn Ferry': A Note on the Catalogue Technique in Whitman's Poetry," *Modern Philology*, 51 (May 1954), 225–232, defends the artfulness of the catalogue as a structural device in terms of a particular example, as I attempt to do in the first section of this paper. Especially stimulating is Coffman's discussion of the progression of tone and idea within and between the

two principal catalogues in "Brooklyn Ferry." Harry R. Warfel, "Whitman's Structural Principles in 'Spontaneous Me,' " *College English*, 18 (January 1957), 190–195, detects unity and movement in the apparent randomness of another catalogue. All four scholars relate Whitman's use of the catalogue to transcendentalist idealism, and their observations—though quite brief, except in Miss Swayne's case—should be compared with mine below, as should Roger Asselineau's interpretation of catalogues as "spiritual exercises" in *The Evolution of Walt Whitman: The Creation of a Book* (Cambridge: Harvard University Press, 1962), pp. 102–103.

2. The following and all subsequent quotations from Whitman are from *Leaves of Grass, Comprehensive Reader's Edition*, ed. Harold W. Blodgett and Sculley Bradley (New York: W. W. Norton, 1967).

3. I cannot believe that "me" in this line is correct. It makes no sense, and it is not to be found in any previous printings of the 1892 or 1860 editions which I have consulted.

4. *The Complete Works of Ralph Waldo Emerson*, ed. Edward Waldo Emerson, 10 vols. (Boston: Houghton, Mifflin, 1903–1904), II, 101–102.

5. The foregoing analysis gives Emerson's essential view of the subject, but there is, we should note, one important inconsistency, due to Emerson's ambivalent and changing philosophy of nature. In *Nature* a rigid conception of nature as a closed system of 1:1 correspondences is adumbrated in "Language," side by side with the more flexible view just analyzed, which is expressed in "Discipline" and "Idealism." The former notion, derived mainly from Swedenborg and his disciples, Emerson never quite outgrew; it comforted him, perhaps, to go on believing that natural objects "are really parts of a symmetrical universe, like words of a sentence; and if their true order is found, the poet can read their divine significance orderly as in a Bible" (VIII, 8). But for the most part, the idea of a symbolic universe was a liberating, rather than a restricting conception for Emerson, and he liked to stress the versatility of the symbol both in nature and in the poet's hands. In "The Poet" he specifically repudiated the point of view of the "mystic," who "nails a symbol to one sense, which was a true sense for a moment, but soon becomes old and false" (III, 34).

6. *Ralph Waldo Emerson* (Boston: Houghton Mifflin, 1915), p. 237.

7. "A Backward Glance o'er Travel'd Roads," p. 563.

8. *Journals of Ralph Waldo Emerson*, ed. Edward Waldo Emerson and Waldo Emerson Forbes, 12 vols. (Boston: Houghton Mifflin, 1909–1914), VI, 47–48, and V, 327.

9. *Symbolism and American Literature* (Chicago: University of Chicago Press, 1953), p. 150. See also René Wellek's section on Emerson in *A History of Modern Criticism* (New Haven: Yale University Press, 1965), III, 163–176. For both scholars, the catalogue and the principle of plentitude behind it seem to represent what is weakest in Emerson's art and criticism. Both discussions, especially Feidelson's, are very provocative, and it will be obvious to the reader that I have been influenced by them even while reacting against them.

10. "A Backward Glance," p. 569.

11. *The Correspondence of Carlyle and Emerson*, ed. Joseph Slater (New York: Columbia University Press, 1964), p. 371.

"Transcendental Antics"

Joel Porte*

I have long nourished a desire—shared, I suspect, by other students of Transcendentalism—to compile what might be called an irreverent anthology of Transcendental humor; to make a collection of writings by and about adherents to the school that would expose the light side of the movement and thus provide some hours of comic relief for sober students of intellectual history. But let me expand a bit on the possible value of such a compilation. I want to suggest that the light-hearted approach to Transcendentalism may be one of the best, as well as one of the most pleasant, ways to understand it. There is, of course, a certain measure of policy in the tactic I am adopting here, since I agree with Lord Bacon that "it is good in discourse and speech of conversation to vary and intermingle . . . jest with earnest, for it is a dull thing to tire"; and nothing indeed can be more tiresome than a large dose of Transcendentalism unrelieved by any glimmer of comedy. As Thoreau noted in his essay on Carlyle, "transcendental philosophy needs the leaven of humor to render it light and digestible."

But, policy aside, I would insist that the comic impulse is a significant component of Transcendentalism: for its abundant presence within the movement itself testifies to a self-awareness, a self-criticism, an ability to see oneself in the round, a fundamental balance and sanity, which are important characteristics of the great burgeoning of American consciousness we know as Transcendentalism. And let me add that the susceptibility of Transcendentalism to comic criticism from the outside is equally important as a reminder that the beliefs and postures of members of the group were frequently, nay usually, extravagant; and extravagance—that quality which Thoreau prayed for—easily lends itself to exaggeration and caricature. But it is also a sign of passion and commitment, of fervent searching and large need to express oneself loudly, and these things, I need hardly say, lie at the heart of the Transcen-

*Reprinted from *Veins of Humor*, ed. Harry Levin, Harvard English Studies 3 (Cambridge: Harvard University Press, 1972), pp. 167–183.

dental ferment. From our point of view, moreover, the ease with which Transcendentalism lent itself to critical lampooning makes such comic criticism an especially useful historical tool, since it brings many of the salient characteristics of the movement into high relief. But enough of prelude. "To use too many circumstances ere one come to the matter," as Bacon observes, "is wearisome." Let us turn directly to an antic portrait of Concord on the Merrymake and environs.

I shall begin with the retrospective glance of a contemporary—a portrait etched in acid from the pen of James Russell Lowell in 1865. Casting his thoughts back some thirty years, Lowell was reminded of the Boston publication of *Sartor Resartus*, and he asserted that Carlyle's "sermon on Falstaff's text of the miserable forked radish gave the signal for a sudden mental and moral mutiny ... On all hands with every variety of emphasis, and by voices of every conceivable pitch, representing the three sexes of men, women, and Lady Mary Wortley Montagues," Lowell continued—with a slighting allusion to the birth of the American blue-stocking—on all hands the cry went out that the time of the Newness had come.

> The nameless eagle of the tree Ygdrasil was about to sit at last, and wild-eyed enthusiasts rushed from all sides, each eager to thrust under the mystic bird that chalk egg from which the new and fairer Creation was to be hatched in due time ... Every possible form of intellectual and physical dyspepsia brought forth its gospel. Bran had its prophets, and the presartorial simplicity of Adam its martyrs ... Everybody had a mission (with a capital M) to attend to everybody else's business. No brain but had its private maggot, which must have found pitiably short commons sometimes. Not a few impecunious zealots abjured the use of money (unless earned by other people), professing to live on the internal revenues of the spirit. Some had an assurance of instant millennium so soon as hooks and eyes should be substituted for buttons. Communities were established where everything was to be common but common sense. Men renounced their old gods, and hesitated only whether to bestow their furloughed allegiance on Thor or Budh. Conventions were held for every hitherto inconceivable purpose ... All stood ready at a moment's notice to reform everything but themselves.[1]

Lowell's description, despite its personal animus and precisely because of its splendid if splenetic sense of comedy, brings clearly before us some of the major impulses, as well as some of the important problems, involved in the ferment of the 1830's and forties. Crusaders burning to remake the world pinned their hopes on dietary reform or the removal of restrictions in dress; others saw the crass commercialism of the State Street bankers as the chief evil of the time. "The Americans

have little faith," Emerson told his audience in 1841; "they rely on the
power of a dollar"[2]—and five years later this lament was expanded into
Theodore Parker's thundering jeremiad, "A Sermon of Merchants."
Lowell also reminds us of the strength of the communitarian impulse,
the hungry search for meaningful society; and his facetious mention of
Thor and Budh only underlines what scarcely needs emphasis—namely,
that the Transcendental movement had its birth in a profound religious
upheaval.

' Here I should like to draw a parallel that I think is too often overlooked by historians of Transcendentalism. I want to suggest a connection between the seriocomic religious fervor of Transcendental reform
and that passionate wave of religious revival which characterized American religion at large during the first half of the nineteenth century. I
believe that both impulses were radically allied, equally expressive of
forces deeply rooted in the American character, and equal sources of
native American humor. "The dominant theme in America from 1800
to 1860," writes Perry Miller in *The Life of the Mind in America*, "is
the invincible persistence of the revival technique...We can hardly
understand Emerson, Thoreau, Whitman, Melville, unless we comprehend that for them this was the one clearly given truth of their society."[3]
The "revolution" of 1800–1801, writes Alan Heimert—referring to the
Second Great Awakening—"reawakened the evangelical hope of the great
community...a nineteenth century in which humanity's social arrangements would be perfected."[4]

This hope, of course, was also that of the Transcendental reformers;
and their community of aspiration and attitude with the Awakening—
the connection between revival and reform—is nowhere better illustrated,
and its problems suggested, than by a section of Constance Rourke's
classic study of *American Humor*. I should like to quote at length a
passage which seems to me worthy of the widest currency and which
points expertly in the direction of some of the notions I am attempting
to develop in this essay. The movement of revivalism, writes Miss Rourke,
"was away from creeds and close formulas, toward improvisation, rapturous climaxes, happy assurances, and a choral strain. In the revivals of
Methodism and the other free new faiths all was generic, large, and of
the crowd; in the end all was wildly hopeful. Rhapsody was common;
the monologue in the experience meeting unfolded those inner fantasies
toward which the native mind was tending in other, quite different
aspects of expression, not in the analytic forms of Calvinism, but as pure
unbridled fantasy and exuberant overflow." And she continues:

> The pattern of comedy appeared again in the innumerable cults
> which sprang up in the '30's and '40's as from some rich and fertile
> seeding-ground. Religious and social traditions were flung to the

four winds. The perfectionists declared that the bondage of sin was
non-existent and that the Millennium had already begun. At Oneida
the bonds of earthly marriage were broken. Spiritualism proposed to
break the bonds of death. The theme of death, which had been a
deep preoccupation in the life of the pioneer, was repeated by these
cults, with a fresh and happy outcome. Life was to be prolonged,
the Millennium had arrived; in the state of perfection death might
never come at all. Most of the new religious communities created
almost overnight in the '30's and '40's agreed to release mankind from
sin, poverty, or mortal care. They all possessed formulas, religious,
economic or social; and they all anticipated conclusions such as the
world had never known. Triumph was their note ... Hysterical,
wrapped in a double sense of national feeling and religious conviction, the believers passed into moods of wildest exaltation. "New,
new ... make all things new." The enchanting cry resounded through
all this ecstasy of faith.[5]

Here I want briefly to break off my quotation from Miss Rourke's
book to juxtapose some sentences from Emerson. Explaining in his lecture
"The Transcendentalist" what were called "new views" in New England,
Emerson said that "Transcendentalism is the Saturnalia or excess of
Faith" and announced that newness was to be the order of the day: "I
do not wish to do one thing but once. I do not love routine."[6] These
mingled themes of newness and ecstasy had already been iterated and
reiterated gaily by Emerson and Margaret Fuller in their high-spirited
introduction to the first number of the *Dial*. Announcing a "new design"
in their opening sentence, they called theirs "a Journal in a new spirit,"
the voice of those making "new demands on literature," eager to express
"new views." Drawing on "the conversation of fervid and mystical pie-
tists," on a faith "earnest and profound," the *Dial* would express "a new
hope," open "a new scope for literature and art," and ultimately through
its perpetually innovational criticism cast "a new light on the whole
world."[7]

Thus does the cry of the cults described by Miss Rourke—"New,
new ... make all things new"—echo through Transcendental writing.
And she continues:

Among all these cults a latent humor broke out; this was clear in
the names which they chose or accepted, such as the placidly humorous variations on Harmony and the grotesque nomenclature of the
Shakers, Groaners, Come Outers, New Lights, Hard Shell Baptists,
and Muggletonians ... A wide level of comic feeling had been
established, sometimes infused with pliant hope, most often with
exuberance. Frequently it was hard to tell when burlesque was
involved, when fakery, when a serious intention. The basic feeling
was romantic, but it crested into a conscious gaiety which raced

beyond the romantic. Even in the most ponderous of these assertions there was something light-hearted.[8]

Now this comic extravagance inherent in and common to American
revivalism, religious cultism, and Transcendentalism clearly assumes in
Miss Rourke's discussion the character of a perennial national habit or
mood, the expression of something fundamental in the American spirit.
First, of course, there is the idea of how necessary has been the cultivation—indeed, the exaggeration—of hope in a land where almost everything had to be done from scratch, whether because of the actual thin-
ness of American culture and tradition or because of the programmatic
assertion that life in the new world had to be purely self-defined and
self-generating. Great hope was needed to sustain a perpetually unrealized and perhaps unrealizable dream of social and religious perfectability; and perhaps just such a great and constantly renewed hope was
the almost conscious counterweight to a gnawing fear that the needful
energy or spirit might flag or disappear. Secondly, the humor associated
with religious and spiritual movements in America since the declension
of the true Bible commonwealth—since the loss, that is, of the Calvinistic
ideal—suggests an anxiety that is being shuffled off in nervous, if not
hysterical, laughter: an anxiety about losing the true faith, an anxiety
about traducing one's forefathers, one's traditions, those institutions and
beliefs that one still half believes in. The American genius for creating
new religions and cults and for throwing oneself into them with exaggerated intensity is matched by a characteristic comic awareness that
incessant newness, the perpetual casting off of yesterday's ideas and
institutions, is a near-relation to faddism and folly. The impassioned
American cry is for something ever new and better, and the American
comic response to that answered prayer represents an awareness that
the promised perfection is and must always be short of its promise.
But the possibility that foolishness or even fakery may crown the irre-
pressible American effort to regenerate or reform must not be taken as
a sign of failure or loss of heart. On the contrary, as Miss Rourke suggests
in her statement about how the comic exuberance of American revivalism
and cultism "crested into a conscious gaiety which raced beyond the
romantic," the very consciousness of gaiety is a final mark of sanity—
a guarantee that wild improvisation and romantic delusion are always
being counterbalanced and corrected by amused self-awareness. Thus,
the ultimate value of American spiritual experimentation may lie in
precisely the kind of sharpened perspective and insight that its comedy
foments.

There is probably no better example of this sort of fruitful interplay between extravagant action or thought to which one is committed
and a simultaneous awareness of comedy than that provided by the

Transcendental ferment. Here, finally, American religious fervor broke the mold of formalized religion, and the passion for reform exhausted the available channels of reformation. The result, at its best, was a literature of witty observations and reflection that has scarcely been surpassed since. And having said that, I must return to Emerson, one of the great American masters of combining participation with ironic detachment. A good place to begin is his own *Dial* essay, "The Comic":

> If the essence of the comic be the contrast in the intellect between the idea and the false performance, there is good reason why we should be affected by the exposure. We have no deeper interest than our integrity, and that we should be made aware by joke and by stroke of any lie that we entertain. Besides, a perception of the comic seems to be a balance-wheel in our metaphysical structure. It appears to be an essential element in a fine character. Wherever the intellect is constructive, it will be found. We feel the absence of it as a defect in the noblest and most oracular soul. . . . The perception of the comic is a tie of sympathy with other men, is a pledge of sanity, and is a protection from those perverse tendencies and gloomy insanities into which fine intellects sometimes lose themselves.[9]

Emerson himself offers us many pledges of his own sanity, examples of how he attempted to enforce the integrity of his being by dissociating himself—now slightly, now pointedly—through gentle humor or mild satire, from some of the more egregious follies of the Transcendental brotherhood. But what is to be noticed is the sharp distinction between Lowell's ill-tempered lampoon of what he considered to be little more than a spiritual disease, and Emerson's delicately managed comic portraits. For Emerson, the perception of the comic side of Transcendentalism was indeed a way of re-asserting his ties of sympathy with other, non-Transcendental men; but he clearly had no intention thereby of denying the bonds of mutual affection and concern that allied him to those fine, though occasionally extreme, intellects among whom he would always be numbered. Leaving the Transcendental club, Emerson could sometimes hear, as others of the group perhaps could not, the voice of nature whispering, "So hot? my little Sir."[10] But this perception of the disparity between the placid calm of nature and the fret and fume of Transcendental disputation, and the comic statement to which such perception gave rise, would not usually cause Emerson to forget or disparage the moral, artistic, or spiritual fervor that produced the heat.

But lest my argument grow too solemn, let me offer some good examples of Emersonian comedy playing over the vagaries of Transcendental reform. Reporting in the *Dial* for July 1842 on "a Convention of Friends of Universal Reform" (otherwise known as the Chardon Street and Bible Conventions), Emerson noted the presence of "men of every shade of opinion, from the straitest orthodoxy to the wildest heresy, and many persons whose church was a church of one member only" and then allowed himself to sketch a consciously humorous portrait of the gathering: "A great variety of dialect and of costume was noticed; a great deal of confusion, eccentricity, and freak appeared, as well as of zeal and enthusiasm. If the assembly was disorderly, it was picturesque. Madmen, madwomen, men with beards, Dunkers, Muggletonians, Come-Outers, Groaners, Agrarians, Seventh-day-Baptists, Quakers, Abolitionists, Calvinists, Unitarians, and Philosophers,—all came successively to the top, and seized their moment, if not their *hour,* wherein to chide, or pray, or preach, or protest."[11]

Carrying the idea of Democratic equality (one man one vote) to its comic conclusion, Emerson has Calvinists and madmen rubbing shoulders—through subtle inference and comic juxtaposition reducing them, as it were, all to one level. In this "Anacharsis Clootz deputation," to use Melville's phrase, tradition and eccentricity have equal rights, but neither has any special privilege. All have the same right to rise momentarily out of the disorderly assembly and try to be heard, but does *this*—Emerson's comic voice seems finally to say to us—constitute an example of the great community? Or of any community at all? A few well-known sentences from *Moby Dick* are especially apposite here: "They were nearly all Islanders in the Pequod, *Isolatoes* too, I call such, not acknowledging the common continent of men, but each *Isolato* living on a separate continent of his own. Yet now, federated along one keel, what a set these Isolatoes were!" What a set indeed is Emerson's nineteenth-century American circus of opinion, and his humor quietly expresses the same uneasiness that laces Melville's sentences. Is this unstable federation really an ecumenical council, or simply a grotesque collection of isolated individuals—"persons whose church was a church of one member only"—who have come to speak but not truly to listen, and who will depart as separate and alone as they have come? Emerson's description of the Chardon Street Convention continues, it must be admitted, in a generally optimistic fashion, but it is surely no exaggeration to see in his humor here a clean sign of that growing distrust of Transcendental reform and ebullient hope that was increasingly to characterize his writing, as well as Thoreau's and that of such demi-Transcendentalists as Hawthorne and Melville. For all of these men, the humor of Transcendentalism became a judgment on the extravagance of its promises—and, perhaps, on the promise of American life generally.

The growth of Emerson's distrust, at all events, is not hard to document. Scarcely two years after reporting on the Chardon Street Convention, he delivered a lecture on "New England Reformers" in which his humor, now sharpened into mild satire, had grown into a pervasive mood of bemused detachment. Speaking of those who had attended the many reform meetings and conventions, he wrote: "They defied each other, like a congress of kings, each of whom had a realm to rule, and a way of his own that made concert unprofitable." The democratic picturesqueness of Chardon Street has become the despotic determination of each to have his own way; and Emerson now views the zeal and enthusiasm of New England reformers as almost pure folly. He continues:

> What a fertility of projects for the salvation of the world! One apostle thought all men should go to farming, and another that no man should buy or sell, that the use of money was the cardinal evil; another that the mischief was in our diet, that we eat and drink damnation. These made unleavened bread, and were foes to the death to fermentation. It was in vain urged by the housewife that God made yeast, as well as dough, and loves fermentation just as dearly as he loves vegetation; that fermentation develops the saccharine element in the grain, and makes it more palatable and more digestible. No; they wish the pure wheat, and will die but it shall not ferment. Stop, dear Nature, these incessant advances of thine; let us scotch these ever-rolling wheels! Others attacked the system of agriculture, the use of animal manures in farming, and the tyranny of man over brute nature; these abuses polluted his food. The ox must be taken from the plough and the horse from the cart, the hundred acres of the farm must be spaded, and the man must walk, wherever boats and locomotives will not carry him. Even the insect world was to be defended—that had been too long neglected, and a society for the protection of ground-worms, slugs and mosquitoes was to be incorporated without delay. With these appeared the adepts of homeopathy, of hydropathy, of mesmerism, of phrenology.[12]

On and on goes Emerson's list of the things that were attacked as being the source of all evil—law, trade, manufacturing, the clergy, academia, marriage—but the conclusion of his wonderfully witty thrust is surprising indeed: the result of this "din of opinion and debate" which he has so wonderfully made sport of he claims to be good, for it asserts "the sufficiency of the private man." The reader, it seems to me, has more justification for feeling that Emerson's treatment of this din of opinion and debate insists rather on the sufficient foolishness of private idiosyncrasy and group hobbyhorses. And so it turns out to be, for the body of his lecture expresses a deep disillusionment with most methods of reform and a belief only in individual *character*. Not the excesses he has pilloried, but rather the humorous detachment—exemplified by his own handling of these things—which sees the world in perspective truly asserts "the sufficiency of the private man." "They are partial," Emerson argues of reformers further on in the lecture, "they are not equal to the work they pretend. They lose their way; in the assault on the kingdom of darkness they expend all their energy on some accidental evil, and lose their sanity and power of benefit. It is of little moment that one or two or twenty errors of our social system be corrected, but of much that the man be in his senses."

Clearly, the only method of reform that Emerson believes in, the only way of forcing men back into their senses, is the use of his own special brand of literary drollery—that Emersonian voice of near-comic exhortation: "Do not be so vain of your one objection. Do you think there is only one? Alas! my good friend, there is no part of society or of life better than any other part. All our things are right and wrong together. The wave of evil washes all our institutions alike. Do you complain of our Marriage? Our marriage is no worse than our education, our diet, our trade, our social customs. Do you complain of the laws of Property? It is a pedantry to give such importance to them. Can we not play the game of life with these counters, as well as with those?"

I suppose there is no denying that Emerson's posture of comic detachment here verges on something close to existential discouragement or even despair. It seems that the habitual perception of humor had itself become Emerson's major defense and the only method of Transcendental reform he still believed in: a conscious gaiety that transformed Transcendental crotchets into whimsical insights and Transcendental querulousness into valuable, if painful, satiric thrusts. "What is it we heartily wish of each other?" Emerson continues. "Is it to be pleased and flattered? No, but to be convicted and exposed, to be shamed out of our nonsense of all kinds, and made men of, instead of ghosts and phantoms. We are weary of gliding ghostlike throughout the world, which is itself so slight and unreal. We crave a sense of reality, though it comes in strokes of pain." Emerson's comic unmasking of folly is his ultimate Transcendental weapon—painful to the point of existential anguish—as it is the major weapon of other great Transcendental writers. This passage from "New England Reformers" clearly looks forward to another satiric thrust, that almost morbid twist of Thoreau's knife in *Walden*, which is meant to impart life though its antic maneuvers toy with death: "If you stand right fronting and face to face to a fact, you will see the sun glimmer on both its surfaces, as if it were a cimeter, and feel its sweet edge dividing you through the heart and marrow, and so you will happily conclude your mortal career. Be it life or death, we crave only reality. If we are really dying, let us hear the rattle in our throats and feel cold in the extremities; if we are alive, let us go about our business."[13]

Well, the chief business of much Transcendental writing and of the criticism which it directly—indeed, defiantly—inspired was precisely that of convicting and exposing folly, of shaming the world out of its nonsense. And such reform had of course to begin at home. Time and time again, the Transcendentalists, and those who remained warily on the fringes of the group, lampooned the extravagances that they mostly all shared—as if to demonstrate that imaginative excess coupled with the ability comically to deflate one's own excesses were the twin characteristics which, precisely through their inseparability, defined the special quality of the intellectual spirit of the times. Melville, for example, alternately attracted and repelled by Transcendentalism, embodied his ambivalent attitude toward the movement in the wide spectrum of his comic response to the Newness—broadly humorous in *Mardi, Moby Dick,* and *Pierre,* but poignantly—almost despairingly—funny in "Bartleby the Scrivener" and savagely satiric in *The Confidence-Man.* Melville chided these "new-light" Apostles, with their "Pythagorean and Shelleyan dietings on apple-parings [and] dried prunes," who "went about huskily muttering the Kantian Categories through teeth and lips dry and dusty as any miller's, with the crumbs of Graham crackers"; but his humor was explicitly meant as a tribute. "Let me here offer up three locks of my hair," Melville exclaimed with gently mocking praise in *Pierre,* "to the memory of all such glorious paupers who have lived and died in this world. Surely, and truly I honor them—noble men often at bottom—and for that very reason I make bold to be gamesome about them; for where fundamental nobleness is, and fundamental honor is due, merriment is never accounted irreverent. The fools and pretenders of humanity, and the imposters and baboons among the gods, these only are offended with raillery."[14] Despite his decidedly irreverent pun on "bottom," Melville had no fear of offending the true Transcendental masters because he knew that what was valuable and noble in them was finally beyond the reach of raillery. Besides, *their* comic self-awareness of folly often easily overmatched his own efforts at friendly satire.

What, in fact, was Transcendentalism at its best, if not a willingness to risk hyperbolic foolishness in the service of truth? Hawthorne could complain good-naturedly of Concord that "never was a poor country village infested with such a variety of queer, strangely dressed, oddly behaved mortals," but he asserted equally: "It was the very spot in which to utter the extremest nonsense or the profoundest wisdom, or that ethereal product of the mind which partakes of both, and may become one or the other, in correspondence with the faith and insight of the auditor."[15] Emerson certainly knew, when he published that first, momentous book in 1836, that his description of himself as a transparent eyeball was comically overdone; but the risk of self-mockery was the price—indeed, the guarantee—of making a serious point with sufficient emphasis. Emerson's object was to convince his audience that spiritual rebirth was contingent on their opening their eyes, literally, to the great new world which was their birthright. Needing more than anything else to behold God and nature face to face, they had—like Emerson—to become transparent eyeballs and *see all.* Then, and only then, would their true *prospects* (the title of the last section of *Nature*) come into focus. "So shall we come to look at the world with new eyes," he concluded headily, insisting that unclouded perception—both *sight* and *insight*—could perform the miracle of turning visions into reality.

Because Emerson's major purpose was to force the sluggard intellect of America to "look from under its iron lids," he had to enact the meaning of his essay by becoming a metaphoric eyeball, even at the risk of seeming silly. Or perhaps becoming metaphorically foolish was the only way of underscoring—indeed, publicizing—his point. Christopher Cranch's now well known and splendidly funny caricature of Emerson as a wide-eyed visual organ on legs takes the author up on his own implicit offer to seem ridiculous. But in this case, to Emerson's ultimate advantage, exaggeration and truth enforce one another, and Emerson's meaning is made certain. Indeed, he would later, in his *Poems* of 1846, reiterate and make further use of this comic self-portrait, ironically allegorizing himself as Uriel, the archangel of the sun, whose "piercing eye" with its "look that solved the sphere" made the stern old Unitarian war gods shudder and helped destroy their bland and complacent Paradise.

Few readers may have noted and truly appreciated the significant comedy of Emerson's eyeball humor, but it was not lost on Henry Thoreau, who continued the jocular tradition in his first book. James Russell Lowell must have been in a particularly dour mood when he wrote, with surprising imperceptivity, that "Thoreau had no humor."[16] But I wonder how many readers of *A Week on the Concord and Merrimack Rivers* have noticed that Thoreau turned Emerson's own favorite literary device against his master when he waggishly "attacked" Emerson in the "Sunday" section of the book:

What earth or sea, mountain or stream, or Muses' spring or grove, is safe from his all-searching ardent eye, who drives off Phoebus' beaten track, visits unwonted zones, makes the gelid Hyperboreans glow, and the old polar serpent writhe, and many a Nile flow back and hide his head! [Then Thoreau broke into a mock-heroic paean.]

> That Phaeton of our day,
> Who'd make another milky way,
> And burn the world up with his ray;
>
> By us an undisputed seer—
> Who'd drive his flaming car so near
> Unto our shuddering mortal sphere,
>
> Disgracing all our slender worth,
> And scorching up the living earth,
> To prove his heavenly birth.

> The silver spokes, the golden tire,
> Are glowing with unwonted fire,
> And ever nigher roll and nigher;
>
> The pins and axle melted are,
> The silver radii fly afar,
> Ah, he will spoil his Father's car!
>
> Who let him have the steeds he cannot steer?
> Henceforth the sun will not shine for a year;
> And we shall Ethiops all appear.

From *his* [quoting Emerson's poem "The Problem"]

> "lips of cunning fell
> The thrilling Delphic oracle."

And yet, sometimes,

> We should not mind if on our ear there fell
> Some less of cunning, more of oracle.

"It is Apollo shining in your face," Thoreau concluded. "O rare Contemporary, let us have far-off heats. Give us the subtler, the heavenlier though fleeting beauty . . . Let epic trade-winds blow, and cease this waltz of inspirations."

It is hard to know where to begin unraveling the complications of Thoreau's wit here. He starts, of course, by hyperbolically verifying the justice of Emerson's metaphoric representation of himself as an "ardent eye," but then Thoreau's humor turns into an expression of anxiety over the danger that this "undisputed seer" may permanently outshine all other Concord literary sights; whence Thoreau accuses the local Apollo of being too clever and smooth in his inspirational music. "Let epic trade-winds blow," exclaims the younger man with over-inflated metaphoric grandeur, commencing to aim his wit against himself as his attack on Emerson turns into a comic advertisement for Ulysses D. Thoreau on the way up—since, naturally, an excellent example of the kind of rough heroic literature being advocated is Thoreau's book itself, an oracular chronicle of Henry the Navigator's brave voyage up these mysterious inland rivers. But, of course, the joke is quite obviously and consciously on Thoreau himself, for his epic journey is no more than a gentle jaunt from Concord to Concord; and the joke will once again be on this self-styled great adventurer when his next contribution to the world's heroic literature documents an errand into the wilderness of Walden Pond—otherwise identifiable as neighbor Emerson's woodlot. Thus, in the very act of lampooning Emerson's own comic literary tactics, Thoreau continues the Transcendental tradition of shrewd and effective self-parody learned from his mentor.

Examples could be multiplied, but I trust my point is sufficiently clear. The Transcendental persuasion, as I see it, was very largely an antic persuasion—an American Renaissance and Reformation of the spirit that owed much of its force to humor. It was a romantic movement endowed with a conscious gaiety that raced beyond the romantic into that realm where the silly and the solemn meet and merge to produce something that begins to resemble truth. Although the comedy of Transcendentalism has often been represented as little more than a merely parochial humorous outburst—Henry James called it "a kind of Puritan carnival" that "produced no fruit"[17]—it was the kind of inevitable comedy that arises from the tensions of a deeply serious human debate. In this case, the debate itself was carried on largely in the spirit of revel. Much of its fruit was therefore unusually sweet—or bittersweet—and it has not all been harvested yet.

Notes

1. "Thoreau," *The Shock of Recognition*, ed. Edmund Wilson (New York: Modern Library, 1955), pp. 229–230.

2. See "Man the Reformer," *Nature, Addresses, and Lectures* (Boston: Houghton, Mifflin, 1890), p. 237.

3. *The Life of the Mind in America: From the Revolution to the Civil War* (New York: Harcourt, Brace and World, 1965), p. 7.

4. *Religion and the American Mind: From the Great Awakening to the Revolution* (Cambridge: Harvard University Press, 1966), p. 544.

5. *American Humor* (Garden City, N.Y.: Doubleday, 1953), pp. 111–112.

6. *Nature, Addresses, and Lectures*, pp. 320, 330.

7. *Dial*, 1 (July 1840), 1–4.

8. *American Humor*, pp. 112–113.

9. *Dial*, 4 (October 1843), 250.

10. See "Spiritual Laws," *Essays: First Series* (Boston: Houghton, Mifflin, 1884), p. 129.

11. "Chardon Street and Bible Conventions," *Dial*, 3 (July 1842), 101.

12. This and other quotations below from "New England Reformers," *Essays: Second Series* (Boston: Houghton, Mifflin, 1897), pp. 240–270.

13. From the penultimate paragraph of "Where I lived, and What I lived for."

14. *Pierre: Or, the Ambiguities*, ed. Henry A. Murray (New York: Hendricks House, 1949), p. 314.

15. See "The Old Manse," *Mosses from an Old Manse.*

16. "Thoreau," *Shock of Recognition*, p. 238.

17. "Emerson," *The Art of Fiction and Other Essays* (New York: Oxford University Press, 1948), p. 236.

"Transcendentalist Literary Method: Inspiration Versus Craftsmanship"

Lawrence Buell*

We have witnessed the Transcendentalists' admiration for the vocation of the poet-priest. But what exactly does such an individual do? What sort of utterance is demanded of him, and what sort of discipline must he master if he is to achieve it?

At first sight, the Transcendentalists' idea about literary method seems rather desultory, even abortive. The couplet inscribed on Emerson's gravestone would have made a good epitaph for the group as a whole: "The passive Master lent his hand / To the vast soul that o'er him planned." All Transcendentalist attempts to describe how art is to be created, and the impact which it should make upon its audience, begin and end with the idea of inspiration.[1] "Genius" is lauded, "talent" disparaged. "There can be no will in composition," Alcott insists. "The spirit within is the only writer" (*JA*, p. 206). The poet "does not seek his song," says Brownson, "it comes to him. It is given him."[2] Jones Very even professed to value his poems "not because they were his but because they were not."[3] Emerson agreed. "A work of art," he says, "is something which the Reason created in spite of the hands" (*JMN*, V, 206), lasting "in proportion as it was not polluted by the wilfulness of the writer, but flowed from his mind after the divine order of cause and effect" (*W*, XII, 466). At such times as these, Emerson sounds like those early protestants who claimed that good works are actually an impediment to salvation.

But even as Emerson seems to be recommending a sort of automatic writing, he is apt to come out with a shrewd remark which suggests the opposite, as in his objections to Very and Ellery Channing: "Is the poetic inspiration amber to embalm & enhance flies & spiders? . . . Cannot the spirit parse & spell?"[4] Although Emerson was a fanciful theorist, he could be a demanding editor and good practical critic. Another example is his mixed opinion of Wordsworth and Tennyson. Wordsworth, most

*Reprinted from *Literary Transcendentalism: Style and Vision in the American Renaissance* (Ithaca: Cornell University Press, 1973), pp. 55–74.

Transcendentalists agreed, had genius;[5] Tennyson had talent; each seemed deficient in the other category. In principle, Emerson was prepared to venerate Wordsworth and disparage Tennyson as "a beautiful half of a poet" (*JMN*, VII, 83). But he did not rest in this view. Picking up a new volume of Wordsworth in 1835, for instance, Emerson reminds himself (as if about to take medicine) that "I may find dulness & flatness, but I 'shall not find meanness & error." But on the next day he exclaims: "What platitudes I find in Wordsworth. 'I poet bestow my verse on this & this & this.' Scarce has he dropped the smallest piece of an egg, when he fills the barnyard with his cackle" (*JMN*, V, 99, 100). After such fatuities, Tennyson comes as "a godsend."[6] In the one essay in which they are compared, "Europe and European Books," Emerson moves with an obvious sense of relief from the former to the latter.

Again, Emerson was often carried away by what he took to be a new genius, in whom he placed "a faith approaching to superstition," as Alcott said;[7] but he was quick to have second thoughts. Alcott, Carlyle, Charles King Newcomb, Walt Whitman, and Emma Lazarus were all warmly praised at first, then coolly reappraised in much the same manner as Very and Channing. The famous letter to Whitman, so often taken as a key link in the great causal chain to which one reduces American literature for mythological purposes, is only one instance of the recurring syndrome, in Emerson's criticism, of high praise giving way to critical reservations followed by qualified respect. Nor was Emerson totally spontaneous when it came to his own writing. No method of composition could have been less spontaneous, indeed, than his practice of piecing together mosaics from journal to lecture to essay.

The same common sense, underneath a rhetoric of inspiration, can be found in all the other Transcendentalists with any claim to literary importance except for Channing and Very, and even Channing revised his manuscripts. Contrasting Byron and Goethe, Margaret Fuller concluded that untutored genius was great but cultivated genius was greater.[8] Thoreau, similarly, accepted the theory of inspiration, but with the proviso that "we blunder into no discovery but it will appear that we have prayed and disciplined ourselves for it" (*JT*, IX, 53). This statement represents pretty well the actual, as opposed to the apparent, consensus among the major Transcendentalists on the subject of inspiration. They were all enamored of the *idea* of inspiration, and hastened to ascribe as much as possible to it, even the literary grubwork. (Witness Emerson's declaration that the process of revising over a period of time does not negate his theory, because each part of the composition comes to the writer in a flash of insight; *JMN*, VII, 216–217). But as refined and sensitive people, they demanded satisfaction from the finished product. Discipline, then, was a hidden but genuine part of the Transcendentalist aesthetic. Even Jones Very served an apprenticeship in sonneteering before he wrote his "inspired" pieces, though he may not have regarded it as such.

In some ways the Transcendentalist view of the creative process resembles the attitude taken toward the workings of grace in the covenant theology of the Puritans.[9] In each case, the individual is theoretically powerless and the spirit does the work. All believe and delight in the absolute sovereignty of God or the Muse as the case may be. But the doctrine of sovereignty is hedged about with qualifications as to the importance of individual preparation. These qualifications were muted enough to expose both Puritans and Transcendentalists to the charge of antinomianism, but distinct enough to allow both to repudiate it.

The analogy must not be pushed too hard, or it will make Emerson, with his fondness for the Plotinian theory of the poet's divine madness, seem altogether too respectable; but the resemblances that do exist are more than coincidental, as the Transcendentalists' use of biblical language to talk about the creative process should have suggested. However much it relies for its expression on such literary jargon as genius/talent, imagination/fancy, and classic/romantic, their theory of creativity begins, like the concept of the poet-priest itself, with their intuitions about religious experience. Inspiration did not mean for them a great idea for a poem or story, so much as the experience of that Truth or Reality of which the finished work was to be the expression. We must bear in mind this equation of creativity with spiritual or intellectual fulfilment if we are to understand not only the theoretical importance they attached to inspiration but also their practical attention to craftsmanship. Though these attitudes might seem incompatible, both are consistent with the Transcendentalists' peculiar beliefs as renegade Unitarians. Their chief weapon against Unitarian "rationalism," as we have seen, was to insist that all men have direct access to the deity. And yet none of them, except Jones Very and perhaps Theodore Parker, seem to have been steady partakers in the divine experience they celebrate. No Transcendentalists wrote diaries like those of many pious evangelicals, with their almost daily attributions of particular events to providence. To be sure, this is explicable partly on technical grounds. The Transcendentalists, like the Unitarians, tended to discount such claims as superstitious, at best quaint, at worst delusive. They viewed spiritual fulfilment in terms of human, natural excellence rather than in terms of supernatural intervention. "Which is greater & more affecting?" Emerson asks, "to see some wonderful bird descending out of the sky, or, to see the rays of a heavenly majesty of the mind & heart emitted from the countenance & port of a man?" (*JMN*, VII, 236). The true mystical experience, that is, is a transfiguration from within and not a message or tuunderbolt from without. But even this sort of experience is rarely recorded by the Transcendentalists. If one excepts their obviously fictitious recreations of ecstasy, like "Bacchus" and "Merlin," as merely vicarious and wish-fulfilling, there are not more than a score of mystical experiences reported by the whole lot of them to rival in emotional intensity the habitual fervor of some of the great American revivalists. Alcott and Fuller each had several; Orestes Brownson had visions in his childhood; Charles King Newcomb and Ellery Channing record none.[10] Emerson gives us something like the real article in "Each and All" and the two anecdotes in the first chapter of Nature—crossing the common and becoming a transparent eyeball; but all three of these are literary elaborations of observations which are reported in a comparatively matter-of-fact way in his journal. The closest thing to a detailed account of an ecstatic experience to be found in all his writing is the description of his illumination in Mt. Auburn Cemetery in 1834 (JMN, IV, 272–273). Thoreau's writings are almost as unmystical. Judging from his frequent complaints in later life of a loss of spontaneous perception, it may well be, as Ethel Seybold says, that he was "a youthful mystic" who later "lost the ability to enter the ecstatic state."[11] In any case, he left little record of such experiences, with the exception of a few journal passages (e.g., JT, VIII, 43–45) and three more literary descriptions, all written during the 1840s: two in A Week (on "Monday" night and "Tuesday" morning) and one in "Ktaadn."[12] For the most part Thoreau's writing conveys the sense of a highly self-conscious and rational intelligence.

This hasty census suggests that despite what the Transcendentalists said about inspiration, they were nearly as Unitarian in their emotional restraint as they were in their distrust of particular providences. Emerson, for example, disliked the "restlessness and fever" of Fuller's religious enthusiasm (Ossoli, I, 309). "He who trusts to sudden flashes of good feeling and excitement, follows no safe guide," says the persona in one of Cranch's parables.[13] Altogether, Transcendentalism was not so much an antirational reaction to Unitarianism as it was, in Clarence Gohdes' admirable phrase, "Unitarianism in the process of 'getting religion.' "[14] Theirs was a highly intellectual, almost a hypothetical mysticism, more talked about than felt. It was not so much that they lacked the emotional capacity for such experience, but that they were too sophisticated to be uninhibited about it, and also too conscientious or unselfish to want to wall themselves up forever with God, without trying to communicate with others. "One must not seek to dwell always in contemplation of the Spirit," Emerson cautioned, lest he become indolent and helpless (JMN, VIII, 188). "The spiritual life," another Transcendentalist minister agreed, "demands, rather contains in itself, the germ which produces . . . utterance of word, utterance of deed."[15] It may be significant that the most passionate men among the Transcendentalists, Brownson and Parker, were also the most committed to logic, as if they felt compelled to rationalize their emotion, and that both found fulfilment in religio-social causes: Catholicism in Brownson's case, theological and social reform in Parker's. Parker's temperament was especially paradoxical. Time and again he insists that belief is a matter of intuition not subject to proof, and from such sermons as "The Delights of Piety" it would seem that he experienced this feeling as much as any man. But at the same time he feels driven to bolster his intuitionalism by copious demonstration and encyclopedic reference. He seems to have had a farmboy's simple trust in the power of knowledge, as well as a farmboy's simple faith. Parker pushes the intuitions still further into the background by insisting upon the moral life as the test of piety. "Parkerism," as a result, is as much rationalism and social gospel as it is Transcendentalism, though the latter is its starting point.

Nowhere are the Transcendentalists' lurking reservations about the validity of inspiration more evident than in their reaction to Jones Very. None of the Transcendentalists were much impressed with Very's messianic claims, not even Alcott, who was most sympathetic. They realized that he spoke reason in madness, but it was still madness. James Freeman Clarke, for instance, draws the following conclusion on Very's insistence to Dr. Channing that he did everything "in obedience to the spirit," even so small an act as walking across the room and leaning on the mantel: "And, indeed, if it has become a habit of the soul to be led in all things, great and small, why not in this too? Only, I suppose, that most of us would not think it worth while to consult the Spirit in such a purely automatic action as this."[16] This is the voice of urbanity curbing the misguided enthusiast, the same voice which speaks in Emerson's comments about Brook Farm, or the Chardon Street Convention, or Edward Palmer, the man who wanted to abolish money. In a way, Yvor Winters was quite right when he said that Very "had the experience which Emerson merely recommends."[17] Emerson admitted as much himself: " 'Tis remarkable that our faith in ecstasy consists with total inexperience of it" (W, VI, 213). Indeed, as his writings show, the faith thrived on the inexperience: after the late 1830s, Emerson's praise of inspiration actually gets more effusive the more he complains about his own lack of it. As he felt his powers of perception wane, inspiration seemed progressively more wonderful.

Still, Emerson sold himself short, with characteristic modesty. Nor should we judge the other Transcendentalists by their reactions to Very. Though they fell short of hierophancy, and were skeptical of Harvard tutors who suddenly claimed to be prophets, there is no question that they experienced inspiration of a sort, perhaps many times. At least they thought so. Emerson, Hedge, Parker, Thomas Stone, and Thoreau all undertook to give a general description of what it felt like.[18] The best-known accounts are Emerson's descriptions of afflatus in "The Poet" and "The Over-Soul." But one gets a better idea of the experiential basis for these idealized pictures if we turn to a passage with a more personal ring.

> We say I will walk abroad, and the truth will take form and clear-ness to me. We go forth, but cannot find it. It seems as if we needed only the stillness and composed attitude of the library to seize the thought. But we come in, and are as far from it as at first. Then, in a moment, and unannounced, the truth appears. A certain wander-ing light appears, and is the distinction, the principle, we wanted. But the oracle comes because we had previously laid siege to the shrine. It seems as if the law of the intellect resembled that law of nature by which we now inspire, now expire the breath . . . , the law of undulation. [W, II, 331–332]

The "inspiration" reported here is modest, but genuine. Everyone has encountered it in some form. It is not the road to Damascus or the Pentacostal fire, but a very natural thing, as natural as breathing, but also mysterious and involuntary, although Emerson is careful to note that we can prepare for it to some extent. It was this sort of phenomenon which formed the primary existential basis for the Transcendentalist theory of literary inspiration. When they talk, that is, of the poet as having direct access to godhead, their confidence derives mainly from having known such flashes of insight. When they talk of the possibility of a "perpetual revelation," they probably have in mind such insight extended and intensified to the nth power—not so much delirious trans-port as perfect powers of perception and sensitivity to one's surroundings. It was the failure to gain this anticipated level of awareness, rather than a deep allegiance to the idea of the divine madness in itself, which led Emerson during his middle years to overdramatize the process of inspira-tion as an almost supernatural event.[19]

Applying the same line of thought to religious experience as well as the intellectual illumination just quoted, one might contend that there was no real difference between the kind of inspiration felt by Transcen-dentalists and by other Unitarians, and by many modern believers, for that matter. This is suggested, for example, by Parker's description of comfort after prayer as a true inspiration. Some conservatives might have quibbled with his definition even as they shared precisely the same experience. Actually, as we have seen, the Unitarians did not categorically deny that there was such a thing as inspiration, and that it might be at work in such a case as Parker cited; they simply claimed less, claimed that it did not imply an identity of the soul with God, that its workings were indistinguishable from other mental acts. Conversely, while the Transcendentalists considered inspiration as a special experience, the most exciting fact of life, they did not think that it should take violent or perverse forms of expression. "It is no turbulent emotion," cautions F. H. Hedge, "no fever of the blood—no unnatural heat. It has nothing of the whirlwind or the tempest, but that repose which belongs alike to nature and to mind in their most healthy moods—the calmness of the sunshine—the tranquillity of intense contemplation."[20] Similarly, for most other Transcendentalists, as Howard Mumford Jones has said, "religion was an experience above, not beneath, the rational faculty."[21] Father Edward Taylor, with his uninhibited sallies of earthy rhetoric, qualified as inspired; Jones Very, when he started to prophesy in garbled Old Testamentese, became suspect.

The fact remains, however, that once the Transcendentalists began to dwell upon the glories of inspiration, they found it hard to apply the brakes. The sense of exuberance one feels in his best moments; the effort of striving to recapture it; the delight of believing that man is truly divine; the awareness that inspiration comes by surprise—all these considerations led them to condone and even to cultivate an extravagance of statement, if not behavior, which goes well beyond what they said in their more sober moments. So it was quite natural that Emerson, in his criticism, should regard genius as implicitly including craftsmanship and yet at the same time choose to view the whole creative process as a divine mystery. Although he knew very well the importance of discipline to writing and to inspiration itself, he believed so strongly that the decisive factor in composition was unpredictable and he attached such a cosmic significance to it that he couldn't bring himself to praise discipline very highly. Though F. O. Matthiessen oversimplifies in saying that the Transcendentalist notion of art as inspiration is necessarily "in sharp opposition" to the idea of art as craftsmanship, such did prove to be the case in some instances, not so much for Emerson and Thoreau as for some of the less gifted Transcendentalists.[22] The reluctance of Very and Channing to comply with Emerson's editorial requests has been alluded to. Alcott and Fuller might also have taken more pains with their writing had they not been discouraged so quickly by the task of getting their insights down on paper. John S. Dwight came to grief as a preacher when, for a time, he took literally the principle of spontaneity and did not prepare. W. H. Channing could deliver beautiful extemporaneous orations but he wrote turgid prose; his biographer rightly says that he dissipated his talents. So did Cranch, who upbraided himself in old age for having "wooed too many mistresses."[23]

Despite this list of casualties, however, distrust of discipline per se was probably less of a problem for the Transcendentalists in the long run than confusion as to the nature of discipline. They recognized no distinction between art and life. They imbibed too eagerly the critical commonplace of their day, that to be a great artist one must be a good man. If an "immoral" person (like Goethe) seemed to have written a great book, then either the man really did have a great soul underneath or the book itself was somehow flawed.[24] This assumption is philosophically defensible; the real difficulty came when the Transcendentalists tried to reverse the idea and claim that the good man will be a good writer. That is exactly the position Emerson takes in "The Poet," in prescribing an ascetic regime for his bard: "Never can any advantage be taken of nature by a trick. . . . The sublime vision comes to the pure and simple soul in a clean and chaste body" (W, III, 28). Thoreau's version of this idea is easier to misread but also adamant: "Nothing goes by luck in composition. It allows of no tricks. The best you can write will be the best you are. Every sentence is the result of a long probation. The author's character is read from title-page to end" (JT, I, 225–226). Here too the speaker dedicates himself to a discipline, and at first it seems to be the craft of writing. But it is not. Sincerity and moral seriousness are really what he is after. "The problem of the artist for Thoreau," Sherman Paul sums up, "was a question of depth," not of expertise,[25] and the same is true in even greater measure of the other Transcendentalists.

Given the times in which the Transcendentalists lived, their viewpoint is not at all surprising. The idea of art as an expression of character was a standard romantic assumption; it was also a classical assumption, and a Christian assumption too. It was drummed into Harvard students by every Boylston Professor of Rhetoric, beginning with John Quincy Adams. What is provocatively unique about the Transcendentalists is the seriousness with which they took it. It was no mere cultural shibboleth with them. Here, as at several other points, what differentiates them from the great English romantics as well as such compatriots as Hawthorne and Poe is not so much their critical principles as the strictness with which they applied them. Thus Coleridge's response to the gap between Wordsworth's theory of language and its practice was to criticize the theory, whereas Brownson's was to criticize the practice, to take Wordsworth to task for writing in a too artificial manner.[26] Likewise, the Transcendentalists took the messianic implications of the poet-priest more seriously than all English romantics except Blake and Shelley.

In their more worldly moments, the shrewdest Transcendentalists conceded that morality and art didn't always go hand in hand, as when Margaret Fuller went out of her way to insist that Byron's dissipation did nothing to impair his power as a writer.[27] Most of them, indeed, were sensitive to the power of language as an independent instrument; they simply considered it trivial if not employed in the service of truth. Such high-mindedness prevented them from grappling with the technical problems of craftsmanship as effectively as they might have otherwise. They preferred to jump from fact to essence, from the nuts and bolts of technique to affirmations like "The true poem is not that which the public read"; "Life is the Poem; Man is the Poet," and so forth. Because of this attitude, they quickly became dissatisfied with art as a whole, for it was obvious that even the greatest works do not fully realize the inspiration that gave rise to them. Not even the writers of the Bible, Andrews Norton had shown, had been able to do that. Like Shelley, the Transcendentalists regarded art as at best a fading coal, a feeble replica of the original experience. They tended to be hardest on the best books, as being the most pretentious.[28] Tennyson was declared lovely but facile, Wordsworth noble but dull, Coleridge and Carlyle provocative but bigoted, Goethe splendid but dilettantish, Shakespeare great but morally unsound. By keeping their eye so scrupulously on the absolute, the Transcendentalists thus short-circuited themselves both as critics and artists. When confronted with a work of art which came close to meeting their standards, which did seem worthy of discussion, they were unable to account for it, let alone rival it. And this, in turn, reinforced their sense of creativity as miraculous.

An interesting case of this sort is Cyrus Bartol's response to a Madonna of Raphael which he saw in Dresden. This picture captivated him, especially the eyes of the child, in which

> there is, in what manner I know not, by what art or inspiration painted I surely cannot tell, a supremacy of control which principalities above or below might well fear to disobey, as though that were the final authority of the universe.
> . . . Long did I inspect, and often did I go back to re-examine, this mystery, which so foiled my criticism, and constrained my wonder, and convinced me, as nothing visible beside had ever done, that if no picture is to be worshipped, something is to be worshipped; that is to be worshipped which such a picture indicates or portrays. But the problem was too much for my solving.[29]

Clearly Bartol *wants* to remain mystified. He wants badly to draw a pious conclusion from this encounter, as he does from all the other "pictures of Europe" presented in his book. But it is clear too that he has approached the picture not just as a minister but as a critic; he has made a great effort to understand it, and failed. His praise of the artist's inspiration is a confession of personal inadequacy as well as an act of reverence.

This very Jamesian image of the preacher-aesthete overcome by the European masterpiece makes a good epitome of the Transcendentalist writer's predicament. His New England background had trained him to be a connoisseur of piety rather than of art, yet led him to the conclusion that great art was a high expression of piety. But how was he to be an artist, or even a critic, when his forte was the moral life? He might be aware that the Madonna was composed of brushstrokes and paint, but he could appreciate it only as the expression of spirit. This dilemma was almost as severe for Thoreau as it was for Bartol. Though Thoreau was a lot closer to being a professional writer and rated D.D.'s lower than chickadees, he could no more than Bartol be satisfied with a conception of art as craft.

Fortunately the problem implied its own solution, namely an expressivist-didactic form of art in which one's thought or experience or perception was uttered and regulated as deftly as possible but was still the dominant element. At best, if one was lucky or worked hard enough, the result would have the roundness of a masterpiece as well as the authenticity of truth. If not, it would at least be heartfelt, which was more than one could say for most art; it would be emancipated from the kind of triviality which the Transcendentalists disparaged in "men of talent" like Longfellow. Indeed a little roughness might be a good thing: "The kingly bard/ Must smite the chords rudely and hard," says Emerson's Merlin (W, IX, 120). One representative literary model for the sort of utterance the Transcendentalists wanted was the ancient bard or prophet, a man of high seriousness, "rude and massive proportions" rather than "smooth and delicate finish,"[30] who would express himself with vehemence and enthusiasm in gnomic, picturesque speech.

> He may not stoop to pander to the herd,
>   Their fickle tastes and morbid appetites,
> He hath upon his lips a holy word,
>   And he must heed not if it cheers or blights,
> So it be Truth.[31]

Thus spake Cranch—a representative view of the poet's role. He himself was not too successful in his imitation of it, to say the least, nor was most Transcendentalist poetry. Thoreau tries in his doggerel:

> Conscience is instinct bred in the house,
> Feeling and Thinking propagate the sin
> By an unnatural breeding in and in.
> I say, Turn it out doors,
> Into the moors.   [Wr, I, 75]

But this sounds less like the bard than like the local crank. Very had a better sense of the prophetic tone:

> Thou art more deadly than the Jew of old,
> Thou hast his weapons hidden in thy speech;
> And though thy hand from me thou dost withhold,
> They pierce where sword and spear could never reach.[32]

But his imagery is usually so derivative that his utterance seems like a pastiche or masquerade rather than the real thing. Perhaps Emerson came closest in his Channing Ode:

> Virtue palters; Right is hence;
> Freedom praised, but hid;
> Funeral eloquence
> Rattles the coffin-lid.   [W, IX, 77]

On the whole, though, prose was a more congenial medium for the Transcendentalists, especially if the occasion happened to be a lecture or sermon:

> Nothing changes more from age to age than the doctrines taught as Christian, and insisted on as essential to Christianity and personal salvation. What is falsehood in one province passes for truth in another. The heresy of one age is the orthodox belief and "only infallible rule" of the next. Now Arius, and now Athanasius, is lord of the ascendant. Both were excommunicated in their turn, each for affirming what the other denied. Men are burned for professing what men are burned for denying.   [Tr, p. 266]

This passage, from Parker's "The Transient and Permanent in Christianity," comes closer than the poetry just quoted to what "Merlin" calls for: artful thunder. It has a truly prophetic sweep and intensity, combined with aphoristic bite. Emerson's Divinity School Address is in the same vein, though Parker is harder-hitting and much more explicit and orderly than Emerson (which explains why Parker aroused more opposition). The pervasiveness of this sort of rhetoric throughout Transcendentalist writing can be seen by glancing through any anthology. It appears in staccato in Brownson's *New Views*:

> I do not misread the age. I have not looked upon the world only out from the window of my closet; I have mingled in its busy scenes, I have rejoiced and wept with it; I have hoped and feared, and believed and doubted with it, and I am but what it has made me. I cannot misread it. It craves union.   [Tr, p. 123]

Where Brownson is merely strident, Thoreau likes to make his point more obliquely, by elaborating his exempla:

The best men that I know are not serene, a world in themselves. For the most part, they dwell in forms, and flatter and study effect only more finely than the rest. We select granite for the underpinning of our houses and barns; we build fences of stone; but we do not ourselves rest on an underpinning of granitic truth, the lowest primitive rock. Our sills are rotten. What stuff is the man made of who is not coexistent in our thought with the purest and subtilest truth? [Wr, IV, 470]

This is the Emersonian technique of showing man's shabbiness by comparison to nature, with the Thoreauvian twist of contrasting the poverty of our inner lives with the quality of our possessions.

The manifesto-note is not the only one the Transcendentalists favored, although it is the easiest to hear. Much of the time, they employed what we would regard as a normative or conventional style of writing. Nor, when they strove for special effects, did they always try to play Jeremiah or Taliessen, any more than Renaissance poets tried to write only epics. Another style, for instance, of which several of them were equally if not more fond, was the ruminative, especially in a pastoral setting. Thoreau's reflection on autumn flowers, in A Week, is an example:

There is a peculiar interest belonging to the still later flowers, which abide with us the approach of winter. There is something witch-like in the appearance of the witch-hazel, which blossoms late in October and in November, with its irregular and angular spray and petals like furies' hair, or small ribbon streamers. Its blossoming, too, at this irregular period, when other shrubs have lost their leaves, as well as blossoms, looks like witches' craft. Certainly it blooms in no garden of man's. There is a whole fairy-land on the hillside where it grows. [Wr, I, 318–319]

This passage gives us the prophet off-duty, so to speak, relaxing. Instead of lofty didacticism for public purposes, we see him playing with the significance of things. His vehemence has diffused into the dreamy atmosphere of fairyland. But it is still moral art: much as he loves nature for herself, Thoreau is not content to stay on the descriptive level alone, even in his later work where there is much less of reverie.

Some other Transcendentalist works which use this style, in whole or in part, are Emerson's "Musketaquid," "Saadi," "Woodnotes," "Stonehenge" (in English Traits), and the second essay on "Nature"; Judd's Margaret; Fuller's Summer on the Lakes; some of Very's nature poems; and much of Ellery Channing's verse. Next to Thoreau, Channing was fondest of pastoral meditation. His poetry in this vein (the best of which is better than it has been given credit for being, as I attempt to show in Chapter 9) ranges widely in content between description and didacticism, and between a leisurely and a compressed style. "Moonlight" is an example of his compression:

> He came and waved a little silver wand,
> He dropped the veil that hid a statue fair,
> He drew a circle with that pearly hand,
> His grace confined that beauty in the air;—
> Those limbs so gentle, now at rest from flight,
> Those quiet eyes now musing on the night.[33]

The stock imagery here is largely redeemed by the poem's compactness and elusive quality: who "he" is is not at first apparent; the last two lines suggest both Luna and someone observing her. As with the passage from Thoreau, the evocation of atmosphere is primary here, but it is an atmosphere in which one is induced to look for meanings.

Prophecy and meditation, manifesto and reverie, the bardic and the pastoral, Merlin and Saadi—much of Transcendentalist writing oscillates between these opposites. The charm of *Walden,* for instance, consists to a large extent in Thoreau's way of alternating between them. Such formulations are simplistic, of course; we shall need to look much more closely at the range of stylistic conventions underlying Transcendentalist literary expression. For now, the point to recognize is that the Transcendentalist idea of craftsmanship, however vaguely articulated, is not a contradiction in terms. Though their theory of inspiration kept them from coping with the practical problems of their craft as clearsightedly as they might otherwise have done, most of the Transcendentalists interpreted the theory as explaining but not precluding literary labor. Although the kinds of expression which chiefly interested them emphasized message and tone at the expense of aesthetic symmetry and logical precision, the Transcendentalists were by no means insensitive in their understanding and use of the intricacies of those points of style best suited to their ends.

Notes

1. For previous discussions of the idea of inspiration and its importance relative to craftsmanship in Emerson's thought, see Norman Foerster, "Emerson on the Organic Principle in Art," *PMLA,* 41 (March 1926), 193–208, rpt. in *Emerson: A Collection of Critical Essays,* ed. Milton Konvitz and Stephen E. Whicher (Englewood Cliffs, N.J.: Prentice-Hall, 1962), pp. 108–120; F. O. Matthiessen, *American Renaissance* (New York: Oxford University Press, 1941), pp. 24–29; Vivian Hopkins, *Spires of Form* (Cambridge: Harvard University Press, 1951), pp. 17–62. For Thoreau, see Paul O. Williams, "The Concept of Inspiration in Thoreau's Poetry," *PMLA,* 79 (September 1964), 466–472. For Very, see Edwin

Gittleman, *Jones Very: The Effective Years, 1833–1840* (New York: Columbia University Press, 1967), pp. 77–79, 87–92, 304–305. For Brownson, see Virgil Michel, *The Critical Principles of Orestes A. Brownson* (Washington: Catholic University of America Press, 1918), pp. 20–21, 37–40.

[The following abbreviations are used for parenthetical citations within the text: *JA: The Journals of Bronson Alcott*, ed. Odell Shepard (Boston: Little, Brown, 1938); *JE: Journals of Ralph Waldo Emerson*, ed. Edward Waldo Emerson and Waldo Emerson Forbes, 10 vols. (Boston: Houghton Mifflin, 1909–1914); *JMN: The Journals and Miscellaneous Notebooks of Ralph Waldo Emerson*, ed. William H. Gilman et al., 14 vols. to date (Cambridge: Harvard University Press, 1960–   ); *JT: The Journal of Henry D. Thoreau*, ed. Bradford Torrey and Francis H. Allen, 14 vols. (Boston: Houghton Mifflin, 1906); *Ossoli: Memoirs of Margaret Fuller Ossoli*, ed. R. W. Emerson, W. H. Channing, and J. F. Clarke, 2 vols. (Boston: Phillips, Sampson, 1852); *Tr: The Transcendentalists: An Anthology*, ed. Perry Miller (Cambridge: Harvard University Press, 1950); *W: The Complete Works of Ralph Waldo Emerson*, ed. Edward Waldo Emerson, 12 vols. (Boston: Houghton, Mifflin, 1903–1904); *Wa*: Thoreau, *Walden*, ed. J. Lyndon Shanley (Princeton: Princeton University Press, 1971); and *Wr: The Writings of Henry D. Thoreau*, vols. I–IV (Boston: Houghton Mifflin, 1906) (Ed. Note).]

2. "Wordsworth's Poems," *Boston Quarterly Review*, 2 (April 1839), 143.

3. Quoted in *The Journals and Miscellaneous Notebooks of Ralph Waldo Emerson*, ed. William H. Gilman et al., 14 vols. to date (Cambridge: Harvard University Press, 1960–   ), VIII, 52.

4. *The Letters of Ralph Waldo Emerson*, ed. Ralph L. Rusk (New York: Columbia University Press, 1939), II, 331.

5. Brownson's review (see note 2 above) was the only dissent.

6. *Letters*, III, 74.

7. *Concord Days* (Boston: Roberts Brothers, 1872), p. 38.

8. *Literature and Art* (New York: Fowlers and Wells, 1852), I, 50.

9. My knowledge of this subject derives chiefly from Perry Miller's discussions in chapter X of *The New England Mind: The Seventeenth Century* (New York: Macmillan, 1939), and in his essay, "The Marrow of Puritan Divinity," in *Errand into the Wilderness* (Cambridge: Harvard University Press, 1956).

10. Odell Shepard, *Pedlar's Progress: The Life of Bronson Alcott* (Boston: Little, Brown, 1937), pp. 437–439; *Memoirs of Margaret Fuller Ossoli*, ed. R. W. Emerson, W. H. Channing, and J. F. Clarke (Boston: Phillips, Sampson, 1852), I, 140–142, 288–289, 308–309; *The Works of Orestes A. Brownson*, ed. Henry F. Brownson (Detroit: Nourse, 1882–1907), V: *The Convert*, pp. 5–6; *The Journals of Charles King Newcomb*, ed. Judith Kennedy Johnson (Providence: Brown University Press, 1946), p. 85; Ellery Channing manuscript journals, bMS Am 800.6, Houghton Library, Harvard University.

11. Ethel Seybold, *Thoreau: The Quest and the Classics* (New Haven: Yale University Press, 1951), p. 73.

12. One cannot dogmatize about Thoreau, however. Some readers might also wish, for example, to include Thoreau's excitement near the end of "Spring" and his moment of comic reassurance in "Baker Farm," although I myself find the first too naturalistic and the second too self-consciously mythical as well as a bit tongue-in-cheek.

13. "The Lightning and the Lantern," *Western Messenger*, 5 (September 1838), 374.

14. Gohdes, *The Periodicals of American Transcendentalism* (Durham: Duke University Press, 1931), p. 10.

15. Thomas T. Stone, *Sermons* (Boston: Crosby, Nichols, 1854), p. 101.

16. Jones Very, *Poems and Essays*, ed. James F. Clarke (Boston: Houghton, Mifflin, 1886), p. xxv.

17. Winters, *Maule's Curse* (Norfolk, Conn.: New Directions, 1938), p. 127.

18. In addition to the previous citations, see Parker, *A Discourse of Matters Pertaining to Religion*, ed. Thomas Wentworth Higginson (Boston: American Unitarian Association, 1911), pp. 203–205; Hedge, "The Transfiguration: A Sermon," *Western Messenger*, 5 (May 1838), 82–88; Stone, *Sermons*, pp. 87–108.

19. For a sensitive account of the contradictions and changes in Emerson's statements about the nature of spiritual experience, see J. A. Ward, "Emerson and 'The Educated Will': Notes on the Process of Conversion," *ELH*, 34 (December 1967), 495–517.

20. Hedge, "The Transfiguration," p. 84.

21. Jones, *Belief and Disbelief in American Literature* (Chicago: University of Chicago Press, 1967), p. 54.

22. Matthiessen, *American Renaissance*, p. 25.

23. Cranch, "Note Book," p. 193, Massachusetts Historical Society; O. B. Frothingham, *Memoir of William H. Channing* (Boston: Houghton, Mifflin, 1886), pp. 7–8, 466–469; George Willis Cooke, *John Sullivan Dwight* (Boston: Small, Maynard, 1898), pp. 35–36.

24. Cf. Margaret Fuller, *Life Without and Life Within*, ed. Arthur B. Fuller (Boston: Brown, Taggard and Chase, 1860), pp. 13–60; and Brownson, "Bulwer's Novels," *Boston Quarterly Review*, 2 (July 1839), 265–297.

25. Sherman Paul, *The Shores of America: Thoreau's Inward Exploration* (Urbana: University of Illinois Press, 1958), pp. 211–212.

26. Brownson, "Wordsworth's Poems," pp. 155–156.

27. Fuller, *Literature and Art*, I, 76.

28. See especially *Literature and Art*, II, 2–4, where Fuller argues that serious literature should be judged by higher standards than popular literature.

29. Bartol, *Pictures of Europe, Framed in Ideas* (Boston: Crosby, Nichols, 1855), pp. 203–204.

30. *The Writings of Henry D. Thoreau* (Boston: Houghton Mifflin, 1906), I, 378–379. See also Nelson F. Adkins, "Emerson and the Bardic Tradition," *PMLA*, 63 (June 1948), 662–677. The *direct* influence of bardic poetry on the Transcendentalists was slight; the bard was important rather as an image of the type of role they envisioned—a combination of artist and lawgiver. Among literary examples of the prophetic mode, the Bible was far more important to the Transcendentalists than any other.

31. "The Poet," *Western Messenger*, 6 (December 1838), 90.

32. Very, *Poems and Essays*, p. 88.

33. *The Collected Poems of William Ellery Channing the Younger*, ed. Walter Harding (Gainesville, Fla: Scholars' Facsimiles & Reprints, 1967), p. 88.

"New England Transcendentalism"

George Hochfield*

I

> The key to the period appeared to be that the mind had become aware
> of itself.
>
> R. W. Emerson

The movement that came to be called, and to call itself, Transcendentalism originated in a conflict within the communion of Boston Unitarianism. Indeed, most of the important Transcendentalist spokesmen
attended Harvard Divinity School, which by the first decade of the
nineteenth century had become a Unitarian seminary, and served for
greater or lesser periods of time as Unitarian ministers. This group included Emerson, George Ripley and Theodore Parker, as well as such
lesser figures as James Freeman Clarke, William Henry Channing, Frederick Henry Hedge, Christopher Pearse Cranch and John Sullivan Dwight.
Orestes Brownson, although self-educated, also occupied a Unitarian
pulpit for several years. Only Bronson Alcott, Thoreau and the feminine
component of the movement, Margaret Fuller and Elizabeth Peabody,
fell outside this narrow pattern, but they too were inextricably part of
the same intellectual and social milieu. Transcendentalism, then, was
an intensely local phenomenon, almost a family affair, and it had its
beginnings in the emotional atmosphere of a family quarrel.

The quarrel arose over the state of religion in the Unitarian churches
of Boston, but it quickly became a contest of much larger scope involving
basic issues of philosophic, theological and social outlook. In the process
of exploring these issues, a literary record of considerable volume was
built up: this is the Transcendentalist contribution to American intellectual history. Given the circumstances, much Transcendentalist writing
has a polemical edge; nor can one overlook the fact that to their contem-

*Reprinted from *American Literature to 1900*, ed. Marcus Cunliffe (London: Barrie
& Jenkins, 1973), pp. 160–193. We have omitted the bibliography of suggested
readings.

poraries, especially in the hectic days of the mid-1830's, the Transcendentalists seemed madmen or fools, perpetrators of a harebrained radicalism that threatened the foundations of society. Of the entire group, only Emerson and Thoreau may be said to have written as literary artists, for the sake, that is, of the work, not necessarily for the sake of the controversy. Even in their writing, however, one almost always finds a vein of practicality and an evident intention to persuade. Transcendentalism, after all, was not primarily guided by aesthetic or speculative ends. Rather it was, in O. B. Frothingham's word, a 'gospel', or as Santayana accurately said of Emerson's thought, 'religion expressing itself as a philosophy'. Nevertheless, Emerson and Thoreau had genuine literary careers and left a deep impression on American letters. They deserve separate treatment. The first step, however, must be an explanation of the Transcendentalist-Unitarian quarrel, and a survey of the body of ideas upon which the Transcendentalist group were in substantial agreement.

Boston Unitarianism in the first third of the nineteenth century was an exquisite socio-theological creation. It had no special ties to the tradition of European Unitarianism (as is shown, for example, in its relative lack of concern with the question of the Trinity), but was the product of a slow century-long evolution in certain churches which had been part of the original orthodox Congregationalism of New England. The chief influence on these churches was Anglican rationalism, and the sharpest lines of division between them and New England orthodoxy were drawn on the issues of innate depravity, the place of reason in Scriptural interpretation, and the character of God. By the beginning of the nineteenth century the principal doctrines of Unitarianism had been hammered out and required only a confident and unified interpretation. This was finally achieved in the work of William Ellery Channing, the spokesman of Unitarianism's golden age from 1819 when he delivered his discourse at the ordination of Jared Sparks ('Unitarian Christianity') to his death in 1841.

Channing's grave, mild, infinitely reasonable voice propounded a set of ideas in which, as Henry Adams remembered many years later, it appeared that Boston had 'solved all the problems of the universe'. He began with a typical eighteenth-century insistence on the rationality of the Christian religion and the perfect adequacy of human reason to interpret its meaning. 'God has given us a rational nature,' Channing said, and this is the foundation of all subsequent intercourse between Him and his creatures. The Bible, despite its entanglements with the history of a former age and its somewhat primitive figurative style which lacks the 'precision of science', is nevertheless 'a book written for men, in the language of men, and . . . its meaning is to be sought in the same manner as that of other books'. God, in other words, 'when he speaks to the human race, conforms . . . to the established rules of speaking and writing'. It is evident, therefore, that men may confidently rely on these rules in extracting universal truths from the knotty, poetical language of Scripture. Channing uses a telling analogy to suggest the nature of this procedure: 'We reason about the Bible,' he says, 'precisely as civilians do about the Constitution under which we live'. Thus doctrinal differences are resolvable on the Highest Authority, just as they are in the Supreme Court, by the exercise of sound reasoning and argumentative skill.

The corollaries are obvious. God, far from being an inscrutable, foreordaining Tyrant as the orthodox would have him, is a benign Parent whose only purpose towards his children is to educate them in the moral conduct necessary for salvation. Nor is man a depraved creature helplessly dependent on God's will. On the contrary, man's reasonable nature is a fundamental ground of unity with God, and in the light cast by reason he may seek to approximate the divine character itself. Christ is the model of perfection towards which he aims, an embodiment of eternal truth in the form of an inspired human teacher. Channing, though he deplored enthusiasm as a false face of piety, was capable of speaking with great warmth on this subject of human capacity and likeness to God:

> Whence do we derive our knowledge of the attributes and perfections which constitute the Supreme Being? I answer, we derive them from our own souls. The divine attributes are first developed in ourselves and thence transferred to our Creator. The idea of God, sublime and awful as it is, is the idea of our own spiritual nature, purified and enlarged to infinity. In ourselves are the elements of the Divinity.

But having come so far, almost to the verge of Transcendentalist heresy, Channing was unable to take the further step by which the 'elements' within man were wholly identified with the divine. He was restrained, in part, by the ancient habit of Christian thought which recoiled from pantheism, but more immediately and consciously by his assumptions about the nature of that very reason from which he derived his exalted idea of human dignity. Like a hundred other versions of rational religion in the eighteenth century, Channing's Unitarianism was grounded in the epistemology of Locke, and thus, as the Transcendentalists were quick to point out, could not help but divide man from God as effectually as Calvinism had done.

Locke had taught that the mind was a blank page upon which only sensations could write. Reason synthesized and abstracted from the ideas produced by sensations, as was evident in the formulation of natural laws, but the mind remained essentially passive and dependent on

external stimuli as the primary source of all knowledge. The attractiveness of this theory lay in its apparently scientific rigour and in the
support it gave to a rational ordering of experience based on the accumulation of hard data. But it created a dilemma for religious writers anxious
to preserve some measure of Christian orthodoxy. They were moved, on
the one hand, to argue the rationality of Christian faith, its basic agreement with natural law and its consistency as a body of doctrine. In this
direction lay deism, to which the Christian revelation was unnecessary
or even suspect. At the same time, Locke's premises contained an implicit
threat to *all* religion, for they could well lead to a thoroughgoing scientific materialism (Holbach) or pure idealism (Berkeley) or to a devas-
tating scepticism which questioned the possibility of any knowledge
beyond what was given immediately to the senses (Hume). Consequently
many rational apologists for Christianity felt compelled to insist as
well on the divine guarantees of faith provided by revelation. Scripture
agreed with reason, but it went beyond reason to record the facts of
supernatural intervention in history. Such facts, it was argued—they were
summed up in the word 'miracles'—buttressed the authority of reason
and at the same time supported the claim of Christianity to unique
status as a vehicle of religious truth. This was the sort of balance between reason and revelation which the New England Unitarians learned
from enlightened Anglicanism, and they took a great deal of satisfaction
in it. Their reliance on Locke assured them of philosophic respectability;
judicious resort to the Bible saved them from deism and maintained a
bond with traditional Christianity. It was an intellectually sound and
serious position: unbigoted, undogmatic, trusting in man and yet careful
in its discrimination between what men might know and what they had
to take on faith. Nevertheless, it was precisely against this admirable
structure that the Transcendentalists declared war, and precisely against
those elements about which the Unitarians felt most secure: the Lockian
philosophy, and miracles.

II

In the decade before 1836, the year when Transcendentalism burst into
public view with a flood of manifestoes, a new sensibility was emerging in the journals and early writings of the young Unitarian ministers.
This sensibility was created in response to the new world of European
Romantic literature just then finding its way to Boston. The major figures
of this period of discovery were Coleridge, Wordsworth and Carlyle in
Britain, Cousin and Benjamin Constant in France, Goethe and Schiller
in Germany, together with certain of the new German theologians like
Strauss and Schleiermacher, and, more dimly, Kant and his philosophic
successors. The upshot of all these influences was a turn towards intro-

spection, towards a new awareness of the self as an object of scrutiny and as a source of insight into the meaning of experience. The whole purpose of modern literature seemed to be an investigation of the inner world and an attempt to relate this world to nature, history and the divine. Simultaneously, there was a growing impatience with the presuppositions of Unitarian thought and the cautious style of Unitarian life. The Lockian image of the mind with its apparently mechanical action and its detachment from the emotions came to seem shallow. Was it not standing in the way of a truer awareness of human potentiality? Was it not having a chilling effect on the religious impulse? Was not Unitarianism, as Emerson said, growing 'corpse-cold'?

These tendencies came to a head in 1836 with the publication of a number of striking documents in which Transcendentalism emerged as a full-blown heresy in the Unitarian camp. Emerson's *Nature* remains the most famous of them, but it was by no means the most controversial. In that year Bronson Alcott issued his first important statement on education, 'The Doctrine and Discipline of Human Culture', and Elizabeth Peabody brought out her *Record of a School* in which she described Alcott's teaching methods to the scandal of Boston. Orestes Brownson published an unapologetic summary of Cousin's philosophy, and went on to a sweeping and radical vision of history in a little book called *New Views of Christianity, Society, and the Church.* George Ripley, too, contributed his earnest and heartfelt *Discourses on the Philosophy of Religion.* These works, and a number of lesser ones, made it clear that a new school had arrived on the New England scene, and that the breach with the old was irreparable.

They all began from the assumption that the root of intellectual evil in their time was Lockian empiricism. The immediate point of attack was miracles. Miracles were an anomaly from a true Lockian standpoint (though Locke himself had accepted them as consistent with reason). So long as the truth of Christianity rested on the evidence of miracles, it was subject to question on the same grounds of empirical validity as all other claims to truth. Nothing might stop the critic hostile to Christianity—David Hume, for example—from demolishing the whole notion of miracles as contrary to experience and thus reducing Christian faith to a childish delusion. In that direction lay the death of religion, for a rigorous empiricism could never admit the possibility of supersensual knowledge. It was very simple as the Transcendentalists saw it: if you relied on the senses, you could never believe in miracles; and if faith depended on miracles, there could be no faith. This was the underlying confusion responsible for the drying up of the Unitarian religious spirit.

The Transcendentalist solution was offered in two ways. On the one hand, they were fond of pointing out that talk of miracles was misleading since God was one will and nature a single act of creation—it was all miraculous if looked at properly. The miracles of the Christian churches, Emerson said in his 'Divinity School Address', were a Monster because they were not 'one with the blowing clover and the falling rain'. But more importantly, the way out of the confusion over miracles was to put Locke in his place, to recognize that the senses had an extremely limited role in the acquisition of knowledge and were irrelevant to the problem of religious truth. To achieve this it was necessary to go back to epistemological beginnings and to discard the apparatus of evidence and argument by which men found it necessary to reason themselves into faith.

The new starting point was a simple idea which proved so gratifyingly effective in solving problems that it became the key to nearly all Transcendentalist thinking. This idea, the distinction between Reason and Understanding, was borrowed most immediately from Coleridge—Brownson got his version from Cousin—who had derived it from post-Kantian German philosophy. In its Transcendentalist form, however, the idea had little relation to any of its possible sources, except for the use of Coleridge's terminology. It was, essentially, the American version of the great Romantic rediscovery of the intuitive and creative powers of the mind. By Reason—with a capital R to distinguish it from the eighteenth-century version—the Transcendentalists meant intuition, immediate knowledge independent of the senses, a grasp of the Absolute arising directly out of the soul or instincts. Understanding was simply the old Lockian knowledge derived from sense perception, but circumscribed by its relevance to the practical world and scientific investigation. To Unitarians, of course, Reason was nothing more than a shameless reversion to the old theory of innate ideas which Locke had demolished, but this criticism was no longer frightening. For the Transcendentalists, it was a way out of the trap of the senses, a fuller, truer description of the powers they knew to be latent within them. It explained the restless human desire for freedom, the sense of an immanent unity with nature, the conviction of transcendent values irresistibly present to the soul. 'Man is conscious,' Emerson said, 'of a universal soul within or behind his individual life, wherein, as in a firmament, the natures of Justice, Truth, Love, Freedom, arise and shine. This universal soul he calls Reason: it is not mine, or thine, or his, but we are its . . .'

The first service of Reason was to clear up the question of miracles by demonstrating their irrelevance to the act of faith. The reality of divine truth, it appeared, was precisely what Reason spontaneously confirmed. Such truth emanated from the 'universal soul' in man; it did not result from his inferences about the relation of certain unusual events to the ordinary course of nature. George Ripley, who was inclined to believe in the reality of miracles, saw them as expressions of the divine character but not in any sense as evidences. 'Our Saviour,' he said, 'explicitly declared that he came into the world to bear witness to the truth, not to exercise a marvellous power over the agencies of physical nature . . . In the final appeal, he rested the claim of his truth on its intrinsic divinity and power'. And these intrinsic qualities are immediately recognizable to man by virtue of the Reason dwelling within him. Thus 'the true manner in which the evidences of Christianity are to be understood . . . is the correspondence between the divine spirit of Christianity and the divine spirit in man . . .'

The claim implicit in words like these extended far beyond the argument over miracles. The idea of Reason contained a dynamic force which often drove cautious men like Ripley and Emerson into positions they had not foreseen but which they arrived at with a sense of exhilarating liberation. Having begun by seeking a way out of the Lockian impasse, they discovered that Reason was not simply a mode of thinking but a fact of consciousness that required a complete redefinition of the nature of man. When they spoke of a 'universal soul within or behind [the] individual life' or of 'the divine spirit in man', the redefinition that was going on in their work becomes apparent. It was carrying them to the point from which Channing had drawn back: the recognition that God was a man, that man was 'a god in ruins', in Emerson's phrase, but a god waiting to be resurrected. Brownson came to this revelation through his reading of Cousin: 'As [Reason] reveals spontaneously in every man's consciousness the vast world of reality, the absolute God, the cause and substance of all that *appears*, it follows that every man has the witness of the spiritual world, of the absolute, the infinite, God, in himself'. And Ripley, in his effort to show that the message of Christ proved itself by its intrinsic divinity and did not depend on inferences from miracles, asserted that 'reason though within us is not created by us; though belonging to human nature, originates in a higher nature; though shining in the mind of man, is an emanation from the mind of God . . .'

The divinity of man was one of the fundamental affirmations of Transcendentalism. Growing out of the idea of Reason, it led directly to the various forms of social, religious and political criticism undertaken by the whole school. This use of Reason differentiated it sharply from Coleridge's and all others'; it was astonishingly naive, peculiarly American, and its implications were revolutionary. The divinity of man was, in effect, an answer to the problem the Transcendentalists had not even known was troubling them but which was, nonetheless, the most important stimulus of their thought. The problem was the meaning of democracy. Transcendentalism sprang up when the eighteenth-century sources of the democratic revolution were running dry. Just as Lockian empiricism no longer satisfied their needs, Lockian contractualism no longer provided an adequate basis for understanding the changed nature of modern society. It was a society in which monarchies and aristocracies had been overthrown, of equality and individualism and freedom, of science and industry. Men's chains had been struck off, and enormous material appetites and energies had been released. Democracy had triumphed—but what was democracy? What was the spirit animating it, and towards what goal?

The answer lay in the nature of man revealed by the idea of Reason. If men indeed shared a 'universal soul' and an inborn 'power of perceiving truth', then the acknowledgement of their value and dignity was a sort of religious obligation. This had been instinctively recognized when, for example, the Declaration of Independence spoke of 'unalienable rights [to] Life, Liberty, and the pursuit of Happiness'. Democracy, it appeared, had its root in a proper estimation of human nature, 'in the sacred truth', as Emerson put it, 'that every man hath in him the divine Reason, or that, though few men since the creation of the world live according to the dictates of Reason, yet all men are created capable of so doing'. Their unrealized capacity for living according to the dictates of Reason, furthermore, defined the ultimate purpose of Democracy. It must be the release and full expression of man's latent powers, his final emancipation from the bondage of historical evil—in a word, his deification. Naturally, the Transcendentalists believed American society to be farther along this path than any others. Although it was already a familiar idea that America was a new beginning for a 'new race of men', the Transcendentalists brought to this dream of national destiny an intensity of hope and a confidence in human nature that have made their statements a *locus classicus* of American idealism. Orestes Brownson had a special penchant for this theme, but his thought was typical when, at the beginning of his essay on Cousin, he justified the new philosophy as serving the needs of the American dream:

> We are beginning to perceive that Providence, in the peculiar circumstances in which it has placed us, in the free institutions it has given us, has made it our duty to bring out the ideal man, and to prove, by a practical demonstration, what the human race may be, when and where it has free scope for the full and harmonious development of all its faculties.

Democracy was thus the link connecting the inner world of man's consciousness with the outer world of his conduct and social relations. It brought into plain view the image of man which the Transcendentalists had discovered in their attempt to restore a 'spiritual' religion, and it provided them with the impetus for a radical criticism of institutions and a utopian view of history that were the first real flowering of democratic ideology produced by the heirs of the American revolution.

III

At the heart of this ideology was a demand for freedom perhaps more insistent and absolute than any made in American history until recent times. The very fact of talking about 'Reason', of imagining its fulfilment in some perfected human individual, compelled the Transcendentalists to see that freedom was an essential condition for them. What they were calling for, in effect, was the *liberation* of mankind, the release of a power everywhere latent but everywhere suppressed or unawakened. The principal cause of human failure seemed obvious to them: it was society, that mass of forms and conventions and institutions by which men were held captive, alienated from their true selves. In the early stages especially, there is an underlying drama in the literature of the Transcendentalist rebellion which gives it its infectiousness. The drama is that of the single individual engaged in a struggle to free himself from the bonds of society. This struggle is intense in Emerson; it comes to a powerful, even ferocious, climax in 'Self Reliance': 'if I am the Devil's child, I will live then from the Devil', and, 'What I must do is all that concerns me, not what the people think'. In Thoreau the same passion for a true identity acquired a relentless and all-consuming force; Thoreau's work is the summit of the Transcendentalist idea of individual freedom.

In part, the pressure behind this idea derived from two other sources. First of all, the movement was nourished in Puritan soil, and it gave vent to some of the most deeply ingrained characteristics of the Protestant temperament. Like their ancestors, the Transcendentalists believed that the essence of religion was an immediate personal relation with the divine, a contact that transformed and sanctified men, purging them of worldliness and infusing them with an ardent, joyful piety. Of course, they cared not at all for the legalism which was the other side of the Protestant mind; in this respect they resembled the antinomians of an earlier day. Reason was their 'grace', and the triumph of divine instincts over social conformity was their 'election'. Although they gave the idea of freedom much wider scope than their Puritan forebears, it still had the central purpose of allowing a return to the primitive source of religion: direct, unmediated apprehension of God's majesty and power. And just as the Puritan longing for a Community of Saints grew out of the extraordinary valuation they placed upon this apprehension of God, so 'democracy' for the Transcendentalists reflected the same impulse to renew society on the basis of the individually redeemed human soul.

In this light, Transcendentalism can be seen to have repeated many of the typical features of Protestant schism. Brownson, who became a Catholic in the 1840s and a violent critic of his own earlier positions, was not wholly inaccurate when in 1846 he characterized the Transcendentalist movement as a desperate attempt to revive the religious spirit in a Protestantism that had been badly weakened by the Age of Reason.

Another source of the radical demand for freedom made by the Transcendentalists was the purely Romantic idea of organicism. This was both a metaphysical and psychological principle, on the one hand an alternative to the Newtonian world-machine and on the other an escape from the Lockian mechanism of idea-formation. Because of their obsessive concern with the evils of 'sensualism', the Transcendentalists were especially drawn to the psychological implications of the organic viewpoint. In general, this meant that they understood the development of the mind by analogy with living creatures, as a process of growth, unfolding and ripening, a gradual realization of inherent qualities latent in the organism from its very birth. As early as 1826 Sampson Reed, the proto-Transcendentalist and Swedenborgian, had said that 'The mind is originally a most delicate germ whose husk is the body, planted in this world that the light and heat of heaven may fall upon it with a gentle radiance and call forth its energies'. Such a view helped the Transcendentalists interpret their own experience in having outgrown Unitarianism, but more importantly it explained how Reason emerged in consciousness, how the mind out of its own elements and independently of the senses could achieve a harmony with nature and an intuition of divine truth.

The organic theory of mental growth was responsible to a considerable extent for the dynamic quality of Reason and inevitably contributed to Transcendentalist radicalism. The 'germ' Reed spoke of was both active and vulnerable. It sought to expand according to the law implanted in it, and hence an impulse was generated in the soul that moved men relentlessly towards awareness of the divinity within them. But needing 'the light and heat of heaven', it was thwarted in its development by a materialistic and conformist society. A sort of biological necessity therefore urged men into conflict with the institutions that surrounded them, and as Reason quickened into life under such influences as nature and the 'Gospel of Christ' the conflict evolved into a full-fledged struggle between individual and society.

A combination of factors then—Reason, the organic metaphor with which it was conceived, and an atavistic Puritanism—pushed the Transcendentalists to an unprecedented demand for individual freedom. In this demand was the burning core of their social criticism. From a somewhat diffident band of ecclesiastical reformers hoping to reawaken the piety of the New England churches, they found themselves transformed by the issue of freedom into radical antagonists of society at large. In a sense, they were compelled to enact the drama which they had first discovered intellectually, the drama of liberation from all that stood between them and 'the dictates of Reason'.

IV

Being churchmen, they turned first to the church. In the controversy over miracles the Transcendentalists had placed their main reliance on the doctrine of Reason which provided them with a new basis for the certainty of religious truth. Ripley, in typical fashion, had insisted that the truth of Christianity was not proved to the Understanding but given immediately to the Reason. The Gospel of Christ which corresponded to 'the divine spirit in man' was its own verification; it did not require learned expositors. But this line of thought cast doubt not only on the rational methods of Unitarian theorists, but on the very idea of a church. If the Christian message and the nature of man were in perfect correspondence, what need was there of an external authority on matters of ritual and theology? Was not such an authority bound to clash with the divinity innate in human consciousness?

Three discourses on these questions are especially memorable: Ripley's 'Jesus Christ, the Same Yesterday, Today, and Forever', Emerson's 'Divinity School Address' and Parker's 'The Transient and Permanent in Christianity'. The burden of all three was that the Word of God had always and necessarily been at odds with the institutions of religion. Between Christ, who had spoken the eternal and immutable truths of Reason, and 'historical Christianity' with its contradictory dogmas and violent idolatries, there was a gulf which no theological casuistry might bridge. In making this distinction the Transcendentalists saw themselves as heralding the ultimate purification of religion: the separating out of the simple Gospel of Christ from the forms which had corrupted it through the ages. It was a task which, they frequently said, was the 'mission of the age', an anarchistic and millennarian dream which had a powerful hold over them, at least in the first flush of their enthusiasm. But it was also closely related to a more immediate social end: the broadening of democracy in the churches and society as a whole. When Andrews Norton, the 'Unitarian Pope', attacked Transcendentalism as 'The Latest Form of Infidelity' on the ground that it claimed a degree of religious certainty beyond the power of human attainment, Ripley replied that Norton's real motive was to keep sacred truth the exclusive possession of a priestly caste. He accused Norton of removing 'Christianity from its stronghold in the common mind, and [putting] it into the keeping of scholars and antiquaries'. But 'The sword of the Spirit,' Ripley went on, 'is not wielded after the tactics of a university', and Christian truth would irresistibly continue to make itself known to the 'intuitive percep-tions' of ordinary men. Brownson was even more vehement against the evils of priestcraft. In his essay on 'The Laboring Classes' he denounced the priesthood as an instrument of human subjugation, and in the name of 'Christian law' asserted that the first remedy for slavery and in-equality was 'to be sought in the destruction of the priest'. In this manner the old quarrel in the church between those who thought man depraved and helplessly dependent on the will of God and those who thought him capable of acting to save himself was converted into a struggle between religious authority and the democracy of universal Reason.

But a new Reformation was only the first step in a much broader prospect of social change. The church was no longer so pivotal an institution as to absorb all the dreams of democratic radicalism. In fact, the very nature of American society had made economic and politi-cal relations the dominant interests of masses of men, and the Tran-scendentalists had from the start been pulled by the same forces that were at work in the world around them. For the sake of economy, we may give special attention to two social questions in which the Transcen-dentalists were particularly interested because of their bearing on indi-vidual freedom: education and work. Education had been a sensitive issue in America ever since the Revolution, when Republican thinkers like Jefferson had proclaimed the necessity for a new system in keeping with the changed political status of the country. Education in this view was to be publicly supported, universal and secular; its subject matter, the real world (as opposed to the classics); its outlook, scientific and practical; and its aim, to create useful and virtuous citizens, able to gov-ern themselves and to share in the government of the nation. To the Tran-scendentalists this ideal represented a sort of educational Unitarianism, degraded by its compromise with 'sensualism' and barely attuned to the needs of democratic man. The discovery of Reason made it possible to imagine a new kind of education, the basic purpose of which was to elicit from the scholar the truths hidden in his own consciousness. As early as 1828, Bronson Alcott, who was to become the chief Transcen-dentalist spokesman on this subject, wrote in his journal that

> The province of the instructor should be simple, awakening, in-vigorating, directing, rather than the forcing of the child's faculties upon prescribed and exclusive courses of thought. He should look to the child to see what is to be done, rather than to his book or his system. The child is the book. The operations of his mind are the true system. . . . Let him follow out the impulses, the thoughts, the volitions, of the child's mind and heart, in their own principles and rational order of expression, and his training will be what God de-signed it to be—an aid to prepare the child to aid himself.

Here is the kernel of Transcendentalist educational thought and the start-ing point, in effect, of American 'progressive education'. The focus is shifted from subject matter or social outcome to the child as an end in himself; the inner world takes priority over the outer; and the teacher's function is to stimulate the independent growth of his pupil rather than force upon him an extraneous burden of learning.

In 1834 Alcott began the Temple School in Boston, an experiment as important in its way as Brook Farm for its revelation of the utopian motives at work in Transcendentalism. The school, in fact, was better served so far as history is concerned than the commune, for its rationale and methods were recorded in great detail by Elizabeth Peabody and Alcott in two books: *Record of a School*, and *Record of Conversations on the Gospels Held in Mr. Alcott's School*. As Miss Peabody pointed out, 'Contemplation of spirit is the first principle of human culture', and Alcott's job was to make his pupils aware of spirit 'as it unveils itself within themselves'. His method was a cultivated introspection in which the chief task was an analysis of language. Like Emerson, Alcott believed that 'Words are signs of natural facts', and since nature is the embodi-ment of spirit, words are ultimately links between mind and matter. Through words the spiritual content of nature is disclosed, as the imag-ination grasps in them the divine meanings hidden in facts. The primary activity of the imagination, for Alcott, was to form language out of nature; hence in the analysis of words the mind is revealed to itself in the mirror of nature as the grand repository and instigator of spiritual insight.

Alcott's teaching was thus designed to be a complete survey of human consciousness, the elements of which he distinguished under such general headings as Love, Conscience, Will, Faith, Judgment, etc. Over and over the lesson was conveyed that in the operation of the soul, as in those of external nature, a divine power was at work which was the fundamental reality of the self and which linked the self to the outer world. A new point of view was thereby inculcated based on man's awareness of 'the true idea of his being', namely that he is divinity incar-nate; he commands a spiritual power capable of recovering his lost Edenic sovereignty over the earth and the flesh.

> In [man's] nature [Alcott said] is wrapped up the problem of all power reduced to a simple unity. The knowledge of his own being includes, in its endless circuit, the alphabet of all else. It is a uni-verse wherein all else is imaged. God—nature—are the extremes of which he is the middle term, and through his being flow these mighty forces, if, perchance, he shall stay them as they pass over his consciousness, apprehend their significances—their use—and then conforming his being to the one, he shall again conform the other to himself.

Alcott's school lasted for about five years. Brook Farm had only a slightly longer life, but its much larger share of public attention and its fame as a communal experiment have seemed to lift it out of the narrow realm of purely Transcendentalist manifestations. Nevertheless, especially in its earliest days before ideological confusion set in, Brook Farm was a direct expression of Transcendentalist concerns. Even in the sharp disagreements that attended its birth, such as that between Emerson and Ripley, we may find an interesting clarification of certain basic Transcendentalist motives and assumptions.

Brook Farm was intended to solve the problem of work, or labour, which was raised in the first place by the Transcendentalist theory of human nature. No one voiced its hopes more simply and eloquently than did George Ripley:

> Our objects, as you know, [he wrote to Emerson] are to insure a more natural union between intellectual and manual labor than now exists; to combine the thinker and the worker, as far as possible, in the same individual; to guarantee the highest mental freedom by providing all with labor adapted to their tastes and talents, and securing to them the fruits of their industry; to do away with the necessity of menial services by opening the benefits of education and the profits of labor to all; and thus to prepare a society of liberal, intelligent, and cultivated persons whose relations with each other would permit a more simple and wholesome life than can be led amidst the pressure of our competitive institutions.

The most important point was the first: 'a more natural union between intellectual and manual labour'. By such a union Ripley intended a good deal more than the simple performance of both kinds of work. He meant that the Brook Farm work would be an integral expression of the soul, an action of the self upon nature consistent with the Transcendentalist vision of organic inter-relatedness between man and nature. Work would not be reduced to a mere economic activity as it was in the world outside, where men cunningly exploited dead matter for the sake of physical survival or material reward. Such work only forced man and nature apart; it turned man either into a machine or, as Thoreau said of the ordinary New England farmer, a 'robber'. At Brook Farm, on the contrary, mind and matter would inter-penetrate; work would be what Emerson had demanded of the American Scholar: 'a total act'.

Emerson, nevertheless, was repelled by the whole idea; 'this scheme of arithmetic and comfort', he called it in his journal—'a room at the Astor House hired for the Transcendentalists'.

> I do not wish to remove from my present prison to a prison a little larger. I wish to break all prisons. I have not yet conquered my own

house. It irks and repents me. Shall I raise the siege of this hencoop, and march baffled away to a pretended siege of Babylon? . . . Moreover, to join this body would be to traverse all my long trumpeted theory, and the instinct which spoke from it, that one man is a counterpoise to a city,—that a man is stronger than a city, that his solitude is more prevalent and beneficent than the concert of crowds.

Emerson's language was ill-tempered because he was on the defensive before people who thought of him as an ally or even a potential recruit. But he saw them as putting their faith in a new institution no better than the old ones and shirking their primary responsibility to free themselves. Emerson's conviction of human separateness was profound. Each man's relation to the universe, he felt, was so absolute that all other relations were essentially trivial. Only through communion with the divine could a man identify himself with other men, since they too possessed divinity within them. To unite with others was possible 'when all the uniters are isolated. . . . The union must be ideal in actual individualism'.

Ripley was the last man in the world to yearn for 'a room in the Astor House', and he was as deeply suspicious as Emerson of institutions. His passion, he said, was 'for being independent of the world and of every man in it'. What, then, induced him to plunge into a communal undertaking like Brook Farm? Why did the problem of work have to be resolved in precisely this way? At bottom, there were three reasons: utopianism, revulsion against capitalism and technology, and the powerful attraction of the American 'pastoral ideal'.[1]

(1) The utopianism of the Transcendentalists was closely related to the millenarian spirit which infused their minds when the core ideas of Reason and democracy were in process of taking shape. Millennialism is evident in a number of enthusiastic passages celebrating the emergence and prospects of divine man; it comes as a burst of vision, a sudden glimpse into the future when the 'god in ruins' shall recover himself and enter into the 'kingdom of man over nature'. These words are from Emerson's *Nature* where they are spoken by the 'Orphic Poet', a persona by means of which the writer is enabled to give vent to the millennialist mood. If so normally restrained a man as Emerson was subject to fits like these, no wonder that others were even more susceptible. Brownson, for example, ended his *New Views* with a rapturous prophecy:

Man is hereafter to stand erect before God as a child before its father. Human nature . . . will be clothed with a high and commanding worth. It will be seen to be a lofty and deathless nature. It will be felt to be divine . . . Man will be sacred in the eyes of man . . . Slavery will cease. Man will shudder at the bare idea of enslaving so noble a being as man. . . . Wars will fail. . . . Education will destroy the empire of ignorance. . . . Civil freedom will become universal. . . .

> Industry will be holy. . . . The universe will be God's temple . . .
> religion and morality will be united, and the service of God and the
> service of man become the same. . . . Church and state will become
> one. . . . God and man will be one.

Millennium, to be sure, is not necessarily the same as utopia either
on the plane of thought or of action; but in the progressive climate of
nineteenth-century America the two could be, and often were, drawn
close together. Brownson's foretaste of the holiness of industry was essentially what Ripley had in mind by 'a more natural union between intellectual and manual labour', and Ripley proceeded to carry the idea into
practice. Furthermore, the millennial vision with its characteristic promise of reconciliation, peace and universal love naturally inspired, as it
had for centuries, a longing for redemptive brotherhood, either as a
portent of the new age or its actual initiation. Hence the inevitably
communal pattern. Brook Farm was thus, in part at least, a translation
of millennial vision into utopian experiment, an attempt to 'combine', as
Ripley said, 'the enchantments of poetry with the facts of daily experience'.

(2) Like most utopias, it was also conceived as a remedy for the
ills of contemporary society. In diagnosing these ills the Transcendentalists made important contributions to American social analysis. At the
heart of their diagnosis was a fear of the growing influence in American
life of the twin forces of capitalism and industrialism. This fear probably had its origin in the old Jeffersonian distrust of urban economic
concentration, but it was also grounded in a new awareness of the
internal contradictions of democratic society. The very freedom on
which democracy was based had unleashed an acquisitive power capable
of endangering freedom itself. The Transcendentalists rightly saw that
this contradiction was the central issue of American history. Since the
Revolution a new class had emerged, not merely of rich men but of
men who controlled society's means of production, and their economic
strength was already undermining the equality and self-sufficiency so
crucial to democratic hopes. Brownson saw the growth of the factory
system as the most ominous development of the period, and he bitterly
compared the dependent condition of the northern workman to that of
the southern slave: 'Wages is a cunning device of the devil, for the
benefit of tender consciences who would retain all the advantages of
the slave system, without the expense, trouble, and odium of being
slave-holders'. In these circumstances the necessity for a second revolution was becoming apparent (at least to Brownson):

> Now the great work for this age and the coming is to raise up
> the laborer, and to realize in our own social arrangements and in the
> actual condition of all men that equality between man and man which

God has established between the rights of one and those of another. In other words, our business is to emancipate the proletaries . . .

Economic inequality had further implications for the critique of capitalism. When labour is a commodity, both buyer and seller are degraded; commercial relations dominate human intercourse and men are reduced to the status of things. Competition becomes a prominent feature of life, and the barbarism of primitive days is revived under the guise of civilization. Political corruption sets in, for the monied class, as Theodore Parker pointed out, 'buys up legislators when they are in the market; breeds them when the market is bare. It can manufacture governors, senators, judges, to suit its purposes, as easily as it can make cotton cloth'. Parker also observed what might be called a general trivialization of consciousness in society. It was manifested in a growing consumer materialism and a hostility to the disinterested culture of science and art. Even the promise of technology was betrayed by its industrial exploitation. The Transcendentalists were theoretically inclined to welcome the machine as an expansion of human power and a relief from drudgery, but they found the actualities of factory production horrifying. Their ambivalence is strikingly illustrated in an article by Parker that appeared in The Dial called 'Thoughts on Labor'. Parker begins by deploring the unnatural state of society in which work brings neither self-fulfilment nor the leisure that permits cultivation. One of the remedies available is the machine, and Parker launches into a conventional celebration of the instruments which 'Genius' has devised to make the river 'turn his wheel' or to 'fetch and carry at his command'. Parker is quite carried away. 'The Fable of Orpheus', he says, 'is a true story in our time', and he suggests that the machine has brought man to the last stage of 'progress in regard to labour' when 'he has dominion over the earth and enjoys his birthright'. But in the next breath he turns to the actual influence of technology as it is felt in the 'village of Humdrum'. Here the machine brings no relief from labour: 'the common people of Humdrum work as long as before the machines were invented, and a little harder'. They are rewarded with the tawdry gratifications of mass-produced consumer goods: 'red ribbons' for their bonnets, 'French gloves', and 'tinkling ornaments' in their ears. The social gulf between them and the vastly richer owners of property has widened, and atomization has increased as men struggle to hold or gain advantage over others. The social state of Humdrum is in fact degenerate, and the mill towns of Massachusetts which are its prototypes seem headed not towards a bright democratic future but a new 'tyranny', a 'feudalism of money'. Brook Farm was thus a remedy for the contradictions of American society and an alternative to capitalism, a political gesture as well as a dream of perfection.

(3) The shape both of the dream and the gesture were determined to a considerable extent by an American ideal that was already, in the 1830's and 40's shifting its location to the past rather than the future. The American imagination had been haunted from the beginning by the image of a pastoral society in a new world, and it was this image more than anything else that guided the founders of Brook Farm. Pastoralism consisted of a few simple elements, although they might be woven into a variety of complex patterns: a rural location midway between the wilderness and the complex city, an agricultural economy, a general condition of equality and independence among men, a prevalence of homely virtue derived from simplicity of life and harmony with nature. These elements belonged primarily to literary tradition, but in America during the eighteenth century they were converted into the stuff of politics. The virgin continent, remote from civilization and untouched by the past, seemed the appropriate place to establish a living pastoral society. Jefferson, in his ambivalent way,[2] was the most influential exponent of this view of American destiny. In his hands the materials of the pastoral tradition were fused with the democractic ideology of the Enlightenment into a permanent symbolism of the American farmer, rooted in his own soil, indebted to no one and the equal of all, his breast 'a peculiar deposit for substantial and genuine virtue'.

The American pastoral ideal was one of the sources of Transcendentalism to begin with, and its symbols were perfectly suited to the individualism and nature-romanticism of the fully developed movement. Thus when Ripley and his friends set out to provide an alternative to capitalist society it was practically foreordained that they would revert to the Jeffersonian model. Instinctively, for example, they turned to the countryside as the proper setting of their utopia, and they did so with the traditional moral associations in mind which came from the ancient pastoral antagonism—given contemporary relevance by Jeffersonian republicanism—between farm and city: innocence vs. corruption, 'naturalness' vs. artificiality, stability vs. disorder, etc. Likewise, agriculture was the form of labour most appropriate to the mission of Brook Farm. As a basis of life, Miss Peabody said, it was 'the most direct and simple in relation to nature'. Agriculture had the double virtue of bestowing physical and spiritual sustenance; it made men independent, and capable of cherishing their independence. The intended effect, therefore, was a heightening of freedom, while the cooperative plan escaped the abuses of freedom induced by capitalism. In all these ways the pastoral idea dovetailed with Transcendentalist attitudes to create a peculiar blend of nostalgia and visionary hope. At Brook Farm, for a brief moment, the American Adam was superimposed on the American farmer; here, perhaps, is the secret of the community's long persistence in the national memory.

V

The Transcendentalist heyday lasted for a little more than ten years, from 1836 to the collapse of Brook Farm in 1847. Even before that time, perhaps in 1844 when *The Dial* ceased publication and Brook Farm went over to Fourierism, Transcendentalism had begun to lose coherence and force. But it remained a strong influence at least until the coming of the Civil War, emerging marvellously in the new forms invented by Thoreau and Whitman. And just as Poe and Hawthorne, contemporaries of Emerson, grew up in an intellectual atmosphere conditioned by the presence of Transcendentalism and were forced to take account of it in their works, so Melville in the late forties and fifties exhibited how deeply it had entered and affected his own mind. Indeed, both to enemies and friends Transcendentalism seemed to strike the keynote of the age. Moreover, the Transcendentalist position exerted its claim not merely on philosophical grounds, but because it had achieved a truly original and impressive literary formulation in the writings of Emerson. When Hawthorne and Melville thought about Transcendentalism, it was primarily Emerson they had in mind. Despite his efforts to avoid publicity and his refusal to assume leadership, Emerson stood at the centre of the movement, brilliant and somewhat ambiguous, compelling a degree of attention well beyond that demanded by his ideas alone. Emerson's distinction was that his writing was more than the sum of his ideas, that in style and spirit he grasped something more profound than the abstractions which for the most part satisfied his colleagues.

Emerson emerged from the same Unitarian cocoon as Ripley, Parker, and so many others. He was born in Boston in 1803, the son of a Unitarian minister and descendant of a long line of New England clerics. His father died when he was young, leaving an impoverished family; his mother ran a boarding-house and educated her sons. In 1821 he graduated from Harvard and spent a few years teaching in a girls' school conducted by his brother. He was sickly, threatened by tuberculosis; in his journals he frequently accused himself of lack of vigour, aimlessness, shyness. Nevertheless, he was ambitious and imagined himself as thriving in the ministry on the strength of his imagination, his love of eloquence and moral truth. In 1825 he entered the Harvard Divinity School and in 1829 became the pastor of the Second Church in Boston. In the same year he married his first wife, Ellen, who was to die only sixteen months after their marriage.

By the time Emerson was ordained the forces were already at work in him and in the Unitarian church which were to make his career in the ministry a brief one. He was ill at ease with the historical evidences and rational proofs of Christianity on which Unitarianism rested. 'Modern philosophy,' as he sensed it, was becoming inimical to 'Bare reason, cold as a cucumber', and was turning to 'blushing, shining, changing Sentiment'. The feelings that welled up in him and could not be denied, the intuitions of the soul—these were more and more the springs of his religious faith. In 1831, during the months succeeding his wife's death, Emerson experienced a profound psychological and intellectual crisis which issued in what ought properly to be called a conversion. As a result, he resigned his ministry in the following year—'The profession is antiquated,' he said—and struck out on a new path, the path of 'self-reliance'.

Emerson's conversion involved a total abandonment of the old props of faith and a surrender to the conviction that the divine was immanent in his own motives—his yearning towards moral purity, for example—and in his capacity to envision the beautiful coherence of nature, a perfect matching of his mind with the great, throbbing order that lay all about him. This identification of himself with God, or absorption of God into himself, filled Emerson with an exultant sense of power and freedom. He had only to trust himself now, brushing aside all intermediaries of church or law or custom, and speak his latent conviction for universal truth to flow from him. In the same month that his resignation from the Second Church became final, he put his daring new credo into blunt verse:

> I will not live out of me.
> I will not see with others' eyes;
> My good is good, my evil ill.
> I would be free; I cannot be
> While I take things as others please to rate them.
> I dare attempt to lay out my own road.
> That which myself delights in shall be Good,
> That which I do not want, indifferent;
> That which I hate is Bad. That's flat. . . .

From this point of view Emerson saw that his way of thinking must be completely reoriented. The cardinal principle, as he told his journal in 1834, was 'Nothing less than to look at every object in its relation to myself'. Just as Alcott had sought a new way to train the attention of his pupils on the spiritual reality that underlay all experience, so Emerson required a mode of perception by which the divinity within him was linked to 'the absolute order of things' in the world outside. But Alcott was essentially a dogmatist; he had only to peel back the skin of phenomena in order to find spiritual reality in its place and waiting. Emerson's insistence upon looking at 'every object in its relation to myself' was a far more demanding intellectual exercise. It required not merely the assertion of metaphysical truths, but a continual re-enactment of the process by which divine man apprehends metaphysical truths. Here was Emerson's real task as a writer: to demonstrate a way of seeing in which the individual eye, free of the constraints of history or culture, achieves ultimate meaning through its perception of the sensible data of the world. Ultimate meaning, for him, was latent in the act of perception, in the link which perception realizes between the self and objects, not in a systemization of abstract ideas derived from the analysis of perception. This is why Alcott's mind seemed at last sterile and monotonous—it had come to rest in ideas. To Emerson rather, 'the one thing in the world, of value, [was] the active soul', that is, the soul engaged in seeing. When he called for 'self-reliance', then, he meant primarily this inward activity; 'self-reliance' was not so much a moral injunction as the beginning of vision.

Another way of putting this would be to say that Emerson was a symbolist and that his chief effort was to recreate the symbolic mode of perception. He was trying, that is, to redeem thought from the empiricism and dualism of the previous century by substituting for them the integrative method of poetry.[3] His use of the idea of Reason, therefore, is more complicated than that of the other Transcendentalists. It is not simply a means of registering intuitive certainties but the power of symbolic insight itself. In symbolic perception the irreconcilable elements of eighteenth-century philosophy—mind and matter, the inner world of value and the outer world of fact—have no separate existences but are ways of talking about a single, unitary act. The distinction between subject and object vanishes, and in its place is an immediate grasp, through the symbols of nature, of the organic relation between human consciousness and what is outside of it, or of the organic unity of all parts of Being. In this way faith is stored as a source of knowledge, and the meaningless universe of atoms projected by the eighteenth-century philosophers is transformed into a vital, coherent order, glimpsed by the imagination in images of a recovered Eden.

Emerson's first major work, *Nature*, illustrates the centrality of the symbolic method to his thought, despite the fact that he seems not to have fully understood what he was driving at. His form betrays his intention in its parody of logical argument, and a vocabulary borrowed from Plato, Plotinus, and Bronson Alcott frequently creates a strong flavour of idealism. But *Nature* is at bottom neither a logical argument nor a case for idealism. Its true motive is clearly stated at the very beginning: 'Why should not we also enjoy an original relation to the universe?' Emerson, in other words, is undertaking 'to look at every object in its relation to myself'. In Section I, 'Nature', he dramatizes the visionary stance which is both key and culmination of his quest. He is alone and under the stars; a mood of 'reverence' is awakened in him which is equivalent to a 'most poetical sense in the mind'. This sense is what enables him to draw his impressions together, to 'integrate all the parts'. A feeling of closeness with nature envelops him to the point of 'exhilaration'. And then his power of insight reaches its climax:

> Standing on the bare ground,—my head bathed by the blithe air and uplifted into infinite space,—all mean egotism vanishes. I become a transparent eyeball; I am nothing; I see all; the currents of the Universal Being circulate through me; I am part or parcel of God.

This seems very near to mysticism, but not quite; or to pantheism, but not quite. It is essentially a vision of nature as symbol, in which the eye has pierced the evil of surfaces to discover the organic unity of Being. Emerson's identity is not wholly dissolved; he becomes 'part or parcel of God' in the act of perception. Nor is nature dissolved. It remains itself, but transparent and meaningful: 'the present expositor of the divine mind'.

The next six sections of *Nature* are devoted to a semi-analytic recreation of the vision with which the book begins. From 'Commodity' through 'Spirit' the brute stuff of nature is gradually metamorphosed until the ordinary world has been made identical with the world of thought. The lesson we arrive at when we finally ask, 'Whence is matter? and Whereto', is that 'the dread universal essence, which is not wisdom, or love, or beauty, or power, but all in one' creates and animates all Being, hence 'does not act upon us from without, that is, in space and time, but spiritually, or through ourselves ... does not build up nature around us, but puts it forth through us. ...' So we come back in the end to the divine soul of man, on the energy of which everything depends. 'The problem of restoring to the world original and eternal beauty,' Emerson says, 'is solved by the redemption of the soul'. The conclusion of *Nature*, filled with the music of the Orphic Poet, is a call for such redemption rather in the style of a Puritan preacher exhorting his congregation to seek the grace of God. But the Puritans knew that grace was given arbitrarily; Emerson was soon to discover that the symbolic method was no more certain than any other means of salvation known to his ancestors.[4]

What he came to realize was that, if he remained true to his own experience, symbolism posed a difficult challenge to the aspiring mind. Emerson, of course, was not always true to his own experience. His conviction of unity was so fundamental and necessary to him that he often permitted himself to touch the spring of faith by which nature's gates were automatically opened. But when he was at his best, when he 'set [his] heart on honesty', he recognized the elusiveness, transiency, and vulnerability of his most satisfying moments. This is Emerson's most impressive theme: not the triumph of insight, but the struggle to recapture and hold it amid the complex antinomies of life. Almost simultaneously with his bold appeal for men to trust their deepest selves, he was forced to admit that the very conditions of human existence interposed obstacles on the way to self-fulfilment. The basic difficulty lay in the indestructible fact of identity; experience always broke apart into the 'bipolarity' of the One and the many. Not long after he published *Nature* he accused himself of being a 'wicked Manichee!' for 'A believer in Unity, a seer of Unity, I yet behold two....' There seemed to be an incredible irony at the heart of life:

> A certain wandering light comes to me which I instantly per-
> ceive to be the Cause of Causes. It transcends all proving. It is itself
> the ground of being; and I see that it is not one, and I another, but
> this is the life of my life, That is one fact then; that in certain
> moments I have known that I existed directly from God ... and in
> my ultimate consciousness am He. Then, secondly, the contradictory
> fact is familiar, that I am a surprised spectator and learner of all my
> life. This is the habitual posture of the mind—beholding. . . .
> Cannot I conceive the Universe without a contradiction?

This contradiction, since he was unable to conceive the universe without it and unable to accept it as an ultimate fact, provides the dramatic tension of Emerson's work. His mind was always seeking to relate the particular to the whole, to convert, that is, every object into a symbol, and so he found himself engaged in a perpetual dialectic in which, as Feidelson says, 'the genesis of symbolism is enacted over and over'.[5] Dialectic is the heart of his method and his style. His essays, especially those written after 1840, are a repeated confession that the world lies about him in disorder, and a repeated struggle to make discernible through the fragments of his experience the order of which they are a part. Here lay Emerson's greatness. Although he comforted himself with the knowledge that the irony of 'contradiction' was not absolute, he did not flinch from confronting that irony with its threat of scepticism and despair. Consequently, his work has real literary and moral distinction. At its best it is a courageous effort to deal with the whole of his experience, not merely those preferred truths which he shared with his fellow Transcendentalists. In his quest for unity he was willing and able to entertain the contradictions engendered by his own thought. In so doing he vindicated his ideal of the 'active soul' and offered a profound insight into the very nature of its activity. Perhaps Melville was thinking of this when, after hearing Emerson lecture for the first time and finding him an 'uncommon man', he said, ' I love all men who *dive*'.

VI

After his resignation from the ministry, a trip to Europe in 1833 during which he was befriended by Carlyle and met Wordsworth, and his remarriage in 1835 to Lydia Jackson, Emerson's life settled into a regular dual pattern. On one side was his home at Concord, his study, and the surrounding woods and fields where he meditated and wrote steadily in his journal, accumulating the material for his lectures and essays. On the other side was his public life of regular forays to the lecture platforms which were springing up all over the country. In this career he visited such provincial outposts as Buffalo, Cleveland, Cincinnati, and St. Louis, and endured the hardships of stagecoach and riverboat travel as well as the courtesies of his often mystified hosts. Gradually his reputation became popular and national, his heresies were forgotten or ceased to matter, and after the Civil War until his death in 1882 he enjoyed the status of an eminent man, the 'American Sage', a representative in the spiritual realm of American progress and success.

Twenty years earlier Thoreau had died of tuberculosis, still relatively unknown as a writer and only forty-five years old. Emerson had given the funeral oration in which, among many words of praise, he expressed his disappointment with Thoreau's accomplishment, and for his condescension history seems to have exacted revenge. In the twentieth century Thoreau's reputation has eclipsed that of his master. Emerson has become blurred to us; his moralism, his personal aloofness, and his association with such vaguely oppressive entities as the Oversoul have contributed to obscure his intellectual distinction. Thoreau, on the other hand, has been ever more deeply etched in our minds, especially in postures of resistance and defiance. He is the writer as hero, whose work and life form an inseparable whole and whose integrity makes every heart vibrate as to an iron string. He has, that is, become an actor in the drama of cultural mythology—a not unsuitable fate for one who was so sensitive to the inner drives of his culture.

Thoreau was born in 1817 in Concord, Massachusetts, the son of a pencil maker. He attended Harvard College where he may have been among the audience of graduating students who heard Emerson deliver his 'American Scholar' address in 1837. After college he returned home and taught school with his brother until 1841 when he joined Emerson's household as a companion and handyman. Though he lived with the Emersons for only two years, and though he came to regard his friendship with the older man as a 'long tragedy', this relationship which began in the mid-1830s and lasted to the end of his life was central in Thoreau's development. He grew eventually to be more than a disciple, which was hard for Emerson to acknowledge, but his indebtedness to works like *Nature* and to the personal stimulus and encouragement of Emerson (which some partisans of Thoreau have questioned) is unquestionable.

In 1845 Thoreau began the adventure which he made exemplary

in *Walden*. He settled by Walden Pond on some land belonging to Emerson and passed about two and a half years there, living not as a hermit—that was not his intention—but essentially as a scholar disengaged from worldly affairs. The time at Walden was an opportunity for communion with nature, but also, and perhaps more importantly, an opportunity for study and a great deal of writing. Thoreau, like Emerson, had kept a journal for many years; at Walden Pond he added to it extensively, and mined it for the composition of his first book, *A Week on the Concord and Merrimack Rivers*, which was published in 1849. Only after he left Walden did he deliberately undertake a book about his experience there, returning to his journals, adding later observations, revising, compressing and shaping his material into an extremely artful record of a single year. *Walden* was published in 1854; Thoreau wrote no other books. In his later years he lived mainly with his family, visited various parts of New England and Canada, and acquired a certain notoriety for his passionate defence of the abolitionist John Brown. The last two years of his life were marked by declining health and in 1862 he died.

Thoreau's fame rests almost entirely on two works, 'Civil Disobedience' and *Walden*. 'Civil Disobedience' was first published in 1849 in the one and only number of *Aesthetic Papers*, a journal edited by Elizabeth Peabody. Its doctrine is that individual conscience takes precedence over all external sources of moral decision: 'The only obligation which I have a right to assume is to do at any time what I think right'. From this Thoreau deduced the necessity, on critical occasions, of civil disobedience such as refusal to pay taxes. (Later, in defending John Brown, he seems to have had no qualms over Brown's acts of violence.) The power of the essay does not arise from its reasoning; indeed Thoreau makes little effort to argue his position. It derives rather from the intensity of his conviction, the courage of his defiance, and the vitriol of his contempt for mere power and numbers. Underlying his attitude is the Transcendentalist image of the self-reliant man, with which Thoreau was prone to identify himself. He conveys this, as he was later to do in the opening chapters of *Walden*, by threading 'Civil Disobedience' with the reiterated use of the word 'man' in a normative sense: 'I think that we should be men first, and subjects afterwards'. The effect is to imply that most men are not men—in Thoreau's imagery they are primarily machines, the passive instruments of state or social power—but that an ideal of manhood remains which will be instantly recognizable when it is appealed to. The doing of 'what I think right' depends almost exclusively upon the acknowledgment of this universally available ideal, for Thoreau does not take great pains to define, except by negation, what he means by 'right'. Yet, despite the great rhetorical force which he achieves by relying on the notion of 'manhood', it seems true that Thoreau no longer shares the older Transcendentalist faith in the divinity of man although it has a strong vestigial influence on his mind. Enough is left of it to goad him to scorn, even fury, towards mankind, but it is evident that he feels himself alone with his burden of conscience, and he slips, somewhat against his own principles, into the role of a Jeremiah crying out against a humanity constitutionally sunk in sloth, habit, cynicism, and docile obedience to the laws.

Thoreau's abandonment of one of Transcendentalism's central affirmations about the nature of man is an important reason for several of the distinctive qualities of his work. Because he is fundamentally sceptical of human nature, his self-reliance is less a means of redemption, as it was for Emerson, than a personal obsession or compulsion, and his moral outrage carries a strong flavour of egotism. The standards of human failure and success are never so clear to his reader as they are to Thoreau himself. This tends to place him beyond the range of criticism, or even of dialogue; one of the peculiarities of Thoreau's books is that they seem to have been written in a world uninhabited by other people. A second consequence of his scepticism was that Thoreau was forced to revert to what, with deliberate paradox, might be called 'Transcendentalist empiricism'. He could not assert the reality of Reason, yet nature remained to him basically the same as it had been for Emerson: 'the present expositor of the divine mind'. His approach to nature, therefore, laid heavy stress upon the senses as the means of receiving precise communication from the natural world. He consciously reversed the terms of censure which had been used by earlier Transcendentalists: 'We need pray for no higher heaven,' he said in the *Week*, 'than the pure senses can furnish, a *purely* sensuous life'. Yet the emphasis indicates that something more was at stake than sensory experience in and for itself. A '*purely* sensuous life' was one in which the senses were pure and so made it possible to '*see* God'. What Thoreau wanted to say was that nature was not 'merely' symbolic, but divine in itself, the actuality of God—God was visible and audible. Without the instrument of Reason, nature was not the rather generalized medium of intuitive vision it had been for Emerson. It was a host of particulars from which the eye and ear, by an alert and disciplined passivity, caught hints of the divine presence. Thoreau's object, then, was a sort of mystical illumination via the senses. He thought that the fact in its very particularity could be induced to yield the secret of its cause and meaning, to 'flower in a truth'. The main concern of *Walden* is just such illumination. It is a book about the attempt to '*see* God'.

Even the most sophisticated readers of *Walden* tend to treat it as literal autobiography, a record of what actually happened to Thoreau while he was living at Walden Pond. There can be no more fundamental mistake, although making it is a tribute to Thoreau's art. *Walden* is an *imagined* work; it is a re-creation of experience in the form discovered by conscious intent. The actual moments of Thoreau's life are quite inaccessible. He is as much, or as little, to be identified with the voice who speaks to us in *Walden* as Henry Adams is with the hero of *The Education of Henry Adams*, or as Whitman with the hero of 'Song of Myself'. *Walden*, then, is not to be read as a validation of Thoreau's hypothesis about the relation of mind to nature, but as an imaginative statement of the hypothesis and an attempt to persuade us of its truth. Only from this perspective can criticism hope to measure Thoreau's achievement without descending into cultural mythology.

So excellent a critic as Perry Miller, for example, writes of *Walden* as if it provided a test of the truth or falsity of the 'Romantic aesthetic':

> If at one and the same time Nature is closely inspected in microscopic detail and yet through the ancient system of typology makes experience intelligible, then Thoreau will have solved the Romantic riddle, have mastered the destructive Romantic Irony. Seen in such a context, his life was an unrelenting exertion to hold this precarious stance. In the end the impossibility of sustaining it killed him. But not until, at least in *Walden*, he had for a breathless moment, held the two in solution, fused and yet still kept separate, he and Nature publishing each other's truth.[6]

The upshot of these remarks is that Miller wishes to admire Thoreau without believing his 'questionable thesis', and he feels constrained to take the thesis seriously in order to admire. Trying to accommodate his conflicting impulses, he talks as if the 'Romantic riddle' were more or less soluble, and as if *Walden* were a successful solution to it. In this light Thoreau takes on the aura of a prophet, and his book the authority of a revelation.

But it is patently absurd to speak of Nature publishing its truth (this language comes from Thoreau himself), or of anyone else doing so on Nature's behalf, for that matter. Only writers publish, and whatever truth they manage to convey is their own. The 'truth' that *Walden* conveys is the truth of Thoreau's attempt to create a language which would embody the mystical illumination he found in natural facts.

In this attempt he was only partially successful. Like other of his contemporaries whose writing began from symbolist premises, Thoreau soon learned that the flowering of fact into truth was an extremely elusive literary subject. The difficulty arose in Thoreau's case chiefly as a result of his unusual fidelity to natural facts. Emerson had, in a sense, stepped back from the issue which Thoreau was determined to face by concentrating on the subjective dilemma of the mind vacillating between unity and duality. Melville, on the other hand, was free to invent a world in which natural symbols were wholly converted into literary symbols. But for Thoreau Concord was his given, and he was committed to making of it what he could. His problem, as he conceived it, was to distil poetry— in practice this meant moral intuition—out of the nearest and most ordinary materials without violating their integrity or super-imposing upon them the law of his own imagination.

The limitations inherent in this predicament may be suggested if we compare *Walden* for a moment with *Moby-Dick*. Both are narrated by an Ishmael who has deliberately removed himself from conventional life in order to confront the truth of direct experience. Both narrators are pursuing a quest in a microcosmic world aimed at penetrating to the 'lower layer' of meaning which is assumed to inform the symbolism of 'visible objects'. Both are impressed by the unexplored territory of the self which this quest reveals, and both are drawn to see the sources of religion in the Orient as a way of restoring the sense of divine omnipresence. But Melville's Ishmael has a mind endowed with enomous associative energy; it draws visible objects into itself, releases their capacity for almost infinite suggestiveness, and finally creates a network of relations that binds them, despite the dissonance or contradictoriness of parts, into a unified whole. Melville makes imagination the furnace and anvil where the materials of the sensuous universe are melted and recast. His white whale is thus the most completely developed symbol ever realized in the pages of a book. All the meanings of the physical world conceivable to Melville are present in *Moby-Dick*, and yet they do not create an impossible incoherence but a grand multi-faceted design.

By comparison, the natural scene in *Walden*, though brilliant in detail and often luminous with an aura of meaning that seems to emanate from within, is thin and fragmentary. The landscape of Concord remains external to Thoreau and finally inorganic. Its major symbol, for example, Walden Pond, fails to exert the unifying and deepening influence on *Walden* that Thoreau's patient attention to it leads us to expect. Thoreau's procedure with respect to the pond is not unlike Melville's: he drinks from the pond, bathes in it, rows on it, fishes in it, measures its dimensions and records its changes in depth, observes its colour and surface and its seasonal variations. All of this scrutiny, so richly expressive of Thoreau's love, leads in Chapter IX on 'The Ponds' to moments of celebration like the following:

> In such a day, in September or October, Walden is a perfect forest mirror, set round with stones as precious to my eye as if fewer or rarer. Nothing so fair, so pure, and at the same time so large, as a lake, perchance, lies on the surface of the earth. Sky water. It needs no fence. Nations come and go without defiling it. It is a

mirror which no stone can crack, whose quicksilver will never wear off, whose gilding Nature continually repairs; no storms, no dust, can dim its surface ever fresh;—a mirror in which all impurity presented to it sinks, swept and dusted by the sun's hazy brush,—this the light dust-cloth,—which retains no breath that is breathed on it, but sends its own to float as clouds high above its surface, and be reflected in its bosom still.

This passage is fairly typical of Thoreau's sensuous mysticism. It is basically an image heightened by metaphor—the pond as mirror—in which the qualities of brightness, clarity, and incorruptible purity are emphasized. These qualities hint at a meaning which is held in suspension by the metaphor, namely that in the waters of the pond man may see reflected the inconstancy and 'meanness' of his own nature. There is, in other words, a moral standard implied by Walden Pond, or a 'truth' referable to man which the divine presence in nature manifests through the symbol of 'sky water'.

Yet when we ask how convincing this symbol is, the answer is in doubt. Can a body of water really offer us moral instruction? Or, to put the question more fairly, has Thoreau succeeded in making his image a vehicle of the relation between man and nature which his whole book implies? For many readers a gap remains between the image and the purpose it is intended to serve. 'Purity' of water and 'purity' of the moral life are essentially so different, and the latter concept remains so vague despite the brilliance of Thoreau's rhetoric in depicting the pond, that the two finally remain unassimilated. The symbol is so to speak, only half-created, and it tends to resemble an allegorical device to which a spiritual meaning has been arbitrarily fastened. The cause of this weakness lies in Thoreau's devotion to fact. Although he is willing to employ metaphors in his rendering of the natural scene, these serve chiefly to reinforce the local impact of sensuous imagery. Thus the descriptive material of *Walden* fails to define the 'higher' reality (spiritual or divine) which is supposed to be present in sensory experience. If it were not for the sermons scattered throughout *Walden* in which Thoreau explicitly states his moral convictions, the reader would be at a loss to find his bearings among the particular details of the book.

Nevertheless, *Walden* achieves another kind of triumph. Taken as a whole, as a fable rather than as an attempt to validate what Perry Miller calls the 'Romantic aesthetic', the final impression made by *Walden* is like that of a myth. In this perspective its basic theme is self-renewal, and its elements are withdrawal from society, isolation, the discipline of poverty, communion with the sacred (nature), and the recovery of a unified and revitalized self. It is an exceedingly simple story that Thoreau tells, and even if the 'Romantic' aspiration of his hero goes unrewarded, a mythic design remains which links his story to other narratives of intense and lonely purpose. The purpose at last dominates the details of *Walden*. In the end one is forced to acknowledge something heroic about Thoreau. His passion to affirm the limitless possibilities and infinite worth of the self, with all his egotism, his facile scorn, and his blindness to the social fabric of life, led him to tell what has proved to be a quintessentially American tale.

Notes

1. For a brilliant study of American pastoralism, see Leo Marx, *The Machine in the Garden* (New York: Oxford University Press, 1964), especially chaps. 3 and 4.

2. Marx, *Machine in the Garden*, pp. 116–144.

3. Charles Feidelson, *Symbolism and American Literature* (Chicago: University of Chicago Press, 1953), p. 121. Chapter 4 of this book is a superb analysis of Emerson's symbolistic outlook.

4. Emerson's religious development, his lapse into scepticism and ultimate resignation to a Fate as uncontrollable and absolute as the Puritan Jehovah, cannot be dealt with here. In any case, it is very well treated in Stephen Whicher, *Freedom and Fate: An Inner Life of Ralph Waldo Emerson* (Philadelphia: University of Pennsylvania Press, 1953).

5. Feidelson, *Symbolism and American Literature*, p. 123.

6. "Thoreau in the Context of International Romanticism," *Nature's Nation* (Cambridge: Harvard University Press, 1967), pp. 177–178.

"Romanticism in America: The Transcendentalists"

Duane E. Smith*

The period from roughly 1830 through the 1860's saw the growth of one of the most exotic intellectual movements ever to take root in American soil. Led by Ralph Waldo Emerson, the New England transcendentalists mounted an attack on the social, intellectual, religious and political beliefs which their fathers, not to mention their contemporaries, had blandly held to represent the ultimate of human wisdom. If the American of the mid-twentieth century sometimes exhibits a distressing fondness for a public recital of national sins and shortcomings, the inhabitants of nineteenth-century Boston revealed an enviable capacity for regional, if not national, self-congratulation. They surely would have agreed with Dr. Pangloss that this was the best of all possible worlds, and why not? Was there not good reason to believe, as Oliver Wendell Holmes was later to suggest, that Boston was the Hub of the Universe?

If this atmosphere of contentment was not totally shattered, it was at least mildly disturbed by the intoxicating speculations of the transcendentalists. In addition to Emerson, people of the caliber of Theodore Parker, William Ellery Channing, Amos Bronson Alcott, Orestes Brownson and Margaret Fuller constituted the phalanx of the movement. Henry David Thoreau was so "transcendent" that he resisted official membership in this, as in any other group. There can be no doubt, however, that for our purposes he must be included.

It would be easy to dismiss these writers with a smile and to adopt a patronizing air toward their efforts, which is what many of their contemporaries did. Even the local wits, however, found it a bit difficult to look upon Alcott with the same condescending manner after his absurdly brave resistance to the mob during the Anthony Burns affair; and it was impossible to ignore Thoreau, that "self-appointed inspector of snow-storms," who calmly but persistently refused to pursue the New England version of the good life. We too could point to their little absurdities, of which there were many, and shake

*Reprinted from *Review of Politics*, 35 (July 1973), 302–325.

our heads at the more amusing extravagances of the transcendental philosophy, but we also would be left with the uncomfortable feeling that these men are not to be so easily dismissed. Exotic and eccentric they may have been, but they also represented "the first outcry of the heart against the materialistic pressures of a business civilization."[1]

The transcendentalists were, of course, a part of that larger movement of nineteenth-century thought which we know as romanticism. It was, however, a curiously American manifestation of the Romantic Movement. It presents us with the odd phenomenon of partaking of the very characteristics against which it was in revolt. For example, romanticism was at least partially a rebellion against the civilization created by the Industrial Revolution. The Europeans, for example, Carlyle, Ruskin, Coleridge, Novalis and Schleiermacher, at least had the virtue of a certain consistency. Enemies of industrialism, they placed their hopes in a nonindustrial civilization. Even where they accepted the fruits of industrialism, as Carlyle did, they attempted to synthesize the existing industrial society and the feudal order which was their ideal. There is no doubt that the transcendentalists, like their European counterparts, were critical of the business civilization which they saw growing up around them. At the same time, however, they were never quite able to conceal their enthusiasm for the possibilities presented by industrial and commercial development. Sounding rather like a spokesman for the Chamber of Commerce, or more to the point, a Manchester economist, Emerson wrote:

> The division of labor, the multiplication of the acts of peace, which is nothing but a large allowance to each man to choose his work according to his faculty,—to live by his better hand,—fills the State with useful and happy laborers; and they, creating demand by the very temptation of their products, are rapidly and surely rewarded by good sale: and what a police and ten commandments their work thus becomes. So true is Dr. Johnson's remark that "men are seldom more innocently employed than when they are making money."[2]

It is doubtful that Ruskin or Novalis would have quoted Dr. Johnson's observation with so much enthusiasm. And yet, it is in the same essay that Emerson advised his reader, "Hitch your wagon to a star. Let us not fag in paltry works which serve our pot and bag alone."[3] Transcendentalism was, then, an unlikely combination of romanticism and the Lockian liberalism against which romanticism rebelled. It is as if we were presented with a collaboration between Bentham and Schleiermacher.

This curious disjunction between their romantic premises and their liberal conclusions becomes especially striking if we compare the transcendentalists with the German romantics. But first it is necessary to state the essential differences between liberalism and romanticism.

Lockian liberalism may be said to have reached its culmination in the utilitarianism of Jeremy Bentham. Bentham's hedonistic calculator is simply an extension of Locke's good bourgeois who leaves the state of nature and enters civil society after a careful calculation of the advantages to be gained. These advantages consist primarily in the attainment of security for the individual and his property.

The basic orientation of liberalism is, of course, individualistic, but it is an individualism of a special and restricted kind. It is commonplace to observe that liberalism lacks any concept of political community. Men are viewed essentially as atomistic creatures, pursuing their goals in isolation from one another. This view of the human condition can be extended in a manner most uncongenial to the liberal temper; it can be infused with an air of grandeur in the style of the Nietzschean hero struggling to make of his life a work of art. Such heroic achievements, however, are not for Lockian man. To the contrary, Lockian man appears to be completely free of such heroic ambitions. He is content with a fairly moderate satisfaction of his material needs, a comfortable satisfaction of his moderate desires. Men who are the causes of few offenses and the recipients of little praise, they are practical, little given to introspection, to the cultivation of the ego. And since this is so, it is not thought that there is really very much difference beween one man and another. Hobbes's denunciation of vanity is typical of the liberal attitude to pretensions of greatness, of genius. Consequently, liberal individualism can hardly be said to represent a celebration of the individual personality and its possibilities. Indeed, personality, in the sense that it distinguishes one man from another, scarcely exists, and individual possibilities are severely restricted by the limited character of the desires and abilities of individual men.

In light of all this, it is hardly surprising that liberal man is not driven by a passion to remake the world, but is, rather, content to achieve that degree of control over the small part of existence which is necessary for the satisfaction of his needs and limited desires. Extravagance has no place in the liberal view of life. Modesty does.

These attitudes are clearly reflected in liberalism's political recommendations. Essentially, the political order is seen as a fairly modest arrangement designed to provide its citizens with a reasonable degree of security. Within this peaceful environment, the individual citizens are free to pursue their interests, to satisfy their needs as they see them. The creation of this political order, as it is described by Locke, resembles, not accidentally, that of a joint stock company. If there is no place for extravagance in the liberal mentality, there is no need for the hero in liberal political theory. This is so because the task of the hero is to struggle against reality in an effort to change it in some fundamental way. In a political theory that is fundamentally devoted to the acceptance of reality, the hero is superfluous.

The characteristics of the romantic style are not as easily defined as those of liberalism. Nevertheless, certain things are relatively clear. Rational calculation is replaced by intuition, analysis and understanding by feeling. This is of fundamental importance, for it helps to explain the difference between liberal and romantic individualism. Romanticism, like liberalism, is fundamentally individualistic, but romantic individualism is very different from liberal individualism. The romantics were preoccupied, indeed obsessed, with the cultivation of the individual ego, the development of the inner life. Rather than the limited individualism of Lockian man, we now encounter the extravagant egoism of the romantic, an egoism restrained only by the limits of his own imagination. And hence, the fascination with genius, the insistence upon the uniqueness of each personality.

At this point, one might assume that the romantic is essentially inward looking, retreating from the external world in order to contemplate the unfolding of his own personality. This, however, is not the case, because ego demands self-expression. It seeks to affect, in one way or another, that which is external to it. Here we encounter what is perhaps the most universally agreed upon characteristic of romanticism: its aestheticism.[4] While Goethe was not a romantic, certain of his ideas were adopted by the romantics and he exemplified romantic aestheticism when he wrote:

> Life lies before us, as a huge quarry lies before the architect: he deserves not the name of the architect, except when, out of this fortuitous mass, he can combine, with the greatest economy and fitness and durability, some form, the pattern of which originated in his spirit. All things without us, I may add, all things on us, are mere elements; but deep within us lies the creative force, which out of these can produce what they were meant to be, and which leaves us neither sleep nor rest, till, in one way or another, without us or on us, that same have been produced.[5]

It comes as no surprise to learn that Prometheus was the romantic ideal[6] and that the romantic enterprise was, in the words of Michelet, "the struggle of man against nature, of mind against matter, of freedom against fate. . . ."[7] The romantic will manifest itself in a determination to wring meaning out of a universe that seems to be beyond understanding, to bring order to a world which seems to be condemned to eternal chaos, and in the process to define and comprehend man's place in the world. In the face of anomie the romantic confronts his environment with a restless striving and nervous search for meaning and order. And it makes no difference that the understanding and order that are sought seem to be forever out of reach, and that liberation is never attained, but always pursued. Emerson understood this when he wrote:

> What is a man good for without enthusiasm? And what is enthusiasm but this daring of ruin for its object? There are thoughts beyond the reaches of our soul; we are not the less drawn to them. The moth flies into the flame of the lamp; and Swedenborg must solve the problems that haunt him, though he be crazed or killed.[8]

Jacques Barzun has written, "But romanticism . . . implies not only risk, effort, energy; it implies also creation, diversity, and individual genius."[9] Given their aestheticism, their emphasis upon creativity and their obsession with individual genius, it was, perhaps, inevitable that the romantics would create a social theory expressing "the artists' demand to dominate society."[10] This demand expressed itself in a variety of ways, one of the most important of which was that the standards of the artists, aesthetic criteria, were applied to the social and political realms. Political judgments were transformed into aesthetic judgments, and the ideal state became a work of art.

One of the curiosities of romanticism is that it is compatible with a relatively broad range of political and social views. Sometimes it results in conservatism. It may, however, give rise to various sorts of radical and utopian theories.

The one political theory which would appear to be incompatible with romanticism is liberalism. And it is here that we encounter the most striking peculiarity of the transcendentalists. There is no question that in their lives and thought they embodied many, perhaps most, of the romantic ideals. Emerson rejected Locke, just as any good romantic should and European romantics did. He said, "the man of Locke is virtuous without enthusiasm and intelligent without poetry," a criticism very much in the romantic mold.[11] Yet, when the transcendentalists turned to politics, they retreated to the safety of the ready-made Lockian liberalism which characterized the environment in which they lived. In short, romanticism in New England took a different path in political theory from that which it pursued in Europe. And thus we are presented with what is perhaps the most striking example of what Louis Hartz has called the irrational attachment of Americans to the principles of Lockian liberalism.[12] In this case, as we have seen, the attachment led to the unlikely synthesis of romanticism and liberalism. Whether it was truly a synthesis, however, remains to be seen. But why the attempt was made is the problem to be examined now, and a comparison of the transcendentalists with the German romantics will help to explain the nature of romanticism in the New England context.

It no doubt came as a shock to the inhabitants of Beacon Street to learn that the apparent security and success of their world were grounded on illusion. This world was, after all, characterized by economic expansion, political stability and social decorum. Economic success, however, was no criterion for the transcendentalists, and they had come to remind their contemporaries that man was made for greater things than were even dreamt of in the law offices of State Street.

It is important to recognize that transcendentalism was an outgrowth of Unitarianism. Several of the leading members of the movement had occupied Unitarian pulpits. Unitarianism was a typically New England blend of eighteenth-century rationalism and Puritanism, an arid blend indeed. If German romanticism was a revolt against the extreme rationalism of the eighteenth century, American transcendentalism was likewise a revolt against the American version of this rationalism. It would be a mistake, however, to leave it at this. Neither the transcendentalists nor their German counterparts rejected reason. What they attempted to do was to enrich the operation of the human reason with a recognition of the importance of the human emotions. It has been said that "German Romanticism was an attempt to create a harmony of intellect and heart. . . ."[13] In a similar fashion, transcendentalism was an attempted union of thought and feeling. William Henry Channing, giving us "A Participant's Definition," wrote:

> In part, it was a reaction against Puritan Orthodoxy; in part, an effect of renewed study of the ancients, of Oriental Pantheists, of Plato and the Alexandrians, of Plutarch's *Morals*, Seneca, and Epictetus; in part, the natural product of the place and time. On the somewhat stunted stock of Unitarianism . . . had been grafted German Idealism . . . and the result was a vague yet exalting conception of the godlike nature of the human spirit.[14]

It is clear that German Idealism must take on somewhat different colors when grafted on the "stunted stock of Unitarianism," and that transcendentalism must differ in crucial respects from German romanticism.

Thoreau calmly observed, "It is not an era of repose. We have used up all our inherited freedom. If we would save our lives we must fight for them."[15] If it was a troubled era, the transcendentalists never lost faith in the final outcome of the battle. It is surely one of the more attractive aspects of their work that they seem to have been sustained by a quiet strength that never left them and thus were saved from some of the more hysterical outbursts of their European counterparts. It must be admitted, however, that this faith arose, at least in part, from the fact that they were so much a part of the society of which they were critics. They may have opposed the crasser manifestations of the business mentality, but at the same time they had a certain admiration for economic progress. Emerson was convinced that if the ruling passions of the moment were "the telegraph, the post-office, the exchange, the insurance company, and the immense harvest of economical inventions," these developments were merely paving the way for the time when Americans would be moved by more elevated passions.[16] He was able to conclude that "We live in a new and exceptional age. America is another word for opportunity. Our whole history appears like a last effort of the Divine Providence in behalf of the human race."[17]

In their approach to the age in which they lived, the attitude of the transcendentalists was in sharp contrast to that of the German romantics. Novalis and Fichte undoubtedly took a less genial view of German society than Emerson and Thoreau were able to take of American society. This may well have been, however, because German society was a less amiable proposition, especially to the critic of the existing political and social order. It has often been held that resentment is one of the central characteristics of the romantic. It is certainly true that all romantics have felt to some degree alienated from their society. One of the curious facts about the transcendentalists is that resentment is totally lacking in their writing and, while they undoubtedly felt some alienation from their social surroundings, they were less conscious of this than were the romantic critics in Germany.

The answer to this discrepancy, as I have suggested, lies in the contrast between German and American society of the nineteenth century. The Germany of Fichte and his colleagues was the same Germany in which Kant had apologized to Frederick William II for publishing views which had offended that reactionary monarch. The episode in which Alcott was arrested for refusing to pay his taxes is instructive; it would have appeared quaint, if not unbelievable, to the Prussian monarchy.

> Alcott was overseeing the children's lessons when Sam Staples, the constable, his neighbor, regretfully came to say that he would have to carry him off to jail. "Very well, Samuel," said Alcott, "if you will wait a moment till Mrs. Alcott can put some food in a basket." The prison fare was too rich for him. Mrs. Alcott brought the basket, and down they walked slowly to the jail. At the door the matron met them and said she was very sorry but Mr. Alcott's cell was not made up yet. "Very well, Samuel," said the sage, "I will go back and resume the children's lessons, and when you want me you can come for me."[18]

It is clear that the transcendentalists enjoyed a security denied to the philosophers of Germany, and that Thoreau knew what he was talking about when he spoke of "our inherited freedoms."

In addition, however, the German writers tended to elevate the importance of intellectual and artistic concerns and to deny the value of more mundane day-to-day activities. This was a reflection of the cultural nationalism which became a mark of the German romantic movement under the pressure of the Napoleonic domination at the same time as it was a manifestation of the rather ambiguous position of the artist and writer in German society. Whatever claims to greatness Germany may have had in the nineteenth century, clearly they did not lie in the political or economic sphere. German culture, however, was a striking contrast. The country defeated by Napoleon was also the home of Beethoven, Goethe, Schiller and Lessing. The elevation of art and the artists was in part a reflection of this condition. At the same time, if Germany had produced great artists, it was not entirely sympathetic to them. The man of letters was almost always on the outskirts of society and, with rare exceptions, the nature of this relationship to the political order is illustrated by Kant's experience. One historian has described their condition in this manner:

> Living outside the realm of political activity, the German intellectuals took their revenge. . . . They considered their purely intellectual pursuits as a higher and purer form of life. They transvalued their exclusion from all political influence into a virtue, the privilege of the scholar or intellectual who lived in "higher spheres," without descending to the lowlands of common humanity.[19]

In contrast to the extreme aestheticism of the German romantics, we find in the transcendental writers an unexpected minimization of the importance of art. They undoubtedly were more conscious of the great cultural achievements of their time than any other single group in America, and someone has remarked that a fondness for Beethoven went along with a commitment to the transcendental philosophy. Margaret Fuller, undoubtedly the most aesthetically inclined of the group, was equally capable of writing an impassioned letter to Beethoven and of advising a young friend that the "love of beauty has rather an undue development in your mind." She goes on to suggest, "I should think two or three hours a day would be quite enough, at present, for you to give to books. Now learn buying and selling, keeping the house, directing the servants; all that will bring you worlds of wisdom. . . ."[20]

One can only guess what the reaction of Schleiermacher might have been. One of Margaret's comrades not only would have agreed, but would have put the point with somewhat greater emphasis. Theodore Parker wrote:

> I can't attend much to the fine arts, painting and sculpture, which require a man to be indoors. And, by the way, the fine arts do not

interest me so much as the coarse arts which feed, clothe, house, and comfort a people. I should rather be such a great man as Franklin as Michael Angelo; nay, if I had a son, I should rather see him a great mechanic, who organized use, like the late George Stephenson in England, than a great painter like Rubens, who only copied beauty. . . . Men talk to me about the absence of art in America . . . I tell them we have cattle-shows, and mechanics' fairs, and ploughs and harrows, and saw-mills; sewing machines, and reaping machines; thrashing machines, plowing machines, etc.[21]

And thus we are presented with the unlikely picture of the transcendentalist as philistine. Parker may have been an extreme example, but his refusal to join the ranks of the aesthetes was typical. Even Thoreau clearly felt that the beauties of Walden Pond were far superior to any that might be found in a museum or a concert hall.

The respective attitudes of the transcendentalists and their German brethren toward art are of more than tangential concern in a consideration of their political attitudes. As we shall see, the Germans revealed in their political thought a tendency to apply aesthetic criteria to politics and revealed a decided contempt for the people. Both attitudes are related to their elevation of art and are important factors in their emphasis on the importance of absolute political authority. The transcendentalists, on the other hand, never departed from their fundamentally liberal beliefs. One of the central reasons for this divergence is the failure of the American writers to develop an exalted view of the artist and to fall into the subsequent resentment which was so typical of the romantic writers in Germany.

The starting point for the political thought of both the transcendentalists and the German romantics is to be found in a radical and thoroughgoing individualism. Thoreau insisted, "The divinity of man is the true vested fire of the temple which is never permitted to go out. . . ."[22] Emerson, going even farther, said, "the individual is the world."[23] The transcendentalists were passionately committed to the integrity of the individual personality, and it was a commitment from which they never swerved. In the case of Thoreau it led to a sort of transcendental anarchism. Thoreau's anarchism was, however, merely the logical extension of the more moderate political views of Emerson. The individualism of Emerson and Thoreau was scarcely more radical than that of Herder, the early Fichte, and the other German romantics. But here, individualism was transformed into the closed commercial state of Fichte and the nationalistic *etatism* of Müller, Novalis and Schleiermacher.

Emerson's political philosophy can be summed up in his contention that "the less government we have the better. . . ."[24] Moreover, the sole purpose of government is to educate men and raise them to the point where no government will be required. Transcendentalist though he might have been, the fact is that Emerson was a true liberal. There is one aspect of his thought where he seems to depart from the tenets of classical liberalism, and his thought appears to take on the tone of the proponents of the ethical state. He argues that the state's purpose is a moral one, that the state exists for the guardianship and education of every man. He gives this proposition a typically liberal twist, however. The state's purpose is moral in that it has the duty to work for its own extinction. Its guardianship is temporary, and the purpose of the state never takes precedence over the purpose of the individual personality.

There is an anarchistic premise in liberal thought, and it was Thoreau among the transcendentalists who made this premise explicit. Proceeding along the same lines as Emerson, he simply carried them farther. If Emerson held that the purpose of the state was in some sense an educative one, Thoreau maintained that the state was not the proper source of education and that politics was not a process through which education was likely to take place. The important problem, the real education of a man, was not concerned with his role in the state. Thus, Thoreau felt little or no necessity for addressing himself to the problems of politics until the state crossed his path. He did not address mankind, he was not concerned with men in groups. Like Nietzsche, he was concerned solely with *"die Frage an den Einzelnen."* He said that politics was superficial and inhuman, and "practically I have never recognized that it concerns me at all."[25] He did not deny that there was a certain necessity for some of the functions of government just as there was for certain other mundane details of day-to-day living. But just as one would not expend more attention than absolutely necessary on these matters, so should politics receive the same minimal attention. Ideally, the functions of government would be "unconsciously performed, like the corresponding functions of the physical body."[26]

If the transcendentalists remained faithful to their individualistic premise, the romantic philosophers of Germany did not. This is not to say that they consciously departed from individualism, but that they transformed it and in the process arrived at a theory of politics quite different from that of their more straightforward American friends. A crucial step in this process was the shift of emphasis from the individual person to the individual nation. In the hands of Herder and his followers, the state was given the attributes of human personality. The state or the nation becomes a gigantic individual and now is the object of the worshipful admiration which previously had been directed at the individual person.

It is clear that this shift of emphasis from the individual to the nation took place under the pressures of the historical situation in which Germany found itself during the early part of the century. It is one of the curious facts of German history that those men who previously had been completely devoid of any patriotic or nationalistic feeling, under the stimulus of the Napoleonic invasion, became the most ardent nationalists. It may be suggested, however, that their nationalism was not solely, nor even primarily, political. As one historian has remarked, "the despotism of Racine [became] as hateful as that of Buonaparte."[27] It was clear, indeed, that the despotism of Racine could not be separated from that of Napoleon, and what was originally a cultural nationalism eventually became a forceful political nationalism.

The final outcome of this shift of emphasis from the individual to the nation was the concept of the organic state. This infatuation with the organic concept of the state may be ascribed to three causes: the historical experience of Germany, the romantic aesthetic theory and the alienation and resentment of the romantic writers. Filled with a passionate desire to see Germany occupy a place of honor on the scene of world politics, they cast about in search of an image of German greatness. Clearly, the great period of German history had been the early feudal period during which a German emperor had ruled Europe. Hence, it may be said that their infatuation with the Middle Ages and with the organic notion of the state was an effort to escape the shabby political realities of the present and recapture the lost greatness of the past.

In addition, however, to the historical situation, we may also see the influence of romantic aesthetics in the organic concept of the state. This influence is clearly shown in a remark made by Schelling: "One of the essential features of beauty is its intrinsic unity, and the State as an organism is the highest possible expression of unity."[28] Thus, the criterion of beauty becomes the standard by which the state is judged, and the perfect state becomes the most beautiful state.

Having elevated the state to this level, clearly they could no longer take the rather matter of fact, pragmatic attitude toward its functions that was characteristic of Emerson and Thoreau. No German could have written, as Emerson did:

> In dealing with the State we ought to remember that its institutions are not aboriginal, though they existed before we were born; that they are not superior to the citizen; and that every one of them was once the act of a single man; every law and usage was a man's expedient to meet a particular case; that they all are imitable, all alterable; we may make as good, we may make better.[29]

This was precisely what the German writer could not remember and would not admit. In the eyes of Adam Müller, Emerson's irreverence toward the state would have seemed like sheer blasphemy. "Where does this mistaken concept come into politics," he demanded, "that the state is a utilitarian device, a mere institution for the common good, a human expedient without which man could live quite well if necessary, though he would live less equally and comfortably?"[30]

Finally, the adoption of the concept of the organic state was a result of the alienation of the German intellectual from the society in which he lived. Surely the organic state would provide him with a sense of belonging to his society, with a clear and well-defined status in the social order, which was absent under existing conditions. One might even go farther and suggest that to advocate a return to the social style of the Middle Ages was a not very subtle way of pulling the rug out from under the feet of the bourgeoisie. If the philistines were in control in the nineteenth century, one sure way to remove them was to return to a social order in which other more admirable qualities prevailed. One may question whether the lot of the intellectuals would have been quite so elegant as they seem to have thought. This idealization of the feudal era by the artists and writers of the nineteenth century is one of the stranger episodes of the romantic movement. I would simply point out here that resentment is not conducive to excessive clarity, and if the idealized image of the Middle Ages seems to be slightly obscured by the mists of literary romance, this, we may suspect, is not totally unrelated to the intense distaste with which the German romantic viewed the society around him.

If it is true that these three factors were crucial in the adoption of the organic view of society, it is clear why the transcendentalists did not move in this direction. It is perfectly obvious that even if Emerson and Thoreau had been forced by a decline in national power and stature to look about for another image of greatness, they scarcely would have turned to the image of a feudal society as their ideal. Both parts of the proposition are, I think, of equal importance. First, they were not forced to do so. Regardless of the critical stance they assumed in relation to American society, the transcendentalists were never able to avoid that typical, and to the European, rather distasteful American conviction that America had been selected for a special and unique fate. Emerson, in particular, often gave expression to that buoyant self-confidence that seemed typical of the American personality. What American in his right mind would have turned to the Middle Ages or any other historical period, when America's greatness clearly was now and in the future? The nostalgic return to past triumphs is motivated by some crisis in the present, and the fact is that, whatever their doubts might have been, the transcendentalists were not aware of any crisis of this order. Moreover, it clearly would have been sheer insanity for an American to attempt to return to a feudal past, for the American past was not feudal. The transcendentalists were saved by their basic assurance regarding the ultimate rightness and success of their cause from the inanity of pursuing that particular blind alley. Of course, their romantic brothers in the South were not to be so fortunate.

While the German romantics judged politics by the standards of beauty, the transcendentalists applied the standards of utility. We have seen that the transcendentalists did not develop the obsessive aestheticism which infected German romanticism. Emerson may have believed that the poet "stands among partial men for the complete man . . . isolated among his contemporaries by truth and his art. . . ."[31] He also was convinced, however, that sooner or later men would recognize the poet and the truths he brings. More significantly, he appears to have thought that the poet's truths were not without danger. Consequently, he cautioned against the "over-refinements and class-prejudices of the lettered men of the world."[32] This curious ambivalence is expressed in the passage where he advises his readers to hitch their wagons to a star. "Work rather for those interests which the divinities know and promote—justice, love, freedom, knowledge, utility."[33] Since utility is one of the interests honored by the divinities—a claim not even Bentham would have made—it is not surprising to learn that "the highest proof of civility is that the whole public action of the State is directed on securing the greatest good of the greatest number."[34]

Finally, if the flight to the feudal past was an expression of alienation and resentment, here, too, the New Englanders failed to measure up to the standard. Why should Thoreau engage in a romanticization of the Middle Ages when he could simply remove himself to Walden? It might be added that his Walden venture was not the result of resentment, and it is doubtful that his sense of alienation was as intense as that of the Germans. As he put it, he simply had some things to do, and they were more easily done at Walden Pond.

Thoreau's preference for Walden reveals that, in spite of his romanticism, he was also a liberal. Liberalism may be said to be an attempt to recapture the state of nature, and what was the Walden episode but such an attempt? The fact is, of course, that going to Walden was the only thing an American could do, and in fact many Americans besides Thoreau were doing it—going not to Walden, of course, but to the Western Frontier. The notion of going *in vacuis locis* may have been a theoretical proposition to Locke, but to the Americans it was of more than theoretical value. How could these natural Lockian men pine for a feudal social order when this was precisely the society from which they had originally fled?

While the Germans bemoaned the atomization of modern society, the transcendentalists not only accepted it but held it up as the ideal. In this, of course, they were true Lockians, but they were more than this.

The transcendental view of man and his self-perfection was one in which society played a relatively minor role. Self-reliance was the theme song of much of Emerson's writing, and if Emerson preached self-reliance, Thoreau practiced it. Elated by the view that man can raise himself by a sheer act of will, Thoreau held that the first step was to free oneself from the claims of the social order. Arguing that one has no duty to eradicate the wrongs that exist in society, he also maintained that one must separate oneself from that society insofar as possible. Society could only interfere with the real business at hand, but before pursuing my own goals I must at least be sure that I "do not pursue them sitting upon another man's shoulders."[35] If I recognize no obligation to society, I must also make certain that I make no demands upon it. In fact, the only demand that one has a right to make is to be left alone. "For government," he wrote, "is an expedient by which men would fain succeed in letting one another alone. . . ."[36] If the German romantics saw isolation as the punishment imposed upon the man of genius by a philistine society, Thoreau saw it as a prize to be won after a long and hard struggle with that society which was prepared to do almost anything except leave one alone.

Thoreau simply could not have understood Novalis when he said, "*Um Mensch zu werden und zu bleiben, bedarf es eines Staates. Ein Mensch ohne Staat ist ein Wilder.*"[37] Thoreau clearly felt that he could manage quite easily to be a man without the state. Adam Müller might insist that "Man cannot be thought of outside the state."[38] Thoreau, however, when he was released from jail after his refusal to pay his taxes, proceeded on his way to the huckleberry patch where, he calmly remarked, "the state was nowhere to be seen."[39]

It is this mild and rather bland dismissal of the state which is one of the most amazing aspects of Emerson and Thoreau's writing. The state for Thoreau is something to be pitied. Emerson informs us that he pays his taxes because the state is "a poor good beast" which means well, and he simply will not begrudge it its rations. Adam Müller would have shriveled at the thought of referring to his beloved state as "a poor good beast."

It must be admitted, of course, that not all of the transcendentalists took the extreme position of Thoreau. Emerson reveals a certain amount of ambivalence on the question of society and solitude. The advocate of self-reliance did not carry his doctrine quite so far as Thoreau did. Nevertheless, he is a far cry from the Germans. He suggests that a somewhat greater degree of cooperation might mark an improvement in American society, but his image of the cooperative enterprise is some distance from the cozy *Gemeinschaft* which the Germans seem to have had in mind. Describing the benefits to be reaped from cooperation, he describes two brothers, one of whom was a brilliant inventor, the other the possessor of considerable business acumen. The inventor by himself was quite helpless, but his brother was able to direct and utilize his talents, making them "instantly and permanently lucrative."[40] We clearly have come quite a way from Schleiermacher's poetic vision of an organic society. It is also obvious that the man who wrote those lines was not as different from his fellow citizens as he sometimes liked to think.

The attitude of the transcendentalists toward the various cooperative experiments of the day was a bit ambiguous. Thoreau, as usual, was direct and straightforward in his opposition. Emerson was cool toward the whole idea. Alcott and his friends at Fruitlands might seem to represent a movement away from the transcendental emphasis on self-reliance and independence. The fact is, however, that any self-respecting organizer of cooperative communities would have been appalled by the anarchy in this effort at communal living. Some of the transcendentalists were to be found at Brook Farm, but one of the more charming aspects of that ill-fated experiment was that it was precisely the transcendental virtues which militated against its success. Men such as Parker and William Henry Channing may have had some sort of vague admiration for the vision of a cooperative community, but when it came to cooperating in fact, the members tended to be excessively tender about compromising the integrity of their personalities.

If the transcendentalists were liberals, they were also democrats. There seems never to have been any doubt in their minds that whatever the weaknesses of the people might have been, when it came to governing, they were to be preferred to any elite that might be imagined. It is true that Emerson maintained that the offices of government should be held by the best men in the community, but when it comes to the problem of locating these best men, he thought that "the community . . . will be the best measure and the justest judge of the citizen . . . the town meeting, the Congress will not fail to find out legislative talent."[41] Lest his point had been missed, in the same essay, called "Aristocracy," he said, "The man of honor is a man of taste and humanity. By tendency, like all magnanimous men, he is a democrat."[42]

In contrast, Schleiermacher said, "there is some truth in the saying that a king must be absolute in order to give liberty to his people; for the liberty of all exists only in the firm unity of the whole."[43] If liberty for the transcendentalists was identified with the absence of political authority, it was, for the German romantics, identified with the centralization of political power. In each case, the writers revealed the historical experience in which they had their roots. The identification of liberty with a strong sovereign was scarcely a new development in German political thought. This notion was bolstered by the idea of positive freedom, a concept that seemed to be especially attractive to the romantic writers. The state is now to insure individual liberty not only by removing external political and economic obstructions but by leading the individual citizen to true freedom which consists in placing oneself under the rule of a higher law. The purpose of the state "is the education of the people to the recognition of the law. This means really the protection of the *inner* freedom of the citizens and implies guardianship."[44] Now of course the transcendentalists also had seen a distinction between a mere absence of restraint and true or moral freedom, but they had not accepted the notion that the state was to lead men to this freedom. The state could only insure certain external conditions and leave men alone so that they would be able to pursue their moral freedom free from interference by the state and society.

One is inclined to feel that Fichte gave the whole thing away when he finally concluded that planned education and planned government are one and the same thing. The ideal state is to be a "Republic of Scholars." Lest anyone think that this new republic will be a more genial affair than the existing political order, he reminds us that "No one has an external right against reason."[45] Fichte, of course, like most of his romantic brethren places considerable emphasis on intellectual freedom. If foreign travel is to be forbidden to the mass of the citizenry in the closed commercial state, this ban is to be lifted for the scholar and the artist.

It is clear that while Emerson and Thoreau were critics of certain features of American society, they were, after all, Americans. Transcendentalism may be a branch of the romantic movement, but it is an American branch. This is not to say that it was impossible for them to escape this fact or to rise above their background. The Southern romantics, for example, managed to do so and bear a much closer resemblance to the European romantics than the transcendentalists do. It is clear from their example, however, that the price to be paid for this departure is enormous. The price is, in effect, to be read out of the American historical experience, to suffer the ultimate indignity of being dismissed as something of an oddity, a sport. It is interesting to note that Orestes Brownson was undoubtedly the most European of the transcendental group and even went so far as to become a Catholic, a conversion very much in the German romantic pattern. Moreover, he turned away from the individualistic and anarchistic path of Emerson and Thoreau and pursued the ideal of the organic society. His fate, however, was typical of that suffered by those who strayed from the approved path. "Thereafter his Transcendental associates entered a spontaneous and tacit conspiracy to forget him, to pretend he never had existed."[46] If the transcendentalists conspired to pretend that he never had existed, it may easily be imagined what his fate was among the rest of the populace.

Thus, while Emerson had a high regard for the unusual man and Thoreau had severe doubts about the wisdom of the general population, neither permitted these doubts to lead to an elitist conception of government. The town meeting was, after all, a reality and the notion of self-government was solidly embedded not only in the political but also in the ecclesiastical organization. Heirs of Locke, they were also heirs of Calvin.

The Germans clearly were dealing with a different situation. Surely one of the outstanding features of the German situation was the total lack of political experience in the population. Moreover, as we have seen, this lack of popular participation in the political rule of the country had been raised to something of a virtue. "Political life and the administration of the state concerned the princes, the *Obrigkeit;* the subject had neither the right nor the knowledge to interfere."[47] Fichte may have been able to imagine a state in which the intellectuals comprised the *Obrigkeit,* but a state without such a ruling elite was completely beyond his ken.

The democratic idea simply was not a part of the German intellectual inheritance. Lutheranism with its emphasis upon the duty of the subject to obey the powers that be had left a legacy of political quietism that was not conducive to the questioning of the validity of political authority. The German liberals of the nineteenth century were not exactly democrats. Even Kant was ambiguous on this point. Making an impassioned plea for personal autonomy, he still was able to counsel submission to the existing political authorities. Here we have a striking example of the tendency that was typical of the German thinkers: the demand for intellectual and internal freedom coupled with the acceptance of external and physical coercion.

Starting out from similar individualistic premises, the Germans and the Americans arrived at radically different conclusions. The romantics, alienated and resentful, developed a political philosophy which revealed their distaste for the bourgeoisie. The transcendentalists were critics of the bourgeoisie, but at the same time they were members of it. One might add that they were almost forced to be. There was no place else for them to go. They were saved by this circumstance from an extreme sense of alienation and the consequent search for revenge in an elitist politics. Emerson and Thoreau both had a profound sense of being born free. The experience of having been born free enabled them to adopt the casual and lightly contemptuous attitude toward the state which would have exasperated their German counterparts. The need for national unification and the search for greatness in Germany's past resulted in the elevation of the state to the mystical status of the supreme individual and the adoption of the organic concept of state and society. The Americans did not feel the need to turn to history for examples of past greatness, but even if they had, they would have arrived at the same liberal conclusions. American history was, after all, liberal from the beginning. Finally, it may be suggested that the somewhat more amiable environment in which the transcendentalists lived contributed not a little to their failure to be impressed with the claims of the political order and their ability to dismiss it in such an offhand manner. They may have had misgivings about John Tyler and some of the other occupants of the supreme office of the land. Bad as he might have been, however, Tyler was no Frederick William II.

In addition, of course, the fact is that the Americans were not confronted with a political problem of the same magnitude as that which faced the Germans. America was, after all, a united nation, and the serious threat of disunity raised by the Civil War had not yet appeared on the horizon. Under these circumstances, it was undoubtedly easier to take a rather cavalier attitude toward the importance of politics. Thoreau's anarchism and Emerson's apoliticism depended in some measure on the political stability which existed at the time.

We can only speculate on Thoreau's response if he had lived to see the Civil War. His essays written under the increasing pressure of the slavery question and the John Brown episode suggest that the benign minimization of politics which characterized *Walden* would have been laid aside and replaced with a more militant pose. In 1862 Emerson felt constrained to say, "Government must not be a parish clerk, a justice of the peace. It has, of necessity, in any crisis of the state, the absolute powers of a Dictator."[48] It would be incorrect to suggest that he was adopting the position of Fichte or Schleiermacher. He was, however, modifying his earlier assertion that "the less government we have the better."

What is one to make of a thinker who, like Emerson, begins by dismissing Lockian man for his lack of enthusiasm and poetry and concludes with the Benthamite recommendation that the political order should secure the greatest good of the greatest number? The student of ideas looks for some kind of unity in thought and, when he reads the German romantics, for example, he finds it. When one turns to the transcendentalists, however, one almost has the sense that one is dealing with schizoid minds. The temptation is great simply to dismiss them as yet another example of the American inability to develop an integrated view of personal aspirations and public issues. The effort to synthesize liberalism and romanticism could then be dismissed simply in terms of the transcendentalists' failure to rise above their inherited political beliefs and to go beyond the counting-house mentality that provided the foundation for these beliefs.

Such an analysis would satisfy the demands of intellectual consistency, but it would leave a nagging doubt, a doubt arising, in part, from an examination of German romanticism in particular and European romanticism in general. The German romantics may have been consistent, but is Fichte's closed commercial state an ideal preferable to the liberal political order admired by Emerson? Moreover, it is not easy to dismiss Camus' charge that romanticism

> inaugurates an aesthetic . . . of solitary creators, who are obstinate rivals of a God they condemn. From romanticism onward, the artist's task will not only be to create a world, or to exalt beauty for its own sake, but also to define an attitude. Thus, the artist becomes a model and offers himself as an example: art is his ethic. With him begins the age of the directors of conscience.[49]

If Camus was right, was Emerson wrong in his suspicion of the lettered men of the world with their overrefinements and class prejudices? One is inclined to think not, and this inclination is deepened by the observations of Malcolm Cowley, who wrote,

> All writers thirst to excel. In many, even the greatest, this passion takes a vulgar form: they want to get rich quick, be invited to meet the Duchess—thus, Voltaire was a war profiteer, Shakespeare disgracefully wangled himself a coat of arms. But always, mingled with cheaper ambitions is the desire to exert an influence on the world outside, to alter the course of history.[50]

The romantic artist who was not invited to meet the Duchess, who was frustrated in his desire to alter the course of history, attempted to take his revenge; he presented himself as one of the directors of conscience.

Even if their refusal to make the artist a model, to judge the state according to aesthetic criticism involved an inconsistency between their fundamental assumptions and their political conclusions, the failure of the transcendentalists to follow the romantic pattern now appears in a different light.

But were they really so inconsistent, is their thought really as schizophrenic as it appears? Thoreau insisted, "We need the tonic of wildness,"[51] and Emerson demanded enthusiasm and poetry. These are romantic qualities which represent the antithesis of the characteristics of Lockian man. More fundamental perhaps was Emerson's claim that "every mind has a new compass, a new north, a new direction of its own, differencing its genius and aim from every other mind. . . ."[52] It was precisely this romantic commitment to the uniqueness of individual genius which led the transcendentalists to the acceptance of Lockian political ideas. Emerson's demand for poetry and his preoccupation with individual genius resulted in his observation that "the State must follow and not lead the character and progress of the citizen. . . ."[53] The transcendentalists' view of the relationship between romantic ideals and liberal political principles is clearly seen in Emerson's description of Thoreau. In *Historic Notes of Life and Letters in New England* he wrote, "Thoreau was in his own person a practical answer, almost a refutation, to the theories of the socialists. He required no Phalanx, no Government, no society, almost no memory. He lived extempore from hour to hour, like the birds and the angels. . . ."[54] To live intuitively, like the birds and the angels, requires no government. Hence, the less government we have, the better.

What the transcendentalists attempted was to use liberal means to achieve romantic ends. In the process they transformed both liberalism and romanticism. The cramped view of human nature associated with Lockian liberalism was enriched by the more expansive view of the romantics. The dangerous extravagance and the obsessive aestheticism of romanticism were moderated by the more sober liberal view of the functions of the political order. What emerged was a peculiarly American ideal, best characterized, perhaps, by Thoreau when he said that, "I do not propose to write an ode to dejection, but to brag as lustily as chanticleer in the morning, standing on his roost, if only to wake my neighbors up."[55]

It has become customary to be at least slightly apologetic when discussing American political ideas. In the case of the transcendentalists it is far from clear that such apologies are necessary. Drawing from two very different traditions of thought, they created a coherent view of man and the political order that was undeniably their own.

Notes

1. *The American Transcendentalists: Their Prose and Poetry*, ed. Perry Miller (Garden City, N.Y.: Doubleday, 1957), p. ix.

2. *The Complete Works of Ralph Waldo Emerson*, ed. Edward Waldo Emerson (Boston: Houghton Mifflin, 1903–1904), VII, 26–27.

3. Emerson, *Works*, VII, 33.

4. "For in its origins romanticism was the revolt of the aesthetic sensibility against the philosophic spirit" (Judith Shklar, *After Utopia* [Princeton: Princeton University Press, 1957], p. 12). See also Arnold Hauser, *The Social History of Art* (New York: Vintage Books, 1958), III, 179.

5. Quoted in Leo Lowenthal, *Literature and the Image of Man* (Boston: Beacon Press, 1957), p. 154.

6. "Not man, the rational animal, but Prometheus, the defiant creator was the new ideal" (Shklar, *After Utopia*, p. 14).

7. D. O. Evans, *Social Romanticism in France* (Oxford: Clarendon Press, 1951), p. 2.

8. Emerson, *Works*, VIII, 260.

9. Jacques Barzun, *Romanticism and the Modern Ego* (Boston: Little, Brown, 1943), p. 193.

10. Shklar, *After Utopia*, p. 66. See also Hauser, *Social History of Art*, III, 179.

11. Quoted in F. O. Matthiessen, *American Renaissance: Art and Expression in the Age of Emerson and Whitman* (New York: Oxford University Press, 1941), pp. 103–104.

12. Louis Hartz, *The Liberal Tradition in America* (New York: Harcourt, Brace, 1955).

13. Allen Wilson Porterfield, *An Outline of German Romanticism* (Boston: Ginn, 1914), p. 177.

14. *The American Transcendentalists*, pp. 36–37.

15. *The Writings of Henry David Thoreau* (Boston: Houghton Mifflin, 1906), IV, 174.

16. Emerson, *Works*, VII, 59.

17. Emerson, *Works*, XI, 279.

18. Van Wyck Brooks, *The Flowering of New England* (New York: E. P. Dutton, 1936), pp. 276–277.

19. Hans Kohn, *The Idea of Nationalism* (New York: Collier, 1944), p. 345.

20. Quoted in Harold Clarke Goddard, *Studies in New England Transcendentalism* (New York: Columbia University Press, 1908), p. 165.

21. Goddard, *Transcendentalism*, p. 165.

22. Thoreau, *Writings*, IV, 278.

23. "Historic Notes of Life and Letters in New England," *The American Transcendentalists*, p. 5.

24. Emerson, *Works*, III, 206.

25. Thoreau, *Writings*, IV, 480.

26. Thoreau, *Writings*, IV, 481.

27. T. S. Omond, *The Romantic Triumph* (Edinburgh: W. Blackwood, 1900), p. 297.

28. Quoted in Rheinhold Aris, *History of Political Thought in Germany* (London: G. Allen and Unwin, 1936), p. 289.

29. Emerson, *Works*, III, 191.

30. Adam Müller, "Elements of Politics," *The Political Thought of the German Romantics*, trans. and ed. H. S. Reiss (Oxford: Blackwell, 1955), p. 144.

31. Emerson, *Works*, III, 11.

32. "Aristocracy," *The American Transcendentalists*, p. 306.

33. Emerson, *Works*, VII, 34.

34. Emerson, *Works*, VII, 37.

35. Thoreau, *Writings*, IV, 365.

36. Thoreau, *Writings*, IV, 357.

37. In Aris, *History of Political Thought in Germany*, p. 277.

38. Müller, "Elements of Politics," p. 145.

39. Thoreau, *Writings*, IV, 380.

40. "Historic Notes of Life and Letters in New England," *The American Transcendentalists*, pp. 19–20.

41. "Aristocracy," *The American Transcendentalists*, p. 297.

42. "Aristocracy," p. 305.

43. Fredrich Ernst Schleiermacher, "On the Concepts of Different Forms of the State," *Political Thought of the German Romantics*, p. 196.

44. J. G. Fichte, "Comments on the Theory of the State," *Political Thought of the German Romantics*, p. 120.

45. Fichte, "Comments," pp. 121–122.

46. *The American Transcendentalists*, p. 340.

47. Kohn, *The Idea of Nationalism*, p. 345.

48. Emerson, *Works*, XI, 282.

49. Albert Camus, *The Rebel*, trans. Anthony Bower (New York: Alfred A. Knopf, 1956), p. 53.

50. Malcolm Cowley, *Exile's Return* (New York: Viking, 1951), p. 101.

51. Thoreau, *Writings*, II, 350.

52. Emerson, *Works*, VIII, 290.

53. Emerson, *Works*, III, 192.

54. *The American Transcendentalists*, p. 19.

55. Thoreau, *Walden and On the Duty of Civil Disobedience* (New York: Harper and Row, 1965), p. 62.

"Transcendentalism: The Metaphysics of the Theme"

Elizabeth A. Meese*

> Let us not underrate the value of a fact;
> it will one day flower into a truth.
>
> Henry David Thoreau,
> "Natural History of Massachusetts"

Since F. O. Matthiessen wrote *American Renaissance* in 1941, we have seen anthologies of primary material like Miller's *The Transcendentalists*, collections of critical essays, fine works on single figures like Paul's *Emerson's Angle of Vision* and *The Shores of America,* and studies of paired figures such as Porte's *Emerson and Thoreau*. Unlike scholars of British romanticism, we have devoted relatively little recent attention to theoretical matters concerning the nature of American transcendentalism as a philosophical and aesthetic movement—as though we feel that matters have been settled, that there is no more to be said. But in other areas of specialization, even with the largest or most ancient concerns—aesthetic design in Shakespeare's plays, for example, or source studies in Chaucer—more is being discovered, perhaps because discovery itself is the offspring of two literary and philosophical sensibilities meeting, one the writer's, the other the reader's.

Although their usefulness has long been noted, obvious limitations mark the variety of area studies which have accrued over the years. Transcendentalists were sometimes religious or literary or political figures. Some were all of these; but, in the strictest senses of the terms, some were none of these. Thus, the investigator concerned to define transcendentalism as being predominantly any one of the above sorts of movements automatically makes exclusions and judgments. As a result, transcendental theory exists in bits and pieces strewn throughout many disciplines and, within those disciplines, throughout many works. While a focused, multidisciplinary synthesis might provide the needed coherence, the versatility demanded virtually foredooms the efforts. Transcendentalism may, however, be defined, and our

*Reprinted from *American Literature*, 47 (March 1975), 1–20.

understanding clarified, through metaphysical or essentially acontextual analysis.

Historical, religious, literary, or political schemata, as compared with metaphysics, limit our view of the transcendentalist movement. We often see more of the paradigm for analysis than we do of the objects of study. Metaphysics, on the other hand, allows us to generate new ways of looking at things. Other schemes may demonstrate the development of religious thought, or how, over time, ideas merged and spread; but they will not and do not show much about the individual consciousness, especially not about the creative imagination as it functions to produce artistic works. Neither do most approaches show what in very basic terms these individuals and works have in common. This last complaint extends as well to literary critics, whose efforts often absolve them of the obligation to discover coherence beyond the works of a single author.

This study is a response to the above inadequacies as well as a corrective to the tendency to read the works of certain transcendentalists either all too literally or in terms of unnecessarily restrictive categories. The approach involves a renaming. It does not necessarily see new things. Neither does it preempt what is already known about transcendentalism as an historical, religious, social, or political movement. Instead, it presents old ideas in new words and new categories in an effort to locate the past within the present, hoping thereby to make each richer.

Despite the fact that we generally have not thought basically or essentially enough, one outstanding study, Kenneth Burke's "I, Eye, Ay—Emerson's Early Essay 'Nature': Thoughts on the Machinery of Transcendence," provides profound insight into the mechanics of transcendence. The uniqueness of Burke's essay resides in his view of transcendence as a purely symbolic operation which involves "the building of a *terministic* [symbolic] *bridge* whereby one realm is *transcended* by being viewed *in terms of* a realm 'beyond it.' "[1] According to Burke, "transcendence involves dialectical processes whereby something HERE is interpreted *in terms of* something THERE, something *beyond* itself" (pp. 22–23). In the simplest of examples, something in the natural world is viewed in terms of its corresponding essence in the spiritual world. When an individual employs this mode of perception, Burke continues, the things of this world "thereby become infused or inspirited by the addition of a *new* or *further dimension*" (p. 8). Such are the very mechanics of the transcendental experience that constitute the metaphysics of the theme.

Ultimately, no single idea or cluster of ideas affords the key to what transcendentalism is. It is, as Burke suggests, a symbolic function, a way of thinking, which results in ideas being put to a peculiarly characteristic use. Herein resides the continuity between seemingly disparate works and writers. And it is the doctrine of correspondence that provides the symbolic structure by means of which these symbolic operations take place; the act of perceiving the corresponding particulars unites, on another level of existence, the observer and the object of perception, and results in revelation. The "bridge-building," which Burke identifies as the "mechanics of transcendence," is actually the perception of the correspondence, which subsequently results in transcendence and therefore in a communion with spirit. For reasons such as these, the idea of correspondence becomes central to the understanding of transcendence.

In any system of cognition which posits man, matter, and spirit as distinct yet interrelated aspects of the cosmos, we may suspect that a correspondential mechanism is operating to bring apparently distinct aspects into interrelationship. As an idea unit, correspondence supplies a structural mechanism—no more than a set of empty blanks—holding in parallel relationship some particular terms which are determined by the specific philosophical or cultural framework within which the idea occurs. In *Emerson's Angle of Vision,* Sherman Paul explains how correspondence functions perceptually: "The universe could be viewed correspondentially because correspondence itself was the prism through which one contemplated—a prism shaped by a temperamental need to see the universe that way."[2] The metaphor of correspondence as prism properly locates the emphasis of the idea's function, both literally and symbolically.

In order to proceed from shared assumptions, as well as to avoid the circularity of deriving the definition from the very material to which it would be applied, the nature and function of correspondence in transcendental literature warrants a redefinition which treats the idea as a structural, metaphysical unit, considered in isolation and in the abstract: *correspondence is predicated upon a belief in more than one level of existence, and presupposes at least two quantities* (meaning, as in logic, any discrete character, material or immaterial)—*objects, ideas, aspects— which are taken from more than one such level and believed to exist in a parallel relationship.* These two particulars, then, can be seen as participating in parallel levels of meaning or being. Correspondence may be operative when an individual employs the One and the Many, the particular and the universal, the subject and the object, or the microcosm and the macrocosm in a way that somehow involves a reference beyond the immediate visible world of the perceiver and the quantity perceived. That is to say, when the One is viewed as the simple, unifying, and ultimate model for the visible world which it generated, analogies are easily drawn between these two realms. Similarly, when the macrocosm is merely a synonym for the One and the microcosm is synonymous with the complex diversity of the Many, correspondence may bridge the particular and the universal. Likewise, in the event of subject-object fusion, the ground of identification here exists on the level of a common denominator in both subject and object—the simple quantity that they share or the relationship between quantities possessed by each in differing degrees. When the simple quantity in the subject is placed in alignment with a simple part in the object of perception, through the operation of correspondence, the subject (and sometimes, through him, the object as well) is referred to the ground of mutual participation in the whole, the One, some universal ground which is the ultimate single unity, a unity so simple that it is contained in all and so much itself that it is not any one thing.

We are best able to recognize the existence of the idea of correspondence in an individual's system of cognition when he expresses a perception of the common reality shared by any set of parallel particulars. This act of perception, whether articulated or assumed, bridges the space between parallel levels of being or meaning. When correspondence is operative, the articulated perceptions reveal the perceiver's awareness of the One in the Many, as well as the diversity which comprises unity. Seen in this way—as a perceptual mechanism—correspondence acquires its full and proper significance as the metaphysical mechanism whereby the individual is enabled to transcend the limitations—the space and time—of human experience, in order then to participate in a higher order of being and meaning.

Correspondence is, as Emerson knew, "an ancient idea"—so pervasive and old that its history cannot be detailed here—but the transcendentalists certainly found reinforcement for their views in their contacts with other literatures, ancient and modern. In *Confrontations*, René Wellek prudently observes that the uncovering of influences on American transcendentalism is extremely problematical, because "the ancestry of Transcendentalism includes almost the whole intellectual history of mankind."[3] In the case of correspondence, however, the contact was in a sense more definitely direct, since Sampson Reed, a purveyor of Swedenborgian ideas—Swedenborg had devoted his life to the elucidation of correspondences between the realms of nature and spirit—resided in the Concord community and was known by major transcendentalists. In this particular instance, with the Swedenborgian tradition alive and current in the figure of Reed, the reinforcing, raw material for art and aesthetic theory flowed from America to England. Here it will be useful to consider Reed's work in terms of the philosophical understanding of transcendentalism previously set down.

Issued a decade before Emerson's *Nature*, Reed's book, *Observations on the Growth of the Mind*, was instrumental in establishing the idea of correspondence as basic to American transcendentalism. Believing that transcendence was dependent upon a state of mind, Reed stressed the power of the imagination in apprehending reality and the infusion of spirit throughout the natural world. The laws of both mind and matter are fixed and perfect in their "immutable relation"[4] to the first cause. Divine truth exists in a transcendent, timeless realm, and when the individual soul embarks upon its progression toward that truth, according to Reed, "there is reason to believe that the past and the future will be swallowed up in the present; that memory and anticipation will be lost in consciousness; that everything of the past will be comprehended in the present, without any reference to time, and everything of the future will exist in the divine effort of progression" (pp. 12–13). In other words, eternity belongs to the mind, as time belongs to nature, and thus the levels of being are mounted in the imagination.

Reed like the Americans after him and like his mentor Swedenborg, felt that "Truth, all truth is practical" (p. 21). The flights of pure mysticism—the direct apprehension of divine truth without the mediation of objects drawn from the visible world—are transitory and elude expression because they are without concrete particulars. If we study truth as it is embodied in objects, "it will form a distinct and permanent image on the mind" (p. 21). Consciousness operates through the agency of the eye. The first form of consciousness entertains one object at a time, the eye being "the point at which the united rays of the sun within and the sun without, converge into an expression of unity" (p. 27). The second form of consciousness "pervades the mind, which is co-extensive with everything it actually possesses" (p. 27). This second power of mind preserves truth "without actually making it the subject of thought; bearing a relation to thought, analogous to what this bears to the actual perception of the senses, or to language. Thus we remember a distant object without actually thinking of it, in the same way that we think of it, without actually seeing it" (p. 28). Because the human mind was made in the image of the divine, the mind's creations were said to mirror the mind itself, in the same way that it and nature mirror the first, creative principle. This is the very basis of all correspondential operations, forming the continuous ground of primal unity. Reed, therefore, observes that when mind "is present in the natural world, feeling the same spirit which gives life to every object by which it is surrounded, in its very union with nature it will catch a glimpse of itself, like that of pristine beauty united with innocence, at her own native fountain" (p. 33).

Reed's view of art emerges from the above context. Poetry is the human analogue of divine creation—"all those illustrations of truth by natural imagery, which spring from the fact, that this world is the mirror of Him who made it. Strictly speaking, nothing has less to do with fiction than poetry" (p. 41). Poetry is not fictional because it presents truth correspondentially, "only dressed in the garments which God has given it" (p. 42). Reed, perhaps under the influence of Swedenborg, praises Baconian science for its focus on fact, on the simple truths of the visible world. The activity of the imagination, when coincident with Divine Being, results in creation. This coincidence with higher being is achieved by aligning the mind "with things as they exist, or, in other words, with the truth" (p. 42). According to Reed, therefore, the "true poetic spirit . . . is the soul of science" (p. 43). The poet deals in facts of the sort that shadow forth "the image of God which is stamped on nature" (p. 43); only the art resulting from such a process is rightfully considered immortal. When the artist learns "a language, not of words, but of things" (p. 46), he has achieved an identification between the thing itself and his own mind on the level of their mutual ground of existence.

Reed further develops this notion in one of the clearest statements of the era on the perceptual process antecedent to transcendental experience: the mind becomes a solvent of the subjects contemplated—

> They fall to pieces as soon as they come in contact with it, and assume an arrangement agreeable to that of the mind itself, with all the precision of crystallization. They are then understood; for the most perfect understanding of a subject is simply a perception of harmony existing between the subject and the mind itself. Indeed, the understanding which any individual possesses of a subject might be mathematically defined
>
> $$\frac{\text{the subject proposed,}}{\text{the actual character of his mind;}}$$
>
> and there is a constant struggle for the divisor and dividend to become the same by a change in the one or the other, that the result may be unity, and the understanding perfect. (p. 69)

Reed conceives of transcendence in terms of the reconciliation of two corresponding particulars; the reconciliation of subject and object produces perfect understanding, which leads the mind to participation in a higher order of being or meaning. Truth is revealed. The activity is self-sustaining in that "every approach to Him, by bringing us nearer the origin of things, enables us to discover analogies in what was before chaotic" (p. 75).

Through the perception of correspondences, the mind penetrates the illusion of separation between internal and external, nature, man and God, visible and invisible, the particular and the universal. Unlike the "pure" mystic, the transcendentalist generally does not seek to annihilate the visible world in a striving after unutterable reality;

instead, he seeks to unify his divided vision in order to see things as they really are—which, for him, means to see them as pure forms or as "things as they are" in relation to other "things." A precarious stance is necessitated by transcendental vision if the perceiver is at once to transcend and to participate in the visible world. Ernst Cassirer explains this balance in *The Individual and the Cosmos in Renaissance Philosophy:*

> "Transcendence" itself postulates and requires "participation," just as "participation" postulates and requires "transcendence." Objectively considered, this reciprocal determination may seem enigmatic and paradoxical; nevertheless, it proves to be necessary and singularly clear, if we take as our point of departure the nature of the Ego, i.e., of the willing and knowing subject. In the free *act* of willing and in the free *act* of knowing, those things are conjoined which in simple *existence* seems always to be fleeing from each other. For both the power of distinction and the power of unification are properties of these acts. They alone can distinguish to the highest degree without, at the same time, letting things distinguished fall into an absolute separation.[5]

The mechanism of correspondence enables the transcendentalist to perform operations of distinction and of unification. It functions conceptually and linguistically as a vehicle whereby man strives to comprehend and articulate his relationship to something beyond himself. The infinite is a mystery for finite man, who nonetheless persists in his desire to know it. To put it most generally, when the individual believes in transcendent power, he may sometimes project it in idealized versions of his own image or of the physical particulars of his world. The process of projection occurs in accord with a perception of or a belief in analogies of correspondences, which function between an implicit assumption concerning transcendent being—its nature and meaning—and an assumption concerning facts similarly derived from the visible world. Transcendence then results from the perception of correspondence between transcendent being and visible fact.

In *The Concept of Truth,* Leslie Armour makes an important observation about correspondential operations:

> We do not compare assertions to sense data or to otherwise "independent" facts. We compare two interpretations—one of the assertion and one of the sense data. But to get an interpretation of the data offered for comparison we need a language with conventions governing identification and classification. In addition, we need a conceptual scheme which will provide enough background so that the two interpretations required can be compared and located in an intelligible scheme.[6]

Thus, the correlations generated by correspondence actually take place between an *interpretation* of phenomena and an *interpretation* of noumena, both equally binding matters of fact or certainty in the perceiver's mind. For the transcendentalist, nothing in the *plenum* exists except by virtue of its relation to the Infinite, which infuses all levels and particulars of the cosmos. For this reason, Emerson chose with care the epigraph (a version of an excerpt from his poem "May Day") to the essay *Nature:*

> A subtle chain of countless rings
> The next unto the farthest brings;
> The eye reads omens where it goes,
> And speaks all languages the rose;
> And, striving to be man, the worm
> Mounts through all the spires of form.[7]

Here the cosmos is represented in terms of spiralling interconnectedness from lowest to highest, a world view which clearly admits of the various levels necessary for universal correspondences to be determined. Given such a cosmic scheme, there are many ways to describe the correspondence of the visible world to the invisible: in terms of the relationship of finite to infinite, particular to universal, microcosm to macrocosm, or subject to object.

Throughout his work, Emerson explored many forms of cosmic interrelatedness. In "Compensation" he explains: "An inevitable dualism bisects nature, so that each thing is a half, and suggests another thing to make it whole; as, spirit, matter; man, woman; odd, even; subjective, objective; in, out; upper, under; motion, rest; yea, nay."[8] The whole is present in every part. Emerson values Plato because he first "domesticates the soul in nature: man is the microcosm.... All the circles of the visible heaven represent as many circles in the rational soul" (*RWE,* IV, 86). The relationship between levels is expressed through corresponding circles, each in relationship to another. As Kenneth Burke observes, "the everyday world . . . is to be interpreted as a *diversity of means* for carrying out a *unitary purpose.* . . . The world's variety of things is thus to be interpreted *in terms of* a transcendent unifier (that infuses them all with its single spirit)" (p. 9). In the example of the rose from *Nature's* epigraph, the spirit is immanent in the flower—a single aspect of the world's diversity. The rose speaks the language of symbol which, through the perceiver's knowledge of spiritual correspondence, the eye transforms into prophecy.

Obviously central here is Emerson's statement that "Every natural fact is a symbol of some spiritual fact. Every appearance in nature corresponds to some state of mind, and that state of the mind can only be described by presenting that natural appearance as its picture" (*RWE*, I, 18). He gives at once a theory of cosmology supportive of the idea of correspondence, the concept of right vision in order to perceive correspondences, and a notion of the language of fact whereby correspondences are to be expressed. Nature is the primary link to spirit, "is thoroughly mediate" (*CW*, I, 25), bridging the visible and the invisible.

Although "Nature always wears the colors of the spirit," the perception of correspondence, of its truth, depends upon man's "angle of vision," or upon a harmony between man and nature.[9] The eye must be in a right relation to the fact under scrutiny, which is why a parallelism (or at least some kind of synchrony) between levels is required for correspondence to be apprehended and for transcendence to occur. In his essay on Swedenborg, Emerson remarks that the doctrine of correspondence itself "required an insight that could rank things in order and series; or rather it required such rightness of position that the poles of the eye should coincide with the axis of the world" (*RWE*, IV, 117). Each natural fact has a corresponding state of mind in the beholder, and both the natural fact and the state of mind correspond to a spiritual truth. From man's position at the center of the visible lower world, Emerson maintains, "a ray of relation passes from every other being to him" (*CW*, I, 19); therefore, man, like a "leaf, a drop, a crystal, a moment of time is related to the whole, and partakes of the perfection of the whole. Each particle is a microcosm, and faithfully renders the likeness of the world" (*CW*, I, 27).

This necessary angle of right vision is both attitudinal and physical. In the contemplation of nature we become cognizant of the angle:

> Nature is made to conspire with spirit to emancipate us. Certain mechanical changes, a small alteration in our local position apprizes us of a dualism. We are strangely affected by seeing the shore from a moving ship, from a balloon, or through the tints of an unusual sky. The least change in our point of view, gives the whole world a pictorial air. (*CW*, I, 30–31)

Theodore Parker makes a similar point in *Lessons from the World of Matter and the World of Man*. Specifically concerned with stripping the transient from the permanent in Christian doctrine, Parker wants a theology to be pure in its relation to higher laws so that it will assist rather than obstruct the soul in its ascent to God:

> In times when no false theology intervenes between the philosopher's cultivated mind and the instinctive religious sense in his soul, then he sees that the laws of heaven are only God's great geometry, and

in the intersecting lines in the section of an elephant's tooth he finds the same thought which God has made fossil in the stones beneath his feet.[10]

Nature offers man a standard for spiritual truth because of its fixity, maintained despite its fluidity. That is, although natural forms are metamorphic, they change in accord with fixed laws, thereby assuring that the things in nature maintain at all times an identical relationship to their correspondent spiritual truth.

Transcendence suggests leave-taking, departure to a realm beyond the temporal and spatial boundaries of the visible world. Nature, though symbolic of truth, remains only a means to another end. The transcendental soul seeks a translucence of its own, wanting to show itself one with the Oversoul, wherein it experiences unity with all being. Similarly, Paul Tillich once noted, "as men we are aware of the eternal to which we belong and from which we are estranged by the bondage of time."[11] When the transcendentalist learns the laws of Spirit by means of their referents in the natural world, as Emerson says, "Time and Space relations vanish" (CW, I, 25). The mind probes the natural particular for its essence; and, finally, in its translucence, the fact gives up the spiritual truth to which it corresponds. In its ascent to Spirit, Emerson tells us in "The Oversoul," man's spirit mounts "through all the spires of form," and "comes out into eternity, and inspires and expires its air. It converses with truths that have always been spoken in the world . . ." (RWE, II, 275). Transcendence has taken place. The perceiver now stands confronting the Absolute: "Standing on the bare ground,—my head bathed by the blithe air, and uplifted into infinite space,—all mean egotism vanishes. I become a transparent eyeball. I am nothing, I see all. The currents of the Universal Being circulate through me; I am part or particle of God" (CW, I, 10). It is this union with divine being, "the bride or bridegroom of the soul," to which the transcendentalist aspired.

Emerson's state of transcendental awareness, when he finds himself "a transparent eyeball," shows how the mind contemplates itself, its own process. The intellect is self-reflexive, as, for example, we find it in some of the best of Wordsworth's poetry. The mind and the mind's content are self-identified, like Walden Pond with the objects mirrored on its surface and the things living in its depth. The mind turns in upon itself. Robert DeRopp calls this the experience of "self-remembering"; the perceiver not only records his perceptions but also experiences himself in the act of perception. This secondary experience contains both the subject and object of the simple act of observation as one single particular of contemplation. DeRopp explains:

> Self-remembering is a certain separation of awareness from whatever
> a man happens to be doing, thinking, feeling. It is symbolized by a
> two-headed arrow suggesting double awareness. There is actor and
> observer, there is an objective awareness of self. There is a feeling
> of being outside of, separated from, the confines of the physical body;
> there is a sense of detachment, a state of nonidentification.[12]

The experience of transcendence may be called nonidentificational
in that it requires a reconceptualization of interrelationships because
conventional categories of perception are destroyed in the experience
of union with transcendent being. When "each" resembles "all," a
new kind of perception occurs in which each, all, self, and other are
no longer what they were. Whether this new mode of perception
precedes or accompanies the transcendental experience is difficult to
determine. Probably a self-reinforcing cycle occurs in which the attitude
of mind is essential to the perception of correspondences prerequisite
to transcendence, and at the same time the individual experiences the
exhilaration of "right vision" when the state of transcendental awareness
is achieved.

Transcendence both challenges and affirms the very human process
of growth in which the "me"-self is delimited necessarily from the
"not-me" outside. The not-me threatens the self as a lover might, by
seducing the self away from itself. To have and retain a sense of self-
definition and simultaneously to transcend that self constitute the
dilemma of transcendence for the American. So Emerson writes in
his first Plato essay: "We unite all things by perceiving the law which
pervades them; by perceiving the superficial differences and the profound resemblances. But every mental act,—this very perception of
identity or oneness, recognizes the differences of things. Oneness and
otherness. It is impossible to speak or to think without embracing
both" (RWE, IV, 48). One necessitates the other: to retain the sense
of the body as the self that sees, hears, smells, tastes, and touches,
allowing one to know the visible, physical world; and to transcend
to a higher self, to the Spirit that knows the larger world beyond
the self. By transcending, the individual becomes larger, knows more,
and more deeply. It is not a matter of "escape from"; rather, it is a
"progress toward."

Transferred specifically to the sphere of art, this metaphysical view
of transcendentalism discloses new insights and problems. Because
the transcendental experience takes the perceiver outside the province of conventional categories of perception and expression, a special
burden falls upon the artistic structure as well as on analogy, metaphor, and symbol in order to represent that experience. When writers

regard the physical world as a symbol for the spiritual world, and when they cultivate a special vision in order to achieve a particular mode of perception, they naturally regard language in terms of its potential for capturing that vision. Transcendental literature characteristically expresses the knowledge of and sometimes simultaneously the process of an accumulating awareness of object, self, and spirit. Likewise, structure, as it is used to approximate this experience which parts time and space, does not necessarily find form in orderly—logical and chronological—progression. Or when it does seem ordered, as in Thoreau's *A Week on the Concord and Merrimack Rivers,* the ordering of the structural units appears arbitrary, like the arrangement of a larger content within a given smaller unit (chapter, essay, or paragraph). At the same time the transcendental writer expects structure to be "natural," "organic," modeling itself on the perfectly integrated formal patterns of nature's fixed fluidity, because nature, as the work of a divine creator, provides paradigms for the perfect (divine) arrangement.

From a conventional point of view, the significance of analogy, metaphor, and symbol to transcendental art results from their shared use of analogical methods. A simple analogy is the expression of a correspondence—a similarity or likeness—between two quantities. When used transcendentally, it expresses a correspondence between particulars drawn from different levels of being or meaning. Metaphor implies an analogy between two terms. Used transcendentally, one term is generally grounded in the more familiar, while the other is located at a correspondent point on a higher level of existence. In this respect the consonance of Kenneth Burke's thought is astonishing when he describes the mechanics of transcendence as "a realm HERE . . . being talked about *in terms of* a realm ELSEWHERE" (p. 5), and in another article defines metaphor similarly as "a device for seeing something *in terms of* something else."[13] By means of metaphor, qualities of the known world may suggest ideas or feelings concerning the unknown. When a metaphor is formed, conventional categories of thought are conjoined, the properties of one expanding those of the other, and vice versa. Thus, the imagination works by violating prior intellectual constructs and by erecting new ones. Metaphor is therefore an exquisite vehicle for the mind that resists the permanence of category, time, and space, as well as for the mind that shuns the chaos of disorder.

In the following passage from *Lessons from the World of Matter and the World of Man,* Theodore Parker fuses man's world and God's world, the world here and the world there, into one unified presence:

> To my religious eye, even if uncultivated by science, the world is the theatre of God's presence. I feel the Father. I see the beauty of His

thought in the morning red, in the mists that fill up the valleys, in the corn which waves in the summer wind, in the billows which dash their broken beauty on every shore, in the stars which look down on the mists of the valley, on fields that wave with corn, on the billows that dash their broken beauty on the shore. I see in the moon—filling her horns with loveliness, pouring out such a tide of beauty as makes the farmer's barn seem almost a palace of enchantment—the thought of God, which is radiating its silver sheen over all the world, and changing it to a wondrous beauty.[14]

Parker weds concrete image and its corresponding spiritual truth. Although the spiritual referents of corn and stars are never specified, in each instance the concrete particular makes its own case. An episode from A Week and one from Walden further illustrates this point concerning the unitive function of metaphor.

In the Wednesday chapter from A Week, Thoreau comes upon a bittern which he says is "the relic of a twilight antediluvian age . . . which may have trodden the earth while it was yet in a slimy and imperfect state."[15] Like the horsetails in the field, it lived in a primal world, there even before man. The thing in the ancient bird lives yet in the one before him:

One wonders if, by its patient study by rocks and sandy capes, it has wrested the whole of her secret from Nature yet. What a rich experience it must have gained standing on one leg and looking out from its dull eye so long on sunshine and rain, moon and stars! What could it tell of stagnant pools and reeds and dank night-fogs! It would be worth the while to look closely into the eye which has been open and seeing at such hours, and in such solitudes its dull, yellowish, greenish eye. Me-thinks my own soul must be a bright invisible green.
(Works, I, 250)

The characteristically transcendental prose of this passage reflects a sense of immediacy, non-rational connections and metaphoric escalation. The accruing emotion culminates in Thoreau's sudden explanation regarding the nature of his own soul. He provides no transition between the discussion of the bittern's eye and of himself; the connection exists only on the level of implicit correspondences. The eye of the bird reflects the Oversoul like the writer's own spirit—the eye and the soul seeming to antedate the bodies which attempt to contain them. On this basis Thoreau concludes that, since all things are in correspondence—"the yellowish, greenish eye" and his soul—his soul must also be "a bright invisible green."

The night-fishing episode in "The Ponds" proceeds similarly. As Thoreau brings in his fish, he remarks,

> It was very queer, especially in dark nights, when your thoughts had
> wandered to vast and cosmogonal themes in other spheres, to feel this
> faint jerk, which came to interrupt your dreams and link you up to
> Nature again. It seemed as if I might next cast my line upward into
> the air, as well as downward into this element which was scarcely
> more dense. Thus I caught two fishes as it were with one hook.[16]

The tug pulls him from spiritual reality, although he realizes that the
physical and spiritual realities are mixed. At the moment of the bite,
the two realities fuse. Through the intersection of self, Thoreau catches
the Oversoul with its correspondent, the horned pout, the catch bringing
him to the realization that the spiritual fish and the physical fish are
one. The Pond is really no different from heaven. The levels of existence
have been transcended, and for that moment, time, space, and physical
mass possess no reality. The identification occurs through the violation
of categories occasioned by metaphorical operation.

The value of symbol to the transcendental artist closely resembles
that of metaphor. Briefly put, symbol is itself and yet more than itself,
retaining its identity value (thus, its permanence) and containing another
or ideal value that comes to it through an analogical aspect of a metaphorical operation. A symbol is metaphor with a time dimension—past
and future—that affords it more potential functions.[17] Of the symbolic
types, the anagogical—symbol in the service of the transcendental—has
the most significance. The symbol as monad, as logos, is symbol as
universal shape or quantity—any, all, or none. It becomes the capsulated
essence which contains all particulars or toward which all particulars
aspire. Thus, Walden Pond manifests a prelapsarian purity; Thoreau
regards it as the "earth's eye," reflecting the sun, or the eye of the Spirit,
in the natural world. As Howard Houston explains, the pond is Thoreau's
"most complex symbol of transcendence[;] . . . it becomes the sacred
center of his world, the focal point through which passes that vertical
axis which joins the self to Brahman or God, the terrestrial to the celestial,
and the creation of the world, through various phases of history, to the
eternal present."[18]

Transcendental theories of art pose real problems which have generally been neglected by critics. How and when, one might ask, does
fact start becoming art? When, in other words, is the Pond not a
pond? Or as Tony Tanner puts it, "If every fact is equally interesting where does one find a criteria [sic] of exclusion, a principle of
abridgement without which art cannot start to be art for it cannot
leave off being nature?"[19] The problem might be further extended:
to what extent are we reading a language of fact and to what extent
a "rhetoric of fiction"? This question warrants extended, careful consideration, and only some of its aspects can be outlined here.

By way of questioning the relationship of raw material to art, of life to language, it seems necessary to ask which passages in transcendental literature are experiential and which cognitive. It should be asked of certain passages, Did the writer really have this experience? Is he recreating something he experienced? And of others, which intuitively seem somewhat different—qualitatively different—it might be asked, Is he dressing up an experience? Is he using language to ornament and improve upon life? Of these latter, "cognitive" forms, we might wonder if the writer hasn't transferred the quality of actually experienced transcendence to other more ordinary events. From their beginning, American writers have somehow had a unique relationship to the facts of the visible world—perhaps by virtue of their relation to the land, perhaps because they struck up a unique and persistent relation to the invisible world. Their words become things: stones, plants, and woodchips. The words are hieroglyphs, pointing backwards and forwards in time; they are signs, perhaps even sacraments. Issuing from this still ambiguous relationship of word, thing, and meaning is the problem of sincerity.

Speaking rather generally, all literature can be seen as moving from the earnest, direct sincerity of sacred and philosophical texts— where words mean what they say—to more elaborate textures of artistic rhetoric. Concerning this earlier language of fact, Martin Price says of Augustine's prose:

> We may see these analogies as commanding metaphors, but we must remember that they are avenues to knowledge of a solemn importance to those who study the rhetoric of the universe. If the rhetoric moves us today less with its persuasive cogency than with its formal richness and imaginative extravagance, we must be all the more careful to recognize these analogies as more than the metaphors of a secular modern poem.[20]

Similarly, in the case of the seventeenth-century artist, Joseph Mazzeo finds that it is necessary to distinguish between two schools of wit: one using wit as ornamentation, the other using it as an activity of discovering and exploring the correspondences believed to exist in the cosmos. Thus Mazzeo maintains that for the artist of the latter school,

> God created a world full of metaphors, analogies and conceits, and so far from being ornamentation, they are the law by which creation was effected. God wrote the book of nature in metaphor, and so it should be read.... Now the poetic involved in this view of the world is not the poetic of ornamental metaphor, but what I call "the poetic of correspondence." ... The universe is a vast net of correspondences which unites the whole multiplicity of being. The poet approaches

and creates his reality by a series of more or less elaborate correspondences.[21]

The same thing might be said of any correspondential artist. Is a particular passage rhetorical or cosmological? Is the function of words
ornamental or is it predominantly an expression of belief in a certain
kind of world? Although such questions have previously been thought
impertinent, they seem the most germane of all in relation to transcendental literature, and especially to its works of intellectual prose.

We must discover what it means to say of language, as Thoreau
does in his *Journal*, "As in the expression of moral truths we admire
any closeness to the physical fact which in all languages is the symbol
of the spiritual, so, finally, when natural objects are described, it is an
advantage if words derived originally from nature, it is true, but which
have turned (*tropes*) from their primary signification to a moral sense,
are used."[22] Language forms the natural intersection between moral
truth and physical reality, the nexus of thing and essence. This forms the
basis, however, for an aesthetic dilemma concerning boundaries between
the "thing as it is" and the "thing as it is said to be," between what is
real and true ("fact") and what is not real and is still true ("art").

Thoreau experienced this dilemma, as he suggests in the following
observation on the relationship of language to life and art:

> I have a commonplace-book for facts and another for poetry, but
> I find it difficult always to preserve the vague distinction which I had
> in my mind, for the most interesting and beautiful facts are so much
> the more poetry and that is their success. They are *translated* from
> earth to heaven. I see that if my facts were sufficiently vital and sig-
> nificant,—perhaps transmuted more into the substance of the human
> mind,—I should need but one book of poetry to contain them all.
> (*J*, III, 311)

Language possesses an ancient relational aspect. Like the woodchip
or the bittern's eye, it has seen more than any one man in its transmission
through time. The poet's words, Thoreau maintains, "are the relation of
his oldest and finest memory, a wisdom drawn from the remotest experience" (*Works*, I, 101–102), perhaps the memory of something never
actually known, but truly known, a logos with potential destiny. According to Charles Feidelson,

> The whole theory of universal language was one way of putting the
> paradoxical relativity and absoluteness of speech, which Thoreau also
> described under the rubric of "correspondence." To speak of "the
> perfect correspondence of Nature to man" was to assert "something

more than association"—was to say that objects affect the poet as language and that the linguistic relation is absolute.[23]

And, finally, we must explore the interrelationship of language, art, being, and meaning, asking the implications of the words like these from Thoreau's *Journal:*

> on the driest parts of the sandy slope, I go looking for *Cicindela,*— to see it run or fly. . . . I am reassured and reminded that I am the heir of eternal inheritances which are inalienable, when I feel the warmth reflected from this sunny bank, and see the yellow sand and the reddish subsoil. . . . The eternity which I detect in Nature I predicate of myself also. How many springs I have had this same experience! I am encouraged, for I recognize this steady persistency and recovery of Nature as a quality of myself." (*J,* VIII, 222–223)

This passage, expressing Thoreau's cognitive awareness, avoids the non-rational ecstasy of transcendence while presenting the intellectual awareness of wholeness and interrelatedness of being. What this means for art has yet to be determined.

Each of these problems points to the fact that American transcendentalism demands a broader understanding which will contribute to the elucidation of art. The idea of correspondence is useful to definition as well as to explication; it is, as Leo Stoller once remarked, "the marrow of transcendental metaphysics."[24] Correspondence functions to express the aesthetic and philosophical relationship governing the transmutation of object or idea into art. Perhaps this means no more than making explicit what has always been known and thought. When transcendence and transcendentalism are synonymized, the predominance of cosmology over rhetoric seems obvious, particularly in instances where the lives and the words of men—men like Parker, Alcott, and Thoreau— coincide so completely. We might now begin to speak in new ways of transcendental rhetoric, aesthetics, and existence, and go on to demonstrate what it means and how it is that fact flowers into truth.

Notes

1. "I, Eye, Ay—Emerson's Early Essay 'Nature': Thoughts on the Machinery of Transcendence," *Transcendentalism and Its Legacy,* ed. Myron Simon and Thornton Parsons (Ann Arbor: University of Michigan Press, 1966), p. 5. All references below are to this edition and are cited in the text.

2. Sherman Paul, *Emerson's Angle of Vision* (Cambridge: Harvard University Press, 1965), p. 2.

3. *Confrontations* (Princeton: Princeton University Press, 1965), p. 164.

4. *Observations on the Growth of the Mind with Remarks on Some Other*

Subjects (1838; rpt. Gainesville, Fla.: Scholars' Facsimiles & Reprints, 1970), p. 6. All references below are to this edition and are cited in the text.

5. *The Individual and the Cosmos in Renaissance Philosophy*, trans. Mario Domandi (New York: Barnes and Noble, 1963), p. 87.

6. *The Concept of Truth* (Assen, Netherlands: Van Gorcum, 1969), p. 58.

7. *The Collected Works of Ralph Waldo Emerson*, ed. Alfred R. Ferguson (Cambridge: Harvard University Press, 1971–   ), I, 7. All references to this edition are cited below in the text as *CW*.

8. *The Complete Works of Ralph Waldo Emerson*, ed. Edward Waldo Emerson (Boston: Houghton, Mifflin, 1903–1904), II, 97. All references to this edition are cited below in the text as *RWE*.

9. For a more complete discussion of "right vision" in Emerson, see chap. 3 of Paul's *Emerson's Angle of Vision*, pp. 77–102.

10. *The Collected Works of Theodore Parker*, ed. Frances Power Cobbe (London: Trübner, 1872), XIV, 267.

11. *The Eternal Now* (New York: Scribner, 1963), p. 123.

12. "Self-Transcendence and Beyond," *The Highest State of Consciousness*, ed. John White (Garden City, N.Y.: Doubleday, 1972), p. 97.

13. *A Grammar of Motives* (Berkeley: University of California Press, 1969), p. 503.

14. Parker, *Works*, XIV, 301–302.

15. *The Writings of Henry David Thoreau* (Boston: Houghton Mifflin, 1906), I, 250.

16. *Walden*, ed. J. Lyndon Shanley (Princeton: Princeton University Press, 1971), p. 98.

17. See Northrop Frye, "Second Essay. Ethical Criticism: Theory of Symbols," *Anatomy of Criticism* (New York: Atheneum, 1969), pp. 71–128.

18. "Metaphors in *Walden*" (Ph.D. dissertation, Claremont Graduate School, 1967), p. 153.

19. *The Reign of Wonder* (Cambridge: Cambridge University Press, 1965), p. 36.

20. *To the Palace of Wisdom* (Garden City, N.Y.: Doubleday, 1964), p. 4.

21. *Renaissance and Seventeenth-Century Studies* (New York: Columbia University Press, 1964), p. 54.

22. Thoreau, *Journal*, ed. Bradford Torrey and Francis H. Allen (Boston: Houghton Mifflin, 1906), XIII, 145. All references below are to this edition and are cited in the text as *J*.

23. *Symbolism and American Literature* (Chicago: University of Chicago Press, 1953), pp. 140–141.

24. In a class lecture.

I am grateful to the Rutgers University Research Council for a grant in support of research contributory to this article.

"The Kinetic Revolution: Transformation in the Language of the Transcendentalists"

Catherine Albanese*

This essay deals with six American Transcendentalists in a way in which they were fond of dealing with life: correspondence. The ancient theory of correspondence antedated its nineteenth-century adherents by long centuries. Chinese sages voiced it in their concepts of the Tao and the Confucian social order which replicated a heavenly model. Indians based the caste system and its Dharma on their perceptions of the structure of the macrocosm. In the Near East correspondence provided the basis for the Babylonians' astrological horoscopes, while in the West it authenticated the sophisticated allegorical musings of medieval churchmen and equally blessed the unlearned superstitions of the poor.

Briefly, the theory of correspondence taught that the universe *answered*, although the answer did not necessarily come in the personal accents of the Christian God. Instead each part of the universe was fitted to a corresponding part in a different plane since each piece of the world participated in the identity of one or several congruent spheres. So a flower told that human life was transitory and at the same time revealed an aspect of eternal beauty. A child born under the sign of Leo shared the way of being in the world which Leo embodied, and a child hiding after a naughty deed behind the sofa in a Puritan parlor repeated the drama of Adam and Eve hiding from God in the garden.

When in 1836 Ralph Waldo Emerson published *Nature*, he was enunciating the transcendental version of the theory. For Emerson, words were signs of natural facts, particular natural facts symbolized corresponding spiritual facts, and nature as a whole could be described as the symbol of spirit. As a man of letters, Emerson was especially interested in words, those signs of natural facts which gave expression to ideas and intuitions. He emphasized the connection between a new word and a new apprehension of an object:

*Reprinted from *New England Quarterly*, 48 (September 1975), 319–340.

> Language clothes nature as the air clothes the earth, taking the exact form and pressure of every object. Only words that are new fit exactly the thing, those that are old like old scoriae that have been long exposed to the air and sunshine, have lost the sharpness of their mould and fit loosely. But in new objects and new names one is delighted with the plastic nature of man as much as in picture or sculpture.[1]

Emerson had stated that language must change with a changing world, and the law of correspondence meant that the best words should reflect nineteenth-century forms of the world. "Old scoriae" had to yield to new images which corresponded to transcendental experience.

Emerson's colleagues agreed. James Freeman Clarke thought that "when men are compelled, by fear of denunciation, to speak their grandfathers' language instead of their own, their words seem empty to themselves."[2] And Frederic Henry Hedge argued that "the mind of a people imprints itself in its speech as the light in a picture of Daguerre."[3]

This study will take the Transcendentalists at their word: it will apply their theory to their own religious language, suggesting that the style of radical ferment and social change which marked the America of the Transcendentalists was paralleled by a preference for motion in transcendental speech. The essay has focused on six men who were nuclear members of the Transcendental Club, a loose association of like-minded spirits which met at irregular intervals for serious conversation, beginning with a gathering on September 19, 1836. Later, from 1840 to 1844, they held a written forum in their periodical, *The Dial.* The possibility of a shared language was therefore very strong.

These New Englanders emerged mostly from the background of Unitarian Boston with its polished intellectual religion, its conservative Whig orientation in politics, and its cool and conservative finishing school at nearby Harvard in Cambridge. Their response was one of impatience and even rebellion against what they considered the outworn and static rigidity of their immediate environment.

Emerson found the established churches "old and ossified under the accumulation of creeds and usages," a collective "corpse" in the hands of retainers.[4] His closest friend, Bronson Alcott, shared the assessment as he denounced preachers who led their congregations "through a bewildering labyrinth of theory, of book-work, far away from the ever-present and all-pervading Deity."[5] "Universal Whiggery," for Emerson, fared little better. The Whig was a hypochondriacal doctor who tended "a universe in slippers & flannels, with bib & pap-spoon, swallowing pills & herb tea, whig preaching, whig poetry, whig philosophy, whig marriages."[6]

Clarke drearily recalled the Harvard education which compelled him and his fellow-students "to wade through Homer as though the Iliad were a bog, and it was our duty to get along at such a rate *per diem*."[7] Hedge voiced his distrust of the "dogmatism of formal metaphysics" at Cambridge,[8] while George Ripley clashed publicly and in print with Andrews Norton, his former professor.[9] Meanwhile even the tolerant Convers Francis observed that the Unitarians must break into an old and a new school "belonging to the spiritual philosophy."

> The last have the most truth; but it will take them some time to ripen, and meanwhile they will be laughed at, perhaps, for things that will appear visionary and crude. But the great cause of spiritual truth will gain far more by them than by the others.[10]

If the past was "corpse-cold" for transcendental believers, we may ask what they put in its place. Emerson, their leader, described his circle as the party of the future. In contrast to Puritan and Unitarian contemporaries who, he said, formed the party of the past, he hailed a new consciousness and celebrated the young men "born with knives in their brain." These blades of the movement, whetted on the documents of German idealism and British romanticism, began to express the "newness" in a religious language suited to its intuitions. Its content included traditional religious symbols used by their contemporaries as well as metaphors and similes from nature, long a source of inspiration for mystics and poets. It is true that the Transcendentalists emphasized the language of nature more than their immediate forebears. But what was new about transcendental language in the context of Brahmin Boston was its *style* more than its content: it was written in the kinetic mode. From the churchly side, the Christian God along with his paraphernalia of word and sacrament joined the camp of motion. From the natural side, water became river, stream, current, ocean, and tide; light became burning flame or fire. Wind or breath; bird or wing; path and journey, sometimes joined to the Christian pilgrim; horse and rider; bow and arrow; circle and circulation; string of beads, thread, and changing garment; birth and nurtured growth—all proclaimed a new religion of process inaugurating a future of eternal energy. God, for the Transcendentalists, was motion.

Emerson's favorite form of expression for the flux of things was moving water. His writings and lectures reveal his keen delight in running water and more often than not the delight possessed religious dimensions. The river expressed Emerson's idea of how an individual human life fitted into the general scheme of humanity and the larger one of the universe. Man's life energy, his being and his thought, was

> . . . a stream whose source is hidden. . . . When I watch that flowing

river, which, out of regions I see not, pours for a season its streams
into me, I see that I am a pensioner; not a cause, but a surprised
spectator of this ethereal water; that I desire and look up, and put
myself in the attitude of reception, but from some alien energy the
visions come.[11]

As each person received the energy, his mandate was not to stand fast
but rather to flow with it:

Nature ever flows, stands never still. Motion or change is her mode
of existence. The poetic eye sees in Man the Brother of the River,
& in Woman the sister of the River. Their life is always transition.
Hard blockheads only drive nails all the time; forever remember;
which is fixing. Heroes do not fix but flow, bend forward ever &
invent a resource for every moment.[12]

Ego melted away into the supra-personal as Emerson confessed:

Above his life, above all creatures I flow down forever a sea of benefit into races of individuals. Nor can the stream ever roll backward
or the sin or death of a man taint the immutable energy which distributes itself into men as the sun into rays or the sea into drops.[13]

Like all rivers, Emerson's eventually met the sea. Time itself was
a sea on which nations and races flitted by without leaving so much as a
ripple, but the "tides of the Infinite" which rolled "their everlasting
circles" lay within.[14] "A man, I am the remote circumference, the skirt,
the thin suburb or frontier post of God, but go inward & I find the ocean;
I lose my individuality in its waves." It was fitter to say "I become" than
"I am," and sun and stars and persons were "the first ripples & wavelets
of that vast inundation of the All which is beyond & which I tend &
labor to be."[15]

The blowing wind fascinated Emerson, and he found in time a
drying wind for the "seedfield of today's thoughts which are dank &
warm & low-bent."[16] The wind brought its secret of new life, so that
"the old things rattle louder & louder & will soon blow away."[17] Emerson
confided to Thomas Carlyle, "The air we breathe is so vital that the Past
serves to contribute nothing to the result."[18]

Clearly, Emerson intended a contrast with the party of memory.
In the opening lines of *Nature*, he measured its living stuff against the
dry and brittle past:

Enbosomed for a season in nature, whose floods of life stream around
and through us, and invite us, by the powers they supply, to action
proportioned to nature, why should we grope among the dry bones

of the past, or put the living generation into masquerade out of its faded wardrobe?[19]

"When a man rests he stinks," Emerson once remarked;[20] and he wrote to his friend, Samuel Ward, telling him that "not in his goals but in his transition man is great, and the truest state of mind rested in becomes false."[21] Transition was the condition of nature, myth, and all of life.

> Nothing is to me more welcome nor to my recent speculation more familiar than the Protean energy by which the brute horns of Io become the crescent moon of Isis, and nature lifts itself through everlasting transition to the higher & the highest. Whoever lives must rise & grow. Life like the nimble Tartar still overleaps the Chinese wall of distinctions that had made an eternal boundary in our geography.[22]

Indeed, the transitive state issued from a divine imperative, for "the voice of the Almighty saith, Onward for evermore!"[23] "God invents, God advances. The world, the flesh, & the devil sit & rot."[24]

The musings of George Ripley expressed the same juxtaposition of death and life. His general portrait of the religious person is a good example. Such a person could not afford to "be so occupied with the mere outside, the dry husk and shell of matter, as to lose sight of the Infinite and Divine Energy, from which it draws the reality of its being." For the man of God, the divine voice would be "heard in the rushings of the wind and the whisperings of the breeze, in the roar of the thunder and the fall of the rain," while the godless person looked "coldly on" at a "mute and dead mass of material forms."[25]

A favorite metaphor for spiritual life was the fountain. Ripley saw that "in the light and strength of the Divine Spirit, which streams forth from the Primal Fountain, on all created things, its [the soul's] divine elements are quickened into life and activity, and it becomes a partaker of the divine nature." "Just as the stream partakes of the qualities of the fountain from which it flows," humanity possessed godlike attributes, and conversely the divine stream in man could "be traced to no other source than to the Eternal Fountain of Truth and Good."[26] Attainment of inner security meant the avoidance of the trap of prevailing opinions in order to "attain to a clear and living system of truth, which shall be to the soul what the blood is to the body,—a flowing fountain of inward strength."[27]

Natural symbols blended with Christian concerns in Ripley's ordination sermon for John Sullivan Dwight. Here Ripley contrasted the rigidity of the past with the present (hopeful) state of affairs in the churches, where the discovery was being made that "other fountains also contain the waters of life."

> A different state of things is now experienced among all the churches of the land. The unlimited freedom of thought which happily prevails in this community, produces a general fermentation; the ancient repose is disturbed; the stagnation of the past has given place to intense mental action; the doctrines of the theologians are brought before the tribunal of the people; a struggle has taken place between the old and the new; the most rigid creeds have been unable to prevent the progress of thought; so that there is scarcely a church of any communion, in which opinion is not divided, and the foundations of ages shaken to their centre.[28]

Later, when Ripley began to conclude that he must leave the Christian ministry, he shared his unrest with his congregation in a letter. He told his community that liberal Christians had "established the kingdom of God, not in the dead past, but in the living present," and insisted on "sweeping away the traditions which obscured the simplicity of truth," urging every soul "to press on to the highest attainments, to forget what was behind, and never to be kept back. . . ." The liberal clergy "could not linger around the grave of the past," and Ripley himself confessed that he could not "stand still."[29] In his vision of the church of the future, "there could be no cold or formal preaching; the instruction would be the outpouring of an individual soul," and, as for topics chosen, "the more exciting and soul-stirring the better." Committed to religious progress, "we should let the dead Past bury its dead," Ripley said; "we should know where we were, by the divine peace and joy, with which our hearts would overflow."[30] Some months after Ripley reluctantly left Purchase Street, his own version of the church of motion commenced at Brook Farm.

Bronson Alcott, in his turn, was a man in love with the symbolism of birth. There was the intriguing passage in his Journal:

> Fluids form solids. Mettle [sperm] is the Godhead proceeding into the matrix of nature to organize Man. Behold the creative jet! And hear the morning stars sing for joy at the sacred generation of the Gods![31]

And there was his custom of sending birthday letters to his daughters as well as Christmas letters to remind them of the birth of Jesus. In *Conversations on the Gospels,* birth emerged as an important theme. Like the rose seed, Alcott told his young students, "so the seed of a human being is placed in the midst of matter which nourishes it, and it grows and becomes perfected." "Where is the Life that causes a seed to spring out and seek the light?" he asked. The answer lay with the spirit which "makes the body just as the rose throws out the rose leaves."[32]

For Alcott, a contemplation of birth should lead to a disclosure of the nature of spirit; and, based on this perception, it would be the task of education to lead forth the spirit implicit in the child and existing still in much of its original state of innocence. Education thus was an active and moving endeavor, a far cry from the humdrum of the recitation system of the Boston Latin School and Harvard University. Alcott explained his notion of education in *The Doctrine and Discipline of Human Culture* (1836). Significantly, the title page bore the quotation of Jesus: "The wind bloweth where it listeth, and ye hear the sound thereof; but ye cannot tell whence it cometh nor whither it goeth; so is everyone that is born of the Spirit."[33]

But the symbol of birth was only one example of Alcott's concern for movement and life in the realm of education. Another favorite was spiritual culture, and in Alcott's mind this abstraction was decidedly kinetic. For Alcott, spiritual culture "lifts the body from the drowsy couch; opens the eyes upon the rising sun; tempts it forth to breathe the invigorating air; plunges it into the purifying bath, and thus whets all its functions for the duties of the coming day."[34] The movement corresponded to the activity of all creation, since "not only the whole universe is in motion, but every thing is in a state of change within it."[35]

Alcott interwove traditional gospel symbols with natural symbols of flux and flow in a view of the world which shared Emerson's basic perceptions. Matter was "like a great sea" moved by the living spirit which pervaded it.[36] "Do you think God flowed through all the forefathers of Jesus down to Joseph," Alcott asked his pupils. "Do you think his spirit flowed on through your ancestors and down to you?"[37] He told of a man in Boston whose spirit could "be made to flow out through his fingers, and make the sick person well."[38] Another time, he recalled for them the effect the sight of the ocean had produced in him when he first saw it at the age of twelve,[39] and again he painted the joy of country life where there were "living springs" from which water sprang up and was never dry. Water meant "Spirit pure and unspoiled," he told them, and asked, "Have you a living Spring?" "The waters become impure by standing still—by your not trying."[40]

Another part of the changing universe which Alcott often noted was light. Religious light was moving light, and in *The Dial* he wrote that the "prophet, whose eye is coincident with the celestial ray, receives this into his breast, and intensifying there, it kindles on his brow a serene and perpetual day."[41] In another offering he pictured inspiration which "darts like lightning, straight to its quarry, and rends all formulas of the schools as it illuminates the firmament of the mind."[42] Again, the soul was a Prometheus who received the divine fires and fashioned them into a man who was image of God and model for all other natural forms.[43] The child was gentle (and sacred) because "there, for a little while, fed by divine fires, the serene flame glows."[44]

Clarke's tracts for the American Unitarian Association revealed his reconstruction of traditional Christian symbols with kinetic material. In *Reconciliation by Jesus Christ*, Clarke began with a reminder of God's work in the natural creation: "The swarming insects who leap in the sunbeam; the free bird, flashing through the wood, or hanging high in the liquid firmament; the fish darting or gliding in the liquid wave,— all are provided for by the Universal Parent." Christianity echoed the movement of nature, for its word was "one which descended from the highest Heaven, far above the reach of the most soaring thought, with which man has ever penetrated the skies." Sin set up a "barrier" to the word and produced a "coldness of heart," which nature, with her "wheels [which] run on iron tracks," could never pardon. But the "awakened conscience" could expect a different reception from the Father, whose "sunshine would break in" at the return of the repentant sinner, and the result would be a renewal of the authentic spirit of Christianity, "love, flowing out of pardoned sin, love to God and man." For the future, "inward peace and joy with God" would strengthen the Christian to "run and not be weary in God's ways." Meanwhile, theology would furnish the "chart by which to guide ourselves through the intricacies of the wilderness, which the soul must traverse in its flight to God." There was only one caution: "we must not study the chart till we forget to go upon the journey."[45]

The motif of the journey was also evident in Clarke's tract, *Repentance toward God*. Life was a Jacob's ladder with the eye of God traveling along the gradation, "along this shining highway of spirits" in which "some had their faces toward him, turned upward and were ascending,—others had their eyes turned earthward, turned from him, and were descending." Man must learn not to walk the broad and easy way, in another metaphor, but he must leave "the religion of ceremony and form" and "walk in the Spirit." The lesson to be learned for the journey was that the doctrines of repentance and faith "moved the world then,—they move it now; they will always move it while man continues to be man." And while man continued to be man, he would know that he needed "a radical change, not a superficial one."[46]

Individual change must proceed in tandem with institutional change, and in *The Unitarian Reform* Clarke turned to the latter. He pondered the nature of the Unitarian movement and paraphrased a typical Unitarian formulation in this way: "Jesus Christ taught no formal system— the Apostles laid down no fixed standard of opinions—they taught the truth in a free, living manner, without any scheme or plan of theology at all." Clarke saw the first great object of Unitarian reform as "Christian

Liberty," which meant living wholly free from "scholastic trammels." He praised the faith "that in the worst of men lay hidden and buried a divine spark, to be kindled by love and truth"; or, put another way, loving sinners involved believing "that there is asleep, under their sin, a spirit of goodness which may be roused at last by our appeals and overcome by our love." Clarke indicated his orientation toward a future of action and democracy as he summarized the Unitarian message:

> Ours is the religion of the future, the religion of progress, the religion for the people. . . . With firm faith in the future triumph of our principles, in deep dependence on the mighty arm of Heaven, and in a strenuous endeavor to live as we profess, we can wait the hour when the truth of our principles will be understood and acknowledged.[47]

Like Clarke, Frederic Hedge was fond of repeating traditional Christian themes in the vocabulary of motion. He was also a spokesman for civil religion in his addresses, and one Fourth of July oration provided an occasion for him to preach the gospel of progress. Hedge looked only briefly at past history, dwelt lightly on the blessings of the present, and then turned full face toward the future, for which all else had been prologue:

> When we contemplate what the last fifty years have done for human culture and human happiness, we involuntarily ask, what the next fifty, or the next one hundred, shall add to the account. It is not till within these centuries, that the idea of progress in human affairs, has dawned upon mankind. . . . that the earth, which witnessed the first unfolding, is destined to witness the final development of all that is in man.[48]

True, there had always been life, whatever the surface stagnation, and "with varying fortunes, in various lands, the unconscious race has crept or sped, but never staid." Now there was a new impetus to the march:

> Six thousand years, the sun and the stars have watched it moving; but never until now—with the momentum acquired in these latter years—has it felt its motion. Now, first awakened to self-consciousness, Humanity is moving on, with new speed and conscious aims, to the fulfilment [sic] of its high calling.[49]

Then manifest destiny erupted for Hedge with a vengeance. The Anglo-Saxon race were:

> . . . the moving force and the last hope of man. . . . climbing the Himmaleh [sic], piercing central Africa, stretching along the Moun-

tains of the Moon, and overspreading Austral Asia, with their beneficent sway,—awakening once more the wizard Genius of the East,
and carrying wherever the sun shines or the winds blow, the sacred
gifts of Freedom.[50]

Progress, process, and democracy in America were linked to education; and, when a new lyceum opened in Bangor, Hedge addressed
the official gathering, using the occasion to sketch his views of learning
in a democracy and the relationship of the quest for knowledge to
spiritual goals. "Earth and sky teem with instruction," he told his audience,[51] and knowledge was a threaded circle in which the student
traced his line from part to whole:

> He who understands one thing thoroughly, holds the threads of all
> knowledge in his hand, and if life were long enough, or circumstances
> and ability would permit us, to follow out to their extremities, the radii
> which centre in any particular branch of knowledge which we may
> have mastered, we might make ourselves masters of the whole circle
> of knowledge, without any instruction from other sources.[52]

Hedge turned to the American situation and commended the absence
of hierarchical structure. Democracy meant a "free and full development" of every man, "where a levelling and radical spirit, of the true
sort, has equalized the human condition by levelling *upward*. . . ."[53] He
ended his speech with an avowal of the quest for spirit as the implicit
goal of knowledge:

> And this, I believe to be the tendency of science, just in proportion
> as inquiry is pushed beyond the visible forms of things, to the inner-
> most laws, and secret life of Nature. The further we explore in this
> direction, the more clearly we discern the ever-present agency of
> Spirit, represented by its highest manifestation—Law. The outward
> form—the mere dead substance, grows less and less; action and life
> fill its place, till at last the whole of being appears to be but an
> aggregate of laws, and nature teems with spirit.[54]

Convers Francis' transcendental colleagues had paid tribute to his
character when they selected him to be moderator of their Club, for
Francis was above all a moderate. Still his preaching revealed the
transformation of the traditional Christian themes characteristic of
Transcendentalism. When his Watertown congregation moved into a new
meetinghouse, Francis greeted the occasion with a discourse on the
significance of a Christian temple, and he shaped the old symbol of
stability to suit his new insights. "Every moment of our lives, we breathe,
stand, or move in the temple of the Most High," Francis told his congregation, "for the whole universe is that temple." He explained:

Ask of the bright worlds around us, and they roll in the everlasting harmony of their circles; and they shall tell you of Him, whose power launched them on their courses. . . . Ask of ocean's waters; and the roar of their boundless waves shall chant from shore to shore a hymn of ascription to that Being, who hath said "Hitherto shall ye come and no further." Ask of the rivers; and, as they roll onward to the sea, do they not bear along their ceaseless tribute to the ever-working Energy, which struck open their fountains and poured them down through the valleys?[55]

Revelation confirmed his interpretation, for the New Jerusalem had no temple—to signify that "the soul shall be emancipated into that world where her whole action will be the true worship, her whole growth the true service." Christian institutions, said Francis, found their true glory in "putting into active forms, and transmitting from mind to mind, from generation to generation, the living spirit, that animates the Kingdom of Christ in the soul."[56]

The Christian case was an instance of correspondence. Matter too was "mutable, transitory, in a state of flux and reflux."

We stand before Nature, as before a passing show. . . . The bubble swelling and bursting on the surface of the water, the vapor ascending and vanishing in the thin air, the dust blown away by the wind,—these are the images by which man represents to himself his brief and broken life.[57]

In this situation it was "refreshing to mount on the wings of that faith, which springs from the constitution of the soul" to the "Fountain of life and blessedness." Ministry itself meant directing the sinner "to the purifying fountain opened in the Gospel,"[58] a work accomplished in harmony with the first disciples who "gave impulses, whose strong vibrations are now spreading through the earth, so that the far distant islands of the ocean, and the tribes of barbarous shores, are listening to the sound as it rolls on."[59]

A consideration of ministry allowed the institutional nature of Christianity to emerge. Here Francis acknowledged that

. . . a power which marshals the world forward on the path of improvement, is down in the depths and abroad over the surface of society, kindles the light of spiritual philosophy, tasks the most gifted intellects to follow its far-reaching revelations of truth, and holds under its reign the nations who march in the van of the world's progress.[60]

Dwelling on the role of the individual Christian in the corporate identity, he continued:

> Whatever may be the measure of our progress in the true spiritual life, it will correspond to the vast expansion of the Divine Nature, as the shadow on the dial corresponds in its motion to the sun in the heavens, though the shadow moves perhaps but a handbreadth, while the place of the great luminary changes by millions of miles.[61]

Christians and their institutions needed grace, Francis reminded his congregation, or they would "sink among the dead things of form, instead of being instinct with a living power." And in a metaphor which vaguely recalled the railroad, he spoke of "preparative influences, which tranquillize and purify our trains of thought by taking them out of their common tracks of worldliness." Too often Francis and his people hastened along, "with . . . eyes on the ground, and . . . hands busy among perishing things" when beauty and light were "bursting forth in the upper region." But grace would bring the soul to that state "when its movements are most free, as the motion of our globe, swiftly as it careers through the fields of space, disturbs not even the slender threads of which the spider weaves her web."[62]

Our six Transcendentalists, then, all shared a preference for the language of motion in their discussion of religious themes. They also shared a platform in their *Dial,* and its pronouncements spoke in the new fashion.[63] *The Dial* aspired to be a vehicle for the communication of those who affirmed a common gospel:

> The pages of this Journal will be filled by contributors . . . whose hearts are more in the future than in the past; and who trust the living soul rather than the dead letter. It will endeavor to promote the constant evolution of truth, not the petrification of opinion.[64]

From the beginning, a thrust toward the future and a concern with time—the duration of that which *changes*—were foremost: "*The Dial,* as its title indicates, will endeavor to occupy a station on which the light may fall; which is open to the rising sun; and from which it may correctly report the progress of the hour and the day."[65]

In a letter to Margaret Fuller, Clarke corroborated the editorial intent, voicing his approval of *The Dial's* name: "I think it excellent—significant of those who believe in the progress of time and who watch it, not in the bustle of a city, but amid the flowers and leafiness of a garden walk. The name speaks of faith in Nature and in Progress."[66] Clarke's *Western Messenger* described what *The Dial* was about: " 'The Dial' marks an Era in American literature; it is the wind-flower of a new spring in the Western world,"[67] an evaluation which was shaped by its kinetic content as well as its conscious articulation of transcendental purpose.

This preoccupation was equally apparent in Emerson's opening chat with readers. The editors, he told them, had obeyed a "strong current of thought and feeling" which had led them to counter "that rigor of our conventions of religion and education which is turning us to stone. . . ." He called it "the progress of a revolution."

> Those who share in it have no external organization, no badge, no creed, no name. They do not vote, or print, or even meet together. They do not know each other's faces or names. They are united only in a common love of truth, and love of its work.[68]

Always *The Dial* must stand for process and progress. It must be "such a Dial as is the Garden itself, in whose leaves and flowers and fruits the suddenly awakened sleeper is instantly apprised not what part of dead time, but what state of life and growth is now arrived and arriving."[69]

The shared gospel and revolution seemed to be an underlying structure of consciousness; in other words, a mental base or foundation of very similar primary perceptions and value judgments. Upon such a base, diverse shapes and forms could rise on the phenomenal level— "special reforms in the state," "modifications of the various callings of men, and the customs of business," "a new scope for literature and art," "philosophical insight," "vast solitudes of prayer."[70] Gospel and revolution, further, were identified not only with the editors but with readers. In a letter to Carlyle in 1842, Emerson described *The Dial's* audience as composed of religious people who hated ecclesial structure and who rejected old manners and mores without offering new ones. The "movement" for Emerson carried a messianic tinge: "Perhaps, one of these days, a great Yankee shall come, who will easily do the unknown deed."[71]

If Emerson's opinion that a revolution was in progress was correct, its prime indicator was language. A common denominator gathered the words of the Transcendentalists and separated them from the established tongue of Cambridge-educated, Unitarian, Whiggish Boston. The common denominator was motion. Though the *content* of transcendental language was Christian tradition or conventional nature, the *mode* of their language had changed from the manner of discourse which was part of their immediate past.

The revolution in words did not go unrecognized by the keepers of the past. In 1837, the scholarly and conservative Francis Bowen penned an article for the Unitarian *Christian Examiner*. "They have deepened the gulf between speculative and practical men," he wrote in horror, "and by their innovations in language, they are breaking down the only bridge that spans the chasm."[72] Bowen's was a feeble disclaimer compared to Andrews Norton's denunciation the following year. Writing

in a widely circulated Boston paper, he castigated an unnamed transcendental writer:

> He floats about magnificently on bladders, which he would have it
> believed are swelling with ideas.—Common thoughts, sometimes
> true, oftener false, and "Neutral nonsense, neither false nor true,"
> are exaggerated, and twisted out of shape, and forced into strange
> connexions, to make them look like some grand and new conception.

Norton continued the attack:

> To produce a more striking effect, our common language is abused;
> antic tricks are played with it; inversions, exclamations, anomalous
> combinations of words, unmeaning, but coarse and violent, meta-
> phors abound, and withal a strong infusion of German barbarisms.[73]

Three days later, the newspaper published, in response to Norton's
diatribe, a letter by Theophilus Parsons pleading for responsible criticism of the "New School." If Norton were to be taken at his word,
Parsons wrote, then "all who believe that the fountains of truth are
neither sealed nor exhausted, are in fact directed to this new school as
to friends who would favor progress." Once antiquity had been the
acceptable standard of truth, but those days were past, and the human
mind was now "abroad upon a pathless sea, and the waves are high, the
sky is dark, and the winds are loud and angry. But for all this, beyond
the clouds the sun still shines; and even the pathless ocean is bounded
by the steadfast land; and who can fear the triumph or perpetuity of
error."[74] Andrews Norton's reaction was angry and immediate. Two days
after the Parsons letter, his condemnation appeared: "A great part of
the Reply consists of remarks concerning old and new opinions, somewhat too extravagantly and poetically expressed, and too much in the
language of the New School."[75]

Transcendental language clearly did not agree with the speech
of former mentors such as Andrews Norton. Yet according to the principle of correspondence, the manner of transcendental speaking should
have been replicated in some part of the macrocosm. The question is
then what other world corresponded? What other world answered?

Outside the neighborhood of Boston, there was the world of
America, and it is the suggestion of this paper that America answered.
Only three decades previously, this world had seemed innocently agrarian. Jefferson had hailed its agricultural flavor and purchased Louisiana
to keep it that way. John Taylor of Caroline, his fellow Virginian, had
theorized on the quality of rural virtue and the stuff of the agrarian
dream. But by 1836 the dream was phasing itself out with incredible

speed. New forces were building mills, importing farm girls as operatives, and settling company towns. Others were dredging canals, harnessing steam which powered boats to sail them, laying the iron and wooden planks which laced the countryside with a path for the speeding locomotive. Meanwhile the motif of speed was echoed in the burgeoning cities which, with ever faster tempo, mushroomed in number and size. While rural migrants and hordes of immigrants settled the cities, others in prairie schooners moved through the plains toward the beckoning frontier. Democratic process took new turns in the Jacksonian era, and a host of reform movements commanded eager followers. The economy spiraled, crashed, then soared to new heights. America was living through a time of ferment and change; it was a time to speed.

Impatient with the formalism of Brahmin Boston, the transcendental heretics had instead chosen fluidity. In doing so they wrote and spoke a language which possessed a strong degree of congruence with the style of their country. While they protested its materialism sometimes, and warned of its frenetic tendencies at others, on the level of style the Transcendentalists had no quarrel with America: they were affirming America's new priority of motion.

When Orestes Brownson wrote his careful evaluation of *The Dial* in the *Boston Quarterly Review,* he commented on the Club members and their endeavor: "On many sides they expose themselves to ridicule, but at bottom there is a serious, solemn purpose, of which even they are but half conscious."[76] Brownson was perhaps more astute than he realized. The Transcendentalists may not have been aware of every dimension in which they were practicing the correspondence which they preached. Yet it has been a useful exercise to pursue the transcendental structure of consciousness further than the Transcendentalists themselves did. A search for correspondences between personal experience and environmental context has given us insights into the formation of religious language which institutional or intellectual history would find more difficult to reach. Correspondence can be a pragmatic tool as well as a poetic vision.

Notes

1. 10 November 1836, *The Journals and Miscellaneous Notebooks of Ralph Waldo Emerson,* ed. William H. Gilman et al. (Cambridge: Harvard University Press, 1960–   ), V, 246. (Hereinafter cited as *"JMN."*)

2. James Freeman Clarke, *The Unitarian Reform,* Tracts of the American Unitarian Association, First Series, XII, no. 138 (Boston: American Unitarian Association, 1839), p. 5.

3. Frederic Henry Hedge, *Conservatism and Reform* (Boston: Charles C. Little and James Brown, 1843), p. 14.

4. "Religion" (19 January 1837), *The Early Lectures of Ralph Waldo Emerson*, ed. Stephen E. Whicher, Robert E. Spiller, and Wallace E. Williams (Cambridge: Harvard University Press, 1959–1972), II, 97.

5. Journal entry, 1828, quoted in Odell Shepard, *Pedlar's Progress: The Life of Bronson Alcott* (Boston: Little, Brown, 1937), p. 126. Unfortunately, the published Journals of Bronson Alcott contain only a small portion of the total material which Alcott left.

6. September 1841, Emerson, *JMN*, VIII, 87.

7. James Freeman Clarke, *Autobiography, Diary and Correspondence*, ed. Edward Everett Hale (Boston: Houghton, Mifflin, 1899), p. 36.

8. "Frederic Henry Hedge," *Unitarian Review*, 34 (October 1890), 295.

9. From 1836 to 1840, Ripley engaged in a literary feud with Unitarian "pope" Andrews Norton concerning the value of miracles as Christian evidence. Norton, as an advocate of Lockean sensational philosophy, found the chief evidence for the truth of Christianity in documented miracles, while Ripley, as a Transcendentalist, found internal evidence from the mind and intuition much more persuasive. For a good discussion of the entire controversy and the specific items of literature it generated, see William Hutchison, *The Transcendentalist Ministers* (New Haven: Yale University Press, 1959).

10. Convers Francis, diary entry, 30 November 1837, quoted in John Weiss, *Discourse Occasioned by the Death of Convers Francis, D.D.* (Cambridge: Privately printed, 1863), pp. 28–29.

11. Emerson, "The Over-Soul," *Essays: First Series* (Boston: Ticknor and Fields, 1865), p. 252. (Originally published in 1841.)

12. 6 December 1840, Emerson, *JMN*, VII, 539–540.

13. 23 April 1841, Emerson, *JMN*, VIII, 435.

14. Letter to Caroline Sturgis, 13 September 1840, *The Letters of Ralph Waldo Emerson*, ed. Ralph L. Rusk (New York: Columbia University Press, 1939), II, 334. (Hereinafter cited as *Letters*.)

15. 17 June 1836, 26 March 1838, Emerson, *JMN*, V, 177, 468.

16. 26 June 1838, Emerson, *JMN*, VII, 36.

17. Emerson to Frederic Henry Hedge, Concord, 23 March 1842, *Letters*, III, 37.

18. Emerson to Carlyle, Concord, 17 September 1836, *The Correspondence of Emerson and Carlyle*, ed. Joseph Slater (New York: Columbia University Press, 1964), p. 150.

19. Emerson, *Nature, The Complete Works of Ralph Waldo Emerson*, ed. Edward Waldo Emerson (Boston: Houghton, Mifflin, 1903–1904), I, 3.

20. 14 April 1839, Emerson, *JMN*, VII, 190.

21. Emerson to Samuel G. Ward, n.d. (ca. 1840), *Letters from Ralph Waldo Emerson to a Friend, 1838–1853*, ed. Charles Eliot Norton (Boston: Houghton, Mifflin, 1899), p. 30.

22. Emerson to Margaret Fuller, Concord, 25 September 1840, *Letters*, II, 337.

23. 28 May 1839, Emerson, *JMN*, VII, 203.

24. 9 March 1839, Emerson, *JMN*, VII, 172.

25. George Ripley, *Discourses on the Philosophy of Religion Addressed to Doubters Who Wish to Believe* (Boston: James Munroe, 1836), p. 24.

26. Ripley, *Discourses*, pp. 42, 53, 74.

27. George Ripley, "Letter to a Theological Student," *Dial*, 1 (October 1840), 183.

28. George Ripley, *The Claims of the Age on the Work of the Evangelist* (Boston: Weeks, Jordan, 1840), pp. 15, 7.

29. George Ripley, *A Letter Addressed to the Congregational Church in Purchase Street* (Boston: [Freeman and Bolles], 1840), pp. 7–8.

30. Ripley, *A Letter . . .* , pp. 22–23.

31. 31 March 1839, *The Journals of Bronson Alcott*, ed. Odell Shepard (Boston: Little, Brown, 1938), p. 121.

32. Alcott, *Conversations with Children on the Gospels* (Boston: James Munroe, 1836–1837), I, 132; II, 15; I, 233.

33. John 3:8, as quoted on the title page of Alcott, *The Doctrine and Discipline of Human Culture* (Boston: James Munroe, 1836).

34. Alcott, *The Doctrine and Discipline of Human Culture*, p. 22.

35. Alcott, *Conversations with Children on the Gospels*, I, 135.

36. Alcott, *Conversations . . .* , II, 27.

37. Alcott, *Conversations . . .* , I, 137.

38. Alcott, *Conversations . . .* , II, 176.

39. Alcott, *Conversations . . .* , I, 229.

40. Alcott, *Conversations . . .* , II, 72–77.

41. Alcott, "Orphic Sayings," *Dial*, 1 (January 1841), 357.

42. Alcott, "Days from a Diary," *Dial*, 2 (April 1842), 416.

43. Alcott, "Orphic Sayings," *Dial*, 1 (July 1840), 97.

44. Alcott, "Orphic Sayings" (January 1841), p. 359.

45. James Freeman Clarke, *The Peculiar Doctrine of Christianity, or Reconciliation by Jesus Christ*, Tracts of the American Unitarian Association, First Series, XVIII (Boston: James Munroe, 1845), pp. 7–24.

46. Clarke, *Repentence Toward God* (Boston: Office of the Christian World, 1843), pp. 10–19.

47. Clarke, *The Unitarian Reform*, pp. 6–15.

48. Frederic Henry Hedge, *An Oration Pronounced Before the Citizens of Bangor, on the Fourth of July, 1838* (Bangor: Samuel S. Smith, 1838), p. 28.

49. Hedge, *An Oration . . .* , p. 29.

50. Hedge, *An Oration . . .* , pp. 30–31.

51. Hedge, *An Introductory Lecture Delivered at the Opening of the Bangor Lyceum, November 15, 1836* (Bangor: Nourse and Smith, and Duren and Thatcher, 1836), p. 4.

52. Hedge, *An Introductory Lecture . . .* , p. 10.

53. Hedge, *An Introductory Lecture . . .* , p. 13.

54. Hedge, *An Introductory Lecture . . .* , pp. 24–25.

55. Convers Francis, Discourse III, *Three Discourses Preached Before the Congregational Society in Watertown* (Cambridge, Mass.: Folsom, Wells, and Thurston, 1836), p. 49.

56. Francis, *Three Discourses*, pp. 66–79.

57. Francis, *Three Discourses*, p. 68.

58. Francis, *Three Discourses*, pp. 70–77.

59. Francis, *Three Discourses*, p. 47.

60. Francis, *Three Discourses*, p. 48.

61. Francis, *Three Discourses*, p. 52. The later title for the Club's journal, the *Dial*, seems suggested here.

62. Francis, *Three Discourses*, pp. 54–67.

63. Convers Francis was the only one of the six Transcendentalists who did

not publish any work in the *Dial*, but he had taken part in preliminary discussions and supported publication of the new journal.

64. The *Dial*, editorial message appearing on the cover of each volume.

65. The *Dial*.

66. Clarke to Margaret Fuller, Louisville, 24 May 1840, *The Letters of James Freeman Clarke to Margaret Fuller*, ed. John Wesley Thomas (Hamburg: Cram, de Gruyter, 1957), p. 138.

67. *"The Dial," Western Messenger*, 8 (April 1841), 571.

68. Emerson, "The Editors to the Reader," *Dial*, 1 (July 1840), 1–2.

69. Emerson, "The Editors to the Reader," p. 4.

70. Emerson, "The Editors to the Reader," pp. 2–3.

71. Emerson to Carlyle, Concord, 15 October 1842, *Correspondence of Emerson and Carlyle*, p. 332.

72. Francis Bowen, "Locke and the Transcendentalists," *Christian Examiner*, 33 (1837), 190.

73. Andrews Norton, "The New School in Literature and Religion," *Boston Daily Advertiser*, 27 August 1838.

74. S. X. [Theophilus Parsons], "The New School and Its Opponents," *Boston Daily Advertiser*, 30 August 1838.

75. Andrews Norton, "On the Article in the *Advertiser* of Thursday Concerning the New School," *Boston Daily Advertiser*, 1 September 1838.

76. Orestes A. Brownson, "Literary Notices: *The Dial*," *Boston Quarterly Review*, 4 (January 1841), 132.

"Individual, Civil Society, and State in American Transcendentalism"

A. Robert Caponigri*

The political and social thought of American transcendentalism retains a double motive of interest. The first motive is historical. Transcendentalism is an episode in the American story. It is an episode of many facets, not the least of which—and in some perspective the most important—is its character as an effort at a crucial moment of our country's development to understand the meaning and assess the character of the American experience. As such it possesses an abiding interest and importance for the American historical consciousness.

The second motive is speculative or theoretical. As a speculative effort, and in virtue of its basic speculative insights, transcendentalism raised anew a most ancient and persistent problem of western political thought. This is the problem of the intricate and dialectical relationships between the individual, the state, and the civil order or civil society. In virtue of its basic speculative insight—which we shall call the transcendentalist principle—transcendentalism effected a radical change in the classic western solution of this problem. Classically, the potentially explosive confrontation between individual and state—or morality and policy, as Thoreau phrases it,[1] conscience and coercive power—was mediated by the civil order, by civil society. At this point the transcendentalist and the classical views were to come into conflict.

Classically, the function of the civil order was mediatorial and constitutive. It comprised a wisdom, as Vico would have called it, or a jurisprudence, an order of civility, which established both state and individual—morality and policy—in the just autonomy of each and in the inter-relations which must prevail between them. It established the ambient in which the just claims and obligations as well as the dynamic interplay of these elements could be realized without violent impact or mutual confusion. This civil order was woven of a public philosophy

*Reprinted from *American Philosophy from Edwards to Quine*, ed. Robert W. Shahan and Kenneth R. Merrill (Norman: University of Oklahoma Press, 1977), pp. 49–77.

reached by open dialogue, of consensus reached on the basis of this philosophy and stabilized in history, tradition, and authority. The concept of this order provided the proper and radical sense of the terms "civil" and "civility." "Civility" resided in the capacity to generate, sustain, and communicate such an order; the civil man, the *civis*, was the man formed and educated to partake in that order in all its aspects.

The radical result of the transcendentalist principle as it entered the world of men and of public action, of policy, to retain Thoreau's term, was the dissolution of the civil order conceived in this sense. It deprived public life of this mediatorial and constitutive principle. As a consequence, it left the other elements of this complex structure, individual and state, in stark confrontation without mediation. This result seriously affected the transcendentalist assessment of the American experience and of the actual condition and tasks of the American polity.

Transcendentalism, as might well be expected, was not unaware of the serious tension created by the dissolution of the civil order and the consequent unmediated confrontation of the elements of individual and state, of morality and policy, or coercive power. As a result, it found itself confronted by the further speculative task of redefining the kind of relations which should prevail between them or, in other words, of finding a principle, procedure, or structure which would fill the vacuum created by the dissolution of the civil order. This effort constitutes the constructive dimension and at the same time the inner speculative movement of transcendentalist political thought.

This is the movement we shall try to trace through its successive stages. The steps which must be taken in this task may be listed in the following manner: (a) the characterization of the transcendentalist principle, or of transcendentalism as principle; (b) the delineation of the process by which the transcendentalist principle entails the dissolution of the concept of the civil order, leaving the elements of individual and state, morality and policy, in unmediated confrontation; (c) the consequences which follow in the transcendentalist assessment of the American policy; (d) the identification of the attempts by transcendentalism to close the gap which has thus been opened by the transcendentalist principle. These, finally, prove to be the Thoreauvian doctrine of resistance to civil power as the means of moralizing policy; the Emersonian doctrine of the elite of character and the educative function of the state; and in conclusion, the Brownsonian rediscovery through the critique of the transcendentalist principle of the concept of civil order and the reassessment of the American political experience in terms of his theory of the constitution. We may begin by formulating in as brief and lapidary a manner as possible the transcendentalist principle.

No word occurs more frequently or is employed with greater emphasis in the idiom of transcendentalism than "principle." Nevertheless, no undertaking seems more resistant to happy results than that of stating the transcendentalist principle itself, although the innermost thrust of transcendentalism is to achieve the status of principle. This is especially true in the present context because the social and political implications of transcendentalism, both theoretical and critical, follow on transcendentalism not as "sentiment" or "enthusiasm," terms frequently employed to characterize it, but as principle. The formulation of this principle, consequently, the transcendentalist principle, though difficult, is imperative. Encouragement is lent by the view of its earliest historian, O. B. Frothingham. Qualifying Emerson's own view, Frothingham writes: "Transcendentalism was a distinct philosophical system. Practically it was an assertion of the inalienable worth of man; theoretically, it was an assertion of the immanence of divinity in instinct, the transfer of supernatural attributes to the natural constitution of mankind."[2]

Transcendentalism as principle concerns in essence man's access to truth. It asserts the direct revelation to the individual, in intuition, of truth of universal range and validity. This direct revelation or communication of truth may come to the individual by either, or both, of two ways. It may come by way of withdrawal to the inner sphere of consciousness (the position favored by Emerson).[3] It may also come by way of the immediate, indeed empathic and not unmystical, communion with physical nature, the Thoreauvian way.[4] These ways, of course, do not exclude each other.

One is assured of the intention of transcendentalism to advance itself as a philosophical principle by Emerson's effort to endow it with a respectable genealogy in the history of philosophy. He employs the distinction, which he asserts to be apodictic, between idealist and materialist to locate it dialectically. He appeals to the authority of Kant for its initial insights and to Jacobi, among others, for its rightness in the moral sphere. Frothingham endows it with an even ampler provenance.[5] The validity of these claims may be debated, especially Emerson's tendency to reduce the process of the critical philosophy of Kant to an assertion of the supremacy of "intuition." One feels that the "tough-minded" Kant, confronted with Emerson's views, would have been tempted to direct against them the heavy-handed satire he directed against Swedenborg.[6] Emerson, incidentally, assigns an extraordinarily elevated status in the history of thought to Swedenborg.[7] But this issue may be left to the historians to judge.[8]

Of greater importance to the character of transcendentalism as principle is the question of the seat and modes of communication of this intuition of universal truth. That seat is the individual, whether through interior illumination or through contemplation and communion with nature. This institution, however, as Emerson explains, is not given the individual as a constant and constitutive element of consciousness. It is granted him, rather, in moments or flashes of interior illumination or insights into the processes of nature which are not his to command. These moments, when granted, lift the transcendentalist to heights of clear vision and wisdom; when they pass or are withheld, they leave him in that penumbral perplexity which Emerson poignantly describes.[9] The transcendentalist, by this account, dwells in a "chiaroscuro" of consciousness, exalted in moments of illumination but resting at other times in a faith that the "blue sky," in Emerson's words,[10] endures beyond the obscuring veils.

The intuitive revelation of truth possesses a purely formal character, for while, as Emerson notes,[11] it touches all that can transpire in experience, no dimension of experience, no content of experience, follows from it with necessity. The salient characteristic of this intuition is that it yields, not a personal and private and hence solipsistic truth, but a transcendental truth, in a sense reminiscent of, but not formally identifiable with, the Kantian meaning of that term as involving universality (that is, normativeness for all individual subjects), and necessity (that is, as involving in some way the inadmissibility of alternate claims).[12] In the introspective or communicative moment the individual is placed in the presence of, even in a kind of possession of, the Fact, the unalterable and all-grounding Fact, in Emerson's term.[13] This presence or possession of transcendental truth (as transpiring *in* but not issuing *from* the individual) lends to the vision and to the utterance (never perfect or even adequate) of the individual a range and authority far outreaching his personal capacity; indeed it makes these utterances normative for all men. In that moment he becomes, as it were, the *medium* of universal truth in a manner which again recalls Swedenborg and the shades of the wrath of Kant.

That everlasting and transcendent Fact is rendered present to the individual through the contemplation of nature, especially contemplation in solitude. Here it is the testimony of Thoreau that is most weighty. Communion with nature opens consciousness to the sense of the great order which informs nature. By reason of this continuity with nature—his indwelling in nature and nature's indwelling in him—indeed its rising to self-consciousness in him, nature ought to find its fullest realization in the human subject. Nature performs all her works, works all her miracles, produces all her effects by the silent outflow of her power from the secret source which is her essence without reliance on aught but herself. Nature works tranquilly and silently; she multiplies her wonders before our eyes with a flow of spontaneous energy which is neither clamorous nor ostentatious. The secret power and silent creative process of nature is also the secret power and the silent inward creative process of the transcendentalist. The rhythm and silent flow of effortless creative energy revealed in nature is the very pattern upon which he would shape his own life. More precisely, perhaps, the vocation of the transcendentalist is to permit the creative energy of nature to release itself in him. He, too, is nature. He is perhaps nature's highest moment—the moment in which the silent outflow of creative energy reaches its culmination, becoming a conscious, a self-conscious, and not merely a physical or animate law.

What is the effect upon the transcendentalist? With what qualities or properties, what potentialities, does this release of the power and the order of nature endow him? These are, saliently, self-reliance and character—two intimately related, but not identifiable, concepts.

The whole ethics of transcendentalism, Emerson writes, is to be self-dependent, on the model of nature.[14] This self-dependence does not, however, immure the individual in a solipsistic isolation. Rather, it arouses an echo of the Kantian categorical imperative: "To believe your own thought, to believe that what is true for you in your private heart is true for all men—that is genius."[15] This self-reliance is not a form of egotism. The transcendentalist is self-dependent precisely because he is not an egotist. He is self-reliant because he humbly recognizes the universal truth which speaks in him and through him, of which he is the bearer but not the source. The self becomes more truly self, the more it recognizes itself as the seat of the epiphany of this universal truth which both annuls and establishes the self—annuls it egotistically to establish it transcendentally.

This self in its transcendentality is not, in turn, given to man as a sure endowment, an abiding gift, a substantial identity. It is countered by a tendency to fly the true universal which speaks in the secret heart and in the miracles of nature, to hearken to the clamorous voice from without, to the babble of opinion—the false universal of Hegel in one of its aspects.[16] Character, the second pillar of transcendentalist ethics, springs from this dialectic: the tension and distension of the self between inner and outer, between society and solitude. Man achieves character to the degree to which he achieves reliance upon the inner light, the inner voice, and resists temptation to seek truth outside himself, in the clamor of the multivoiced world of opinion. To the degree to which he achieves character, he becomes the lawgiver to himself, not subservient to any outer law.[17]

The crucial test of this view of man and of his access to truth, of the transcendentalist principle, arises at the point at which the self-reliant man leaves his solitude and enters the world of civility, of public truth and action. The most sweeping consequence of this encounter is the ideal dissolution, that is, the dissolution in its idea, of the civil order, or civil society.

Interestingly enough, this consequence is contrary to a first expectation aroused by the transcendentalist principle. The natural expectation is that universal truth, speaking in the private heart (in Emerson's phrase) of each man on issuing into the world of men would find a universal echo and generate that domain of public truth which constitutes the elemental structure of the civil order. Thus a civil world would eventuate, a world of civility, of consensus, founded on the fact that each man, speaking his own, utters also the universal truth. Within the framework of this discourse the institutions of civility, which mediate all claims and obligations and dialectically relate morality and policy, individual and state, would arise. Emerson hints as much in his short verse: "Character":

> He spoke, and words more soft than rain,
> Brought the Age of Gold again,[18]

that golden age which forms one of the most enduring and cherished myths of mankind.

This expectation, however, is frustrated. Carried to its conclusion, the transcendentalist principle effects rather the ideal dissolution of the concept of the civil order, making of that golden age a delusion rather than a myth. Our concern now is with the steps by which this dissolution is effected. These steps involve one by one the processes by which the civil order is constituted and sustained; these are: the public philosophy, history, tradition, and authority. To comprehend more clearly this process of dissolution, it may be worthwhile, before taking up these steps in turn, to delineate more precisely, but briefly, the notion of the civil order, of civility, and its function.

The notion of the civil order rests on the perception of that distinction between morality and policy which Thoreau recognizes. It rests further on the perception that these two factors have a very particular characteristic: they cannot be resolved without residue the one into the other, nor can they exist and function in sheer confrontation or juxtaposition. The reason lies in the fact that they both, morality and policy, come to focus in a single point, human action, alike individual and group, and both establish claims upon and generate obligation, erecting normative principles for such action. Finally, the civil order rests upon the reality of the public sphere, in which the consequences of morality and policy meet and intermingle.

The consequence of this characteristic is that morality and policy must be mediated. The civil order is precisely that order in which such mediation between morality and policy, between individual and state is effected, and effected in such wise that the native autonomy of each and the intricate interplay of both is established. Civility is that condition, or quality, of human association in which such mediation is effected and prevails. Civil wisdom, or prudence, is the process of establishing the principles, norms, and procedures of such mediation between morality and policy and of translating these into the complex institutions of civil society.

It is to be noted that the civil order, while it generates the order of institution, is not to be identified without residue with any particular set of institutions. It is transcendent to all such sets and is the norm by which they are judged in their various qualities. The civil order is essentially an order of principles, the specific force of which is to generate the highly dialectical unity between thought and action under diverse conditions of time and of necessity in such wise that the quality of civility endures through changes. The fact that the civil order is essentially an order of principles does not, however, preclude the quest for the common or normative institutions of civility. This is a quest which has always beguiled philosophers and while the prey is elusive, the quest goes on. The ideal state of Plato, the religion, solemn marriage, and the burial of the dead in the genial insights of Vico, and the many other such insights which history records, are legitimate terms of this quest, though the claims of any one cannot be allowed as absolute.

By reason of its character as a mediatorial process, the notion of the civil order involves certain presuppositions as the basis of its actualization, exhibits certain properties which cannot be destroyed without involving the destruction of that order itself and hence returning morality and policy to that unmediated state in which they confront each other as hostile and mutually exclusive elements. The first of these conditions is the public character of truth and the capacity of establishing a public philosophy on the public character of truth. The second is that the social processes in which this public philosophy is realized exhibit a time-ideal dimension, that is, that the ideality and normative force of the principles of civility emerge in human consciousness and inform human action in an historical process in which the ideal principles and the demands of concrete action are temporarily mediated. History and civility, as Vico has demonstrated, are indissolubly linked. The third condition is tradition. Tradition is the dimension of civility in which the principles established in the time-ideal order of history are given effective continuity and are communicated. Tradition is essentially an economic process; that is, it reduces the mediatorial principles of the civil order to forms in which they can be communicated and perpetuated without a re-enactment of the process by which those principles were formed. Finally, the civil order is marked by the character of authority. Authority is not an unmediated act of will, but an act mediated by the public philosophy.

The transcendentalist principle effects the ideal dissolution of the civil order because its theory of man's access to truth through private revelation (the term is Emerson's own: "We distinguish the announcements of the soul, its manifestations of its own nature, by the term Revelation"; again, "Revelation is the discourse of the soul"[19]) more or less directly undermines each of these elements of the civil order in turn.

In the first place the transcendentalist principle inhibits the formation of a truly public philosophy. Emerson speaks of the encounter of private insight with private insight and their coincidence:

> . . . tomorrow a stranger will say with masterly good sense precisely what we have thought and felt all the time and we shall be forced to take with shame our own opinion from another.[20]

Such coincidence, however, is merely occasionalistic. It does not constitute a public truth because it exhibits no law or principle by which this coincidence is regulated and assured. A public philosophy, such as the civil order requires, demands just such a principle and all the great civil philosophers have directed their enquiries toward the discovery of that principle.

In similar fashion the historical basis of civil order is undermined. No better example of this process can be found, perhaps, than Emerson's own essay on history. While opening the essay with the sage remark that "man is explicable by nothing less than all his history,"[21] as the exposition proceeds, this position is entirely reversed. It proves to be that man, the individual man, in the light of his inner revelation, deciphers history: "Civil and natural history . . . must be explained from individual history or remain mere words. . . ."[22]

The individual gives meaning and reality to history by discovering in it the confirmation of what is original in himself. History is thus transformed from time-ideal process to symbolic enactment of the universal mind present wholly in the individual. From history the individual draws comfort and illumination, but no original truth. The essence of the civil order, however, is the capacity of the time-ideal process of history to generate a normative and mediating truth which is not antecedently accessible to the individual.

The transcendentalist principle, in like manner, transforms tradition from a living mediating force into an incubus upon the individual which alienates him from himself, blinding him to the inner light and burdening him with a dead wisdom which he cannot inform with new life. It forces him to imitate himself and not to live in that eternal present which is the native milieu of the transcendentalist.[23]

This process of the annulment of the elements of the civil order culminates in the rejection of authority. Authority, in the light of the transcendentalist principle, becomes the royal questioner of Diogenes; it stands between him and his sun, the inner light. It is the complete annihilation of his self-dependency, for in the view of the transcendentalist principle authority is the complete other, with which there can be no compromise or conciliation. Authority is the ideally unmediated will of the other and carries with it no warranty from the universal mind. It comes close to being that practical lie of which Emerson speaks, and which has its paradigm in the dogma of Plato's *Republic*.[24]

If this is the process by which the civil order is dissolved in its idea by the transcendentalist principle, what are the consequences of this dissolution? The principal consequences are two: the first is the reduction of the principle of the state as the agent of policy to expediency; the second is the reduction of morality and polity to that original condition of unmediated confrontation and alienation which the civil order was meant to heal.

"Government is at best but an expedient," Thoreau says in the lecture "Resistance to Civil Government."[25] This sentiment becomes the leitmotiv, not only of this, but of all his essays and lectures germane to the question. The state, the institutional agency of government or public policy, does nothing of its own initiative; rather it is an impediment to the initiative of individuals and groups acting on their own.[26] The state is not for all that without a principle of necessity, but this necessity is only the need of the people for some complicated machinery to satisfy their idea of government.[27] The state, despite this necessity, has no ideal principle proper to itself; when its true character is revealed, as in the idea or the practice of majority rule, its only principle proves to be superior force.[28] At best government and the state are an expedient by which men would fain succeed in leaving each other alone; and when government is most expedient, the governed are most let alone by it.[29]

Emerson is no less, but perhaps even more, emphatic in his affirmation of this same idea. For him it is unintelligent brute force which lies at the basis of the society.[30] Society everywhere is in conspiracy against the manhood of every one of its members.[31] Man to be a man must be a nonconformist; no law can be sacred save that which he legislates to himself. The civilized man has built a coach and lost the use of his legs; society is good when it does not violate me, best when it is most like solitude; he who has the Lawgiver (the inner light) may with safety not only neglect, but even contravene, every written commandment; the transcendentalist shuns society and finds his tasks and his amusements in solitude: he is not a good citizen, and Emerson is completely at one with Thoreau in the resounding assertion that the less government the better and that the government is best which governs not at all.[32]

Expressions such as these, reiterating in various ways the single idea of government and of the state as mere expediency, could be multiplied. It is more important, however, to examine the basis and import of this assertion than to review such expressions. What is the essential meaning of expediency in this context and in what sense does it properly define the principle of the state? The reply to this query cannot be drawn from the general language of political thought but must be sought within the proper idiom of transcendentalism.

Expedience in that idiom means an order of thought and action unilluminated by the inner light and hence containing no ideal principle, no gleam of the universal truth. It is thought and action ordered to mere contingency and utility. The opposite of the expedient is the moral, which is the will illuminated by the universal mind. As the state is the organ of expediency, conscience is the organ of moral insight and will. The expedient possesses no ideality in itself; it arises, rather, in those moments of the obscuring of the inner light which we have noted in Emerson's exposition of the transcendentalist principle. When that inner illumination is enkindled anew, the essential unreality of the expedient becomes apparent. In this sense, proper to transcendentalism, the notion of expediency is applicable to the state in two ways. The state is mere expediency in its origin and it is mere expediency in the range of the claims it can make, the obligation it can engender.

Expediency lies at the basis of the state, is its origin, because the realm of morality, of illumination by the inner light of universal mind, contains intrinsic limits. That illumination is given to man, as we have seen, not as a constant and constitutive element of his being, but intermittently in those "gleams of the light within" for which, as Emerson writes, man must watch and which he must learn to detect. It is in the moments of obscurity, induced by the intermittency of this inward illumination, that the expedient appears. Expedience is, therefore, essentially a negative or limiting concept in the transcendentalist context; it is not ideality but the absence of ideality. In these moments of obscurity, of the absence of inner illumination, the expedient appears in two forms, as force and as utility. These, rather than conscience and morality, become in those moments the motive principles of human action, and the state (government) policy is but the institutionalized form of this activity.

For this reason, as Emerson writes,[33] the state is by its nature meant to disappear, as wisdom in the person of the wise man broadens the range of illumination and extends the sway of universal truth, though this disappearance, as Thoreau notes, is a horizon concept, since man has no power to evoke that inner revelation of universal mind. As a consequence the authority of the state is an "impure" one, not a moral authority transcendentally grounded.[34] Policy is the organized form of public action on the ground of expedience, of force and utility, in the absence of the illumination of conscience. The state is the organ of policy. In view of its basis in expediency in this sense Thoreau's notion of the necessity of the state, noted earlier, must be revised. Expedience, the state and government, policy have a deeper necessity than he there assigns them, precisely because of those intrinsic limitations of the inner light. Policy has its necessity in the very dialectic of transcendentality.

The state is mere expediency also in the range of claim it can advance, in the range and quality of the obligation it can engender. Thoreau quotes Paley on this point,[35] though with qualified approval. The state can make no claims upon the individual save those which fall within the range of expediency, which are matters of pure policy, that is, where action is dictated by utility or force and not by the guidance of conscience. Beyond the realm of expedience and the power of the state lies the vast realm of justice, and Thoreau accuses Paley of limiting his vision to that of expedience alone. He is at one with Paley, however, that in this range of expedience the claims of the state are valid. His point ultimately will be that in matters of justice the state cannot prevail; a higher obligation appears which may take the phenomenal form of resistance to the state—a notion which must be clarified.

These reflections lead us to the second consequence of the definition of the state as mere expedience. The situation of direct, unmediated confrontation, between morality and policy is reintroduced. The essential point is that each of these, morality and policy, contains a principle or ground of necessity, and both come to focus at the point of human action. Their direct, unmediated confrontation constitutes the essential ambiguity, the inner tension, of the human situation in the transcendentalist context, because the transcendentalist principle establishes no process of mediation between them. It is Manichean in this aspect, dividing human action into two realms of light and darkness which are essentially at war.

The transcendentalists were most sensitive to the condition of American society. Their animadversions upon it touch the most sensitive points: slavery, the problem of states rights, the emergence of class tensions, and others. It would be an undertaking of considerable interest to review and evaluate these animadversions in detail. Of greater importance for our theme, however, is to try to reach the root criticism and to determine in its light the penetration of transcendentalist criticism into the actual condition and needs of American society.

All of its single criticisms of American society and its political system, which culminate in the extreme statement of Thoreau that a man cannot without disgrace be associated with it,[36] add up to a single censure, which is never stated by the transcendentalist in explicit terms: American society, the American political system, provides no principle for the mediation of morality and policy, conscience and expedience; that is to say, it is unsustained by a civil order. As a consequence, the transcendentalists' assessment of the American system appears astigmatic. Its vision does not come to focus on the true situation of American society, namely, that such a civil order was its basic need, its absence the source of all the flaws they detected in it, and that its internal struggles could be justly evaluated only as efforts to generate such an order. This astigmatism was no accident; it was induced by the transcendentalist principle.

To this point it is the *pars destruens* of the transcendentalist approach to society and politics which has been emphasized: namely, the dissolution of the concept of the civil order, the reduction of the state to expediency (in the transcendentalist sense defined above), the indiscernment of the true situation and basic need of American society. But this *pars destruens* does not exhaust the transcendentalist effort. It too has its *pars construens* in the light of which alone its character can be fully delineated.

The starting point of the *pars construens* of transcendentalism is its recognition that, while morality and policy are, as Thoreau affirms, different and distinct, they cannot be left in that state of hostile confrontation in which the transcendentalist principle has placed them. The mediation of morality and policy, of conscience and expediency, individual and state, is a speculative imperative which transcendentalism accepts. The effort to meet this imperative constitutes the *pars construens* of transcendentalist thought. The fruit of these efforts can be traced in three conceptions of that principle of mediation: the notion of resistance to civil government in Thoreau, the elitism of character, or the wise man, of Emerson, and finally, in the rediscovery of the civil order by Brownson and his effort in *The American Republic* to make it the interpretative key to the true structure and dynamics of the American constitution.

A serious editorial error was committed when the title of Thoreau's celebrated lecture was altered from "Resistance to Civil Government" to "Civil Disobedience." This alteration obscures the force and intent of Thoreau's thought. It slants that intent in a negative direction, toward an ultimate anarchism. The true thrust of Thoreau's thought is positive. It lies in the direction of the discovery of a principle of mediation between morality and policy not toward anarchy. In Thoreau's own words he demands "not at once no government, but *at once* a better government."[37]

The clue to the positive element in Thoreau's position, we believe, is to be found in two passages of the lecture "Resistance to Civil Government." The first is the qualification which he places on Paley's view on civil obligation. The second is the visionary passage with which the same lecture closes. In the first passage he notes: "Paley never appears to have contemplated those cases in which the rule of expediency does not apply, in which a people, as well as an individual, must do justice, come what may."[38] In the second he writes. "I please myself with imagining a state at last which can afford to be just to all men. . . ."[39] Somewhere between these two points the positive emphasis of the notion of resistance to

civil government, that is, its character as a principle of mediation between morality and policy, falls.

To seize this point it is necessary to recur to the transcendentalist
principle itself: that the individual is the repository of the revelation of
universal mind and its truth and that the source of the expediency of the
state lies in the limits inherent in this revelation. The positive duty of the
individual is to make justice prevail over expediency, as the example of
the drowning men illustrates.[40] But what channels are open to him to this
end? One is the path of reform on which Thoreau looks with jaundiced
eye.[41] The other is the path of resistance, which may take either a passive
or an assertive form. While Thoreau himself is little inclined to the latter
in any extreme form, his impassioned apology for John Brown is proof
that for him even violence can be a justifiable form of resistance.[42]

Resistance, however, is but a phenomenal form. It is the form in
which, under the given condition that the higher truth is revealed to the
individual, that truth can be made to appear as the transcendental limit
to the expediency of the state. But the noumenal principle of resistance
is the extension of that universal truth. The positive function of resistance is not to pose a limit to the state as expedience, but to release the
power of truth into the realm of policy. Gandhi, whose debt to Thoreau
has often been remarked and explicitly acknowledged by himself, interpreted resistance in this fashion. He recognized the phenomenal form
of resistance, seeing behind it and informing it, a positive principle, his
own notion of "Satyagraha," the "force of truth."[43] Resistance to civil government is the channel for the release of this force of truth into the world
of policy. It brings the moral conscience to bear upon the calculations
of expediency and extends the realm of universal mind and its truth beyond the limits inherent in the basic mode of its revelation to the individual. Actually, resistance is positive, for it opposes force to force, the
force of truth to that brute force in which, as Emerson says, the ultimate
basis of the state is to be found. Conscience and expediency, morality
and policy, individual and state are thus mediated, though the form of
mediation is tense and falls short of synthesis.

The negative attitude of Emerson toward the state, harsh as it at
times appears, is, nevertheless, only the obverse side of his integral position. The positive aspect of his thought is an effort to establish a principle
of mediation between morality and policy. This principle takes the form
of his concept of the elitism of character and of the myth of the wise
man. The state will take on moral stature and become a moral force from
a merely brute force, its enactments will reflect the illumination of universal truth rather than the dictates of mere expediencey, when character
prevails in public life, when the wise man and the man of policy are one.
The passage in which this conception is expounded deserves to be

quoted directly, for no paraphrase can achieve the suavity of Emerson's own expression:

> Hence the less government we have the better—the fewer laws and the less confided power. The antidote to this abuse of formal government is the influence of private character, the growth of the individual; the appearance of the principle to supersede the proxy; the appearance of the wise man, of whom the existing government is, it must be owned, but a shabby imitation. That which all things tend to educe; which freedom, cultivation, intercourse, revolutions, go to form and deliver is character; that is the end of Nature, to reach unto this coronation of her king. To educate the wise man the State exists, and with the appearance of the wise man the State expires. The appearance of character makes the State unnecessary. The wise man is the State. . . . The power of love, as the basis of a state, has never been tried. . . . According to the order of nature . . . it stands thus; there will always be a government of force where men are selfish; and when they are pure enough to abjure the code of force they will be wise enough to see how . . . public ends . . . can be answered. . . . There is not, among the most religious and instructed men of the most religious and civil nations, a reliance on the moral sentiment and a sufficient belief in the unity of things, to persuade them that society can be maintained without artificial restraints as well as the solar system. . . .[44]

This is his version of the reign of the philosopher-king. In a sense this vision goes beyond mediation, or more accurately perhaps, reaches the state of pure mediation in the reign of love.

The flaw in this vision is apparent and not unlike the flaw which mars its remote prototype: the reign of the philosopher-king in Plato. This flaw is a circularity which negates the power of the original assertion. Emerson holds that the total mediation of morality and policy would flow from the presence and sway of the wise man, and the state would be thus redeemed from its condition of expediency, not in the half-hearted manner of the reformers (all of whom admit in some manner the supremacy of the bad state[45]) but completely. At the same time he holds that "to educate the wise man the State exists, and with the appearance of the wise man the State expires"[46]. The state must educate the wise man and in that very process prepare its own demise and dissolution. This circularity is paradoxical. Whence would the state, at whose basis lies brute power and whose whole principle is expediency, draw the resources to educate the wise man? Does not the notion of the self-dissolution of the state violate the deeper law of power (to which theorists of politics almost unanimously attest), namely, that power ends not only to preserve itself but to extend its sway? The presence of the wise man is the precondition of the state's transformation from force and expediency; yet the state itself has the mission of forming the wise man. The remedy of this paradoxical circularity is nowhere to be found in Emerson. The positive thrust of his thought, nevertheless, appears here: It is to find a principle by which the stark confrontation of morality and policy, of conscience and expediency, of state and individual, is mediated.

The strength of a philosophical system is evidenced nowhere so clearly as in its capacity for self-criticism. By this standard transcendentalism must be recognized as a strong system, for in the thought of Orestes Brownson it exhibits this capacity in a marked degree. From within transcendentalism itself Brownson initiates a process of criticism of its principle, which leads eventually to a recovery of the concept of the civil order as the mediating principle of morality and policy, of the relation between citizen and state. This recovery is effected through the reestablishment of those principles, public truth, history, tradition, and authority, upon which civil society rests. In another context the effort has been made to retrace the stages through which these principles are reestablished by Brownson.[47] In the present context, it would seem more relevant to indicate briefly the way in which Brownson invokes the notion of the civil order, of civil society, in his theory of the American polity and its constitution, because in this theory all of those principles are seen at work.

The crux of Brownson's theory of the American constitution lies in his distinction between the written and the "unwritten" constitution.[48] It is a fallacy, to which the founding fathers of the Republic, in Brownson's view, had fallen victim, to imagine that the Republic rests upon the written constitution, that it has been called into being by an act of convention or contract. The act of convention, from which the written constitution eventuates is preceded by a process far more profound, the establishment of the American people or *civil society*.[49]

This people, or *civil society*, is to be distinguished both from the government and from the abstract individual, whose notion underlay the theory of the origin of the nation by convention. Government is rather the ordination of civil society.[50] The formation of civil society is a long and complex historical process. Only the historical identity thus established empowers the sovereign people, civil society, to establish in turn the constitution of government and the status of the individual as citizen. This civil society establishes both state and citizen in their respective autonomy and in their relationships vis-à-vis each other and mediates the interplay of claim and obligation between them. The function of civil society is to secure at once the authority of the public order and the freedom of the individual citizen, the sovereignty of the people without social despotism and individual freedom without anarchy.[51] Its function is to bring into dialectical union authority and liberty, the natural rights of man and the rights of society.[52]

A constitution in which this ideal has been realized has not, before the American experience, appeared in history. Ancient republics asserted the state to the detriment of the individual; modern republics either repeat this error or assert the individual to the detriment of the state. It is the particular mission, providentially ordained, of the American republic to actualize this ideal, to realize in its polity the freedom of each, individual and state, with advantage to the other.[53]

This unique character and mission of the United States has been overlooked and misunderstood by the great majority even of our own statesmen.[54] Indeed, the very men who composed the written constitution exhibit this lack of understanding. They misprised the character of their own action; as a consequence, the theoretical concepts by which they sought to explain and justify that action and define its consequences cannot be taken as clues to the interpretation of the constitution.[55] This miscomprehension can be traced to no other source than a failure to understand the notion of civil society, the historical process which gives rise to it, and the exclusive capacity with which it is endowed to establish both government and citizen. Through this civil order alone can their respective claims and the respective claims of morality and policy be mediated, for it is the civil order which establishes each and defines their respective spheres.

A dual weakness, consequently, seems to afflict the political and social thought of transcendentalism as represented by Thoreau and Emerson. The first is a deficiency at the level of theory, the second, at the level of the concrete analysis and evaluation of the American experience. These deficiencies are closely related.

At the level of theory, the elaboration of the basic principle of transcendentalism—its theory of man's access to truth—leads to serious imbalance and internal divorcement among the elements: citizens, civil society, and state. Individual and state are brought into sharp confrontation because of the absence of a valid principle of mediation. This line of thought leads in turn to the concept of the state as pure expediency, harboring no ideal principle in itself. Classically, this principle of mediation is the civil order, civil society. The transcendentalist theory of Thoreau and Emerson leaves the concept of the civil order undeveloped; it is forced to excogitate alternate principles of mediation on whatever basis the transcendentalist principle could provide.

This theoretical deficiency or limitation accounts for the corresponding limitation at the level of the concrete assessment and characterization of the American polity. A more nearly adequate conception of the civil order would have indicated to Thoreau and Emerson at what point the actual weakness of American polity lay; namely, that it had not, after its revolutionary origins (which, in the last analysis, could only be justified on the basis of a sound notion of the civil order) adequately comprehended its civil origins and that the real task before it was to redefine its own character on the basis of that order. Only thus could it truly understand the perplexing and harassing problems which bedeviled it, specifically those of slavery and states rights.

The political and social thought of Brownson, specifically his theory of the American polity, suggests itself as an effort, with its roots in transcendentalism itself, to correct both these deficiencies. Brownson, through his critique of the transcendentalist principle, rediscovered the concept of the civil order with its constitutive and mediating functions. On this basis he was able to offer an assessment of the American experience and a theory of the American polity in which the sharp unmediated confrontations of transcendentalist theory were transcended and the speciously conflicting claims of state and individual, conscience and policy, reconciled.

Notes

1. "Will mankind never learn that politics is not morality?" in "Slavery in Massachusetts" in *The Writings of Henry David Thoreau, Reform Papers*, ed. Wendell Glick (Princeton: Princeton University Press, 1973), p. 104 (hereafter cited as *Reform Papers*).

2. *Transcendentalism in New England* (New York: Putnams, 1876).

3. "His thought—*that* is the universe. His experience inclines him to behold the procession of facts you call the world as flowing perpetually outward from an invisible, unsounded centre in himself, centre alike of him and of them, and necessitating him to regard all things as having a subjective or relative existence, relative to that aforesaid Unknown Centre of him" ("The Transcendentalist" in *Essays and Poems*, ed. G. F. Maine [London: Collins, 1965], p. 299 [hereafter cited as *Essays and Poems*]).

4. Cf. Norman Foerster, *Nature in American Literature* (New York: Macmillan, 1923), p. 101. "Thus it was not to study the fauna and flora of Middlesex County that Thoreau spent his life. . . . What . . . brought him out in all weathers . . . was the mystic's hope of detecting 'some trace of the Ineffable.' . . . This Izaak Walton of the soul" (p. 102).

5. Cf. "The Transcendentalist," *Essays and Poems*, pp. 301–302, for Kant; p. 300 for Jacobi; and Frothingham, *Transcendentalism*, Ch. 1–5 inclusive.

6. Cf. Immanuel Kant, *Dreams of a Ghost-seer Explained by the Dreams of a Metaphysician* (1766).

7. "The Moral Insight of Swedenborg, the correction of popular errors, the announcement of ethical laws take him out of comparison with any other modern writer, and entitle him to a place, vacant for some ages, among the lawgivers of mankind" in *Representative Men* ("Swedenborg: The Mystic," *Essays and Poems*, p. 364).

8. Cf. Lewis White Beck, *Early German Philosophy: Kant and His Predeces-

sors (Cambridge: Harvard University Press, 1969), passim but especially Ch. 8, Part 2, and Ch. 17, Part 3.

9. Cf. "The Transcendentalist," *Essays and Poems*, p. 307.

10. "What am I? What but a thought of serenity and independence, an abode in the deep blue sky? Presently, the clouds shut down again; yet we retain the belief that this pretty web we weave will at last be overshot and reticulated with veins of blue. . . . Patience . . . is for us. . . . Patience, and still patience" ("The Transcendentalist," *Essays and Poems*, pp. 307–308).

11. *Essays and Poems.*

12. For the Kantian sense of transcendentality, cf. Beck, *Early German Philosophy*, pp. 409–437, passim, especially pp. 413–414.

13. ". . . I feel like other men my relation to that Fact which cannot be spoken, or defined, or even thought, but which exists and will exist" ("The Transcendentalist," *Essays and Poems*, p. 299).

14. "From this transfer of the world into consciousness, this beholding all things in the mind, follows easily his whole ethics. It is simply to be self-dependent" ("The Transcendentalist," *Essays and Poems*, p. 299).

15. "Self-Reliance," *Essays and Poems*, p. 38.

16. "I was at my old tricks, the selfish member of a selfish society. . . . I wish to exchange this flash-of-lightning faith for continuous daylight, this fever glow for a benign climate" ("The Transcendentalist," *Essays and Poems*, p. 307). For the "false universal" in Hegel cf. J. N. Findlay, *The Philosophy of Hegel* (New York: Collier Books, 1966), pp. 227–230.

17. "No law can be sacred to me but that of my nature" ("Self-Reliance," *Essays and Poems*, p. 40).

18. "Character," *Essays and Poems*, p. 501.

19. "The Oversoul," *Essays and Poems*, pp. 136–137.

20. "Self-Reliance," *Essays and Poems*, p. 38.

21. "History," *Essays and Poems*, p. 21.

22. "History," *Essays and Poems*, p. 27.

23. "What have I to do with the sacredness of tradition, if I live wholly from within?" ("Self-Reliance," *Essays and Poems*, p. 40).

24. Cf. *Essays and Poems*, p. 262.

25. "Resistance to Civil Government," *Reform Papers*, p. 63.

26. "This government never of itself furthered any enterprise, but by the alacrity with which it got out of its way" ("Resistance to Civil Government," *Reform Papers*, p. 64).

27. "But it is not the less necessary for this; for the people must have some complicated machinery or other, and hear its din" ("Resistance to Civil Government," *Reform Papers*, pp. 63–64).

28. "After all . . . when . . . a majority are permitted . . . to rule, [it] is not because they are most likely to be in the right . . . but because they are physically the strongest" ("Resistance to Civil Government," *Reform Papers*, p. 64).

29. "Resistance to Civil Government," *Reform Papers*, p. 64. The Paley quoted on p. 67 by Thoreau is William Paley (1743–1805), British theologian and moralist (*Principles of Moral and Political Philosophy* [1785]).

30. "Self-Reliance," *Essays and Poems*, p. 43.

31. "Self-Reliance," *Essays and Poems*, p. 40.

32. Cf. for Emerson, *Essays and Poems*, pp. 40, 55, 299, 300, 302, 305, 366; for Thoreau, *Reform Papers*, p. 63.

33. Cf. *Essays and Poems*, p. 263.

34. Cf. *Reform Papers*, p. 89.

35. Cf. "Resistance to Civil Government," *Reform Papers*, pp 67–68.

36. "How does it to become a man to behave toward this American government today? I answer that he cannot without disgrace be associated with it" ("Resistance to Civil Government," *Reform Papers*, p. 67).

37. "But to speak practically and as a citizen, unlike those who call themselves no-government men, I ask for, not at once no government, but *at once* a better government" ("Resistance to Civil Goverment," *Reform Papers*, p. 64).

38. "Resistance to Civil Government," *Reform Papers*, p. 68.

39. "Resistance to Civil Government," *Reform Papers*, p. 90.

40. "Resistance to Civil Government," *Reform Papers*, p. 68.

41. Cf. "Reform and Reformers," *Reform Papers*, pp. 181–197; "The Reformer, the impersonation of disorder and imperfection" (p. 182); "The modern Reformers are a class of *improvvisánti* more wonderful and amusing than the Italians" (p. 185).

42. Cf. *Reform Papers*, pp. 111ff, especially p. 124.

43. For Gandhi, cf. B. R. Nanda, *Mahatma Gandhi: A Biography* (Boston: Beacon, 1958); Horace Alexander, *Gandhi Through Western Eyes* (New York: Asia Publishing House, 1969); E. H. Erikson, *Gandhi's Truth: On the Origins of Militant Non-violence* (New York: W. W. Norton, 1969).

44. Cf. *Essays and Poems*, pp. 263, 264.

45. Cf. *Essays and Poems*, p 265.

46. Cf. *Essays and Poems*, p. 263.

47. Cf. A. Robert Caponigri, "Brownson and Emerson: Race and History," *American Transcendentalism*, ed. Brian M. Barbour (Notre Dame: University of Notre Dame Press, 1973); Thomas I. Cooke and Arnaud B. Leavelle, "Orestes A. Brownson's *The American Republic*," *Review of Politics*, 4 (January, April 1942), 77–90, 173–193.

48. "The constitution of the United States is twofold: written and unwritten, the constitution of the people and the constitution of the government" (Brownson, *The American Republic*, ed. Americo D. Lapati [New Haven: College and University Press, 1972], p. 143 [hereafter cited as *American Republic*]).

49. "The constitution of the people as one people . . . precedes the convention and it is the unwritten constitution, the providential constitution of the American people or civil society, as distinguished from the constitution of the government, which . . . is the ordination of civil society. . . . The unwritten constitution is the creation or constitution of the sovereign [people] . . . which constitutes, in turn, the government . . . which is clothed with just so much . . . authority as the sovereign . . . ordains" (*American Republic*, p. 156).

50. Cf. *American Republic*, p. 156.

51. "Secures . . . the true idea of the state which secures at once the authority of the public and the freedom of the individual—the sovereignty of the people without social despotism and individual freedom without anarchy" (*American Republic*, p. 33).

52. *American Republic*, p. 33.

53. "The Greek and Roman Republics asserted the state to the detriment of individual freedom; modern republics either do the same or assert individual freedom to the detriment of the state. The American republic has been instituted by Providence to realize the freedom of each with advantage to the other" (*American Republic*, p. 33).

54. *American Republic*, p. 33.

55. "But the philosophy, the theory of government, the understanding of the

framers of the constitution, 'must be considered . . . *obiter dicta.* . . . Their political philosophy, their political theory . . . forms no rule for interpreting their work. Their work was inspired by and accords with the historical fact and is authorized and explained by them" (*American Republic*, p. 155). (One recalls the *"ipsis rebus dictantibus"* of Tacitus and Vico and the *"come stanno le cose"* of Machiavelli.)

"The Ideology of Brook Farm"

Richard Francis*

It is difficult to define exactly what one means when referring to the phenomenon of New England Transcendentalism. Hawthorne well illustrates the movement's paradoxical combination of bulk and intangibility when he portrays Giant Transcendentalist in "The Celestial Rail-road" as "a heap of fog and duskiness."[1] A more recent student, William R. Hutchison, points out in his book *The Transcendentalist Ministers* that a description broad enough to accommodate the full complexity of the movement will also admit "all philosophical idealists from Plato through Bradley," while any attempt to be more specific will tend to disqualify various of the active participants: and he mentions that Orestes Brownson, Thedore Parker, Bronson Alcott, and even Ralph Waldo Emerson himself, have suffered this fate at different hands.[2] It is obviously much easier to make certain assumptions about the movement than to attempt a satisfactory definition of it. This can be an equally dangerous activity, however. Two of the most common assumptions about the Transcendentalists are that they were individualists, and that they tended to adopt a stance of genteel Bostonian aloofness toward society at large. Clearly there is a substantial amount of evidence to support these closely related points of view; and yet the picture they give us of the movement is not, finally, an accurate or even a helpful one. The Brook Farm experiment provides a perfect example of the difficulties such preconceptions can get us into.

One can easily establish that Brook Farm was born out of the authentic Transcendentalist impulse; the problem here is one of mapping the community's later route. The best way of validating the community's original claims is to sidestep the vexed question of ideology for a moment, and to follow Hutchison's example by pointing toward the participants involved. George Ripley, the founder and leader of the movement, had unchallengeable Transcendentalist qualifications. He had been one of the

*Reprinted from *Studies in the American Renaissance 1977*, ed. Joel Myerson (Boston: Twayne, 1978), pp. 1–48. A section dealing with William Henry Channing (pp. 31–41) and two photographs have been omitted.

leading campaigners in the attack on Andrews Norton and orthodox Unitarianism since what Perry Miller calls the "annus mirabilis" of 1836; indeed his review of Martineau's *Rationale of Religious Enquiry*, published in the *Christian Examiner* during that year, was one of the central documents of the miracles controversy.[3] He was one of the four graduates who originated the idea of the Transcendental Club during the bicentennial celebrations—also in 1836—of Harvard College.[4] It is true that when the Club heard his plan for a community in October 1840, the interest expressed by the members present was not supplemented by active support.[5] However, many other prominent Transcendentalists involved themselves in the community to a greater or lesser extent. John Sullivan Dwight, who had begun his career as a Unitarian minister and who was destined to become the most influential music critic in America; George P. Bradford, another disillusioned minister; and the young G. W. Curtis were among the members of the community, while William Henry Channing, nephew of the great Unitarian divine and precursor of Transcendentalism, William Ellery Channing, played an important part in its development, as we shall see later, even though he never took up full-time residence at the Farm. Margaret Fuller's younger brother and the children of George Bancroft and Orestes Brownson boarded at the Farm and attended the school. Theodore Parker had the neighboring parish of West Roxbury until 1845, and was frequently calling upon his friend Ripley. Emerson, Bronson Alcott and his English colleague Charles Lane, Fuller, Brownson, and C. P. Cranch were among the many visitors.[6]

However, once scholars have accepted that Brook Farm was a manifestation of Transcendentalism, they have had some difficulty in coming to terms with the implications of its conversion to the doctrines of the French utopian thinker, Charles Fourier, in 1844. The problem revolves round the question of the Farmers' commitment to social reform. Put crudely, the difficulty seems to be this: if the community was a thoroughgoing Transcendentalist enterprise, then it had no business allying itself with a movement that aimed at complete (not to say half-baked) social reorganization. Alternatively, if the Farm is accepted as being sincerely committed to the establishment of a new order, then its links with Transcendentalism must be seen as rather tenuous, the result of a kind of historical and geographical coincidence.

Charles Crowe, in his excellent biography of George Ripley, inclines toward the latter view. He takes for granted that Ripley and the others were sincere in their desire to reestablish the whole of society on a different basis. He provides us with a well-balanced account of the history of the experiment, and devotes a chapter to showing how much time and energy the leading members of the community allocated to the administration and publicization of Fourierism on a national scale, and to allied radical movements like the National (Land) Reformers and the "Cooperators."[7] At the same time, he regards Transcendentalism and individualism as synonymous, and therefore detects a contradiction, or at least an inner tension, in the ideology of the Brook Farmers. "If they embraced Fourierism completely," he asks, "what became of the much-vaunted Transcendentalist individualism?"[8] His answer is, very little. He implies a development from Transcendentalism toward social radicalism and indeed, in an earlier article, he claims that the "ideology of the Brook Farm leaders was from the beginning closer to Fourierism than to Trancendentalism."[9] While we are invited to consider the members as serious social reformers, therefore, we are for that very reason expected to conclude that they had in some way grown out of their earlier allegiances. We are left with a feeling that something fortuitous and unexpected has happened—that a group of Transcendentalists has revealed much more sense of responsibility than we, or they, thought they possessed.

Perry Miller in effect agrees with this verdict—although his allegiances are different from Crowe's. In one of the connecting passages of his anthology *The Transcendentalists* he claims that "Nobody knows what went on in Ripley's mind as he consented, by 18 January 1844, to change Brook Farm from a Transcendental picnic into a regimented Phalanx." He goes on to quote Lindsay Swift to the effect that Ripley must have come "to lay more stress on the method by which individual freedom was to become assured, than on the fact of personal liberty in itself."[10] In other words, the Farmers have given up their privileged and charming existence and for no good reason have imposed upon themselves a disciplined and even constricting way of life. Miller and Swift disapprove; Crowe applauds. But the three commentators agree that Transcendentalism and Fourierism do not really mix. This alleged incompatibility reflects no credit on either party. The assumption is either that the Transcendentalists were too frivolous, or that Fourierism was inhuman and bizarre—Miller describes the Brook Farm Phalanx as sitting "foreign and forlorn in West Roxbury."[11]

Neither charge is altogether baseless. It is clear that the Brook Farmers tended to have a good time, as Charles Lane's jaundiced account reveals when he describes going with Alcott "one evening to Roxbury where there are 80 to 90 persons playing away their youth and daytime in a miserably joyous and frivolous manner."[12] At the same time it is easy to find something at least un-American about the further reaches of Fourier's imagination—his notion that the seas will eventually change into lemonade, for example, or that a supple and elastic anti-lion will one day take people on long journeys at high speed.[13] We could, perhaps, total the main objections to the reconciliation of Fourierism with Transcendentalism by claiming that the escapism of the Brook Farmers, and the insane fanaticism of the proto-socialist were opposites which would naturally repel each other.

They did not, however, and for a number of very good reasons. For one: throughout its history Brook Farm represented a sincere attempt to remove social injustice. It was, it is true, a middle-class enterprise in its conception and realization, a joint-stock company rather than a communist society. Like most attempts at reform via utopia, it was the inspiration of those with adequate means and education. But during both its phases it represented bourgeois ideals at their most generous: it was an attempt to extend the ranks, not to defend them. Moreover, the community's conversion into a phalanx was a perfectly logical development, and it can be understood not merely in the light of the social commitment of the Transcendentalists, but in that of their psychological, historical, and even religious preoccupations as well. A close examination of Fourier's basic ideas reveals that there are a number of inner connections between them and the beliefs of the Transcendentalists generally. Fourier's plan of labor organization locked much more neatly than might be expected into the pattern of behavior—of both work and play—that can be detected at the Farm during its earlier phase. Moreover—and this of course is a closely related point—his analysis of human identity, both individual and social, was closer than it might appear to certain lines of Transcendentalist inquiry, and it provided a relevant solution to some of the paradoxes encountered in the latter. Similarly, Fourier's account of the historical process chimed in harmoniously with a particular trend in the Transcendentalists' thinking of the subject.

Of course, Fourierism could not be swallowed by the Farmers in one monolithic mouthful—although Fourier himself, along with his American disciple, Albert Brisbane, took a firm take-it-or-leave-it attitude to prospective adherents. Despite their protestations, the Farmers were not quite able to accept Fourier's sternly utilitarian pursuit of happiness at all costs. Nevertheless, and this is probably as good a testimonial as any, Fourierism proved that it could accommodate a moral superstructure. The work of William Henry Channing—not a member, but an important influence on the intellectual and religious life of the community—shows perhaps better than any of the rather thin contemporary material pertaining to the experiment, how Fourierism looked to formerly Unitarian eyes.

In 1895 Charles Anderson Dana, then an old and famous journalist and reactionary, was invited by the University of Michigan to give an address on Brook Farm. He had joined the community as a young man in 1841, after his eyesight had been damaged by an overindulgence in Dickens while a Harvard student. He rapidly became Ripley's right-hand man and was one of the most important members of the Farm throughout almost the whole of its history. He was therefore well qualified to pass a verdict, and his later career as an aggressive polemicist for the political right indicates that he was under no temptation to exaggerate the community's reforming verve. And yet he is unequivocal in his judgment that the initial impulse and central doctrine of Brook Farm was an egalitarian one. The community was an essay in applied democracy:

> In this party of Transcendental philosophers the idea early arose— it was first stated by Mr. George Bancroft, the historian . . . that democracy, while it existed in the Constitution of the United States, while it had triumphed as a political party under Jefferson, and while it was then in possession of a majority of the governments of the States, and at times of the government of the United States, was not enough. . . . If democracy was the sublime truth which it was held up to be, it should be raised up from the sphere of politics, from the sphere of law and constitutions; it should be raised up into life and made social.[14]

Of course, there is no way of fully substantiating this claim that the Farm represented a deliberate and consistent attempt to interweave democratic ideals into the very texture of social life. To do so would require the kind of empirical approach that historians simply cannot achieve. It is impossible to know what the day-to-day experience of the Farmers was like—how, in the impromptu moment, the different elements of their society really treated each other. It certainly appears that from the beginning there were serious problems. Ora Gannet Sedgwick, who was present during the first years as a boarder at the school, unconsciously reveals the patronization and tension that must have been current during the pre-Fourierist period:

> Besides those whom I have mentioned others joined us, with well-trained hands, but not of such good New England blood. I recall among them two Irishwomen, one of whom, a fine cook, had lived with the Danas and others of the best families of Boston. This woman came to Brook Farm for the sake of her beautiful young daughter, an only child, who looked like a madonna and possessed much native delicacy. Her mother was desirous that she should be well educated. These women were perfectly welcome to sit at the table with us all, but they preferred not to sit down until the two courses had been put upon the table, if at all.[15]

The scope for the kind of unpleasant situation that Sedgwick describes was of course widened by the change to Fourierism. A certain amount of reshuffling inevitably occurred, and one assumes that among the departing were included the more troglodytic of the middle-class members.[16] However, the influx of a high proportion of "mechanics," as they were usually described, in turn served to increase the potential for social unrest. The adult male signatories of the Fourierist Constitution of 11

February 1844, which is now in the possession of the Massachusetts Historical Society, were required to record their previous work. Of the forty-nine occupations listed, there were two clergymen, three teachers, one student, one attorney-at-law, one clerk, and one broker. All the remaining previously employed members had been tradespeople, artisans, and laborers.[17] Some kind of class confrontation was at least in the cards, and if Arthur Sumner, who was about sixteen at the time, is to be trusted, the internecine social conflict rose for a time to a fairly serious level:

> Soon after this Fourierist agitation began, some very unpleasant people appeared upon the scene. They seemed to us boys to be discontented mechanics. They soon fell into a group by themselves. After dinner, they would collect together in the great barn, and grumble; and when the others passed through, the malcontents eyed them with suspicion, and muttered, "Aristocrats!" All because they knew themselves to be less cultivated and well-bred.

He adds innocently, "Yet there was the kindest feeling of brotherhood among the members; and it did not need that a man should be a scholar and a gentleman to be received and absorbed."[18]

A more mature and perhaps more representative attitude is provided by Marianne Dwight, sister of J. S. Dwight, in a letter to her friend Anna Q. T. Parsons. She is describing the wife of one of the community's carpenters, a Mrs. Cheswell, who was pregnant at the time:

> We have noble spirits here at Brook Farm. I have been much affected lately, by the noble devotedness of our good Mrs. Cheswell. This coarse woman, as I once thought her, and as she was, is really becoming very charming—a most zealous and untiring worker, full of nobleness and enthusiasm in a good cause, sweet and cheerful too, so that it does one good to look upon her. In her, we see what Association is going to do for the uneducated and rude.[19]

It is clear that working-class members were not to be accepted on their own terms. They were, however, to be accepted—and then manipulated and "improved" until they became more nearly the social equals of the middle-class members. Marianne Dwight is writing in 1845, a year into the Fourierist period, but her assumptions are those on which the community had rested from the beginning. They are stated in 1842 by the "distinguished literary lady" whose report on the Farm, together with an introduction by Orestes Brownson, appeared in the *Democratic Review* for November of that year. The Brook Farmers, we find, are not hastening, lemming-like, toward a social lowest common denominator; instead, "true democratic equality may be obtained by *levelling up*, instead of *levelling down*."[20]

It is easy to see this aspiration as an example of Brahminesque paternalism at its most naïve. From our present perspective we cannot automatically achieve imaginative sympathy with an egalitarian ideal that involves the extension, rather than the questioning, of bourgeois values. And yet an examination of the Brook Farm material reveals not merely that the members were dedicated to this cause, but also that their commitment involved a certain amount of courage, and the sense that they were taking up a revolutionary stance.

The school provides an excellent example of Brook Farm's good intentions, and its problems, since quite apart from being, throughout the history of the community, the most important of its "industries," it was also the one which involved the most give-and-take with the outside world. It provided education for children from four to college level; students could select the courses of study they wanted to take (the possibilities ranged from agriculture to "Intellectual and Natural Philosophy"); and it was a basic principle of the school that mental and manual labor should be combined.[21] Naturally, a progressive institution of this sort tended to attract parents who were themselves well educated, but this was certainly not exclusively the case. We have already seen in the Ora Gannet Sedgwick passage that the madonna-like daughter of the Irish cook had been brought to the Farm to get an education. A couple of months after the conversion to Fourierism, Charles Anderson Dana stated the principles of the school in his address to the General Convention of the Friends of Association in the United States (4 April 1844). It is clear that he is describing, not a new theory, but established policy. He affirms that every child, irrespective of his social and financial background, is entitled to a complete education at Brook Farm. Moreover, "It is not doled out to him as though he was a pupil of orphan assylums [sic] and almshouses—not as the cold benefice and bounty of the world—but as his right—a right conferred upon him by the very fact that he is born into this world a human being—and here we think we have made great advances."[22]

That these words are more than oratorical liberalism is implied in some interesting comments by James Kay of Philadelphia, one of the Farm's most important supporters and Ripley's business adviser. In a letter to J. S. Dwight dated 10 May 1844, he offers some proposals designed to aid the community in its fight for survival. He urges that the school should dismiss (among others) "those 3 or 4" pupils who are receiving board and education at half price. The numbers might seem rather insignificant, although it must be remembered that the older children could work in exchange for their education anyway (and their contribution perhaps represented a higher value in principle than in hard cash). Certainly Kay sees the assistance provided as a blind defiance of the rules of success ("No business in civilization could withstand such a drain").[23] However, his real worry becomes evident when he turns to a rather different question:

> I have one remark more to make, and that is, respecting the presence of impure children. My views, I know, are well understood; but I must claim the privilege of friendship to insist on them—if you will, "in season & out of season." Little importance as you attach to them, I am a true prophet when I say, that indifference or contumacy in this matter will break you down, if all other conditions were excellent. You cannot know how much harm has been done to you from this cause already; nor do you seem to be aware that the public are perhaps over-well informed of past events. I have heard much from time to time on the subject in Massachusetts; and strange as it may seem, more than a few here are better informed than they are willing to say. I know not where or from whom they procured their knowledge or whether it is of truth; but the story is here. I say that this enormous evil ought to be abated.[24]

It is clear that Kay is alarmed because his son is a fellow pupil of these undesirables, and also annoyed that the Farmers have ignored his previous remonstrances on the subject. But even taking these two provocations into account, his expression still seems unduly violent and testifies to the amount of popular hostility, in this and other respects, that the community must have had to face. His mention of impurity, of "enormous evil," his setting himself up as a "true prophet," implies that much more than economic efficiency, mere success, is at stake. His language is that of a man afraid in the presence of radical social change—of a man who views association from a certain aesthetic distance. In an earlier letter, he expressed his admiration of the new Fourierist constitution, "the beautiful structure which you have erected." He goes on to claim that "If it were simply a literary exercise, with no particular object, it would win universal applause for its author."[25] We get the picture of a dilettante at bay—a picnicking Brook Farmer. Kay, however, was a valetudinarian publisher from Philadelphia, and not a member of the community. Amelia Russell, who really had been one, confirms that he was not letting his imagination run away with him—talking of public suspicion of the school she says:

> People were shy of us; we were supposed to nourish some very fantastic views which encroached much on the decencies of society. I will not enumerate all the absurd stories which were circulated with regard to us; and although our outside friends, who still continued to feel an interest in us, paid no heed to these ridiculous inventions, there were thousands who looked upon us as little less than heathens, who had returned to a state of semi-barbarism.[26]

It is clear that the Brook Farmers were willing, for the sake of their ideals, to take a certain number of risks, to occupy exposed ground.[27] Perhaps the reason why they have never really been given the benefit of the doubt—why, apart from the relevant chapters in Crowe's book, no serious and sustained treatment of the enterprise has been published since 1900[28]— is that there is so little primary material which sets out the aims and achievements of Brook Farm. Amelia Russell, writing on the *Home Life of the Brook Farm Association* more than thirty years after its collapse, poses a problem noticed by Hawthorne in his Preface to the *Blithedale Romance*[29] and by many of the other less important members when the time came for them to pen their memoirs:

> I cannot understand why no one of those who better comprehended all the machinery which kept the wheels going through many trying vicissitudes (though I suspect sometimes the operators themselves felt doubtful how it was done) has ever brought its interior life to view, since a real history of its aims and endeavours after a truer life has been asked for.[30]

Some years later, Arthur Sumner suggested that the cause of this lapse was "that it never had any result except upon the individual lives of those who dwelt there."[31] It is an answer that certainly plays into the hands of those who wish to see the community as symptomatic of a kind of death-wish, an attempt to "banish the world,"[32] particularly as he goes on to say: "It was a beautiful idyllic life which we led, with plenty of work and play and transcendentalism; and it gave place to the Roxbury poor-house."[33]

The opposition established between "transcendentalism" and the "Roxbury poorhouse" is a suggestive one, but Sumner's explanation is not entirely satisfactory. For one thing, even in 1841 there were complaints that Ripley was not being audible enough on the subject of the experiment. In a letter to John Sullivan Dwight (who had not yet become a member) written in June of that year, a couple of months after the community was inaugurated, Elizabeth Palmer Peabody remarks of Ripley: "He enjoys the '*work*' so much that he does not clearly see that his plan is not in the way of being demonstrated any farther than that it is being made evident."[34] Moreover, although there were over six hundred articles by Brook Farmers in the *Harbinger*, a Fourierist journal which was published by the community every week between June 1845 and June 1847, only two give a direct account of Brook Farm, and they concern the calamitous destruction by fire of the nearly completed phalanstery in 1846.[35] This policy of omission is a deliberate one, and testifies not to any halfhearted-ness but, on the contrary, to the depth of the institution's commitment to Fourierism, and to the cause of Association generally. The journal is devoted to all the "socialisms" then prevalent, its articles and reviews covering the whole gamut of social wrongs and reforming possibilities.[36] In the first volume alone there are articles on, for example, capital punishment, the encroachment of capital upon labor, the abandonment of children in Boston, prisons and the reforming of criminals, the influence of machinery, the superiority of justice to charity, the conditions in Lowell, the advantages of a short working day, slavery, the Working Men's Association, the wrongs of women, and many other similar causes. Ripley explains the position in an editorial in the third issue:

> We trust that our brothers of the different Associations in the United States will not regard the Harbinger as the exclusive organ of the Brook Farm Phalanx. Although issued from its press, it is intended, that it should represent, as far as possible, the interests of the general movement which is now spreading with such encouraging progress throughout the land.[37]

The likeliest explanation of the subsequent silence on the part of the Farm's leaders is not that they did not want to break a butterfly upon a wheel, but that the almost simultaneous collapse of the community and of the national impetus toward Association must have had a traumatic effect on those who had invested their emotional and intellectual capital in the movement. By 1850 Ripley, Dwight, and Dana had embarked on careers which bore little or no relationship to their earlier ideals[38]—and to put a psychological distance between themselves and their unsuccessful experiment was a natural, and perhaps even necessary, undertaking.

By an irony that seems rather appropriate in view of Brook Farm's precarious stance between the world of fantasy and that of harsh social realities, one of the effects of this uneasy silence is that we have to rely heavily for information about the daily life of the community on writers who lay great stress on the fun they had during their time there. It is small wonder that Lindsay Swift should claim that "Enjoyment was almost from the first a serious pursuit of the community,"[39] when we see the emphasis laid on entertainment in most of the reminiscences. John Van Der Zee Sears devotes a whole chapter to the subject—it seems a long way from the *Harbinger's* gritty sociology to his inauspicious opening: "Our slide down the knoll proved very popular"—and John Thomas Codman has one entitled "Fun Alive" which deals almost exclusively with the community's addiction to punning. The quantity, if not the quality, of this word-play inevitably bathes the Farm in an Illyrian glow. Ora Gannet Sedgwick, Amelia Russell, George P. Bradford, and Arthur Sumner all add their own lists of pleasures to the register.[40]

This apparent sybaritism can be explained away to some extent by pointing out that most of these writers were looking back to their youth from the standpoint of old age—indeed, all of them except for Amelia Russell and George P. Bradford, were teenagers during their time at the Farm. In any case, despite Charles Lane's grumbling, there is no real need to excuse the fact that there were pleasures available at the community—unless, like one commentator, you object to the fact that the members allowed only ten hours a day for work.[41] Perhaps the best defense of all is to point out that if one compares the kind of play the Farmers enjoyed with the way they organized their work, it becomes clear that the two activities were not merely compatible, but were each controlled by the same overriding concern. Whether they were at work or at play the Farmers were attempting to cement the bonds that joined them together and to create a new kind of communal consciousness.

It is worth looking at Brook Farm entertainment more closely. Probably the most vivid picture we have of it occurs in Hawthorne's *Blithedale Romance*. Of course, Hawthorne warns the reader in his Preface about taking his romance to be a record of the actual experiences of the Brook Farmers, and it would be an act of critical insensitivity to look too closely for parallels between the work of the imagination and historical reality. Particularly dangerous perhaps would be any attempt to manipulate the masks of Hawthorne's characters until they fit the known features of individual communications. At the same time it is fair to remark that Hawthorne's very obsession with masks, with play-acting, with the relationship between public and private identity, reflects one of the central features of Brook Farm life. For this reason it is worth looking at the scene presented in the chapter "The Masqueraders," particularly as there is substantial evidence that the masquerade described here actually took place.

Coverdale has been away from the community, and in this chapter we are given a rather odd description of his return. As he approaches Blithedale he begins to suspect that the farm has been abandoned. His anxiety is not a serious one, however, but a form of self-teasing which somehow serves to increase the shock when he finds that the buildings are actually deserted. His anticipation had resulted from his feeling that the community could hardly have existed in the first place:

> I indulged in a hundred odd and extravagant conjectures. Either there was no such place as Blithedale, nor ever had been, nor any brotherhood of thoughtful labourers, like what I seemed to recollect there, or else it was all changed during my absence. It had been nothing but dream work and enchantment. I should seek in vain for the old farmhouse, and for the greensward, the potato-fields, the root-crops, and the acres of Indian corn, and for all that configuration of the land

which I had imagined. It would be another spot, and an utter strangeness.[42]

The community is still there, as it turns out, but Coverdale is right to anticipate "utter strangeness": he discovers "a concourse of strange figures beneath the overshadowing branches. They appeared, and vanished, and came again, confusedly, with the streaks of sunlight glimmering down upon them." This description, taken out of context, has a quality of Gothic menace about it. Rather uncharacteristically, however, Hawthorne has taken pains to drain the uneasy overtones from the situation—the wood "seemed as full of jollity as if Comus and his crew were holding their revels in one of its usually lonesome glades." When, therefore, we abruptly come across the masqueraders, the effect is one of benign surrealism (if the two terms do not cancel each other out):

> Among them was an Indian chief, with blanket, feathers, and war-paint, and uplifted tomahawk; and near him, looking fit to be his woodland bride, the goddess Diana, with the crescent on her head, and attended by our big lazy dog, in lack of any fleeter hound. . . . Another party consisted of a Bavarian broom-girl, a negro of the Jim Crow order, one or two foresters of the middle ages, a Kentucky woodsman in his trimmed hunting-shirt and deer-skin leggings, and a Shaker elder, quaint, demure, broad-brimmed, and square-skirted. Shepherds of Arcadia, and allegorical figures from the Faerie Queen, were oddly mixed up with these.[43]

Coverdale is more conscious than ever of being an outsider and while it is obviously simply chance that he should happen to return while the members of the community are merry-making in this fashion, the accident is of a deliberate and significant kind. These strange and apparently arbitrary juxtapositions, which he finds so alien and confusing, are characteristic of the community; in fact it was the intention of the Brook Farmers to create just such atmosphere of cheerful, if slightly self-conscious, role-playing as that established in this scene.

Many of the reminiscences discuss the masquerade which provided the source of Hawthorne's description. Codman appends to his book a letter signed "Charles" which obviously describes the actual event: "One of the ladies personated Diana, and any one entering her wooded precincts was liable to be shot with one of her arrows." Ora Gannet Sedgwick attempts to correct the record in her version—apparently Hawthorne's "one variation from the facts was in making me, both there and in the American Note-book, the gypsy fortune-teller, whereas that part was really taken by Mrs. Ripley, and I was merely the messenger to bring persons to her," while Arthur Sumner, who actually joined the Farm after Hawthorne had left, remembers attending "a fancy dress picnic in the woods, which might have furnished Mr. Hawthorne his scene in the Blithedale Romance."[44]

There were many similar events, and they are recalled with a graphic detail which suggests the importance of the part they played in the life of the community. John Van Der Zee Sears claims that

> The first pageant we ever had was arranged by the Festal Series, after the reorganization into a phalanx. It was historic in design, illustrating the Elizabethan period in England. Dr. Ripley personated Shakespeare; Miss Ripley, Queen Elizabeth, in a tissue paper ruff, which I helped to make; Mr. Dana, Sir Walter Raleigh; Mary Bullard, the most beautiful of our young women, Mary Queen of Scots, and Charles Hosmer, Sir Philip Sidney.[45]

Similarly, Amelia Russell describes another one, held at Christmas time, at which were impersonations of Hamlet, Greeks and Circasians, an Indian, Little Nell and her grandfather, and Spanish bolero dancers.[46] We also hear about other tableaus, charades, rural fetes, and a prodigious list of plays and operas performed in whole or in part by the Farmers: Byron's *Corsair*, Douglas Jerrold's *The Rent Day*, *The Midsummer Night's Dream*, the *Caliph of Baghdad*, *Zampa*, *Norma*, and so on. Of course, other activities—music, tobogganing, dancing—are mentioned, but those requiring acting of one sort or another seem to have been the most important, and the ones that had the deepest effect on the minds of the participants.[47]

We are already familiar with the equation Transcendentalism equals play. However, the significance of the kind of play described in the *Blithedale Romance* and in so many of the reminiscences is that it relates this formula to what could otherwise seem the opposing one of Fourierism equals work. There are interesting connections between the assumptions underlying masquerade and those that determine the Fourierist theory of labor; and the source of these connections can be traced to the inception of the community. From the very beginning, the Farmers were conscious that the individual's identity, or rather his sense of it, was unduly restricted by the rigidity of the social role that was forced on him in "civilization." They were aware of the problem of the dissociated sensibility and sought to solve it by creating a balance between physical and intellectual labor in the community. As a sympathetic contributor to the *Monthly Miscellany of Religion and Letters* demanded, in a very early account of the Farm, "How dare I sacrifice not my own, but others' health, in sequestrating myself from my share of bodily labour, or neglecting a due mental cultivation?"[48] The descriptions we have of the pre-Fourierist period show us what this involved—we find Hawthorne uneasily shoveling manure or dealing with the transcendental heifer, and trying desperately to keep his writing going; George Ripley teaching in the school, administering the Farm, discussing intellectual topics with his neighbor Theodore Parker, and contemplatively milking cows; Charles Anderson Dana teaching, laboring, and organizing a corps of waiters; George P. Bradford leaving his hoeing to go and teach, only to find his pupil was still out hunting, and had forgotten the lesson.[49] Frothingham tells us that "When convenient, the men did the women's work,"[50] and indeed there are accounts of them doing the laundry, cooking, washing up, and hanging out the clothes. In any case, we are told, the women were able to cope with their duties because "By the wide distribution of these labors, no one has any great weight of any one thing."[51]

It is clear that the community was trying to make available to each member as wide a range of experience as possible. George Willis Cooke quotes Charles Anderson Dana as saying of the Brook Farmers that "in order to reform society, in order to regenerate the world and to realize democracy in the social relations, they determined that their society should first pursue agriculture, which would give every man plenty of out-door labor in the free air, and at the same time the opportunity of study, of becoming familiar with everything in literature and learning."[52] This desire to run the gamut of occupations and identities, to be everything from Diana to a schoolmarm, from a woodsman to an intellectual, is the Brook Farmers' most noticeable characteristic. It was one that could find complete fulfillment in Fourier's scheme. After the reorganization we find, by looking at the Brook Farm Account Book for June 1844 to April 1845, that, for example, C. A. Dana's typical working month (this one is May 1844) is divided up as follows: ten days (of ten hours each), three hours, agricultural; one day seven hours, domestic; six days nine hours educational; one day, six and a quarter hours miscellaneous; two days, eight and three-quarter hours, functional.[53] The women, needless to say, have a more restricted range of opportunities; indeed Marianne Dwight describes in a letter to her brother Frank, dated 14 April 1844, what would appear to be a desultory round of domestic occupations—if it were not for the manner in which she writes about them—:

> Now my business is as follows (but perhaps liable to frequent change): I wait on the breakfast table (½ hour), help M. A. Ripley clear away the breakfast things, etc. (1½ hours), go into the dormitory group until eleven o'clock,— dress for dinner— then over to the Eyrie and sew until dinner time,—half past twelve. Then from half past one or two o'clock until ½ past five I teach drawing in Pilgrim Hall and sew in the Eyrie. At ½ past five go down to the Hive, to help set the tea table, and afterwards I wash teacups, etc., till about ½ past seven. Thus I make a long day of it, but alternation of work and pleasant

company and chats make it pleasant. I am about entering a flower
garden group and assisting Miss Russell in doing up muslins.[54]

The precision of the times, the reference to "groups," above all the praise
of "alternation of work" identify the Fourierist structure behind Marianne Dwight's working day. Fourier's scheme of industrial organization
(like the rest of his universe) is based on the operation of series and
groups, and these, with a gallant defiance of the laws of time and
motion, dictate that all labor shall be broken up into small units, so
that the individual can go from one occupation to another before he
grows stale.

Oddly enough, this apparent dispersal of energies and indeed of
identities in the Fourierist scheme is balanced by a doctrine which
claims the underlying unity of all men and things. In fact, the latter
is a necessary prelude to the former. The "Introductory Statement" to
the second Brook Farm constitution states that "while on the one hand
we yield an unqualified assent to that doctrine of Universal unity which
Fourier teaches, so on the other, our whole observation has shown us
the truth of the practical arrangements which he deduces therefrom."
These practical arrangements boil down to "The law of groups and
series," which "is, as we are convinced, the law of human nature,
and when men are in true social relations their industrial organization will necessarily assume these forms."[55] At this point, it is
worth looking closely at Fourier's doctrines in order to find out exactly
what the Farmers mean when they talk about the "doctrine of Universal unity," the "law of groups and series," and so on. The best
source of information, for us as well as for them, is undoubtedly the
writings of Albert Brisbane, Fourier's most prominent American disciple.
Because of the orthodoxy built into Fourier's scheme, almost all the
material on him takes the form of translations or summaries. This means,
of course, that there is a finite amount of work for his American protégés
to produce. Brisbane cornered the market, as it were, and his *Social
Destiny of Man*, his four *Democratic Review* articles on "Association
and Attractive Industry," and his *Concise Exposition of the Doctrine of
Association* provide a comprehensive account of the social implications
of Fourierism.[56]

Brisbane was well qualified to be the leading American authority on
the subject, since he was one of the few admirers to have seen the
light while the master was still alive. He was born in upstate New York,
of a well-to-do family, and spent a good part of his youth on a grand
tour of Europe and Asia, during which he attended Cousin's lectures in
Paris and Hegel's in Berlin. He became interested in St. Simonianism,
and then Fourierism, and in 1832, shortly before the master's death, he
actually met and studied with Fourier himself. On returning to America,

he published *Social Destiny of Man* in 1840, and followed it with innumerable articles, including a weekly column in Greeley's *Tribune*.[57]
His efforts brought a rich, if short-lived, harvest. John Humphrey Noyes,
the founder of the Oneida Perfectionists, uses the data left by A. J.
Macdonald, a contemporary student of Association, to show that there
were approximately thirty-five phalanxes scattered about the country,
with a total membership of over 3,000 people during the 1840s.[58] This
takes no account, of course, of the many who were interested in, or even
committed to, Fourierism, but who never put their beliefs to the test.
Greeley, and indeed Brisbane himself, belong to this group. Nevertheless
the latter was a frequent visitor to the Farm, staying there on one occasion for several months, and he was one of the editors of the *Harbinger*.
Codman tells us that he did not regard Brook Farm as an ideal Fourier-
istic experiment (any more than did Ripley), but his influence on the
later path of the community was enormous.[59] It may not have been
exactly what he wanted, but he was responsible—to a large degree—for
what it actually was.

Brisbane tells that a perfect society is possible as a result of Fourier's theory—or discovery, as the latter complacently put it[60]—that attractions are proportional to destinies. In other words, each individual has a
certain number of drives or "passions"; each of these directs him
toward a certain objective which has only to be achieved and he will
be perfectly happy.[61] These passions can be analyzed and tabulated.
They are as follows: five sensitive passions, one arising out of each of
the senses, which have as their object "Elegance, Riches and Material
Harmonies"; four affective passions—friendship, love, ambition, and
paternity—which tend toward "Groups and passional Harmonies"; and,
more obscurely, three "Distributive and Directing Passions," the "Emulative," "Alternating," and "Composite." These are, respectively, the
desire for intrigue and rivalry; for variety of occupation; and for the
double enjoyment of intellectual and emotional satisfaction; and they
lead to "Series and Concert of Masses." This whole nexus of desires can
receive fulfillment only if work is arranged according to Fourier's
blueprint.[62]

The Harmonies— social and otherwise—are distributed according to
groups and series. "Nature employs Series of Groups in the whole distribution of the Universe; the three kingdoms,—the animal, vegetable
and mineral,—present us only Series of Groups."[63] In other words,
despite the apparent variety of existing things, their composition and
relationship to each other conforms to a consistent law. In his autobiography Brisbane describes the moment when he achieved an imaginative
grasp of what this meant:

I perceived that there was unity of law with great diversity of phenomena; that the laws manifested themselves differently according to the differences of the material spheres in which they acted. Hence unity of law and variety in manifestation. The same law, for instance, which governs the distribution, co-ordination, and arrangement of the notes of music governs the distribution, co-ordination, and arrangement of the planets and the solar system. As sounds are notes in musical harmony, so the planets are notes in a sidereal harmony. Continuing the analogy: the species in the animal or vegetable kingdom are the notes of a vast organic harmony; the bones in the human body are the notes of an osseous harmony, and these, with the muscles and other parts of the human organism, are the notes of a physical harmony. *Law is unchanging,* but there is infinite variety in its manifestations;—such manifestations being as rich and complex as are the varied spheres or departments of the Universe.[64]

I have discussed elsewhere the Transcendentalists' fascination with the concept of "unity of law with diversity of phenomena."[65] Thoreau's assertion that the "Maker of this earth but patented a leaf," Emerson's gleeful account, in his essay on Swedenborg, of what appears to be the same osseous harmony that Brisbane describes—"spine on spine to the end of the world"—indicate the centrality of that "cordial truth" to be found in the "fable of Proteus." As Emerson's multi-tongued and athletic Sphinx (a creature as supple, surely, as Fourier's anti-lion) puts it:

> Through a thousand voices
> Spoke the universal dame;
> "Who telleth one of my meanings,
> Is master of all I am."[66]

Naturally, since Fourier's law is unchanging, it must apply to industrial organization as well as everything else: labor is miserable and inefficient because it has not so far obeyed it. All working men are to be divided into groups, and series of groups. A group is the basic unit of labor and "should be composed of at least seven persons." These

form three divisions or three sub-groups, the centre one of which should be stronger than the two wings or extremes. A group of seven persons will furnish the three following divisions: 2-3-2 (two persons at each wing and three in the centre). Each division would be engaged with some department of the work with which the Group was occupied.

A series is made up of groups in the same way that a group is composed of individuals. It "must contain at least three Groups—a Centre and two Wings: twenty-four persons is the least number with which a Series can be formed. The Central Group should be stronger than the Groups of Wings."[67] This structure enables one's emulative passion to be fully engaged.

> The ascending wing will be occupied with the heaviest branch of a work, if the Series be engaged in manufactures, and with the largest variety, if engaged in the cultivation of grains, fruits, vegetables or flowers; the centre will be occupied with the most elegant and attractive branch or variety; and the descending wing with the lightest and smallest.[68]

The idea is that the two wings will unite to excel the center; they will have numbers on their side, while the center will have the satisfaction of producing the highest quality of article. This careful discrimination of function avoids the danger of easily resolved and therefore ineffective competition.

This organization of labor caters not merely for Emulation, but for all the other passions as well. One will never spend more than an hour or two on any particular activity: that deals with Alternation; the industrial system will be so highly specialized that each person will be able to do exactly the work he wants to do and will do it in the company of those who are also happy in their jobs: this provides the Composite Pleasure of interesting employment and good company. Friendship, Love, and Paternity are kept at full stretch because the mobility of the worker enables him to choose his company: he can work side by side with his wife if he wants to—and for as long as he wants to. Ambition is catered for by the possibilities of rivalry, and because the individual is making maximum use of his abilities. The five Sensitive Passions—Sight, Hearing, Smell, Taste, and Touch—can play on the beautiful environment that is the natural result of living in a community and thereby breaking down the distinction between home and work, and of the joint-stock system by which everyone receives his share in the whole and therefore possesses both the worker's needs and the proprietor's powers.[69]

Perhaps the oddest assumption behind this whole system is not that the deepest wishes of individuals can be identified and provided for, but that we are capable of achieving all the tasks we want to perform. Brisbane deals with this question in a passage in his *Concise Exposition*:

> It will be objected that if an individual takes part in so many branches of Industry, he will become perfect in none; this difficulty will be entirely obviated by the minute *division of labor*, which will take place, and by assigning to each individual of a Group the performance of a detail of the work with which it is engaged. In a Group

of fruit-growers, for example, a person will attend to the grafting; now an intelligent person can learn to graft as well in a few days as in a lifetime, and his knowledge in this branch will enable him to belong to several Series of horticulturists. Thus, while changes of scene and company would prevent monotony and apathy, the same detail of a work could be performed. A skilful turner could belong to Groups of chair-makers, without varying materially the nature of his work; a person skilled in working leather could belong to the Series of saddlers, glove-makers, and shoe-makers, and the part in which he excelled might be performed in each of the branches of Industry.[70]

The "division of labor" (technically speaking "parcelled exercise") is very minute indeed: one does not just want to work with, say, a flower, but with a specific part of a tulip, and one's taste will exactly complement that of one's colleagues: "for among twelve persons with a passion for the tulip, none of the twelve will have a lot of love for the twelve functions connected with its cultivation; therefore unless they make a parcelled division of their work and distribute functions according to tastes, disagreements and discord will break out."[71]

After focusing on one's work with such microscopic intensity one would expect to feel something of a jolt when it came to switching occupations at the rate that is suggested:

> A man, for example, may be
> At five o'clock in the morning in a Group of Shepherds;
> At seven o'clock in a Group of gardeners;
> At nine o'clock in a Group of fishermen.[72]

However, Fourier is confident that the individual will fit exactly into each of the niches that have been made available for him. He asserts that "THERE IS NOTHING ARBITRARY IN THE SYSTEM WE PROPOSE, we resort to no laws or regulations of human invention; we make use of three of the twelve passions to direct the other nine with the freest and most economical of systems, that of Series of Groups, which system is a universal desire of the human heart, as well as the distribution followed in the whole order of known Nature."[73] The point is that the configuration of the individual's passions actually corresponds—on its own small scale—with the intricate topography of the natural order. He is like a piece of jigsaw puzzle, and when he interlocks with the other members of the phalanx, they provide together a miniature reproduction of the world itself. The phalanx is a self-sufficient community, able to cope with all of life's needs. As Emerson sarcastically expressed it:

> It takes sixteen hundred and eighty men to make one Man, complete in all faculties; that is, to be sure that you have got a good joiner, a

good cook, a barber, a poet, a judge, an umbrella-maker, a major and alderman, and so on. Your community should consist of two thousand persons, to prevent accidents of omission.[74]

Despite Emerson's sneer, however, the premise on which the phalanx is based has its points of resemblance with that underlying the individualistic variety of Transcendentalism. In this connection, it is worth looking at the following extract from a letter to John Sullivan Dwight written by George William Curtis, an ex-Brook Farmer who disapproved of Fourierism:

Raphael could have sung as Shakespeare, and Milton have hewn as many forms as Angelo. Yet a divine economy rules these upper spiritual regions, as sure and steadfast as the order of the stars. Raphael must paint and Homer sing, yet the same soul gilds the picture and sweetens the song. So Venus and Mars shine yellow and red, but the same central fire is the light of each. In the capacity of doing all things well lies the willingness to serve one good. The Jack of all trades is sure to be good at none, for who is good at all is Jack of one only. It seemed a bitter thing to me, formerly, that painters must only paint and sculptors carve; but I see now the wisdom. In one thing well done lies the secret of doing all.[75]

The letter is dated 25 November 1843, shortly after Curtis left the community, and shortly before what he (as a Transcendentalist of the picnicking type) was to term the "earlier, golden age of the colony" gave way to the Fourierist period.[76]

Curtis has come to accept—at first unwillingly—that in order to achieve anything one must confine oneself strictly within a single discipline. Obviously, this is very different from Fourier's attitude, and yet there is a point in common. Curtis has an atomic view of the structure of the universe. Things are inextricably connected with each other in such a way that even though each of us deals with only a single point in the large pattern, the reverberations of our actions run right through the whole framework so that "In one thing well done lies the secret of doing all." Fourier believes that the basic unit of the social universe is an organized system which is composed of almost 2,000 people and which can be reproduced in the form of the phalanx; Curtis pins his faith on the individual. Both, however, assume that once you have mastered the part you have access to the whole. Both believe that the material and social universe has a consistent and repetitive order. Curtis sees the lowest common denominator of this system as an atom; Fourier finds that it is a molecule. The two men are simply disagreeing over the size and complexity of the basic component.

Curtis' description is the one we have come to associate with Transcendentalism: it is the Emersonian position. And yet Fourier's account, with its emphasis on communal identity, offered certain rewards that individualism could not provide. Emerson himself gives negative evidence of this, when he states in his "American Scholar" address that

> there is One Man,—present to all particular men only partially, or through one faculty; and ... you must take the whole society to find the whole man. Man is not a farmer, or a professor, or an engineer, but he is all. Man is priest, and scholar, and statesman, and producer, and soldier. In the *divided* or social state these functions are parcelled out to individuals, each of whom aims to do his stint of the joint work, whilst each other performs his. The fable implies that the individual to possess himself, must sometimes return from his own labor to embrace all the other laborers. But, unfortunately, this original unit, this fountain of power, has been so distributed to multitudes, has been so minutely subdivided and peddled out, that it is spilled into drops, and cannot be gathered. The state of society is one in which the members have suffered amputation from the trunk and strut about so many walking monsters,—a good finger, a neck, a stomach, an elbow, but never a man.
> Man is thus metamorphosed into a thing, into many things.[77]

The phalanx admirably fulfills the implications of the fable. It provides a place where the individual can "return from his own labor to embrace all the other laborers." Actually, it does more even than that. The variety of occupations provides the individual with the opportunity of fulfilling so many different functions that he is no longer a mere member, but a man—or at least, more nearly one than he is in civilization. It is interesting to compare Emerson's metaphor of dismemberment with a much more matter-of-fact remark by Brisbane. He is pointing out that many kinds of work lead to physical illness—hernias, obesity, and so on—but that this danger will be avoided by the short occupations of phalansterian life. He goes on to say, almost in answer to Emerson's complaint, that the "health of man is promoted by this perpetual variety of functions, which exercising successively all parts of the body, all faculties of the mind, maintains activity and equilibrium."[78]

The attraction of role-playing for the Brook Farmers—whether it took the form of masquerade or of manual labor—becomes obvious. A simple accumulation of diverse activity frees the individual from a fixed and arbitrary social function, and enables him to become more nearly a whole person. Moreover, the phalanx integrates its members into a new unity—helps them to become what Emerson so much wanted everyone to be: one man. When one considers the latter's doctrine of a racial consciousness to which we all contribute, it seems odd that he should have been so unsympathetic to Fourierism. After all, the phalanx is a limited manifestation of that collective mind—a kind of finite over-soul.[79]

Fourier clearly had something to offer the Transcendentalists in his account of human identity and the relationship between the individual and the rest of society. He proved equally useful in another respect. The most difficult problem utopians are faced with, no matter where or when they perform their experiment, is that of the relationship between the good society and the historical process. Fourier, in his usual punctilious manner, showed the Brook Farmers exactly how such a relationship could be established.

Harold Clark Goddard, in his elderly but still useful *Studies in New England Transcendentalism*, puts his finger on the problem faced by the Transcendentalists. He exclaims at the fact that "at the very time when the historical way of regarding things was grounding itself in the minds of men, a movement should occur whose very essence was a denial of history," and remarks that while the world was learning that "society and civilization are the products of an evolution," the Transcendentalists were propounding the thesis "that both may be brought, outright, into perfect being."[80] Goddard's account is an over-simplification, of course, but an awareness of the full complexity of the Transcendentalists' position serves to deepen the paradox he has stated, rather than to solve it. The Newness, as its proponents were well aware, was not as new as all that. The Transcendentalists were much influenced by French and German thought and were perfectly *au fait* with doctrines of historical evolution. George Bancroft, who hovered on the periphery of the movement for a time, put the evolutionist's case succinctly:

> The world cannot retrograde; the dark ages cannot return. Dynasties perish; cities are buried; nations have been victims to error, or martyrs for right; Humanity has always been on the advance; its soul has always been gaining maturity and power.[81]

It is probably fair to say that Theodore Parker's great projected work on the history and development of religion is as much a product—or would have been, if he had completed it—of the movement's afflatus as Thoreau's wooden hut by Walden Pond.[82] Actually the famous last sentence of *Walden*—"The sun is but a morning star"—could stand as an assertion of progressivism if it were not qualified by the preceding passage:

> I do not say that John or Jonathan will realize all this; such is the character of that morrow which mere lapse of time can never make to dawn. The light which puts out our eyes is darkness to us. Only that day dawns to which we are awake.[83]

As it is, Thoreau seems to leave us with the doctrine of the "angle of vision": do not change things, just look at them aright. Nevertheless, in his notion that the light originally appears to be darkness, he is pointing toward a solution already adopted by many of the evolutionists, as we shall see shortly.

Emerson's essay on "History" plunges us into the very heart of the problem. By establishing an analogy between the growth of the individual and the development of civilization he implies an evolutionary view. The ancient Greek army, for example, is "a gang of great boys, with such a code of honour and such lax discipline as great boys have."[84] Different phases of civilization reflect different periods in an individual's life. Therefore the student of history "interprets the age of chivalry by his own age of chivalry, and the days of maritime adventure and circumnavigation by quite parallel miniature experiences of his own."[85] At the same time, however, there is a dimension of human experience which takes place outside the realm of history. Man "is the compend of time; he is also the correlative of nature."[86] Emerson appears to visualize a coming time that will be emancipated from the temporal order, a human destiny that will take place outside the historical process. Nature and history have been at odds; the latter does not participate in the harmonies which are embodied in the former. Emerson foresees a new historiography, one which will release man from the burden of his past by reestablishing him in the eternal natural world. This new perspective will bring about human redemption:

> Broader and deeper we must write our annals,—from an ethical reformation, from an influx of the ever new, ever sanative conscience,— if we would trulier express our central and wide related nature, instead of this old chronology of selfishness and pride to which we have too long lent our eyes. Already that day exists for us, shines in on us unawares, but the path of science and of letters is not the way to nature. The idiot, the Indian, the child and the unschooled farmer's boy stand nearer to the light by which nature is to be read, than the dissector or the antiquary.[87]

Emerson has in fact extended his argument from history to human knowledge in general. Civilized man is out of step with the rest of creation, and therefore only those who by an accident of birth find themselves outside our cultural frame of reference can have access to nature. There is not much comfort to be derived from this diagnosis despite the hopeful rhythms of Emerson's prose. All may be well for the idiot and the Indian but for the rest of us, for John and Jonathan as Thoreau rather patronizingly put it, the future looks somewhat bleak.

At this point it is worth referring to one of the earlier products of the Transcendentalist movement: a review (published in the *Christian Examiner* in March 1834) by Frederic Henry Hedge of an address by Edward Everett on the subject of social progress.[88] Hedge's discussion of the problem involved in the progressive view of history deserves some respect, if for no other reason than because he was a central enough figure in the movement for the Transcendental Club to be frequently referred to as "Hedge's Club." There is another reason, as it happens: his account of historical development points toward the manner in which the utopian impulse could be accommodated in the evolutionary system.

Hedge admits that "Alternate civilization and barbarism make up the apparent history of man."[89] Nevertheless, he goes on to claim that society has never actually gone backward; at the worst it has stood still for a time. The point is that progress is not a consistent, accumulative phenomenon but is a matter of sporadic evolutionary developments. He calls these phases of growth "impulses" or "pulsations." They occur in a specific context and then, by a kind of chemical process, communicate themselves to society at large: "Each pulsation [of the human mind] has sent forth into the world some new sentiment or principle, some discovery or invention, which like small portions of leaven, have successively communicated their quickening energy to the whole mass of society."[90] Just as, in the natural world, the maker had to do no more than patent a leaf, so in society a single "invention" can gain universal currency. The utopian microcosm, if only it is correctly formulated (and the possibilities were to range from Thoreau alone in his hut to the plans for a full-scale phalanx), has the power of redeeming the macrocosm. Moreover, a sense of dissatisfaction with the modern world, a feeling that civilization is aimless and sterile, need not cast a shadow over the evolutionists' perspective— Hedge's theory of the alternation of civilization and barbarism sees to that. As Bronson Alcott expressed it in one of his "Orphic Sayings":

> The hunger of an age is alike a presentiment and pledge of its own supply. . . . Now, men are lean and famishing; but, behold, the divine Husbandman has driven his share through the age, and sown us bread that we may not perish.[91]

It is not difficult to understand the appeal of Fourier's account of the historical process when one looks at the way in which certain of the Transcendentalists were grappling with the conflict between evolutionism and utopianism. Although Hedge was confident that there was nothing irregular or arbitrary about the occurrence of "pulsations," he did not pretend to have deciphered the historical pattern of which they formed part. Instead, he awaited the coming of a "philosophic historian" who would be able to "trace and exhibit these successive impulses. He who can do this, and he only will be able to furnish a systematic history of Man: something very different from, and infinitely more important than the histories we now have of dynasties and tribes."[92] Fourier provides just such a "systematic history of Man."

Fourier's series do not simply extend vertically as hierarchies of phenomena, and horizontally as equivalences between those different hierarchies: they have a third dimension, too—existence in time. Needless to say, the "Formula of the Movement of a Serie" (Brisbane sometimes found it convenient to distinguish between a singular and plural form of the word "series") is itself a "serie":

Ascending Transition	or *Birth*
First Phasis	or Infancy
Second Phasis	or Youth
Apogee	or MATURITY
Third Phasis	or Decline
Fourth Phasis	or Decrepitude
Descending Transition	or *Death*[93]

Human history has consisted of four of these temporal series so far: savage, patriarchal, barbarian, and civilized. The movement of the fourth civilization, can be tabulated as in the table printed on p. 586.

A clear indication of the way Fourierism manages to have the best of both worlds is that Brisbane can follow his account of this elaborately structured past by dismissing the confidence in "progress" that he detects in the contemporary historians of France and Germany because they "sanction the history of the past, the principles of which they wish to be the basis of all future improvement; they admire the dreary career of mankind as a magnificent achievement, and endeavour to read in their annals of blood a wisdom, which they claim to be Providence, but which is an illusive chimera of their own erroneous speculations."[94] The reason this attitude is possible is that the temporal serie has what may be called organic form: in other words, it possesses a beginning, a middle, and an end, and serie follows serie, as generation follows generation. Thus history is not a simple success story, a matter of the cultural survival of the spiritually fittest. Instead, new stages of human development arise phoenix-like out of the ashes of the old. The structure of the serie is admirably suited to recording the successive "pulsations" of the human mind, while at the same time it provides a satisfactory explanation of the imperfections of the present social state. We are, in fact, in a period of decline; but for that very reason we are entitled to look forward to a more glorious future.

Another problem the evolutionary view of history brought with it was that of the status, and the freedom, of the individual. Fourier's

TABLE OF THE MOVEMENT OF CIVILIZATION, WITH
ITS FOUR AGES OR PHASES[95]

FIRST AGE. *Infancy.*
Exclusive marriage or Monogamy.
Feudality of the Nobles.

PIVOT: CIVIL RIGHTS OF THE WIFE.
Federation of the Great Barons.
Illusions in chivalry.

SECOND AGE. *Growth.*
Privileges of free Towns and Cities.
Cultivation of the Arts and Sciences.

PIVOT: ENFRANCHISEMENT OF THE SERFS OR LABORING
CLASSES.
Representative System.
Illusions in Liberty or Democratic Agitations.

MATURITY: { EXPERIMENTAL CHEMISTRY: ART OF NAVIGATION.
NATIONAL LOANS: CLEARING OF FORESTS WITHOUT
EXCESSES.

THIRD AGE. *Decline.*
Commercial and Fiscal spirit.
Stock companies.

PIVOT: MARATIME MONOPOLY.
Anarchical Commerce.
Financial Illusions.

FOURTH AGE. *Decrepitude.*
Agricultural Loaning Companies.
Associated Farms; discipline system of
cultivation.

PIVOT: COMMERCIAL AND INDUSTRIAL FEUDALITY.
Contractors of Feudal Monopoly: Oligarchy of
Capital.
Illusions in Association.

ASCENDING MOVEMENT.

DESCENDING MOVEMENT.

position on this issue was not so easy for the Transcendentalists to accept. The Unitarianism on which they had been brought up may have been dry and inconsistent, but it represented a reaction against Calvinism and embodied Enlightenment values: it taught a respect for the power of the human mind, man's ability to choose between good and evil, and his right to select his own destiny. The Transcendentalists emphasized these features, diminishing the power of authority in favor of a doctrine of personal responsibility. Although too much can be made of their individualism, it would be just as false to assume that they were blasé about free will. "Nothing can bring you peace but yourself," proclaims Emerson at the end of "Self-Reliance." "Nothing can bring you peace but the triumph of principles."[96] And yet it is very difficult to combine a belief in the possibility of moral choice with a doctrine of the approaching social millennium.

Since the human race is proceeding inevitably, if not necessarily on the most direct route, toward a heaven on earth, then surely, by taking our own contribution seriously, we are participating in the youthful error of Hawthorne's Holgrave "in fancying that it mattered anything to the great end in view, whether he himself should contend for it or against it."[97] It is a short step from saying, with Bancroft, that the "world cannot retrograde" to claiming that everything we do must be for the best; and an even shorter one from there to the belief that we are simply tools in the hands of Providence, without free will of our own. As usual, Emerson is a good representative of Transcendentalist confusion on the subject. His essay "The Over-Soul" provides an example of the ambiguous nature of the individual's status. Here we find that men possess enough independence of will to be able to "forsake their native nobleness" in "habitual and mean service to the world."[98] At the same time, however, we are told that the facts of experience, intractable though they may appear, will finally give way before our true destiny. We can be optimistic because "the argument which is always forthcoming to silence those who conceive extraordinary hopes of man, namely the appeal to experience, is forever invalid and vain. We give up the past to the objector, and yet we hope."[99] Despite everything—ourselves included—we have access to a higher life, the over-soul:

> By virtue of this inevitable nature, private will is overpowered, and maugre our efforts or our imperfections, your genius will speak from you, and mine from me. That which we are, we shall teach, not voluntarily but involuntarily. Thoughts come into our minds by avenues which we never left open, and thoughts go out of our minds through avenues which we never voluntarily opened.[100]

Emerson has provided us with a kind of inverted fatalism: the individual is part of the "eternal ONE," whether he chooses to be so, or not.

Fourier shares this belief in insurmountable good. According to his table (see above), we are now in the third age of civilization, rapidly approaching the fourth. The new age will dawn because businessmen and speculators, unphilanthropic though they may be, will begin to find that Association is the most profitable social form. After a period of misguided experimentation (Owen's work at New Harmony, if not

the more successful attempt at New Lanark, suggests an example), they
will introduce the new order. It is not the over-soul, but the forces
of history, as he interprets them, that will bring it about: "Thus the
human race, to accomplish their Destiny, have to be urged on by
force; the paths which lead to it are so rugged and the obstacles to
be overcome are so great, that the attainment would be abandoned, if
the double power—the political and monied, and the interest of those
who wield it—did not force the mass to surmount these obstacles."[101]
This being the case, there was not much point in doing anything
except wait for things to happen. Fourier took little interest in the
"partial" experiments done in his own time, just as, no doubt, he
would have taken little interest in Brook Farm, the North American
Phalanx, and the other American communities which attempted, im-
perfectly, to carry out his precepts. Instead, "Every day on the stroke
of twelve he made a point of returning to his lodgings to wait for
the appearance of the Maecenas who would somehow, of his own
accord, arrive to consult with him on the practical details for the
establishment of a model."[102]

The Transcendentalists were obviously impressed by the inexorable
progress of Fourier's juggernaut. Its independence of individual volition
appealed to that side of their thinking which viewed human history as
the manifestation of God's will. But Fourier's answer could not satisfy
them completely. The willingness to muddle through, with inadequate
numbers and occupations, and only a vague approximation of Fourier's
model, testifies to their continuing faith in the role of the individual in
the broad historical effort, to their belief that one could exert leverage
on the course of events by the power of one's will. The Transcendentalists'
problem was basically that they suffered from an excess of optimism,
which led simultaneously to confidence in a benevolent destiny, and
at the same time to an increased respect for the individual's powers.
The writings of Theodore Parker provide a particularly acute example
of this paradox. The problem in his case was accentuated because he
had to reconcile the Transcendental variety of optimistic evolutionism
with his role as a deeply committed social agitator.

Parker shares Emerson's inability to take the possibility of evil
completely seriously. When cornered, Emerson was quite prepared to
pretend to be above the whole business: "if I am the Devil's child, I
will live then from the Devil." Parker's equivalent gesture is to refer
to sin, contemptuously, as "ngnsin-n-n-n."[103] As a result he is able to
achieve an admirably ecological perspective on the natural world:
"Earthquakes, volcanoes, hurricanes, tigers, lions, rattlesnakes, vipers—
nobody has ever pretended that they did more harm than good; the
leaning of science is quite the other way, to suspect that what we call
evil is good in reality, only not comprehended yet."[104] The development

of civilization takes place within the same comforting parameters that shield the natural world from the forces of evil, waste, and chaos. Parker asks: "How has the civilization of the world thus far been achieved?" and answers himself by claiming that it "has taken place in the providence of God, who, from perfect motives, of perfect material, for a perfect purpose, as a perfect means, created this human nature, put into it this reserve of power, put about it this reserve of material elements, wherewith to make a Jacob's ladder to clamber continually upwards towards God, our prayer being the hand which reaches up, while our practice is the foot which sustains the weight."[105] The occasional shuddering of this apparently perfect machinery is explained away by the fact that the Almighty has built a "margin for oscillation" into the system.[106] Human evolution is a conscious process and the mind can make mistakes. None of these can be crucial, however—they are part of the process of mankind's self-education:

> Look at the human race as one person: from the beginning till now man has been devising an instrument to produce welfare. Every experiment has been a partial success; each also a partial failure. So far as the attempt succeeded the result has been delightful; so far as it failed, painful. Suffering follows error; man abandons the error, abolishes the mischief, tries again, making out better next time. The pain has only been adequate to sharpen his wits, like hunger and thirst to make him work in other forms. Thus man gets political education and political enjoyment.[107]

When it comes to assessing an individual's behavior, therefore, the notion of sin has to be replaced by that of "wrong choice" because "No man loves the wrong for its own sake, but as a means for some actual good it is thought to lead to."[108]

The only trouble with this account of human behavior is that it does not seem to explain the stance that Parker himself took on issues that affected his society. Despite the rational framework which he provides for the historical process, Parker's temperament and his respect for human rights made it impossible for him to tolerate the social abuses of his own time and place. The upholders of the Fugitive Slave Law in Massachusetts are not allowed to get off as lightly as the volcanoes and rattlesnakes.

> Where shall I find a parallel with men who will do such a deed,—do it in Boston? I will open the tombs, and bring up the most hideous tyrants from the dead. Come, brood of monsters, let me bring you up from the deep damnation of the graves wherein your hated memories continue for all time their never-ending rot.[109]

A man who is prepared to speak in these terms is not merely one who is deeply concerned about the state of the society in which he finds himself, but also one who is willing to award the individual the privilege of being evil if he chooses to be so. A good example of this moral perspective is the memorial address on Daniel Webster in which Parker makes his subject a tragic figure, and clearly reprimands error— and thus acknowledges the possibility of waste and evil in a way that appears incompatible with his general account of human destiny.[110] This problem is a central one in Parker's philosophy, just as it is, in different ways, in the thinking of other Transcendentalists, including the Brook Farmers.[111]

❋   ❋   ❋   ❋   ❋   ❋   ❋   ❋   ❋   ❋   ❋   ❋   ❋   ❋   ❋   ❋   ❋   ❋   ❋   ❋

It is ironic that the community should fail as it was on the point of achieving the kind of "life" which Elizabeth Peabody had claimed it originally lacked. The reasons for the collapse have frequently been discussed: the fire, and its economic consequences; the increasing notoriety of Fourierism; the lagging enthusiasm of Brisbane and the movement's loss of impetus at the national level; the effect on the school of an outbreak of smallpox at the Farm; the disillusion of many of the members—a whole complex of factors led to the breakup.[112] A final evaluation will, however, have to take into account the fact that during its short existence it embodied, and indeed extended, some of the basic Transcendentalist ideas. As a phalanx it put into action a belief which individualistic members of the movement like Emerson and Thoreau manifested in a more passive mood when they set themselves up as representative men. The community assumed, with a literalness that is hard to take completely seriously now, that it constituted a perfectible microcosm of society, and that once Brook Farm was in proper running order it would inaugurate the reformation of the social macrocosm. This optimism may have been mistaken, but this does not mean that we are entitled to dismiss the experiment as a frivolous or escapist enterprise. Brook Farm was both a manifestation of the Transcendentalist impulse and an attempt to create a better world—there is no need to see a conflict between these two descriptions. Underlying the efforts of its members was a confidence in man: the Brook Farmers believed that the human race was adequate to its work, that people had only to behave as they were designed to and they would achieve a glorious destiny. For a short time near the end of the community's life, the Fourierist and Transcendental doctrine that man only had to express his innermost being—to be himself—in order to be perfect, was deepened under the influence of Channing. His contribution was the notion of self-sacrifice. The welfare of the many depended on the correct organization of the one: the complex harmony of the phalanx was provided by the appropriate relationships being maintained between its individual components. But for those relationships to be established, other possibilities, other rewards, had to be abandoned. Phalansterian man was called upon to sacrifice something for his fellows. Adherence to the law of the universe was, finally, not merely an evolutionary imperative but a moral one as well.

Notes

1. "The Celestial Rail-road," *Mosses from an Old Manse* (Columbus: Ohio State University Press, 1974), p. 197. Vol. X of *The Centenary Edition of the Works of Nathaniel Hawthorne,* ed. William Charvat et al.; future references to Hawthorne's writings are to this edition unless otherwise indicated.

2. William R. Hutchison, *The Transcendentalist Ministers* (New Haven: Yale University Press, 1959), pp. 22, 28.

3. *The Transcendentalists: An Anthology,* ed. Perry Miller (Cambridge: Harvard University Press, 1950), pp. 129–132.

4. Charles Crowe, *George Ripley: Transcendentalist and Utopian Socialist* (Athens: University of Georgia Press, 1967), p. 81.

5. Crowe, *George Ripley,* p. 137.

6. See Lindsay Swift, *Brook Farm: Its Members, Scholars, and Visitors* (New York: Macmillan, 1900), for further details of these and others involved in the experiment.

7. Crowe, *George Ripley,* pp. 143–223.

8. Crowe, *George Ripley,* p. 173.

9. Charles R. Crowe, "Fourierism and the Founding of Brook Farm," *Boston Public Library Quarterly,* 12 (April 1960), 87. Morris Hillquit makes the same point in his *History of Socialism in the United States* (New York: Funk & Wagnalls, 1903), p. 103.

10. Miller, *The Transcendentalists,* p. 469. Swift's remark is from his *Brook Farm,* p. 135.

11. Miller, *The Transcendentalists,* p. 464.

12. Letter to the *New Age,* 30 July 1843, reprinted in F. B. Sanborn and William T. Harris, *A. Bronson Alcott: His Life and Philosophy* (Boston: Roberts, 1893), II, 382–383.

13. See the Introduction by Charles Gide to *Selections from the Works of Fourier,* trans. Julia Franklin (London: Swan-Sonnenschein, 1901), pp. 14–16.

14. "Brook Farm," an address delivered at the University of Michigan on 21 January 1895, printed as an Appendix to James Harrison Wilson, *The Life of Charles A. Dana* (New York: Harpers, 1907), p. 517. Besides Wilson's book there is a good account of Dana's later career in Candace Stone, *Dana and the Sun* (New York: Dodd, Mead, 1938), and a brief summary of his life in Swift, *Brook Farm,* pp. 145–152.

15. "A Girl of Sixteen at Brook Farm," *Atlantic Monthly Magazine,* 85 (March 1900), 396.

16. See, for example, John Thomas Codman, *Brook Farm: Historic and Personal Memoirs* (Boston: Arena, 1894), pp. 31, 57.

17. The manuscript does not provide information on the occupations of female members of the community.

18. "A Boy's Recollections of Brook Farm," *New England Magazine*, n.s. 16 (May 1894), 310.

19. Summer 1845, Marianne Dwight Orvis, *Letters from Brook Farm 1844–1847*, ed. Amy L. Reed (Poughkeepsie, N.Y.: Vassar College, 1928), p. 104.

20. "Brook Farm," *United States Magazine and Democratic Review*, n.s. 11 (November 1842), 491.

21. See Codman, *Brook Farm*, pp. 10–11.

22. *Phalanx*, 1 (20 April 1844), 114.

23. Letter to John Sullivan Dwight, 10 May 1846, Clarence Gohdes, "Three Letters by James Kay Dealing with Brook Farm," *Philological Quarterly*, 17 (October 1938), 383.

24. Gohdes, "Three Letters," p. 383.

25. Letter to Dwight, 14 March 1845, Gohdes, "Three Letters," p. 379.

26. Amelia E. Russell, *Home Life of the Brook Farm Association* (Boston: Little, Brown, 1900), p. 24. This book collects her articles originally published in the *Atlantic Monthly Magazine*, 42 (October, November 1878), 458–466, 556–563.

27. The Brook Farmers had to put up with a considerable amount of hostility as a result of their adoption of a Fourierist constitution. John Van Der Zee Sears, in his book *My Friends at Brook Farm* (New York: Desmond FitzGerald, 1912), claims that "there was bitter feeling against us among the old Puritans of Roxbury. They hated us and took occasion to annoy us and injure us in many mean ways" (p. 169). Codman mentions the press campaigns that were conducted against the community—usually on the grounds that Fourierism threatened the sanctity of marriage, which indeed it did, although not at Brook Farm (*Brook Farm*, p. 204).

28. That is since Lindsay Swift's book. Like other manifestations of Transcendentalism, Brook Farm has tended to invite superficial and gossipy treatment. See, if examples are required, Katherine Burton, *Paradise Planters: The Story of Brook Farm* (New York: Longmans, 1939), and Edith Roelker Curtis, *A Season in Utopia: The Story of Brook Farm* (New York: Thomas Nelson, 1961). A hostile but stimulating study of Brook Farm is contained in Jane Maloney Johnson, "'Through Change and Through Storm': A Study of Federalist-Unitarian Thought, 1800–1860" (Ph.D. diss., Radcliffe College, 1958).

29. *The Blithedale Romance* (Columbus: Ohio State University Press, 1964), p. 3.

30. Russell, *Home Life*, pp. 1–2.

31. Sumner, "A Boy's Recollections," p. 313.

32. Johnson, "'Through Change and Through Storm,'" p. 277.

33. Sumner, "A Boy's Recollections," p. 313.

34. 24 June 1841, Zoltán Haraszti, *The Idyll of Brook Farm* (Boston: Boston Public Library, 1937), p. 18.

35. George Ripley, "Fire at Brook Farm," *Harbinger*, 2 (14 March 1846), 220–222; Ripley, "To Our Friends," *Harbinger*, 2 (21 March 1846), 237–238.

36. The plural of "socialism" is used in the title of John Humphrey Noyes, *History of American Socialisms* (Philadelphia: J. B. Lippincott, 1870). Virtually the only light relief for readers of the *Harbinger* was a translation of George Sand's *Consuelo*, running in an almost interminable serial.

37. "To Our Friends in Association," *Harbinger*, 1 (28 June 1845), 47.

38. Ripley became a journalist on Horace Greeley's *New York Tribune*, and, with Dana, edited the *New American Encyclopedia*, 16 vols. (New York: D. Appleton, 1858–1863); see Crowe, *George Ripley*, pp. 224–263. Dwight edited *Dwight's*

Journal of Music from 1853 to 1887; for information on his life see George Willis Cooke, *John Sullivan Dwight* (Boston: Small, Maynard, 1898).

39. Swift, *Brook Farm*, p. 53.

40. Sears, *My Friends*, Ch. 6, "Entertainments," pp. 80–106; Codman, *Brook Farm*, Ch. 5, pp. 172–185; Sedgwick, "A Girl of Sixteen," esp. p. 402; Russell, *Home Life*, esp. pp. 15–17, 43–44; George P. Bradford, "Reminiscences of Brook Farm by a Member of the Community," *Century Magazine*, 45 (November 1892), 141; Sumner, "A Boy's Recollections," esp. pp. 311–312.

41. Johnson, " 'Through Storm and Through Change,' " p. 198.

42. *The Blithedale Romance*, p. 206.

43. *The Blithedale Romance*, p. 209.

44. Codman, *Brook Farm*, p. 260; the letter is dated "Oct. 27th, B. F. Mass.";
Sedgwick, "A Girl of Sixteen," p. 402; Sumner, "A Boy's Recollections," p. 311.
Hawthorne's account of the original event can be found in his *American Notebooks*, ed. Randall Stewart (New Haven: Yale University Press, 1932), entry for 28 September 1841, pp. 78–79.

45. Sears, *My Friends*, p. 101.

46. Russell, *Home Life*, pp. 15–17.

47. See, for example, Bradford, "Reminiscences," p. 142; Sears, *My Friends*, pp. 80–106; Codman, *Brook Farm*, pp. 53–68.

48. "The Community at West Roxbury, Mass.," *Monthly Miscellany of Religion and Letters*, 5 (July 1841), 113–118, introduced by the editor as being "an extract from a letter written by a friend—not a member of the new Community—to a lady in England" (p. 114).

49. The Brook Farm material is strong on anecdotes of this kind. See, for example, Hawthorne, *Passages from the American Notebooks*, ed. Sophia Hawthorne (Boston: Houghton, Mifflin, 1893), p. 229: this material is not included in more modern editions—see the prefatory note to Stewart's edition, pp. vii–viii; Swift, *Brook Farm*, passim; Bradford, "Reminiscences," p. 144; Sumner, "A Boy's Recollections," p. 311.

50. Octavius Brooks Frothingham, *George Ripley* (Boston: Houghton, Mifflin, 1883), p. 128.

51. "Brook Farm," *United States Magazine*, p. 494.

52. George Willis Cooke, "Brook Farm," *New England Magazine*, n.s. 17 (December 1897), 395.

53. Massachusetts Historical Society. Despite the title, the book begins with information for May 1844.

54. Orvis, *Letters*, pp. 7–8.

55. *Constitution of the Brook Farm Association for Industry and Education, West Roxbury, Mass., with an Introductory Statement. Second Edition with the By-Laws of the Association* (Boston: I. R. Butts, 1844).

56. *Social Destiny of Man; or, Association and Reorganization of Industry* (Philadelphia: C. F. Stollmeyer, 1840); "On Association and Attractive Industry," *United States Magazine and Democratic Review*, n.s. 10 (January, February, April, June 1842), 30–44, 167–182, 321–336, 560–580; *A Concise Exposition of the Doctrine of Association or Plan for the Reorganization of Society* (New York: J. S. Redfield, 1843).

57. For his life, see the account he dictated to his wife, *Albert Brisbane, a Mental Biography*, ed. Redelia Brisbane (Boston: Arena, 1893).

58. Noyes, *History of American Socialisms*, pp. 15–18. Noyes offers a perceptive, if not always accurate, account of Brook Farm.

59. He quotes a revealing letter from Brisbane, 9 December 1847 (Codman, *Brook Farm*, pp. 144–146).

60. See, for example, Brisbane, *Mental Biography*, p. 184: "It is interesting to remark in this connection how emphatically he [Fourier] condemns every semblance of speculation. In a hundred places in his works he asserts that he gives no theory of his own. 'It is not by speculation and theorizing,' he says, 'that men are to discover the normal organization of society: it is by going back to eternal laws in nature.'"

61. Brisbane, *Social Destiny*, pp. 245–252.

62. Brisbane, *Social Destiny*, Ch. 12, "The Passions," pp. 157–180, esp. the table on p. 160.

63. Brisbane, *Social Destiny*, p. 185.

64. Brisbane, *Mental Biography*, p. 258.

65. See Richard Francis, "Circumstances and Salvation: The Ideology of the Fruitlands Utopia," *American Quarterly*, 25 (May 1973), 213–215.

66. *Walden*, ed. J. Lyndon Shanley (Princeton: Princeton University Press, 1971), p. 308; "Swedenborg; or, the Mystic," *The Complete Works of Ralph Waldo Emerson*, ed. Edward Waldo Emerson, 12 vols. (Boston: Houghton, Mifflin, 1903–1904), IV, 107; "The Sphinx," *Works*, IX, 25.

67. Brisbane, *Concise Exposition*, p. 44.

68. Brisbane, *Concise Exposition*, p. 44. The work distribution within the groups is exactly the same.

69. Brisbane, *Social Destiny*, pp. 119–127.

70. Brisbane, *Social Destiny*, p. 47.

71. Brisbane, *Social Destiny*, p. 147.

72. Brisbane, *Social Destiny*, p. 184.

73. Brisbane, *Social Destiny*, p. 189.

74. "Historic Notes of Life and Letters in New England," *Works*, X, 350.

75. *Early Letters of George Wm. Curtis to John S. Dwight*, ed. George Willis Cooke (New York: Harpers, 1898), pp. 127–128.

76. Curtis, *Early Letters*, quoted from an "Editor's Easy Chair" essay, p. 9.

77. *Works*, I, 82–83.

78. Brisbane, *Social Destiny*, p. 154.

79. Crowe has some interesting comments on Brook Farm as an answer to Emerson's diagnosis of the divided personality of modern times. However, he is talking about Ripley's intentions at the time of the founding of the community, so that his discussion takes a rather general form (*George Ripley*, pp. 140–141).

80. Goddard, *Studies in New England Transcendentalism* (New York: Columbia University Press, 1908), p. 10.

81. George Bancroft, "On the Progress of Civilization," *Boston Quarterly Review*, 1 (October 1838), 389–407, excerpted in Miller, *The Transcendentalists*, p. 429.

82. John Weiss, *Life and Correspondence of Theodore Parker* (New York: D. Appleton, 1864), II, 50–52.

83. *Walden*, p. 333.

84. "History," *Works*, II, 25.

85. "History," *Works*, II, 27.

86. "History," *Works*, II, 35–36.

87. "History," *Works*, II, 40–41.

88. Hedge, "Review of Address . . . by E. Everett," *Christian Examiner*, 16 (March 1834), 1–21, excerpted in Miller, *The Transcendentalists*, pp 72–74.

89. Miller, *The Transcendentalists*, p. 73.

90. Miller, *The Transcendentalists*, p. 73.

91. "Orphic Sayings," No. XXIV, *Dial*, 1 (July 1840), 91.

92. Miller, *The Transcendentalists*, p. 73.

93. Brisbane, *Social Destiny*, p 228.

94. Brisbane, *Social Destiny*, p. 200.

95. Brisbane, *Social Destiny*, p. 284.

96. "Self-Reliance," *Works*, II, 90.

97. *The House of the Seven Gables* (Columbus: Ohio State University Press, 1965), p. 180.

98. "The Over-Soul," *Works*, II, 278.

99. "The Over-Soul," *Works*, II, 287.

100. "The Over-Soul," *Works*, II, 286.

101. Brisbane, *Social Destiny*, p. 344.

102. Frank E. Manuel, *The Prophets of Paris* (Cambridge: Harvard University Press, 1962), p. 203.

103. "Self-Reliance," *Works*, II, 50; Parker's comment quoted in John White Chadwick, *Theodore Parker: Preacher and Reformer* (Boston: Houghton, Mifflin, 1900), p. 196.

104. "God in the World of Matter," *The Works of Theodore Parker*, 15 vols. (Boston: American Unitarian Association, 1907–1916), VI, 263.

105. *Lessons from the World of Matter and The World of Man*, ed. Rufus Leighton (Boston: C. W. Slack, 1865), pp. 29–32.

106. "Of Justice and the Conscience," *Ten Sermons of Religion* (Boston: Crosby, Nichols, 1853), pp. 52–53.

107. Parker, *Works*, II, 301.

108. Parker, *Works*, II, 379.

109. "The Chief Sins of the People," *Works*, IX, 37.

110. *A Discourse Occasioned by the Death of Daniel Webster* (Boston: B. B. Mussey, 1853).

111. I have discussed his role very briefly in "Circumstances and Salvation," pp. 215–216.

112. See, for example, Sears, *My Friends*, p. 166; Russell, *Home Life*, pp. 126–127; Swift, *Brook Farm*, pp. 280–281.

"A History of the Transcendental Club"

Joel Myerson*

The Transcendental Club, along with the Town and Country Club, the Saturday Club, and others, was one of the important forums where writers could exchange views in mid-nineteenth-century America. Yet until 1972, when a calendar of its meetings was published, surprisingly little of substance was known about the Transcendental Club beyond the reminiscences of Bronson Alcott and the often inaccurate accounts of F. B. Sanborn.[1] Alcott's comments were published some twenty-five years after the Club disbanded and are understandably hazy in particulars. Sanborn had access to both Alcott's and Theodore Parker's private journals but misquoted them and supplied false information in preparing his own studies of the Transcendental period. By using those manuscript sources and others, it is possible to flesh out the bare outline of the Club's history by reconstructing its meetings.[2] And a study of the Club also sheds light on the often overlooked social side of early New England Transcendentalism.

The Transcendental Club began in June 1836 when Frederic Henry Hedge, a Unitarian minister in Bangor, Maine, sent Ralph Waldo Emerson a letter proposing the formation of a "symposium" to discuss the mood of the times.[3] Hedge had talked with George Putnam, minister at Roxbury, and George Ripley, Emerson's cousin and minister at Purchase Street in Boston, all of whom wished to assemble "certain likeminded persons of our acquaintance for the free discussion of theological & moral subjects." The three had recently attended a meeting of the Unitarians where they had all been struck by "the lamentable want of courage shown by the members in their discussion of subjects, & the utter neglect of truth for expedients." The proposed "symposium" would be informal: "No constitution, no offices, no formal debates were deemed expedient, conversation alone is contemplated, which an occasional 'reference to the side table' might perhaps render more glib."[4] Emerson

*Reprinted from *ESQ: A Journal of the American Renaissance*, 23 (1st Quarter 1977), 27–35.

agreed, and they planned to use the celebration of Harvard's bicentennial in September as the occasion of their first meeting.

On 8 September 1836, Emerson (whose first book, *Nature*, would be published the next day) met with Hedge, Putnam, and Ripley at Willard's Hotel in Cambridge immediately following the festivities at Harvard. Agreeing that the present state of philosophy and theology was very unsatisfactory, they wished to examine what, if anything, could be done to protest the old ideas and promote the new ones. Specifically, they objected to the sensuous philosophy of John Locke, the prevailing belief, preferring instead the transcendental or spiritual philosophy of Coleridge, which had "created a ferment" in their minds, and they wished to see whether and how these new ideas could be given a wider circulation. Toward this end, Ripley volunteered his home for the next meeting, to which more people were invited.[5]

The new participants at the second meeting were all ministers except Amos Bronson Alcott, a self-educated farmer's son who had raised himself from a pedlar to an educator and was now running the innovative Temple School in Boston. Emerson, a good friend, sponsored him for membership. Orestes A. Brownson, a vigorous reformer, was invited, despite the common knowledge of his egotism and intolerance of opposing views. Also added were James Freeman Clarke, in town during his annual trip from Ohio, and Convers Francis, a Unitarian minister at Watertown and Emerson's long-time friend who, at forty-one, was the oldest member of the group.

At three o'clock on Monday, 19 September, this group of seven men (Putnam had been unable to come) met at Ripley's house in Boston "to form a sort of society for the discussion of great subjects in theology, philosophy, and literature."[6] Emerson, recalling Hedge's original invitation, dubbed the group the "Symposeum."[7] The tone of dissent, the hallmark of these meetings, was quickly established when Emerson described the best talents of the day—Washington Allston and Horatio Greenough in art, William Cullen Bryant in poetry, and the Reverend William Ellery Channing in religion—as having a *"feminine* or receptive" cast as opposed to a "masculine or creative" one.[8] Francis, who as eldest member had been given the position of moderator, asked the various members for their opinions; as Alcott noted, "there was seldom an inclination on the part of any to be silent."[9] The only steadfast rule adopted was that "no man should be admitted whose presence excluded any one topic." Emerson liked the group's earnestness and felt that the conversation inspired hope. One promising sign was the decision to extend invitations to a number of people whose views the Club as a whole opposed. They invited the Reverend Channing, who was wary of the new forces arising in the Unitarian church, the aristocratic Jonathan Phillips, and James Walker, another conservative Unitarian.[10] Significantly, Walker, whose position as editor of the *Christian Examiner* made him a major force of the day, was asked after the Club had tried, without success, to decide between starting a journal of its own in which to forward its views and working through existing ones.[11] Other ministers, more friendly to the Club's aims, were also invited. Alcott volunteered his house for their next meeting and at seven o'clock, four hours after the conversation had started, they adjourned.[12] After arriving home, Alcott entered into his journal: "What good may come to us, and to our *people*, time must unfold."[13]

When the third meeting convened at Alcott's on the afternoon of 3 October, a program of sorts had been planned and the discussion centered around the topic, "American Genius,—the causes which hinder its growth, and give us no first rate productions." Again the meeting was a success: Alcott considered the discussion lively and interesting, and Francis thought that many admirable points had been made.[14] Emerson was favorably impressed, especially liking Alcott's statement that every man is a genius. He must have given Alcott support during the discussion, for Alcott thought well of Emerson's contributions. Before the company broke up they decided to meet two weeks hence to discuss the "Education of Humanity."[15]

After another meeting in November, the Club's activities began to decline. Some members returned to their homes for the winter while others, like Emerson, had their own projects to occupy them. The next major gathering was not until the following spring when Hedge came to Boston for a few weeks. Ripley and Francis then suggested that the Club re-assemble, and Alcott set about gathering together the old members and inviting new ones.[16] Except for himself, Alcott again limited the company to ministers, hoping that their interaction would be healthful and would "give unity to the action of all." Personally, Alcott felt very privileged, for he was in touch with the finest minds of the time.[17] As soon as the date for the meeting had been decided upon, Alcott informed Emerson who would attend and urged him to come "prepared to give us free and bold speech as usual."[18]

When the Club met at Ripley's on 29 May 1837, all of the regular members were among the eleven men present. Because Hedge's appearance in Boston had provided the spark for the meeting, others followed Emerson's lead in referring to the group as "Hedge's Club."[19] This meeting was really the first one of important consequences. While earlier discussions had been general, now matters which deeply involved all were taken up: "What is the essence of *religion* as distinct from morality, —what are the features of the present time as to religion." Emerson's answer that religion was "the emotion of shuddering delight and awe from perception of the infinite" pleased many but not all. Disturbed by the group's interest in reform, George Putnam left and never returned.

Brownson, whose personality had proved abrasive, did not disappoint many when he too withdrew after this meeting. To him, their philosophy sounded like pantheism, which would eventually lead to infidelity. Because only two men were lost owing to disagreement over ideas, Emerson felt that "rivers of encouragement" flowed from this meeting.[20]

But opposition to the Club's ideas was forming. Alcott's book of conversations with his pupils, published earlier that year came under vicious attack by the Boston press. Parents withdrew their children and Alcott was forced to close his Temple School. The city's teachers and preachers continued to revile a deeply despondent Alcott for most of the summer. At about the same time, Margaret Fuller invited Emerson to address the school in Providence, Rhode Island, where she was teaching. His 17 June lecture on education was poorly received. A correspondent for the *Providence Daily Journal* said that while he had admired its "intelligible parts," he could not possibly understand those sections tainted with "Germano-*Sartor-Resartus-ism*." Others agreed, Fuller told Alcott, and she thought that Emerson's "good words" had fallen on "stony soil."[21]

Also during the summer of 1837, Francis Bowen criticized Emerson's *Nature* scathingly in the *Christian Examiner* and, in passing, generally condemned the American Transcendentalists. Emerson's controversial address on "The American Scholar," delivered at the end of the summer before Harvard's Phi Beta Kappa Society, served to harden the opposition. Although the twenty-eight-year-old Oliver Wendell Holmes jokingly considered the address further evidence that "the transcendental nose was one that stretches outward and upward to attain a fore-smell of the Infinite," others were seriously offended.[22] As the tolerance between Unitarians and Transcendentalists disintegrated, the conservative Unitarians closed the pages of their influential journals to the Transcendentalists. Thus forced back upon their own resources, the rebellious ministers turned to the Club as their forum.

The Club held four meetings during this summer, one of which was a picnic at the Emersons' on the day following his address, 1 September, for members and other of Emerson's friends. The host felt that under such circumstances the "rules" of the Club might be let down, and "who knows but the . . . more timid or more gracious may crave the aid of wise & blessed women at their session." Thus when the Club met on 1 September, its ranks temporarily swollen by the addition of Emerson's friends, Margaret Fuller attended her first Transcendental Club meeting. Lidian Emerson felt herself to be "honoured with the opportunity of administering to the earthly comfort of the whole transcendental coterie," and she believed that her "all-day party," which seated eighteen at the dining table, went off "very satisfactorily."[23]

Favorably impressed by Fuller, the Club members invited her to their next meeting on 6 September. Soon afterwards the Club again disbanded for the winter. During this period of inactivity, the public began to ridicule Transcendentalism as well as show its indignation. While previously the public really did not know what Transcendentalism was, except that it was "dreamy, mystical, crazy, and infidelitous to religion," now people such as Almira Barlow described it, "with a wave of her hand," as "A little beyond." Each member had a distinct idea, plan, or project, on which no two persons agreed. With so many people pursuing such varied courses of action, it was inevitable that some should go down poorly chosen paths. Such did Alcott, who called himself, while passing out copies of his and Emerson's writings in backwoods areas, a "Missionary of Human Culture."[24] The Transcendentalists thought of themselves as members of a "New School" in literature, philosophy, and religion, inside of which each individual had the right to pursue his own goals. To them, Transcendentalism was the collective name applied to the views of those who opposed existing institutions, especially within the church, which stood in the way of progress. Since members had different means of approaching their ultimate goals, they rejected any attempt to link their disparate methods together under one glib appellation. When the Club reconvened, most of the subjects were ones the general public had complained about. By discussing these criticisms of their actions, the members hoped to defend themselves better in the future.

Consequently, when the Club met on 20 May 1838, one of the subjects it took up was "Is mysticism an element of Christianity?" Most of those present agreed that in the broadest sense Jesus was a mystic who used a "universal tongue" that was understood by all honest men. Yet as the conversation wore on, the participants also agreed that Jesus technically was not a mystic, since he "did not impose his own special views of things on others, by means of special symbols." Alcott was particularly elated at this meeting because his statements were heard with some degree of respect and not with the ridicule which he had become accustomed to since the Temple School episode. The young radical preacher Theodore Parker was also favorably impressed with this and the "noble" meeting held a week later.[25]

Summer again brought with it a number of upsetting events. Concerned by his congregation's complaints over his association with the Transcendentalists, Hedge elected to stay in Bangor. Alcott, who usually made arrangements for the Club's meetings, was depressed at Emerson's recent decision not to publish his "Psyche," a description of the spiritual development of his young daughters. A sense of foreboding hung over the Club when it met in June to discuss "the character and genius of Goethe." Although Alcott found the discussion "animated and prolonged," it was also "quite miscellaneous and desultory."[26]

The major incident this summer was Emerson's Divinity School Address, delivered on 15 July. As soon as the oration was published in August, the conservative Unitarians, led by Andrews Norton, lashed out at it. Although Emerson himself remained aloof from the resulting controversy, both Parker and Ripley leaped into the fracas on behalf of the New School.[27]

One common charge brought against the Transcendentalists was that of Pantheism. Not surprisingly, then, when the Club met in mid-November this topic was the subject for a discussion which Alcott thought "free, bold, and, sometimes, profound," with himself, Emerson, and J. S. Dwight illustrating the "doctrines of the Godhead."[28] The meeting began with Alcott defining three forms of Theism: anthropomorphism ("The affections craving something to rely upon; & create a god like themselves"), pantheism ("The senses, & the verifying reason, see identity everywhere"), and deism ("The intellect attempts the problem & makes a god of abstractions"). Most of the company seemed pleased with these statements, but Parker remained unsatisfied, for he could not discern in Alcott's comments the existence of "an objective god" who was both "*intelligent & conscious.*" Alcott replied that "*Justice, Love Truth* &c" were, collectively, God. The company disagreed, saying these were qualities, but Alcott insisted they were entities. As Alcott continued, more objections were raised. His statement that God was always in a state of "*becoming*" being every day "more perfect than heretofore," drew this derisive comment from Parker: "a progressive god, a triangle becoming a ◯ circle yet continuing a △ !"[29] Alcott went even further in saying that a man who does a good deed *is* God, and "not merely *divine* godlike." To this the company replied, "the new god means the totality of perfection. You do a just act—are you conscious you are its Totality of Perfection?" Dwight answered that he was, but most remained skeptical, asking, "will you give us a rule whereof we may verify it ourselves, in the next good act we do?" This question was, Parker noted, "like asking Mahomet for a miracle," and no satisfactory answer was forthcoming. When the meeting broke up Parker was still worried. He knew that Alcott's concept of the self verifying its own divinity could easily lead to egotism and dogmatism, and he felt that Alcott's general beliefs did indeed resemble Pantheism.[30] Alcott too was upset and entered into his journal his opinion of his questioners: "Traditions and usages still dominate over the minds of these priests of the modern temples. They fear full, bold, fair, entire statements. The mind is cowed. Men dare not utter what they believe."[31]

The talk on Pantheism was carried over into the Club's next meeting on 5 December, when Alcott revised his position somewhat by proposing that life was "the primary fact" from which "sprang Light, Intellect, and Sense." In making these qualities the manifestations of a central force rather than that force itself, he avoided much of the cross-examination which had been directed at him at the previous meeting. The next week the Club met at Alcott's house to discuss "miracles, mysticism, [and] conditions of approaching the views of another" before adjourning to hear one of Emerson's lectures.[32]

On 5 March 1839 the Club met for an "unbroken, lively, and bold" discussion of "Wonder and Worship." Alcott felt he had trouble discoursing on "such high matters before a popular circle, just breaking off from small talk," but soon he "rose above all these embarrassments and felt free and in my own province: enjoying the prerogative of my gift. . . ."[33] Another meeting, on "Innocence and Guilt," was held later in the month.[34]

When Hedge reached Boston in May, Emerson set about gathering the Club's members. This time it took up more concrete subjects: journals, property, and Harvard College. Alcott began the discussion by taking the position that, with the sole exception of William Lloyd Garrison's Liberator, contemporary journals were "destitute of life, freshness, [and] independence." Alcott attributed the uniqueness of the Liberator to the fact that abolition was "the true Church" and "constituted Christendom," its sympathy with the sentiment of freedom being embraced by "true men of all sects and parties." He also took the lead in discussing property, and when he proposed that it be distributed according to the moral worth of each individual, he was pleased by the general assent. Parker, though silent, believed that the basic concept of property would continue to exist, and that the best that could be hoped for was its distribution in a wiser way. Harvard, the group felt, was not living up to their expectations for it. They held that the college, as the leading educational institution in the country, should show the way in reform and innovation instead of mocking the independent spirit of the young as it was then doing. The conversation went well, thought Alcott, but Emerson was somewhat disappointed. He wished to hear "the thoughts of men which differ widely in some important respect" from his own, not merely the "varied garb" of his own "daily thoughts."[35] Such an occasion was presented by the Club's next meeting.

The subject proposed when the Club met again later in May was "the Genius and Claims of Jesus," but most of the conversation centered about "the doctrine of Innocence." Francis was not alone in differing with Emerson's and Alcott's denial "of any such thing as a struggle or combat with sin, in the phenomena of human consciousness." Alcott was disappointed at the adverse reaction of "this circle of men, the freest, the most erudite, truest men of the time," to the "grandeur" of his purpose. But when he found it necessary "to recur quite often to those universal principles, which . . . are intuitive," the more learned members of the Club demanded that his propositions be "laboriously demonstrated" before being admitted into discussion. Since many of Alcott's "universal principles" were unique, the Club's reticence to accept them is understandable; and what resulted was, in Francis' view, merely Alcott's singing "the same monotone" which he always sang, "absolutely ignoring everything but his own view."[36]

Despite recognizing that Alcott monopolized the conversations, Francis had faith in the Club and offered his home for its next gathering. The meeting was postponed until Hedge arrived from Bangor, and in early September Francis sent out invitations for the sixteenth.[37] Alcott had proposed "the Esoteric and Exoteric doctrine" for discussion, but the talk soon came around to "whether men shall speak freely, or with reference to the fears & the sleep of others." Parker thought it was a good meeting, and Alcott considered it "one of our best interviews." He was only sorry that the group lacked the ability to execute works worthy of the position in which "the good Soul" had placed it.[38] The next meeting would see the beginnings of the solution to that problem.

The Club met again two days later, on 18 September, at Cyrus Bartol's house in Boston. Although Emerson did not come, Hedge, Ripley, Francis, Dwight, Alcott, Parker, and Margaret Fuller were all there. A letter from the English reformer John Marston was read, thereby launching a discussion of English reform movements. Alcott mentioned his great respect for John A. Heraud's *Monthly Magazine* in England, and soon a topic which many had been discussing privately came out into the open: "the subject of a Journal designed as the organ of views in accordance with the Soul." Although much was said about the possibility of such a journal, no definite action was taken. Even so, Parker commented privately, "There will be a new journal I doubt not. Emerson Miss Fuller & Hedge alike are confident to the birth." And Alcott even proposed a title for the magazine, "The Dial," named after the heading he had given a collection of thoughts which he had been assembling from his journals and from "Psyche" over the past few years.[39] When the meeting broke up, it was understood by most that the Transcendentalists would soon have their own journal. The Transcendental Club, having provided its members with a body of sorts, was now preparing to supply them with a voice with which to be heard.

Soon Fuller was appointed editor of the new journal, *The Dial*, and it was undoubtedly discussed when the Club came together at Ripley's on 5 December. This meeting was the first the Reverend William Ellery Channing attended; he had not come earlier both because he disagreed with the Transcendentalists on many points, and because a severe winter cold had recently limited his activities.[40] Channing was especially interested in hearing about *The Dial*, feeling a new periodical to be a necessity after Norton had intensified his attacks on the Transcendentalists.[41]

In May 1840, the Transcendental Club reconvened for three meetings. On the fifth they met at Caleb Stetson's house in Medford to discuss "the doctrine and rites of Worship, and the indications of the new Church and ritual of the present time." Emerson found the meeting so agreeable that he volunteered his home for the next gathering and even sent out letters of invitation.[42] Meeting the next week, the Club discoursed on "the Inspiration of the Prophet and Bard, the nature of Poetry, and the causes of sterility of Poetic Inspiration in our age and country."[43] The last meeting that month, at Bartol's in Boston on 27 May, was both enlivened and upset by the presence of a "hardfeatured, scarred, & wrinkled Methodist," Father Edward Taylor of the Seaman's Bethel. When Taylor entered the discussion on the influence of preaching and the administration of religion, he rebuked the shortcomings of the various religious sects, including his own, with such "sarcastic wit" and "grim but fervent satire," that the Club was unable to resume the discussion, for "all other speech seemed so cold and hard after the glowing words they had heard."[44] *The Dial* was not a major topic of discussion at any of these meetings, thus eliminating whatever hopes may have been held for the Transcendental Club as a whole supporting it. *The Dial* existed—its first number was published in July—without the formal backing of the Club.[45]

On 2 September the Club met at Parker's to discuss "the organization of a new church." Hedge, Francis, and Caleb Stetson supported the Unitarian Association with vigor, causing Parker to complain that they were wedded to the past. Now he loved the past, Parker said, but he would "as soon wed [his] grandmother whom [he] love[d] equally well." Together with Ripley, Parker supported "a new church but a Christian Church," while Emerson, Fuller, and Sophia Ripley proposed a universal creed and church. Both Parker and Emerson were disappointed in the company's response to their arguments. Emerson felt that their "distrust that the Divine Soul would [not] find its own organs" was "the essence of Atheism," and he complained that important questions went untouched. Only the young ministers William Henry Channing and Christopher Cranch seemed to be satisfied with the discussion, for they had wished to let the matter take care of itself.[46]

When the Club reconvened in late September, the church was again discussed. Since Emerson was absent and Fuller mostly silent, the discussion moved towards an exposition of the present conditions of the church rather than towards alternatives to it. Ripley started the meeting by proposing that "the ministers & Church are upheld in order to uphold a society vicious in its foundations." The inherent evil, he went on, resulted from the multitude's desire that the church "should continue in its present conditions." Hedge defended the church by pointing to its past accomplishments, but Ripley finally made him confess that the "Social Principle" had "yet to be educated," and therefore the "Church of Humanity" has "yet to grow." The meeting broke up, as usual, with all sides still far apart.[47]

The late September meeting was probably the Club's last. What had originally been organized for informal discussion among a small, uninfluential group of dissidents now found itself containing some very important and very opinionated members who wielded real power. Parker and Ripley had become leaders of the radical element within the Unitarian church, and the latter would soon resign his pastorate to put his ideas into action at Brook Farm. Emerson was established as a successful lecturer and was preparing his first book of essays for publication in 1841. The younger Transcendentalists who lived in Ohio—Henry Channing, Clarke, and Cranch—were returning to the east with less enthusiasm for Transcendental reforms than they had left with a number of years earlier. With other forums and careers to occupy its members, who were beginning to differ sharply and often harshly among themselves, the Club, after more than thirty meetings, was silently disbanded.

Later memories of the Club were mixed. Alcott considered it "a fine whetstone for the wits, and served us higher ends than we all were conscious of at that time."[48] But Emerson and Parker took it less seriously. Even in 1844 Emerson had considered the Social Circle at Concord "the best society I have ever known," for "Harvard University is a wafer in comparison with the solid land which my friends represent."[49] In 1883 he remembered that the Club had had "some notoriety, and perhaps wakened curiosity," but, he concluded, "Nothing more serious came of it than the modest quarterly journal called The Dial."[50] And Parker looked back at the Club meetings as mere "aesthetic teas."[51] But the contemporary impact of the Club cannot be denied. In an era of "Conversations," such as those made famous by Alcott and Fuller, the opportunity to freely discuss and exchange ideas was important. In addition, the Club provided a focal point for Transcendentalism and the Transcendentalists and, in turn, produced another uniting force, The Dial. If for nothing else than this, the Transcendental Club is worth remembering.

Notes

1. See my "A Calendar of Transcendental Club Meetings," *American Literature*, 44 (May 1972), 197–207, which also includes a history of previous accounts of the Club, and details of attendance at individual meetings.

2. I am grateful to the Andover-Harvard Theological Library, the Boston

Public Library, and the Houghton Library of Harvard University for permission to quote from manuscripts in their possession.

3. Emerson to Hedge, 20 July, *The Letters of Ralph Waldo Emerson*, ed. Ralph L. Rusk (New York: Columbia University Press, 1939), II, 29. Hereafter cited as *L*.

4. Dated 14 June, Myerson, "Frederic Henry Hedge and the Failure of Transcendentalism," *Harvard Library Bulletin*, 23 (October 1975), 400–401.

5. Hedge to Cabot, n.d., James Elliot Cabot, *A Memoir of Ralph Waldo Emerson* (Boston: Houghton, Mifflin, 1887), I, 244–245.

6. "Extracts from the Journal of C. Francis," 19 September, Houghton Library, Harvard University.

7. Dated 11 September, Myerson, "Bronson's Alcott's 'Journal for 1836,'" *Studies in the American Renaissance 1978*, ed. Myerson (Boston: Twayne, 1978), pp. 71–72.

8. Dated 20 September, *The Journals and Miscellaneous Notebooks of Ralph Waldo Emerson*, ed. William H. Gilman et al. (Cambridge: Harvard University Press, 1960–   ), V, 195. Hereafter cited as *JMN*.

9. Alcott, "The Transcendental Club and the Dial," Boston *Commonwealth*, 24 April 1863, p. 1.

10. Dated 20 September, *JMN*, V, 194–195.

11. Hedge to Cabot, n.d., Cabot, *Memoir of Emerson*, I, 245.

12. Emerson to Margaret Fuller, 20 September, *L*, II, 37.

13. Dated 19 September, Myerson, "Alcott's 'Journal for 1836,'" pp. 76–77.

14. Alcott, October, "Autobiographical Index," Houghton Library, Harvard University; entry dated 3 October, Myerson, "Alcott's 'Journal for 1836,'" p. 80; entry dated 3 October, "Extracts from the Journal of C. Francis."

15. Entries dated 6 October, *JMN*, V, 218; and 3 October, Myerson, "Alcott's 'Journal for 1836,'" p. 80.

16. Alcott to Emerson, 9 May, *The Letters of A. Bronson Alcott*, ed. Richard L. Herrnstadt (Ames: Iowa State University Press, 1969), p. 32.

17. Alcott, Week XXI, "Journal for 1837," pp. 381–382, Houghton Library, Harvard University. The dating by weeks is Alcott's.

18. Alcott, 24 May, *Letters*, p. 33.

19. Dated 30 May, *JMN*, V, 338. "Symposeum" (Alcott's spelling), "Transcendental Club," and "Hedge's Club" were used interchangeably in describing this group. I have chosen to use the most common designation, "Transcendental Club," throughout this article.

20. Dated 29 May, "Extracts from the Journal of C. Francis"; Henry F. Brownson, *Orestes A. Brownson's Early Life* (Detroit: H. F. Brownson, 1898), p. 308; Emerson to Margaret Fuller, 30 May, *L*, II, 78.

21. W. V., "Opening of the Greene-St. School," 17 June, p. 2; 27 June letter, Annie Russell Marble, "Margaret Fuller as Teacher," *Critic*, 43 (October 1903), 340.

22. Quoted in Madeleine B. Stern, *The Life of Margaret Fuller* (New York: E. P. Dutton, 1942), p. 153. But Holmes later denied saying this: see Moncure Daniel Conway, *Autobiography, Memories, and Experiences* (Boston: Houghton, Mifflin, 1904), I, 384.

23. Emerson to Fuller, 17 August, *L*, II, 95; Lidian Emerson to Elizabeth Peabody, 22 August, and to Lucy Brown, 2 September, Houghton Library, Harvard University.

24. Charles Godley Leland, *Memoirs* (New York: Appleton, 1893), p. 77;

dated 6 October 1836 in *JMN*, V, 218; Alcott, Week IV, "Journal for 1838," p. 81, Houghton Library, Harvard University.

25. Alcott, Weeks XVIII-XXI, "Journal for 1838," pp. 251–254; Parker to George E. Ellis, 27 May, Massachusetts Historical Society.

26. Alcott, Week XXII, "Journal for 1838," pp. 255–256.

27. The best discussions of the Unitarian controversy are in Charles Crowe, *George Ripley: Transcendentalist and Utopian Socialist* (Athens: University of Georgia Press, 1967), pp. 97–123; and William R. Hutchison, *The Transcendentalist Ministers* (New Haven: Yale University Press, 1959), pp. 64ff.

28. Alcott, Week XLVIII, November, "Journal for 1838," pp. 411–412.

29. Parker was very well read and capable of supporting his arguments with documentation; Alcott, whose reading was erratic, felt that his "divine" inspiration provided documentation enough for his generalizations. Emerson told George F. Hoar of one occasion when Parker "wound himself round Alcott like an anaconda; you could hear poor Alcott's bones crunch" (Hoar, *Autobiography of Seventy Years* [New York: Scribners, 1903], I, 74).

30. Parker also entered this in his journal: "When examined to the bottom is [Alcott] anything more than a very spiritual & highly religious Dogmatist" (entry ca. 15 November, "Journal," I, 74–75, Andover-Harvard Theological Library).

31. Alcott, Week XLVIII, November, "Journal for 1838," pp. 412–413.

32. Alcott, Weeks XLIX, L, December, "Journal for 1838," pp. 427–428, 449–450.

33. Alcott, 5 March, "Diary January–June 1839," pp. 433–435, Houghton Library, Harvard University.

34. Editors' statement, *Journals of Ralph Waldo Emerson*, ed. Edward Waldo Emerson and Waldo Emerson Forbes (Boston: Houghton Mifflin, 1909–1914), V, 168.

35. Emerson to Hedge, 5 May, *L*, II, 199, and Emerson to Cyrus Bartol, 2 May, Barrett Library, University of Virginia Library; Parker, 9 May, "Journal," I, 144; Alcott, 8 May, "Diary January–June 1839," pp. 745–748; 10 May, *JMN*, VII, 194.

36. Francis to Parker, 24 May, Clarence L. F. Gohdes, *The Periodicals of American Transcendentalism* (Durham: Duke University Press, 1931), p. 223; Alcott, 22 May, "Diary January–June 1839," pp. 745–748; Francis to Parker, 24 May, Gohdes, *Periodicals*, p. 223.

37. J. S. Dwight to Alcott, 12 September, copy, Alcott, "Diary July–December 1839," p. 239, Houghton Library, Harvard University.

38. Parker, [16 September], "Journal," I, 232; Alcott, 16 September, "Diary July–December 1839," p. 242.

39. Alcott, [18 September], "Diary July–December 1839," p. 249; Parker, [18 September], "Journal," I, 232; Alcott, February, in Myerson, "Bronson Alcott's 'Scripture for 1840,'" *ESQ: A Journal of the American Renaissance*, 20 (4th Quarter 1974), 242.

40. Alcott, 5 December, "Diary July–December 1839," p. 456; Channing to Peabody, [summer 1840], Elizabeth Palmer Peabody, *Reminiscences of Rev. Wm. Ellery Channing* (Boston: Roberts Brothers, 1880), p. 411.

41. Peabody, *Reminiscences*, p. 370.

42. May, Myerson, "Alcott's 'Scripture for 1840,'" p. 245; 6 May, *JMN*, VII, 346; see Emerson to Fuller, 8 May, *L*, II, 293, and Emerson to Bartol, 8 May, Barrett Library, University of Virginia Library.

43. May, Myerson, "Alcott's 'Scripture for 1840,' " p. 245.

44. 28 May, *JMN*, VII, 360; George Ripley and George P. Bradford, "Philosophic Thought in Boston," *The Memorial History of Boston*, ed. Justin Winsor (Boston: James R. Osgood, 1881), IV, 323n.

45. For a further discussion of the *Dial* and the role played by Transcendental Club members in it, see Myerson, *The New England Transcendentalists and the Dial: A History of the Magazine and Its Contributors* (Rutherford, N.J.: Fairleigh Dickinson University Press, 1980).

46. Parker, 1–2 September, "Journal," I, 442; Peabody to Dwight, 20 September, Boston Public Library; Emerson to Peabody, 8 September, *L*, II, 329; Cranch to Dwight, 12 September, F. DeWolfe Miller, "Christopher Pearse Cranch: New England Transcendentalist" (Ph.D. dissertation, University of Virginia, 1942), pp. 126–127.

47. Peabody to Dwight, 20 September, Boston Public Library.

48. Dated 5 March 1850, *The Journals of Bronson Alcott*, ed. Odell Shepard (Boston: Little, Brown, 1938), p. 228.

49. Letter to [Samuel Gray Ward], 17 December, *Letters from Ralph Waldo Emerson to a Friend*, ed. Charles Eliot Norton (Boston: Houghton, Mifflin, 1899), pp. 58–59.

50. "Historic Notes of Life and Letters in Massachusetts," *Atlantic Monthly*, 52 (October 1883), 535.

51. Letter to Emerson, 11 October 1853, *L*, IV, 390n.

"The Transcendentalists and Language: The Unitarian Exegetical Background"

Philip F. Gura*

Scholars of Transcendentalism recognize the importance of language in the early nineteenth century, and point to the "Language" section of Emerson's *Nature* and the manifold punning in Thoreau's *Walden* as evidence of a widespread concern with the significance of words.[1] Recent critics have gone further afield and discovered in Thoreau an obsession with the speculative philological theories of Europeans such as Charles Kraitsir and Walter Whiter, and have demonstrated Emerson's indebtedness to Sampson Reed and Guillaume Oegger, who showed how Swedenborgian correspondence was applicable to the study of language.[2] But there has been no explanation *why* this concern with language was so widespread in Transcendentalist circles. One answer lies embedded in the theological controversies in which New England divines were engaged.

Between 1820 and 1850 New England witnessed a lively debate over the origin and meaning of language, with roots in the dialogue which began when Immanuel Kant rejected Lockean sensationalism as a satisfactory epistemological model. This debate was most noticeable in the conflict between the Unitarians, who championed an empirical reading of scripture, and the Trinitarians, who attempted to defend a more orthodox reading of the Bible by adopting a "symbolic" view of its language.[3] The issues of this debate suggest not only why the study of language was taken seriously by contemporary theologians, but also how such people as Emerson, Theodore Parker, Bronson Alcott, and Henry Thoreau were linked through their belief that many of the important philosophical problems of the early nineteenth century stemmed from differing conceptions of language and its uses.

The study of language in that age was part of a rational climate of philosophical and religious thought with humanistic implications difficult for our generation to comprehend. As Hans Aarsleff has noted,

*Reprinted from *Studies in the American Renaissance 1979*, ed. Joel Myerson (Boston: Twayne, 1979), pp. 1–16.

in the nineteenth century the budding science of philology attempted to answer such questions as "What was the origin of thought?" "Did the mind have a material basis?" "Did mankind have a single origin?" "Was the first language given by revelation, or had man invented it in the process of time?"[4] But historians seeking an explanation for the Transcendentalists' interest in the philosophy of language, do not acknowledge how many of the main figures of the movement were themselves exposed to just such questions, and that the terms of this theological debate, especially with respect to the accuracy and relevance of language to eternal matters, were of considerable importance to many Transcendentalists.[5] As the conversations over exegesis became more stringent, and as the participants read more widely in European philology, what had begun as an attempt to discredit the interpretations of scriptural language which gave rise to denominational bitterness opened the doors to a novel theory of literary symbolism, which had its counterpart in the thought of the European Romantics.[6] But this transformation had its beginning in the early 1800s, when liberal ministers resorted to the philosophy of John Locke in order to buttress their theology against attacks by Trinitarian opponents.

The belief in religious voluntarism—developed as a corollary to the United States Constitution—provided the starting point of a fifty-year debate over the nature and meaning of language. Attempts to interpret certain biblical texts bred a widespread concern with exegesis; and, although theologians and philosophers had earlier recognized that many of their disagreements stemmed from questions of interpretation, never had there been such a plethora of readings of important biblical passages. What was the proper form that baptism should take? Would there be everlasting damnation for all sinners? How much free will does man possess?[7] Similar questions agonized the consciences of many Americans who had never known so chaotic a religious situation; and, while such controversies excited many denominations, the issue of immediate concern here is the Unitarians' extended defense of their own methods of biblical exegesis. Here we can locate the formulation of the philological premises against which many Transcendentalists later rebelled.

By 1820, "liberal Christianity" had emerged as a separate and powerful denomination with a philosophical framework built on the empiricism of John Locke, but this proto-Unitarian group soon came under increasing attack by those who found its principles fatal to vital religion. The reaction of Sampson Reed, the Swedenborgian druggist whose *Observations on the Growth of the Mind* (1826) was one of the earliest premonitions of dissent within the liberal ranks, serves as an example. In his "Oration on Genius" delivered in 1821 when he received his

M.A. from Harvard, he irreverently declared that Locke's mind would not always remain "the standard of metaphysics." Nurtured on "common sense" empiricism when he was at Harvard, Reed (through the aid of Swedenborg's works) already had begun to pierce the shallowness of empirical philosophy.[8] He reminded his listeners that, given the developments in philosophical Idealism, "had we a description of it [the mind] in its present state, it would make a very different book from 'Locke on the Understanding.'" His tone was belligerent, and the next twenty years saw a major assault against the Unitarians stem precisely from his observation. And Reed's judgment was no exception; for, as a recent critic has noted, as long as the debate over Transcendentalism raged, "the name of John Locke" remained "integral to its philosophical history . . . a symbol of commitments too diverse and too profoundly rooted to permit facile compromise."[9] Among the various constrictions of the Lockean mind, the men who later came to be called "Transcendentalists" discovered a conception of language which did not square with their philosophical Idealism.

In many of the religious controversies of the 1820s, the age-old argument of how the written or spoken word impressed its significance upon men, of how language made its meaning, had resurfaced. Even in America this question was not new, for a hundred years earlier Jonathan Edwards had confronted a similar query and, with the aid of the then-novel Lockean epistemology, had refashioned Calvinism into a profoundly emotional, yet intellectually respectable, system.[10] But in the next century men began to re-examine the relationship between word and thing, and the theory of language outlined in the "Third Book" of Locke's *Essay Concerning Human Understanding* seemed appropriate only when they professed to live by their rational understanding alone. When some dissidents began to speculate that some of man's thoughts were intuitive, Locke's theory came under increasing criticism, even though, as Perry Miller has pointed out, such attacks did not immediately demolish his well-wrought edifice.[11]

Locke's declaration of how *arbitrary* words were is what appealed to the Unitarians. In the empirical system words were perceived merely as external stimuli, and the "truth" of language consisted of its utility. The source of meaning was simply "rational usage derived from sensory perception." Words were a contrivance designed for human convenience and, if they came to be used by men as the "*signs* of their *ideas*," this was not through any "natural connection, that there is between particular articulate sounds and certain ideas," but only through a "voluntary imposition, whereby such a word is made arbitrarily the mark of such an idea." The languages of the world thus had no underlying unity, and words "in their primary or immediate signification" stood for nothing universal, but only for the ideas "in the mind of him that uses them." If men employed terms for which they had not experienced some sensory analogue, they could not know the meaning of what they said. Conversely, words themselves were not universal symbols, for the truth of each idea had to be learned empirically by each man to whom the word-idea was expressed.[12]

The implicit analogy between Locke's theories on government and language is evident and has been recognized. Both were artificial constructs resting upon a contract voluntarily entered, or, more precisely, upon a *contextual* arrangement. As with the rules of a political state, "neither vocabulary nor syntax had an inherent or organic rationale" but were created to serve particular needs—in this case, communication. Words were not gifts from God standing as precise ciphers to reality but only "noises, having no transcendental or preternatural correspondence with what they name." The meaning of meaning was a private or, at best, a narrowly cultural experience, and acts of human communication were only approximations of ideas experienced, not magical incantations of the ideas themselves.[13] Language, then, was to be interpreted by the intellectual tools given men as rational creatures. Words were implements forged for a particular situation, and the continuity of meaning from generation to generation came through the agreed upon usage of articulate men.

In the early nineteenth century, when such theoretical premises were applied to the religious situation in New England, the issues grew thornier. What happened when one tried to explain the words of Scripture? Could the word of God merely be contextual and not possess some further, or absolute, significance? According to Lockean premises, if the Bible was the word of God, it was the word of God understood *as set down by men in a particular place at a particular time* and so had been affected by the vagaries of historical circumstance. Language was not divine inspiration but inspiration affected by the limitations of time and chance above which no human being could rise. Thus the Unitarians' main interest was in the reliability of the empirical evidence surrounding scriptural testimony. It never occurred to them that words themselves could be viewed as vitally provocative symbols that transported men to an awareness of secrets which had no relation to their sensory experience.

While some New England liberals—most noticeably Joseph Stevens Buckminster—had become interested in the "higher criticism" of the Bible developed by such European scholars as Johann Jakob Griesbach and J. G. Eichhorn, what these Americans neglected to realize was that the recent scholarship in the German universities came as a result of the intellectual freedom Kant's distinction between the real and phenomenal worlds had given men who sought an accurate transcription of the Bible.[14] Within a few years the corollaries to Kant's system opened a Pandora's box for American biblical commentators who failed to consider the epistemological consequences of Kantian idealism. Only the more resilient among them could adjust their beliefs to those propositions which suggested that the key to man's spiritual existence was found in his Reason. A look at the controversy over scriptural testimony between the Unitarian Andrews Norton and the Trinitarian Moses Stuart illuminates how such a glaring philosophical oversight contributed to the Unitarians' already crabbed intellectual position.

Norton, who subsequently achieved fame for his attack on Emerson's "Divinity School Address" (1838), was a chief expositor of the Unitarian view of the Bible. He had read theology with Henry Ware, who in 1805 had been appointed to the Hollis Chair of Divinity at Harvard, a gesture that assured the Unitarian ascendency at that institution. Earlier, Norton had been under the tutelage of Buckminster himself, whose large library offered a solid introduction to contemporary European theology. Installed the Dexter Professor of Sacred Literature at the Harvard Divinity School, Norton had by 1819 read enough German criticism to begin his lifelong project of proving the "genuineness" of the Gospels.[15]

His chief gadfly, Moses Stuart, an orthodox Trinitarian, held the Chair of Sacred Literature at Andover Theological Seminary, the institution founded to counter Harvard's liberalism. Stuart was "probably the best read scholar" in biblical criticism in New England, and his saturation in the German scholarship was so profound that at one point the Andover trustees began to fear for his orthodoxy. They investigated his beliefs but, because they realized that if their clergymen were to maintain the orthodox position against the Unitarians they had to adopt similar methods of textual scholarship, Stuart escaped with merely a censure.[16] When in 1819 William Ellery Channing delivered his famous sermon on "Unitarian Christianity" at the ordination of Jared Sparks in Baltimore, Stuart was presented with the opportunity to attack the Unitarians head-on.

The heated exchange, which began when Stuart attempted to refute the arguments Channing had advanced against the "unscriptural doctrine of the Trinity," revolved around the ultimate authority invested in scriptural language. For Stuart the question was, "what did the writers mean to convey" in the biblical passages? Once the textual scholar had treated the Bible with the same grammatical and literary tools he would bring to any other ancient book, that is, once he had discerned the words' *meaning*, the text, being the word of God, was authoritative. "It is orthodoxy in the highest sense of the word," Stuart declared, and "everything which differs from it, which modifies it, which fritters it away, is *heterodoxy*, is heresy." His only query was what thought the language of this or that passage conveys. When this was answered "philologically," a Christian "had to believe what is thought, or else to reject the claim of divine authority." Simply stated, scriptural studies were to be conducted by one's philology independent of one's philosophy. But after that investigation, the truth discerned was a binding truth, for the Bible was an inspired text.[17]

Channing contended that, before any text could be considered as authoritative as the Trinitarians suggested, it had to agree with the general spirit of the Bible and be part of the universal truth revealed by Christ and His disciples in the New Testament. The question he posed was not only what the original writer meant to convey but whether his text had validity for all ages or merely applied to the local, temporal situation. The underlying assumption was that the *interpreter himself* could distinguish between what Theodore Parker later called "the transient and permanent" in Christianity. Channing maintained that in parts the Bible was composed of other than divine utterance, and in many places dealt with subjects on which men received ideas "from other sources besides itself," subjects such as the "nature, passions, relations, and duties of man." Moreover (and this was blasphemy to any Trinitarian), man was expected to "restrain and modify" scriptural language "by the known truths which observation and experience furnish."[18] Trinitarians like Stuart rejected this idea because it gave final authority to man's reason rather than to divine revelation; to Stuart's thinking no one had the authority to modify propositions to make them agree with man's limited experience. God's word had a divine significance which did not change over time. Truth remained constant, and to assert the contrary was only one more display of man's sinful nature.

In opposition to the Unitarian position, Stuart sought to establish the theological authority of the Bible by using exegetical scholarship *within* the tradition of orthodox Calvinism. Just as Edwards had adopted Lockean epistemology for his own purposes, Stuart went to the German scholars to reinforce beliefs he already held. The Unitarians broke new ground with their conception of Christ as human being and not part of the Godhead in the orthodox sense, a suggestion that Stuart regarded as heretical arrogance, the rash judgment of men trying to ascertain too much through their rational faculties. In a crucial admission, Stuart stated that many of his fellow Trinitarians who still believed in the inscrutability of God would never undertake (as the Unitarians did) to "describe affirmatively the distinctions of the Godhead." Such terms as "the proceeding from the Godhead" and "the Logos made

Flesh" were merely "a language of approximation," feeble attempts to describe the indescribable. Men of humility made no claim to know the literal significance of such terminology; and, while language expressed enough of the truth to "excite our highest interest and command our best obedience," its function was only suggestive. Men had to realize that the final truth at which language hinted emitted a constant light only partially disclosed through the symbolism of words.[19]

Channing was not an outstanding textual scholar and did not reply directly to Stuart's attack on his sermon, but the redoubtable Norton needed no prompting to enter the fray. A *Statement of Reasons for Not Believing the Doctrines of the Trinitarians*, the *locus classicus* of the Unitarians' understanding of language, appeared that same year, 1819, and was reprinted several times, achieving its final form in 1833.

Norton's arguments were patently simple. Supporting his position through the German higher criticism, he restated Locke's principles of language and suggested that even biblical words were only "human instruments for the expression of human ideas." It was impossible that words should express anything else but an "idea or aggregate of ideas which men have associated with certain sounds or letters." Thus, the word had no other meaning, was not inherently symbolic. Words always had to represent something which "the human understanding is capable of conceiving." Thus, all that had ever been written down (in scripture and elsewhere) could be understood rationally by intelligent men: so far as any words have meaning, he declared, "they are intelligible." And while Norton was generous enough to admit that there were some truths that finally were incomprehensible, they were such as could not be expressed through verbal signs. It was not his purpose to speculate on such hypothetical matters: his research led him to grapple only with the "historical circumstances surrounding scriptural language, its peculiarities of idiom, and the prepossessions of writer and audience." *How* divine wisdom was transmitted to earthly creatures, especially when that wisdom contradicted "common sense," was something he did not condescend to consider.[20]

Norton thought that the art of interpreting the Bible derived its origin mainly from what he termed "the intrinsic ambiguity of language." But rather than maintaining, as Stuart did, that some important concepts were to be approached only through figurative or symbolic forms, Norton resolved questions of ambiguity in a straightforward, unimaginative way. He declared that "when the words which compose a sentence are such that the sentence may be used to express more than one meaning, its meaning is to be determined SOLELY by a reference to EXTRINSIC CONSIDERATIONS." Stated more bluntly, this meant that one's intuitions, the flights of imagination during a state of inspiration, had nothing to do with understanding the truth of a scriptural passage. Cultural differences accounted for most misrepresentations of language because "figures and turns of expression familiar in one language are strange in another"; and proper interpretations of passages that seemed to "bear a Trinitarian sense" could be achieved definitely through a consideration of "the character of the writer, his habits of thinking and feeling, his common state of expression...his settled opinions and beliefs...the general state of things during the time in which he lived [and] the particular local and temporary circumstances present to his mind while writing."[21] The words chosen by a writer thus were the result of his social and historical context. It never occurred to Norton that in a transcendent moment a man might be aware of things never perceived before, or that such visions might become an unshakable part of his faith, Christian or otherwise. To Norton's mind, intuitive principles, and symbolic representations, had no place in the life of the rational individual.

Norton's intellectual tragedy was his profound inability to fathom how language, if understood in a more figurative sense, extended the boundaries of the religious sensibility. If language were more than just the fabrication of human minds, if it were also an image or shadow of a divine thing, could it not be that through a wise submission to his intuition man could discover new dimensions to his religious experience? Norton and other Unitarians would not accept this. They believed that God's revelation to man did not extend to language. Revelation was conceptual rather than verbal, and the recovery of those concepts that would return men to the purity of the original churches was the exegete's primary goal. That this conceptual truth was available to rational man and that language was of secondary importance and not within its very self the embodiment of truth were cardinal assumptions of the liberal Christians of the day.

This brief survey of a complex field is meant to suggest that speculative minds in the early nineteenth century found themselves in a crisis of rhetoric similar to that which preceded the Great Awakening a century earlier, and that by the 1830s the debate over language had become centered on the authenticity of words in the Bible. Soon there arose yet another school of thought, the members of which declared that, contrary to what both the Trinitarians and Unitarians held, verbal communication among men was based on more than an arbitrary imposition of meaning upon sound by man himself. As one critic of the symbolic mode in American literature has suggested, this new group, composed mainly of disaffected young Unitarians, was engaged in nothing less than an attempt to rescue the sterile intellect of the day from Lockean sensationalism by showing how "controversy grew out of the nature of logical language," thus implying that "the full substance of theology could never be rendered in creeds at all, but only in complex symbols."[22]

By the 1830s these men had begun to adhere to an idealistic philosophy offering them what seemed a more convincing description of the human mind than that proposed by Locke. They understood that Unitarianism needed a new emotional and spiritual foundation, one offering the recognition that the divine worked in and through the world; and they found that they could provide this basis by incorporating the twin streams of German Idealism and English Romanticism into their faith. Along with Coleridge and Wordsworth, these young men came to believe that nature, more than the Bible, displayed the revealed will of God, and that, as Kant had suggested, one had to respond to nature, as well as to Scripture, with one's intuitive faculty.[23] Once the value of this "Reason," as the intuition came to be known, was recognized, it followed that, if man's verbal signs came from his observation and understanding of the natural world, there might be some reason *why* a word meant such a thing. From the higher critics they had learned to read Scripture for its conceptual truth, but the emotional response necessary for genuine religious sentiment was to be provided by their grasp of how Reason assimilated the language of nature, which in turn corroborated the truths of the Christian religion.

The subtlety here is that the controversy over scriptural language was resolved tangentially as younger Unitarians flocked to the New Thought and became aware of a "language of nature." This does not assert that any man read his Coleridge or Swedenborg primarily to discover a new way to structure his understanding and usage of language. But once Americans understood the new philosophical propositions which allowed them emotional faith, they also discovered the implicit connections between the new epistemology and religious language. In the idealistic system, for example, transcendental knowledge was defined as "theoretical knowledge about the necessary principles of all knowledge."[24] The way man encountered the world was necessarily founded upon *a priori* principles which Kant defined as in advance of any experience understood in the strictly empirical sense. This was a declaration that man saw differently than any Lockean had ever imagined; and, if one *saw* differently, did not this also imply that these sights and insights might be *communicated* differently as well? If a realm of intuitive knowledge did exist, could it not be that, just as nature derived its meaning from its relation to that ineffable Oversoul, so too did language have its roots in that universal ether?

Emerson's struggle with the tenets of his Unitarian faith serves as an example of the manner in which many Transcendentalists had to reconsider the premises of language in their attempts to overcome the Lockean epistemology absorbed from their mentors. His sermon on "The Lord's Supper," delivered in 1832 after he had decided that he no longer could administer that sacrament in good faith, is based upon the exegetical principles of the very Unitarians whose judgment in matters of doctrine he was beginning to question. As he explained, his rejection of the ordinance of the Lord's Supper came from a rational examination of the scriptural evidence for administering the sacrament; and, after carefully examining the texts, his heartfelt conclusion was that "Jesus did not intend to establish an institution for perpetual observance when he ate the Passover with his disciples." Emerson decided that the ritual of the Lord's Supper was based on local, Hebraic custom, and that Christ's followers (especially St. Paul) erred in their assumption that Christ meant the institution to be maintained permanently after His death. The historical evidence from the Evangelists suggested that "we ought to be cautious in taking even the best ascertained opinions and practices of the primitive church for our own." Moreover, ironically displaying true Unitarian colors, Emerson warned his contemporaries that on such doctrinal matters they should "form a judgment more in accordance with the spirit of Christianity than was the practice of the early ages."[25] Sifting through the historical and textual evidence, he had used the Unitarians' exegetical principles against them and decided that the commonly accepted practice of Communion was not in line with the deeper, more intuitive truths of the Christian religion. But by the time he came to address the graduating class of the Divinity School in 1838, his reasoning on matters of scriptural language had evolved in new directions, marking a more decisive break with the faith of his fathers. His exposure to Swedenborgian and Coleridgean thought already had produced new fruit in his first book, *Nature* (1836), in which the section on "Language" spoke his interest in an organic language of natural forms. The new principles he brought to his understanding of the nature of theological language, however, are more evident in his interpretations of the functions of the ministry outlined in the later address.

The key proposition concerning language that Emerson advanced in the "Divinity School Address" was akin to Stuart's sense that the literal, contextual meaning of scriptural language was not as important as its more symbolic function, its ability to suggest truths beyond the ken of man's rational understanding. Speaking of Christ, whom Emerson here began to describe as a divinely inspired poet, he noted that "the idioms of His language and the figures of His rhetoric" had "usurped" the place of His "truth," resulting in churches being built on His "tropes" rather than on His "principles." More important, however, was that men had to derive His principles *intuitively*, and not merely through the study of the historical context of scriptural words. Emerson believed that the revelation to the present age was that the laws of God, best expressed in human terms in the life of Christ, were also reflected through all nature and so were not just the property of men who, once upon a time, had captured Christ's "tropes." The man who attempted to speak the truths of the Christian religion "as books enable, as synods use, as fashion guides, and as interest commands," merely "babbles," for the true seer had to attend to the language of nature as well as to the contextual base of biblical language. Rather than seeking biblical exegetes, in the class of 1838 Emerson sought "the new Teacher that shall follow so far those shining laws [of nature] that . . . he shall see the world to be the mirror of the soul" and "the identity of the law of gravitation with the purity of the human heart." Truth, then, was not the truth because the Evangelists so recorded it, but because the men "to whom the soul descends, through whom the soul speaks," had witnessed it and spoke it in words which were themselves the expression of the laws of nature and God.[26]

Emerson's later essay "The Poet" developed further this concept of inspired language; but, rather than just serving as an example of his own conception of language, what is most important about the arguments Emerson initially made against "historical Christianity" in this address is their similarity to those advanced by other members of the Transcendentalist circle. For example, Theodore Parker's reaction to the Unitarian creed, best studied in his *A Discourse of Matters Pertaining to Religion* (1842), was based largely on his understanding of the distinctions between those parts of the Bible he termed "transient," that is, the rituals and myths which reflected the time at which the scriptural evidence was compiled, and the "permanent," those sections where the truth and beauty of the passages overrode any temporal references. He sought "to recall men from the transient Form to the permanent Substance"; and, taking the Unitarians' biblical criticism as a starting point, he demonstrated that they simply had not been honest to the principles of their theory. All that mattered was the "Substance" of the language, the higher truths which scripture suggested. These transcended earthly bounds and were what was *suggested* by the poetry of the Bible. "Man is greater than the Bible," Parker concluded. It was the "inward Christ" (by which Parker meant man's intuition), and not His words, "which alone abideth forever."[27]

Parker's understanding of the transcience of men's words was shared by Bronson Alcott, who was so moved by his new understanding of biblical language that in his Temple School he trained his young scholars to be aware of the deeper significance of words—that is, to comprehend the truths that went beyond the mere temporal significance given them. After the children had gone through their elementary philological exercises (a daily event in his school), Alcott never failed to remind them that "the contemplation of Spirit in God is necessarily wrapt up in a study of language" and leads upward to "the study of the Soul." He was so convinced of the importance of a true understanding of the language of natural forms that his description of Jesus was as a "Teacher" who sought to "renovate" humanity through a "genius" which depended on language that was like "the living Word, rising spontaneously in the soul, and clothing itself" in images taken from "majestic Nature."[28] From people like Sampson Reed and Coleridge, Alcott learned to read the scriptures through his intuitive faculty and had to leave behind his conservative friends in his search for a true life of the Spirit.

Even Henry David Thoreau, whom we do not usually number as one deeply concerned with scriptural exegesis, did not escape the influence of the debate over biblical language. His *A Week on the Concord and Merrimack Rivers* (1849) contains a long section (in the "Sunday" chapter) in which he expresses his disgust at the current state of Christianity, a disenchantment stemming from his recognition that, because men had become so involved with the logical consistency of their creeds and language, they neglected the essence of Christ's message. He sarcastically asked if contemporary theologians had "learned the alphabet of heaven," so sure were they about the nature of that spiritual realm. He continued: ". . . and can you count to three? Do you know the number of God's family? Can you put mysteries into words? Do you presume to fable the ineffable? Pray, what geographers are you, that speak of heaven's topography? Whose friend are you that speak of God's personality?"[29] His contemporaries labored over such propositions because they assumed that their logical faculties could define the precise meaning of God's wisdom, when, as Thoreau well knew, the substance of it was never to be truly comprehended. "Think of repeating these things [God's truths] to a New England audience!" he exclaimed. Christ's statements "never were read, they never were heard," because men refused to pierce the rotten diction to the truth behind, a truth as often indicated in the language of nature as through the words of men. "I believe in the forest, and in the meadow, and in the night in which the corn grows," he later stated. It was only when men used the alphabet of nature for understanding God's wisdom that the spiritual life became readily apparent.[30]

Coming under the influence of novel philological theories, Thoreau went on to use the American language with rare integrity. But, like Emerson, Parker, and Alcott, he was drawn to reconsider the premises of vocabulary because of the culture-wide concern with the power of language to convey the truths of the Christian religion. Emerson redefined the meaning of symbolic discourse for later American writers; Parker, in his insistence on the substance rather than the forms of religion, developed a theology beyond dogma; Alcott used the study of language as a startling educational tool; Thoreau energized his prose style until it became memorable in American literature.

There were also many other significant figures, from Elizabeth Palmer Peabody to Horace Bushnell, whose thoughts on language were greatly influenced by the contemporary debates over scriptural exegesis and each of whom needs more scholarly treatment.[31] Anyone seriously undertaking a study of the philosophy of language in nineteenth-century America has to deal with the peculiarly religious basis of that interest. Once men began to leave behind the premises of Lockean sensationalism and posited that the language they used was not totally arbitrary, and, moreover, that the word of God bore some relation to the language of nature from which man's vocabulary came, the enterprise of scriptural exegesis, especially as practiced by the Unitarians, proved woefully inadequate. It is, indeed, a long way from the Divinity School in Cambridge to the shores of Walden Pond, but, at least where language is concerned, the path is not as indirect as one might first think.

Notes

1. On Emerson, see for example, Vivian Hopkins, *Spires of Form: A Study of Emerson's Aesthetic Theory* (Cambridge: Harvard University Press, 1951); Sherman Paul, *Emerson's Angle of Vision: Man and Nature in American Experience* (Cambridge: Harvard University Press, 1952); and *Emerson's* Nature—*Origin, Growth, Meaning*, 2d ed., rev., ed. Merton M. Sealts, Jr., and Alfred R. Ferguson (Carbondale: Southern Illinois University Press, 1979). On Thoreau, see David Skwire, "A Checklist of Wordplays in *Walden*," *American Literature*, 31 (November 1959), 282–289; Gordon Boudreau, "Thoreau and Richard C. Trench: Conjectures on the Pickerel Passage in Walden," *ESQ: A Journal of the American Renaissance*, 20 (2d Quarter 1974), 117–124; and Christopher Collins, *The Uses of Observation: A Study of Correspondential Vision in the Writings of Emerson, Thoreau, and Whitman* (The Hague: Mouton, 1971).

2. See Michael West, "Charles Kraitsir's Influence Upon Thoreau's Theory of Language," *ESQ: A Journal of the American Renaissance*, 19 (4th Quarter 1973), 262–274; West, "Scatology and Eschatology: The Heroic Dimensions of Thoreau's Wordplay," *PMLA*, 79 (October 1974), 1043–1064; West, "*Walden's* Dirty Language: Thoreau and Walter Whiter's Geocentric Emtyological Theories," *Harvard Library Bulletin*, 22 (April 1974), 117–128; and my "Henry Thoreau and the Wisdom of Words," *New England Quarterly*, 52 (March 1979), 38–54. On Emerson and Reed, see Clarence P. Hotson, "Sampson Reed: A Teacher of Emerson," *New England Quarterly*, 2 (June 1929), 249–277—still the starting point for examining

Reed's influence; and on Oegger, see Kenneth Walter Cameron, *Emerson the Es-sayist* (Raleigh, N.C.: Thistle Press, 1945), I, 295–302.

3. Jerry Wayne Brown, *The Rise of Biblical Criticism in America: The New England Scholars* (Middletown, Conn.: Welseyan University Press, 1965), is the best introduction to the topic of scriptural interpretation in the nineteenth century. Also see Daniel Walker Howe, *The Unitarian Conscience: Harvard Moral Philosophy, 1805–1861* (Cambridge: Harvard University Press, 1970), for a brilliant analysis of the philosophical position of the Unitarians.

4. Hans Aarsleff, *The Study of Language in England, 1780–1860* (Princeton: Princeton University Press, 1965), p. 4.

5. Clarence Faust, "The Background of Unitarian Opposition to Transcenden-talism," *Modern Philology*, 35 (February 1938), 297–324, offers aid in locating the first points of tension between the two groups. Lawrence Buell, *Literary Transcen-dentalism: Style and Vision in the American Renaissance* (Ithaca: Cornell University Press, 1973), has important sections on the Unitarian background (see especially part 1), but Buell stops short of discussing the connections between scriptural exegesis and language theory.

6. See, for example, M. H. Abrams, *Natural Supernaturalism: Tradition and Revolution in Romantic Literature* (New York: W. W. Norton, 1971), especially pp. 17–71, where he argues that "the characteristic concepts and patterns of Romantic philosophy and literature are a displaced and reconstituted theology." What has not yet been demonstrated is how a similar transformation was occurring among the American Romantics.

7. The bibliography on these topics is lengthy; as good a starting point as any is Sydney Ahlstrom, *A Religious History of the American People* (New Haven: Yale University Press, 1972). William R. Hutchison, *The Transcendentalist Ministers: Church Reform in the New England Renaissance* (New Haven: Yale University Press, 1959), is a good source from which to begin study of the theological divisions between the Unitarians and the Transcendentalists, but Hutchison does not stress the difficulties over the differing epistemologies.

8. Sampson Reed, "Oration on Genius," *The Transcendentalists: An An-thology*, ed. Perry Miller (Cambridge: Harvard University Press, 1950), p. 55.

9. See, for example, Cameron Thompson, "John Locke and New England Transcendentalism," *New England Quarterly*, 35 (December 1962), 435–457.

10. For Edwards' use of Lockean epistemology in his reinvigoration of lan-guage, see Perry Miller, "The Rhetoric of Sensation," *Errand into the Wilderness* (Cambridge: Harvard University Press, 1956), pp. 167–183, and his *Jonathan Ed-wards* (New York: William Sloan, 1949), pp. 43–70.

11. Miller, "Rhetoric of Sensation," p. 168.

12. John Locke, *Essay Concerning Human Understanding*, ed. Russell Kirk (Chicago: Gateway, 1956), pp. xlii, 132, 137, 141, 172.

13. Miller, "Rhetoric of Sensation," p. 169.

14. Brown, *Biblical Criticism*, chaps. 1 and 2, offers a good understanding of the European exegetical background that affected the figures discussed in this essay. The school of "Higher Criticism" treated the Bible like any other ancient text and sought to establish definitely the temporal and grammatical context of scripture. In the hands of the "higher critics" the Bible became more of a sourcebook for moral illustration than the unadulterated words of God. In this matter, the influence of J. G. Herder was profound; see Robert T. Clark, *Herder: His Life and Thought* (Berkeley: University of California Press, 1955), especially pp. 295–297.

Joseph Stevens Buckminster was a brilliant Unitarian clergyman installed at the Brattle Street Church in Boston who had assembled a large collection of European theological works. His early death, at the age of twenty-eight, robbed Unitarianism of one of its most articulate spokesmen.

15. See Brown, *Biblical Criticism*, pp. 29–39, for background on Norton.

16. Brown, *Biblical Criticism*, pp. 45–47, 58. For background on Andover's founding, see Daniel Day Williams, *The Andover Liberals* (New York: King's Crown Press, 1941). For the story of the controversy over Stuart's orthodoxy, see Henry A. Pochmann, *German Culture in America: Philosophic and Literary Influences* (Madison: University of Wisconsin Press, 1957), pp. 128–131.

17. See Brown, *Biblical Criticism*, p. 44, and Moses Stuart, *Letter to Channing* (Andover, Mass.: Flagg and Gould, 1819), p. 11.

18. Brown, *Biblical Criticism*, p. 65. Channing, quoted in Faust, "Unitarian Opposition," pp. 302–304.

19. Stuart, quoted in Williams, *Andover Liberals*, p. 19.

20. Andrews Norton, *A Statement of Reasons for Not Believing the Doctrines of the Trinitarians* (Boston: Walker, Wise, 1859), p. 162. Norton first responded to Stuart in two reviews in the *Christian Disciple* for 1819, and later expanded one of these pieces into *A Statement of Reasons*. Also, see Hutchison, *Transcendentalist Ministers*, pp. 14, 54. The Unitarians' main premise here was that man's means of perception were not impaired at the Fall—hence, he was capable of ascertaining truth through his rational faculties.

21. Norton, *A Statement of Reasons*, pp. 138, 149, 148.

22. Charles Feidelson, *Symbolism in American Literature* (Chicago: University of Chicago Press, 1953), p. 97; also all of chap. 3, in which he discusses the American symbolist tradition. He does not satisfactorily explain, however, the immediate *origin* of the nineteenth-century American symbolists' concern with language.

23. Good general studies of the Transcendentalists' philosophical beliefs are Harold Clarke Goddard, *Studies in New England Transcendentalism* (New York: Columbia University Press, 1908), and Alexander Kern, "The Rise of Transcendentalism," *Transitions in American Literary History*, ed. Harry Hayden Clark (Durham: Duke University Press, 1953).

24. See Walter Leighton, *The French Philosophers and New England Transcendentalism* (Charlottesville: University of Virginia, 1908), p. 1; and Kern, "Transcendentalism," p. 252.

25. "The Lord's Supper," *Miscellanies* (Boston: Houghton, Mifflin, 1884), pp. 10–11, 21.

26. Divinity School Address, *Nature, Addresses, and Lectures, The Collected Works of Ralph Waldo Emerson*, ed. Alfred R. Ferguson et al. (Cambridge: Harvard University Press, 1971–   ), I, 81, 84, 93.

27. Theodore Parker, *A Discourse of Matters Pertaining to Religion* (New York: Putnams, 1876 [1842]), pp. 7, 354ff. All of "Book IV"—"A Discourse of the Bible"—is pertinent here.

28. On Alcott's use of the philosophy of language in his Temple School, see Odell Shepard, *Pedlar's Progress: The Life of Bronson Alcott* (Boston: Little, Brown, 1937), pp. 112–218. Alcott, quoted in Elizabeth Palmer Peabody, *Record of a School, Exemplifying the Principles of Moral Culture* (Boston: James Munroe, 1836), p. vi; and Alcott, *Conversations with Children on the Gospels* (Boston: James Munroe, 1836–1837), I, xxxiv.

29. *A Week on the Concord and Merrimack Rivers, The Writings of Henry David Thoreau* (Boston: Houghton Mifflin, 1906), I, 71, 73.

30. "Walking," *Excursions and Poems, Writings*, V, 225.

31. On Peabody's interest in language, see her "Language" in *Aesthetic Papers* (Boston: E. P. Peabody, 1849); John B. Wilson, "Grimm's Law and the Brahmins," *New England Quarterly*, 38 (June 1965), 234–238; and my "Elizabeth Palmer Peabody and the Philosophy of Language," *ESQ: A Journal of the American Renaissance*, 23 (3d Quarter 1977), 154–163. On Bushnell, see H. Shelton Smith, *Horace Bushnell* (New York: Oxford University Press, 1967), a fine critical anthology with frequent mention of Bushnell's theory of language; Frederick Kirschenmann, "Horace Bushnell: Cells or Crustacea?" *Reinterpretation in American Church History*, ed. Jerald Brauer (Chicago: University of Chicago Press, 1968); and Harold Durfee, "Language and Religion: Horace Bushnell and Rowland G. Hazard," *American Quarterly*, 5 (Spring 1953), 57–70.

INDEX

625